Oxford Archaeological Guides

General Editor: Barry Cunliffe

Ireland

Andy Halpin is Assistant Keeper of Irish Antiquities at the National Museum of Ireland. Educated at University College, Dublin and at Trinity College, Dublin, his research interests include the archaeology of medieval Dublin and medieval weapons and warfare. He is the author of numerous papers in scholarly journals and of *The Port of Medieval Dublin* (2000).

Conor Newman lectures in Archaeology at the National University of Ireland, Galway. He was director of the Discovery Programme's acclaimed archaeological survey of Tara. His publications concern landscape archaeology and art-history and he is the editor of the *Journal of Irish Archaeology*.

Barry Cunliffe is Professor of European Archaeology at the University of Oxford. The author of more than forty books, including *The Oxford Illustrated Prehistory of Europe* (Oxford University Press, 1994), he has served as President of the Council for British Archaeology and the Society of Antiquaries, and is currently a member of the Ancient Monuments Advisory Committee of English Heritage.

Oxford Archaeological Guides

Ireland

An Oxford Archaeological Guide to Sites from Earliest Times to AD 1600

Andy Halpin and Conor Newman

OXFORD

UNIVERSITY PRESS

Great Clarendon Street, Oxford OX2 6DP

Oxford University Press is a department of the University of Oxford.
It furthers the University's objective of excellence in research, scholarship,
and education by publishing worldwide in

Oxford New York

Auckland Cape Town Dar es Salaam Hong Kong Karachi
Kuala Lumpur Madrid Melbourne Mexico City Nairobi
New Delhi Shanghai Taipei Toronto

With offices in

Argentina Austria Brazil Chile Czech Republic France Greece
Guatemala Hungary Italy Japan Poland Portugal Singapore
South Korea Switzerland Thailand Turkey Ukraine Vietnam

Oxford is a registered trade mark of Oxford University Press
in the UK and in certain other countries

Published in the United States
by Oxford University Press Inc., New York

British Library Cataloguing in Publication Data

Data available

Library of Congress Cataloging in Publication Data

Data available

Typeset by RefineCatch Limited, Bungay, Suffolk
Printed in Great Britain
on acid-free paper by
Clays Ltd, St Ives plc

ISBN 0–19–280671–8   978–0–19–280671–0 (Hbk)
ISBN 0–19–288057–8   978–0–19–288057–4 (Pbk)

1

Series Editor's Foreword

Travelling for pleasure, whether for curiosity, nostalgia, religious conviction or simply to satisfy an inherent need to learn, has been an essential part of the human condition for centuries. Chaucer's 'Wife of Bath' ranged wide, visiting Jerusalem three times as well as Santiago de Compostela, Rome, Cologne, and Boulogne. Her motivation, like that of so many medieval travellers, was primarily to visit holy places. Later, as the Grand Tour took a hold in the eighteenth century, piety was replaced by the need felt by the élite to educate its young, to compensate for the disgracefully inadequate training offered at that time by Oxford and Cambridge. The levelling effect of the Napoleonic Wars changed all that and in the age of the steamship and the railway mass tourism was born when Mr Thomas Cook first offered 'A Great Circular Tour of the Continent'.

There have been guidebooks as long as there have been travellers. Though not intended as such, the *Histories* of Herodotus would have been an indispensable companion to a wandering Greek. Centuries later Pausanias' guide to the monuments of Greece was widely used by travelling Romans intent on discovering the roots of their civilization. In the eighteenth century travel books took on a more practical form offering a torrent of useful advice, from dealing with recalcitrant foreign innkeepers to taking a plentiful supply of oil of lavender to ward off bedbugs. But it was the incomparable 'Baedekers' that gave enlightenment and reassurance to the increasing tide of enquiring tourists who flooded the Continent in the latter part of the nineteenth century. The battered but much-treasured red volumes may still sometimes be seen in use today, pored over on sites by those nostalgic for the gentle art of travel.

The needs and expectations of the enquiring traveller change rapidly and it would be impossible to meet them all within the compass of single volumes. With this in mind, the Oxford Archaeological Guides have been created to satisfy a particular and growing interest. Each volume provides lively and informed descriptions of a wide selection of archaeological sites chosen to display the cultural heritage of the country in question. Plans, designed to match the text, make it easy to grasp the full extent of the site while focusing on its essential aspects. The emphasis is, necessarily, on seeing, understanding, and above all enjoying the particular place. But archaeological sites are the creation of history and can only be fully appreciated against the *longue durée* of human achievement. To provide this, each book begins with a wide-ranging historical overview introducing the changing cultures of the country and the landscapes which formed them. Thus, while the Guides are primarily intended for the traveller they can be read with equal value at home.

Barry Cunliffe

Contents

Acknowledgements

Our first debt of gratitude is to our respective families, for their support and forbearance. We wish to thank our colleagues at the Department of Archaeology, N.U.I., Galway and the Irish Antiquities Division of the National Museum of Ireland. Special thanks go to John Waddell for providing practical help when it was needed. Thanks are also due to Dara Keane, Roseanne Schot, Eamonn O'Donoghue, and Edel Bhreathnach for assistance at various stages of the project, and to the many other friends and colleagues who so kindly granted us permission to reproduce images from their own publications: Stefan Bergh, John Bradley, Barrie Hartwell, Brian Lacey, Jim Mallory, Tom McNeill, Billy O'Brien, Celie O'Rahilly, Tadhg O'Keeffe, Elizabeth Shee-Twohig, David Sweetman, and John Waddell. We also acknowledge the generous permission of the following institutions to reproduce drawings: the Society of Antiquaries of London, the Collins Press (Cork), the Discovery Programme (Dublin), Dundalgan Press (Dundalk), Government Publications/Stationery Office (Dublin), HMSO (Belfast), Kells Region Economic & Tourism Enterprise Ltd, Ordnance Survey Ireland (Dublin), Ordnance Survey of Northern Ireland (Belfast), the Royal Archaeological Institute (London), the Royal Irish Academy (Dublin), the Royal Society of Antiquaries of Ireland (Dublin), the Cork Archaeological and Historical Society and the Ulster Archaeological Society (Belfast). Many of the photographs credited to the Department of Archaeology, NUI, Galway, were taken by Professor Etienne Rynne.

While it has not been possible to consult with the experts on each and every place or monument, we have picked their brains in different ways and hope that in so doing we are not too far off the mark! Finally, we are grateful to the dozens of landowners and local enthusiasts who gave us directions and permission to visit the monuments in their care. While the State has statutory responsibility for the care of ancient monuments, the great legacy of field antiquities in Ireland is the product of the respect accorded to them by generations of landowners. This is a tradition that must endure, for we are but temporary custodians of Irish and world heritage.

How to use this Guide

It would not be possible to write a complete guide to the archaeological and historical sites of Ireland. The best we can do is to guide you to as broad a cross-section of sites as possible in the hope that what you learn from them will whet, and educate, your appetite for more. An enduring attraction of touring archaeological sites is the fascinating people and places you find along the way. And though we have tried to make our directions as clear as possible, it has been our experience that losing yourself in the Irish countryside is the surest way of finding the real Ireland. Irish people have a deep pride in, and sense of ownership of, their own history, and respond with enthusiasm to enquiries about local archaeological and historical sites; so do not be afraid to ask! As often as not, people will share with you some of their own local knowledge and traditions, and direct you to yet further places of interest.

The forging of individual and social identities compels people to erect monuments. Just as today we try to accommodate—or sometimes disregard—ancient relics and traditions, so too did people long ago carve out lives amongst the monuments and memories of the past. This convergence of old and new is what creates historical meaning in human society. Thus, cultural landscapes are made up of monuments of different periods. This is why archaeologists routinely examine whole landscapes that together comprise the homes, neighbourhoods, and territories of the past. For this reason, instead of simply describing individual monuments, in this guidebook we have attempted to guide the reader to landscapes of the past, rural and urban. The monuments and places described in this book are, therefore, a combination of accessible National Monuments and others on private land. Monuments on private land should never be visited without the permission of the landowner and the usual rules of the countryside apply such as always closing gates behind you, never entering a field with cattle or horses, and telling someone where you are going.

Human society is often shaped by the overriding character of the landscape it inhabits, the mountains, wetlands, and sea shore. A number of more or less distinct adaptive niches existed in Ireland, from the wet, flat, and boggy midlands, to the upland peninsulas of the south-west, and these surely affected aspects of behaviour and cultural identity. In an attempt to reflect this we have arranged this guidebook into seven regions, choosing sites and monuments that reflect the character and cultural history of each area from prehistory to the end of the Middle Ages. As far as possible, these regions correspond with those administered by the regional tourism boards. Within each regional section, individual monuments or landscapes are arranged in alphabetical order.

We have also attempted to include monuments that are of importance to the history of Irish archaeology: though not necessarily the finest specimens of their type, the names of these sites and their excavators resonate for students of Irish archaeology. In some cases, such as the few Mesolithic sites that are included, there are no monuments to see, just the landscape setting and a sense of place.

1 North-east: Antrim, Armagh, Down 2 North-west: Derry, Donegal, Tyrone 3 North Midlands: Cavan, Fermanagh, Leitrim, Longford, Monaghan 4 West: Galway, Mayo, Roscommon, Sligo 5 East: Dublin, Kildare, Laois, Louth, Meath, Westmeath, Wicklow 6 Shannon: Clare, Limerick, Offaly, N. Tipperary 7 South-east: Carlow, Kilkenny, S. Tipperary, Waterford, Wexford 8 South-west: Cork, Kerry

This guidebook is written during a period of massive growth in the Irish economy, which has placed many archaeological and historical sites in jeopardy. Of more immediate concern to the readers of this book is the unprecedented level of road construction and the difficulty of keeping road directions and even Ordnance Survey maps up to date. We have used the latest edition of the Discovery (Republic of Ireland) and Discoverer (Northern Ireland) Series maps (abbreviated Disc. Ser.), and each site entry records the Sheet Number. These maps are available in most bookshops and newsagents and are a worthy investment in their own right.

Introduction: Ireland from first settlers to the seventeenth century AD

First settlers

While there are tantalizing hints of a possible human presence in Ireland during the Palaeolithic period, the earliest definitive evidence of settlers in Ireland dates from around 9,000 years ago, during the Mesolithic or Middle Stone Age. Radiocarbon dates of remains from Irish cave sites indicate that animals exploited by Palaeolithic hunters elsewhere in Britain and Europe, such as the woolly mammoth, brown bear, reindeer, red deer, horse, and Arctic fox (along with the indigenous Giant Irish deer), inhabited the Irish countryside during warm interstadials. Many, however, did not survive the dramatic and rapid temperature fluctuations that mark the stuttering end of the Ice Age. A landscape of juniper and birch copses, which characterized the Woodgrange interstadial, was converted into grasslands by a 1,000-year cold 'snap' around 12,000 BP. Great herds of reindeer and Giant Irish deer roamed over these grasslands and it is quite possible that they were followed by Palaeolithic hunters. Frank Mitchell, the doyen of Irish quaternary studies, picked up a Clactonian-style flake in glacial deposits at Mell, near Drogheda, Co. Louth. The flake was probably transported there during the Munsterian glaciation (200,000–130,000 BP) from a settlement in what is now the Irish Sea. Less store is placed in a handaxe found among the *chevaux de frise* around **Dún Aonghasa** on Inis Mór, as this may have been a recent deposit. The last cold phase, the so-called Nahangan stadial (*c.*11,000–10,000), saw the demise of the Giant Irish deer, leaving Ireland with only fourteen native mammals, four of which, the wild boar, the wild cat, the brown bear, and the wolf, are now extinct. This naturally impacted on the first settlers and may explain, to some extent, their apparently heavy reliance on aquatic resources, which is indicated by the coastal and riverine distribution of Mesolithic sites.

Equipped with a tool kit that included microliths, the first settlers arrived, probably from Britain, into a quite heavily wooded landscape. Vast stands of hazel scrub were gradually giving way to pine, elm, and oak forests, forcing these first inhabitants to hug the coastlines and river valleys. Changes in relative sea level (post-glacial isostatic and eustatic responses to the melting ice sheets) have since submerged many coastal sites. Others were pushed up several metres above present sea levels, creating 'raised beaches' particularly around the north-east coast at places like Larne and Glenarm, Co. Antrim. Indeed, archaeological labels like 'Larnian Industry' and the 'Bann Flake' testify to the concentration of Mesolithic remains in the north-east, the birthplace of Irish Mesolithic studies. But this concentration may be partly due to a bias in fieldwork, as research in other areas, as far south as **Ferriter's Cove**, Co. Kerry, has demonstrated a Mesolithic presence there too. Few intact settlement sites are known and there are no burials of this period.

Two phases are distinguished in the Irish Mesolithic based on a change in tool production techniques that resulted in two quite different assemblages. In general the early (c.7000–5500 BC) assemblage is characterized by microliths such as points, scalene triangles and rods (parts of composite implements) and a variety of axes, some partly polished. Only the most durable material survives and we must remember that a host of organic implements (antler, leather, wood, etc.) were also used. The later assemblage is characterized by altogether larger, broad-blade pieces produced by direct percussion. These include butt- and distally trimmed blades and the leaf-shaped, butt-trimmed Bann flake. Sometimes found in caches or hoards, it has been suggested that these heavier flakes were designed for transport into areas lacking in suitable stone and that they were worked up into more dedicated tools on the spot. Despite these differences, there is no evidence of any major behavioural change.

At **Mount Sandel**, Co. Derry, Woodman excavated a base camp, dating from around 7,000 BC. Situated on a bluff overlooking the lower reaches of the river Bann, the occupation area was peppered with postholes from as many as fourteen huts. Four were capable of reconstruction as flimsy, dome-shaped, hide-covered structures about 6 m in diameter and each with a central hearth. Year-round but nonetheless seasonal occupation is suggested in the food remains of a healthy and well-balanced diet. Wild pig and fish (principally salmon and eels which are still harvested here during their autumn migration) were the primary foodstuffs and these were supplemented by a great variety of wildfowl and fruits, including hazelnuts, crabapples, and water-lily seeds. Exploiting a 10 km radius, the inhabitants of Mount Sandel had access to forest, river, and coastline. No structures were found at the midlands site of Lough Boora, Co. Offaly, where Ryan excavated a lakeshore settlement roughly contemporary with Mount Sandel. Food remains suggest a greater reliance on wild pig but fish and birds contributed substantially to the diet. Neither site produced remains of red deer and it is suggested that this animal must have been a later arrival.

Later Mesolithic sites or findspots are rather more numerous and more widely distributed. Once again, the stone industry was based principally on flint and chert, its development revealed by an impressive one-and-a-half-thousand-year sequence at Newferry, Co. Antrim. Many of the best-known sites are raised beaches such as **Cushendun**, Co.

Antrim, where excavation is complicated by geological factors that have altered and eroded the original environment. No hut structures are known from this period. A number of coastal shell middens date from the 6th and 5th millennia BC. At two such middens on Dalkey Island, Co. Dublin, domestic ox was included in the faunal assemblage, and this is interpreted as the interface between hunter-gatherers and the first farmers.

First farmers

The first farming activities in Ireland are evidenced in the pollen record around 4300 BC (though dates as early as 4950 BC have been advanced) at a time when annual temperatures may have been warmer by about 1 or 2 degrees centigrade. Cores from a number of locations around the country record a noticeable drop in arboreal pollen coinciding with a rise in herb taxa and the first appearance of cereal pollens, implying the widespread and more or less contemporaneous appearance of this new approach to food production. The first farmers were probably immigrants, arriving here from Britain or possibly even directly from continental Europe. Their way of life, a combination of farming and foraging, may not have been immediately attractive to indigenous hunter-gatherers who only slowly acculturated towards predominantly sedentary ways over the succeeding centuries. They arrived into a heavily wooded landscape, which they set about clearing with, among other things, the ubiquitous polished stone axe. Over 18,000 axes have been recorded by the Irish Stone Axe Project, nearly 54 per cent of which are made from porcellanite which outcrops at **Tievebulliagh**, Co. Antrim, and on **Rathlin Island** where major axe factories were located. Porcellanite axes were highly valued and were exported to the Isle of Man and Britain as status items. The movement was not all one way, and axes were imported from Britain also. Magnificent translucent green jadeite axes are also known. They were clearly of ceremonial importance and may ultimately have been sourced in Alpine Europe.

Apart from pigs which, as we have seen, were already native to Ireland, all other domestic livestock, including cattle, sheep, goats, and possibly horses, were introduced, along with seed-grain, by the first farmers. The preservation of over 1,000 ha of field walls beneath a bog at **Céide**, Co. Mayo, provides a unique insight into land management and settlement dispersal between about 3700 and 3200 BC. A coaxial system of long, parallel field walls divided off at intervals into rectangular fields of up to 7 ha, the **Céide** field system was evidently planned and executed cooperatively by a sizeable community. Caulfield suggests that both live-stock and tillage were integrated at **Céide**, though it has been recently argued that if these were originally rubble rather than upright walls (peat was not found under the stones), they are unlikely to have contained livestock. Dispersed at regular intervals are settlement enclosures and megalithic tombs (Court tombs and Portal tombs) suggesting that in addition to areas of commonage, each family had ownership of part of the field system and it was here that they lived and buried their dead. Tombs such as these became, in time, deeds of ownership.

In contrast to the dispersed settlement of north Co. Mayo are the enclosed, hilltop settlements of **Donegore** and Lyles Hill, Co. Antrim, and Feltrim Hill, Co. Dublin, where there were evidently population nodes. Similar enclosures have also been discovered at **Tara** and **Knowth**, Co. Meath, and concentrations of hut circles of Neolithic date have been recorded on the eastern flank of **Knocknarea**, Co. Sligo. Excavation of two of them revealed quite flimsy oval-shaped structures (7 m × 5 m), possibly rebuilt a number of times, which may have been temporary or seasonal dwellings. More permanent occupation is implied in the case of substantial rectangular houses at Ballynagilly, Co. Tyrone (6 m × 6.5 m), Ballygalley, Co. Antrim (13 m × 4.5 m), Ballyglass, Co. Mayo (13 m × 6 m), Newtown, Co. Meath (10 m × 6.9 m), and Tankardstown, Co. Limerick (7.4 m × 6.4 m). Walls were often made from split planks and corner entrances are common. At **Lough Gur** in Co. Limerick both round and rectangular houses were found together. Two of the round houses had double walls, the cavity having been originally insulated with plant material. Hearths were typically centrally placed and in addition to refuse pits, areas devoted to specific activities, such as knapping, are also evidenced. Despite a spate of recent discoveries, Neolithic houses are an ephemeral species and megalithic tombs remain the 'public face' of Neolithic Ireland.

There are basically five types of megalithic tomb in Ireland: Court tombs, Portal tombs, Passage tombs, Linkardstown-type tombs (sometimes called Single Burials), and Wedge tombs, the latter connected to the first metal users. Recent analysis has tended to emphasize the similarities rather than the differences between the various tombs. This is most apparent in contemporary critiques of the elevated status accorded to Passage tombs and their builders in traditional archaeological literature which treated them as a somewhat exclusive, not to mention superior, type of monument. Although they employed exclusive funerary goods, in day-to-day living the builders of Passage tombs appear to have had largely the same pottery and flint tools as everybody else.

Some of the earliest dates have been returned for Court tombs (e.g. **Ballymacaldrack**, Co. Antrim, *c.*4000 BC), so named because of their arcuate, megalithic forecourt prefacing the compartmentalized burial chamber. Sub-classifications are based on variations of the court area. **Audleystown**, Co. Down, with its back-to-back tombs is an excellent example of a dual-court tomb; **Creevykeel**, Co. Sligo, on the other hand, with its almost complete oval court, is a fine full-court tomb.

Cairns are trapezoidal and this, and aspects of the burial rite and protracted architectural development evidenced at some sites, connects
Irish Court tombs with the long barrow tradition of Britain (Cotswold–
Severn and Clyde tombs) and western Europe. The court and burial
chambers are located at the broad end of the cairn and usually face
eastwards. A mixture of cremation and inhumation, the burial rite also
involved the provision of grave goods such as round-bottomed, handmade pots, leaf- and lozenge-shaped arrowheads, javelin points, and
hollow scrapers, as well as polished stone axeheads and occasionally
stone beads. The 390 or so Court tombs are distributed over the northern third of the island. An especially dense concentration of classic, two-
chambered open-court tombs along the Mayo/Sligo coast prompted de
Valera to suggest a point of entry around Killala Bay with a gradual
spread across to eastern Ulster. This hypothesis has never garnered much
support, most commentators finding the idea of a British connection,
and an easterly origination, more persuasive.

There are around 174 Portal tombs in Ireland, distributed across
Ulster, Leinster, and north Munster. This is the 'cromlech' of old. The
principal structural components of a Portal tomb are tripod-like, consisting of a massive capstone which rests on two large portal stones and
a smaller endstone. The capstone is, therefore, invariably tilted upwards
towards the entrance which can face any of a number of different
directions, although a significant proportion are orientated eastwards.
Sidestones and entrance-blocking stones also occur. Evidence for cairns
is quite limited and in ground plan they appear to range from round to
rectangular. A connection with Court tombs seems plausible particularly
in light of the addition of 'façade' stones at the Welsh Portal tombs at
Dyffryn Ardudwy. Indeed, the portal stones are often turned to present a
broad, flat face outwards.

Few Portal tombs have been fully excavated and knowledge of the
burial rite is incomplete and confusing. Ironically, the most informative
picture comes from excavation of Ireland's most photographed megalith, Poulnabrone, Co. Clare, located in the heart of the karst Burren
flagstones. Here, the remains of 22 individuals were found jammed into
the limestone crevices within the burial chamber. Mixed with them were
sherds of plain, coarse pottery, a polished stone axehead, stone beads, a
mushroom-headed bone pin, and a wide range of animal bones. Disarticulated, though quite complete, the remains were evidently exhumed
from elsewhere before being placed in the Portal tomb. Radiocarbon
dates suggest that this took place over a 600-year period, between 3800
and 3200 BC.

Present estimates put the number of Irish Passage tombs at around
230. A classic Passage tomb comprises a kerbed, round mound covering
a burial chamber which is approached by a passage. There is, however, some variability of form, particularly amongst the more simple

specimens which can look rather like small Portal tombs. The more complex tombs have cruciform chambers and some can achieve quite enormous proportions—**Knowth**, Co. Meath, being the largest megalithic tomb in western Europe. Passage tombs are often sited on hill- or mountain tops where they often occur in groups referred to as cemeteries, such as in the **Boyne Valley** and **Loughcrew**, Co. Meath, and at **Carrowmore** and **Carrowkeel**, Co. Sligo. Famous for their complex curvilinear art, some of the best examples are found in the Boyne Valley, Knowth alone having over 300 decorated stones. Impressive formality of ceremony is indicated by a strict adherence to cremation and consistent use of a select assemblage of grave goods which includes bone and stone beads, enormous mushroom-headed bone and antler pins, and distinctive, stab-decorated round-bottomed pots (Carrowkeel ware). Occasionally, objects of exceptional artistic beauty such as the flint macehead from **Knowth** (*on display in the National Museum of Ireland*) are also found. That these are more than just tombs is evidenced by the relatively few burials found within (compared with the enormous amount of labour involved in their construction) and the fact that so many of them have proven astronomical alignments.

Passage tombs have a very similar distribution pattern to Portal tombs, though they are absent from north Munster/south Connacht. The main cemeteries have a markedly linear distribution north-west to south-east, from Sligo Bay to the **Boyne Valley** in Co. Meath, and they are intervisible. Invariably, these cemeteries provided the focus for subsequent religious endeavours and are often at the heart of complex 'ritual landscapes'. The debate surrounding the origins of the form remains at stalemate. The intriguing possibility of external impetus raised by Breton and Iberian comparanda remains quite unresolved and as the picture grows ever more complex, the possibility of a native evolution has gained considerable support. The suggestion that the simple Passage tombs of **Carrowmore**, Co. Sligo, are the earliest, dating

▼ Fig. 1. Carrowkeel ware pot (photo: Dept. of Archaeology, NUI, Galway)

from around 4000 BC, and that the larger, more elaborate tombs are an essentially contemporaneous phenomenon appears plausible but cannot be taken to imply that all simple tombs are early. The focus of much current archaeological analysis of Passage tombs is on the economy and settlement patterns that lay behind the construction of such enormous religious architecture.

Though the recent identification of a possible Passage tomb on Cape Clear, West Cork, has raised intriguing possibilities, it is fair to say that megalithic tombs are a largely northern phenomenon and that comparatively little is known of burial traditions in the Neolithic south. This situation is redressed somewhat by the ten or so Linkardstown-type burials extending from south Leinster to north Munster. These rich, usually lone male burials may belie a quite different social organization. Named after a type site at Linkardstown, Co. Carlow, these tombs consist of a megalithic cist, polygonal or rectangular, centrally placed within a low circular cairn. Burial rite is flexed inhumation (at Ardcrony, Co. Limerick, the disarticulated bones of two men were found) and includes the provision of a range of personal items and a distinctive, highly ornate, round-bottomed shouldered bowl. All known examples have been excavated and an impressively consistent list of radiocarbon dates places these tombs between 3600 and 3300 BC. A connection has been posited between these and Passage tombs, on the basis of enigmatic arcuate and radial stone settings found beneath the cairns at Jerpoint West, Co. Kilkenny, and **Baunogenasraid**, Co. Carlow, and cognate specimens beneath some of the Passage tombs at **Knowth** and Townley-hall, Co. Meath, and **Carrowmore**, Co. Sligo.

The middle of the 3rd millennium BC saw some substantial developments in Irish Neolithic society, manifest most clearly in the development of a new lexicon of religious architectural motifs. The most impressive of these new monuments, embanked enclosures and stone and timber circles, are often closely associated with Passage tombs. This suggests general social, and to some extent religious, continuity. There are about 25 embanked enclosures in Ireland. They are thought to be the equivalent of the British henge except that the large, flat-topped bank is comprised of material scarped from the interior, so they lack an internal ditch. They are among the largest Irish field monuments; Rath Maeve near **Tara**, Co. Meath, has a maximum diameter of 270 m, one at **Dowth**, Co. Meath, is around 180 m maximum diameter and the so-called 'Giant's Ring' at **Ballynahatty**, Co. Down, has a diameter of around 225 m. There is a particular concentration of such monuments in the catchment area of the river Boyne in Co. Meath and Stout has suggested a possible connection with copper ores in the region. One of the more problematic aspects of these monuments concerns the relationship between them and smaller internally ditched enclosures and barrows. The concept of an extended family of internally ditched ritual enclosures of widely varying sizes is generally accepted but the question of whether these large enclosures should be distinguished as a class apart is hotly debated.

Thus far, excavation has taken place at just three embanked enclosures; Monknewtown, in the **Boyne Valley**, **Ballynahatty**, Co. Down, and **Grange**, near **Lough Gur**, Co. Limerick; and though inconclusive, the weight of the evidence favours a religious explanation for these monuments. The Giant's Ring, for instance, is constructed around a small Passage tomb and is surrounded by religious monuments and burials. At Monknewtown, Sweetman uncovered a range of burial evidence, including a burial in a Carrowkeel pot and, at the centre of a small ring-ditch, a flat-bottomed coarse pot. A small hut with associated Beaker pottery, dated 2456–2138 BC, may indicate some settlement activity. Ó Ríordáin's interpretation of the five ring-ditches within the enclosure at **Grange** as 17th-century bell-tent surrounds is unconvincing—they are far more likely to have been for burial. **Grange** differs from these other examples because there is a stone circle around the internal perimeter of the enclosure, a juxtaposition which serves to emphasize the familial relationship that exists between embanked enclosures and stone and timber circles.

The number of recorded timber circles (sometimes referred to as timber henges) in Ireland has grown dramatically over the last decade or so and it is now clear that they range in date from the Neolithic to the later Iron Age. Associated with both Grooved Ware and Beaker pottery assemblages, early prehistoric timber circles vary enormously in size, two recent discoveries at **Knowth** and **Tara** ranging from 8 m to 180 m in diameter respectively. Once again, they are frequently associated with Passage tombs. At **Newgrange**, for example, Sweetman uncovered part of a large timber circle hard by the south-eastern side of the Passage tomb, the two forming a giant figure of eight. Ongoing excavations by Barrie Hartwell at **Ballynahatty** have revealed a fascinating complex of temple, timber circles, and part of a potentially enormous timber enclosure. The circle at **Tara** deliberately surrounds a small Passage tomb there (the 'Mound of the Hostages').

The foreign parallels for this new religious architecture hint at an international dynamic acting on Irish society. The cup-and-ring compositions in Irish rock art, for example, are strikingly similar to those of Portugal and north-west Spain and seem to outweigh comparisons that exist with indigenous Passage tomb art. Rock art, so-called because of its occurrence on rock outcrops, is most frequent in the south-west of the country, but scattered examples occur in Ulster, Leinster, and Connacht. Over 100 examples are known. Siting is frequently on hillsides that have commanding views and this might belie an important territorial dimension. The style combines a narrow range of motifs such as concentric circles, cup shapes, and dots into compositions of varying densities, from the crowded Reyfad, Co. Fermanagh, stones to apparently isolated motifs such as at Ballinvally stone circle beneath the **Loughcrew** Passage tomb cemetery. Territoriality cannot have been the sole motivation behind the creation of these enigmatic carvings, and of the various suggestions that have been advanced, aspects of sun worship seem the most convincing.

The earlier Bronze Age

On Ross Island, **Killarney**, Co. Kerry, O'Brien has uncovered the oldest known copper mine in north-western Europe, dating from between 2400 and 2000 BC. Here, arsenical copper was mined from short shafts tunnelled more or less vertically from the surface. Inside these cramped tunnels fires were lit to fracture the parent rock which was then dislodged using stone mauls or hammer stones. It is very difficult to estimate how much ore was extracted from Ross Island, or indeed Mount Gabriel, Co. Cork, which was exploited between about 1700 and 1500 BC, but the work was clearly labour intensive and the resultant copper extremely valuable. Tin may have been mined across the country in Wicklow, or might have been imported from Cornwall in south-west Britain. Combined, these two metals produced bronze.

Associated with the copper mine on Ross Island was Beaker pottery, a fine, often highly decorated, flat-bottomed drinking vessel which is irregularly distributed throughout western Europe where it has a recurring association with the first use of metal. Consequently, the Ross Island assemblage is central to the question of how knowledge of metallurgy first arrived in Ireland. The traditional view connects the spread of the use of copper with 'Beaker Folk' whose migrations were revealed in the distribution of their distinctive material assemblage (which includes conical, V-perforated buttons, barbed and tanged arrowheads, and stone archers' wristguards) and the appearance of copper metallurgy among the furthest outposts of north-western Europe. Many scholars today, however, question the plausibility of such folk movements. Emphasizing the regional diversities throughout north-west Europe in the Late Neolithic/Early Bronze Age, they suggest that rather than people, what spread was a new concept in social organization: the distinctive artefacts are simply internationally recognized symbols of social status. Accordingly, they would argue that the technical know-how required to mine and process copper, and later (c.2200 BC) bronze, could have been passed on by word of mouth along traditional Late Neolithic trade routes.

In Ireland Beaker pottery is often associated with Wedge tombs, built between about 2300 and 2000 BC. Along with embanked enclosures and stone and timber henges, they represent the earliest elements in the lexicon of ritual architecture in Bronze Age Ireland that, over the course

▲ **Fig. 2.** Gleninsheen, Burren, Co. Clare: Wedge tomb (photo: Dept. of Archaeology, NUI, Galway)

of a thousand years, came to include Single Burials, cemetery mounds,
standing stones, stone alignments and stone circles, boulder burials, and
rock art. With the relative dearth of settlement sites these confusing
and often enigmatic monuments have come to dominate our analyses
and perception of this period. Though Wedge tombs, of which just over
500 examples are known, are the most numerous Irish megalithic tombs,
their origins are shrouded in obscurity. While sharing certain characteristics with Neolithic tombs, their closest parallels are with the *allées
couvertes* of north-western France, and so a connection with that area
cannot be ruled out. Wedge tombs have a decidedly western distribution,
with notable concentrations in south-western and northern Munster
and again along a band curving from north Mayo and Sligo across south
Tyrone and into east Donegal. This contrasts with the generally more
eastern distribution of the Single Burial tradition of pit and cist burials
and introduces the possibility of distinct socio-cultural provinces in
early Bronze Age Ireland. Analysis of the mutually distinct Wedge tombs
and Single Burials in Munster, for example, suggests to O'Brien that
Wedge tomb builders controlled access to ores and distribution of
metal, which their Single Burial neighbours in central and eastern
Munster could only acquire through barter. Such monopolies led to the
emergence of what are known as 'Big Man' elites, while down-the-line
exchange gave rise to specialized middlemen who must have played a
pivotal role in the acquisition of tin, which was not available in Munster.

From the outset (*c.*2350 BC) there was tremendous variability among
the Single Burials which outlasted the use of Wedge tombs by some

centuries. During this time the accompanying bowl- and vase-shaped funerary vessels developed from grave good to urn. As the name implies, Bowls are essentially round-bellied pots, highly decorated with impressed and incised ornament that owes much of its inspiration to the Beaker tradition. They are found mainly in the north and east of the country and so complement the distribution of Wedge tombs. The vast majority occur in small, stone-lined cists and more than half accompanied cremated burials. Occasionally, other artefacts such as plano-convex flint knives, leaf-shaped arrowheads, and polished stone artefacts have been found along with Bowls and at Corkey, Co. Antrim, and Carrickinab, Co. Down, riveted bronze daggers were also found. Miniature Bowls (sometimes called Pygmy Cups) are also known. The contemporary Vase Tradition is characterized by tapered bi- and tripartite pots, 11 to 16 cm tall. Handmade, they too are highly decorated and although they share the same northern and eastern distribution, there is a significant grouping in Galway and Mayo. Most Vases have been found with cremated burials and the range of associated grave goods compares to that accompanying Bowls. From around 1900 BC we see the emergence from the indigenous Vase Tradition of two types of large funerary pot (i.e. up to 40 cm tall), the Vase Urn and the Encrusted Urn, types which feature in the burial tradition for about two centuries. They share the stage with two British-inspired urn types, the impressive Cordoned and Collared Urns.

Cordoned Urns are found in simple pits, inverted over the cremated remains of the dead (usually one individual, sometimes more) which were presumably sealed in place with a cloth before the pot was turned upside down. They occur in the east of the country with a particular concentration in the north-east. Associated finds include exotica, such as small oval-shaped bronze knives or razors, which may be symbols of masculinity, and beads of faience, a blue vitreous paste, originating in the Near East. However, the most impressive artefacts to have been found with Cordoned Urns are the so-called battleaxes. Beautifully carved, waisted, and perforated, these stone axes were clearly for ceremonial use and, like the urns, originate in Scotland. Sixty or so burials with Collared Urns have been found in Ireland and these date from between 2000 and 1500 or 1400 BC. Concentrated in the north-east, they too are most frequently found in simple pits, associated grave goods being quite rare. There are noteworthy exceptions, however, as at the Mound of the Hostages, **Tara**, Co. Meath, where a battleaxe and a riveted bronze dagger were found with a Collared Urn and an inverted Vase.

The forty-plus burials in the Mound of the Hostages at **Tara** comprise a cemetery mound. As at **Tara** and **Baunogenasraid**, Co. Carlow, occasionally Neolithic tumuli were reused as cemetery mounds during the earlier Bronze Age but in other cases, such as at Knockast, Co. Westmeath, new mounds were built. Flat cemeteries are evidently far more difficult to recognize and are usually found by chance during ploughing. Consequently, there has been little concerted excavation of such sites. At Urbalreagh, Co. Antrim, three burials were demarcated by a small penannular ditch. A similar ring-ditch was excavated at Bally-veelish, Co. Tipperary, and was found to encircle a porched mortuary house in the centre of which was a polygonal cist containing the remains of two adults, a young teenager, and two children, as well as an Encrusted Urn and two Pygmy Cups. Many such ring-ditches date from the earlier Bronze Age, though as a type simple ring-ditches were built throughout prehistory. Burials such as those at Tara and the Bowl burial at **Knockaulin** represent one aspect of the continuing investment into complexes that would, in time, become the royal sites of later prehistoric and early historic Ireland.

Recent re-examination of the cemeteries indicates a predominance of male burials suggesting a stratified society in which not everyone was accorded the formal rite of cist or pit burial. The rich burial of a young teenage male at **Tara**, complete with a necklace of jet, amber, bronze, and faience and a bronze dagger and awl, demonstrates, for example, that for some aristocracy was a birthright. Further indication of the wealth to which people might aspire, and the international tenor of the trappings of status, is seen in the corpus of sheet goldwork which includes 85 crescentic gold collars or lunulae, 20 decorated sun-discs, and 2 basket-shaped earrings: all types known from Britain and indeed further afield. No doubt bronze objects, such as axes, halberds, and, as we have seen, daggers, belonged to only the richest in society. All that glitters is not gold!

Funerals represented only one facet of ritual activity during the 2nd millennium BC. Communal ceremonial monuments were also created. Although many of these have associated burials, it seems that this was not their primary role, instead the burials may have connected, symbolically, the cycle of human life and death with the cosmological order. In addition to the large embanked enclosures, or henges, which continued to be used into the first few centuries of the second millennium BC, smaller henges and hengiform barrows now appeared throughout the country (indeed, as we shall see, in Ireland the tradition of defining sacred space with a hengiform enclosure continued in various guises into the 1st millennium AD). And, whereas previously henges might have been associated with timber circles and temples, during the 2nd millennium these circles were increasingly made from stone, a development exemplified in the case of **Newgrange** where the massive pit circle once attached figure-of-eight style to the site was replaced by a great stone circle encircling the mound itself. By their very nature, stone circles are difficult to date but appear to have been built throughout the 2nd millennium BC. Major concentrations occur in Ulster and Munster, with over 90 examples recorded in Cos. Cork and Kerry alone where the dominant type is the 'recumbent' circle. Such circles, consisting of five or more stones, are entered between two matching portal stones, the largest in the circle, on the opposing side of which lies the recumbent or axial stone. The axis between the portals and recumbent stone is consistently aligned south-west/north-east, i.e. on the rising and setting sun. Few circles have been excavated. At **Drombeg**, Co. Cork, five pits were uncovered in the central area. One contained the cremated remains of an adolescent and a sherd of coarse pottery which yielded a date of 1124–794 BC. Similar 'token' deposits of cremated human bone were uncovered at Bohonagh and Reanascreena, Co. Cork, and at Cashelkeelty, Co. Kerry. Some of these circles appear to be associated with stone alignments, that is rows of standing stones that can stretch for considerable distances across the countryside. Analysis has demonstrated that many alignments 'point' towards important solar and lunar positions or to places where sun and geography combine to curious affect, as at Lough Inagh, Co. Galway, where the alignment points to a corrie that is illuminated by the last rays of the setting sun during the winter solstice. Alignments may also have defined territorial boundaries across large tracts of open countryside.

As in Munster, the stone circles of Ulster are also associated with stone alignments, and this is nowhere better illustrated than at **Beaghmore**, Co. Tyrone, where seven circles and at least eight alignments comprise one of the most enigmatic archaeological landscapes in Ireland. Unlike the Munster circles, these northern specimens consist of vast quantities of small, portable stones arranged in concentric circles and radial lines. A spectacular group has recently been exposed in cut-away peat at Copney Hill, about 11 km from **Beaghmore**.

Pollen evidence tells us that these people lived in a still largely forested environment, practising agriculture in clearings on lighter, drier soils, although a general increase in ash from about 2300 BC suggests that forests were lighter than previously. Throughout the course of the 2nd millennium there was progressively more settlement on the uplands. It has been argued that in such a context agriculture was merely an adjunct to the exploitation of the greater ecosystem. So, while the underlying trend is of a steady increase in arable agriculture and increasing reliance on farm produce, the macrofossil evidence indicates that substantial quantities of wild foods continued to be collected. Movement was along trails and droveways and, over boggy ground, on wooden trackways such as those uncovered at Corlea and Annaghbeg, Co. Longford. There are very few settlement sites of the period. Most consist of habitation deposits uncovered during the excavation of multi-period sites with few or no surviving structural remains. A series of possible postholes at Monknewtown, Co. Meath, has been speculatively reconstructed as the outline of a conical, wigwam-type house. There is evidence, however, that the first fulachta fiadh date from around

2300 BC. These are cooking pits where meat was broiled in water-filled, sunken wooden troughs, brought to the boil by having hot stones dropped in. Over 2,000 are known throughout the country and they are an important indicator of the whereabouts of Bronze Age settlement. What are to all intents and purposes identical installations are described in documentary sources of the early medieval period, suggesting extraordinary longevity.

Until recent radiocarbon programmes began to push forward the dates of stone circles and alignments and pull back the dates of fulachta fiadh and widely spaced multivallate hillforts, the archaeology of Middle Bronze Age Ireland (c.1500–900 BC) was dominated by artefact studies. Substantive technological advancements, such as the development of sockets, were made during these centuries. A unique set of stone moulds from Killymaddy, Co. Antrim, bear the matrices of socket-looped spearheads and a dirk or rapier, the first of such weapons in the Irish arsenal, along with tanged knives and a sickle. The problems of mounting a flat axe were overcome by creating axes with side flanges and a stop-ridge which ultimately led to the development of the palstave, principally a woodworker's tool, which was produced in huge numbers. Indeed, the whole bronze industry had moved onto an altogether more industrial plane, though unfortunately most of the vast quantity of Middle Bronze Age metalwork comprises stray finds. Significant percentages of these, however, come from wet contexts and this suggests that many were votive deposits, with an apparent preference for rivers over and above lakes and bogs. The tools of the bronzesmith's trade are preserved in a slightly later hoard from Bishopsland, Co. Kildare, and these include among other things a double-sided saw, an anvil, a selection of chisels, bronze socketed hammers, and a vice. This hoard connects the Irish bronze industry with the so-called Taunton Phase of the British Bronze Age, dated to between 1350 and 1200 BC. In addition to the new tool and weapon types, new types of jewellery appeared also, including a variety of twisted gold torcs, or neckrings, and similarly made earrings. Most common, however, are penannular bronze bracelets.

The dearth in burials of this period is compensated for, in some measure, by numerous recent discoveries of settlement sites. At both Ballyveelish (c.1130–810 BC) and Chancellorsland, Co. Tipperary, the habitation area was located within a large oval enclosure (both around 40 m × 30 m) and this suggests that other enclosures of the same size and shape might also date from this period. Although no house structures survived in the excavated part of the Ballyveelish enclosure, a considerable amount of pottery and organic refuse was recovered from the surrounding ditch. Cattle accounted for 43 per cent of the livestock, pig nearly 36 per cent, and sheep/goat 17 per cent, the remainder comprising horse, dog, and red deer. Slaughter patterns suggest that the cattle were reared primarily for beef. Barley and wheat were also grown.

The pottery consisted of plain coarse, flat-bottomed ware, probably used for cooking, a type that would dominate the domestic scene until at least the 4th century BC. At Chancellorsland a succession of small oval and sub-rectangular huts was uncovered. Again, there was excellent survival of organic material in the fosse. House plans were also uncovered at Curraghatoor, Co. Tipperary, **Lough Gur**, Co. Limerick, and Carrigillihy, Co. Cork, and these consist of relatively small circular or oval shaped dwellings around 5 m or 6 m in diameter with walls that are likely to have been of wicker, possibly covered in clay daub or animal skins. At **Lough Gur** pig dominated the faunal assemblage, with cattle coming in at around 38 per cent. Tillage was also important as attested at Belderg, Co. Mayo, where Caulfield uncovered 'lazybeds' in a field system associated with a small round house. With an economy so rooted in the land, O'Sullivan has suggested that wetlands sites, such as those uncovered at Cullyhanna Lough, Co. Armagh, and Lough Eskragh, Co. Tyrone, might only have been seasonally occupied, thus accounting for their comparatively small assemblages.

The later Bronze Age

Haughey's Fort in Co. Armagh is on an altogether different scale. Here, around 1100 BC, a hillfort was constructed comprising three widely spaced concentric ramparts, covering an area c.340 m by c.310 m (roughly 10 ha). Notwithstanding the military character of the defences, the material assemblage, which includes coarse pottery, some tiny fragments of gold, bronze artefacts, glass beads, and a group of the largest canine skulls known from prehistoric Europe, indicates that this was once a high-status settlement. Cattle and pig bones dominated the faunal assemblage. The widely spaced ramparts at **Haughey's Fort** are paralleled at two other excavated sites, **Mooghaun**, Co. Clare, and **Rathgall**, Co. Wicklow (or three if one includes **Dún Aonghasa** on the Aran Islands), which have produced late 2nd- to early 1st-millennium BC dates and assemblages. These should be considered as nothing less than regional capitals and are probably at the head of a complex settlement hierarchy.

That such hierarchies were upheld by martial law is perhaps illustrated by the increasing amount of weaponry, including the first Irish swords (the Ballintober type), from these centuries. Further technological and social advancements during the 9th and 8th centuries BC heralded the onset of the later Bronze Age. Our perception of this period is dominated by vast quantities of bronze- and goldwork, much of which occurs in hoards, the largest of which, comprising over 200 objects, came from Dowris, near Birr, Co. Offaly, and gave its name to the industry. What proportion of these were votive offerings is unclear but the fact that so many come from wet or boggy places illustrates the broad range of environments that were being exploited. Indeed, throughout these centuries wetlands settlement was a legitimate alternative to upland locations, and excavations at Cloonfinlough and Ballinderry No. 2 in Co. Offaly and around the shore of Lough Gara, Co. Sligo, prove that despite obvious inconveniences, here too people lived in quite sizeable communities. Material associated with these sites demonstrates that they were in no way cultural backwaters. On the contrary, nearby trackways, or *toghers*, indicate that such sites were probably associated with a network of communications across the otherwise impassable midlands bogs. The three Cloonfinlough houses were circular, 7 m to 9.5 m in diameter, and enclosed within an irregular oval palisade. They appear to date from around the beginning of the 8th century BC. The settlement at Ballinderry comprised two unenclosed, square house platforms, around 11 m square. Here the rich assemblage comprised coarse pottery and a range of bronzes that included both tools and ornaments. A hoard of nine Dowris-phase bronzes was found nearby and is plausibly connected with the settlement in some way.

The image thus presented of later Bronze Age society in Ireland is one of old wealth, stability, and cultural homogeneity. But all this was about to change, precipitated perhaps by events in 6th-century Europe which saw the rise of Halstatt warrior aristocracies and the beginning of the European Iron Age. Catastrophe theorists have argued for the almost overnight demise of Irish Later Bronze Age society in the face of a dramatic downturn in the weather, resulting in famine and poverty— though pollen diagrams have not always borne this out. Others have postulated a more direct connection with iron itself, suggesting that if the *ancien régime* was underpinned by its control of copper and tin resources, the ready availability of iron ores throughout Ireland and Britain would have brought to an end such monopolies. The cessation of hoard deposition around the 6th century BC is often taken to signify the break-up of later Bronze Age society. That there were significant behavioural changes is not in dispute but whether these were of sufficient moment to completely overturn society is uncertain. Prestige architecture, mode of burial, and the type of pottery people used appear to have remained largely unchanged into the last few centuries BC. So, despite the obvious importance of hoard deposition, other equally fundamental aspects of life went on as usual.

The Iron Age

The new metal iron appears to have been introduced to Ireland sometime between the 6th and 3rd centuries BC. The manner of its arrival, whether the technical know-how was simply passed on by word of mouth through contacts with iron-using communities abroad, or whether it arrived in the minds and superior arsenal of a foreign force with its own language, religion, and material culture, remains unknown but yet is central to the veracity of the Irish claim to a Celtic identity. The traditional view is of a Celtic invasion and a rapid replacement of the indigenous, later Bronze Age culture with the Celtic cultural package. This idea was, in fact, first promulgated by linguists, who postulated a diffusionist explanation for the spread of the Celtic languages: where there is a Celtic language (in this case Irish), they argued, there were Celts. Part of the attraction of the theory was that Irish pagan mythology seemed to acclaim the same type of heroic ethos attributed by classical commentators to the continental Celts. Further comparative details such as the peculiar way chariots were deployed both in the Gallic wars (as documented by Julius Caesar) and in the tales of the Ulster Cycle, the predilection among Celtic men for spiked hair, punk-style, and the tradition of going into battle naked, seemed to copper-fasten the case. Supplied with such an eminently plausible theory archaeologists sought, in vain, for evidence for this putative invasion, only to conclude that it did not happen and that, with some spectacular exceptions, the Irish Iron Age material assemblage is essentially Irish, of clearly indigenous manufacture and at some typological remove from its British and continental progenitors.

There are, nonetheless, traces of direct contact with Iron Age Britain and Europe, as in the case of a gold torc or neckring from Ardnaglug, Co. Roscommon (originally thought to have been from near **Clonmacnoise**, Co. Offaly), and an anthropomorphic sword hilt dredged up at Bally-shannon, Co. Donegal. More recently, excavation of a small ring-ditch cemetery at Ballydavis, Co. Laois, uncovered a cremation burial with an inlaid cylindrical bronze box of a type known from a chariot burial at Wetwang Slack, Yorkshire, dating from around the 1st century BC. Connections such as this remind one of the tribal names recorded on the mid-2nd-century AD map of Ireland compiled by the Greek geographer Claudius Ptolemaeus (Ptolemy), some of which, such as the Brigantes, Manapii, and Voluntii, raise the intriguing but yet unproven possibility that parts of Ireland were settled by European and British tribes. So, it seems that rather than being invaded, Ireland experienced generations of mostly indirect acculturation, through trade between the elites in society, of European and British Celtic (i.e. barbarian) traditions, which only become manifest in the archaeological record from about the 3rd century BC, as well as the occasional immigration of people of more mainstream Celtic background. Insofar as it embraced important aspects of the Celtic cultural package (in fact creating its own version) Iron Age Ireland can be described as Celtic. But this, for now, is a scholastic definition (equivalent to describing today's Irish population as European, or, better still, American because we have bought into that cultural package), and does not necessarily describe our genetic stock.

The most discernible changes occurred in the artefact assemblages, where, apart from the continued use of coarse, bucket-shaped pottery, an entirely new range of weapons and jewellery arose, owing nothing to the foregoing Bronze Age traditions. Moreover, these were decorated not with the repetitive geometric patterns of the Bronze Age but instead with bold, flowing curvilinear art and red enamel settings inspired by the La Tène style of Celtic Europe. In a number of cases Bronze Age types were rendered in iron in what have been interpreted as the first faltering use of iron by bronzesmiths. These include a truly magnificent iron version of a Bronze Age cauldron found at **Drumlane**, Co. Cavan, and looped socketed axeheads from Toome and Lough Mourne, Co. Antrim. Such axes were quickly superseded by the shaft-hole axe (like the ones in use today), a design more suited to the forge. Swords too were now forged in iron, though the elaborate washers and guards of the hilt were still made in bronze, which remained the decorative metal. Scabbards were also made in bronze and could be highly decorated, their inscribed scrolls comprising the first integrated school of Insular La Tène art. Details such as parallel or very gradually tapering blade form, the bell-shaped quillons, and nests of three almost microscopic dots recall the European background of these swords which were, arguably, weapons destined for the parade ground rather than for the battlefield.

There appears also to have been a dramatic fall-off in the amount of jewellery in circulation, as the mass production of the later Bronze Age gave way to what appear to be individual commissions, often decorated with raised, cast ornamentation and red enamel, which made its appearance in Ireland at this time. Here too, demand outpaced technical know-how with bronzesmiths resorting to riveting the enamel into place. Neckrings and bracelets were replaced as the dominant form by safety-pin brooches and later curved-shank ring-headed pins. Neck ornamentation persisted in the form of collars (or torcs), symbols of high, possibly priestly office, including the spectacular Broighter collar, one of the masterpieces of Irish La Tène art. The same style is also found in other media, including stone, the best-known example at **Turoe**, Co. Galway.

Whatever may be the mobility of portable objects such as horse-trappings, swords, or brooches, monoliths like the Turoe and Castle-strange stones and the 200 plus beehive-shaped rotary querns (which also made their first appearance during the Iron Age) are not so easily moved and their distribution is thought to reflect the true extent of the Irish Celtic, or La Tène, province. They, like most of the material of the La Tène tradition, occur to the north of a line roughly from Dundalk to Galway Bay. So, what was happening in the south? The suggestion of a protracted later Bronze Age retains some of its merit only if 'Bronze Age' is used in its broadest, socio-cultural sense. Married to Caulfield's suggestion of a non-La Tène Iron Age, the result is an iron-using society still structured along age-old, early 1st-millennium hierarchies utilizing a material assemblage that lacks the trademark La Tène veneer and so remains archaeologically anonymous. It was once thought that the answer to this conundrum might lie among the hillforts which appeared to have a largely complementary distribution to that of the La Tène material. Hillforts, however, are by definition an upland phenomenon and their distribution was determined at least as much by geography as by cultural groupings; although there are more hillforts in the southern half of Ireland (where, as it happens, there are also more mountains), there are many fine examples in the north. Furthermore, by over-emphasizing the upland component in the definition of a hillfort we run the danger of ignoring similarly functioning monuments in lowland areas and thus of defining cultural provinces on the basis of geography, not archaeology. These are just some of the problems surrounding the study of Irish hillforts. The single greatest obstacle, however, is the lack of excavation. As we have seen, hillforts with widely spaced ramparts have consistently returned later Bronze Age dates, and while there are virtually no dates from univallate and promontory forts it is reasonable to regard them as Iron Age, possibly centring around the Birth of Christ.

The burial record is equally nebulous, with cremation being the principal burial modus until about the 2nd century AD when the Romano-British tradition of inhumation began to appear. Skull veneration and burial continued to be practised and barrows also continued in use. It is possible that a new form, the ring barrow, consisting of a small, externally embanked circle with a low internal mound, made its first appearance at this time. Burials were typically placed, cuckoo-style, in the ditches of these and earlier barrow types and might be accompanied by safety-pin brooches and minuscule glass necklaces.

The centuries around the Birth of Christ also saw the grand finale of some of the so-called 'royal' sites such as Emain (**Navan**) and Dún Ailinne. Here, huge wooden temples were built, circles of wooden poles were erected, and prestige objects, and probably people too, were sacrificed to the gods. At **Tara**, which outlasted such complexes, the great internally ditched enclosure of Ráth na Ríg was built and huge ring barrows were constructed, consuming ancestral burial mounds in an attempt to capture something of their prestige. And in the surrounding countryside further ritual and military monuments were built as the landscape became increasingly politicized. Borders were defined with linear earthworks and strategically sited fortifications. However, all this monumental industry may, in reality have amounted to nothing more than a last desperate attempt to appease the forces of nature and defend what little was left, because the pollen record tells a quite different story. Massive woodland regeneration was precipitated by an increase in annual rainfall between 200 BC and AD 200, and this meant the collapse of agriculture and depopulation. Irish society must have been on its knees by the time of the Roman conquest of Britain in AD 43, and Agricola's observation that Ireland could have been taken with one legion was no idle boast but rather was a statement of fact. Ireland did not sufficiently interest Rome and, somewhat paradoxically, the Roman conquest of Britain may have been what ultimately sparked a recovery, for it brought the Mediterranean to Irish shores.

The 3rd to 6th centuries comprise a formative period in the evolution of Irish culture, a time of profound change that heralded the birth of a new and invigorated social order. Yet, these centuries are also obscure, yielding little to traditional archaeological approaches and leading to their virtual abandonment as a subject of research. Many historians too have of late effected a hasty withdrawal from this period as their confidence in the relevance of documentary sources to late prehistory wavers. Despite this, however, recent years have seen a revival of interest and a number of significant advances, some of which have been fostered by a theoretical climate that favours, rather than discourages, the notion that Ireland learned much from Britannia and partook, in its own way, in the so-called Migration period.

The later Iron Age

Tree-ring analysis tells of a general improvement in climate, less rain, and a rise in annual temperatures of about one or two degrees centigrade from about AD 300: ameliorations were recorded faithfully by trees but enjoyed by fewer and fewer of them, as attested by pollen diagrams for the period, which show a dramatic decline in arboreal taxa, indicating that woodland was turned back into farmland. Ireland underwent something of an agricultural revolution during the succeeding centuries as the Roman coulter plough, possibly introduced by the Church, allowed heavier, root-matted soils to be tilled for the first time, and developments in livestock management saw a shift from beef to dairy farming and an immediate sevenfold increase in the calorific output of the herd. Developments such as these doubtless led to improved standards of living, better diet, longer life expectancy, and an inevitable increase in population. Moreover, as Roman Britain gradually disintegrated during the second half of the 4th and early 5th century, so the opportunities for personal and tribal aggrandizement increased as Ireland's persona changed from that of market to pirate den. Precious metals were of limited practical value in a coinless economy; more useful were slaves and these were kidnapped in their hundreds, if not thousands. The bottom rung in society, slaves provided a ready-made, low-maintenance workforce who, critically, were educated in Romano-British agricultural know-how. Like Patrick, the most famous among their number, many slaves were Christian and it is they who probably comprised the core of the first Christian communities in

Ireland to whom Pope Celestine sent Palladius as first bishop in 431. Christianity is a religion based on the written word and consequently played a key role in the spread of literacy throughout Ireland, manifest first on ogam sticks and stones and later on wax tablets and church manuscripts.

Clearly then, Ireland borrowed—and stole!—much from Roman Britain. The Roman conquest of Britain was rapid and the first Irish people heard of it was probably in the testimonies of British refugees such as a group of Brigantians who found safe haven on Lambay Island, among familiar trading partners. It is worth recalling that the conquest probably impacted heavily on traditional lines of overseas exchange and communication, networks that heretofore had sustained Irish Iron Age aristocracies, rendering them even more vulnerable to the changes that were afoot. Artefacts recovered from Drumanagh promontory fort (almost opposite Lambay), from **Newgrange**, and from **Tara** testify to a maturing of relations, leading ultimately to commerce, the wheels

▼ **Fig. 3.** Araglen, Mount Brandon, Co. Kerry: cross-inscribed ogam stone (photo: Dept. of Archaeology, NUI, Galway)

of which were oiled by gift exchange and propitiatory offerings at key religious locations. A copper cake of typical Romano-British shape was found at Damastown, Co. Meath, a short distance to the north-west of Drumanagh. Rather than being an import, however, this copper cake may indicate a connection between the entrepôt at Drumanagh and an ancient copper mine that lies a couple of kilometres to the north of the promontory fort. Evidently, Imperial citizens traded and lived in Ireland. An oculists' stamp from Golden, Co. Tipperary, tells of a qualified optician working in the south midlands and completes the picture provided by other surgical instruments and ointment bottles known from elsewhere. The cremation burial in a glass urn from Stoneyford, Co. Kilkenny, suggests the possible existence of a trading post on the river Barrow during the 1st or early 2nd century, a place where traders picked up the type of geographical and anthropological information drawn on by Ptolemy when he compiled the first map of Ireland, annotated with tribal and river names, around AD 150.

Familiarity resulted in mimesis, as the traditional Iron Age dress-pins (the ring-headed pins) were gradually replaced during the course of the 5th century by the Roman penannular brooch which, in the hands of British and, later, Irish bronzesmiths, had its terminals manipulated to look like highly abstract animal heads, enhanced sometimes with red enamel and millefiori. Weaponry too changed as the short Roman *gladius* and the longer *spatha* influenced not just the shapes of Irish swords but also possibly the nature of military engagement. On this point, it may be significant that only a handful of horsebits are known from the 5th to 9th centuries, in sharp contrast to the dozens known from Iron Age Ireland. It is possible, though by no means proven, that closely set multivallation made its first appearance in Ireland around this time, coastal promontories providing some of the best examples. Whatever its genesis, this defensive technique was eventually adopted wholesale by the builders of ringforts, some of which may date from as early as the 6th century. Throughout the second half of the 4th and early 5th century Irish raids on a weakening Roman Britain were endemic. The most infamous of them was christened the 'Barbarian Conspiracy', a joint assault by Picti, Scotti (Irish), and Saxons in AD 367. In addition to archaeologically invisible slaves, coin and hack silver hoards such as those from Balline, Co. Limerick, and Ballinrees, Co. Derry, probably represent the divided spoils of successful raids. Silver was abundant and some of it was turned into finely cast dress-pins (proto-hand-pins and hand-pins) in north Britain and Ireland, types that represent the final stage in the devolution of the Iron Age ring-headed pin. Perhaps significantly, penannular brooches appear not to have been made in silver (at least in Ireland). Some of the silver came from classically decorated plates and dishes which, before their consignment to the furnace, exposed Irish artisans directly to the art of the classical world and was one of the means by which classical and antique motifs found their way into the native artistic repertoire.

If it was Roman Britain, as the target for Irish raiding parties, that supplied the catalyst for change, the absence of Rome from Britain brought its own consequences as the warlords turned their attentions inwards, attacking the bastions of the ancient, quinary polity. The old lands were carved up and new kingdoms and chiefdoms created. Time may have distanced us from the people who lived through these upheavals but their totemic names, Cunocenni ('the hound of Cenni'), Branaddov ('black raven'), Cunagsusus ('possessing the strength of a wolf'), preserved on ogam stones, reach across the centuries to proclaim their individuality and pathos. Ogam inscriptions, almost always in the genitive case, are formulaic, drawing on a variety of link words to describe different sorts of relationship, *maqqi* (of the son), *mucoi* (of the tribe), and *avi* (of the grandson), e.g. Doveti maqqi Cattini ('of Doveti of the son of Cattini'), and, in some rare cases, profession, e.g. Qrimitir Ron[a]nn Maq Comogann ('of Ronan the Priest of the son of Comogann'). However, despite the commemorative tenor of the inscriptions, the true function of ogam stones remains uncertain. In general, they do not appear to have been grave markers. The alternative suggestion that they were territorial markers, although borne out in the law tracts, has yet to be rigorously tested. Nevertheless, this hypothesis has the potential to cast some light on dispossession, migration, and the emergence of new kingdoms.

Historical accounts of the reshaping of Irish society in the 5th and 6th centuries are fraught with difficulty. Transcribed retrospectively in the 7th century and later, the kingdoms they describe were already long established, their bloody ascents obscured behind semi-legendary heroic origin tales, a veritable Gordian Knot of truth and fabrication. Change was aggressively achieved over the northern half of the country. The ancient territories of the Ulaid were taken over by Niall Noígiallach (Niall of the Nine Hostages) and his sons—founder of the Uí Néill dynasty, the most powerful political block in early medieval Ireland, and great-grandson of Cormac mac Airt, king of **Tara**. Around Emain Macha (**Navan**), tribes that had been subordinate to the Ulaid joined to form a confederation of nine petty kingdoms. Known collectively as the Airgialla, 'the hostage-givers', they each surrendered as surety a hostage to Niall who afforded them the protection of allies. Three of Niall's sons, Conall, Endae, and Eógan, are reported to have carved up Donegal and north Tyrone. The Ulaid contracted east of the Bann to join the Dál Riata, Dál nAraide, the Uí Echach, and the Dál Fiatach (whose capital was at **Downpatrick**), the dominant force in this area. Others of his sons, Maine, Conall Cremthainne, and Fiachu—the 'Southern Uí Néill'—swept down into the midlands, wresting Brega and Mide from the Laigin. Overlordships were also established closer to the ancestral base at Cruachu, by Niall's brothers Brión and Fiachra west of the Shannon—the Uí Briúin and the Uí Fiachrach respectively.

The story of the Laigin Fifth is also one of contraction and reordering, details of which are contained in regnal poems and the genealogies of seventeen Leinster tribes. All but a handful of these tribes lay claim to being of true Laiginian stock, tracing common ancestry to one Sétna Síthbacc, descendant of Labraid Loinsigsech, mythological king of the Laigin who is said to have led them from Gaul into Ireland, destroying Dinn Ríg, stronghold of Cobthach, king of Brega. Shared ancestry such as this is a common expediency of Irish medieval genealogists and is of dubious historical and chronological value. Nonetheless, relics of former glory days, when Laigin territories encompassed the whole of the midlands (including **Tara**) and stretched into Connacht, are preserved in a thread of connections maintained by key Laiginian monasteries across the midlands bogs to the Shannon basin and on an ogam stone in Painestown, Co. Meath, 11 km north–east of **Tara**, which commemorates *MAQI CAIRATINI AVI INEQAGLASI* ('Mac Cairthinn grandson of Enechglass'), once king of **Tara**. As we encounter the Laigin in the later 5th century the political reordering has acted like a centrifuge, dispelling successive leading tribes to the periphery of the territory. The Uí Garrchon of the Dál Messin Corb, 5th century kings of the Laigin and defenders of the north-western frontier against the Southern Uí Néill, were marginalized to the corridor between the mountains and the coast of south Wicklow. A similar fate awaited their 6th-century successors, among them the Uí Bairrche, Uí Enechglaiss, Uí Failge (from whom the Uí Néill wrested the plain of Mide and with it, significantly, **Tara**), and Uí Máil who were in turn subjugated by the Uí Dúnlainge and Uí Cheinnselaig during the 8th century. The Dál Cairpre Arad, cousins of the Uí Garrchon, suffered a similar decline in fortune, finding themselves subject tribes of the kings of Mumu who annexed their lands in Limerick and Tipperary. A cursory glance at the relevant Irish telephone directories shows how many of these tribal names, now surnames (e.g. Kinsella), are still concentrated in these areas and serves to explain why so many Irish families claim descent from kingship.

Comparatively little is known of the fragmentation of the Fifth of Mumu. Here, in the 6th century, arose the Eóganachta, a hegemony of dynastic families tracing common descent from a legendary Eógan Már, grandson of Mug Nuadat. Their origin tales suggest an ancestral home around Cnoc Áine (Knockainey), Co. Limerick, but it was the Eóganachta Chaisil who secured the most famous stronghold, the spectacular Rock of **Cashel**—proclaimed, at least, as seat of the high-kings of Munster. Alongside the Eóganachta, and enjoying unprecedented independence, were the Múscraige, the Osraige (bordering the Laigin), the Éli in the north, and the Déisi and Uí Liatháin in the south-east, an area corresponding to modern-day Waterford and south-east Cork. The

Déisi were a vassal tribe, mercenaries whose military prowess doubtless contributed to the success of the Eóganachta. It is in their territories and, further west, in the territory of the Corcu Duibne on the Dingle and Iveragh peninsulas of Kerry, that we find the greatest concentrations of ogam stones. Sometime during the 5th century the Déisi, possibly accompanied by their neighbours the Uí Liatháin, established a kingdom in southern Wales (modern-day Dyfed), an area they may formerly have visited as raiders, where their story is taken up not by history or archaeology but by palaeography, for here is found a unique group of ogam stones, some bilingual, comprising inscriptions in both Latin and Irish, containing the names of Irish leaders, including Votecorigas (Goutepir) whose exploits as 'protectoris' appear to have included adultery, incest, and murder!

The impact of Christianity

Given the level of social turmoil during the 5th and earlier 6th centuries, the survival of Christianity is no small miracle in itself and can be credited to the political astuteness of early church leaders, their pragmatism and doggedness. The 5th-century Palladian/Patrician church in Ireland appears to have followed the diocesan system of bishops, priests, and deacons, adopted in the Roman provinces where Christianity was a predominantly urban religion. The names of a number of 5th-century saints and bishops, both foreigners and Irish, come down to us and some may be linked to specific sites. Churches were founded by Secundinus at Dunshaughlin, Co. Meath, Auxilius at Kilashee, Co. Kildare, Iserninus at Kilcullen, Co. Kildare, Declan at **Ardmore**, Co. Waterford, and Ailbe at Emly, Co. Tipperary. Some of these were located, probably deliberately, close to the major pagan centres. Thus Dunshaughlin is close to **Tara** and Kilashee close to Dún Ailinne. Overshadowing them all, of course, is the figure of St Patrick. Paradoxically, probably the most nebulous and enigmatic of the early church founders, Patrick may well have been a slave in Ireland at the time of the Palladian mission, but when he returned as a churchman his mission was not to the south, where the others had operated, but to the north, where he is indelibly associated with **Armagh**, a religious counterpoint to Emain Macha. Through the 4th century, however, developments took place in church organization in the eastern Mediterranean that would soon add a new dynamism to the fledgling Irish Christian Church. The monastic regime, based on communal asceticism and isolation, spread westwards, arriving in Gaul with the foundation of monasteries by St Martin at Marmoutier and Ligugé near Poitiers, c. AD 375, by Honoratus at Lerins, and John Cassian further south. Much faith has been placed in the theory that the absence of towns in 5th- and 6th-century Ireland stunted the growth of the Irish diocesan Church, which was dependent on such environments for its survival, but presented no obstacle to the monastic orders who positively thrived in the rural Irish countryside. Recent historical analysis maintains a less pedantic definition of the early diocesan Church and has demonstrated the continued existence and importance of bishops throughout the early medieval period, emphasizing, moreover, the fact that Palladius and his colleagues came from a Gaul where monasticism was already well established.

The Church is likely to have played an important role in the 6th-century consolidation of Irish agriculture, climaxing around AD 600. A measure of the strength of the new economy was its ability to survive three major crises, the first centring around 540 when the northern hemisphere was plunged into a nine-year winter following a major volcanic eruption in 536. At the same time, coincidentally or otherwise, 'Justinian's Plague' (so called because it was first reported in Constantinople) swept across Europe, striking Ireland in 544–5. By 550 the crisis had passed and, as attested by a sudden increase in the occurrence of archaeological oak timbers, a major building programme, detectable across Europe, was set in motion. A second plague struck between 664 and 668 only to return in 698. The effect was devastating as whole monastic communities were wiped out. It was around this time that ringforts began to appear in abundance on the Irish landscape. The ringfort, an enclosed farmstead, is the most common Irish monument type. With a little over 45,000 recorded examples, the ringfort was the dominant rural settlement type until at least the coming of the English.

Early medieval settlement and society

There have been three formative phases in the ebb and flow of research into ringforts over the last sixty years or so. Seminal excavations during the 1940s at sites such as Garranes, Ballycatteen, and Garryduff (all in Co. Cork), Carraig Aille and Cush, Co. Limerick, and at Letterkeen, Co. Mayo, suggested general cultural, functional, and chronological homogeneity, conclusions that had the effect of temporarily halting, rather than inspiring, further research. Though far less numerous, excavations of cashels, e.g. **Leacanabuaile**, Co. Kerry, **Cahercommaun**, Co. Clare, and **Drumena**, Co. Down, indicated that they too were contemporary, the stone equivalents of the earthen ringfort or rath. Dating was based solely on analysis of the artefact assemblages. The next major phase of archaeological activity surrounded the excavation, during the 1970s and early 1980s, of three raised raths at Gransha and Rathmullan in Co. Down, and Deer Park Farms, Co. Antrim, and a ringfort at Killyliss, Co. Tyrone. These excavations produced a suite of radiocarbon and dendrochronological dates which, when added to dates returned from other sites, suggest that the most intensive period of ringfort construction was between AD 600 and 900. Arguing from this restricted chronological range to the likely contemporaneity of many of the surviving ringforts, Matthew Stout has recently postulated that their present distribution preserves more or less intact the settlement pattern of early medieval Ireland, where rigid hierarchies of social rank were maintained by force of law. According to Stout, patterns in ringfort distribution and the size of associated land holdings adhere closely to the directives contained in medieval law tracts and the late 7th-century *Críth Gablach*, which itemize in great detail the material possessions appropriate to the different social grades, the species and gender profile of their livestock holdings, the size of their farms, the number of ramparts encircling their ringfort, what sort of houses they should live in, and the correct number and rank of clients. That the laws were not simply an intellectual abstraction is attested at Deer Park Farms where superbly preserved buildings, dating from around AD 700, correlate closely in form, layout, and size to the figure-of-eight, wattled houses, outbuildings, and pens accredited in *Críth Gablach* to the *mruigfer* or 'strong farmer', the highest grade of free landowner. Here, in waterlogged deposits, were uncovered, at one level, no fewer than three contemporary circular wicker huts, two of which were of figure-of-eight design, consisting of a smaller room (about 5 m diameter) attached to the rear of a larger one (about 7 m diameter). The houses were all double walled for insulation (with grass) and rigidity, the collapsed wall of one of them measuring more than 2.5 m in height.

But Deer Park Farms is unique among ringforts for its preservation of organic remains. Normally on these dryland sites buildings survive only as postholes or wall footings, bone assemblages are severely compromised, and leather and plant remains are well-nigh non-existent. Assemblages thus typically consist of durables such as corroded ironwork, bronzes, glass beads, crucibles, whetstones and querns, etc. Pottery is rare for, remarkably, Ireland was virtually aceramic during this period. Apart from coarse, tub-shaped Souterrain Ware found only in the north-east of the island, the three other forms of pottery were imported. Wine, and possibly also olive oil, was imported from the eastern Mediterranean in large amphorae, probably via entrepôts in Cornwall (possibly Tintagel), along with fine, red slip bowls from western Turkey, both types found predominantly at ecclesiastical sites. More common on secular sites is E ware, a buff-coloured domestic ceramic of suspected French origin. These imported pots are important for dating purposes.

The picture is balanced somewhat by the evidence from wetland settlements. The term 'crannóg' has traditionally been applied to man-made, palisaded living platforms that date from the early medieval period. As we have seen, however, there is a considerable history of exploitation of and settlement on Irish wetlands and so the distinction between these and living platforms of prehistoric date is becoming increasingly difficult to apply in the field. In Connacht and west Ulster, for instance, crannógs can take the form of stone platforms (some quite small), wholly or partially man-made. They resemble the crannógs of Highland Scotland, many of which date from the later Bronze Age. A number of such sites were excavated around the shore of Lough Gara, Co. Sligo, where the evidence was indicative of repetitive usage over extremely long periods from at least the later Bronze Age to the medieval period. Apart from these sites, the Irish excavation record is biased in favour of crannógs of early medieval date from the midlands, following the excavation of three such sites in the 1930s by the Harvard Archaeological Mission. Midlands crannógs are quite uniform: they are more or less circular (30 m to 40 m in diameter) and, as far as we know, are always surrounded by a palisade or stockade of wooden posts. Their construction involved the deposition of vast amounts of brushwood and peat, more than is usually found on prehistoric sites, and comparatively little stone. Among those excavated by the Harvard team was Lagore crannóg. Within shouting distance of the important monastic site of Dunshaughlin, Lagore was the chief royal residence of the Uí Néill kings of southern Brega and is arguably the single richest site of this period. An equally impressive and possibly better preserved crannóg is currently under excavation at Moynagh Lough, just below the village of Nobber in north-central Meath. It too is a royal site. In the centre stood a double-walled circular wattle house which at 11.2 m in diameter is the largest house of the period.

Apart from fine brooches and dress-pins, the former an acknowledged symbol of high office, the archaeological value of these sites lies in the survival of more mundane organic materials and very delicate metalwork: the lathe-turned wooden bowls and stave-built buckets and churns, wool and silk textiles, bronze needles, leather moccasins, fine-toothed bone combs, parallelepiped dice, and beautifully crafted pegged gaming pieces. These inform us of daily routine and pastimes and also of the range of crafts, lowliest among which was the comb-maker, lampooned as one who could race a dog for a bone, straighten the horn of a ram with his breath (without fire), and chant on a dunghill to summon to the top what there was below in the way of antlers, bones, and horns! Almost all of the excavated sites have produced extensive evidence of fine metalwork, a craft that was doubtless controlled by the wealthiest families. Thus, far from being sidelined on the boggy periphery of early medieval Ireland, crannógs, particularly the midlands sites, were home to some of the most influential people in society. Indeed, only the most wealthy could have tolerated the inconvenience of life on a crannóg, which, separated from the farmlands, was, more so than any other type of settlement, reliant on the institution of clientship.

An ingenious system of loans and repayments, involving grants of stock in return for rent and services, clientship maintained the social hierarchy of early medieval Ireland, whilst at the same time allowing for just the right amount of scope for personal advancement. Grants were determined by the rank of both the grantor (lord) and the client and on the basis of the number of lords to whom a client was already indebted. Two types of client are distinguished in the law tracts, free and base. Free clientship (*sóerchéile*) was the more desirable form of contract because it involved no surrender of independence on the part of the client and either party could terminate the contract without penalty. However, it was also more taxing. For example, a free client who received a grant of three milch cows paid an annual rent of one milch cow, or its equivalent, for six years and in the seventh and final year returned the same number of cows as in the original grant. Free clients appear also to have been obliged to provide labour to their lord, two labourers every third year for each milch cow given in the original grant. Base clientship (*dóerchéile*) was probably more common. It too involved a grant of stock, and sometimes land, in return for which the client paid an annual food-rent proportional to the size of the grant as well as providing manual labour around the lord's house, at harvest time, and in the construction of the ramparts around his ringfort. Clearly, then, the scale and numbers of banks—sometimes referred to as the ramparts of vassalage—surrounding a ringfort were a direct indication of the wealth of the lord. The lord also purchased his base client's 'honour-price' and this entitled him to a share in any compensation paid to the client in the event of his being injured by a third party. In return, the base client enjoyed the protection of the lord.

It seems that most contracts operated within the *túath* or tribe, of which there were up to 150 at any given moment in time. At the head of each *túath* was a king. Thus, the tribal lands constituted independent territorial units, petty kingdoms beyond the borders of which ordinary freemen forfeited their normal legal rights: only a handful of learned men (*sóernemed*), poets and clerics, travelled freely. Occasionally a number of *túatha* were ruled over by one king, a *rí túaithe* who commanded an honour-price of eight cumals, which by the 7th century was the equivalent of twenty-four milch cows. Such a system—and we can really only touch upon it here—was clearly designed around these hierarchical rural economies, where the two most valuable commodities were cows and land. Land was divided into units called cumals, the exact size of which is unknown. The value of a cumal was estimated in terms of cows, then of similar size and shape to the diminutive Kerry cow, the best land being worth twenty-four milch cows per cumal, the worst only eight dry cows. Ownership and division of land were, naturally, issues of the utmost importance and are dealt with at length in the law tracts. When it came to questions of ownership, inheritance, farming, and protection the basic legal unit was the close kin group or *derbfine*, i.e. descendants of a common great-grandfather. Most land was *fintiu* 'kin-land', held in common by the tribe and divided among the heirs according to their social rank, the *ócaire* or small farmer receiving land worth seven cumals, the *bóaire* or strong farmer inheriting land worth fourteen cumals. The kin group had a say in the management of such allocated land, making sure that it was properly farmed, that the fences were maintained, and, above all, that it was not sold outside the kin group without permission. This level of interest in common land is to be accounted for by the strain that partible inheritance inevitably placed on each *túath* to provide sufficient land to maintain the legal status of its members. Land could also be held in private ownership having been purchased with surpluses accruing from the farming of inherited land or in exchange for specialist services.

From the outset, monastic founders were dependent on grants of land from the laity and so often found themselves initially on rather marginal ground. However, by adhering to the principle that heirs to the office of abbot were to be sought among the family of the founding saint, or, if that was not possible, from among the family of the man who gave the land to the monastery, the donation of land was made an attractive proposition since it offered a way of keeping land permanently in the family. Unlike *fintiu*, monastic lands were not redistributed following the death of the abbot. It was to the advantage, therefore, of the leading families to provide both land and abbot who was thus often of royal descent. Moreover, through the establishment of daughter monasteries in other territories, the Church could acquire lands beyond the confines of the original *túath*, and this led to the emergence of *paruchia* or monastic confederations ruled over by the abbot of the primary monastery. These were powerful men, occasionally kings, who could command the honour-price of a *rí ruirech* (provincial king), fourteen cumals. One such person was Colmcille (Columba: 'little dove').

In form and layout, Irish monasteries of the period combined both Mediterranean and indigenous elements and are identifiable in the field as large circular enclosures (*termon*) defined by a bank or wall. Some of the larger monasteries such as **Nendrum**, **Armagh**, and **Kells** had three widely spaced concentric enclosures (in the case of the latter two now preserved in the modern street layout) and these divided the monastery into three distinct areas of increasing sanctity, the *sanctus, sanctior*, and *sanctissimus*. The interior of smaller enclosures, such as Reask, Co. Kerry, has a diagonal wall running across the enclosure and this may have fulfilled a similar function. The most important building was the church. In larger sites this is centrally placed, at the smaller sites it is often to one side. While only stone examples survive today, both history and archaeology attest to the former existence of wooden churches which, during the 5th to 7th centuries, may have been the norm. Surviving examples are usually very simple, lacking in any diagnostic architectural features. It would be naive, however, to equate extreme simplicity with earliness of date, though given the durability of stone some specimens

▲ **Fig. 4.** Kiltiernan, Co. Galway: early medieval monastic enclosure (photo: Conor Newman and Eamonn O'Donoghue)

are likely to be very old indeed. Furthermore, it has been suggested that certain features, such as *antae* (i.e. where the side walls project beyond the gables creating a sort of shallow canopy) and inclined door jambs, are a throwback to the design and joinery of wooden buildings. *Clochán* or beehive-style construction was used in the building of both churches and domestic quarters, typically small circular buildings hugging the periphery of the enclosure.

The cemetery is often right beside the church and is usually demarcated by a bank wall or sometimes slabs set on edge. The burial rite consisted of supine inhumation, orientated east–west, head to the west, and burials, apart from the occasional shroud-pin, are almost always unaccompanied. The fact that churches are frequently found to overlie earlier burials suggests that many graves remained unmarked (or ended up unmarked if originally marked with a wooden cross). Others were proclaimed by cross-inscribed slabs—up to four per grave—and these occur in a multitude of designs from simple linear crosses to complex interlaced forms, probably inspired by the interlace crosses of early medieval Italy. Cross-inscribed slabs were also used to mark the stations and sometimes also the *termon* of the monastery and other important places associated with it such as holy wells. The *termon* could also be marked with a bullaun stone, i.e. a stone with a hollow in it. Many cross-slabs bear commemorative inscriptions, the finest collection of which is preserved at **Clonmacnoise**, Co. Offaly, beginning with the words *ór do*, meaning 'a prayer for . . .'. At the other end of the sculptural range are the high crosses (popularly, though somewhat erroneously, known as Celtic crosses), which rank among the most impressive of the Irish field monuments. Henri's 1960s suggestion of a Darwinian-style evolution of the free-standing high cross from cross-slabs has been overturned in favour of an origin among processional crosses and an iconographical formula for the Resurrection assembled from various Christian monuments in Jerusalem, such as the Crux Gemata and the Aedicule of the Anastasis. Features of processional crosses encased in precious metal plates appear on many of the earlier high crosses, including the decorative rivet heads (bosses) and the C-shaped edgings which would have held the plates in place. The dating of high crosses is largely art-historical and typological, though some of the later crosses can be dated by inscription. In the decoration of earlier crosses, such as those at Ahenny dating from the 8th century, abstract decoration predominates, with figural scenes being confined to the base-stone. Through time, figural scenes begin to appear with greater frequency on the shaft of the crosses until, by the 10th century, the two broad faces of the shaft are given over to biblical scenes from the Old and New Testaments.

From the 7th century onwards the Church became the major patron of the arts in Ireland, as witnessed not only as we have seen in stone sculpture, but also in fine metalwork and illuminated manuscripts. In addition to classical influences, the establishment of monasteries with important scriptoria in parts of Germanic Europe gave rise to a unique blend of art styles known as Insular Art. The evolution of the style can be traced through the Book of Durrow (mid-7th century) and the Book of Lindisfarne (early 8th century) culminating in the magnificent Book of Kells (late 8th/early 9th century). No less awe-inspiring is the surviving altar ware of this Golden Age, the Ardagh and Derrynaflan chalices and the unsurpassed artistic and technical excellence of the Derrynaflan paten.

The Viking period

At the end of the 8th century Ireland, like much of north-western Europe, experienced a new phenomenon in sudden attacks by seaborne raiders from Scandinavia. Although not as large or as devastating as elsewhere, in many ways the Viking onslaught had a particularly profound effect on Ireland—precisely because it was a relatively closed society with little exposure to the outside world, and especially to foreign aggression. This effect was not specifically military, but rather social, economic, and political. It is one of many paradoxes in the Viking experience in Ireland that they had such a profound influence on the development of Irish society, despite being far less successful in military terms than elsewhere. Unlike in France, England, and Scotland, for instance, the Vikings never conquered a substantial part of Ireland, and while the full extent of Viking settlement in Ireland is still uncertain, it seems clear that it never amounted to more than a number of discrete and relatively small coastal kingdoms. These Vikings were, in Ireland, almost entirely of Norwegian background, although there has been some debate about whether they came directly from Norway or indirectly, via Norse settlements in Scotland.

The earliest recorded raid in Ireland was in 795, on **Rathlin Island**, off the north coast of Co. Antrim. Historians see subsequent Viking activity in Ireland as falling into a number of broad phases, with the first forty years characterized by widely scattered small-scale raids, largely on coastal targets. Monastic sites were the objects of particular attention almost from the outset, as the Vikings quickly realized that these—especially the larger sites such as **Armagh**, **Clonmacnoise**, **Glendalough**, and **Kildare**—were the major foci of wealth and population in an island with few other nucleated settlements. From the late 830s a new phase of more large-scale raiding began, penetrating the interior of the island and accompanied by the building of defensive fortifications, referred to in the Irish annals as *longphoirt* (literally, 'ship forts'). The erection of the first of these is recorded in 841, at Linn Dúachaill and Duiblinn, two sites whose subsequent history forms a stark contrast. Linn Dúachaill rapidly disappears from history and even its location can only be tentatively identified as an earthwork overlooking the river Glyde at Annagassan, Co. Louth. Duiblinn, on the other hand, developed into the most important Scandinavian town in Ireland and ultimately into modern Ireland's largest city. Viking raids lost momentum in the later 9th century, partly due to a more aggressive and organized Irish response and also, perhaps, because of new opportunities in England,

Scotland, and especially in Iceland. In 902 **Dublin** was destroyed by the surrounding Irish kingdoms and this is taken to mark the end of the second phase of Viking activity in Ireland.

The archaeological evidence for the first century of Viking activity in Ireland is meagre. The only possible settlements are a number of suggested *longphort* sites which have recently been identified in the field. Some tentative conclusions have been drawn about their morphology and siting, but the fact that no such site (with the exception of **Dublin**) has been excavated is a serious hindrance to useful discussion. Burials are often seen as the best indicator of the distribution of Viking settlement (or at least activity) in Ireland, but even the burial record is quite poor, outside of **Dublin**. **Dublin** has yielded a considerable number of Viking burials, probably of 9th-century date—notably the cemeteries at Kilmainham and Islandbridge—but practically all of these are old finds which were never scientifically excavated. Some idea of the extent of early Viking activity in Ireland can be gleaned from the combined distribution of Viking burials and artefacts (mainly hoards of silver ornaments and coins), which show definite concentrations in the east midlands, the north–east, and the Shannon estuary.

The effects of the Viking raids on Irish society are still being debated, but older views of an entirely negative impact have generally given way to more sanguine assessments. It is impossible to deny that the Vikings killed, raided, and plundered—the contemporary Irish annals are full of accounts of this—but some scholars argue that such violence was not unprecedented. They also question the argument that the Viking attacks ended the 'Golden Age' of the Irish Church, with its marvellous artistic achievements. It seems clear that literature and metalwork of high quality were still being produced by the churches, even in the 9th century. The great series of high crosses, notably the scripture crosses such as those at **Clonmacnoise**, **Monasterboice**, and **Kells**, also began to be produced during the 9th century, although some have argued that stone crosses were being carved at this date precisely because they were of no value to the Vikings and thus likely to be left alone. What is beyond dispute is that the Vikings had a profound, if largely unintentional, impact on the politics and economy of early medieval Ireland. The need to defend their kingdoms from Viking aggression forced Irish kings to improve their military organization and tactics, and to adopt better weaponry. The international activities of the Vikings also introduced new wealth into Ireland, most clearly seen in the occurrence of large quantities of silver from about the middle of the 9th century onwards. A significant part of this new wealth found its way into the hands of the greater Irish kings, either through trade or tribute. The increased military and economic power of these kings was used not just to repel the Vikings, but also to dominate less powerful neighbours. It is no coincidence that succeeding centuries saw the growing ascendancy of a small number of powerful provincial kingships, which controlled large areas, including the Viking settlements.

The Irish Church, too, was witnessing significant changes, at least as far as the surviving buildings—churches and round towers—are concerned. Almost certainly the building of stone churches first became widespread during this period, although this is a highly controversial area among scholars; a church such as **Gallarus**, Co. Kerry, for instance, has been dated as early as the 8th century and as late as the 12th. The early dating of **Gallarus** and similar churches has been criticized for the unsubstantiated assumption that their simplicity of form and construction indicates an early date. This is probably fair criticism, but many modern scholars are guilty of an equally unfounded assumption, that these churches must be late—probably 12th century—in date because they are located in (to modern eyes) remote parts of the south-west. Once again, much of the difficulty arises from the scarcity of properly excavated sites, but an additional problem in this case is that many stone churches, even when excavated, yield little conclusive evidence of their date. The extreme simplicity of most early Irish stone churches leaves little for architectural historians to get their teeth into, and thus without hard archaeological evidence of date we are all too easily left in the kind of stalemate exemplified by the debate over **Gallarus**.

Many excavated sites have yielded evidence for early wooden churches which were later replaced by stone buildings, but exactly when this happened is rarely certain. Some stone churches display features best explained as skeuomorphic hangovers from timber construction. These include *antae*, thought to mimic the appearance of cruck construction in a timber church, and gable finials that seem to imitate the crossing of gable rafters on a wooden roof. The best examples of this are **St MacDara's** church, Co. Galway, and **Kilmalkedar**, Co. Kerry, where the antae are continued right up the gables to the apex of the stone roofs. Other examples can be found, for instance, at **Fore, Glendalough, Inchcleraun, Inishcaltra**, and Liathmore. Here too, however, there is debate over whether such features necessarily indicate an early date.

Many modern scholars are probably too cautious about accepting pre-12th-century dates for surviving churches. Historical sources make it clear that stone churches were in existence not later than the 8th century on at least some sites, notably **Duleek** and **Armagh**, although no visible traces of these churches remain. Radiocarbon dates (from the mortar) suggest a 9th-century date for the church ('St Columb's House') at **Kells** and the possibility of an 8th-century date for a church at **Inishmurray**, Co. Sligo. Opinions are still divided over the level of confidence to be placed in such results, but other evidence is less open to doubt. The cathedral at **Clonmacnoise** almost certainly represents the substantial remains of the church built by the high-king,

Flann Sinna, in 909, while even at the remote western hermitage of High Island, excavation has indicated that the surviving stone church was built not later than the 10th century. The cathedral at **Clonmacnoise** is not only the earliest, but the largest surviving early medieval church in Ireland, and if a date at the beginning of the 10th century is accepted for it there is no reason why many other churches might not be similarly early.

The most distinctive building of the early Irish church is the round tower, a tall, narrow, free-standing tower designed primarily as a bell-tower and status symbol and not, as popular opinion has it, as a place of refuge from Viking raiders. The bells used in these towers were hand-bells, presumably rung through the openings at the top of the tower, rather than being hung within the tower as in later centuries. Round towers are not as ubiquitous as churches—only sixty-five examples are known from surviving remains, while there is evidence for the former existence of towers in about another twenty-five locations. The surviving towers share a remarkably consistent range of features: externally, the walls are slightly battered (i.e. inclined inwards rather than truly vertical) as they rise to a conical cap of corbelled stone. Internally, the tower is usually divided into a number of storeys by means of offsets in the wall. Both the floors themselves and whatever ladders or stairs were used to ascend the tower were presumably of wood and do not survive (modern replacements are present in many towers, including **Devenish, Kildare, Kilkenny,** and **Monasterboice**). Normally each storey is lit by a single window, apart from the top storey which has several (usually at least four) evenly spaced windows. A characteristic feature is the placing of the sole doorway above ground level, usually between 1.5 m and 4.5 m above ground, which is probably the main reason for the towers being considered as places of refuge. Security is the obvious explanation for the curious placing of the doorways, although it has also been suggested that the doorways may have been raised to avoid weakening the remark-ably shallow foundations of the towers. The most obvious feature of the towers, of course, is their height and here there is rather more diversity than in the other structural features. Most towers are now incomplete, but of those that are at least reasonably complete it appears that the typical height is 25 m to 35 m, although some may never have been more than 15 m high.

The origins and chronology of round towers has also been disputed and, as with churches, there is a dearth of hard dating evidence pro-duced by excavation. Older suggestions of a very early date (7th, or even 6th century) have little support today, and in general the debate tends to run along much the same lines as for the churches. A number of towers display Romanesque features, indicating a 12th-century date, while others (such as **Monasterboice**) can be dated to the 10th and 11th centuries by references in historical documents. As with the churches, it is likely that most round towers date to the 10th–12th centuries. There are two main schools of thought about their origins; one sees them as an indigenous Irish development, based on the corbelling technology used in traditional *clochán* structures, while the other sees them as based on round stair turrets or belfries built as part of 9th- and 10th-century churches in Carolingian Europe.

Alongside round towers, high crosses have become internationally recognized icons of early medieval Ireland. These tall stone crosses, with their characteristic ringed cross head, are found on many early church sites and can be either plain or decorated. They served a variety of functions—devotional, liturgical, ceremonial, and symbolic, as markers of the *termon* or area of sanctuary around a church, and even as focal points for the markets which grew up at many of the more important church sites. The apogee of the high cross tradition is the great series of 'scripture' crosses, that is crosses decorated with biblical scenes. A pattern has been recognized on many crosses where the east face tends to bear scenes from the Old Testament and the Book of Revelation, while the west face bears scenes from the New Testament, specifically the life of Christ. A number of these crosses can be dated reasonably closely by inscriptions which they carry. The earliest of these, at Kinnity, Co. Offaly, has been dated 846–62, while two of the great masterpieces of the series, Muiredach's cross at **Monasterboice** and the Cross of the Scriptures at Clonmacnoise, can be dated *c.*900–20. Most of the other scripture crosses probably date to the period from 850 to 950, but there is less certainty about the date of other crosses, especially the relatively large number of plain, undecorated crosses. The smaller group of crosses decorated with abstract or geometric ornament, such as those at **Ahenny** and Kilkieran, are also more difficult to date but it is likely that they are, on the whole, earlier than the scripture crosses—possibly of the 8th century. They also tell us something about the origins of the high crosses as they are, quite clearly, stone versions of decorated metal crosses.

Despite a shortage of excavated evidence, analysis of surviving remains on church sites has revealed certain patterns in the layout of the structural elements within the monastic enclosures. The enclosures themselves are usually of earthen bank and fosse construction, although drystone walling is also used, and tend to be roughly circular, topography permitting. The maximum diameters can vary between 200 m and 600 m; where an inner enclosure is present it tends to be between 100 m and 200 m in diameter. The main ecclesiastical structures—churches, round towers, high crosses, or cross-slabs—are contained within the inner enclosure, with the principal church usually fairly centrally located. A feature of many Irish sites is the proliferation of church buildings; at **Clonmacnoise** there are visible remains of at least eight churches and evidence for at least four more, while at

Glendalough, too, there are the remains of at least eight churches. Churches are invariably aligned east–west, with the main entrance at the west end. Where a round tower is present, it is generally located to the west, south-west, or north-west of the principal church, with its doorway facing the doorway of the church, and on or near the perimeter of the inner enclosure. Crosses, too, tend to be located on or near the perimeter of the enclosure, often at cardinal points. The main entrance to the enclosure seems generally to have been on the east, and this probably explains the frequent evidence for the existence of a market place on the eastern side, located either within or just outside the outer enclosure and often associated with an eastern cross (which may well have been primarily associated with the entrance). It is also noticeable that subsequent urban development on such sites is often focused on the area east of the original monastic enclosure.

Hiberno-Norse Ireland

Viking fleets returned to Ireland after 914, apparently in greater strength than previously. Settlements were established or re-established at **Dublin, Waterford, Limerick, Cork**, Wexford, and probably at other locations also, and these developed fairly rapidly from fortified bases for raiding and trading into the first true towns in Ireland. From the later 10th century they were effectively absorbed into the Irish political system, generally being controlled by one or other of the greater provincial kings—which increased their economic and cultural impact within Ireland. The process and extent of cultural (and ethnic) assimilation is difficult to measure, but it is clear that the Viking towns of the 10th–12th centuries were neither wholly Scandinavian nor wholly Irish; for this reason their culture is usually described as 'Hiberno-Norse'. Archaeological excavation in **Dublin**, in particular, has revealed an extraordinary quality of evidence that has revolutionized our understanding of these settlements. They quickly developed into well-planned urban centres with an ordered regularity in the layout of property plots and streets, and a set range of building types which was used with remarkable consistency. A wide range of trades and crafts was pursued, including fine craftsmanship in metals, wood, bone, and stone which borrowed from both Scandinavian and Irish artistic traditions, eventually fusing the two into a distinctive regional style. **Dublin** was primarily a trading town, and evidence has been recovered for widespread trading contacts, stretching from the Arctic to the Mediterranean. With the exception of **Waterford** (at a slightly later date), the other Hiberno-Norse towns have so far not produced comparable archaeological evidence but there is little doubt that they were similar to **Dublin** both in form and economy; it is likely, however, that **Dublin** was always the wealthiest and most important of these towns.

One difficulty in assessing the relative importance of the Hiberno-Norse towns in Ireland lies in the fact that so few other sites of comparable date have been excavated. Only a handful of sites, including ringforts such as **Beal Boru**, Co. Clare, and Ballynarry and Rathmullan, Co. Down, and the crannóg of Ballinderry, Co. Westmeath, provide evidence for the continued use of the major traditional settlement types. Ballinderry produced a rich 10th- and 11th-century artefactual assemblage, in many respects so similar to contemporary material from **Dublin** that one might be tempted to suggest its occupants were themselves Hiberno-Norse. More likely, however, it illustrates the extent to which the wealthier Irish families and the Hiberno-Norse were coming to share a largely common material culture. Much the same might be said of the extensive, apparently undefended settlement on the great mound at **Knowth**, Co. Meath, a royal site probably of the 10th to 12th centuries which yielded the stone foundations of at least nine rectangular houses and several souterrains. **Knowth** may represent something new in Irish settlement patterns—a move away from dispersed, single dwellings to more nucleated settlements. Until more sites of this period are excavated, however, it will not be possible fully to understand either **Knowth**, or the role and impact of the Hiberno-Norse towns in their Irish context.

The impact of the Vikings extended far beyond the towns, however. Large quantities of silver were clearly in circulation from the late 9th century onwards, indicated in the archaeological record by many hoards of coins and ornaments, and by the production of new ornament types in silver (mainly brooches and armrings). Much of this wealth originated in the Viking towns, but it clearly did not stay there. In fact it provided the financial base for new developments in many areas of Irish society, particularly in the Church and among the great provincial overkings. The 11th and 12th centuries were a period of fundamental change in Ireland, as political power was increasingly concentrated among a few royal dynasties who not only dominated the smaller kingdoms but began to challenge each other for overall control of the island as a whole. To support their military ambitions kings seem to have fostered some fundamental changes in social organization that have been described—not without reason—as the effective feudalization of Irish society. It has also been suggested that these social changes may be behind one of the most significant features of medieval Ireland: the apparent demise of the ringfort. By far the most common field monument in the Irish landscape, ringforts are the classic settlement form of early medieval Ireland, but evidence for construction of ringforts is extremely rare by the 11th century and completely lacking thereafter. Radical changes were also taking place in the Church, especially in the 12th century and largely under the patronage of the great provincial kings. The Hiberno-Norse towns were vital catalysts in these changes.

Their economic and military resources became essential assets for the provincial kings in their quest for hegemony, and their wide trading networks were hugely important in opening Ireland up to outside influences and contacts. **Dublin, Waterford,** and the other towns had increasingly close contacts with England in the 11th and 12th centuries, and the English model of a unitary state with a centralized monarchy may well have inspired the greater Irish kings in their pursuit of overall dominion—the so-called 'high-kingship' of Ireland.

The greatest exponent of the new realpolitik (and one of the earliest), was Brian *Borumha* (Ború). Originally a relatively minor mid-western king, he exploited the new possibilities to achieve unchallenged pre-eminence by the beginning of the 11th century—helped by his control of **Limerick** and later of **Waterford** and **Dublin**. Brian was, perhaps, the closest to an effective ruler of the entire island that medieval Ireland ever knew, but the cost of his final, Pyrrhic victory at Clontarf in 1014 (in which he died) meant that his heirs were unable to maintain his dominant position. For most of the 11th and 12th centuries they fought for dominance along with the other provincial kings. This struggle for dominance involved radically new developments in military organization and strategy, including the possible beginnings of castle construction. During the first half of the 12th century the Irish annals begin to use the terms *caistel* and *caislén*, translatable as 'castle', to describe fortifications erected by some of the great provincial kings, especially the Uí Conchobhair kings of Connacht. These are not easily traced in the modern landscape, however, and McNeill's recent assessment suggests that possible traces of such early castles can be discerned only at **Downpatrick**, Co. Down, and in excavations at the later castles of **Limerick** and **Dunamase**, Co. Laois.

The best surviving evidence for the changes of this period relates to the Church. The late 11th and 12th centuries saw a fundamental and thorough reform of the Church, the impulse for which came originally from within the Church itself, but which was powerfully supported by several of the great provincial kings. Many churchmen recognized that the Irish Church had become spiritually lax, largely because of political involvement and the attendant abuses such as hereditary lay abbacies. They saw the solution to these problems in terms of integrating Ireland more closely into the general European religious model, which was itself undergoing profound changes with the rise of new religious orders. The major Irish kings had their own reasons for supporting the reform movement, the main features of which were the establishment for the first time of a regular diocesan structure throughout the island and the introduction of continental monastic orders such as the Augustinians, Benedictines, and Cistercians.

Culturally, the reform was mirrored by renewed activity in many areas. There was a literary renaissance, based largely on vernacular texts

rather than Latin learning, and a revival in the production of illuminated manuscripts. A revival took place in the production of high crosses
which, together with the fine metalwork of the period, feature new
artistic expressions based on contemporary Scandinavian styles. The
12th-century crosses are quite different from those of the 9th and 10th
centuries. They tend to occur on sites which do not have earlier crosses,
and are largely confined to Munster and Connacht, which may well
reflect the dominance of the Uí Briain and Uí Conchobhair kings.
The characteristic ringed cross head is either played down or absent
altogether and the biblical scenes so characteristic of the earlier scripture
crosses are also absent. Instead, the iconography of the crosses is
dominated by two figures, the crucified Christ and an ecclesiastic (often
identifiable as a bishop), displayed either on opposite sides of the cross
or one above the other on the same side. Other decoration is largely
confined to panels of interlace based on an Irish version of the Scandinavian Urnes style. The apparent prominence of bishops is almost
certainly linked to the reform movement of the time and so, in a sense,
the crosses can be seen as part of the reform. Another characteristic of
this period was the enshrinement of relics of the early church founders,
including both corporeal relics and the quintessential symbols of the
Irish ecclesiastic, book, bell, and crosier. Major pieces of craftsmanship
were produced in the 11th and 12th centuries, including the shrines of
the *Cathach*, of St Patrick's bell, and of the Lismore and **Clonmacnoise**
crosiers, St Manchan's shrine, and the Cross of Cong. In contrast to the
stone crosses, the production of many of these reliquaries can be linked
to traditional centres such as **Kells, Armagh**, and **Clonmacnoise**, and
often involved the patronage of the great provincial kings. Like the
crosses, however, the metalwork displays a combination of traditional
artistic idioms and techniques with new influences, ultimately derived
from the Scandinavian Ringerike and Urnes art styles. The channel for
these new influences was clearly the Hiberno-Norse towns.

The architecture of the Church also shows changes and new influences. In the spirit of the age, the Irish Church looked to what
was happening in the rest of Europe, and in architecture this meant
Romanesque. From the early 12th century many Irish churches begin to
display features of the Romanesque architectural style. Most of these
churches (such as **Ardfert, Clonfert, Killaloe**, and **Roscrea**) are associated with the reform movement, in that they are the centres of the new
dioceses created as part of the reform. The most important Romanesque
building in Ireland—and generally accepted as probably the earliest—is
the church known as Cormac's Chapel at **Cashel**, dedicated in 1134.
Both English and continental inspirations have been claimed for the
Romanesque elements in this remarkable building, and their relative
importance is debated. It is indisputable, however, that these features
are applied to a building that is substantially traditional in plan, size, and

structure. Other Irish Romanesque buildings tend to be even more conservative, with the Romanesque influence confined to details such as
doorways, windows, and chancel arches. Nevertheless, even in this
limited expression Romanesque architecture clearly represents something new in Ireland and reflects a receptivity to contemporary
developments elsewhere. It has been suggested that one avenue for these
influences may have been the traffic in Irish monks to and from Irish
monasteries in Germany, the *Schottenkloster*. However, English contacts
are likely to have been more substantial and more important and here
again, the Hiberno-Norse towns may have been of central importance as
the gateways for these contacts.

A final development linked to the church reform movement was the
introduction of continental monastic orders. Some Augustinian communities seem to have been introduced from the late 1120s and many
Irish monasteries adopted the Augustinian or Benedictine rule, but the
major event in this process was the introduction of the first Cistercian

▼ **Fig. 5.** Killeshin church, Co. Laois: Romanesque doorway (photo: Conor
Newman)

community at **Mellifont** in 1142. The abbey of **Mellifont**, which was finally consecrated in 1157, was an even more revolutionary departure in the Irish landscape than Cormac's Chapel had been twenty years previously. The new abbey was laid out in the mid-12th century along standard Cistercian lines, the first appearance in Ireland of the European model of an abbey church (probably the largest church in Ireland at that time) with cloister to the south, surrounded on the other three sides by ranges of buildings. This highly structured plan became standard, not only for other Cistercian abbeys, but for most other monasteries subsequently established in medieval Ireland. Daughter houses of **Mellifont** were fairly quickly established in many parts of the country and were to introduce not only a new form of church life and organization but also, in time, a new architecture: Gothic. The first true Gothic building in Ireland was probably erected by the Cistercians at **Grey abbey** (Co. Down) in the 1190s, but elements of Gothic were being introduced even earlier. The influence of Cistercian architecture in Ireland was profound and has been detected in many other churches, ranging from the cathedral in **Limerick** to the parish churches of **Carrickfergus** and **Fethard**, to the Augustinian priory of **Ballintubber** (Co. Mayo).

The coming of the English

The English conquest of Ireland after 1170 is rightly seen as a defining moment in Irish cultural and political history, but recent research has tended to stress that it was not a bolt from the blue; rather, it was almost the inevitable outcome of increasingly close contact with England. The crucial role of the Hiberno-Norse towns in this process is also becoming clearer. Archaeological excavation in **Dublin** and **Waterford** has produced evidence for strong trading links with England in the 11th and early 12th centuries. From the mid-12th century these links become even stronger and focus increasingly on the Bristol area, which was to be the cockpit of the initial conquest. The towns had also aligned themselves with the English Church, rather than the Irish, when they became fully Christianized in the 11th century; most of the early bishops of **Dublin, Waterford**, and **Limerick** were consecrated in Canterbury. Several Irish provincial kings of the late 11th and 12th centuries had their own political contacts with England and, indeed, this was to be the immediate cause of the English conquest when Diarmait Mac Murchada, the deposed king of Leinster, turned to Henry II of England for help in recovering his kingdom in 1166. In a broader European context, the English conquest can be seen as a local expression of a widespread phenomenon of conquest and colonization, from rich centres out to more peripheral areas. This in turn was driven by a prolonged period of agricultural and economic expansion, coinciding with optimal climactic conditions and leading to rapid population growth over much of Europe from the mid-11th to mid-13th centuries.

Mac Murchada brought English forces to Ireland from 1167 to 1170, but the English conquest really begins in 1171, when Henry II invaded Ireland. Ironically, he seems to have been concerned not so much to conquer the Irish as to prevent his own vassal, Richard de Clare, earl of Strigoil—better known as Strongbow—from setting up an independent lordship in Ireland. Strongbow had inherited Mac Murchada's kingdom on the latter's death in 1171. Be that as it may, Henry's arrival initiated a thorough conquest of much of the island, although its progress was complex, haphazard, and ultimately incomplete. In addition to Strongbow's new lordship of Leinster in the east and south-east, a power vacuum in the once-great midland kingdom of Meath (modern Cos. Meath, Westmeath, Longford, and parts of Cos. Offaly, Cavan, and Louth) allowed a rapid English takeover. The new lordship of Meath was granted to Hugh de Lacy, who was to be the king's man and a counterbalance to Strongbow. In 1177 the kingdom of Ulaid (in effect modern Cos. Antrim and Down) on the north-east coast was captured in a largely private operation by John de Courcy, a Cumbrian baron with strong connections in north-west England and the north Irish Sea area. At much the same period the Hiberno-Norse town of **Cork** and an area around it were successfully captured, but an attempt to do the same in **Limerick** had to be abandoned. Further expansion in the south and south-west began in the late 1180s, helped by the death in 1194 of the powerful king of Thomond, Domhnall Mór Ó Briain. By the early 13th century much of the modern counties of Tipperary, Waterford, Limerick, and east Cork was being occupied. Thrusts into west Cork and north Kerry followed from c.1215, but those areas north and west of the river Shannon—almost half of the island—remained effectively unconquered for some time. In the 1230s and 1240s considerable parts of Cos. Galway, Roscommon, Mayo, and Sligo were occupied and in the 1250s an ultimately unsuccessful attempt was made to penetrate the heartland of the Ó Briain kingdom of Thomond in modern Co. Clare. Most of Co. Clare, along with much of west Cos. Galway and Mayo, was never effectively occupied. The same was true of a considerable part of west Cos. Cork and Kerry (the Mac Cárthaig kingdom) and of a vast area in the north, comprising most of Ulster and adjoining areas of Cos. Leitrim and Sligo.

The English colony in Ireland

Historians have documented in considerable detail the processes by which the new English lords occupied their lands and subdivided them among lesser tenants, who in turn established their manors and villages and settled them with colonists from Britain. More recently historical geographers and archaeologists have begun to examine the physical expressions of this process—castles, manors, towns, villages, and churches. Earthwork castles, particularly mottes, have been assumed to be the earliest form of English fortifications in Ireland and this is probably true, in broad terms. It is now clear, however, that Ireland's two finest stone castles, **Trim** and **Carrickfergus**, were under construction by 1180, well before most mottes. These are exceptional structures in many respects but the possibility that other stone castles were being built at this early date cannot be ruled out. There is also reason to believe that many mottes (especially in Ulster) may have been built by Irish, rather than English or Anglo-Irish lords. With few excavations (most of which are concentrated in Co. Down), study of Irish mottes has been largely survey based, focusing on the issues of form and distribution. Ireland has an unusually large proportion of mottes without baileys, and there have been several attempts to explain the significance of the presence or absence of baileys. In Leinster, it is suggested that relatively large mottes, especially those with baileys, may indicate manors of the major lords (the tenants-in-chief of the king) and of their principal tenants. Elsewhere, however, especially in the north-east, mottes with baileys seem to be located with great frequency on the supposed peripheries of lordships, suggesting a military function. Various attempts have been made to reconstruct the developing frontiers of lordships by linking together lines of mottes supposedly guarding the borders, but few convincing conclusions can be drawn.

One thing that is clear from the overall distribution of mottes is their scarcity in some areas known to have been intensively settled by the English, such as Cos. Cork and Limerick. This may be partly an issue of chronology—there is little evidence for motte-building after the early 13th century (**Roscrea** in 1213 being perhaps the latest recorded example), and 'blank' areas may have been settled mainly after this. It has also been suggested that these gaps may be filled by another English earthen fortification type, the ringwork. A long-running debate over the reality of the ringwork as a type has effectively been settled by the discovery of physical evidence for ringworks under stone castles such as **Trim** and **Kilkenny**. This overdue confirmation has led in some quarters to an overly optimistic reaction, with 'ringworks' being recognized in the field in large numbers and with absolute confidence. This may be an inevitable phase in the development of research, but greater caution might be called for, in view of the dearth of excavation and the difficulty of distinguishing ringworks (without excavation) from the earlier, and much more numerous, ringforts. To date it has not been possible to map the distribution of ringworks in Ireland, even in the most preliminary manner, and thus the relationship between ringworks and mottes cannot be established.

Large castles of stone, on the European model, are chronologically confined in Ireland mainly to the late 12th/13th centuries. It has recently been suggested that the earliest castles were built by the new English lords as confident statements of their new status in the conquered land, designed to impress, rather than primarily as defensive strongholds. Some castles of the later 13th/early 14th centuries show more evidence of a concern for defence and incorporate new developments in castle architecture, notably a move away from keeps and strong points within a castle, to an integrated system of curtain walls, flanking towers, and strong gatehouses providing overall strength. It has even been suggested that the royal castle of **Roscommon** may actually anticipate Edward I's more famous Welsh castles, such as Harlech, Conway, and Beaumaris, in this respect. Nevertheless a feature of most Irish castles, throughout the Middle Ages, is their relatively weak military aspect. On close examination even the most impressive castles, such as **Trim** and **Carrick-fergus**, often provide the appearance of great defensive strength more than the reality. This, however, probably reflects a fairly accurate risk assessment—given the nature of the Irish tradition of warfare, these castles were unlikely to face prolonged sieges by large armies. Warfare in medieval Ireland was generally small scale and highly mobile. The classic expression was the cattle raid, rather than the siege or pitched battle. Indeed, the few major sieges of English castles in Ireland were almost invariably undertaken by other English or Anglo-Irish armies, as part of some internal conflict. Gaelic lords rarely had any interest in such undertakings.

Recent years have seen prominence given to another 13th-century castle type, the hall house. These are relatively small, rectangular two-storey structures, usually with a defensive lower floor and a more open, hall-like upper floor. They are not very common, and occur mainly in the western half of the country rather than in the east. Many can best be interpreted as the defended manor houses of the first English lords, and it is a moot point whether they should properly be considered as castles at all. In many respects they are probably analogous to the far more numerous moated sites. These are enclosures, mainly rectangular, with external fosses designed to hold water from a nearby stream or spring. Excavation of a small number of sites has usually revealed evidence for a large house or hall internally. Moated sites are normally interpreted as the settlements of English or Anglo-Irish tenants of some substance, but there are suggestions that some may also have been built by the (Gaelic) Irish. They are distributed fairly widely over the island but especially densely in the south-east; by contrast they are largely absent along the western seaboard and, above all, in the north. Dating usually centres on the period from the mid-13th to early 14th centuries, and it has been suggested that (at least in the heavily colonized south-east) moated sites represent a secondary colonization of marginal lands. In other areas, notably the west midlands, which were not occupied by the English until the mid-13th century, the moated sites are presumably associated with the primary colonization.

At a level below the great lords in their castles and the minor lords in their manors, moated sites, and hall houses were the ordinary people, the farmers and labourers who worked the fields. It is clear that large numbers of English and Welsh settlers were brought to Ireland in the late 12th/13th centuries to populate the new manors, although many Irish were also incorporated into the system. Little work has been done on the villages and field systems which the English established to exploit the agricultural potential of their new lands. Ireland has its manorial villages and even classic deserted medieval villages, but there are suggestions that there were, in fact, relatively few villages and that settlement retained a dispersed pattern of pre-conquest origin. There are many obvious manorial centres, usually identified today by the ruins of a parish church and perhaps a motte, castle, or tower house. However, scholars disagree over whether these centres should automatically be seen as the last remnants of once-thriving villages. In the present state of knowledge it might be premature to argue strongly in either direction.

Markets were vital to the new landowners in realizing the value of their agricultural produce, and markets meant towns. Possibly the most remarkable achievement of the English conquest was the manner in which, within a century (c.1170–1270), a wide network of towns was established, which still forms the basis of Ireland's modern urban framework. On closer examination it is striking how many of these towns were located on pre-existing settlement sites. The most obvious example is the takeover of the 'Viking' port towns such as **Dublin, Waterford**, and **Limerick**. Many others were sited at monastic centres, such as **Ardfert, Cashel, Castledermot, Downpatrick, Duleek, Kells, Kildare, Kilkenny, Kilmallock, Kinsale, Roscrea**, and **Trim**. Less certain, but quite likely, is an association with earlier secular sites or strongholds; possible candidates include **Carrickfergus, Dunamase, Ferns**, and **Rindown**.

A large amount of development-driven archaeological excavation has taken place in Irish towns but, with the exception of **Dublin, Cork**, and **Waterford**, has yet to result in substantial published results. Unfortunately, for a complex variety of reasons, archaeological deposits of the 13th and later centuries rarely survive in such spectacular quality and quantity as for Hiberno-Norse **Dublin** and **Waterford**. Nevertheless, what is available from these towns has greatly amplified the historical record, particularly in relation to the industries and crafts pursued in the towns and to their trading contacts. Aside from excavation, much work has been done on the analysis of surviving buildings (mainly castles, churches, and town defences) and of the basic form and layout of medieval towns. Not surprisingly most Irish towns were, by European standards, small and simple. Most were laid out in a linear pattern along a single main street, widening at one end to form a market place; good examples include **Carrickfergus, Fethard**, and **Kilkenny**. More complex street patterns occur, such as in **Athenry** and **Galway**, where there appears to be a form of chequer pattern. Town defences were also usually simple; in many cases it appears that they consisted of earthen banks rather than stone walls, perhaps with stone gateways, which were important as much for collection of tolls as for defence. A feature of several larger towns (such as **Athenry, Carlingford, Carrick-fergus, Trim**) is the presence of the feudal lord's castle, usually occupying one corner of the town where it could either protect or dominate the town, as occasion demanded. Parish churches and friaries also occupied corners of the town, on occasions. By the later 13th century the English conquest was faltering and so, too, was town foundation. **Roscommon**, in the late 1270s, was probably the last English town founded in medieval Ireland; for the remainder of the Middle Ages any new towns were developed by Irish lords.

The introduction of Gothic architecture is traditionally seen as one of the tangible legacies of the English conquest. This is undoubtedly true, in broad terms, but recent research stresses that one did not automatically follow the other. The first churches built by the English in Ireland, such as the rebuilt east end of Christ Church cathedral in **Dublin**, were late Romanesque in style, and the earliest Gothic elements are not seen for almost a generation after 1170. In the first half of the 13th century—when the English colonization of Ireland was in full spate—several fine structures were erected in the current Gothic style, but thereafter Irish architecture departs from contemporary European styles. The development of Gothic architecture in Ireland parallels that of Romanesque, in many respects. In most cases the 'Gothic' elements consist merely of individual features such as doors, windows, and arcades set within relatively small and extremely simple buildings, such as nave-and-chancel churches. The number of genuine essays in Gothic architecture is very small—the early 13th-century cathedrals of Christ Church and St Patrick's in **Dublin** and Holy Trinity in **Waterford** (now destroyed), and perhaps a few abbey churches elsewhere. This was largely an inevitable effect of the nature of Irish society—there simply was neither the population to justify, nor the wealth to support, the construction of large and elaborate churches. Even where Gothic elements are employed, they are frequently outdated by European standards. In areas not controlled by the English, architecture often developed along more idiosyncratic lines—a notable example being the early 13th-century regional style known to modern scholars as the 'School of the West'. This was a transitional late Romanesque/early Gothic style, characterized by an extremely high standard of carving, both in animal, human, and foliage ornament and in the setting of feature windows in ashlar masonry. Good examples are found at **Killaloe, Abbeyknockmoy, Boyle**, and **Ballintober**.

By the late 13th century there were even fewer opportunities for building new cathedrals or monastic foundations. The main growth area in church architecture was the friaries, which by their very nature were not given to extravagance. The main orders of friars, the Franciscans and Dominicans, established their first Irish houses c.1224 at **Youghal** and **Dublin**, respectively. Other orders such as the Augustinian and Carmelite friars were later arrivals and less numerous. Friary foundations of the 13th/early 14th centuries were almost invariably founded in towns by English or Anglo-Irish patrons. These urban friaries were usually located on the periphery of the town, such as at **Athenry, Carlingford**, and **Kilmallock**. Their churches typically began life in the 13th century as long, narrow rectangular structures, divided into the nave (for lay people) and choir (for friars), usually by a screen of stone or wood towards the middle of the church. Side aisles and 'preaching' transepts, usually on the south, were frequently added in the 14th/15th centuries as the friars' pastoral ministry developed. These tended to provide opportunities for greater architectural elaboration than in the original church. Distinctive slender towers were also often added in the middle of the church; these were not true crossing towers (most friary churches did not have a crossing, as such) but replaced the screen which originally divided nave and choir.

And what of the Irish—the indigenous population—during this period? This is one of the most intractable issues facing medieval archaeology in Ireland today, for we have practically no Irish sites to set against the explosion of Anglo-Irish activity in the late 12th/13th centuries. This problem probably has little to do with the English conquest, being due largely to the apparent abandonment of ringforts which, as we have noted, occurred in the 11th/12th centuries. Well before 1170 a gap has appeared in the archaeological record—a lack of secular settlement sites—which we are still struggling to fill. Some have looked to the ubiquitous ringfort to fill this gap, but it now seems clear that there is no evidence for the construction of ringforts after 1100 (if not earlier), and little enough for the occupation or reoccupation of earlier ringforts. Whatever was happening, the English conquest may have had little effect—particularly in those large areas of the island (mainly in the north) which remained outside English control. However, there are suggestions that some of the typical 'English' site types, such as mottes, moated sites, and even stone castles, may have been built by Irish lords. In English-controlled areas, historical records point to Irish people integrating in Anglo-Irish society, working as labourers on the manors and even being active in the towns, but it is unclear what proportion of the Irish population can be accounted for in this way.

Later medieval Ireland

Throughout northern Europe the 14th century is seen as a period of downturn after the boom years of the 12th/13th centuries. Ireland was no exception, but the period has an extra dimension as the first signs become evident of a decisive shift in the balance of power between the Irish and Anglo-Irish communities. By the end of the 14th century the Anglo-Irish colony was in retreat and even strong English castles such as **Roscommon, Dundrum**, and **Bunratty** were in Irish hands. The ultimate physical manifestation of this process is the Franciscan friary of **Quin**, founded in the early 15th century by an Irish lord and literally built on the ruins of a 13th-century English castle. There are two aspects to this process: first, a series of setbacks which particularly affected the Anglo-Irish colony and, secondly, an apparent growth in the military power of the Irish lords, often referred to as the 'Gaelic military revival'. The Anglo-Irish colony stopped expanding in the later 13th century— probably because most of the best agricultural land had been occupied and there was little interest in the remainder. Towards the end of the 13th century climatic conditions, which had been unusually favourable for over a century, began a gradual deterioration which had a particular impact on the arable-based agriculture of the Anglo-Irish colony. In the 1290s and early 1300s the colony was drained by financial and other demands made by Edward I for his wars against the Scots. From 1315 to 1318 Edward Bruce's Scottish army campaigned in Ireland with highly destructive effects, particularly for the Anglo-Irish colony. A series of plagues, most notably the Black Death of 1347–9, was especially devastating in the towns of the colony.

Large-scale English intervention was required to bolster the colony, but royal preoccupation with wars in Scotland and France meant that there was little appetite for this. Instead, the colony gradually shrank as considerable areas reverted to the control of Irish lords, while many Anglo-Irish lords effectively ignored the weak central government. The persistent small-scale warfare between the lordships—of whatever racial background—was incompatible with the orderly agricultural economy introduced by the English, and manors and villages were abandoned on a large scale. Physical evidence of declining communities can be seen in abandoned or shrunken towns such as **Rindown** and **Athenry**, or in the many churches which were reduced in size in the late Middle Ages. This includes both secular churches, such as the cathedral at **Newtown Trim**, and monasteries such as **Athassel, Holycross**, and **Kilcooly**. By contrast, traditional Irish agricultural, economic, and social patterns were more resilient and better adapted to such conditions, and were embraced by many Anglo-Irish lords. By the later 15th century the area effectively controlled by England had shrunk to a narrow coastal strip bordering **Dublin**, known as the Pale (after the earthen rampart built to defend it in the 1490s), and a few large towns elsewhere.

Notions of a late medieval Gaelic military revival are largely based on an underestimation of earlier Irish military capacity. In fact the militarization of the Irish lordships in the late Middle Ages was largely a continuation of a long-standing process, although there is evidence for new military approaches, seen particularly clearly in the attitude to castles. English castles were no longer simply destroyed, but occupied. Even more significantly, from at least the mid-14th century Irish lords were building their own castles, two of the earliest known examples being **Harry Avery's** castle and **Dunluce**, both in the Irish stronghold of Ulster. Relatively large castles of this type were rarely built by Irish lords, but they can definitely be associated with another type of castle, the tower house. Tower houses are by far the most common late medieval monument in Ireland; they are typically small, rectangular fortified buildings of three or four storeys, often surrounded by a small walled enclosure. Several hundred are known today and estimates of the original total run as high as 3,000. They are found throughout the island (although much less common in Ulster than elsewhere) and cross all boundaries—they occur in Irish and Anglo-Irish areas, in urban and rural forms, and even on church sites. Some of the heaviest concentrations of tower houses occur in areas clearly controlled by Irish lords, and Irish lords built some of the finest individual examples such as **Bunratty** and **Blarney**.

Leask sought the origins of the tower house in early 15th-century Exchequer grants to Anglo-Irish settlers in the Pale who built fortified residential towers on their lands. Undoubtedly the structures envisaged in this scheme would today be recognized as tower houses, but this does not necessarily mean that tower houses only began to be built at this date. Like most government initiatives, this probably reflected the existing reality on the ground, rather than giving rise to it. Leask's theory was an inevitable corollary of his view of an almost total hiatus in building activity in Ireland between c.1320 and c.1420. This theory is being increasingly challenged, however, and there have been several suggestions of an earlier, 14th-century origin for the tower house. Derivation from the rectangular keeps of 13th-century castles, or from hall houses, has been suggested. It has also been suggested that tower houses replaced moated sites as the defended homesteads of the Anglo-Irish minor nobility in the south and east of the island. All of these theories would tend to favour an earlier date for tower houses, but they lack the crucial supporting evidence of actual tower houses securely dated to before 1400. This is used by traditionalists to shoot down arguments for early date, but the crux of the problem with tower house origins is that very few examples can be securely dated at all. Until this situation improves through further research and excavation, the debate is unlikely to progress very far.

Other aspects of tower houses also need to be followed up, such as

McNeill's suggestion that their proliferation reflects a fragmentation of lordship and authority in late medieval Ireland. Certainly the proliferation of tower houses points to an atmosphere of insecurity, in which every man of property had to look to his own defence. On the other hand, the very limited defensive capabilities of most tower houses reminds us that warfare in medieval Ireland, although frequent, was usually very small scale. Regional variations in tower house design are evident, although they have not been analysed to any great extent. What is perhaps more striking, however, is the broad similarity of tower houses in all areas, regardless of cultural background. By the 15th century, if not earlier, the culture of Irish and Anglo-Irish (outside of the Anglicized core of the Pale) had largely merged so that, for example, it is difficult to determine whether a tower house or church is 'Irish' or 'Anglo-Irish' from its form alone. Late medieval culture is a hybrid. Official English sources speak dramatically of the Anglo-Irish having 'gone native', adopting Irish language, dress, military practices, and even Irish law, but it could equally be argued that the Irish had been Anglicized to some extent. Their lords were living in tower houses or castles, and were founding houses for friars on their lands and even (on admittedly rare occasions) founding towns.

Architectural evidence indicates that the 15th/16th centuries were actually a period of relative prosperity. In church architecture, the major focus of activity was the friaries. Existing friaries were frequently enlarged, but a large number of new friaries were founded, mainly in the western half of the island. Some, such as the Franciscan friary at **Adare**, were founded by Anglo-Irish patrons but most—such as **Quin, Muckross, Roscrea, Donegal**, and **Creevelea**—were founded by Irish lords. This activity was not confined to the friaries, however, taking in cathedrals such as **Limerick** and **Clonfert** and abbeys such as **Kilcooly** and, above all, **Holycross**. It has been pointed out that late medieval Irish architecture is strangely archaic, being largely based on early 14th-century styles of Decorated Gothic, with an almost complete absence of the Perpendicular style current in contemporary England. Whereas much of the best 13th-century work was quite possibly executed (or at least directed) by English masons, or at least masons who were quite familiar with developments in England, the architecture of late medieval Ireland seems to be the product of local masons who drew their inspiration from within Ireland. Although conservative, it is a distinctive, rather eclectic and lively style, frequently executed with great confidence and accomplishment, and with no major differences between Irish and Anglo-Irish areas. Other evidence for the prosperity of the period includes the wealth of monumental funerary sculpture, especially in the south-east, best represented by the marvellous collection in St Canice's cathedral, **Kilkenny**.

This architectural tradition came to an abrupt end with the Reformation of the mid-16th century, which brought with it the dissolution of the monasteries (although this did not take effect in some parts of the island until much later in the century) and many changes in the secular cathedrals and parish churches. In Ireland, the Reformation was essentially part of a larger process—the veritable reconquest of the island by the Tudor rulers of England. Although more effective than the original English conquest, this was also far more destructive and ushered in a period of unparalleled turbulence lasting until the end of the 17th century. The devastating wars of the late 16th and 17th centuries finally destroyed the medieval Irish social order along with its economic, cultural, and religious systems, and left England in unchallenged control of Ireland. But they also had a disastrous effect on the island's medieval heritage. The built fabric typically survives today only as bare shells without any trace of internal features and furnishings. Of the hundreds of castles and tower houses only one—at Dunsoghly in north Co. Dublin—retains its original roof timbers. Scarcely a church survived unscathed—most were in ruins by the end of the 17th century, leaving almost no furniture or internal features. The late medieval wooden misericords in **Limerick** cathedral, and even a carved wooden chest in St Patrick's cathedral, **Dublin**, are unique survivals, while wall painting is virtually non-existent, apart from faded traces such as at **Holycross** and

▼ **Fig. 6.** Castlederg Castle, Co. Tyrone: cobbled entrance to plantation-period castle overlying bawn wall of an O'Donnell tower house (photo: Conor Newman)

Abbeyknockmoy. The vital historical documents of medieval Ireland, which were normally kept either in churches or in castles, have also fared badly. This heightens the apparent gulf between Ireland and other areas where medieval buildings are better preserved. Undoubtedly this gulf is real, in many respects—Ireland was a poor, remote place in the later Middle Ages. Yet this remoteness, along with its unique cultural mix, made Ireland a distinctive place and this is reflected in its archaeology, which the writers hope will be enjoyed by many visitors.

North-east: Antrim, Armagh, Down

Introduction

The north-eastern corner of the island comprises two upland areas—the Antrim plateau in the north and the Mourne Mountains in the south—with a relatively low-lying area in between. These lowlands in Cos. Down and Armagh form the eastern terminus of the north midland drumlin belt and much of the land is of limited use. There is, however, a lot of highly fertile land along the south Co. Down coast, in north Co. Armagh, and in west Co. Antrim. The mountainous mass of Co. Antrim (described as 'Switzerland in miniature' by Thackeray) provides less in the way of fertile land. It does, however, boast the closest point in Ireland to Britain—Torr Head being only 20 km from the Mull of Kintyre. This proximity to Scotland was to have a profound impact on Antrim in particular, and the north-east in general. To the west, Co. Antrim and most of Co. Down are separated from the rest of Ulster by Lough Neagh and the upper and lower branches of the river Bann, which forms one of the most enduring political boundaries in Ireland. It still divides the Protestant/Unionist-dominated north-east from a Catholic/Nationalist majority to the west. In the thirteenth century it marked the western limit of the English earldom of Ulster. Even before this, in the earlier Middle Ages, it separated the lands of the Ulaid, to the east, from those of the Uí Néill to the west. The Ulaid are the heroes of Ireland's greatest mythological cycle (the 'Ulster cycle') and at the dawn of history there are indications that they had once dominated the whole of the north. Ironically, the fact that Ulster is named after them is due, not to this semi-mythological greatness, but to the fact that their later, much reduced kingdom subsequently became the English earldom.

The north-east is, in many ways, the home of Mesolithic and Neolithic studies in Ireland. Naturally occurring flint deposits, combined with a small army of enthusiastic antiquarian collectors, who came together formally in 1821 to found the Belfast Natural History and Philosophical Society, led to the assemblage of vast collections of lithics and ceramics. This momentum was maintained by archaeologists like Estyn Evans and Oliver Davies who undertook comprehensive excavation and survey campaigns in the 1930s, and by Hallam Movius of the Harvard Archaeological Expedition to Ireland who excavated key later Mesolithic sites at **Cushendun**, Glenarm, and Curran Point, Co. Antrim. Early and late Mesolithic sites are known from the Bann Valley

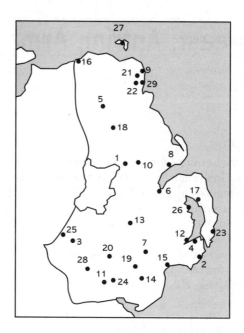

▲ Map 1
Key:

1. Antrim, Co. Antrim
2. Ardglass, Co. Down
3. Armagh, Co. Armagh
4. Audleystown, Co. Down
5. Ballymacaldrack, Co. Antrim
6. Ballynahatty, Co. Down
7. Barnmeen, Co. Down
8. Carrickfergus, Co. Antrim
9. Cushendun, Co. Antrim
10. Donegore Hill, Co. Antrim
11. Dorsey, Co. Armagh
12. Downpatrick, Co. Down
13. Dromore, Co. Down
14. Drumena, Co. Down
15. Dundrum, Co. Down

16. Dunluce, Co. Antrim
17. Grey Abbey, Co. Down
18. Harryville, Co. Antrim
19. Legananny, Co. Down
20. Lisnagade, Co. Down
21. Lubitavish, Co. Antrim
22. Lurigethan, Co. Antrim
23. Millin Bay, Co. Down
24. Narrow Water, Co. Down
25. Navan, Co. Armagh
26. Nendrum, Co. Down
27. Rathlin Island, Co. Antrim
28. Slieve Gullion, Co. Armagh
29. Tievebulliagh, Co. Antrim

and around Lough Neagh, in both coastal and inland Antrim, and around the coast of Co. Down, particularly at the top of Strangford Lough.

The wealth of natural resources in this region sustained comparatively large Neolithic populations. There are megalithic tombs of all main types, including, on the summit of **Slieve Gullion**, Co. Armagh, the highest Passage tomb in Ireland. It has been argued, *pace* de Valera who postulates a western origin of the form, that Court tombs in Antrim and Down belong to the Scottish chambered tomb tradition.

Wonderful examples of Court and Portal tombs, such as **Audleystown**, **Legananny**, and **Clontygora**, congregate in particular in south Armagh and south Down and again in north-east Antrim. There is, however, more to the Neolithic of this region than just megalithic tombs. At **Donegore** is a substantial hilltop settlement compared to British causewayed enclosures, and in Antrim are the porcellanite axe factories at **Tievebulliagh** and on **Rathlin Island**. There is also a very impressive collection of field monuments of later Neolithic date, including the great henge at **Ballynahatty**.

The number of Bowl Tradition funerary pots reported from these counties compares favourably to the rest of Ulster, but there is a distinct concentration of Vase Tradition pots, particularly to the immediate east of Strangford Lough. These demographic patterns are also reflected in the general north-eastern bias in the distribution of Cordoned, Collared, and Encrusted cinerary urns. Whereas these ceramic assemblages indicate social stability, finds such as the stone moulds from Killymaddy, Co. Antrim, demonstrate local production, on an industrial scale, of bronze objects. The occurrence on the Killymaddy moulds of matrices for looped, socketed spearheads, razors, and dirks provides vital clues as to the contemporaneity of different middle Bronze Age types. Settlement sites of the later Bronze Age are quite rare and the discovery and excavation of the trivallate hillfort at **Haughey's Fort**, just to the south of **Emain Macha**, Co. Armagh, is an important addition to the corpus. It is associated with the **King's Stables**, a ritual pond in which votive offerings, including human heads, were thrown, and with **Navan** Fort. Ritual deposition is a characteristic of later Bronze Age Ireland and was as common in the north-east as elsewhere. An intriguing combination of Dowris-phase bronzes and glass and faience beads, the hoard from Derryhale, Co. Armagh, contains no fewer than fourteen so-called sunflower pins and testifies to both wealth and far-flung connections. Another hoard, from Cromaghs, Co. Antrim, included a number of pieces of woollen cloth and a unique ornamental tassel made from horsehair. In a period dominated by gold and bronze objects, these pieces of cloth are hugely informative about the more basic needs of society.

The practice of hoarding continued into the Iron Age and is evidenced in the north-east by, for example, the discovery of an undisclosed number of ribbon torcs at Ballylumford, Island Magee, Co. Antrim, in 1817 and 1824. The same motivation might explain some of the La Tène swords and scabbards recovered from the river Bann but should not be applied too readily to the remarkable assemblage of swords, scabbards, spearbutts, etc, found at Lisnacrogher, Co. Antrim, because there was a considerable amount of associated structural evidence as well. This material comprises not only one of the biggest assemblages of La Tène objects in Ireland but also one of the oldest—the swords and scabbards are considered to be among the first native productions of La Tène forms. Indeed, in terms of both artefacts and monuments, the north-east has emerged as one of the key areas for the study of La Tène Ireland. The importance of monuments like **Navan** Fort (Emain Macha) and the **Dorsey**, and the connection between them, cannot be overstated. Finds of Romano-British material are confined to the north coast of Antrim and south Co. Down. Antrim and Down have quite dense populations of ringforts and a series of modern excavations by Chris Lynn of sites like Ballyhenry and Deer Park Farms in Co. Antrim and Rathmullan, Co. Down, has made a considerable contribution to our understanding of this settlement form, as well as providing a suite of well-contexted radiocarbon dates. In contrast, there has been comparatively little modern examination of crannógs in the north-east, though a dendrochronological sampling initiative in the 1980s indicated that most crannógs were built in the late 6th and early 7th century.

Legend (possibly with some historical basis) places the fall of the Ulaid capital **Emain Macha** and the break-up of their kingdom, under pressure from the Uí Néill, in the 5th century. Thereafter Ulaid power was effectively confined to this region. The earlier ascendancy of the Ulaid was indirectly reflected, however, in the primacy of **Armagh** in the Irish Church. Armagh was clearly chosen (whether by Patrick or another founder) for its proximity to Emain Macha, but unlike Emain, **Armagh** survived the destruction of Ulaid power and thrived under Uí Néill patronage. The early ecclesiastical history of the region is dominated, almost exclusively, by the cult of St Patrick. Through their tireless promotion of Patrick, the church at **Armagh** relegated to the position of also-rans many contemporary and later clerics operating in this area. St Mochaoi, the founder of **Nendrum**, Co. Down, is described as having been one of Patrick's converts, while St Darerca (also known as Monnena and Bline), founder of Cell-Sléibhe-Cuilinn (**Killevy**, Co. Armagh), is said to have been baptized and instructed by him as a child.

Across northern Antrim, however, the cult of St Patrick came into direct competition with that of St Columba (Colmcille) of Iona and the growing political might of the Uí Néill. Iona, off the west coast of Scotland and just beyond the visible horizon from north Antrim, was the premier church site of Dál Riada (Dál Riata), an Irish maritime kingdom, established in the 5th or 6th century, encompassing both the north-east of Antrim and south-west Argyllshire in Scotland. The proximity of the two countries at this point led to close cultural connections from prehistoric times that became even closer during the early medieval period. Though their kings resided at Dunadd, in Scotland, the Dál Riada belonged to the contracted Ulaid confederation, which included to the south the Dál nAraide and the Dál Fiatach, whose capital was at **Downpatrick,** and extended into north Louth. At one stage they seem to have exercised control over the Isle of Man. The Ulaid remained a powerful force in east Ulster until the 11th century, but by the early 12th century they were effectively under the control of the Cenél nEógain branch of the Uí Néill. This region experienced a great deal of Viking raiding but surprisingly, in view of its position on the Irish Sea, there is no evidence for any significant Viking settlement—probably because of the dominance of **Dublin.**

In 1177, however, a new threat suddenly appeared. An ambitious English baron, John de Courcy, took advantage of a period of division and weakness among the Cenél nEógain to attack the Ulaid from the south, defeating the Dál Fiatach. This led to the creation of an earldom of Ulster, which essentially followed the lines of the old Ulaid kingdom, but with a new centre at **Carrickfergus,** where de Courcy built a large castle and founded a town. Attempts to extend the earldom west of the Bann, into the Cenél nEógain heartland, were largely unsuccessful. In 1205 the earldom passed to Hugh de Lacy, younger brother of the lord of Meath, and in 1264 to Walter de Burgh, who was already lord of Connacht. During this period most of Cos. Antrim and Down was occupied, and this is reflected in the relatively dense distribution of motte castles, most of which were probably erected between 1177 and 1250. The mottes point to the subdivision of the earldom into a network of smaller lordships, but unlike other parts of the island this was probably not accompanied by large-scale Anglo-Irish settlement on manorial farms. The other monument types typical of Anglo-Irish rural settlement—moated sites and manorial villages—are virtually absent. The lack of moated sites (which elsewhere seem to represent a slightly later, secondary phase of Anglo-Irish colonization) may also be due to the fact that the earldom began to experience pressure from neighbouring Irish lordships at an earlier date than other parts of the colony.

Despite growing Irish pressure, the earldom remained relatively stable under the strong hand of the de Burghs. In 1315, however, Edward Bruce (brother of the Scottish king Robert) landed in Ulster with a large Scottish army. In the three-year campaign that followed, the earldom probably suffered more than any other part of Ireland. The murder of the last de Burgh earl in 1333 was another major step in the decline of the earldom, leading almost immediately to the collapse of the limited Anglo-Irish settlement west of the Bann. After the ravages of the Black Death (1348–9), even the core of the earldom came under increasing pressure, especially from the Ó Néill. In the late Middle Ages it is uncertain whether any significant Anglo-Irish settlement survived in Ulster, outside of coastal strongholds such as **Carrickfergus** and **Ardglass.** Much of Cos. Antrim and Down was taken over by a branch of the Ó Néill, the Clann Aodha Buidhe, and in north Co. Antrim lordships were established by Gaelic families from Scotland, chiefly the

MacDonnells. The classic late medieval monument type, the tower house, is common in south-east Co. Down where it seems to reflect the adaptation of the lesser Anglo-Irish landowners to more insecure times. Elsewhere in the region, however, tower houses are relatively rare and most of these were clearly built by Irish lords. Most of the region remained in Irish hands until the early 17th century. Although most of the region was not formally included in the government's Plantation of Ulster, it was still subject to a massive influx of British settlers which radically changed almost every aspect of society and settlement—with effects that are still felt today.

Antrim, Co. Antrim Round tower

28 km north-west of Belfast, in the grounds of Antrim Borough Council offices on the north side of Antrim town. Disc. Ser. 14.

The town of Antrim [*Aontroim*, 'one holding'], from which the county takes its name, was founded in the wake of the English conquest in the late 12th century, but ultimately owes its existence to the presence there of an earlier monastic site. Little is known about this foundation, which was possibly founded by St Comgall of Bangor (Co. Down) and seems to have been closely connected with that more important monastery. Indeed, the relics of Comgall were taken to Antrim after a Viking raid on Bangor in 824. Antrim itself was plundered in 1018 and burned in 1147. The only visible traces of the monastery are a large bullaun stone and the well-preserved round tower, complete at 28 m high (the roof was restored in the 19th century). The tower is a good example of its type, six floors high and built of local basalt with granite mouldings for the doorway and some windows. Its most important feature is a ringed cross, carved in a stone above the lintel of the raised doorway. The doorway on the north-east side presumably faced a church, of which no trace is visible.

Ardglass, Co. Down Medieval port

10 km south-east of Downpatrick on A2 (Belfast–Newry coastal route); signposted. Disc. Ser. 21.

Ardglass [*Aird Ghlais*, 'grey/green point'], today a fishing village on the Irish Sea coast, was an important late medieval port for the north-east of Ireland and preserves several monuments of that period. Although King John landed here during his visit to Ireland in 1210, there is no definite evidence for a medieval town at Ardglass or for any substantial settlement before the 15th century. The apparent absence of any medieval church also indicates that Ardglass was not actually a town. The surviving monuments reflect the prosperity of the port in the 15th and 16th centuries but this was brought to an end by the wars of the late

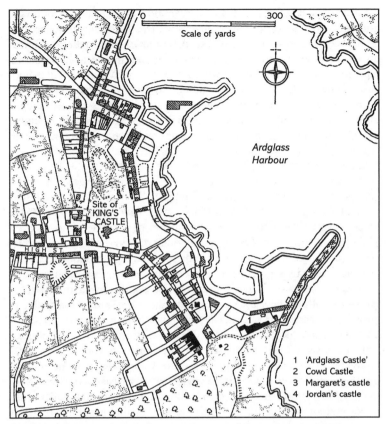

▲ **Fig. 7.** Ardglass: map showing location of the main monuments (HMSO)

16th and 17th centuries. Ardglass declined significantly before being revived and largely rebuilt in the 19th century. This revival removed much of the evidence for the layout of medieval Ardglass but the distribution of the medieval monuments suggests that it was concentrated around the southern end of the present harbour.

'Ardglass Castle' (now the golf club) incorporates substantial remains of a unique building, probably of early 15th-century date. It is essentially a medieval fortified warehouse block, built to provide secure storage spaces beside the quay and protected by towers at either end. Such buildings were probably common in medieval Irish ports, but this is the only one surviving. Many of its original features have been removed or are obscured by extensive alterations since the 18th century. It can be reconstructed, however, as a two-storey building, c.65 m long and c.9 m wide, with projecting three-storey towers on the north side at either end and near the centre. It seems originally to have had a series of

15 pairs of alternating pointed doorways and square-headed windows in the north wall, at ground floor, suggesting that there may have been up to 15 separate units in the block, to be rented to merchants. Few of these openings survive, however. The other sides seem to have had no openings, apart from narrow window loops at ground- and first-floor level in the south wall. Above the first floor was a wall walk, protected by a crenellated parapet. Immediately to the north-west is a much-altered, three-storey rectangular building, probably a late medieval tower house.

South-west of Ardglass Castle, on the golf course, is Cowd Castle, a small, simple tower house of late 15th/16th-century date which was presumably a merchant's residence. It is two-storeyed with an attic above, and the walls have an external base batter and (largely destroyed) parapet on top. The entrance is a rebuilt doorway on the west side, immediately inside which a mural stairway (now blocked) led to the upper levels. The accommodation consists of a single almost square chamber on each floor. The ground floor, lit only by a number of narrow loops (mostly blocked), was probably intended for storage, whereas the first floor is lit by slightly larger rectangular windows, set in embrasures with seats, and was clearly residential. Two further tower houses, both probably 15th century, are of a characteristic Co. Down form, with two projecting turrets on one side united by a high-level arch. This arch formed a machicolation, clearly designed to defend the entrance, which is located between the turrets. The smaller of the two buildings, Margaret's castle, is located south-west of Cowd Castle, at the extreme southern end of the village. It was originally of at least three storeys but only the lower two survive, barrel vaulted over ground floor. There is a modern doorway in the east wall, but the original entrance is a doorway (now rebuilt) in the north wall, set between the turrets and defended by a murder hole overhead, internally. Each floor has one main chamber and the north-west turret contains a spiral stair giving access to the upper levels.

The other tower house, known as Jordan's castle (after the medieval merchant family who lived there), is the northernmost of the surviving medieval buildings, on the east side of Kildare St. *c.*30 m north of Cowd and Margaret's castles. It was restored early in the 20th century, when new timber floors were put in at the upper levels. It has four storeys with a wall walk above and is almost identical in plan to Margaret's castle, with a single chamber on each floor (barrel vaulted over ground floor) and a spiral stair in the north-west turret. The entrance is not between the turrets but in the east wall of the north-west turret, and is defended by a machicolation, high above over third-floor level. The doorway is rebuilt, but note the bar-hole on the south side, which held a bar to secure the door. Similar bar-holes can be seen in each of the doorways leading from the stairs to the upper chambers. The ground-floor chamber is typically poorly lit; the upper chambers are only slightly better lit but the presence of fireplaces in the south wall, latrines in the north-east turret, and seats in most windows clearly indicates that these were residential chambers. The stairs rise to a continuous wall walk at roof level, which communicates via stone stairs with turrets at each angle, protected by a battlemented parapet. The north-west turret rises an extra storey, the upper chamber originally providing access to the machicolation over the entrance, but subsequently converted to a pigeon loft.

Armagh, Co. Armagh Monastic enclosure and town

55 km south-west of Belfast on A3 (Belfast–Monaghan). Disc. Ser. 19.

Armagh [*Ard Mhacha*, 'Macha's hill'] is the ecclesiastical capital of Ireland and was probably the most important early medieval monastic site in the country—a position based on its claim to be St Patrick's primary foundation in the 5th century. Unfortunately, its status is not adequately reflected in the surviving archaeology. Several early manuscripts can be reliably attributed to the Armagh scriptorium, the most important being the Book of Armagh, copied by the scribe Ferdomnach in 807–8 (*on display in Trinity College, Dublin*). Within the present Church of Ireland cathedral are fragments of the shafts of two high crosses and a cross head, all carved with scriptural scenes. Although worn and damaged, they represent at least two impressive, probably 10th-century high crosses. The shrine of St Patrick's bell (*on display in the National Museum of Ireland*) was almost certainly made in and for Armagh in *c.*1100. A Franciscan friary was founded in 1263–4; dissolved in 1542, it was in ruins by 1600 as a result of the Nine Years War, and never recovered. The 13th-century church (*in the grounds of the former Archbishops' Palace, now the District Council offices, off Friary Road*) was the longest friary church in medieval Ireland, but the surviving remains are disappointing. It had a south aisle and there are traces of a tower, added in the 15th century.

For the most part, however, we can only speak of what once existed at Armagh. One of the earliest documented stone churches in Ireland was at Armagh, in 788. A priory of *Célí Dé* existed here from at least the 10th century until the 16th century. There was also a round tower, referred to as early as 998, which probably stood north of the cathedral. This disappeared in the 17th century and, as with the other early buildings, no trace survives today. The community of Armagh was a leading force in the church reform movement of the early 12th century, as a result of which Armagh became an archbishopric and its position at the head of the Irish Church was confirmed. Unfortunately for Armagh, this was followed soon afterwards by the English conquest, which was to prove disastrous—because it stopped just short of Armagh itself. By the late 13th century the diocese was effectively divided between 'English'

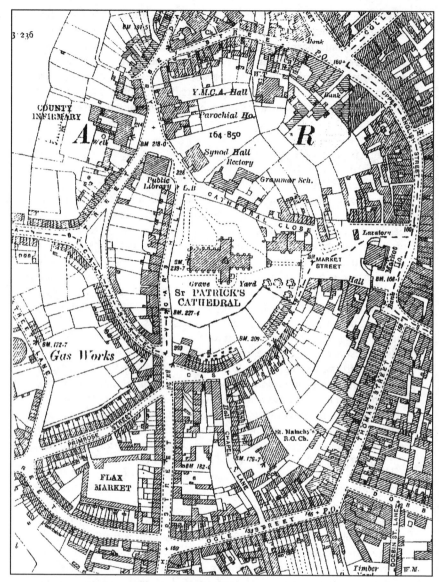

▲ **Fig. 8.** Armagh: map of town centre (OSNI)

and 'Irish' areas. Armagh, in the 'Irish' area, was cut off from valuable English patronage while her traditional Irish patrons were greatly weakened. Later archbishops, who were largely non-Gaelic, tended not even to reside in Armagh but based themselves within the English colony. Thus Armagh did not prosper as might be expected in the later

Middle Ages, but this in itself makes the town significant. It is a prime example of a settlement that developed from an early monastic site, without any significant involvement either by Vikings or English.

While the visible archaeology is scanty, the modern town preserves a highly distinctive urban form rooted in its early medieval origins. At the centre of the town, crowning the hill from which it takes its name, St Patrick's cathedral (Church of Ireland) occupies the site of the principal church of the early monastery. Although preserving the form and probably some of the fabric of a later medieval cathedral, the present building is mainly the product of 19th-century restoration. Surrounding the cathedral, and forming the core of the modern street pattern, are two concentric rings of streets that clearly reflect the enclosures of the early monastery. An inner enclosure, up to 250 m across, is reflected in the curving line of Callan St./Castle St., while the Abbey St./English St./Thomas St./Ogle St./Navan St. line reflects an outer, oval enclosure up to 480 m across. These features survived, in a sense, in the urban framework, even after the plantation of the town with English and Scottish settlers in the 17th century. Excavation has revealed the presence of a ceremonial or ritual enclosure on the hilltop before the coming of Christianity, probably in the very early 1st millennium AD. Earlier pre-historic activity has been revealed by excavation in Scotch St., down-hill to the east. This was succeeded by Christian burials, probably of the 5th/6th centuries, and later (probably in the 8th/9th centuries) by an area of craftsmen's workshops.

While in Armagh, be sure to visit the County Museum (*on the Mall, at the east side of the town*), which has good archaeological displays. St Patrick's Trian (*English St.*) is an interpretative centre focusing on the development of Armagh from pre-Christian times.

Audleystown, Co. Down Court tomb

Third turn on the left on the Castleward–Audleystown road. Signposted at Carrowcarlan on the A25 north-west of Castleward. Disc. Ser. 21.

This is one of the classic examples of a dual-court tomb. It is situated in a slight hollow one field in from the tidal mudflats around Jackdaw Island on the southern shore of Strangford Lough. The cairn is trapezoidal in plan and is orientated north-east/south-west, with the wider end facing south-west. It is revetted with a drystone wall of shale slabs and outside this again is a unique 'buttress' of shale and red soil. The 'court' façade at the south-west end is comparatively shallow, or flat, and only a selection of the façade stones survives, including just one jambstone. Behind this is a four-chambered gallery. The north-eastern 'court area' is rather more concave and it too gives onto a 10-m long gallery of four regularly sized, roughly paved chambers. In this case the end chamber has an *in situ* corbel stone revealing something about

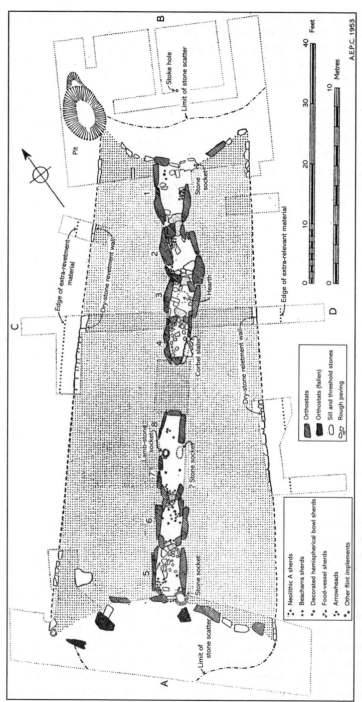

▲ Fig. 9. Audleystown: plan of Court tomb as excavated (after Collins)

the original method of roofing. The site was excavated by Pat Collins in 1952, six years after its discovery.

The burial assemblage was really quite remarkable. Only the inner two chambers of the north-eastern gallery were empty; instead of burials there was a fire pit and evidence of intense burning. The remains of about 34 people were found in the remaining chambers, comprising men, women, and children. They were either inhumed, partially burnt, or fully cremated. The majority of inhumations were of women and children and these burials were disarticulated and occasionally collected into groups, such as the selection of small long bones, a jaw fragment, and a pig's jaw arranged in the second chamber of the south-western gallery. This is clear indication of exhumation or excarnation. There were also animal bones, including the earliest evidence of horse. Throughout these deposits were sherds of pottery and lithics. The pottery assemblage included round-bottomed, plain and carinated bowls, decorated Goodlands-style sherds, and some Carrowkeel ware. The burial deposits were sealed beneath a packing of soil and stones and it has been suggested that the remains represent one episode of collective burial. A Bowl Tradition pot was also found and represents secondary funerary activity.

There is an interesting collection of field monuments, of all periods, in the immediate vicinity, including two round cairns to the east and a standing stone near Castleward to the south-east (all privately owned). There is another concentration of prehistoric monuments around Lough Money, about 5 km to the south-west, including, to the south of the Lough, Ballyalton Court tomb itself.

Ballymacaldrack, Co. Antrim Court tomb

10 km south-east of Ballymoney, off B16 (Ballymoney–Cullybackey); take minor road to west 1.2 km south of Dunloy; signposted. Disc. Ser. 8.

Affectionately christened 'Dooey's Cairn' after its 1930s landowner, the discovery of a pre-megalithic 'cremation passage' (*sic*, Evans) is one of the most significant pieces of evidence connecting Irish Court tombs with the British long barrow tradition. This rather unprepossessing open-court tomb was excavated in 1935 by Estyn Evans and again in 1975 by Pat Collins, to retrieve samples for C14 dating. It is orientated north-east/south-west, with the paved 'court' area opening to the south-west. There is one megalithic chamber opening onto an earlier, paved and stone-lined trench, about 1 m deep and 6.5 m long. Evenly spaced along the bottom of the trench were three large pits. These appear to pre-date the trench lining (and probably even the trench itself) and represent the earliest phase of activity, around 4000 BC. They are interpreted as possible upright supports of a mortuary structure or ossuary. After this the pits were cleared of the posts and were reused for funerary deposits. In addition to the original packing stones, the outer two pits also contained sherds of a carinated pot while the innermost pit contained the cremated remains of five adults (male and female), a burnt arrowhead, and sherds of pottery.

A second major structural phase (Evan's 'cremation passage' proper) was initiated with the digging of the trench, which, though clipping all of the pits, was deliberately positioned on the same line. The sides of the trench were lined with a rough stone walling, and the bottom was paved over. There may have been a small surface cairn at this stage. Above the paving was a layer of charcoal (evidence of *in situ* burning was unequivocal) and 45 cm of burnt earth and stones. This phase is radiocarbon dated to between about 3800 and 3600 BC and has strong parallels with the Scottish sites of Lochill, Pitnacree, and Slewcairn.

The chamber and forecourt were added during a third structural episode. No human remains were placed in the chamber but instead a handful of animal teeth, some potsherds, two lozenge-shaped arrowheads, and a serpentine bead. During the fourth phase the whole court area was filled with loose stones and the entrance proper was blocked off with more formal walling from which were recovered two porcellanite polished stone axeheads. Sherds of small, globular pots were found throughout the court blocking material. That this occurred relatively late in the history of the site is suggested by the fact that one of the 'court'

▼ Fig. 10. Ballymacaldrack: plan of Court tomb as excavated (after Collins)

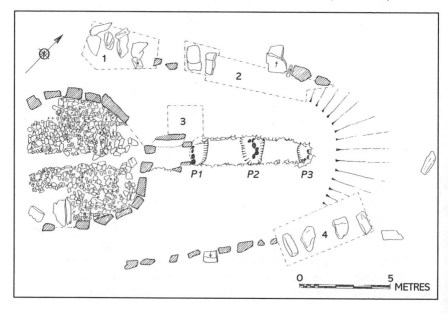

orthostats had already collapsed at this stage and by a radiocarbon date of 3690–2920 BC from under the pile of stones. Two sherds of a Vase, unstratified in the court area, indicate some ritual activity during the earlier Bronze Age.

The site is situated on the gently inclined western side of the valley of the river Main and below the five peaks of Long Mountain. At around the same contour line on the western side of the mountain (south at Mullan Head crossroads on the Dunloy–Finvoy road) is another fine Court tomb known as the Broadstone. It is a traditional meeting point for games and coursing.

▼ **Fig. 11.** Ballymacaldrack: excavated pottery (after Collins)

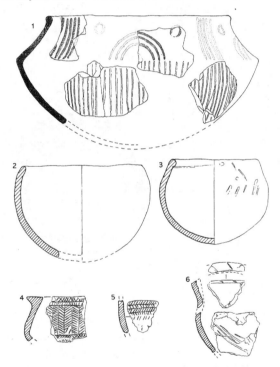

Ballynahatty ('the Giant's Ring'), Co. Down Henge

complex

South side of Belfast, 7 km from city centre; approached via Malone Road and Milltown Road; signposted. Disc. Ser. 15.

The 'Giant's Ring' is a hugely impressive henge on a bluff overlooking the middle reaches of the Lagan Valley. The gravel and earth bank survives to a height of 4 m and encloses an area some 190 m in diameter.

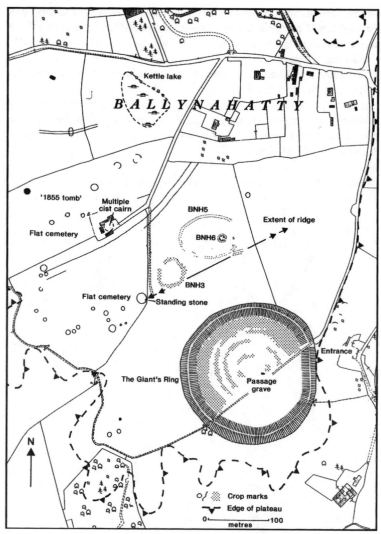

▲ **Fig. 12.** Ballynahatty: plan of ceremonial landscape associated with the 'Giant's Ring' (after Hartwell)

Of the five gaps around the circumference, only the one approached directly from the car park (to the north-east) is original. Excavations by Henry Lawlor (1917) and Pat Collins (1954) proved that the banks (16 m wide) were constructed with material dug from a wide, shallow quarry ditch (20 m wide; 1 m deep) around the internal perimeter. The inside of the bank was revetted by a low boulder wall, the outside by a low, primary embankment. Slightly off-centre are the remains of a Passage tomb, comprising a short passage and polygonal chamber with one *in situ* capstone.

To the north of the Ring is a significant ridge that runs across the bluff, from north-east to south-west. From about halfway along this ridge one can actually see into the great henge. The south-western terminus of the ridge is marked by a standing stone, the sole survivor of a once great complex of prehistoric funerary monuments concentrated to the north of the ridge in the area around Edenderry Farm. The first recorded of these (1855) was a small subterranean burial chamber, about 150 m north-east of the farm. It comprised a circular, radially stalled, corbel-roofed chamber marked by a small surface cairn. In the middle of the chamber was a standing stone. The burial deposit consisted of cremated human remains and four Carrowkeel pots of Passage tomb tradition. Another of these 'passage grave cists' (*sic*, Hartwell 1998), which are so far unique to Ballynahatty, was found some years previously and a third was found during Barrie Hartwell's 1994 excavations. In it were two cremation-filled Carrowkeel pots. Investigation of a multiple cist cairn in the grounds of Edenderry House was reported by O'Laverty in 1878 and later still an associated flat cemetery was identified. Specific details are lacking but there are reports of urns, arrowheads, and two so-called 'battleaxes' of earlier Bronze Age date.

By far the most exciting discoveries, however, have been made through aerial photography and follow-up excavations in the early 1990s by Barrie Hartwell. BNH3 (after Hartwell) is probably a small penannular henge. BNH5 and 6 are palisaded enclosures, one inside the other. Excavation of these latter has revealed a complex sequence of building, dismantling, and reassembly. The first phase at BNH6 is represented by a simple timber circle entered from the south-east. Inside this was a square setting of four posts and a smaller, centrally positioned square post setting (the 'western setting'), possibly an excarnation platform. All these posts were removed in the second phase, the holes were re-dug and still larger posts erected. The four posts around the 'western setting' are estimated to have risen 7 m above the ground. Plank shuttering was erected between the posts on either side of the entrance. A second timber circle, the entrance of which was also formally defined by plank shuttering, was erected around the first one. About 10 m in front of this, two open-ended rhomboid post settings were built (the 'eastern settings'). The purpose of these latter remains a mystery but Hartwell has carefully recreated the elliptic geometry connecting them to the circles. The whole ensemble was then set alight after which the stumps of the four largest posts and those of the inner circle and both entrances were levered out of the ground and the holes filled with the charcoal and ashes of the remaining posts. Burnt stones were piled up to mark the former positions of the main posts. BNH5 is radiocarbon dated to 3018–2788 BC.

BNH6 occurs near the eastern side of a huge, oval-shaped enclosure demarcated by a double palisade that was built sometime after the 'eastern settings'. It is estimated that at least 260 mature oak posts were felled in its construction. A complex annexe was built on the eastern side of this magnificent monument in order to define a formal approach to the Giant's Ring from the eastern end of the ridge. Fragments of up to 26 Grooved Ware pots were found here.

Barnmeen, Co. Down Standing stone

3 km south-west of Rathfriland; off A25 (Newry–Rathfriland); on roadside, behind Barnmeen village. Disc. Ser. 29.

This very fine, granite standing stone stands 3.6 m high and is one of the most impressive of the Mourne monoliths. Known as 'The Long Stone', it evidently lent its name to Longstone Hill, on which it stands, and is probably the most accessible of a host of standing stones and hilltop cairns around the north-west foothills of the Mournes. This specimen belongs to a group that is strung out along the meandering Clanrye river valley. There is a particular concentration around the village of Mayobridge about 6 km south of Barnmeen, including the 2.7 m high stone on the summit of Slievecarnane, another 3 m tall granite stone about 0.8 km south of the village (also known as 'The Long Stone'), and a third, in between these two. There is a denuded but nonetheless quite impressive cairn on the summit of Carmeen Hill to the north-east. On the other side of this mountain is Hilltown, and nearby Goward Portal tomb.

Carrickfergus, Co. Antrim Medieval town, castle

16 km north-east of Belfast, on A2 (Belfast–Larne). Disc. Ser. 15.

Carrickfergus belies its history; it is of little importance today but for some 500 years, from the late 12th century until the end of the 17th century, it was Ulster's main town. When John de Courcy carved out a lordship on the east coast of Ulster in the late 1170s, he chose this place as his capital. The name [*Carraig Fhearghais*, 'the rock of Fergus'] may well indicate that there was already a stronghold on the site. A castle had probably been begun by 1180 and a Premonstratensian priory was established soon afterwards. The foundation of St Nicholas's parish church in 1185 is clear evidence that the town was also in formation by this date. The town flourished despite de Courcy's downfall in the early 13th century and a Franciscan friary was founded in the 1240s. Carrickfergus suffered severely in 1315–16 when Edward Bruce's Scottish army besieged the castle for over a year. It was burned by the

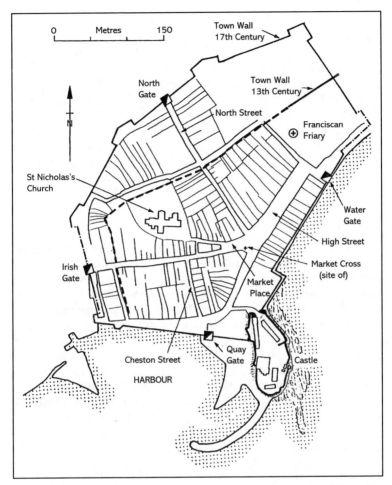

▲ **Fig. 13.** Carrickfergus: outline map of town showing medieval and Plantation features (after Bradley)

Irish in 1374 and 1403, but survived as an embattled outpost of the much reduced earldom of Ulster throughout the late Middle Ages. In the early 17th century Carrickfergus was largely rebuilt by the English planter Arthur Chichester, one of the most powerful men in Ireland. A new town wall was built, enclosing a much larger area. St Nicholas's church was also substantially rebuilt and Chichester erected a new mansion (Joymount) for himself on the site of the Franciscan friary.

Town

The medieval town occupied a roughly rectangular area fronting Belfast Lough, north of the castle, and was laid out along a single main street (High St./West St.), which widened into a market place near the middle of the town. St Nicholas's church occupied most of the north-western corner of the town while the Franciscan friary was located just outside the defences, at the east end. Excavation has shown that the town was enclosed in the 13th century by an earthen bank surmounted by a timber palisade, with an external fosse *c.*4 m in width. The early 17th-century town wall had six bastions and four gatehouses, of which only the North Gate survives, although substantial portions of the wall survive.

Parish church

St Nicholas's church (*entrance off the Market Place; open to visitors each morning*) was the largest parish church in medieval Ulster and, probably, the effective cathedral of the diocese of Connor (since Connor itself was outside English control). It dates to the late 12th century, but its present form owes much to the rebuilding of *c.*1614 by Chichester, whose tomb occupies the north transept. Chichester rebuilt most of the nave and transepts, which were probably in ruins at the time. He greatly reduced the length of the nave to the three easternmost bays that can be seen in the blocked aisle arcading (piers and fragments of round arches) in the north and south walls. The original length of the nave cannot be determined, but it was clearly considerably longer than at present and the blocked arcades show that it originally had side aisles. In the angle between the choir and the north transept are the remains of the north-east pier of the original crossing, clear evidence that the late 12th-century church was cruciform with a nave, chancel, and north and south transepts. The church seems to have been considerably enlarged in the 14th century. In the west wall of the south transept are two blocked arches of this period, indicating that the aisle on the south side of the nave was enlarged to a double aisle. The east end of the chancel is also probably of 14th-century date—the western part, and all of the window tracery, is 17th century. The tower is late 18th century, probably replacing an earlier structure.

Castle

Carrickfergus Castle (*visitor centre; admission charge*) is one of the earliest and finest stone castles in Ireland. De Courcy built it on a spur of volcanic rock projecting into the Lough (presumably the original 'rock of Fergus'), which would have been almost entirely surrounded by water at that time. Its earliest sections (*c.*1180–1200) are at the southern end, consisting of a small, polygonal walled enclosure with an impressive square keep at its northern end. The castle was expanded to the north in two main stages during the first half of the 13th century, so that today the visitor sees the more recent parts of the castle first. The entrance is through a large gatehouse that, along with the adjoining curtain wall, was built c.1226–42 to enclose the whole of the rocky spur on which the castle was located, and to provide a strongly defended entry point. The gatehouse has twin towers, three storeys high, flanking the short entrance passage. These were fully round originally but in the 16th century they were truncated internally and reduced in height. The entrance passage had previously (c.1300) been strengthened by vaulting it in stone, with a new chamber overhead, and adding a gate and portcullis at each end. The gatehouse gives access to the outer ward, at the southern end of which is a fragmentary curtain wall dividing the outer and middle wards. This curtain wall was built around the outside of the original castle (now the inner ward) in c.1215–23, when the castle was under royal control. Its function was to defend the approaches to the castle from the landward side (to the north) and across the sands exposed at low tide (to the east). Squared towers on the north (beside the entrance, now levelled) and east, with multiple loops for archers, provided flanking fire along the outside of the wall.

The inner ward—the original castle—is now entered through an opening beside the keep, but the original entrance was a simple arched gateway in the curtain wall, near the south-east corner. This gateway, and the late 12th-century castle generally, is notable for its lack of defensive features other than the massive keep itself. The great hall was probably built against the east side of the courtyard, where there are two windows with seats in the curtain wall, but no other trace of it survives. The keep is entered at first-floor level through a doorway near the south-east angle, beside which is a spiral stair leading to the other floors. Internally, a simple rectangular chamber occupies the entire interior at each level, now divided in two by a 16th-century spine wall which perhaps replaced an original wooden wall or arcade. The chambers are lit by windows set mainly in the south and east walls, which face into the courtyard below. The poorly lit first-floor chamber was probably a guardroom, and contains a well and a double latrine in the south-west angle, reached through a mural passage in the south wall. The second floor is also poorly lit but unlike the floor below has a fireplace, as well as a latrine in the south-west angle. It may perhaps have been designed for the lord's household and officials. The third floor has windows in all walls, including good two-light windows in the south wall, and seems to have been a double-level chamber with a wooden gallery above. These features mark it out as the lord's residential chamber.

Cushendun, Co. Antrim   Raised beach

15 km south-east of Ballycastle; located on a newly constructed riverside path along the west side of the Glendun river just before the bridge. Disc. Ser. 9.

At the end of one of the famous Glens of Antrim, the village of Cushendun nestles under the cliffs at the east end of a pebble beach where the Glendun river issues into the sea. Most of the houses belong to the National Trust, which is at present constructing a pathway along the west side of the river that, as it rounds the first bend in the river, will bring the visitor to the site of Hallam Movius' 1934 excavations of later Mesolithic sedimentary deposits. Here, the complex interaction of isostatic and eustatic responses saw Boreal Horizon peats (9000–5800 BC) covered over by 5 m of gravels and silts deposited by rising sea levels. Scattered through these latter were implements of late Mesolithic character. At the lower levels the flint implements were both water rolled and undamaged, suggesting that the material accumulated from the erosion of a number of sites. The upper gravel levels comprised a raised beach, above which was found a hearth and some scrapers.

At the other end of the bay, in Ballycleagh townland, are two standing stones alongside the driveway to a private house. A third stone is incorporated into the field fence. The stones are aligned roughly south-east/north-west. Nearby are the remains of an unusual little castle about which virtually nothing is known except that it is popularly held to be where Shane O'Neill attempted to negotiate an alliance with MacDonnell in 1567, only to end up murdered. A few miles north of Cushendun, in the townland of Altagore is a very fine cashel (*in private ownership*).

Donegore Hill, Co. Antrim   Causewayed camp; standing stone; early medieval settlement

7 km north-east of Antrim, off the M2; signposted. Disc. Ser. 14.

Rising to heights of 210 m and 234 m, the twin peaks of Donegore Hill are a prominent landmark to the north-east of Antrim town. The hill overlooks the upper reaches of Six Mile Water Valley and across to Lyles Hill, only 6 km to the south-east. To the west is Lough Neagh. There is a long history of diverse human activity here, even if only a small selection of the sites is accessible to the visitor. Systematic field-walking on the highest summit of Donegore in the early 1980s produced thousands of sherds of Neolithic pottery and lithics, including several porcellanite axes. A short exploratory excavation followed in 1983. At the same time, aerial photography by Barrie Hartwell revealed crop-marks of an interrupted, double-fossed (1–2 m deep, 3 m wide) enclosure, measuring about 200 m by 150 m. This was Ireland's first, and so far only 'causewayed camp', a classic site type of the English Neolithic

▲ Fig. 14. Donegore Hill (photo: Barrie Hartwell)

(*nothing remains to be seen of this monument and the land is in private ownership*).

Early prehistoric remains are not confined to the summit. An enormous motte beside the church near Nettlebush Bridge, at the south-western foot of Donegore Hill (*access through the Garden Centre*), was trenched to a depth of about 1 m in the early part of the 20th century and pockets of cremated human bone were found. This has led to the suggestion that the builders of the motte commandeered a prehistoric cemetery mound. In addition to this, fragments of Neolithic pottery were recovered from a now blocked-up, rock-cut 'souterrain' a few metres south-east of the mound.

A number of interesting sites are also reported on the summit of Browndod Hill, immediately north of Donegore Hill, including a fine Court tomb which was excavated in 1934. On the next peak to the north-west is a standing stone. Finally, west of the crossroads between Donegore Hill and Ballywoodock, in the townland of Tobergill, are the remains of a much denuded stone circle which early reports claim was approached by no less than two avenues of standing stones (*all these sites are on private land*).

Ballywee

Early medieval activity in the area is attested in the settlement at Ballywee on the north-east side of Donegore Hill, about 2 km north of Parkgate (*not signposted; access across one field opposite white-gabled*

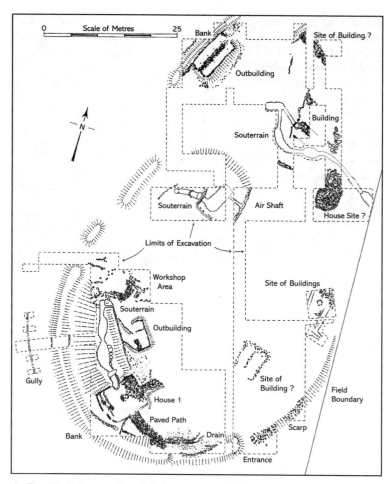

▲ Fig. 15. Ballywee: plan of site as excavated (after Lynn)

house hard by Ballywee Road). Excavations here in 1974 resulted in the discovery of an unusual but nonetheless substantial, enclosed settlement. The archaeology of early medieval secular settlement in Ireland is dominated by two monument types—ringforts and crannógs. It has long been suspected that there must have been many other, less formally defined settlement sites, but identifying these has proved difficult. Ballywee [*Baile Uaimh*, 'homestead of the caves'] seems to be such a site—not a ringfort, although clearly closely related. It consists of an oval area, *c.*90 m by 50 m, informally enclosed by a low, double earthen bank that can hardly have served any defensive purpose. An entrance gap in the south-east gave access to the interior, where excavation has revealed traces of at least nine structures, probably occupied in the 10th/11th centuries. The visible remains belong to the latest phase of occupation, as excavation revealed hints of an earlier phase of activity associated with a series of wooden buildings.

The embankments comprise a figure-of-eight shape (hard to discern on the ground) with the larger, primary enclosure to the south. They are comparatively slight and, unlike those of a conventional ringfort, appear to have been built solely to deflect surface water away from the interior. The entrance to the main enclosure is in the south-east, to the left of which is a drain and a kerbed and paved path, leading to the main house, a rectangular, sod-walled building (7 × 4 m internally) with a central hearth. The sods were retained at ground level by stone revetting. The south wall may have been of wood, possibly wicker, and there is a second paved entrance in the north-east wall. Much of the floor area was paved and the material assemblage, including pottery, jewellery, and a quernstone, is indicative of considerable wealth. Opposite the main entrance is a 16 m long souterrain, the lintel stones of which were buried beneath a bank. The northern side of the bank was revetted and about halfway along it are the remains of a rectangular outbuilding. Coterminous with the northern end of this embankment was a roughly paved workshop area with crucible fragments, burnt soil, and charcoal. About 20 m north of this is another partially buried souterrain with a large, rectangular chamber and stone-lined air vent. The trapdoor entrance is to the west. There are slight indications of an associated building on the surface. The incomplete outlines of a further two buildings in the eastern quadrant were also found.

Apart from the arcuate embankment of its north-western quadrant, the smaller, northern enclosure is quite incomplete. A well-preserved, rectangular building, interpreted as yet another outbuilding, abuts the interior face of the bank. The entrance is in the north wall and running down the middle of the building is a paved surface on each side of which were regularly spaced posts. Traces of three other buildings were found within the northern enclosure. One of them is associated with a long and sinuous souterrain. Although in a collapsed state, the remains of at least four rectangular chambers were uncovered. To the south of this is an oval-shaped paved area, possibly a floor surface. An ornate bronze belt buckle with blue glass studs was found nearby.

Dorsey, Armagh Linear earthwork

15 km south-west of Newry; off A29 (Newtonhamilton–Dundalk), 2 km north-west of Silver Bridge. Disc. Ser. 28.

The linear earthworks known as 'The Dorsey' lie on the west-south-western perimeter of the Ring of Gullion in South Armagh. For a long time it was considered to be a great, trapezoidal enclosure between the

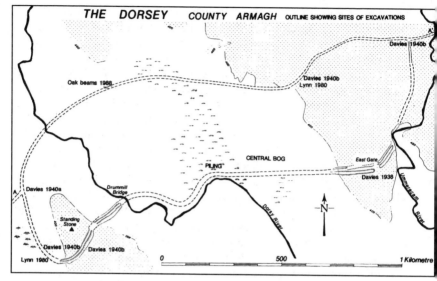

▲ **Fig. 16.** The Dorsey: plan of earthworks (after Lynn)

Ummercam and Dorsey rivers, though overlapping the latter. Recent excavations and a programme of dendrochronology have, however, radically altered this interpretation. Updating a theory advanced by Chart in 1930, Chris Lynn has cogently argued that the southern side is a supersession of the northern side. In other words, the original configuration of the earthwork proved unsatisfactory and so it was remodelled by building a new linear embankment, parallel to the first, a little less than 0.5 km to the south. Whether by design or default, the net result is actually an enclosure, and at times it may indeed have been utilized as such.

This theory is supported by constructional differences between the northern and southern sides, and in the dating evidence. The mid-point between the two rivers is quite boggy and here, instead of an earthen embankment, a palisade of oak piling was erected. Piles from the northern section returned dates centring on the 140s BC whereas those from the southern section are dated to a little after 100 BC. This latter date is sufficiently close to the 95/94 felling date of the central post of the Forty Metre Structure at **Navan Fort**, 26 km to the north, to suggest a direct connection. The Dorsey is traditionally considered to be part of the Black Pig's Dyke, or Worm Ditch, and the connection therefore carries with it the implication that this critical section was renovated under the authority of Emain Macha. The east–west long axis of the earthwork does indeed suggest a southern borderline, in many ways taking up where the **Ring of Gullion** leaves off. Where it survives, the southern earthwork is quite massive, rising about 8 m above the bottom of the ditches. A genuine entrance, the so-called 'East Gate' is located overlooking the Ummercam river.

The earthwork is substantially overgrown. It can be accessed in two places. Both difficult of access, the earthwork is perhaps at its most impressive where it is crossed by the tertiary road from Drummill to Coulter's Bridge, off the A29.

Downpatrick, Co. Down   Medieval town, cathedral

33 km south-east of Belfast on A7 or take A25 east from Newry; signposted. Disc. Ser. 21.

The name of Downpatrick [*Dún Pádraig*, 'the fort of Patrick'] reflects its main claim to fame—as the burial place of St Patrick. In the cathedral graveyard, on the south side, is a large slab inscribed with the name *PATRICK*, marking the saint's traditional resting place, although the slab itself is modern. However, both the name *Dún Pádraig* and the Patrician tradition only appeared after the English conquest in the late 12th century, and seem to have been deliberately engineered by the new lord, John de Courcy. The previous name for the place was *Dún dá Lethglais* and under this name it became the main residence of the Dál Fiatach, the ruling dynasty of the displaced Ulaid, possibly as early as the 5th/6th centuries. The *dún* element may have an even older ancestry, as excavation has revealed that the present Cathedral Hill is the site of a prehistoric hilltop enclosure that was refortified and reoccupied on several occasions from the Late Bronze Age through the Iron Age. Two hoards of Late Bronze Age gold bracelets have been found on the hill. There is also evidence for an early monastic site, which is first recorded in the 8th century and was presumably established by the Dál Fiatach. Thanks to Dál Fiatach patronage, it replaced the much older foundation at Bangor as the main church site of eastern Ulster and was chosen as an episcopal see in the early 12th-century church reforms. After de Courcy captured Downpatrick in 1177, the cathedral was reconstituted as a Benedictine priory with monks from Chester (dedicated no longer to the Holy Trinity but to St Patrick) and a town was subsequently established to the east of Cathedral Hill.

Very little survives of medieval Downpatrick. The present cathedral is largely a late 18th-/early 19th-century restoration, but seems to incorporate significant remains of an early 13th-century structure, especially in the choir. The present tower at the west end of the cathedral is entirely 19th century. The medieval cathedral, which was ruined *c.*1540, seems to have been a relatively small, rectangular building of five bays, with a central nave and side aisles extending the full length. In the choir, with its very attractive late 18th-century wooden stalls and box pews, the columns of the aisle arcades bear decorated capitals which seem to be original 13th-century work, although heavily restored in the 19th century. In the porch (under the tower) are fragments of two 9th/10th-century crosses and other early carved stones, while fragments of two 12th-century crosses are inserted in a wall in the south aisle. Just inside the cathedral proper is a large granite font of medieval (possibly 13th-century) date; although it was found in the town in the early 20th century, it probably belonged to the medieval cathedral originally. Outside the east end of the cathedral are the weathered remains of another large cross. A round tower, which was burnt by lightning in 1015–16, stood to the south-west of the cathedral until the late 18th/early 19th century.

North-east of Cathedral Hill is a large enclosure known as the Mount, or Mound of Down (*access via Mount Crescent, off English St.*), measuring *c.*175 m by 100 m with massive earthen defences. Internally there is a mound built against the bank of the enclosure, which may be an unfinished motte. On the assumption that the mound is a motte of late 12th-/early 13th-century date and is later than the enclosure, it has been suggested that the enclosure is a royal residence of the 11th/12th-century Dál Fiatach kings of Ulaid. This remains to be confirmed by excavation. On the Mall, at the foot of Cathedral Hill, the Down County Museum occupies the historic County Gaol site and is worth visiting.

Dromore, Co. Down Motte-and-bailey castle, high cross

25 km south of Belfast off A1 (Dublin–Belfast); signposted. Disc. Ser. 20.

Dromore [*Druim Mór*, 'the great ridge'] is a small, sleepy town but is worth visiting for probably the finest motte-and-bailey castle in Ulster. It was also an early church site, said to have been founded by St Colmán *c.*600 and which became the see of a diocese at the end of the 12th century. The present cathedral is mainly early 19th century, but nearby (*beside the Lagan bridge*) is a restored high cross of granite, the original parts of which are 9th/10th century. The 'cushioned' form of the base is unusual and the surviving part of the shaft is decorated with fretwork designs within sunken panels, framed by interlace panels. The upper part of the shaft is modern but the cross head, with its unpierced ring, is original and has worn interlace decoration on the west face.

The motte sits high over the town at the east end (*south side of Mount St.*). Surprisingly little is known of its history—it may have been erected by de Courcy after 1177, but this is not certain as Dromore never really formed part of the English earldom of Ulster. An Irish king may have erected it, although this seems unlikely. Limited excavations in the 1950s shed little light on the castle's origins. The motte is up to 20 m in diameter at the summit and rises 12 m above the base of the surrounding fosse. A low earthen bank surrounds the summit (excavation showed this to be a replacement for an original palisade) and a narrow berm is present about two-thirds of the way up the mound. The surrounding fosse is up to 12 m wide and 3.5 m deep; to the south it extends in a roughly square shape to enclose a bailey c.30 m wide. Most of the motte and the east side of the bailey are further defended by an outer bank and fosse, while the interior of the bailey also has a low earthen bank, best preserved on the south.

Drumena, Co. Down Cashel

23 km north-east of Newry, off A25 (Newry–Downpatrick); beside tertiary road, 3.6 km south-west of Castlewellan, signposted from A25. Disc. Ser. 29.

This is a fine example of a cashel, dating from early medieval times. It is situated on an unnamed hill at the north-eastern foot of Slievenaman, looking across Lough Island Reavy to Tullynasoo Mountain. It is somewhat pear shaped in plan and the original entrance is facing east-south-east. The walls average about 3 m in thickness. The cashel was investigated, and partially restored in 1925–6. It has been suggested that the undulating ground south of centre indicates the foundations of secondary buildings. Behind these, in the south-west quadrant is a fine T-shaped souterrain in which sherds of Souterrain Ware were found.

Dundrum, Co. Down Castle

33 km north-east of Newry on A25 (Newry–Strangford); on a hill overlooking Dundrum village; signposted. Disc. Ser. 21.

This important early 13th-century castle replaced an earthwork castle built by John de Courcy soon after 1177, which itself probably stood on the site of an earlier stronghold [*Dún Druma*, 'the fort on the ridge']. Strongly sited on a hilltop overlooking Dundrum Bay, the castle was probably intended mainly to dominate the land route along the east Ulster coast. The stone walls and buildings were probably also begun by de Courcy and continued by successive 13th-century earls of Ulster, but by the mid-14th century the castle was in the hands of the Mac Aonghusa (Magennis) lords, who held it for the remainder of the Middle Ages. The castle consists of upper and lower wards joined in a rough figure-of-eight plan. The upper ward is the earlier, but the visitor enters through the lower ward, probably a late medieval Mac Aonghusa addition, of which little survives other than the curtain wall. The original entrance is a simple gateway, with machicolation above, in the north-west angle, and there is a blocked postern gate on the east side. In the southern angle are the ruins of an inserted L-shaped 17th-century house.

The upper ward is surrounded by a large, rock-cut fosse, within which is a late 12th-century curtain wall following the natural contours of the hill. Just below the parapet (where it survives) small square holes

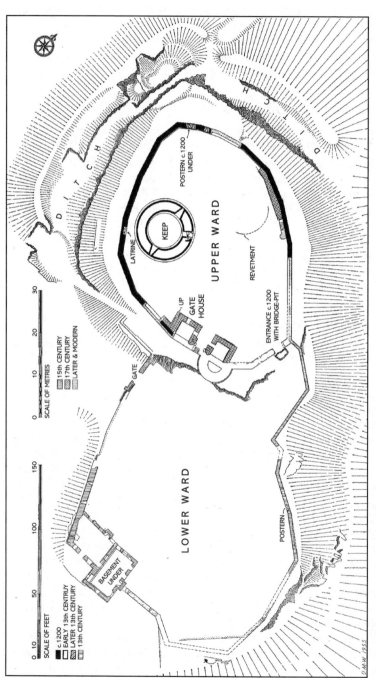

▲ **Fig. 17.** Dundrum Castle: plan (HMSO)

in the curtain wall held beams supporting a wooden hoarding from which defenders could repel attackers. The original entrance is on the east, beside the junction with the wall of the lower ward, and was clearly defended by a drawbridge across the fosse, as the bridge pit is visible externally. To the west of this entrance are the ruins of a large gatehouse erected *c.*1260 to replace the earlier one. It consists of twin square towers, originally of two storeys, built against the inner face of the curtain wall and flanking an entrance passage running through an opening inserted in the curtain wall. The foundations of the semicircular outer face of the eastern tower are visible in the fosse, but there is no evidence for a similar forework to the western tower.

On the west side of the upper ward is a great circular keep, built early in the 13th century. It is 15 m in internal diameter, with walls up to 3.4 m thick, and has two storeys above a basement that contained a rock-cut cistern to collect the castle's water supply, by natural seepage. The keep is entered at first-floor level by a doorway on the east. Just north of this a spiral stair within the thickness of the wall gives access to the other floors; on the west another narrower doorway gave access (via some form of bridge) to the curtain wall walk. The first floor is lit by two rectangular opes set in large embrasures with window seats, on the north and south walls, and was originally vaulted. The second floor may have been partly rebuilt in the 15th century and contains a series of chambers within the thickness of the wall on the north, west, and south sides. Above this was a wall walk, with parapet.

Dunluce, Co. Antrim   Castle

10 km north-east of Coleraine, on A2 coast road (Portrush–Bushmills); signposted. Visitor centre; admission charge. Disc. Ser. 4 and 5.

Dunluce is perhaps the most dramatic of Irish castles, perched on a high rocky promontory overlooking the North Channel. It is also important archaeologically as an example of a relatively large castle built by a Gaelic lord, probably first built by the MacQuillans in the late 14th century. The name [*Dún Lios*, 'strong fort'] suggests that it was the site of an early medieval fort or *dún*, and this is borne out by the discovery of a souterrain beneath the north-eastern tower of the later castle. In the late 16th century it was occupied by the MacDonnells from nearby western Scotland, who created a late medieval lordship in north-eastern Ireland, largely at the expense of the MacQuillans. They built most of what is visible at Dunluce today, probably after the castle had been badly damaged by the English Lord Deputy, Perrott, in 1584. The MacDonnells also established a small town to the south-west of the castle in the early 17th century but this did not survive long, as part of the castle collapsed into the sea in 1639 and the remainder seems to have gone out of use soon after this.

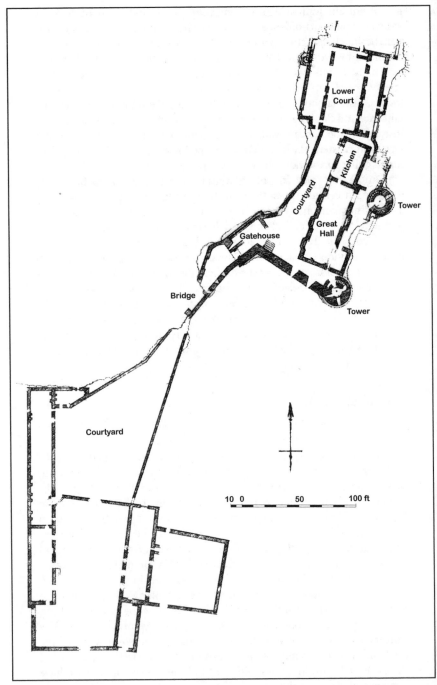

▲ **Fig. 18.** Dunluce Castle: plan by Du Noyer, 1839

Dunluce is approached through a large house and court, built by the (MacDonnell) earl of Antrim for his wife, the duchess of Buckingham, whom he married in 1635 and who did not like to live in the castle itself. Strong converging walls protect the approach from this house to the castle, which sits on a rock-stack and is only accessible via a narrow bridge, which would have been a drawbridge in the Middle Ages. The rectangular gatehouse was built by the MacDonnells shortly before 1600 and, like much of the castle, shows strong Scottish influence (for instance in the corbelled-out turrets). The rest of the castle stretches northwards along the rock and consists of a series of buildings of different dates. To the rear (east) of these are two circular towers that, along with the curtain wall on the southern edge of the site, are the oldest surviving features, probably representing the southern and eastern sides of an original roughly square 14th-century castle. From the gatehouse one enters a narrow courtyard, on the east side of which are the pillars of a late 16th-century Italian-style *loggia*—a north-facing open-sided arcade—unique in Ireland at this period. This was largely replaced in the early 17th century by a fine two-storey house, with mullioned windows and an interesting fireplace in the great hall on the ground floor. North-east of this is a kitchen with two ovens, to service the great hall. At the north end of the site is a lower court with domestic quarters originally arranged around three sides of a courtyard.

Grey abbey, Co. Down Cistercian abbey

25 km south-west of Belfast on A20 (Newtownards–Portaferry); at east end of village of Grey Abbey; signposted. Disc. Ser. 15.

This fine Cistercian abbey was founded in 1193 by Affreca, wife of John de Courcy—one of a series of monasteries established in de Courcy's new lordship of Ulster in the late 12th century. It was not part of the Irish Cistercian community derived from **Mellifont**, but was colonized by Cistercian monks from Holm Cultram abbey in Cumbria, reflecting de Courcy's probable Cumbrian origins and his desire for a loyal English church. The abbey functioned throughout the Middle Ages, despite serious damage during the Bruce invasion (1315–18) but was dissolved *c.*1541 and in 1572 the buildings were burned by Brian Ó Néill. The nave of the church was restored for use as a parish church for much of the 17th and 18th centuries.

Grey abbey is one of the earliest examples of true Gothic architecture in Ireland, probably built by masons from northern England, and almost all of the surviving fabric appears to be original, late 12th-/early 13th-century work. It is relatively simple architecturally, and only a restricted range of Gothic elements was employed; thus, for example, there is no evidence for vaulting. Like all Cistercian abbeys it conforms to a standard plan, with the church and three ranges of buildings arranged

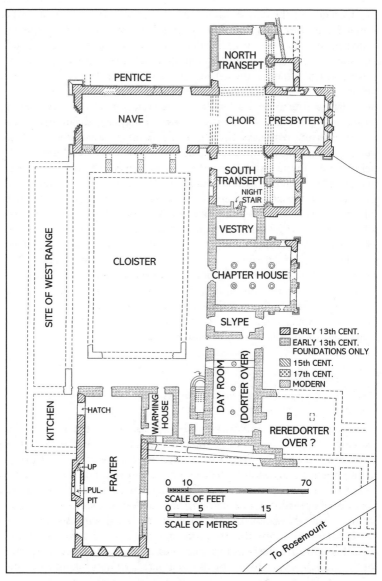

▲ Fig. 19. Grey abbey: plan (HMSO)

around a central cloister garth. The lack of architectural ornamentation is also characteristically Cistercian. The church occupies the north side of the cloister and consists of an aisleless nave with relatively short choir, north and south transepts (each with two chapels on the east side), and a typically low, squat tower over the crossing. It seems clear (from the relationship of the nave to the cloister) that the church was originally intended to be much longer than actually built, but was scaled down for financial or other reasons. The west doorway is a fine, rather squat early Gothic composition of four orders, dating to c.1220, which suggests that construction lasted over 20 years. It was reconstructed in the 19th century and may not be in its original location. The east end is lit by two storeys each of three lancet windows and similar lancets in the north and south walls light the nave. The roof of the presbytery and two of its windows were remodelled in the 15th century, when the corbel table with carved heads was added to the exterior of the north wall. In the choir are a piscina and sedilia, as well as a tomb recess containing a female effigy. A male effigy of a knight in armour, once very fine but now much eroded, is located in the north transept chapel and the two effigies are traditionally said to represent John de Courcy and his wife Affreca. This may be the case, but the effigies themselves are much later—late 13th/early 14th century.

In the south wall of the south transept are the foundations of the night stairs, which led to the monks' dormitory at first-floor level over the east range of claustral buildings, and provided ready access to the church for night offices. The cloisters are arranged on an unusually narrow rectangular plan, rather than the normal square. This, together with the disproportionately small nave of the church, suggests that the original plans (which presumably would have extended much further to the west) had to be drastically scaled back during construction. The main building on the east side of the cloister is the chapter house, where the community held their chapter and business meetings. It is divided by pillars into three aisles and was lit by lancet windows in the east wall and at the east ends of the north and south walls. The other buildings in the south-eastern sector of the abbey are poorly preserved or completely vanished, as is the entire range of buildings on the west side of the cloister. On the south side there are substantial remains of the monks' refectory, a projecting rectangular building with fine early Gothic lancets in the south wall. Note the pulpit midway along the west wall, where a brother read devotional literature to the monks as they ate. An opening in the north-west corner led to the kitchen, to the west. Immediately east of the refectory was the *calefactory* or 'warming house', a simple room which was the only chamber of the abbey (apart from the kitchen) with a fireplace—and no doubt eagerly sought out on many cold days!

Harryville, Co. Antrim Motte-and-bailey castle

On south side of Ballymena, take the A36 towards Ballygreggy, or the Toome Road (B18) off Queen Street. Disc. Ser. 14.

This tall, flat-topped motte-and-bailey castle is prominently located on a ridge overlooking the river Braid, although now rather incongruously bordered by modern housing. The motte is *c.*13 m high and is separated from the raised bailey by a deep fosse; a large earthen bank surrounds both motte and bailey. It is a fine example of a motte-and-bailey castle, but what is of most interest about it is its location, in an area that seems never to have formed part of the English lordship of Ulster. It has therefore been suggested that it was built by an Irish lord, to fortify his lordship against English aggression, in the late 12th/13th centuries.

Legananny, Co. Down   Portal tomb

20 km west of Downpatrick on south-west side of Slieve Croob, midway between Castlewellan and Dromara; approached on tertiary road off the B7 (Ballynahinch–Rathfriland) between Gransha and Massford, or off the A50 between Castlewellan and Ballyward. Disc. Ser. 20.

Very little is known about Legananny dolmen but it is worth a visit on aesthetic grounds alone. It is the most elegant tripod Portal tomb (or dolmen) in Ireland. The capstone is supported on three strikingly tall orthostats. It is located on a 250 m shoulder about 3 km to the south-east of the summit of Slieve Croob. From here are spectacular views of the Mountains of Mourne to the south. Cairn stones protrude from the grass around and William Gray reported that 'urns' of unspecified type were recovered from the tomb in the late 19th century.

▼ **Fig. 20.** Lisnagade: sketch plan of earthworks (HMSO)

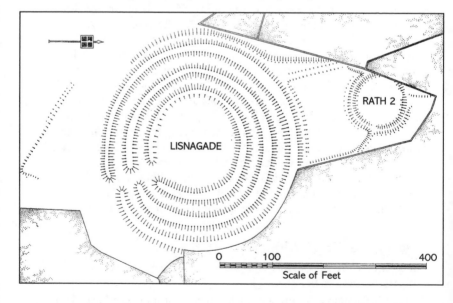

RATH 2

LISNAGADE

0   100   400

Scale of Feet

Lisnagade, Co. Down Ringfort

2 km south-west of Banbridge; turn south off B10 (Banbridge–Scarva) at Ballyvarley School; beside the avenue leading to Lisnagade House. Disc. Ser. 20.

According to the law tracts, great triple-ramparted raths such as this one were the homes of kings, one of a number scattered across the *túath* or petty kingdom. The far smaller, univallate rath appended to the back of it is probably the equivalent of a servant's quarter. The site was cleaned up in 1852, when a cauldron, a spear, and some arrowheads (now lost) were unearthed. Excavations in 1951 were unrewarding. The earthwork is about 120 m in diameter and the interior about 55 m. The entrance faces south-east. It was planted with trees as a landscape feature and is a little overgrown, but the scale of the ramparts alone makes this site worth a visit. In addition to these two, there are four other raths in this townland, including (*on the far side of Lisnagade House*) the huge, oval-shaped, bivallate rath of Lisnavaragh. This too was excavated in 1951 but again no structures or datable artefacts were found.

These sites occur on the east side of the middle reaches of the Newry river valley, just to the north-east of Lough Shark. This is a very significant natural corridor from Carlingford Lough to Lough Neagh and is partially bridged by a section of the so-called 'Dane's Cast' or Black Pig's Dyke. No great leap of the imagination is required to assemble these raths and the dyke into a defensive line along the valley. Indeed, Lawlor suggested that Lisnagade Fort was one of a series of enormously defensive earthworks on the east side of the 'Dane's Cast'. If contemporary, however, their classification as ringforts may need to be reconsidered.

Lubitavish, Cloghbrack, Co. Antrim Court tomb

Between Cushendun and Cushendall, signposted on A2 (Belfast–Ballycastle); up a laneway off tertiary road. Seek parking in the farmyard at the start of the laneway as there is no turning at the top. Disc. Ser. 5.

Known as 'Ossian's Grave', this open-court tomb is on the north-eastern shoulder of Tievebulliagh Mountain. It is positioned on an almost level platform below the summit of a small hill that obscures the view of Tievebulliagh itself. Instead, the landscape comprises the back of Tieveragh hill and Cushendun Glen to the north-east. The tomb is reasonably well preserved and has two burial chambers opening towards the east-south-east. The chambers are separated by well-defined jambstones, but one or two of the sidestones are missing or rolled over. About 20 m downhill, to the north, are two standing stones, aligned on Cushendun. Below these again are numerous loose and seemingly randomly scattered boulders. The alignment of the two standing stones is taken up by two further stones spaced about 20 m apart in the

▲ **Fig. 21.** Lurigethan promontory (photo: Conor Newman)

next field higher up the hill, from where the summit of Tievebulliagh is visible.

Lurigethan, Co. Antrim Promontory fort

3 km south-west of Cushendall, on link road to Red Arch off the B14 to Ballymena; not signposted. Disc. Ser. 5.

Overlooking Glenarriff, Red Bay, and the town of Cushendall, Lurigethan is one of the most spectacularly situated promontory forts in Ireland. To the north is Tievebulliagh Mountain and across the sea are the Western Isles of Scotland. As elsewhere in Antrim, the headland comprises an escarpment of peat-covered, basalt cliffs over deep deposits of chalk and steeply inclined scree slopes. Direct access to the summit is from the northern foot along the zigzag paths, clearly visible from the bottom but difficult enough to follow on the ground. These are best approached through or alongside a recent plantation of fir and silver birch trees on the west side of the tertiary road to Red Bay, off the Ballymena Road from Cushendall. Not for the faint of heart, nor indeed the weak of heart, this is a very steep climb and the return journey downhill is treacherous in wet weather. Approaching the base of the cliffs swing left towards a line of fence posts and follow these to the top. Once there, follow the stone wall along the headland to the ramparts (by way of an alternative the site can be approached inland, from the west; it is, however, a long walk). They are best preserved in the area where they are intersected by the wall, surviving to well over 1 m in height. There are typically four closely spaced ramparts but from time to time an extra one or two are added. The entrance is south-east of the wall and is marked by an inward-turning of the banks and an alignment of small boulders.

There are numerous thought-provoking undulations in the area behind the ramparts, including what looks like a somewhat oval-shaped ring barrow and a series of sub-rectangular hollows that might be the remains of sunken houses. The view, of course, is awe-inspiring; particularly evocative is the Eilse Bute off the west coast of Argyllshire, south-west Scotland, from where the stone for curling balls is quarried. At the northern foot of the mountain, almost opposite the above-mentioned plantation, is an unusual monument comprising a circular embankment surrounding a rock outcrop that rises to a distinct, soil-covered point. It is probably a form of burial mound and has a close parallel near Nobber in Co. Meath. A race is held annually from the watchtower on the beach at Cushendall to the summit. The record currently stands at about 26 minutes!

Millin Bay, Co. Down Prehistoric burial site

Near the tip of the Ards peninsula. Off A2 (Bangor–Portaferry coast road), 4 km south-east of Portaferry, overlooking Millin Bay; signposted. Disc. Ser. 21.

Millin Bay opens onto the Irish Sea, about 4 km south-east of Portaferry on the east coast of the Ards peninsula. One end of the bay is marked by Millin Hill overlooking the village of Tara, the other by a standing stone. The long cairn itself is more or less in the middle. About 1 km to the south is a prominent hill on the top of which is Tara Fort. While there may not be much to see at Millin Bay today, this complex monument occupies an important place in the study of early prehistory. Even if it remains something of an enigma, the excavation was exemplary. Prior to its excavation in the summer of 1953 by Pat Collins and Dudley Waterman, the monument presented as a low, oval mound of sand (23 m × 15 m) partly surrounded by standing stones. In the centre, beneath the mound was uncovered a long, narrow cist (5.5 m × 0.6 m). Some of the slabs were decorated with pecked symbols, similar to Passage tomb art, and cupmarks and at least half of the lintel slabs were intact. There were at least 16 disarticulated burials and one cremation packed into the southern end of the cist. Bones were, to an extent, sorted according to type (long bones, skulls, etc.) and in a couple of cases dislodged teeth were inexpertly and inaccurately refitted into the empty sockets. The cist was in turn surrounded, eccentrically, by a façade of contiguous upright slabs, many of which bore decoration. These were supported from behind by a small bank of shingle. A second, semi-circular orthostatic façade occurred around the north end of the bank. This whole ensemble was surrounded by an incomplete ring of large orthostats, some of which had pecked ornamentation. Three so-called

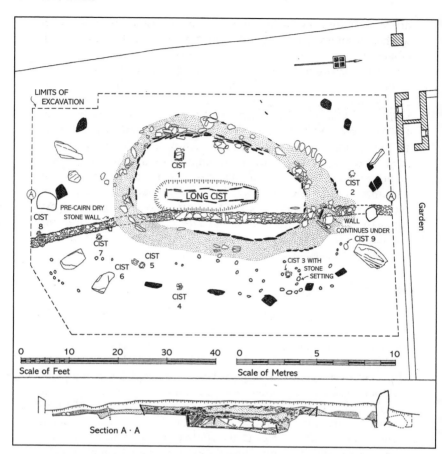

▲ **Fig. 22.** Millin Bay cairn: plan of site as excavated (after Collins & Waterman)

'axial stones' were also erected at either end of the cairn. In addition
to this nine smaller, box-like cists were also found. One was close to the
long cists and the remaining nine occurred between the embanked,
orthostatic façade and the stone circle. Five contained cremated adult
remains. There were also a number of cobblestone arrangements in
this area, comprising rows or arcuate settings. One in particular all but
surrounded cist no. 3. In marked contrast to the angular slabs employed
elsewhere, these were all water-rounded whitish Silurian cobbles. The
embanked central area was filled in with a cairn of shingle, sand, and
stones many of which bore pecked ornamentation. Fragments of a
Carrowkeel pot were found near the north end of the monument,
though the rim has affinities with a pot from the nearby Court tomb at
Audleystown and the **Ballynoe** stone circle and cairn. Over 300 struck
flints were found and part of a partially polished flint axe. Part of a

drystone wall was exposed during excavation running from north to south across the site and under the burial monument. Although clearly of considerable antiquity, the excavators argued against a practical or agrarian explanation because it was built on a developing sand dune.

Narrow Water, Co. Down Tower house

7 km south of Newry on A2 (Newry–Warrenpoint); signposted. Disc. Ser. 29.

This three-storey tower house is picturesquely situated on the estuary of the Newry River, just above its entry into Carlingford Lough. It was probably built *c.*1560 by John Sancky and was clearly intended to control traffic on the river. The three floors each contain a single main chamber, with an attic above, and it is vaulted over the first floor. The ground-floor entrance is protected by a murder hole overhead. There are latrine chambers in the south-west angle at first- and second-floor levels, and two other mural chambers at second floor. Surrounding the tower house is an irregular bawn, substantially restored. Nearby (*c.400 m south-east*) is a small motte.

Navan complex Late prehistoric settlement/ritual landscape

2.6 km west of Armagh; signposted. Disc. Ser. 19. Note: at time of writing, the visitor centre has ceased trading.

The Navan complex is one of Ireland's premier prehistoric ritual and settlement landscapes. Over 40 sites have been identified in an area of about 6 km², most notable of which are Navan Fort itself, the ritual ponds of Loughnashade and the King's Stables, the hillfort known as Haughey's Fort, two destroyed stone circles or megalithic tombs, and numerous ring-ditches, linear earthworks, and mounds. Excavations at some of the principal sites suggest that the area achieved something approaching regional prominence during the later prehistoric period (*c.*1200 BC to AD 500). This wealth and achievement is reflected in the range of stray finds of high-class metalwork from the vicinity, including four magnificent Iron Age bronze trumpets recovered during the 18th century from Loughnashade, where they had been votively deposited with a large quantity of bones including human skulls.

It has been suggested that the later Bronze Age sites of Haughey's Fort (which appears to have been a settlement site) and the King's Stables were abandoned in favour of Navan Fort and its ritual pond, Loughnashade, during the Iron Age. Even before this changeover took place, however, Navan Fort may already have been a major ritual site, associated with Haughey's Fort, and some of this early ritual prestige was doubtless conferred on those who lived there during the Early Iron Age. This may well be reflected in the mythology that has grown up around it. Recent dating of the linear earthwork at Tray Bog, between

Navan Fort and Haughey's Fort, suggests that it too relates to this period of activity.

Navan Fort (Emain Macha)

Navan Fort is a site of immense importance, not only in archaeological terms but also in early Irish history and mythology. There is little doubt that Navan Fort is the *Emain Macha* described in early mythology as the capital of the Ulstermen (Ulaid). *Emain Macha* plays a central role in the earliest Irish heroic literature, the Ulster Cycle of tales, including the *Táin Bó Cuailgne* (The Cattle Raid of Cooley). It was the seat of the legendary king Conor Mac Nessa and home to the Red Branch Knights and the Ulster hero Cú Chulainn. The meaning of the name *Emain Macha* is uncertain but apparently derives from Macha, one of a triad of war goddesses associated with fertility and valour. One popular explanation is that the name means the twins of Macha, for legend has it that in spite of being nine months pregnant, Macha was forced into a race against the king's horses around the ramparts of Navan Fort. Naturally, she won but upon crossing the finish line gave birth to twins and died. She also gave her name to the area around Emain, *Mag Macha* (the plain of Macha) and to the hill on which is built the city of Armagh (*Ard Macha*). Emain may be the *Isamnion* listed by the 2nd-century AD Greek geographer Ptolemy. Ptolemy locates Isamnion in the area of a tribe known as the Voluntii (derived from the Celtic *Ulunti*, whence Old Irish *Ulaid*).

The fort is defined by a massive circular bank with internal fosse, about 290 m in diameter, enclosing the top of a small drumlin. Various dates (from Late Neolithic to Iron Age) have been advanced for its construction but the only independent evidence, until very recently, was a radiocarbon date of 766–398 BC for peat from the base of the fosse, extracted by pollen core. This suggested that the enclosure was built sometime before 400 BC. In 1999–2000, however, Jim Mallory cut a series of sections across the fosse and discovered, at the base, large oak timbers that are dated dendrochronologically to the later 2nd and early 1st century BC, contemporary with the construction of the Forty Metre Structure (see below).

There are two circular monuments (referred to as sites A and B) within the fort, both of which were excavated by D. Waterman 1963–70 (neither has been fully published). Site A, located a little to the south-east of centre, is a ring barrow and Site B, some 40 m to the west, is a large circular mound.

Site A

A ring barrow, some 50 m in diameter, with a central mound surrounded by a fosse and external bank. Excavation revealed three phases of development: the **first phase**, dating from the Late Bronze/Early Iron Age, is evidenced by three closely set concentric foundation trenches which have been interpreted as three successive, very large, circular wooden buildings. Alternatively, they may represent a single, triple-walled structure. It is not known whether these were domestic buildings or not. A recent geophysical survey has revealed what appear to be the foundation trenches of a double-walled enclosure/building about 30 m in diameter to the west. This may have been attached to the phase 1 buildings in a figure-of-eight arrangement identical to the buildings and compounds erected during the third phase of activity at Site B.

The **second phase** saw the construction of an unusual circular building whose double walls were set about 2 m apart. This building overlapped with the eastern half of the phase 1 buildings and was provided with an east-facing entrance flanked by two extended burials. It has been suggested, principally on the basis of the burials, that the building dates from the Early Christian Period, but this could be seen as anomalous in view of the subsequent construction of a ring barrow—which is essentially a pagan burial monument—in phase 3. Assuming that the burials are related, it is likely that this building had some ritual function. The ring barrow was constructed during the **third phase**, its fosse cutting through the phase 1 trenches. The mound is something of a *trompe l'œil*, and while a ritual function must be presumed, there was no evidence of how this monument functioned, though ploughing in the recent past may have removed much of the evidence.

Site B

This large mound, 6 m high and 50 m in diameter at the base, was constructed at the beginning of the 1st century BC, but excavation revealed a fascinating sequence of earlier activity. The earliest remains (**phase 1**), dating from the Neolithic period, survived only as a collection of pits and some pottery, having been greatly disturbed by later activity. The first major structural feature (**phase 2**), dating from around the 8th century BC, can be interpreted as a type of henge consisting of a circle of large timber poles (evidenced by a ring of 34 large postholes), 35 m in diameter, encircled by a broad, shallow, penannular fosse opening to the east. Relatively little attention has been focused on this important ritual structure, which attests to ceremonial activity at Navan Fort from at least this period.

During the **third phase** (4th to 1st century BC) a succession of circular wooden buildings (evidenced as groups of concentric and overlapping foundation trenches) were erected on the same spot towards the southern side of the earlier enclosure. Depending on whether these are interpreted as double-/triple-walled buildings, or as successive single-walled buildings, anything from four to twelve successive houses may have been built. To the north of these, in some cases physically attached to them, stood another series of larger circular enclosures, interpreted as compounds with fenced avenues approaching from the east, across the gap in the later Bronze Age enclosure. A close comparison exists with the ground plan of the buildings of the 'Rose Phase' at Dún Ailinne (**Knockaulin**, Co. Kildare) which, though far larger and obviously of ritual significance, are essentially contemporary. The structures at Dún Ailinne may be ceremonial renditions of conventional domestic buildings of high status such as those at Navan. The material assemblage from this phase at Navan includes a winged chape of Hallstatt C type, a finely decorated ring-headed pin, and the skull and mandible of a Barbary ape (suggesting that the ape was either alive or not long dead upon its arrival), implying contact with the Mediterranean world and indicating that these were high-status—perhaps royal—residences.

Very shortly after the abandonment of these buildings (perhaps even precipitating it) a highly elaborate and quite unique ritual structure was built (**phase 4**) in three successive stages. The first stage saw the erection of a multi-ringed timber circle consisting of five concentric rings of posts arranged around a massive central oak post (felled in 95–94 BC) with an 'entrance' from the west. This edifice was contained within a double wall, about 37 m in diameter, composed of stout posts connected by horizontal split timbers, and may have been roofed. Soon after its completion, while the posts were still standing, the interior was filled with limestone blocks to a height of nearly 3 m. The whole structure was then set alight and covered with a mantle of soil, producing the mound visible today (reconstituted after excavation). Lynn suggests that this ritual sequence may be an elaborate offering to the Celtic sky or thunder god, Taranis, whose symbol, the wheel, is represented by the radial pattern of the stone cairn as seen from the air. In a complex thesis, he suggests that the three basic elements of the structure, wood, stone, and soil, were meant to symbolize the three castes in Celtic society, druids, warriors, and farmers, united in a ritual analogous to a holocaust rite described by Posidonius and Caesar which apparently involved setting alight enormous wicker effigies filled with living sacrificial victims. However, rather than burning people alive, it is suggested that the limestone blocks, which were possibly removed from an earlier burial cairn nearby, were used instead to represent the souls of the dead. The great timber structure (the central post of which is the *axis mundi*) represents a *bruiden*, presided over by Donn, lord of the otherworld.

These represent the latest structures identified at Navan Fort. Although *Emain Macha* continued to occupy a prominent place in early

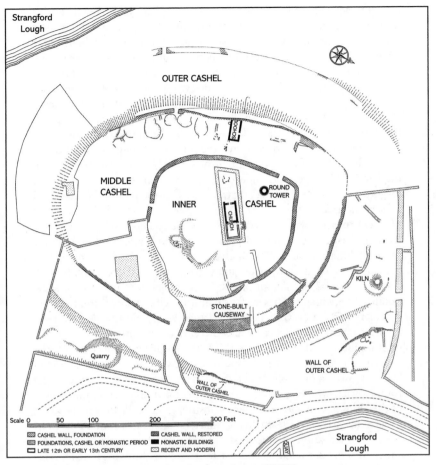

▲ **Fig. 23.** Nendrum: plan of monastic enclosure (HMSO)

medieval literature, there is little evidence for sustained activity at Navan in the Christian era.

Nendrum, Co. Down Island monastery

25 km south-east of Belfast; take A22 (Comber–Downpatrick) and minor road to east; signposted. Visitor centre on site.

Nendrum [probably *Naendruim*, 'nine ridges'] is an early monastic site on an island in Strangford Lough. Although it was never a particularly important foundation, it is significant as probably the most extensively excavated such site in Ireland. Unfortunately the main excavations in the 1920s fell far below modern archaeological standards, so that less is known about the site than might be expected. Despite this (and some unfortunate restoration), Nendrum is one of the best sites to get an impression of the layout and appearance of an early medieval monastic site. The traditional founder was the 5th-century St Mochaoi (after whom the island, Mahee Island, is named) although a somewhat later foundation date is perhaps more likely. The monastery was clearly in existence by the early 7th century, however, as recent excavations have revealed a tide mill on the island shore that has been dated by dendro-chronology to 619. Two later mills were built on the site, the latest phase being dated to 789. Little is known of Nendrum's later history until 1179 when John de Courcy gave the site to an English Benedictine community. This foundation in turn probably ceased to function in the late Middle Ages and, indeed, the site was entirely abandoned and forgotten until the 19th century, which accounts for its exceptional preservation.

Nendrum displays the classic morphology and layout of an early Irish monastic site, divided by concentric enclosing walls into three zones of differing status. The innermost and smallest zone, at the crest of the ridge, is *c*.75 m in diameter and surrounded by a stone wall (largely restored), over 2 m thick in places. It contained the main ecclesiastical buildings, of which the bases of a small stone church and a round tower, together with a graveyard, survive. The west wall and lintelled doorway of the church are restored, while the eastern extension was probably built by the Benedictines in the late 12th century. At one corner of the church is a restored sundial (one of the few early medieval examples known), used to mark the times of the main daily religious services. The round tower, which survives to a height of 4 m, is located north-west of the church. Outside the inner enclosure, the middle enclosure seems to have been used both for living quarters and craft production. Con-siderable excavation on the west side revealed foundations of several small structures, including at least four circular buildings of drystone walling, interpreted as workshops, and a rectangular building inter-preted as a school. Much of the middle enclosure wall on the west side appears to be a modern restoration, and the original enclosure probably ran some distance to the west. Lawlor (the 1920s excavator) suggested that there was evidence in this area for earlier, pre-Christian and secular occupation, and indeed that the enclosure itself was pre-Christian. However, modern scholars believe the 'earlier' material represents simply an earlier phase of the monastic occupation. Neither earlier nor later occupation material can be securely dated. Only fragments of the outer enclosure wall survive, and little investigation of this area has taken place.

Rathlin Island, Co. Antrim

Access by ferry from Ballycastle. Disc. Ser. 5.

First recorded as *Ricina* on Ptolemy's mid-2nd-century AD map, this narrow, L-shaped island, 10 km off the north coast of Antrim, is the only inhabited island in Northern Ireland. It has a rich natural and historical heritage and boasts spectacular coastal scenery. The sea between the island and the mainland is notorious in myth and legend for its currents and whirlpools and is called *Sloch na Mara* or the 'Cauldron of Brecán'. Brecán, son of Partholon (the first mythological invader of Ireland), is said to have perished here with a fleet of 50 curraghs. St Columba (Colmcille) is said to have had a lucky escape, too—but do not let that put you off!

Early prehistoric activity is in evidence at the porcellanite axe factory in Brockley townland, towards the west end of the island near Ballygill. This is now inaccessible, but once rivalled **Tievebulliagh** in terms of gross output. Just behind the south side of Church Bay harbour, which is in the 'elbow' of the island, is a cemetery area that Richard Warner has speculated stretches from the Bronze Age to the Viking period. Tumuli and cist graves have been reported in this area since 1784 and numerous cist burials were recorded during quarrying in the early 1980s. One of them contained the remains of five people. In the same area is a standing stone which is said to mark a 9th-century cist-like grave, dated by the finding there of a splendid silver penannular brooch (*on display in the National Museum of Ireland*). It was probably the grave of a Viking. To the north-east, in Ballycarry townland, is 'Bruce's castle', a high promontory fort (*dangerous to access*) defended on the island side by a stone wall. The date of the remains is not known. It was to a cave below the promontory (*accessible only by boat*) that Robert Bruce retreated in 1306, only to find inspiration in the determination of a spider to cast its web between two rocks. Thus girded, he returned to Scotland and success at the Battle of Bannockburn. There is another promontory-like fort, Doonmore, at the north-west end of the island, about 3.2 km from Bull Point, with remains of a stone-faced rampart, 4 m wide. Contact with the Roman Empire is attested to in the discovery of a 1st century AD patera near Church Bay and a sherd of diagnostic pottery from Bruce's castle on the east coast.

The early ecclesiastical history of the island is quite confusing. Columba is said to have stopped over at Rathlin on his way to founding Iona off the nearby west coast of Scotland. However, he is not credited with the founding of a church here. His biographer Adomnán relates, instead, how the saint assumed the role of patriarchal marriage counsellor in a domestic dispute. Some sources attribute the first monastery to Comgall of Bangor but the *Annals of Ulster* credit Lugadius with this foundation at about the beginning of the 6th century, reporting also that

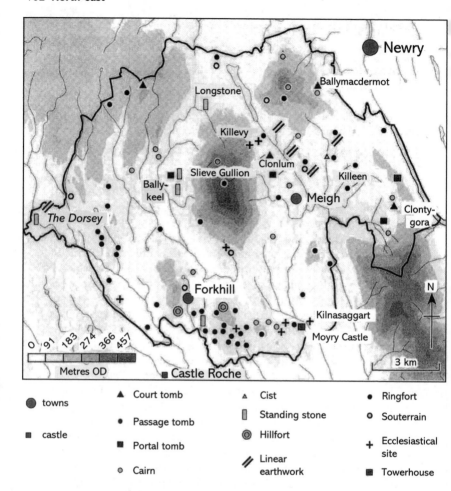

▲ **Fig. 24.** Ring of Gullion: map showing location of sites (after Aalen, Whelan and Stout).

the parish church was established by Sigenius about fifty years later. And though there are no early ecclesiastical remains, the monastic community on Rathlin have the dubious distinction of having been victims of the first Viking raid in Ireland in AD 795. The church was burned on two subsequent occasions. For those interested in industrial archaeology, it was from here too that Marconi succeeded in transmitting the first maritime wireless radio transmission, contacting a station at Ballycastle. More about the archaeology and history of the island is available at the Boat House Visitor Centre at Church Bay.

Slieve Gullion and the Ring of Gullion,

Armagh Archaeological landscape

6 km south-west of Newry, approached on various roads, access to summit from B113 (see below). Disc. Ser. 28 and 29. A dedicated map is available from the St Patrick's Trian in Armagh.

Slieve Gullion, in south Co. Armagh, is as much a geological spectacle as an archaeological one. The mountain itself is a massive, 53-million-year-old volcanic intrusion, rising to a height of 577 m. It is surrounded at a distance, varying from less than 2 km to over 10 km, by a remarkably

▼ **Fig. 25.** Slieve Gullion: map showing location of megaliths (after Collins & Wilson)

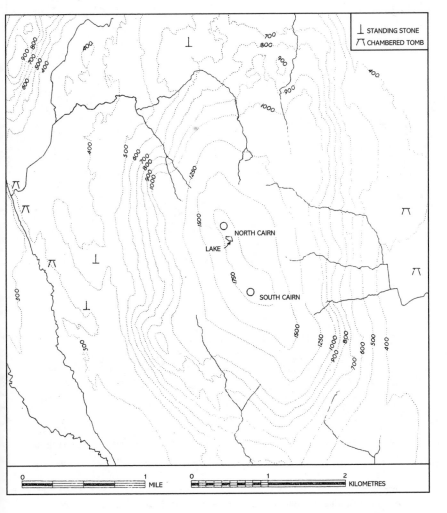

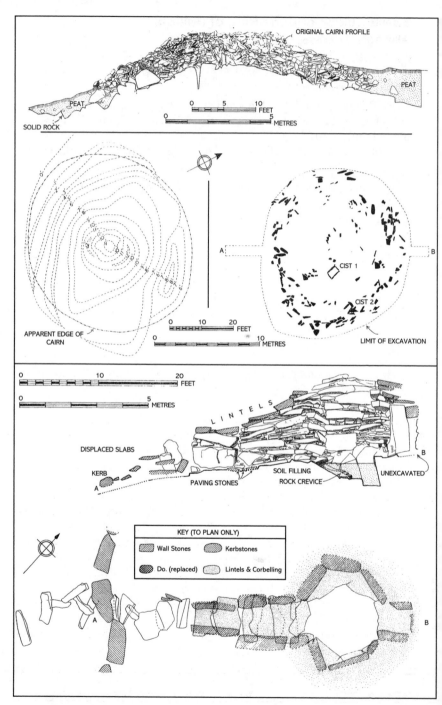

ORIGINAL CAIRN PROFILE

PEAT

PEAT

SOLID ROCK

0   5   10 FEET

0   5 METRES

APPARENT EDGE OF
CAIRN

CIST 1

CIST 2

A   B

0   10   20 FEET

0   10 METRES

LIMIT OF EXCAVATION

0   10   20 FEET

0   5 METRES

L I N T E L S

DISPLACED SLABS

KERB

A

PAVING STONES

SOIL FILLING

ROCK CREVICE

UNEXCAVATED

B

KEY (TO PLAN ONLY)

Wall Stones   Kerbstones

Do. (replaced)   Lintels & Corbelling

A   B

▲ **Fig. 26.** Slieve Gullion: plans of North and South Cairns as excavated
(after Collins & Wilson)

complete granitic ring-dyke of craggy pinnacles, about 11 km in overall diameter. The intervening lowlands are fertile and well drained. Like an enormous natural ring barrow, the geological ensemble is known as the Ring of Gullion. It is designated an Area of Outstanding Natural Beauty and is packed with interesting archaeological sites. It is an integrated archaeological landscape and will reward a full day of touring.

The Passage tomb on the summit of Slieve Gullion has the distinction of being the highest in Ireland, a well-deserved accolade, demanding fortitude of those who would visit it. It is approached via the Slieve Gullion Courtyard Centre off the B113 (Newry–Forkhill) on the south-east side of the mountain. This leads to the Forest Drive, a one-way road around the west side of Slieve Gullion. From the second car park (with the picnic tables), follow the red and white posts to the summit, a steep, 40-minute climb. Its local name, 'Cailleach Birra's House', is somewhat at odds with its geographical location given that the *Cailleach Bhéarra* ('the Hag of Beara') is directly associated with the Beara peninsula in distant west Cork. However, like many mythological earth goddesses, she reappears in different guises throughout the country (and in Scotland) and is attributed with the creation of specific land formations. Both the Passage tomb and a nearby cairn were damaged during an impromptu hunt for the hag in the 1780s. The tomb, which is at the south end of the ridge, was excavated in 1961 by Pat Collins and Basil Wilson. The cairn is about 60 m in diameter—one of the largest in the country—and 5 m high and is surrounded by some barely visible kerbstones. The tomb opens from the south-west and is more or less cruciform in plan, with a distinct end chamber and two vestigial side chambers, the left-hand of which is bigger. It is built entirely of horizontal slabs and has a corbelled roof. The passage has a lintelled roof, gaining in height towards the chamber, and was foreshortened in the recent past. Three basin stones were found, two in the chamber (still *in situ*) and one, broken, near the entrance. Only a handful of cremated human bone survived. The arte-fact assemblage comprised a round scraper, a barbed-and-tanged arrowhead, and a selection of struck flints.

At the north end of the ridge, overlooking a small lake, is another cairn, about 14 m in diameter. Built on an outcrop, it appears much taller than its 1.5 m of cairn material would otherwise suggest. A halo of irregularly spaced, large stones set on edge, four or five deep, serves as a quasi-kerb. Two cists were found in the eastern quadrant. The more central, and better constructed, of them was empty, whereas the other had a fill of fine black soil containing the cremated remains of one adult. Near the bottom of this deposit were fragments of a pot of the Bowl Tradition.

Standing stones

There are numerous standing stones around the mountain. One, 2.5 km due north of the Passage tomb, is known as the Long Stone. On private land off the tertiary Milltown road, it lies midway between the Passage tomb on Slieve Gullion and Sugar Loaf Hill on the south side of Sturgan Mountain, and there can be no doubt that these are its axial points. At the south-eastern foot of Sturgan Mountain, in the townland of Aghmakane, is an arrangement of three tall standing stones. Known as the 'Hag's Chair', they are possibly the portal and entrance stones of a Portal tomb.

Ballykeel

A genuine Portal tomb occurs just south of Ballykeel Bridge, 2.3 km south-west of the Passage tomb on Slieve Gullion. The site was excavated in 1963 by Pat Collins and its unique importance lies in the fact that the tomb is at the southern end of an extant, sub-rectangular cairn, 28 m long. Some of the stones have been re-erected and the remains comprise a near complete set of features including entrance stone and forward-tilted capstone, but no sidestones. The finds consist of a range of Neolithic pottery forms, including Lyles Hill-style carinated pots, a highly decorated necked vessel, and coarse ware similar to Lough Gur Class II. No burials were found. At the other end of the cairn was a cist. Despite having been robbed out, it yielded a Neolithic bowl and a flint javelin-head and is, therefore, regarded as being contemporary. Further sherds

▼ **Fig. 27.** Ballykeel, Ring of Gullion: Portal tomb, with Slieve Gullion in the background (photo: Conor Newman)

were found in the cairn material and on the old ground surface. There are two more Portal tombs in the immediate vicinity of Ballykeel Bridge, but they are on private land.

There are yet more megalithic tombs on the east side of Slieve Gullion. There is a small Portal tomb at Clonlum, literally in the shadow of the mountain, midway between Killevey Castle and Meigh. Like the tomb at Ballykeel Bridge, that at Clonlum is in an intact cairn. Again, there was no burial but sherds of a possible earlier Bronze Age pot and a stone bead were found. A further 4 km to the north-east is the spectacular Court tomb of Ballymacdermot. This very well-preserved, three-chambered tomb is situated in a commanding position on the south side of Ballymacdermot Mountain, from where one gets a magnificent vista over the eastern side of the Ring of Gullion (a little further to the east is the famous viewing point of Bernish Rock). Ballymacdermot Court tomb was first recorded and investigated in 1816 by John Bell and Jonathan Seaver and scientifically excavated in 1962 by Pat Collins and Basil Wilson. The 'court' area faces upslope and is at the head of a kerbed, trapezoidal cairn. There were relatively few artefacts and very little cremated bone (high phosphate levels indicate the former presence of bone), though the strata were compromised by the 1816 interference. Finds included, in primary contexts, evidence of limited flint-knapping in the end chamber associated with round-bottomed, plain Neolithic pottery. A flint blade was found in the first chamber and two sherds of Neolithic pottery came from the middle chamber. Further to the south-east in Clontygora, at the foot of Anglesey Mountain on the east side of the Dundalk–Newry road, there is a very fine Court tomb and a Portal tomb, both of which were excavated in 1937 by Davies and Patterson.

Clontygora

The Court tomb at Clontygora (*9 km south of Newry, turning east at Killeen Bridge*) is known as the 'King's Ring'. The 'court' area is comparatively deep and opens towards the north. An area in the middle was roughly paved and sherds of Neolithic pottery were found there. Only one of the three original gallery chambers survives intact and its roofstone is intact, along with a lintel stone connecting the two portals. One adult was buried in the first chamber along with sherds of several Lyles Hill-type bowls, numerous hollow scrapers, and a polished stone axe. Though disturbed, the second and third chambers also produced cremated human remains, three leaf-shaped arrowheads and sherds of a variety of Neolithic vessels (round and flat bottomed), and sherds of two earlier Bronze Age vases.

Kilnasaggart

Hillforts have been recorded at the north and south ends of Tievecrom and Croslieve, either side of the Forkhill river valley, possibly guarding the southern 'entrance', as it were, to the Ring of Gullion. The **Dorsey** is south-west of Slieve Gullion and, though *sensu stricto* it is outside the Ring of Gullion, it may well guard the Cashel Lough Upper pass into the Ring. There is also a standing stone in the pass, a dense concentration of ringforts and a number of church sites. Another river valley breaches the Ring at Kilnasaggart, a little further to the east, between Slievenabolea and Feede Mountain. This is reputed to be the route taken by the *Slígh Midluachra* (one of Ireland's ancient routeways) from Tara to Dunseverick. Kilnasaggart (*signposted*) is a monastic site, the outstanding feature of which is a tall monolith decorated with thirteen circled crosses and a very clear inscription in Irish, which translates as 'Ternoc son of little Ceran bequeathes this place under the protection of Peter'. Ternoc's *obit* appears in the *Annals of the Four Masters* under the year AD 714, which is generally accepted as dating the stone to the early 8th century. There is a series of blade grooves on one side of the stone. The purpose of these is uncertain but they are known from other early Christian sites and may be related to some regularly enacted ritual involving remarking of the boundaries. The stone stands in the middle of a slightly raised, round cemetery platform, with a unique configuration of two concentric rings of radial long-cist graves (no longer visible). Around the base of the slab is a group of small, cross-inscribed stones and two hollow ones. The cross slab is signposted across two stiles and is enclosed in a hawthorn hedge ring.

Killevy

If Ternoc remains a little anonymous, the life of St Darerca (also known as Monnena, and locally as St Bline), foundress of *Cell-Sléibhe-Cuilinn* ('the church of the mountain of Cuilinn') at Killevy, is rather better documented. Founded *c.* AD 450, this important monastery stood in the north Louth/south Armagh territory of the *Conaille Muirthemne* (possibly of Pictish extraction, one of whose ancestors is commemorated on an ogam stone in the Isle of Man) who, according to a remarkable and unbroken succession list from the 5th to the 15th century, maintained firm control of the monastery throughout its history. Darerca's biography tells of the oak-plank wooden church built with her saintly intervention by her third successor Derlasre, and of how her hoe and spade were passed on as relics. Rightly or wrongly, St Darerca is attributed with a foundation at Burton-upon-Trent. The monastery was plundered by the Norsemen in AD 923. Nothing remains of the original foundation but there are two ruined medieval churches near Killevy Castle and there was once the remains of a round tower there.

Tievebulliagh, Co. Antrim Stone axe factory

4.5 km west of Cushendall along Gaults Road, off the Cushendun–Cushendall road (A2), at the sign for Cullentra House and right at the first Y-junction. Disc. Ser. 5.

Porcellanite outcrops on the eastern side of Tievebulliagh Mountain were mined in the Neolithic period for the production of thousands of highly prized polished stone axeheads, making this arguably the most important axe factory in Ireland and Britain. Rising to a height of 402 m, it is a good 20-minute walk from the first gate to the rough path leading around the east face of the mountain. The best and safest way to reach the top is alongside the wire fence on the north face. There are three porcellanite outcrops on the steep, east side of the mountain. The most accessible and largest one is about halfway up the enormous pile of dolerite scree directly below the summit (*a steep and quite dangerous climb*), and comprises a vein 1.7 m thick and about 5.5 m long. The scree below this was peppered with waste flakes and axe rough-outs. The 'factory' was first identified around 1900 by the collector William Knowles (who carried off around 4,000 flakes and rough-outs) and since then there have been a number of surveys and a series of exploratory excavations by Jim Mallory in 1984. Three stages of production are in evidence at different locations, from extraction to primary and secondary working to rough-out stage. The axes appear to have been finished elsewhere, such as at Culbane, Co. Londonderry, where six axes were found with a sandstone grinding block. No associated settlements have yet been found.

Axes made from the blue-grey volcanic porcellanite outcropping here and at Brockley on **Rathlin Island** were greatly sought after, and have been found as far afield as south-east England and the Orkney Islands (about 180 are known from Britain), their presence there explained by down-the-line exchange. That axes had international currency is demonstrated by the one hundred or so tuff axes found in Ireland that can be traced to an axe factory in Great Langdale, Cumbria. **Rathlin** and **Tievebulliagh** are, with some justification, referred to as factories, accounting for nearly 54 per cent of the 18,000 polished stone axeheads known from Ireland. Not all of them were for chopping; some are so large (up to 38 cm long) that, like the fabulous green jadeite axes, they must have been symbols of power and may even have had religious functions—as the discovery of some in Court tombs (e.g. **Ballymacaldrack**) would suggest. Smaller axes were also ascribed symbolic importance. Geochemical analysis, which is the only way of distinguishing between the Tievebulliagh and Brockley porcellanites, indicates that though less well known nowadays, the factory at Brockley was at least as important as the mainland site.

The summit of Tievebulliagh is small and rather marred by television aerials. The view, however, is spectacular. To the north-east and south-east are the bays of **Cushendun** and Cushendall; between them is Tieveragh Hill and overlooking Cushendall is the huge, foreboding mass of **Lurigethan**. Through a dip in the mountains due north **Rathlin Island** can be seen and, to the north-west, the huge white quartz summit cairn of Knocklayd. In the distance to the north-east and east are the Western Isles of Scotland. The view, therefore, is of the uniquely important prehistoric landscape of mid-coastal Antrim. We would recommend it to be treated as such and for the reader to spend at least a day here.

North-west: Derry, Donegal, Tyrone

Introduction

The north-west of Ireland is in many respects a rugged region with large areas of uplands, focusing on three main mountain ranges—Derryveagh in the north-west, the Blue Stacks in the south-west, and the Sperrins in the east. These uplands are dissected by river valleys, notably those of the Bann, forming the region's eastern boundary, and of the Foyle and its tributaries in the centre of the region. The lowlands bordering these

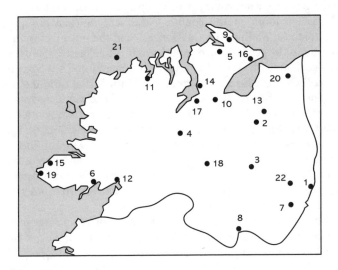

▲ Map 2

Key:

1. Ardboe, Co. Tyrone
2. Banagher, Co. Derry
3. Beaghmore, Co. Tyrone
4. Beltany, Co. Donegal
5. Carndonagh, Co. Donegal
6. Casheltown, Co. Donegal
7. Castlecaulfield, Co. Tyrone
8. Clogher Valley, Co. Tyrone
9. Clonca, Co. Donegal
10. Derry, Co. Derry
11. Doe, Co. Donegal
12. Donegal, Co. Donegal
13. Dungiven, Co. Derry
14. Fahan, Co. Donegal
15. Glencolumbkille, Co Donegal
16. Greencastle, Co. Donegal
17. Grianán Ailech, Co. Donegal
18. Harry Avery's castle, Co. Tyrone
19. Malin More, Co. Donegal
20. Mount Sandel, Co. Derry
21. Tory Island, Co. Donegal
22. Tullaghoge, Co. Tyrone

river systems contain substantial areas of fertile soils, but elsewhere land use capability is quite limited, with extensive peatlands on the mountains. The region also boasts a long and rugged coastline which, together with the ocean beyond, has been a very important factor determining the patterns of human activity and settlement. Evidence for the earliest human colonization of this region is confined to the lower Bann Valley, and includes the famous riverside settlement at **Mount Sandel**, Co. Derry. A shell midden recently excavated by Peter Woodman and Nicky Milner on the south side of Inch Island, Lough Swilly, Co. Donegal, attests to movement further westwards. Later Mesolithic lithics have been found as far afield as the sand dunes at Horn Head, north-west Donegal, and there is a concentration of finds to the immediate south of the Inishowen peninsula.

A strong and permanent Neolithic presence is attested to in the impressive corpus of megalithic tombs in this region. There are excellent examples of all four main types, including the now fragmentary Passage tomb at **Knockmany**, Co. Tyrone (the most northerly decorated Passage tomb in the country), the very unusual grouping of Portal tombs at **Malinmore**, Co. Donegal, and the nearby monumental Court tomb. In general, such tombs avoid the highest uplands of the Derryveagh and Bluestack Mountains in Donegal and the Sperrins in Tyrone. Prehistoric field walls have also been reported from the region, including extensive remains of stone walls, an enclosure, and standing stone at Kindroghed and Knockergrana, just over 3 km south-east of Culdaff, Co. Donegal. Nearby is a Court tomb and a cupmarked stone. Perhaps even more unusual, however, is a report by Kinahan in 1889 of the discovery of an upstanding wattle fence under about 4 m of bog. In the 1960s Arthur ApSimon excavated remains of a large rectangular house (6.5 m × 6 m) of early Neolithic date that had been exposed under a bog at Ballynagilly, Co. Tyrone.

Bogs have also preserved a fascinating array of Bronze Age material, including the amazing circle, cairn, and alignment complex at **Beaghmore**, Co. Tyrone, and the recently uncovered circles at Copney Hill, a little further to the east. There is an interesting distributional overlap between this north-western group of stone circles and Bowl Tradition urns, in particular tripartite vessels that are densely concentrated in this area. There are comparatively few later Bronze Age hoards from the region, a pattern that is all the more intriguing given the apparent concentration of such hoards in neighbouring counties. The possibly that this region was somewhat marginalized during the later Bronze Age is further emphasized by the fact that only one Class 4c sword (i.e. swords that are heavily influenced by the Gündlingen sword associated with the first iron users in central Europe) is known from here. However, against this can be marshalled the magnificent Castlederg, Co. Tyrone, class 2 cauldron which, as a type influenced by Hallstatt C forms, indicates contact between late Bronze Age Ireland and the first iron users on the Continent.

An intriguing mystery surrounds the discovery and survival of two ostensibly separate hoards of ribbon torcs reported from Inishowen and Largatreany, Co. Donegal. Between them they account for an unprecedented twenty-one torcs, but Eogan has suggested that some of the Inishowen specimens may in fact be missing torcs from the Largatreany find. The Inishowen find, of course, is a very short distance across Lough Foyle from the findspot of the famous Broighter, Co. Derry, hoard of gold objects which includes, *inter alia*, a magnificent repoussé-ornamented torc and two knitted gold necklaces. Richard Warner has argued that it was an offering to the Celtic sea god Mannan Mac Lir, whose home was in Lough Foyle. These are really torc hoards, and their deposition is equivalent, in behavioural terms, to multitudinous torc depositions elsewhere in the Celtic world. Further west, an anthropoid sword hilt of 1st-century BC date was trawled from Ballyshannon, Co. Donegal; it probably originated in south-western France. Evidently, the region was of considerable standing during the Iron Age and was not just a landfall for people travelling from north Britain, but from further afield as well. Indeed, in positioning the hillfort at **Clogher**, Co. Tyrone, regionally, Warner emphasizes the international flavour of the archaeological record of the region, particularly during the first few centuries AD. There is a notable concentration of Roman objects from the north coast, including a massive hoard of silver coins, ingots, and cut plate from Ballinrees, Co. Derry. Indeed, Warner has argued that the *regia* marked on Ptolemy's map is none other than **Clogher**.

By the 4th century, **Clogher** had become a stronghold of the Airgialla who, according to tradition, carved out a kingdom of 'swordland' from the more ancient Ulaid, whose capital at **Emain Macha** they overthrew. It emerges into the light of history as caput of the Uí Cremthainn and their lands probably occupied all of present-day Tyrone, Monaghan, and much of Fermanagh. To the north, dominating all of Donegal and Derry, were their traditional overlords, the Uí Néill. They traced their descent from Niall *Noígiallach* (Niall of the Nine Hostages), whose great grandson was Columba (Colmcille; AD 521–97). Columba became the most important ecclesiastical figure in the north-west and his *paruchia*, which included Durrow and Iona (and in time Lindisfarne and **Kells**), was in direct competition with **Armagh** and its promotion of the Patrician Church. Traditionally, Columba's first foundation was at **Derry** and his footsteps can be traced all over this region. A Columban heritage trail has been created with, as its centrepiece, Columba's retreat at **Glencolumbkille** in south-west Donegal. Here as elsewhere in the region (e.g. **Carndonagh**), there is a fine collection of Early Christian sculpture.

There are comparatively few ringforts in these counties and the

▲ **Fig. 28.** Drumhallagh, Co. Donegal: cross-inscribed slab symbolizing a jewelled cross (photo: Conor Newman)

majority of those are cashels. Their distribution follows that of later prehistoric material in avoiding the boggy uplands, concentrating instead on the relatively good lands around south Tyrone and east Derry. Likewise, there are also very few crannógs (the magnificent cashel of O'Boyle's Fort on Lough Doon, just south of Portnoo, Co. Donegal, is built on a natural island). However, over the years an eclectic and highly interesting corpus of material, of all periods, has been collected from sand dunes along the north coast. One such location is at Dooey peninsula, which juts out into Gweebarra Bay, west Co. Donegal. Here Rynne and Ó Ríordáin unearthed an extensive settlement while excavating a mound on which a very large standing stone had collapsed. During the latest phase the site was used as a cemetery.

The fragmentation of the ancient province of Ulster in the 5th century is attributed to the expansion of the Uí Néill dynasty, pressing northwards from Connacht into the north-west. One branch, the Cenél Conaill, dominated most of modern Co. Donegal—still known as *Tír*

Conaill ('the land of Conall'). The other main branch, the Cenél nEógain, initially occupied the north Donegal peninsula of Inishowen [*Inis Eógain*, 'the peninsula of Eógan'], but expanded south-eastwards into central Ulster in the 7th and 8th centuries, dominating most of Cos. Derry and Tyrone [*Tír Eógain*, 'the land of Eógan'] from their centre at **Aileach**. This effectively confined the Cenél Conaill to the Donegal area, whereas the Cenél nEógain could extend their influence into the north midlands and frequently held the high-kingship. By the 11th/12th centuries two main dynasties competed for the kingship of Cenél nEógain—Mac Lochlainn and Ó Néill (O'Neill who, confusingly, must be distinguished from the wider grouping of the Uí Néill, of which they formed part). After the downfall of Muirchertach Mac Lochlainn in 1166 the Ó Néill were almost undisputed rulers of Cenél nEógain. In Donegal, the kingship of Cenél Conaill was dominated throughout the later Middle Ages by one dynasty—the Ó Domhnaill (O'Donnells).

The first half of the 13th century saw several English attempts to subdue both Cenél Conaill and Cenél nEógain, with little effect. The kings of Cenél nEógain were notionally subordinate to the Anglo-Irish earls of Ulster (at least in English minds), but there was no significant colonization of the region. As a result, typical Anglo-Irish monuments such as mottes and moated sites are virtually non-existent. After the earldom of Ulster passed to the de Burghs in the later 13th century, considerable parts of north Co. Derry seem to have been colonized, and as late as 1305 the earl built a castle at **Greencastle**, as a foothold in Ó Néill territory. However, the double setback of the Bruce invasion in 1315–18 and the death of the last de Burgh earl in 1333 meant the end of any attempts to expand the earldom into this region. Similarly, attempts by the FitzGeralds in **Sligo** to extend their control northwards over Cenél Conaill came to nothing. Throughout the late Middle Ages the north-west was by far the largest Gaelic-controlled bloc in the country, dominated by the Ó Néill and Ó Domhnaill. At the end of the 16th century a (rare) alliance of both dynasties led to the greatest of all uprisings against the English government. Despite some remarkable successes the Nine Years War (1594–1603) ended in defeat for the Gaelic lords, and the ultimate English response—the Plantation of Ulster—changed the region irrevocably.

Ardboe, Co. Tyrone Early church site; high cross

15 km east of Cookstown, off B73 to Lough Neagh; take minor road south 7 km west of Coagh; signposted. Disc. Ser. 14.

Ulster's finest high cross is located on a promontory called Ardboe [*Ard Bó*, 'the hill of the cows'], overlooking Lough Neagh. The sandstone cross probably dates to the 10th century and is the only definite trace of a monastery, said to have been founded by the 6th-century St Colmán Mac Aed. Two church ruins also survive, but one (*in the graveyard to the east of the cross*) is post-medieval while the other, known as 'the Abbey' (*to the north of the graveyard*), is featureless and not easily dated. The high cross is one of the tallest of all the Irish crosses, and although badly weathered near the top, it is a good example of the great series of scripture crosses. Scriptural scenes are carved in panels on the cross and are carefully arranged, with Old Testament scenes on the east face and south side, and scenes from the life of Christ on the west face and north side, as follows (from base to top):

East face: *Adam and Eve*
               Sacrifice of Isaac
               Daniel in the Lions' Den
               Three Youths in the Furnace
               Second Coming of Christ
               The Last Judgement (on the cross head)
South side: *Cain and Abel*
               David/Samson and the Lion
               David and Goliath
               Paul and Anthony in the Desert
West face: *Adoration of the Magi*
               Marriage Feast of Cana
               Miracle of the Loaves and Fishes
               Christ's Entry into Jerusalem
               The Crucifixion (on the cross head)
North side: *Baptism of Christ*
               Child Jesus in the Temple?
               Slaughter of the Innocents
               Birth of Christ Announced to Shepherds
               Uncertain

Banagher, Co. Derry   Early church site

3 km south of Dungiven; turn south off A6 (Derry–Belfast) in centre of Dungiven, for Magheramore; signposted. Disc. Ser. 7.

Banagher is an early church site, with an interesting group of surviving monuments, sited on a surprisingly prominent hillock [the name, *Beannchar*, means 'peaked hill'] on the west side of the Dungiven–Magheramore road. The origins of the site are uncertain, but the church is probably of the mid-12th century, roughly contemporary with the earliest phase of the church at **Dungiven**. Its main feature is the west doorway, a form characteristic of early Irish churches with inclined jambs and a massive flat lintel, but highlighted by an external architrave. Unusually, it has a round rear arch. The original church was typically plain, with two small round-headed windows in the south wall, again outlined by architraves. The church was later extended—probably in the early 13th century—by adding a chancel at the east end, with a chancel arch opened in the original east wall. In the south wall of the chancel is an impressive window, outlined (externally) with multiple continuous mouldings. Beside it (internally) is the base of another opening, possibly a sedilia, outlined with similar mouldings. Although the form of the window is still definitely Romanesque, the mouldings suggest a Transitional (Romanesque/Gothic) background. This is also indicated by the decoration of two capitals surviving on the east gable, externally. Some remodelling of the east end of the chancel was later carried out, probably in the 15th century.

South-east of the church is a stone shrine, built in the shape of a church or gabled sarcophagus, perhaps the best of a few surviving examples of characteristic Irish form. On the west gable end is the figure of a bishop or abbot, possibly representing the reputed founder of Banagher, Muiredach O'Heney, and it is likely that the shrine was erected as his tomb, although the shrine itself is hardly earlier than the 12th century (and may even be early 13th century). Two rough stone crosses also survive, one in the churchyard beside the entrance, to the east of the church, and the other to the north-west, near the road. There are also the remains of a late medieval building, known as the 'Residence', beside the churchyard gate west of the church. Originally a semi-fortified three-storey structure—possibly a priests' residence—only the ground floor now survives.

Beaghmore, Co. Tyrone Stone circles, alignments, cairns

13.5 km north-west of Cookstown, north of the A505 to Omagh in the direction of Dunnamore, from where it is signposted. Disc. Ser. 13.

The spectacular stone circle and alignment complex at Beaghmore is in the foothills (195 m) of the Sperrin Mountains, east Co. Tyrone. Seven great stone circles, nine alignments, and numerous cairns and barrows, all in close proximity to one another, were uncovered here in the 1930s during turf cutting and were systematically cleared of peat a decade later. Some of the sites have been formally excavated. The components are arranged in triads, typically comprising a pair of closely adjacent circles with a small cairn mound tucked into the junction and from which emanates the alignment or alignments. This is a pattern repeated elsewhere, e.g. **Drumskinny**, Co. Fermanagh. At the north-east end of the Beaghmore complex Circles A and B comprise a pair, separated by a small cairn containing a cist which held a porcellanite axehead. No fewer than four stone alignments radiate north-eastwards from this point of junction. Likewise, a little further south-westwards, Circles C and D, the largest in the complex, are contiguous (with C flattening out where it comes closest to D). Once again on the northern side of this junction is a small

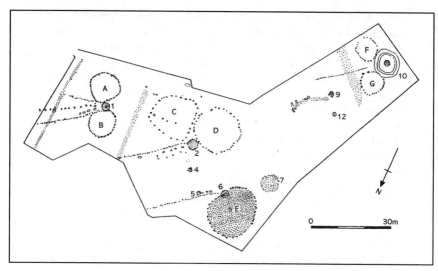

▲ **Fig. 29.** Beaghmore: plan of part of the complex (after May)

cairn (3 m in diameter) From the north-east side of the cairn emanates a long stone alignment and two shorter ones. This cairn also had a cist and some unidentified potsherds. Pits inside Circle C were found to contain round-bottomed, carinated bowls referred to as Lyles Hill ware. There are two further cairns to the north, between the C–D couplet and Circle E which is also known as the Dragon's Teeth. One of these (no. 4) contained a cist in which was placed part of the trunk of a oak tree.

Oval shaped, Circle E differs from the others in that the interior of the circle is filled with smaller stones (over 880 of them) arranged in closely spaced, concentric circles. A cairn (no. 6) was incorporated into the south-eastern side of the circle and it contained two burials. From it another two alignments emanate in a north-easterly direction. A hearth near Cairn 6 was dated to 2900–2500 BC. Behind it, to the south-west, is the smallest circle, no. 7 (less than 10m in diameter). Described elsewhere as a rockery, it consists of at least three densely compact, concentric circles. At the south end of the complex are Circles F and G. They appear to have entrance gaps facing south-east. From between them emerges an alignment (running north-east to south-west) and immediately adjacent on the other side is an elaborate ring barrow-like structure, comprising a small soil-covered, boulder-kerbed cairn surrounded by a fosse and external bank (about 10 m in diameter). A cist in the cairn contained some cremated bone; another outside it was empty. Charcoal from under the cairn returned a date of 1950–1684 BC, while the fosse dated to between 990 and 808 BC. A little cache of struck flints was found near the alignment.

Detailed palynological analysis has demonstrated tree clearance starting from around 3800 BC, which in turn suggests that some of the earlier dates may relate to pre-circle activity. Moreover, some of the field boundaries may belong to this agricultural phase as they, too, pre-date the circles. Consequently, it is suspected that the circles themselves date from between about 1500 BC and 800 BC. It is possible that the alignments are directed towards the midsummer sunrise. More recently, nine multi-ringed circles (like Circle E) have been uncovered and mapped at Copney Hill, 11 km to the east.

Beltany, Co. Donegal Embanked stone circle

3 km south of Raphoe (junction R236/264), from where it is signposted. Veer right off the Castlefinn road 0.5 km from the aforementioned signpost. Informal parking area on eastern flank of hill from which it is a 10-minute walk to the top. Disc. Ser. 6.

▼ **Fig. 30.** Beltany: plan of stone circle (after Boyle-Somerville)

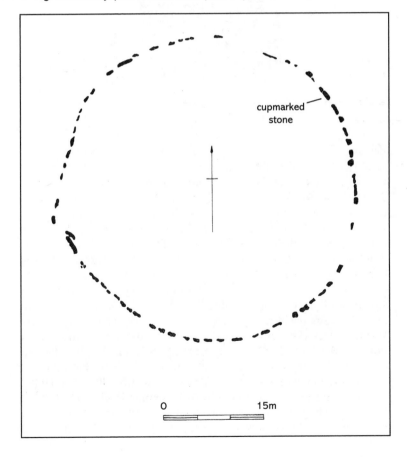

cupmarked stone

0   15m

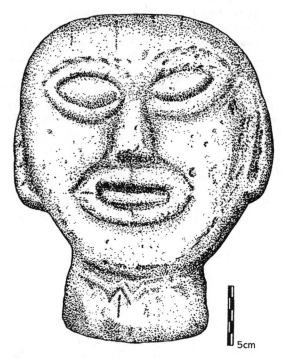

5cm

▲ **Fig. 31.** Beltany: stone head (after Rynne)

Beltany, or Tops Stone Circle, is prominently sited overlooking the south-westerly end of the Deele river valley and the middle reaches of the Foyle. The view to the north is quite compromised by afforestation. There is some debate as to whether this site is a conventional stone circle or a cairn with an orthostatic kerb. To be sure, the 64 surviving kerbstones are the most impressive and distinguishing feature but this is partly because the cairn has been so badly disturbed and survives to a height of only about 50 cm. Indeed many of the cairn stones have been thrown out from the centre into a kind of bank around the orthostats. In the south-west quadrant of the interior a tall, triangular-sectioned stone protrudes from the cairn and beside it is a long, recumbent stone which may indicate the existence of a cist or chamber. Working clockwise from the somewhat pyramidal stone at the extreme north of the kerb, there is a series of cupmarks on the seventh stone after this. An outlying stone, about 2 m tall, stands to the south-east and on the opposite side of the circle are the two tallest, but slightly overlapping, stones suggesting an axis of orientation. There are three further standing stones on this hill, two of which can be seen on the north slope, and there are still more in fields off the Castlefinn road.

On the opposite side of the Deele Valley is Croghan Hill but the prominence on the top, which looks for all the world like a cairn, is actually a natural outcrop.

The so-called Beltany stone head (*now in the National Museum of Ireland*) was found either in the circle or nearby. Rynne has identified a particular concentration of stone idols in the Raphoe area, of which the Beltany head is the best-known example. Its stylized features and the presence of a neckring or torc suggest an Iron Age date.

Carndonagh, Co. Donegal   Early medieval sculpture

30 km north of Derry; the sculpture is located at the west end of the town, near the junction of the R238 and the R244. Disc. Ser. 3.

Carndonagh, near the top of the Inishowen peninsula, is home to one of the most important, thought-provoking, and indeed beautiful collections of early medieval sculpture in Ulster, yet virtually nothing can be

▼ **Fig. 32.** Carndonagh: interlaced cross symbolizing the Resurrection (photo: Dept. of Archaeology, NUI, Galway)

said about the history of the site. There must have been a significant ecclesiastical centre here, but of this nothing remains apart from the five pieces of sculpture. The centrepiece of the present composition, known as 'St Patrick's Cross', has dominated discussion of the collection, to the extent that dates proposed for it are, by inference, applied to the other pieces. There may, however, be some justification for this, as there are common details of execution. St Patrick's Cross is a tall free-standing monument with short, slightly upturned arms and rounded angles. It is decorated on one face with a broad ribbon interlace design and on the opposite face with an interlace cross above a rather moon-faced Christ, flanked by four smaller figures. Below this is a procession of three figures. Three profiled birds with interlocking beaks occupy each of the 'armpits' of the interlace cross and the sides of the shaft are also decorated. Henry believed this, and the slab at Fahan, to be early specimens and accordingly dated it to the earlier 7th century. More recently, most scholars opt for a 9th-century date. There is no doubt that Henry's rather Darwinian typology of the insular high cross is fundamentally flawed, but it is also possible that the alternative dating is too late. Broad ribbon interlace is primarily a 7th-century phenomenon and the interlace cross is a very specific and deliberate development. It occurs in Coptic Egypt, on Anglo-Saxon coins from the 7th century onwards, and in 7th- and 8th-century Lombardic Italy, where the finest specimens date from the reign of Luitprand, in the early 8th century. In execution, however, the Carndonagh sculpture conforms to a regional style extending southwards towards the Erne basin and northwards to the Western Isles of Scotland.

The two small pillars, or stelae, on either side of the high cross are the most enigmatic pieces, each one decorated on all four sides. Ecclesiastical figures are distinguished by crosiers, bells, and books and the figure with a harp is probably David. Another of the figures is clearly a warrior, equipped with Viking-style sword and round shield, and on yet another face is a bird of prey catching a fish, a well-known motif in Germanic art adopted into Christianity as a symbol of Christ saving a sinner from the sea of despair. A triple pelta motif occurs on another of the faces and is comparable to designs in the termini of 7th-century zoomorphic penannular brooches. The most unusual figure is said to have catlike ears, but these are more likely to be part of a hood because conventional, round ears are also present. Between the rabbit-like ears is a triquetra knot and across the torso are two hands clutching an axe or hammer-like object. There are also two large discs.

A few yards away, in the graveyard, stands the unique Marigold Stone. The marigold has seven petals, rather than the usual six, indicating that it was drawn freehand. It dominates the round disc of a flabellum, or liturgical fan, and is flanked by two ecclesiastics. Below them is a quatrefoil knot and circle. On the opposite face, less well preserved, is the crucified Christ with two ecclesiastics standing at the bottom of the cross and, below this, an interlace cross. Most of the panels above and below the arms of the crosses bear some ornamentation. The basic motif on both sides are two crosses, one above the other, symbolizing the Resurrection using a formula found on 6th-century Palestinian pilgrim's flasks. Finally, near the church is an important carved lintel stone, a rare find that really deserves more attention. In the middle stands a ringed cross. To the left of this is a group of figures, and to the right an undeciphered motif connected to a panel of narrow band interlace. It

▼ **Fig. 33.** Casheltown: plan of tombs (after Cody)

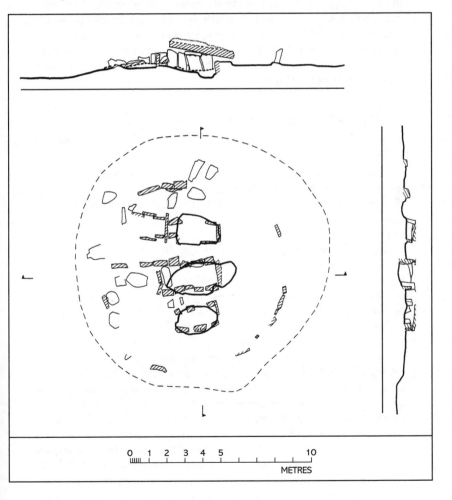

0 1 2 3 4 5 10
METRES

has been dated to the 9th century. A small bullaun stone has been incorporated into the south wall of the graveyard.

Casheltown, Co. Donegal   Wedge tombs

20 km west of Donegal town on the N56 (Donegal–Ardara); signposted from the Killybegs side of Dunkineely and part of the Donegal Heritage Trail; a short climb through forestry is involved. Disc. Ser. 10.

The three Wedge tombs at Casheltown are unique in that they were enclosed within the one cairn. The tombs are arranged side by side with the largest one in the middle and all of them are orientated southwards in the direction of St John's Point. Around them is the outline of a D-shaped cairn, flat at the front end and demarcated by orthostats, a number of which survive around the north side. They are located below the summit of the hill overlooking the short Bunlacky river valley, which opens into Inver Bay. The hill is now planted with conifers and the once terrific views over the valley and the sea are all but lost, but they probably explain the siting.

Castlecaulfield, Co. Tyrone   Post-medieval house

3 km west of Dungannon, on east side of Castlecaulfield village; take minor road north/north-west off A4 (Dungannon–Enniskillen); signposted. Disc. Ser. 19.

Castlecaulfield is named after its builder, Sir Toby Caulfield, an English soldier who administered substantial lands in the O'Neill territory, Tír Eoghan, following the flight of Hugh O'Neill in 1607. The house was built in the years after 1611, when Caulfield was granted 400 ha of O'Donnelly land, probably on the site of a bawn of the O'Donnellys. The house was essentially unfortified, reflecting the confidence of the new English planters, but this confidence was misjudged and the house was burned by the O'Donnellys in the revolt of 1641. Although reoccupied by the Caulfields in the 1660s and 1670s, the house never really recovered from the burning of 1641, traces of which can still be seen on the masonry.

The house is U-shaped, consisting of a rectangular main block with two projecting wings on the north-east and north-west. It is three storeys high throughout, with a basement under part of the main block, and is lit by numerous large transomed and mullioned windows. Entry was by two doorways placed opposite each other, roughly in the centre of the north and south sides of the main block. Access to the upper floors must have been by wooden stairs, no trace of which survives. The massive fireplace in the east wall of the north-east wing suggests that this was the location of the kitchen. Immediately north-east of the house is a two-storey rectangular gatehouse, with round turret on the north side. Traces of an enclosing bawn wall run north-west and south-east from the

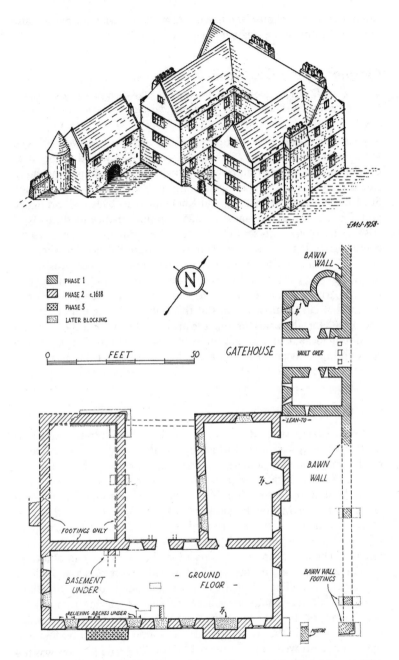

Labels within figure:

PHASE 1
PHASE 2 c.1618
PHASE 3
LATER BLOCKING

N

0 — FEET — 50

BAWN WALL

GATEHOUSE — VAULT OVER

LEAN-TO

BAWN WALL

FOOTINGS ONLY

BASEMENT UNDER

– GROUND FLOOR –

BAWN WALL FOOTINGS

RELIEVING ARCHES UNDER

MORTAR

·EMJ·1958·

▲ Fig. 34. Castlecaulfield: plan and isometric reconstruction of house (after Jope) gatehouse. The gatehouse and bawn wall are earlier than the main house and may belong to the original O'Donnelly residence.

Clogher Valley, Co. Tyrone Archaeological landscape

40 km west of Armagh; Clogher is on the A4 (Enniskillen–Dungannon), just south of the junction with the B83 (Omagh–Monaghan), about 22 km south of Omagh. Disc. Ser. 18.

The Clogher Valley is the principal natural corridor east–west between the Dungannon–Armagh region, east of Lough Neagh, and the necklace of lakes between Upper and Lower Lough Erne. The longer, northern side is defined by a string of uplands from Cappagh Mountain through Slievemore, Shantavny Scotch, and Knockmany to Ballyness, Brougher, and Topped Mountain—most of them familiar names to students of Irish archaeology. The south side comprises principally Slieve Beagh, overlooking Clogher, and Burnt Hill south-east of Ballygawley where the valley bifurcates, north-eastwards to Dungannon and south-eastwards, following the course of the river Blackwater, through Aughnacloy towards Armagh. Clogher is midway along the valley, facing two narrow valleys that cut north-westwards at this point, opening out at Fintona and on to Omagh. It was for long the principal town in the area and was no doubt located to take advantage of this location. The valley and surrounding hills are rich in archaeological remains from all periods, some placed to exploit the landscape, others to demarcate it.

Creggandevesky

The earliest activity is attested to in the dense concentration of Court tombs, the best-preserved of which is actually outside and to the north of the valley at Creggandevesky. There are no fewer than 11 Court tombs within a 10 km radius of Creggandevesky. This is a very fine example of an open-court tomb on a small hill overlooking the south shore of Lough Mallon (*4 km north-east of Carrickmore, off the B4 (Omagh–Pomeroy)*). It was shrouded in peat before rescue excavations by Claire Foley between 1979 and 1982 revealed the full extent of the remains. The east-facing court is positioned at the wide end of a trapezoidal cairn (18 m long and up to 13 m wide) with a kerb of boulders and drystone walling. It opens, via a rather squat portal with lintel stone, into a three-chambered gallery decreasing in height from front to back. Some of the original corbels are still *in situ*. Cremated human bone was found in the greatest quantities around the entrance; acid soils may have destroyed any inhumed burials. Three flint arrowheads, a scraper, and a piercing implement were found together in the second chamber and elsewhere was found a necklace of 112 stone beads, a flint javelinhead, scrapers, and sherds from seven round-bottomed, carinated bowls. The remains of 21 individuals could be distinguished, of which seven were positively identified as women, five as men, and one as an unsexed adolescent. The bone was dated to around 3500 BC. Further activity during the Bronze Age is attested to by disturbance at the west end of the cairn.

Knockmany

Neolithic activity is also attested by the Passage tombs that are dotted along the high ground either side of the valley. According to tradition, the Passage tomb at the top of Knockmany Forest Park (*reached by turning at the obelisk in Clogher*), just north of Augher and overlooking the Clogher Valley, is the burial place of Báine, wife of Tuathal Teachtmhar. According to propagandist legends, Tuathal returned from exile and carved out Ireland's fifth province of Mide (Meath). Knockmany is one of the more northerly of the decorated Passage tombs and this is its principal claim to fame. The covering mound is an entirely modern protection (glass covered and inaccessible) and gives access to the polygonal chamber and a possible short and denuded passage leading from the south. An interesting design feature is the way in which the orthostats alternate through 90-degree angles, a pattern of broad and narrow faces. Four of the stones are decorated with concentric circles, zigzag lines, and lozenge nests (and no little amount of modern graffiti). The site was excavated in 1951 by Collins and Waterman, prior to conservation. They traced the original outline of the cairn (about 25 m in diameter) and found a small amount of cremated bone in the chamber. From both within and outside the chamber were retrieved flints (some burnt), including blades, scrapers, and a fine leaf-shaped arrowhead, and an unclassified sherd of pottery, possibly Lyles Hill type. This tomb is to some extent an outlier of the tombs on Shantavny, visible to the north-east, and Sess Kilgreen, in a little valley at the foot of Shantavny between Errigal and Tycanny.

Crockgallows Hill

The area is also rich in standing stones, which are dotted along the course of the Blackwater (*all on private land*). On Crockgallows Hill, Altanagh, about 3 km south of Carrickmore (which is also known as Termon with its obvious early ecclesiastical connotations) Brian Williams excavated an enigmatic, multi-period ritual and domestic site. The earliest activity is represented by a series of pit burials accompanied by plain and decorated Neolithic bowls, arrowheads, and personal ornaments. Later a Court tomb was built here formalizing, as it were, the burial tradition. Cists and pits with Vase, Bowl, and Cordoned Urn burials followed and these date from between around 1700 and 1500 BC.

After this the site was abandoned until a rath was constructed here around AD 500. It was evidently a significant ironworking centre.

Clogher

However, metalworking of an entirely more refined type was carried out at around the same time at Clogher hillfort (*signposted at the west end of the village*). Situated on a small hill at the south-east end of Clogher Demesne behind the Bishop's Palace, it is by far the most important site in the Clogher Valley. The remains comprise a modest hillfort (about 2 ha in area) with faint traces of multiple ramparts at the north end only—though apparently not all erected at the same time. The summit is crowned by a later ringfort, outside and to the south of which is a small but prominent triangular mound, partly enclosed by the outer bank of the ringfort. To the south of this again is a very well-preserved, penannular ring barrow. The site was excavated by Richard Warner between 1969 and 1974. It was the seat of the Síl nDaimíni, of the Airgialla. The Airgialla were a subject tribe of the Ulaid, but shifted allegiance to the up and coming Uí Néill, and by *c.*800 they ruled over large parts of the north midlands, from near Louth to Fermanagh. Clogher also has the distinction of having been marked out as *regia* on Ptolemy's mid-2nd-century map of Ireland. However, in reality, these events occurred comparatively late in the history of the site, which saw activity from the Neolithic period onwards. The hillfort, comprising a bank and external fosse, may have been constructed during the Late Bronze Age and may be associated with some large pits in the interior and a cashel-like wall, which appears to have been strengthened with horizontal timbers. The importance of the site as *regia* is reflected in the material assemblage including an exquisite rod-bow safety-pin fibula (interestingly, the concentration in the Clogher Valley of such brooches with leaf-shaped bows suggests a specialist workshop in the area). A platform built over the hillfort defences in the eastern quadrant between AD 400 and 610 was used for metalworking. At around the same time an unusual enclosure, 50 m in diameter, was built on the summit, consisting of a palisade surrounded by a fosse and palisade-topped bank. Imported and native artefacts were found in this, including detritus from the manufacture of zoomorphic penannular brooches and sherds of a Mediterranean wine amphora. The ringfort was built on top of this, probably during the 7th century, and is associated with imported E-ware pottery. It has been suggested that the triangular mound to the south of the ringfort is an inauguration mound. The hillfort overlooks a natural amphitheatre to the west, at the bottom of which is an area of wet/boggy ground. The area is also very rich in ringforts. Within 3 km of Clogher village are up to 28 raths. There is also a souterrain, due south of the royal site, and about 3 km to the south-west (*on the A4* *towards Fivemiletown, on the right-hand side of the road*) is a large mound.

A church was also established nearby by St Mac Cairthinn, said to be a contemporary of St Patrick, in deliberate counterpoint to the seat of pagan power. Evidence of the later monastery includes the remains of three 9th–10th-century crosses, now erected near the cathedral. Inside the cathedral is a 7th–8th-century sundial. In the 12th century Clogher became the see of the diocese of the kingdom of Airgialla. Another important but undocumented monastic site was found by chance on a hill at Dunmisk, near Carrickmore, which, as we have seen, is also called Termon (indeed, a second townland of this name occurs still nearer to Dunmisk). Excavations by Richard Ivens within the sub-triangular enclosure here uncovered the remains of a wooden building, probably a church, two areas for specialized craft working, and a densely packed cemetery of over 400 graves. The most elaborate burials were in the south-east, near the building. Analysis revealed interesting life-expectancy details; a quarter of the population were dead by 15 years of age, the average age of death was 25 years, and only 2.5 per cent lived to be 40; cold comfort, then, in the fact that they enjoyed near cavity-free teeth. One of the craft workshops was for metalwork only, the other for metal and glass, including working with millefiori. Ivens has speculated that this could be the missing *Domnach Mescáin* of the *Vita Tripartita* (one of the early biographies of Patrick). Indeed this area is also rich in places associated with the Patrician mission. A Neolithic chambered cairn on the south-west summit of Knockroe, to the south-east of Clogher, is called Carnfadrig [*Carn Phádraig*, 'Patrick's mound'], and due east of this, at Altadaven, is St Patrick's Chair and Well, the latter comprising a large cupmark in a rock.

Clonca, Co. Donegal   Early church site; high crosses

23 km north-east of Buncrana, off R238 (Moville–Culdaff); take minor road to west 1.7 km south of Culdaff. Disc. Ser. 3.

High up on the Inishowen peninsula, near the northernmost point in Ireland, is Clonca [*Cluain Catha*, 'meadow of the battle'], an early monastic site said to have been founded by St Buodan. The surviving church is 17th century, but there is evidence of the earlier monastery—a reused, probably 12th century, lintel with worn figure carvings over the doorway, and parts of two high crosses. One (*in the field west of the church*) is almost complete at 3.95 m high, carved from a single slab of stone, and is probably of 10th–12th-century date. Its unringed cross head is mainly a modern replacement. Most of the surface is decorated with panels of interlace and geometric ornament, but some figure carving is present, including a *Miracle of the Loaves and Fishes* at the top of the east face. Further west in the same field is the head of a second cross, possibly of 9th–10th-century date, another fragment of which lies inside the church. The cross head is ringed, but not pierced, and is decorated with roundels of C-curves. Further to the south-west is a fallen standing stone. Within the church, near the north-east corner, is an elaborate 16th-century grave slab with a central cross, foliage decoration, and a sword, hurley stick, and ball. An inscription at the top reads FERGUS MAK ALLAN DO RINI IN CLACH SA MAGNUS MEC ORRISTIN IA FO TRL SEO ('Fergus Mac Allan made this stone; Magnus Mac Orristin under this [stone]'). This slab is strongly Scottish in style and almost unique in Ireland, although it is definitely Irish and not Scottish.

Derry, Co. Derry Early monastic site; plantation town

Historically, Derry is one of the more important settlements in Ireland, though this is hardly reflected in the visible archaeology. Like so many other Irish towns, it originated as a monastic site, *Doire Cholmchille* ('the oak grove of Colmcille'), closely associated with the 6th-century saint Columba. Derry became an important monastery, controlled by the Cenél Conaill until the 11th century, when it passed into the control of the rival Cenél nEógain. This led to a significant expansion and in the mid-12th century Derry replaced **Kells** as the chief monastery of the entire Columban federation. Unfortunately, this highpoint of Derry's development was short-lived, as by the end of that century the federation itself had been substantially destroyed by the English conquest. This was a major blow to Derry's prestige and during the 13th century the community adopted the Augustinian rule, subject to the authority of **Armagh**. Derry continued to function in relative obscurity for the remainder of the Middle Ages, although it probably remained the largest settlement of north-west Ulster. This made it a target for the English, culminating in its capture by Sir Henry Docwra in 1600, which marked the effective end of the monastic settlement. As part of the plantation of Ulster James I granted Derry to the London companies in 1613. The result was the new plantation town of Londonderry. The new town, populated with British Protestants, was laid out on contemporary (probably French) principles and enclosed with walls in 1618—possibly the last Irish town to be walled. It was intended to act as a stronghold for the English crown in the wild north-west, but ironically the walls of Londonderry were most famously employed to defy the king of England, when James II was refused admission by the Protestant townspeople in 1688, leading to a prolonged and ultimately unsuccessful siege. Such are the vagaries of history.

Effectively, no trace remains today of the medieval monastic site, but the original layout of the plantation town survives almost intact, with four axial streets leading from a central square (the 'Diamond') to gates in the walls. The original gatehouses have been replaced by arches, but the circuit of walls is practically complete and makes an interesting and enjoyable walk, providing a unique vantage, not only on 17th-century history but also on more recent events. The walls are quite different from those found in earlier, medieval towns—relatively low but very broad, designed both to accommodate artillery and to withstand it. In the south-eastern angle of the walled town stands St Columb's cathedral, which has the distinction of being the first Protestant cathedral built in Ireland—indeed, it may well be the oldest post-Reformation church on the island. Although some restoration and other works were carried out in the 19th century, the church is still substantially as it was built *c*.1630. At the northern end of the walled town stands a modern version of a medieval tower house, housing the Tower Museum, which contains interesting displays on the history of the city and surrounding area, from earliest times to the present.

Doe, Co. Donegal Tower house and bawn

22 km north of Letterkenny, off N56 (Letterkenny–Dunfanaghy); take minor road to east at southern edge of Creeslough village, then to north-east after 400 m; signposted. Disc. Ser. 2.

Doe was a stronghold of Mac Suibhne *na dTuath* ['of the territories'— Anglicized to Doe], a lordly family who originally came to Ireland from Scotland as gallowglass mercenaries. First documented in 1544, Doe was

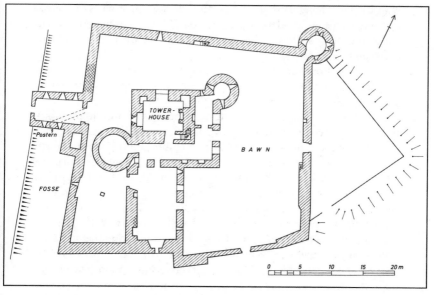

▲ **Fig. 35.** Doe Castle: plan (after OPW)

probably built in the early 16th century, and figured prominently in the wars of the early 17th century and of the 1640s. Extensive restoration was carried out in the early 19th century, which is not always easily distinguished from original work. Doe is a relatively elaborate castle, by late medieval Irish standards, well sited on a promontory in Sheephaven Bay. The tower house is surrounded by a rectangular walled bawn (c.34 m east–west by c.33 m north–south), which in turn is protected by the sea on three sides, and by a rock-cut fosse on the west. A causeway over the fosse leads to the main entrance, which is defended by a projecting turret on the south side. The causeway is defended by crenellated walls that are clearly later than the bawn wall. There are also doorways in the south and east bawn walls—the latter defended by a machicolation. The bawn wall, probably much rebuilt, is battered externally and has a wall walk defended by a crenellated parapet—probably added in the 19th century. The bawn is defended by a three-storey round turret at the north-east corner and by bartizans at the other three corners.

The tower house is surrounded on the east and south by an L-shaped building with a projecting, two-storey, circular turret at the north-east corner. The turret has a conical corbelled roof and has gun loops, providing flanking fire along the north and east sides of the main building. Another round turret stands at the south-west angle of the tower house, but may not be original. A 16th-century grave slab has recently been built into the external face, on the north side. Opening off the L-shaped building to the south (and probably contemporary with it) is a rectangular hall; the north wall and upper parts of the east and west walls are modern replacements. The south wall is offset over corbelling at first-floor level, and is defended by a machicolation externally.

The four-storey tower house has a single chamber on each floor, and is entered through a doorway in the south wall, immediately inside which a mural stair gives access to the upper floors. The ground-floor chamber was probably used for storage and/or servants' accommodation. The present east wall is an addition, inserted to accommodate corner fireplaces. In the west wall a large embrasure contains three gun loops, and the opening in the north wall probably contained a similar embrasure. There are wall cupboards in the north-west and north-east angles. The first-floor chamber is accessed from the mural stairs through a doorway in the east wall, and was lit by windows (now merely rectangular openings) in the other three walls. A doorway in the north-east corner gives access to a garderobe—a clear indication that this was a residential chamber. However, it was less important than the chambers above and was probably used for servants' accommodation. The second-floor chamber could only be accessed from the third floor—a security feature indicating that we are approaching the lord's quarters. The third floor is reached via the mural stair in the east wall, which rises to third-floor level as a spiral stair in the north-east angle, leading into a passage in the east wall, from which a doorway gives access to the main chamber. Doorways in the north-west and south-east corners lead to short spiral stairs descending to the second floor. This design ensured that a single door, across the eastern mural passage, could have effectively protected access to both second- and third-floor chambers. The third-floor chamber had windows in the other three walls, of which original trefoil- and ogee-headed windows survive. The quality of the windows suggests that the third-floor chamber was the lord's hall, while the second floor below may have contained his family sleeping quarters. Another mural stair in the east wall gave access to an attic floor above the third-floor chamber.

Donegal, Co. Donegal Castle, friary

55 km north-east of Sligo; on N15 and N56. Disc. Ser. 11.

A Viking origin for Donegal has often been suggested, on the basis of its name [*Dún na nGall*, 'the fort of the foreigners'], but there is no evidence to corroborate this. In fact, apart from one doubtful reference in the late 12th century, the name is first documented in the late 15th century, and this suggests that it has nothing to do with Vikings. A Franciscan friary was founded here *c.*1473 by Aodh Ruadh Ó Domhnaill, who is also credited with building the castle of Donegal prior to his death in 1505. In the late 16th century this was the main residence of the Ó Domhnaill lords of Tír Conaill (roughly modern Co. Donegal), including the famous Red Hugh O'Donnell. After O'Donnell's flight from Ireland in 1607, Donegal was granted to the English planter Basil Brooke, who was responsible not only for extensive alterations to the castle, but also for the establishment of the modern town.

Castle

The fine castle is built on a rock outcrop, overlooking the river Eask. Its centrepiece is a four-storey tower house, quite possibly built by Aodh Ruadh Ó Domhnaill before 1505, occupying the north-east corner of a polygonal walled bawn. The bawn is protected by the river on the north and east, and is entered on the south through a gateway, defended by a two-storey tower with bartizan. This tower and most of the bawn wall date to Brooke's rebuilding in the early 17th century. The rectangular tower house consists of a single chamber on each floor, vaulted over ground-floor level. The original entrance was on the south—it's now obscured by the bay front, which was added by Brooke. The ground-floor chamber was lit by six narrow window loops, one of which was later enlarged into a doorway communicating with the house built to

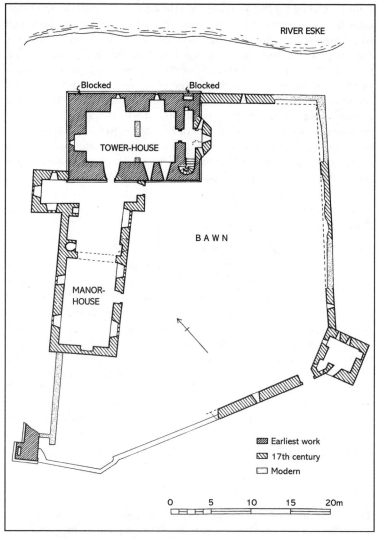

▲ Fig. 36. Donegal Castle: plan (OPW)

the west. The other loops all received new jambs in the 17th century. A spiral stair in the south-west corner leads to a small mural chamber over the original doorway, which it probably helped to defend. The rest of the first-floor level is occupied by the vault over the ground-floor chamber. The spiral stair continues to second-floor level, which was clearly the main chamber of the tower house—at least in the time of Brooke, who added a bay window (now restored) on the south side, and inserted large transomed and mullioned windows in the west and north walls. In the east wall he inserted a large, ornate fireplace with Renaissance decoration and bearing the arms of Brooke and Leicester (his wife's family). Another fireplace near the north-east corner (blocking the entrance to a mural stair) suggests that the chamber may once have been divided into two. Later, when the adjoining house was built, a doorway was inserted in the west wall (probably in a window embrasure) to provide access to it. There was originally a third-floor chamber, reached via a mural stair in the north-east corner, but this was blocked—presumably when the adjoining house was built. This chamber is also lit by large transomed and mullioned windows in the south, west, and north walls. One of these, near the north-west corner, was later partly blocked to accommodate the roof line of the adjoining house. Again there are two fireplaces in the east wall, suggesting that the chamber was divided into two by Brooke. The 17th-century building originally had an attic floor above this, lit by three-light windows set within dormer gables (recently restored). It was probably divided into several small rooms. At each end of the south wall are large, square bartizans (also restored), apparently designed to protect the original doorway below, which must have been still in use when the attic floor was added.

On the west side of the tower house Brooke built a large Jacobean gable-fronted house or wing of three-storeys and five bays, clearly added after most of the alterations had been made to the tower house. The wing is lit by fine mullioned windows of two, three, and four lights (rather unevenly distributed over the elevations), and can be entered through two doorways at ground-floor level. A large fireplace and oven in the north wall indicate that much of the ground floor was taken up by the kitchen, and the remainder was probably used for storage. Doorways were opened in the west wall of the tower house at ground- and second-floor levels, and it was presumably at this stage that the original doorway of the tower house was replaced by the bay front. There is also a finely decorated round-headed doorway at first-floor level in the south wall of the new wing (obviously approached via a vanished external stair), which clearly became the main entrance. It must have led to a wooden stair, rising from first- to second-floor level, and leading to the new doorway in the west wall of the tower house, which still contained the most important rooms. The upper floors of the new wing were probably taken up mainly with offices and accommodation for Brooke's household.

Friary

The Franciscan friary, on the seashore south of the town, was probably built *c.*1473–88. Founded by the Ó Domhnaill, and apparently staffed by friars from **Ross** (Co. Galway), it is most famous as the home of the friars who compiled the *Annals of the Four Masters* in the early 17th century. Occupation by English forces in 1601 resulted in an explosion and fire, leading to the current fragmentary condition of the remains. The church was originally a typical long, narrow nave-and-choir structure with central tower, south aisle, and south transept, but little more than the choir survives above ground. This was lit by four windows in the south wall, of which the two central windows have been partially blocked, reducing them from three to two lights. In the north-east corner are a piscina (in the east wall) and sedilia (in the south wall). The claustral buildings, on the north side of the church, are slightly better preserved. Sections of the cloister arcade survive on the east and north sides, along with traces of the surrounding ranges of buildings on the north, east, and west sides.

Dungiven, Co. Derry Medieval church

25 km south-east of Derry off A6 (Derry–Belfast); turn south 1 km east of centre of Dungiven village; signposted. For access to the chancel, the Environment and Heritage Service should be contacted in advance. Disc. Ser. 7.

Dungiven is believed to be the site of an early monastic foundation associated with the 7th-century St Neachtain, although the name [*Dún Geimhin*, 'Geimhean's fort'] suggests an earlier, secular site. It probably became an Augustinian priory in the mid-12th century, after the Ó Catháin became lords of the region. The church, located on a height overlooking the river Roe, is a much rebuilt nave-and-chancel structure. At the west end of the church are the foundations of a late medieval tower house, probably erected by the Ó Catháin. In the early 17th-century plantation of Ulster Dungiven passed to the English planter Edward Doddington. Doddington converted the church into a parish church and built his manor house and outbuildings, arranged around a courtyard, on the south side. Only the foundations of these survive. Perhaps the earliest of all visible features on the site is the 'holy well' beside the pathway, a short distance east of the church. The well is actually a bullaun stone and overhanging it is a thorn bush festooned with rags—testimony to the continuing tradition of seeking a cure at the well.

The earliest part of the church is the nave. A mid-12th century date is indicated by possible antae (externally) and traces of blank arcading (internally) at the east end, and a small round-headed window in the south wall. This probably reflects a rebuilding of the church after the monastery adopted the Augustinian rule. Most other features of the church are later. A later wall has replaced the original west wall, including the main doorway, and the fine traceried window in the north wall of the nave was inserted in the 15th century. The chancel was added in the 13th century. It had a ribbed vault and twin lancet windows in the east wall. A similar window in the south wall is probably a 17th-century rebuilding, inserted into a blocked doorway. The chancel arch was rebuilt, and a new north door and porch added in the early 17th century. The most important feature of the church is the (restored) Ua Catháin tomb, set in a pointed recess in the south wall of the chancel, with a fine traceried canopy overhead. On the mensa of the tomb is the effigy of a warrior, holding his sword and wearing an aketon—a padded garment usually worn under mail armour, but here worn without any mail covering apart from the neck and shoulders. The head, with its unusual head covering, is a relatively modern replacement. Beneath the mensa, the tomb front features six armoured figures (in place of the traditional weepers) in cusped niches. The tomb is traditionally said to be that of Cumhaige na Gall Ó Catháin (d. 1385) and it could be of the late 14th century, although a 15th-century date is perhaps more likely.

Fahan, Co. Donegal Early medieval sculpture

15 km north-west of Derry, on the R238 (Derry–Buncrana); signposted. Disc. Ser. 3.

The fishing village of Fahan is picturesquely situated on the east shore of Lough Swilly, opposite Inch Island and about midway up the Inishowen peninsula. The suffix *Mura* is often applied and refers to the first monastery founded here in the 6th century by St Muru. It was an offshoot of the Columban foundation of Derry, in which context it is not irrelevant that its founder, like Columba (Colmcille), was of the house of Cenél nEógain. In the old graveyard, near the ruins of a 15th-century abbey, stands an important grave slab, which according to local tradition marks the grave of St Muru. It is 2.1 m tall with a triangular canopy and is decorated with an accomplished interlace cross carved in false relief on each face. Below the cross on the west face are two ecclesiastical figures. The pattern on their cloaks is a very worn inscription, partially read and then imaginatively reconstructed by Macalister. Vestigial cross arms project from either side. An inscription on the northern edge of the slab, in Greek lettering, is far clearer and was deciphered by Macalister to read ... *ΔOEA KAI TIME* (*sic*) *ΠATPI KAI YIΩ KAI ΠNEYMATI AΓΩ*, which translates as 'Glory and honour to Father and to Son and to Holy Spirit'. In dating the slab to the earlier 7th century, Henry placed great store in the sanctioning of this doxology (with its unusual addition of 'and honour') by the Council of Toledo in AD 633. However, it has recently been shown that this formula was in use for some time before this and therefore its value as *terminus post quem* is reduced. The Fahan inscription is, however, the only Greek inscription on an Irish cross. The inscription in Irish across the robes of the two ecclesiastics on the west face of the slab has not been fully deciphered but appears to commemorate an otherwise unidentified archbishop Marga ua Rinagain or Rindagain: Marga may be a variation of Múra.

As with the high cross at Carndonagh, Henry regarded the Fahan slab as an embryonic stage in the development of the free-standing cross. Most commentators now date it to the 9th century (but for an alternative view, see the entry for **Carndonagh,** which is further north along the peninsula). Nothing else of the original foundation survives. The southern horizon is dominated by **Grianán Ailech**, traditional capital of the northern Uí Néill and ruled by the saint's family, Cenél nEógain. Further along the Buncrana road, just after Fahan House, are the remains of Muru's Well.

Glencolumbkille and the Columban Heritage Trail, Cos. Donegal, Derry, and Tyrone

45 km west of Donegal town, on the R263 from Killybegs. Disc. Ser. 10.

The north-west, in particular Donegal, is closely associated with St Colmcille (Columba: 'little dove') and a Columban heritage trail has been established. Although at the most westerly point of the trail, Glencolumbkille, an elaborate penitentiary, remains one of the most important places associated with Colmcille. Glencolumbkille is a remote valley underneath Glen Head in south-west Donegal. It opens out into a sandy beach swept by great Atlantic breakers. On either side are huge cliffs. It is here, according to tradition, that Colmcille defeated a host of demons who had proven too powerful even for St Patrick, and where a *turas* or pilgrimage is held on Colmcille's Day (9 June) around fifteen penitential stations spread out across the valley. All of the stations are of interest for one reason or another. Some are marked by cross-slabs, some of them highly accomplished, others by cairns. 70 km to the north-east is Columba's birthplace, Gartan (*10 km west of Letterkenny on the R251 (Letterkenny–Gweedore), just west of Churchill*), where there is an interesting and worthwhile heritage centre dedicated to the saint, including an audio-visual show, tea rooms, and lakeside walks (*open during the summer months only*).

Greencastle, Co. Donegal Castle

38 km north-east of Derry; take R238 coastal route to Moville, then R241 coastal route to Greencastle village; castle is 200 m beyond village, to north-east. Disc. Ser. 3 and 4.

This once-fine castle, now sadly neglected, is probably the last great English castle built in Ireland. It was built in 1305 by Richard de Burgh, earl of Ulster, to command the entrance to Lough Foyle, as part of an unsuccessful attempt to bring north-west Ulster under English control. It also served as a supply base for English armies attacking Scotland in

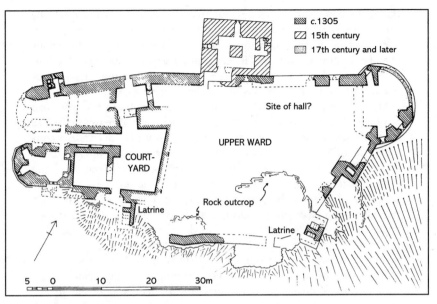

c.1305
15th century
17th century and later

Site of hall?

UPPER WARD

COURT-
YARD

Rock outcrop

Latrine

Latrine

5 0   10   20   30m

▲ **Fig. 37.** Greencastle: plan (after Waterman)

the early 14th century and was briefly captured by the Scots under
Edward Bruce in 1316. It was probably designed for de Burgo by a
mason who had worked on Edward I's great castles in north Wales. The
layout of the gatehouse is very like that at Harlech (built 1283–9), but
the closest parallels are with Caernarfon (built 1283–1330). The plan is
similar, with a massive gatehouse at one end and a large polygonal
tower at the other, but the most striking comparison is in the use of
banded polychrome masonry—i.e. horizontal bands of alternating
light- and dark-coloured stone. This is a feature of Caernarfon, ultimately derived from the walls of Constantinople, and de Burgo (a close
ally of Edward I) may have imitated it to associate himself with Edward
I's successful conquests in north Wales. If so, it was not effective. By the
15th century the entire Inishowen area had reverted to Ó Domhnaill
control and the castle was occupied by their allies, the Ó Dochartaigh.
It was seriously damaged, with the aid of artillery, by Calbhach Ó
Domhnaill in 1555, and although it was granted to the English planter
Chichester in the early 17th century, there is no sign of later rebuilding.
The only significant later addition at Greencastle is the large square
tower of two storeys (possibly three storeys originally) on the north
side. It is probably 15th century and must have been added by the
Ó Dochartaigh.

The castle is built on a rock outcrop, but extends beyond it at the
west end, where the twin-towered gatehouse is at a lower level than

the main courtyard. Thus on entering through the gatehouse, one arrives at a small courtyard, enclosed by outcropping rock, from which steps lead up to the main upper ward, at the level of the first-floor chambers of the gatehouse. The gatehouse itself consists of twin towers with polygonal fronts flanking a central, vaulted entrance passage with two doorways. Each tower was of three storeys, with two chambers, one behind the other, on each floor—but only the southern tower is even remotely intact. The ground-floor chambers would have served as guardhouses, defending the entrance passage, but the upper floors contain residential suites that could only be accessed from the interior of the castle, to the east. On the north side of the gatehouse is a projecting square turret with garderobes. Another garderobe turret stands at the south-east corner of the gatehouse. The upper ward is roughly trapezoidal, with a large polygonal tower of three storeys at the north-east angle and a later square tower midway along the north side. The polygonal tower was originally enclosed on the inner (west) side by a stone wall, now missing, along with the stairs that would have provided access to the upper floors. There was presumably a great hall, but no definite trace of it survives. It was probably located along the north side of the upper ward, most likely at the east end where six relatively small windows survive in the curtain wall.

Grianán Ailech, Co. Donegal Royal enclosure

8 km north-west of Derry; take minor road to south off N13 (Derry–Letterkenny); signposted. Disc. Ser. 7.

Grianán ('sunny/important place') was the residence of the Uí Néill kings of Ailech, one of the most powerful dynasties in early medieval Ireland. The annals record its destruction, possibly in 676 and certainly in 1101, when Muirchertach Ó Briain, king of Munster, is said to have had each of his soldiers carry away a stone from the walls, in revenge for the destruction of his capital *Ceann Córadh* (Kincora) at **Killaloe** in 1088. The site of the *Grianán* of Ailech is traditionally (and, for most people, unquestioningly) identified with the magnificent stone fort, set within a much larger earthen enclosure, which crowns the top of the hill known as Greenan Mountain. It has recently been suggested that the actual site of the *Grianán* is now occupied by a 13th/14th-century castle at Elagh More (5 km to the north-east), but definitive proof will be required to have any hope of shifting the long-standing and widely accepted identification with the fort on Greenan Mountain.

The fort is prominently located with commanding views over Lough Foyle, Lough Swilly, and the adjacent countryside. It consists of a circular area *c.*24 m in diameter, surrounded by a massive drystone wall up to 5 m high and 4.6 m thick. The wall is battered externally and terraced

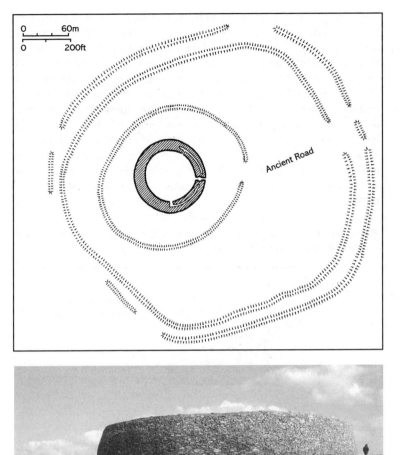

▲ **Fig. 38.** Grianán Ailech: plan showing surrounding earthworks (after Lacy); photo: Conor Newman

internally, with sets of steps giving access to the top at five main locations around the perimeter. Unfortunately, the wall was heavily restored in the 19th century and it is impossible to know how accurately it reflects the original form. A lintelled entrance passage on the eastern side gives access to the interior, which is featureless on the surface. On either side of the entrance, passages have been incorporated in the thickness of the wall. The stone fort is surrounded, at a distance of *c*.25 m, by a low, worn, roughly concentric earthen bank with slight traces of an external fosse. Outside this again, at distances varying between 20 m to the west and 70 m to the east, is a much larger enclosure, defined by two very eroded earthen banks 10–15 m apart with probable internal fosses. Both inner and outer enclosures seem to have entrance gaps on the east, roughly corresponding to the entrance to the stone fort. These enclosures are probably the remains of a hillfort substantially older than the stone fort, perhaps of the Late Bronze Age or Iron Age, although this has yet to be confirmed by excavation. As with a similar structure at **Staigue**, Co. Kerry, the date of the stone fort is debated, but an early medieval date (*c.* AD 500–1000) is most likely. The association with an earlier enclosure is characteristic of other high-status early medieval sites.

▼ **Fig. 39.** Harry Avery's castle: overall plan showing stone curtain wall as revealed by excavation (after Jope)

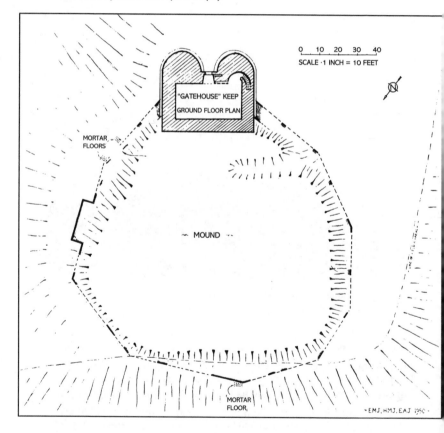

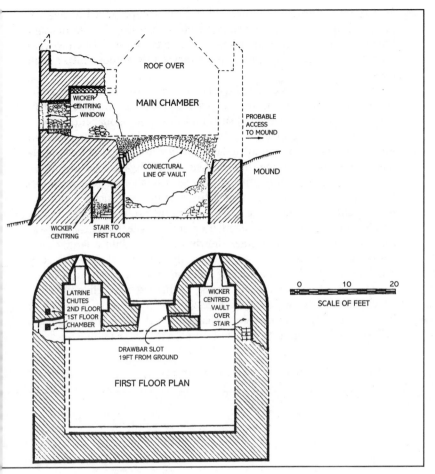

▲ **Fig. 40.** Harry Avery's castle: plan of first floor and section through the 'gatehouse' (after Jope)

Harry Avery's castle, Co. Tyrone Castle

15 km north of Omagh, off A5 (Omagh–Derry); take minor road to Rakelly at Newtownstewart. Disc. Ser. 12.

This castle is significant both architecturally and historically—as one of the earliest surviving castles built by an Irish lord. It bears the name of Henry *Aimhreadh* ('unsmooth') Ó Néill, a brother of the lord of Tír Eógain, who died in 1392 and is thought to have built the castle to consolidate his hold on an area disputed by the great rival dynasties of Ulster, the Ó Néill and the Ó Domhnaill. The castle cannot be firmly dated, but there is no good reason to doubt the traditional, later

14th-century date. Its structure, although poorly preserved, is of great interest. While it has been considered a poor imitation of a 13th-century English castle, it is in many respects something quite different, which actually looks forward to the late medieval tower house rather than backwards.

The castle consists of a substantial gatehouse with a large polygonal walled enclosure to the north, occupying a prominent hill that was artificially scarped and raised, and surrounded by a polygonal curtain wall. Little more than foundations of the wall survive, but there are traces of projecting towers to the north-east and north-west. Although superficially resembling an English-style twin-towered gatehouse of the late 13th or early 14th century, the 'gatehouse' actually functions quite differently, as a self-contained unit incorporating the functions of gatehouse, hall, and residence. Instead of having an entrance passage, leading between the twin towers to the interior of the castle, its central gateway (originally reached by an outer drawbridge) leads into a large chamber—originally vaulted—that occupies the entire width of the gatehouse. Access to the remainder of the castle was by means of a mural stair in the south-west corner, leading to the first-floor chamber from which, apparently, was the only access to the large enclosed bailey or bawn to the rear. The first-floor chamber itself was a large hall, with private chambers in the two tower fronts for the lord's family.

▼ **Fig. 41a.** Malin More: plan of megaliths (after Cody)

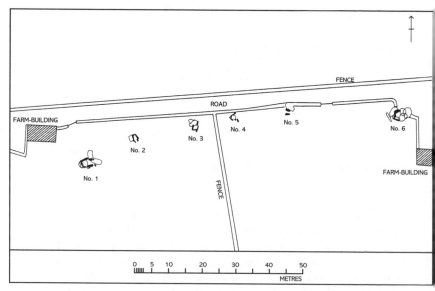

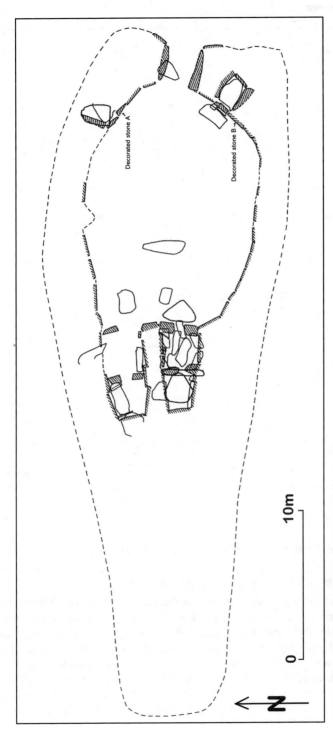

▲ Fig. 41b. 'Cloghanmore', Malin More: plan (after Cody)

Decorated stone A

Decorated stone B

0   10m

N

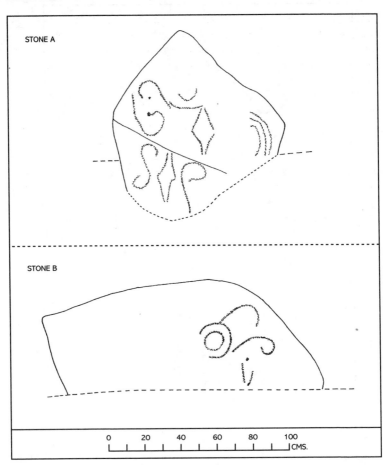

▲ **Fig. 42.** 'Cloghanmore', Malin More: decorated stones of Court tomb (after Cody)

Malin More, Co. Donegal Megalithic tombs

50 km west of Donegal town, off the link road from the R263 (Killybegs–Rocky Point) to Malin More; not signposted. Disc. Ser. 10.

Malin More (quite distinct from Malin Head, on Inishowen) is the most westerly point of Donegal and boasts a dense concentration of megalithic tombs. Near the seaward end of Malin More Valley is a unique configuration of six Portal tombs arranged in a more or less straight line, east–west. These are approached down a lane on the Malin Beg side of the Malin More–Carrick road, and are now somewhat compromised by modern houses. The tombs at each end are the largest and are orientated towards the east. Between these, but displaced northwards, are four very small tombs, some of which are orientated northwards. It has been suggested that all of these tombs may once have been enclosed under one long (approx. 90 m) cairn, thus explaining the displacement of the small chambers which, according to this theory, would have opened off the north side of the cairn.

The westernmost tomb originally had two capstones but following the cracking of the northern portal the massive front capstone has tumbled forwards and now blocks the entrance. About 8 m to the east is the first of the diminutive tombs, which is in a fairly dilapidated state. The next one along (about 17 m to the east) is in far better condition; only the western portal has collapsed, causing the roofstone to become displaced. The third of the small tombs is 3 m away in the adjacent field and nearly all the supporting stones have shifted or fallen over causing the capstone to dislodge and collapse. The last of the small tombs is 13 m away to the east, and comprises two portal stones and a capstone, which is supported between one of them and an adjacent field fence. The large tomb at the east end has been described as 'deranged' (possibly because the whole ensemble looks rather like a parade of drunken megaliths) and is indeed difficult to decipher, not least because it has been incorporated into a field fence. The two portal stones have folded over under the front capstone but would have originally stood an impressive 2.6 m tall. The rear of the tomb is more intact and still has its capstone, albeit leaning at an odd angle.

A little distance to the north-east is a fabulous Court tomb known as Cloghanmore. It lies in boggy ground (*small car park; wellington boots a must!*) about 110 m south-west of the road and close to the stream that runs through the valley. It is a well-preserved, full-court tomb opening from the east end of a 40 m long, somewhat coffin-shaped cairn that is revetted with a drystone wall (much of which is the result of early restoration). The huge, oval-shaped court is entered through a 3 m long passage. At the opposite side, announced by quite majestic orthostats, are *two* parallel galleries (5 m long), a development paralleled only at Deerpark, Co. Sligo. Each one is divided by jambstones into two chambers. Smaller, single chambers open into the court area on either side of the entrance and two of the court orthostats next to these are decorated with faintly incised curvilinear designs—the only decorated stones associated with this class of tomb. This tomb has not been excavated.

Mount Sandel, Co. Derry Mesolithic settlement

On the southern outskirts of Coleraine, signposted off the A26 to Ballymoney or on link road to Knockantern from town centre. Disc. Ser. 4.

Known since the 1880s to have yielded Mesolithic artefacts, and more recently threatened by the suburban sprawl of Coleraine, the field immediately north-east of Mountsandel Fort was excavated between 1973 and 1977. These excavations, directed by Peter Woodman, uncovered a miraculously intact Mesolithic settlement, dating to between 7000 and 6500 BC. The settlement was located on a bluff on the east bank of the river Bann, south of Coleraine, and was traced over an area of about 7,000m². The best-preserved remains occurred in a slight hollow. Here were found dozens of stake-pipes, from which four sub-oval huts about 6 m in diameter could be distinguished, four large hearth pits and a multitude of pits, representing episodic reoccupations. The stake-pipes were driven into the ground at 60 degree angles and are thought to have been saplings, bent over to form dome-shaped huts. Thousands of flint microliths were found, the business end of composite tools and hunting weapons. Organic remains from the numerous pits provided insights into the subsistence economy of this settlement. The main animal foods were young pig, flounder, bass, salmon, and eels, when in season, and these were supplemented with hare, wolf, and wild cat and a wide variety of birds including divers, mallards, teal, eagle, grouse, woodcock, etc. Hazelnut shells, being durable, were found in considerable quantities and of course could also be stored. The seasonality of these different resources suggests the main occupation was between autumn and early winter, but could easily have sustained early and late summer occupancy as well.

Mountsandel Fort is a type of promontory fort and dominates the river from a height of about 50 m. The headland is defended on the east side by a fosse. Above this is a terrace surrounding the hollow summit. The site is undated, but generally considered to be medieval. However, it is not to be confused with Kilsantel Castle, built by de Courcy, which is identified as a motte-and-bailey and ruined castle at Camus, 5.5 km south of Coleraine, where St Comgall founded a monastery.

Tory Island, Co. Donegal Island monastery

Access by boat only; ferry available daily, June–September, from Bunbeg and Magheraroarty (both on R257 coastal route, off N56 west of Gortahork). Disc. Ser. 1.

Tory is a small island 15 km off the north-west coast of Co. Donegal. While it may appear bleak and isolated today, Tory [*Tóraigh*, '(island) of the towers'] has been occupied since prehistoric times and was the site of an important early medieval monastery. Prehistoric settlement is demonstrated primarily by the promontory fort, at the extreme eastern end of the island. It has not been excavated or definitely dated, but is probably late prehistoric. The fort was formed by cutting off the tip of the island by means of four large, parallel earthen banks with intervening fosses; the remaining three sides of the headland are naturally defended by cliffs. Several rounded hut sites are visible in the southern and eastern parts of the interior.

The main settlement on the island today, West Town on the south coast, occupies the site of an early monastery said to have been founded by St Colmcille (Columba) in the 6th century—it was certainly in existence by 612, when its church was destroyed in a marine attack. It probably functioned, in some form, until the end of the 16th century, before being destroyed by the English in 1595. Today there are traces of two churches and an incomplete round tower, which suggests that Tory was a site of some importance, at least in the 11th/12th centuries. The tower is 12.8 m high and was apparently never much taller than this, although much of the west side was rebuilt in the 19th century. It is built of rounded granite boulders, with a round-headed doorway facing south-east, set 2.6 m above ground. On the third floor are the remains of two (originally four) windows, indicating that this was the top floor, while a fragment of the roof survives on the east side. Unusually, there is evidence for a stone vault between the second and third floors. Nearby, to the east, is 'St John's altar', with a number of interesting carved stones including a small stone cross. Many of these stones may have been associated with St Colmcille's church, possibly the principal church of the monastery, which stood near this spot but has now vanished.

Perhaps the most interesting feature of Tory, however, is the tau (T-shaped) cross, located south-west of the round tower, near the pier in West Town. Carved from a single slab of stone, it is 1.9 m high and plain. Only two of these unusual stone crosses are known in Ireland and they are difficult to date, but this one may well be roughly contemporary with the round tower, i.e. 11th/12th century. Further west, outside West Town are the remains of the church of the *Mórsheisear* ('six persons'), a small, simple, and probably early church with an altar at the east end and a bullaun stone near the entrance.

Tullaghoge, Co. Tyrone Inauguration site

4 km south-east of Cookstown, off B162 (Cookstown–Stewartstown); take minor road east 3.5 km south of Cookstown; signposted. Disc. Ser. 13.

Tullaghoge [*Tulaigh Óg*, 'mound of the warriors'] is famous as the inauguration site of the Ó Néill (O'Neill) kings of Cenél nEógain, who were generally the most powerful dynasty in medieval Ulster. This area only came under direct Ó Néill control in the 11th century, and it is not known whether the earthwork was built by them or was already in existence. It is located on the summit of a prominent hill, with magnificent views in all directions. The earthwork has the general appearance and proportions of a ringfort, consisting of a hillock fortified by two earthen banks, possibly with a wide, shallow fosse in between. However, it is not certain that it should be considered a ringfort, as the widely spaced banks seem to be designed for ceremonial, rather than defensive purposes. Only excavation will confirm whether the site was ever occupied, in the sense that a normal ringfort was, or whether its function was exclusively ceremonial. A large stone chair or throne was located here and used in the inauguration ceremonies of the Uí Néill, but was destroyed by the English general Mountjoy in 1602.

North Midlands: Cavan, Fermanagh, Leitrim, Longford, Monaghan

Introduction

This region is characterized topographically by lakes, drumlins, and small bogs and, as such, it defines the northern edge of the Central Plain. The principal drainage systems are the Erne and upper Shannon in the mid-west and the Dromore and Annalee rivers in Monaghan. Although Leitrim proudly defends its short Atlantic coastline, sandwiched

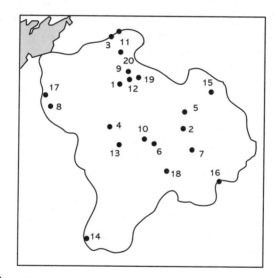

▲ Map 3
Key:

1. Aghnaglack, Co. Fermanagh
2. Black Pig's Dyke, Scotshouse, Co Monaghan
3. Boa Island, Co. Fermanagh
4. Burren, Co. Cavan
5. Clones, Co. Monaghan
6. Cloughoughter, Co. Cavan
7. Cohaw, Co. Cavan
8. Creevelea, Co. Leitrim
9. Devenish, Co. Fermanagh
10. Drumlane, Co. Cavan
11. Drumskinny, Co. Fermanagh
12. Enniskillen, Co. Fermanagh
13. Fenagh, Co. Leitrim
14. Inchcleraun, Co. Longford
15. Monaghan, Co. Monaghan
16. Mullagh, Co. Cavan
17. Parke's castle, Kilmore, Co. Leitrim
18. Shantemon, Co. Cavan
19. Topped Mountain, Co. Fermanagh
20. White Island, Co. Fermanagh

between Sligo and Donegal, these are really inland counties. A drumlin belt extends across Cavan and Monaghan, but the main areas of high ground lie further to the west in Leitrim and Fermanagh. At the eastern extreme of the region are acid brown earths, whereas gleys and peats dominate the remainder. Farming is cattle-dominated and, on account of the topography, of comparatively small scale.

Apart from the county inventories and sub-regional and site-specific analyses, the region has not been treated, as such, archaeologically. Clearly, however, it has tremendous potential in this regard, not least because the topography has put the brakes on development and so the largely rural landscape has not been spoiled. A thin scatter of stray finds of later Mesolithic tools are the oldest evidence of a human presence. In view of the behavioural bias among early hunter-gatherers in favour of freshwater resources, this region must have been very attractive. Most of the region lies between the lines of Passage tomb cemeteries running diagonally from the Boyne to Ballisadare Bay and from Armagh across south Tyrone and into south-east Donegal. This probably says more about the topography of this region than about its cultural history, for it is very well populated with Court and Portal tombs. Indeed, some seminal work on these types has been carried out in this region, including Howard Kilbride-Jones's excavation of the dual-court tomb at **Cohaw**, Co. Cavan, Oliver Davies's excavations at **Aghanaglack**, Co. Fermanagh, and Gabriel Cooney's analysis of the siting of megalithic tombs in Leitrim. Earlier Bronze Age populations are represented primarily in the funerary record. Wedge tombs are found mainly in the western part of the region, but flat cemeteries, cemetery mounds, and cist graves, while not found in great numbers, have been reported from the rest of the region. Curiously, cist graves appear to be all but unknown in Longford. One of the more important cemetery mounds in Irish archaeology, however, is on the summit of **Topped Mountain** in Fermanagh. The region does not boast the massive quantities of later Bronze Age material found elsewhere, but the Erne waterway seems to have been an important trade area and has a particularly high density of socketed axeheads.

Notwithstanding the general dearth of Iron Age settlement sites, from an analysis of artefact distributions this region emerges as one of the core areas of La Tène culture in Ireland, a conclusion underwritten by Raftery's excavations of a series of Iron Age toghers at Corlea, Co. Longford. The area was also densely populated in the early medieval period. It is the core area of crannóg distribution in Ireland and has an above-average density of ringforts. The northern part of this region—Cos. Fermanagh and Monaghan—formed part of the early Ulster kingdom of Airgialla, a confederation of vassal peoples under the overlordship of the northern Uí Néill. Further south, in the Cos. Leitrim/Longford area, was the Uí Néill kingdom of Tethbae, but by the

11th century it had been absorbed—along with most of Co. Cavan—into the kingdom of Bréifne. The Ó Ruairc (O'Rourke) kings of Bréifne were one of the Uí Briúin dynasties of Connacht but lost out to another Uí Briúin dynasty, the Ó Conchobhair (O'Connors), in the struggle for the kingship of Connacht. Turning their attention to the midlands, they carved out a new kingdom for themselves in the 9th/10th centuries and were particularly prominent in the 11th and 12th centuries.

Following the English conquest there were attempts to colonize Bréifne, chiefly by the de Lacy lords of Meath. The most serious of these attempts was in the early 1220s, when it seems the de Lacys substantially controlled most of Cos. Cavan, Leitrim, and Longford. This expansion effectively ended, however, with the death of William de Lacy in 1233, after which this area reverted to the control of Irish lords. Much of the Co. Monaghan area was granted to the English baron Peter Pipard, *c.*1190, but only the southern part of the county seems to have been actively colonized at this date. A motte-and-bailey castle was erected by the English at **Clones** in 1212, as part of a wider campaign against the Irish kings of the north, but the campaign soon petered out—as did English efforts at settlement in the area. The Co. Fermanagh area was relatively unaffected by the English conquest, although Hugh de Lacy, earl of Ulster, granted lands in south-west Fermanagh to Maurice FitzGerald, who was already lord of Sligo. Maurice's attempts to enforce this claim came to nothing, however, and there was no further serious effort at English colonization until the 17th century. For the remainder of the Middle Ages this region was almost entirely dominated by Irish lords such as the Ó Raghallaigh (O'Reillys) in the Co. Cavan area, the Ó Fearghaill (O'Farrells) in the Co. Longford area, and the Mac Uidhir (Maguires) in the Co. Fermanagh area. As a result the region is almost entirely lacking in the standard forms of medieval Anglo-Irish monuments—mottes, moated sites, manorial villages, boroughs, or towns. Stone castles and even tower houses are relatively scarce, but there are several important church sites, notably **Devenish**, **Fenagh**, and **Inchcleraun**. In the early 17th century much of the region, especially Cos. Cavan, Monaghan, and Fermanagh, experienced a substantial influx of English and Scottish settlers as part of the plantation of Ulster, although this was less thorough than in areas further north.

Aghanaglack, Co. Fermanagh   Court tomb

12 km south-west of Enniskillen, to the west of link road between Boho and Belcoo; turn off at Dooletter, following the Ulster Way, until the first cross, at which go straight ahead (path veers right) for 0.9 km. Disc. Ser. 17.

This fine dual-court tomb was excavated by Oliver Davies in 1938. It is located on a rocky bluff about two-thirds of the way from Belcoo to

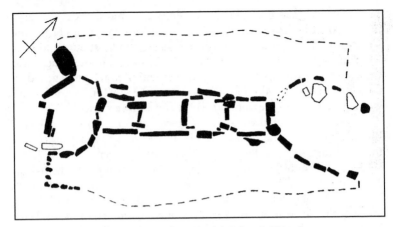

▲ Fig. 43a. Aghanaglack: plan of court tomb (after de Valera)

Boho, between Dooletter Lough and Lough Blocknet. It overlooks a river valley that descends through Boho towards Ross Lough. The tombs are end to end, each comprising a megalithic forecourt and dual-chamber gallery. The galleries share a backstone. The cairn is about 24 m long and is orientated north-east/south-west. The only burial remains comprised the cremated remains of a child and a youth, the latter associated with pig and deer teeth. The lithic assemblage included hollow scrapers, two barbed and tanged arrowheads, a javelinhead, and a bead, and the ceramics comprised sherds of round-bottomed bowls and chord-impressed bowls. The assemblage is therefore mixed and suggests primary use in the earlier Neolithic and secondary use in the early Bronze Age.

The valley was evidently an important communication between the Derrygonnelly region south-west of Lower Lough Erne, and the neck of land at Belcoo, between Upper and Lower Lough Macnean, and thence to Leitrim. This is corroborated by the location of a cairn to the north-west of and overlooking Boho, and a possible stone circle with cupmark and cashel overlooking Mullylusty and the head of the Lurgan river at the south-western end of the valley. Boho is famous in archaeological circles because of the recovery from a bog nearby of a decorated spearhead of Iron Age date.

Black Pig's Dyke, Scotshouse, Co. Monaghan Linear
earthwork

18 km north-east of Cavan; best approached from Scotshouse, following the signpost for Drum off the R212 (Scotshouse–Cavan); exactly 2.15 km from Connolly's pub in Scotshouse. Not signposted. Disc. Ser. 28A.

Attributed to the rootings of a mythological schoolteacher-turned-pig and traditionally interpreted as the border of ancient Ulster, the Black

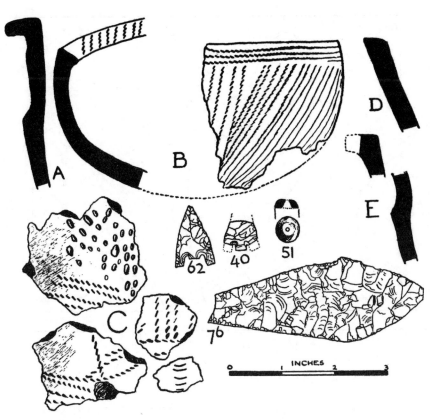

▲ **Fig. 43b.** Aghanaglack: excavated finds (after Davies)

Pig's Dyke is a series of linear earthworks (Claí na Muice Duibhe) running from north Sligo to south Armagh. The earthworks go under various names including the Dane's Cast, Worm Ditch, and the **Dorsey**, which is in south Armagh. In so far as the earthworks connect together natural impediments such as lakes, bogs, and high ground, they are manifestly defensive in aspect. This does not, however, mean that they are all contemporary, nor does it mean that collectively they constitute one border for one people. That said, the general coincidence with the present borders of the province of Ulster should not go unremarked. Moreover, it is not known how much of the earthwork has been destroyed. Excavations have been undertaken on two locations, here near Scotshouse, Co. Monaghan, and at the **Dorsey**, in Co. Armagh.

Aidan Walsh excavated two sections across the Black Pig's Dyke south of Scotshouse, Co. Monaghan, near to where the Scotshouse–Drum road crosses the earthwork. Here, in the heart of drumlin

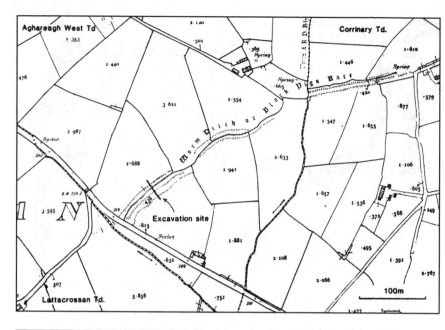

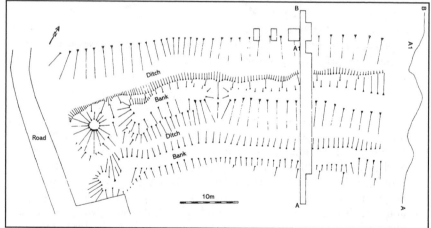

▲ **Fig. 44.** Black Pig's Dyke: map (after Lynn) and plan of excavated section (after Walsh)

country, the earthwork curves through a small valley around the northern foot of Callowhill in the direction of Drumcot Lough. Part of it has been fenced off and is preserved for public access, though it is hopelessly unkempt and overgrown. There is a small overgrown car park space beside it. Here the earthwork comprises two parallel banks with

intervening fosse and an outer fosse on the north side and a contemporary palisade 1 m behind the southern bank. C14 dates indicate
an early Iron Age date (390–70 BC; 487–100 BC). Samples from an
accidentally exposed section of the earthwork in nearby Aghnaskew
townland returned a date of 390–100 BC, demonstrating contemporaneity of these two sections. Another section of the earthwork occurs
about 1 km due east in Corrinshigo townland, where it crosses the
upper reaches of the Bunnoe river.

Boa Island, Co. Fermanagh   Figure sculpture

25 km north-west of Enniskillen, on the A47 (Kesh–Beleek); signposted. Disc. Ser. 17.

A long, narrow island at the north end of Lough Erne, Boa Island is
home to two remarkable pieces of stone sculpture. The oldest monument is a denuded cairn near the southern tip of the island at Inishkeer-
agh Bridge. East of this is Caldragh cemetery. Before having been cleaned
up this was a most evocative place, overgrown and leafy, wherein the
visitor came face to face with one of the most striking and enigmatic
stone figures in Ireland, the so-called Boa Island figure. Surprisingly big
and described as a double-sided Janus, the bearded faces are pointed-
oval in shape, with large, staring eyes, straight noses, and half-open
mouths, joined together with a basketry of hair. The head rests directly
on the torso, which is really just a square block. The arms are crossed
stiffly across the belted torso and the shoulders are hunched. Comparisons have been drawn with the Tanderagee figure, now in the Armagh
cathedral collection, and another from Holzerlingen in Germany, thus
raising the possibility of an Iron Age date and with it insoluble art-
historical contradictions as the figure is closely comparable to that on
the 9th-century bucket from Oseberg, Norway. This latter comparison
has the merit of contextualizing the figure in the same family as the
White Island collection of sculpted figures, a 5 km boat ride to the
south-east. The lower section of the stone, with two hands and elongated
fingers carved in relief, was discovered recently, half-buried in the
ground beside the figure. The second figure is called the Lustymore Idol
because it was moved here from Lustymore Island, which is due south of
Boa Island. With its back to the 'Janus', it is far less impressive though
nonetheless comparable in some ways to the **Beltany** and Tanderagee
idols. The arms and hands are directed, sheela-na-gig style, towards the
genitals and there is a slight hint of folded, lotus-like knees. An Iron Age
date has been suggested.

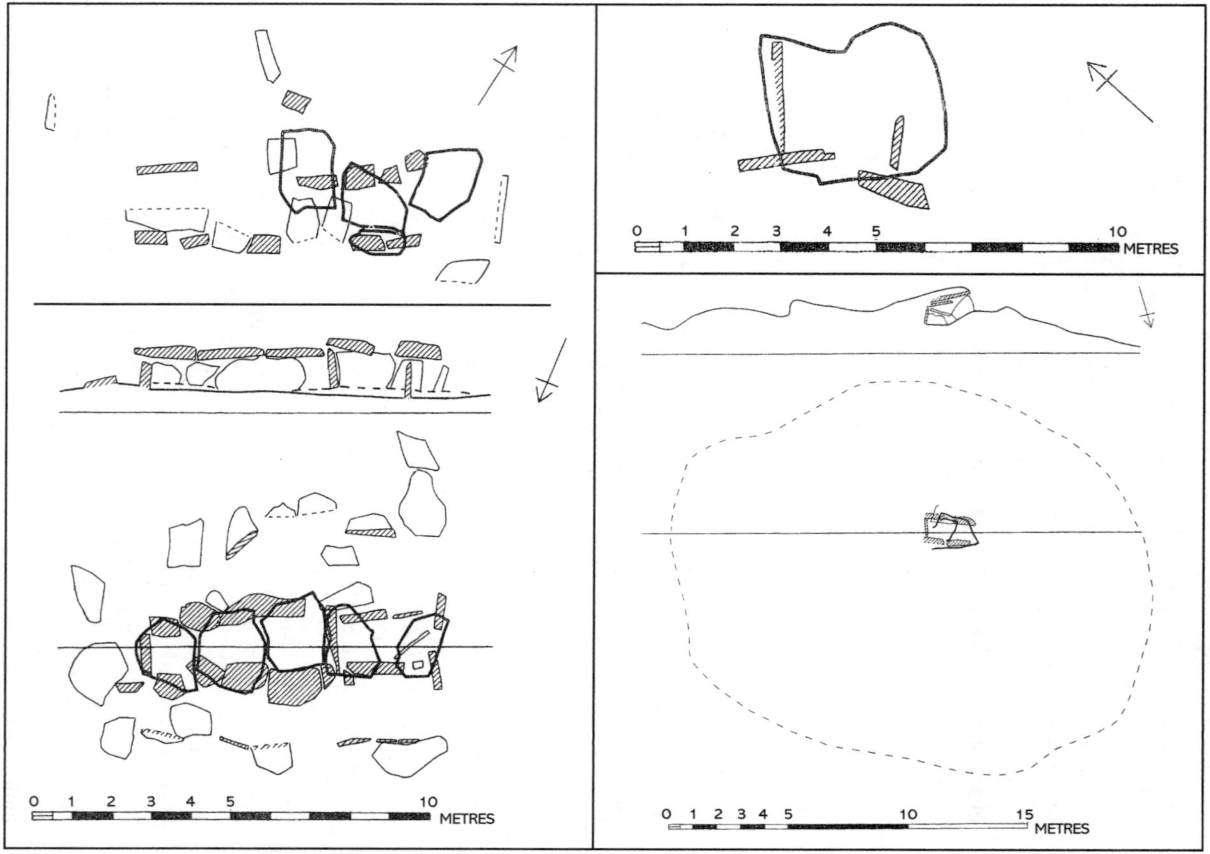

Fig. 45 Burren: plans of megalithic tombs (after de Valera & Ó Nualláin)

Burren, Co. Cavan   Upland archaeological landscape

Along the Cavan Way, south of Blacklion. South from the crossroads in Blacklion,
first left and veer right; signposted 'Cavan Way'. Disc. Ser. 26.

This group of megalithic tombs is strung out across Burren Hill and
Legalough at the north-western end of the Cuilcagh Mountains on the
Cavan–Fermanagh border. Burren Hill overlooks Blacklion and Belcoo
and the neck of land between Upper and Lower Lough Macnean, and
the monuments are sometimes referred to as the Blacklion Group. The
hill is planted over with forestry and this makes it difficult to find some
of the sites, and the landscape is rough underfoot, steep, and has some
upland cliffs along the north and east sides.

This is an area with a high concentration of megaliths and no fewer
than six tombs have been identified between Burren and Legalough.
Those at Burren are rather more accessible and comprise two Portal
tombs and two Wedge tombs. The best-preserved specimen is a Wedge
tomb in a forest clearing a little to the east of the summit and immediately south of a gorge called the Giant's Leap. It comprises a roofed
gallery 7.5 m long with a large portico at the west-south-west end
fronted by two massive portal stones. A U-shaped kerb of large stones,
some still erect and visible through the peat, has been identified. South-
west of this, and closer to the summit, is another, badly disturbed tomb
partially incorporated into a field wall and farm building. It is difficult to
interpret but may be a Portal tomb. North-west of this, on the eastern
bluff of the highest hill, is a reasonably intact Wedge tomb, again
deprived of its spectacular views over Lough Macnean by afforestation.
The gallery is about 14 m long and has three extant roofstones. The
fourth tomb lies some distance to the south-west and is a well-preserved
Portal tomb, somewhat enveloped in peat. The chamber has two
overlapping roofslabs and is surrounded by a large, oval-shaped cairn
(*c.*20 m in maximum length). A funerary urn of unspecified type is said
to have been found in the chamber. There is an enclosure to the north-
west of this tomb but it is entirely hidden by vegetation.

Clones, Co. Monaghan   Church, round tower, high crosses

20 km south-west of Monaghan town on N54 (Monaghan–Cavan). Disc. Ser. 28A.

Now a busy market town, Clones [*Cluain Eois*, 'the meadow of Eos']
originated as a monastery apparently founded by St Tighearnach in
the 6th century. Like many other early monasteries it adopted the
Augustinian rule from *c.*1140. The abbey was burned by the English in
1207 but seems to have been rebuilt by them in 1212, when a motte-and-
bailey castle was also erected. English control of Clones was short-lived,
however. The castle was burned by Aedh Ó Néill in 1213 and for most of
the Middle Ages both the monastery and the settlement that developed
around it were decisively Irish. In 1414 an indulgence was granted to

raise funds for repairs to the abbey church. It was dissolved *c.*1585. The features of the early monastic site have largely been obliterated by the modern town and it is now difficult to get any impression of its original form. Nevertheless there are several visible remains, including two 9th/10th-century high crosses, a 10th–12th-century round tower, a 12th-century stone sarcophagus, and a 12th-century church. In the National Museum of Ireland is a fine book shrine of 8th- to 15th-century date, known as the *Domnach Airgid* ('silver church'), which was associated with Clones. There is also an early 13th-century motte-and-bailey castle. By analogy with other sites, the motte-and-bailey may have been erected on the perimeter of the monastic enclosure. This would suggest that much of the present town centre, from the motte on the west to the east side of the Diamond, is within the original enclosure.

In the Diamond stands the 'high cross'—actually composed of fragments of two 9th/10th-century crosses mounted together. The lower portion was clearly part of a large and impressive cross. Both fragments bear geometric decoration on the sides and scriptural scenes on the broad faces, with Old Testament scenes on the west face and New Testament scenes on the east face. These can be identified as follows (from base to top):

West face:	*Adam and Eve*
	The Sacrifice of Isaac
	Daniel in the Lions' Den (on shaft)
	Daniel in the Lions' Den (on cross head)
East face:	*Adoration of the Magi*
	Marriage Feast at Cana
	Miracle of the Loaves and Fishes
	Crucifixion (on cross head)

Originally, both crosses probably stood closer to the church that still stands in a graveyard on Abbey Street (*south side of the Diamond*). Only the nave of the church survives, but traces of a chancel arch at the east end indicate the presence of a chancel. The Romanesque style of the chancel arch and of a well-carved round-headed window in the south wall suggests a 12th-century date. In a larger graveyard to the south-east (*off Ball Alley St.*) stands a round tower, missing its roof but still 23 m high and dating to the 10th–12th centuries. The flat-headed doorway faces east and is 1.7 m above ground. Nearby is a remarkable gabled stone sarcophagus or shrine. Carved from a single block of sandstone, the sarcophagus is shaped like a miniature church, with gabled roof having finials at each end, similar to the gable finials found on many early churches. It may be a copy in stone of a metal sarcophagus or shrine—on the south side are traces of three projecting elements that are best interpreted as imitating the clasps or locks on a metal shrine. In the eastern gable is a worn figure wearing a mitre and possibly carrying a torso, probably representing the founding saint, Tighearnach, whose shrine this may be. However, the form of the sarcophagus and the details of the very worn decoration, on the roof and elsewhere, suggest a 12th-century date, much later than Tighearnach's time. It has been suggested that the heavy stone sarcophagus was made during a period of insecurity in the 12th century, perhaps following the English invasion, to replace a precious metal shrine as the holder of the founder's relics.

The motte-and-bailey castle on the west side of the town is interesting in that we know exactly when it was built, in 1212. The motte is surrounded by a fosse at its base; its present terraced profile is the result of landscaping in relatively modern times. The attached sub-rectangular bailey is defended by an earthen bank and preserves traces of a causeway linking it to the motte. In the north and west corners of the bailey are traces of two possible stone towers, which may be connected with the building of a stone castle there in the 17th century.

Cloughoughter, Co. Cavan Castle

7 km west of Cavan in Killykeen Forest Park; take R198 (Cavan–Arvagh/Killeshandra) and take minor road to west after 6 km; site is accessible by boat only, available nearby.

This unusual circular keep stands in ruins on a tiny island in Lough Oughter. The castle was probably built *c.*1220 by Walter de Lacy, lord of Meath, or his half-brother William, and was strategically sited to dominate both vessels on the lake, and the nearby crannóg of the Ó Raghallaigh (O'Reilly) lords of east Bréifne. By the 1230s, however, the English attempt to conquer Bréifne had collapsed and the castle was in Ó Raghallaigh hands for the rest of the Middle Ages. Partly rebuilt in 1610–20, the castle was used during the wars of the 1640s and is perhaps best known as the place where the Irish general Owen Roe O'Neill died in 1649. In 1653 it was the last Irish garrison to surrender to the Cromwellian army, who then demolished much of the south side of the tower.

The tower survives to full height (over 18.3 m) on the north side, and is 10.5 m in diameter internally, with walls *c.*2.5 m thick. It had two storeys originally but this was later raised to four, with parapet and wall walk above—probably done as an afterthought by the original builders. As with many 12th/13th-century keeps, the original entrance was at first-floor level on the south-west side, but another doorway was inserted directly below this at ground-floor level in the 17th century. Two original embrasures with arrow loops survive at ground-floor level, as well as an inserted 17th-century cross-wall, with a doorway and fireplace. A series of square holes which held the beams supporting the first floor are clearly visible. Only one side of the original main doorway survives, along with two windows and traces of two other doorways—that on the south-east probably gave access to a wall walk on a vanished curtain wall. The other doorway, on the north, led to a vanished stair turret which was added when the height of the tower was increased; the existing window embrasure was blocked and a new opening inserted on the east side. The stair turret gave access to the parapet above, via a doorway of which only traces survive. The added second and third floors are strangely featureless, with only two inserted 17th-century windows on the second floor and one on the third.

Cohaw, Co. Cavan Court tomb

25 km south of Monaghan town, off the R192 (Cootehill–Shercock). 4 km south-east of Cootehill, near school building; signposted. Disc. Ser. 28A.

Cavan boasts quite a high density of megalithic tombs, of which around 18 can be positively identified as Court tombs. Cohaw is a very fine example of a dual-court tomb and was excavated by Howard Kilbride-Jones in 1949. The tombs are aligned north–south and are set within a rectangular cairn with orthostatic kerb, about 24.5 m long and 13.5 m wide. The two 'court' areas are connected by a long, five-chambered burial gallery. The middle chamber, however, is sealed off and the remaining chambers are defined in more orthodox manner by sillstones and jambs into two distinct chambers each. The burial assemblage comprised teeth and skull fragments and the cremated remains of a child. A fine, carinated, round-bottomed Neolithic bowl with a perforation

▼ **Fig. 46.** Cohaw: plan (after Kilbride-Jones)

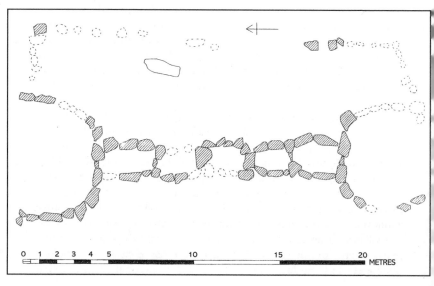

0 1 2 3 4 5   10   15   20 METRES

under the rim was also found. An unusual feature of this site was the arcuate bank across the entrance to the northern court. Beneath it were postholes (now marked out with stones). Equivalent postholes were found in the southern court area and they are tentatively interpreted as the remains of temporary screens. Two slender pillar stones once stood within the northern court area. This tomb, on the side of a ridge, overlooks a small tributary of the Annagh river and is otherwise lost in a maze of drumlins and small lakes.

Creevelea, Co. Leitrim Franciscan friary

11 km south-east of Sligo, just west of Dromahair off R287 (Dromahair–Collooney/ Sligo); reached by riverside path from Dromahair; signposted.

Creevelea [*Craobh liath*, 'grey sacred tree'] has the distinction of being the last Franciscan friary founded in medieval Ireland and its well-preserved remains have interesting architectural details. It was founded in 1508 by Eoghan Ó Ruairc, lord of Bréifne, and his wife Margaret (both of whom were subsequently buried there) and staffed by friars from **Donegal**. The friary suffered serious fire damage in 1536 but was rebuilt by the Ó Ruairc. It was officially dissolved in 1541, but England had little control over this part of Ireland and the friary continued to function until the 1590s, when English forces occupied and burned it. Although reoccupied sporadically by Franciscan friars at various times in the 17th century, it never really recovered from this setback. The surviving remains consist of the church with nave and south transept, choir, tower, and cloister on the north side. Many of the architectural details seem to date to a rebuilding of the friary, presumably after the 1536 fire.

The nave is entered by a simple but attractive west doorway, above which is a two-light window with simple reticulated tracery. The arches to the south transept—like those under the tower—are round headed rather than pointed, which in this case indicates a late date (16th century) rather than an early, pre-Gothic one. The transept was lit by a three-light traceried window in the south gable and by simpler round-headed twin-light windows in the east wall. The east wall is unusually thick, to accommodate two altar recesses—again round headed—each containing an altar with a piscina to the side. The tower is unusually wide and shallow (from east to west) for a Franciscan structure; it was mainly for residential use but was substantially modified in the 17th century. There are three floors above the vault, reached by a spiral stair in the south-east angle. The choir is lit by four twin-light round-headed windows, similar to those in the transept, and by a four-light east window. This was apparently rebuilt—perhaps after the fire of 1536—as the profiles of the simple flamboyant tracery do not match those of the sills and jambs. In the upper level of the north wall, near the east end, is a

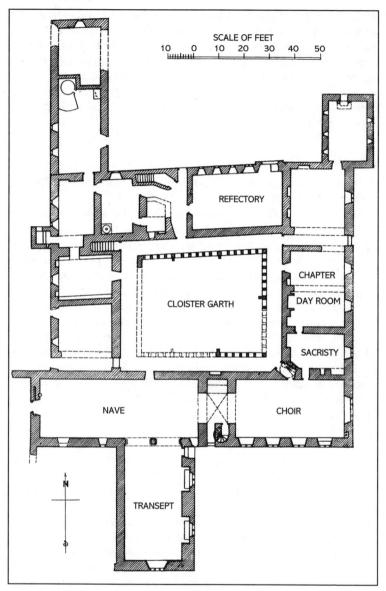

▲ Fig. 47. Creevelea: plan of friary (OPW)

small opening allowing bedridden friars a view of the high altar from the dormitory.

Doorways in the north walls of nave and choir led to the cloisters, arranged around a rectangular garth. The ambulatory was built in lean-to fashion against the surrounding buildings, rather than being integrated into them as is common in many western friaries. The cloister arcade survives on three sides (it was possibly never built on the west side) and has pointed arches on the north and east sides, but round-headed arches on the south. On one of the arches of the north arcade are some rare low-relief carvings; one (on the soffit of the arch) appears to show a cowled St Francis with the stigmata and has a crude black-letter inscription on a scroll, which appears to read *H. E. QARTA FR* (possibly 'this is a picture of Francis'). Another carving shows St Francis preaching to the birds; his pulpit is the calyx of a flower, on the stalk of which the birds perch. The east range comprises four small chambers at ground-floor level, with a long dormitory overhead. The room nearest the church was clearly the sacristy. The next was possibly a residential apartment (perhaps for the guardian), as it has a fireplace. This is followed by the chapter room and, in the north-east angle, a large room with a fireplace, probably the friars' day room. Adjoining this, to the north, is a projecting two-storey building with a garderobe at the north wall, probably the main latrine building servicing both the day room and the dormitory overhead. In the north range is the refectory and kitchen, probably with another dormitory overhead. The enlarged window at the east end of the refectory contained the *pulpitum*, from which a friar read devotional literature as the community ate meals. The functions of the rooms in the west range are uncertain but the presence of a two-level garderobe tower on the west side suggests that at least some rooms were residential. Built onto the north end of the west range is a long, single-storey extension, in two parts. It is clearly a later addition, although its date is uncertain.

Devenish, Co. Fermanagh Island monastery

3.2 km north-west of Enniskillen in Lough Erne. Access by ferry from Trory Point—take minor road from junction of A32 (Enniskillen–Irvinestown) and B82 (Enniskillen–Castle Archdale). Ferry charge includes admission. Museum/visitor centre on site.

Devenish is an important example of how an early medieval monastery survived, albeit in altered circumstances, in the later medieval period. Beautifully located on an island [*Daimhinis*, 'ox island'] in Lough Erne, it is thought to be a 6th-century foundation of St Laisre (or Molaise), and was the victim of several Viking raids. The earliest buildings on the site are the round tower and the small church known as 'St Molaise's House' (a mistranslation of *Tech Molaise*, which in this context refers to a church). Both date to the 12th century, but the earliest surviving archaeology of Devenish is an important piece of early 11th-century metalwork, the shrine of the *Soiscél Molaise* ('gospel-book of Molaise'), commissioned by the abbot Cenfaelad between 1001 and 1025 (*now in the National Museum of Ireland*). An Augustinian priory was founded in

1130 but unusually, the Augustinians seem to have functioned alongside the older monastery, both physically and metaphorically, rather than taking it over. Both the original foundation (now a *Céli Dé* community) and the Augustinian priory were suppressed at the beginning of the 17th century.

The first structure encountered from the jetty is the *Teampull Mór* ('great church'), probably built in the early 13th century, to judge by a round-headed window of 'Transitional' (Romanesque/Gothic) form in the south wall. It may have replaced an earlier church and served as the parish church in the later Middle Ages, administered by the *Céli Dé* community. It is a narrow rectangular building, which was extended to the east probably in the 14th century. On the north side are late medieval residential quarters for the clergy serving the church, and on the south side the 'Maguire Chapel' with 17th-century armorial slabs. At the west end of the church is 'St Molaise's Bed', probably the base of a sarcophagus of uncertain date.

South-west of the *Teampull Mór* is 'St Molaise's House', actually a small 12th-century church or shrine. Only the lower courses of the thick walls survive, but it seems to have had a very fine, high-pitched stone roof, of which some worked stones remain. The moulded pilasters at the angles, rising from decorated bases, provide another indication that this was a particularly fine building, despite its small size.

To the west is the well-preserved round tower, complete at 25 m high, with five floors that can be climbed to the top, thanks to modern flooring and ladders. It has a unique cornice or frieze, carved with a human head with interlaced hair and beard above each of the four windows on the top floor. The doorway is round headed, 2.6 m above ground level, and faces north-east, possibly towards an earlier church where the *Teampull Mór* now stands. Traces of iron door hinges are visible on the south jamb. The foundations of another round tower were discovered just north of the present one in the 1970s and it takes little imagination to suppose that this tower collapsed and was replaced by the intact tower in the mid-12th century.

The largest church on Devenish is St Mary's Augustinian priory, founded in 1130 on the highest point of the island, south-west of the old monastic enclosure. The church is recorded as having been rebuilt in 1449 and most of the present fabric is 15th century. It is small for its period, with a particularly short nave having no aisles, and it is clear that this was never a wealthy house. The low crossing tower was added in the late 15th/early 16th century, as was the west doorway of the nave. Traces of a small cloister, with a sacristy and refectory, are visible on the north side of the church. The doorway from the church to the sacristy has a fine ogee-shaped hood moulding featuring two birds pecking at the vine-leaf finial, and flanking pinnacles. There was also a good two-light east window with flowing tracery, which is now mounted in the Church of Ireland parish church at Monea (*c.*5 km to the north-west). In the nearby graveyard is an important and elaborately decorated 15th-century high cross with a *Crucifixion* on the eastern face, while in the small museum are several decorated stones.

Drumlane, Co. Cavan Monastic site

10 km north-west of Cavan town; take minor road south at Milltown on R201 (Belturbet–Killeshandra); signposted. Disc. Ser. 27A.

Drumlane [*Droim Leathan,* 'wide ridge'] is the site of an early monastery associated with the 6th-century St Maedhóg (or Aidan) of **Ferns**, and located prominently on a ridge at the north-western end of Lough Oughter. The monastery became an Augustinian priory, probably in the 12th century, and was subsequently taken over by Augustinian canons from **Kells**. The *Breac Maedhóg,* an important metalwork shrine of *c.*1100 (*now in the National Museum of Ireland*) is associated with this monastery, but the only remaining trace on the site is the round tower. The tower now stands 11.6 m high but is obviously incomplete, and is distinguished by two weathered carvings of birds (possibly a cock and a hen) on the north side, *c.*2 m above ground. The round-headed doorway is outlined with a plain, flat moulding and faces south-east, towards the adjacent church. This suggests the church, which is clearly much later than the round tower, occupies the site of an earlier structure. The tower shows a clear break in the limestone masonry about halfway up, where the well-shaped and smoothly dressed blocks give way to much rougher rubble masonry, similar to the fabric of the church. It is possible that the round tower was rebuilt at the same time as the church was erected, probably in the late 13th century.

Most visible architectural features of the church are 15th century and may reflect its rebuilding following appeals for alms in 1431 and 1436. It is a rectangular building with well-carved 15th-century windows and west door, displaying carved heads of kings and abbots or bishops. The tomb niches in the south wall are probably also 15th century, and an interesting medieval grave slab is mounted on the north wall, externally. The external buttresses are post-medieval and much of the west end of the church was probably reconstructed in the 17th century. Another fragment of a cross-inscribed grave slab is built into the northern pier of the gateway into the graveyard. Some 150 m south of the church, on the lakeshore, are a series of earthworks with some standing masonry, possibly the remains of the Augustinian abbey or of a hospital, known to have existed here until the 16th century. An important iron cauldron of later Bronze Age form [*now on display in the National Museum of Ireland*] was found in the vicinity.

Drumskinny, Co. Fermanagh   Stone circle; alignment; cairn

11.5 km south of Castlederg, Co. Tyrone, off the B72 (Kesh–Castlederg); sign-posted. Disc. Ser. 12.

A little complex comprising a stone circle, a cairn, and an alignment was reclaimed from cut-away bog at Drumskinny, 7 km north of Kesh. The site was excavated by Dudley Waterman in 1962 and is now restored and open to the public. Here, in miniature, is the same composition as at **Beaghmore**, Co. Tyrone, namely a stone circle (39 stones, three of them modern replacements), nearly 13 m in diameter, to the north-west

▼ **Fig. 48.** Drumskinny: plan (after Waterman)

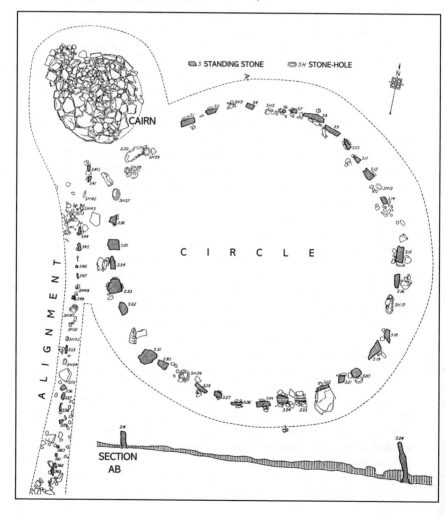

of which is a small cairn from which emanates a 24-stone alignment running in a southerly direction for about 7.5 m. The stones are all relatively small. Drumskinny is at an elevation of about 130 m, overlooking a natural amphitheatre created by a great arc of higher ground running from Pettigo, Co. Donegal, eastwards around by Derrynashesk, Lough Lack, Tappaghan Mountain, and southwards towards Irvingstown. In fact, here again is a case of topography influencing political boundaries, as this arc of high ground today determines the Fermanagh–Donegal and Fermanagh–Tyrone border. Such borders were often marked out in antiquity with burial mounds and standing stones and this is quite apparent here. For example, there is a ruined Wedge tomb on the summit of Keeran Hill, which marks the south-east tip of the 'amphitheatre'. This overlooks the complex at Kiltierney Deer Park, 3.5 km south-east of Kesh. Here, Brain Williams (last in a long line of antiquarians and archaeologists to excavate here) found the Passage tomb to be surrounded by a ring of 21 smaller mounds, seven of which contained Iron Age burials, making them contemporary with a remodelling of the main mound into a sort of giant ring barrow. Nearby is a linear earthwork called the 'Friar's Walk', which is now thought to be a cursus.

The 'amphitheatre' opens south-westwards onto Lough Erne and Boa Island. There are numerous monuments in this area and Drumskinny is more than likely to be related to the rather more elaborate complex in Montiaghroe townland, 1.5 km to the south, where there are four stone circles and various standing stones and alignments. Three standing stones occur immediately opposite Montiaghroe Roman Catholic church and it has been suggested that they may be related to a stone circle poking out from the bog a further 20 m or so to the south. Another such complex occurs 3 km south-west in Formil townland, about 2 km north-east of Clonelly bridge. There is a fine standing stone 70 m or so to the north of the old railway station in Kesh. This ritual landscape extends down to the lake, as attested to by the presence of a denuded round cairn on **Boa Island**.

Enniskillen, Co. Fermanagh Castle, County Museum

55 km west of Sligo on A4 (Belfast–Sligo); signposted.

Enniskillen was the main stronghold of the Mac Uidhir (Maguire) lords of Fermanagh in the late Middle Ages, located on a small island [*Inis Ceithleann*, 'Ceithleann's island'—no longer visible] in a strategically important position at the top of Lower Lough Erne. It figured prominently in the wars of the late 16th century, and in the early 17th century it was granted to the English planter William Cole. The development of the town of Enniskillen dates from this period. The castle was originally built by the Maguires, probably early in the 15th century, and consisted of a strong tower house set within a stone-walled bawn. The only surviving part of the Maguire castle is the ground floor of the tower house, with its very thick walls and pronounced basal batter. The upper floors were rebuilt by Cole *c.*1610. Between 1610 and 1620 Cole also added the curtain wall surviving on the west side and the distinctive 'Watergate' (actually not a gate), a three-storey structure with twin Scottish-style round turrets at the angles of the front façade. Most of the rest of the enclosure consists of 18th/19th-century barrack buildings, within which is located the fine Fermanagh County Museum, well worth a visit.

Fenagh, Co. Leitrim Monastic site

20 km north-east of Carrick-on-Shannon at junction of R209 (from Carrick-on-Shannon) and R202 (Dromod–Ballinamore).

Fenagh [*Fiodhnach*, 'woody place'] is an early church site, said to have been founded by St Caillin, a disciple of Colmcille (Columba), in the 6th century. The church is recorded as being unroofed in 1244, and the monastery was burned in 1360. Nevertheless the monastery continued to function until the 16th century, when the Book of Fenagh (*now in the Royal Irish Academy*) was copied there from an earlier manuscript. Two late medieval churches stand on the site of the monastery, 300 m south of the modern village of Fenagh and *c.*120 m apart.

It is possible that only the southern church (the larger of the two) occupies the early monastic site, as it is located within a roughly circular earthen enclosure with traces of other structures. The architectural features of the church suggest a 14th/15th-century date and it is possible that it was erected after the fire of 1360. It is a rectangular building with a pointed west doorway and a fine traceried east window, having an unusual centrepiece of six trefoils arranged in a circle. Later doorways are inserted in the middle of the north and south walls. Externally, on the east wall, a rope moulding runs below the east window, ending in an animal carving at the north end, while there are carved gable brackets at the north-east and south-east angles. The western end of the nave is barrel vaulted, with a gallery or residential chamber above reached by a stair against the north wall. This structure is clearly a later insertion, although how much later is uncertain. At the east end are a piscina (below the window) and sedilia in the south wall.

The smaller northern church is also a simple rectangular building, with an inserted barrel-vaulted western section which can only be entered from the east end, through two pointed doorways. These are set in two parallel cross-walls, within which is a stair leading to the chamber or gallery above the vault. The church has a blocked doorway in the north wall, and originally had another in the south wall. On the south side is a long narrow aisle or corridor, contemporary with the church, and entered through a doorway in the east end. This building is difficult to date but is probably late medieval, perhaps 15th century.

Inchcleraun, Co. Longford Island monastery

Access by boat only; no regular service, but boats may be hired at Portrunny (off N61 on Roscommon shore of Lough Ree) or Collum (off R392 on Longford shore).

Inchcleraun is an island in Lough Ree, said to be named after a sister of the legendary Medb, queen of Connaught [*Inis Clothrann*, 'Clothra's island']. It is better known locally as Quaker Island. It was the site of an early monastery, said to have been founded by a St Diarmait in the mid-6th century. The monastery adopted the Augustinian rule in the 12th century, probably soon after 1140, becoming the priory of St Mary. It was dissolved in 1541. The surviving remains, consisting of six churches, are mainly later medieval, but the multiplicity of small churches is typical of an early medieval monastery. An oval-shaped enclosure on the east shore of the island may well preserve the line of an early medieval predecessor, but only slight traces of the original enclosure are visible, including fragments of a 12th-century stone gateway having jambs decorated with chevron bands and beading.

Within this enclosure four churches are located close together, including 'St Diarmait's church', a tiny oratory or shine with a lintelled doorway and pronounced antae at the gables—probably the earliest church on the island. It may have been stone roofed and dates to the 10th–12th centuries. Just to the north, the *Teampull Mór* ('great church') is a simple rectangular church with a paired east window of twin lancets, suggesting an early 13th-century date. It was presumably the Augustinian priory church. In the 15th century a cloister was added on the north side of the church, of which only parts of the east range survive. Adjacent to the *Teampull Mór* are the small, rectangular *Teampull na Marbh* ('church of the dead') and another small nave-and-chancel church.

There are two further churches outside the enclosure. On the highest point of the island, to the north-west, is the 'Belfry Church' or *Clogás an Oileáin* ('the belfry of the island'). Its round-headed east window suggests a 12th-century date and it has a number of unusual (and probably later) architectural features, including the belfry tower at the west end and the stairs in the north wall. South of the main group is another church, known as *Teampull Mhuire* ('St Mary's church') or the 'Women's Church'.

Monaghan, Co. Monaghan County Museum

On N2 (Dublin–Derry); Disc. Ser. 28.

The county town of Monaghan [*Muineachán*, 'place of the thickets'] contains no archaeological sites of importance, but the County Museum (on Hill St.) has interesting archaeological displays (including the 14th-century processional Cross of **Clogher**), as well as more recent history.

Mullagh, Co. Cavan Ogam stone

10 km north-west of Kells, Co. Meath; take R164 (Kells–Kingscourt) to Moynalty, turn west onto R194 to Mullagh; stone is in Heritage Centre at north end of village. Disc. Ser. 35.

Probably the only surviving ogam stone from Co. Cavan, this specimen was apparently removed the short distance from an ecclesiastical site at Rantavan to the graveyard in Mullagh and thence indoors to the new visitor centre across the road. The inscription reads *OSBBAR*. While ogam stones are exceedingly rare in Co. Cavan, it is reasonable to suggest that this one is at the northern limit of a group of ogam-inscribed pillars concentrated in the Blackwater Valley (roughly between **Kells** and Navan), a corridor to the north-west from the Boyne–**Tara** area. There is a promontory fort on the north shore of nearby Mullagh Lough, guarding the narrow corridor of shoreline between the lake and Mullagh Hill. This pass is called the 'Gates of Mullagh' and is one of the few access points to the Blackwater Valley from the north-west. Another such pass on the east side of Screebog Hill is also defended by a promontory-like enclosure.

Picturesquely situated on a slight rise overlooking the north-east shore of the lake, and hard by the Protestant church, are medieval church remains associated with St Kilian, who was born in nearby Mullagh in AD 640. Travelling with eleven companions to the Continent around AD 686, he established a successful monastery at Würzburg, earning for himself the title 'Apostle of Franconia'. He was martyred, along with two companions, Colman and Totman, in AD 689 and his tomb is still venerated in Würzburg.

Parke's castle, Kilmore, Co. Leitrim Plantation castle

10 km east of Sligo town on R286 (Sligo–Dromahair); signposted. Visitor facilities; admission charge.

This 17th-century plantation castle on the shores of Lough Gill, which figured in the wars of the 1640s, has recently been restored and opened to the public. Excavation in the 1970s showed that it was built on the site of an earlier tower house of the Ó Ruairc (O'Rourke) lords of Bréifne, set within a stone-walled bawn with round towers at two corners and a gatehouse in the centre of one side. Tradition suggests that this tower house was destroyed by the English as a reprisal for the O'Rourkes giving refuge to a Spanish officer of the Armada, shipwrecked in 1588. In the early 1620s the English planter Robert Parke took over the site. He built a new three-storey residence, incorporating the original gatehouse, and later extended this as a semi-fortified house running between the gatehouse and one corner tower of the bawn.

Shantemon, Co. Cavan   Stone alignment

6 km north-east of Cavan town, off the link road running south of and parallel to the R188 (Cavan–Cootehill); in forest clearing on the east side of the northern shoulder of Shantemon Mountain, uphill and to the right of the forestry track. Disc. Ser. 34.

This five-stone alignment is known as 'Finn McCool's Fingers'. The stones are aligned from north-west to south-east and are graded in height from 2 m down to 0.5 m. The hill is the traditional inauguration place of the Ó Raghallaigh of Bréifne (whose seat was for a time the island stronghold of **Cloghoughter**) and was, within living memory, a station on a pattern that took place annually on Bilberry Sunday, a Lughnasa festival celebrated at the beginning of August. On the summit of the hill, commanding a fine prospect, is a D-shaped enclosure comprising a raised platform surrounded by a denuded bank.

Topped Mountain, Co. Fermanagh   Bronze Age cairn

Approach from south on B80 from Enniskillen in the direction of Tempo, turn right at the first crossroads (with church) 2 km on the Tempo side of Garvary village, straight at the next crossroads (with school), and left at the third crossroads. 3.5 km further on, just past Topped Mountain Lough, is a trackway to summit. Disc. Ser. 18.

Topped Mountain ranks as one of the more famous type sites of the Early Bronze Age. Situated in the uplands between Enniskillen and Tempo, Topped Mountain (275 m) is the highest and most northerly of three peaks and is crowned by a cairn about 36 m in diameter and over 3 m high. It was partly excavated by Coffey and Plunkett in 1897 and three burials were found. One of these, near the eastern edge of the cairn, was in a sub-rectangular cist and consisted of a much decayed adult male inhumation accompanied by a decorated vase and a riveted, bronze dagger with a grooved, triangular blade and a gold pommel binding (*now on display in the National Museum of Ireland*). A cremation burial was found in the same grave beneath two slabs. The inhumation was one of the test samples used in Brindley and Lanting's collagen dating programme undertaken at Groningen, returning a date of 3460 ± 50 BP (*c.*1900–1700 BC). Retracing your steps and following the road around the east side of Topped Mountain Lough brings you around the back, as it were, of Cloghtogle Mountain towards Lough Skale, into an area peppered with standing stones and megalithic tombs. All are privately owned but some, such as the standing stone immediately south of Lough Skale, can be seen from the roadside.

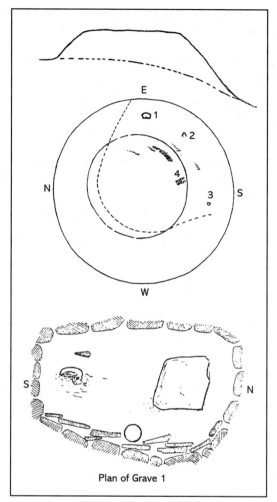

E

⌂1

∧ 2

N

4

3

S

W

Plan of Grave 1

▲ **Fig. 49.** Topped Mountain: plan (after Plunkett & Coffey)

White Island, Co. Fermanagh Church and sculptures

18 km north-west of Enniskillen, in Lower Lough Erne; accessible by ferry from Castle Archdale on B82 (Enniskillen–Kesh); signposted.

On an island in Lough Erne stands a late 12th-century church with a (restored) Romanesque south doorway, with worn interlace ornament on the capitals. Excavation has shown that this church replaced an earlier wooden one, but little is known of the history of the site. Its main interest lies in a unique series of stone sculptures now mounted within the church, although they are considerably older than the church—

probably dating between the 8th and 10th centuries. There are six complete figures and an unfinished one, which indicates that they were actually carved on the island. The complete figures are finely carved and beautifully preserved, with distinctive features characterized by large, rounded eyes and mouths open in expressions that have been described variously as 'grimacing' or as a 'stylized pout'. One clearly represents a noble warrior (possibly a king), armed with sword and shield and dressed in a long tunic and cloak, which is held in place by a penannular brooch, a type that can hardly be later than the 10th century. Another figure represents an abbot or bishop, also dressed in long tunic and cloak and carrying the symbols of his office, a crosier and handbell. The other figures are not so easily interpreted. There may be a second abbot or bishop, possibly also holding a crosier in one hand and with the other hand to his mouth. A fourth figure holds two birds by the necks. The two smallest figures comprise one sitting cross-legged and the other with its hands in what looks like a muffler.

The function of the figures remains a mystery. They were probably inserted into the north wall of the present church when it was built in the late 12th century, but this is not their original position or function. They may have stood in the earlier wooden church. Two significant features can be noted—first, that the complete figures form three pairs, respectively $c.60$ cm, $c.80$ cm, and $c.100$ cm in height, and secondly, that they have sockets in the top as if to receive tenons or wooden beams of some sort. The stepped heights of the three pairs has led to suggestions that they may have been supporters for a set of steps, but this cannot be confirmed.

West: Galway, Mayo, Roscommon, Sligo

Introduction

The western province of Connacht is often considered the poor relation among Ireland's regions. Physically, it tends to be characterized in terms of the mountainous landscapes of the western parts of Cos. Galway and Mayo. Nevertheless there is a lot of quite fertile land, especially in south Co. Galway, north-east Co. Mayo, and east Co. Roscommon. Because its essentially rural character remains largely intact, the west of Ireland is a veritable treasure chest of well-preserved archaeological sites, with still more awaiting discovery, particularly in upland areas. Nowhere is this better illustrated than at the famous **Céide** Fields in north Mayo where Séamus Caulfield has mapped out an extensive Neolithic field system beneath a thick layer of blanket peat. Pre-bog archaeology is frequently reported, and the stumps and roots of prehistoric pine and oak woodlands are a regular feature of cut-away bogs in the west of Ireland.

There is no evidence of early Mesolithic settlers in this region and less than half a dozen later Mesolithic findspots. However, these latter include interesting collections of lithics from the shores of Lough Corrib, near Oughterard, Co. Galway, and at Lough Gara, Co. Sligo, where they may be connected to the so-called platform crannógs, of which there are scores of examples around the lakeshore. Evidence of early farming communities is attested, not just in pollen records from the region but also by a multitude of settlement and funerary monuments. There is a full range of conventional megalithic tomb types, including the two Passage tomb cemeteries at **Carrowmore** and **Carrowkeel**, Co. Sligo, the latter with an associated settlement complex. Between them these counties boast the densest concentration of Court tombs in Ireland, including the spectacular full-court variety at **Creevykeel**, Co. Sligo, and one with a central court at **Ballyglass**, near Céide, Co. Mayo, that overlay one of the first Neolithic house sites excavated in Ireland. A Court tomb is also incorporated into the **Céide** field system revealing a close intellectual integration between the sacred and the secular. The same association between settlement sites and funerary monuments is repeated at **Knocknashee**, Co. Sligo.

Religious monuments also dominate the corpus of early Bronze Age sites in the west, such as the stone circles and cairns at **Nymphsfield**, Co. Mayo, standing stones and alignments, e.g. Loughinagh, Co. Galway,

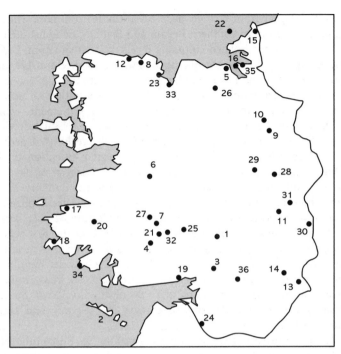

▲ Map 4

Key:
1. Abbeyknockmoy, Co. Galway
2. Aran Islands, Co. Galway
3. Athenry, Co. Galway
4. Aughnanure, Co. Galway
5. Aughris Head, Co. Sligo
6. Ballintubber, Co. Mayo
7. Ballynagibbon, Co. Mayo
8. Ballyglass, Co. Mayo
9. Boyle, Co. Roscommon
10. Carrowkeel, Co. Sligo
11. Castlestrange, Co. Roscommon
12. Céide, Co. Mayo
13. Clonfert, Co. Galway
14. Clontuskert, Co. Galway
15. Creevykeel, Co. Sligo
16. Cúil Irra, Co. Sligo
17. Derryinver, Co. Galway
18. Doonloughan, Co. Galway

19. Galway, Co. Galway
20. Gleninagh, Co. Galway
21. Inchagoill, Co. Galway
22. Inishmurray, Co. Sligo
23. Killala, Co. Mayo
24. Kilmacduagh, Co. Galway
25. Knockma, Caltragh, Co. Galway
26. Knocknashee, Co. Sligo
27. Nymphsfield, Co. Mayo
28. Rathcroghan, Co. Roscommon
29. Rathra, Co. Roscommon
30. Rindown, Co. Roscommon
31. Roscommon, Co. Roscommon
32. Ross, Co. Galway
33. Rosserk, Co. Mayo
34. St Macdara's Island, Co. Galway
35. Sligo, Co. Sligo
36. Turoe, Co. Galway

and Wedge tombs, such as those on the **Aran Islands**. However, the region is not without artefacts of the period. A hoard of thick-butted, flat axes of Early Bronze Age date found at Knocknague, Co. Galway, has given its name to the type, and two gold lunulae were found buried together near Ballina, Co. Mayo. Finds such as these and a six-riveted dagger from Grange, near Tulsk, Co. Roscommon, which is of a type known from southern Britain and Brittany, demonstrate that this region was not isolated culturally by its western situation. Distribution maps of later Bronze Age hoards, which are a reasonable indication of the locus and extent of human activity around the beginning of the 1st millennium BC, reveal a slight concentration of activity towards the east of the region. This contraction of settlement—which of course is by no means proven—may represent a gradual depopulation of upland areas along the western littoral, precipitated perhaps by the development of blanket bog. A spectacular exception to this is Dún Aonghasa, a cliff-edge fort on Inis Mór, the largest of the **Aran Islands**, and one of Ireland's most westerly monuments. Excavations here have yielded a considerable amount of later Bronze Age evidence. Impressive, military-style forts are a feature of later Bronze Age Ireland and are paralleled by the appearance of the first serious weaponry, including slashing swords, the earliest type named after a findspot at Ballintober, Co. Mayo, and shields. A wooden mould for producing leather shields was found at Churchfield, Co. Mayo, while an actual wooden shield was found near Swinford, Co. Mayo. Smaller, bronze shields were also found at **Athenry**, Co. Galway, and Lough Gara, Co. Sligo.

The gold, fused-buffer torc from Ardnaglug, Co. Roscommon (*on display in the National Museum of Ireland*), is a direct import from early Celtic Europe. Dating from the late 4th to early 3rd century BC, it is the oldest La Tène decorated import into Ireland. There is a considerable corpus of La Tène material from the west of Ireland, including the remarkable decorated monoliths at **Turoe**, Co. Galway, and **Castlestrange**, Co. Roscommon. Rynne's excavation of a ring barrow with cremation burials, glass beads, and fibulae at Grannagh, Co. Galway, indicate that such monuments, which occur in quite high numbers in the region, are of Iron Age date. However, not everyone died of natural causes at this time; it is possible that the man found in a bog at Castleblakeney, Co. Galway, was garrotted and pinned down under water by a withy around his neck. He wore a knee-length dress, or tunic, laced up at the front, and was bearded. While the practice of making votive offerings at bog holes persisted into the Iron Age, a considerable amount of effort also went into constructing trackways for pedestrians and carts across these otherwise impassable wetlands. The oldest pair of wheels in Ireland were found in a bog at Doogarymore, Co. Roscommon. These three-part block wheels are made from alder, with dowels of yew, and date from the early Iron Age. Centres like **Rathcroghan**, Co. Roscommon, probably attained the zenith of their importance during the Iron Age, with the construction of massive ceremonial monuments like Rathcroghan Mound. **Rathcroghan**, or Cruachain Aí, is the traditional royal centre of the Connachta, an affiliation of tribes claiming descent from the mythical Conn *Céad-chatach* ('of the hundred battles'), which included the Uí Néill.

Moreover, the historical record—especially in the early Middle Ages—gives the lie to any notion of Connacht as a peripheral backwater. The Uí Néill—the greatest of all early Irish royal dynasties—originated in the west, probably in the region of Cruachan (**Rathcroghan**), before moving north-eastwards into Ulster at some point around the 4th or 5th century. In their wake they left a region without any dominant kingdom. From the 5th to mid-8th centuries the most important dynasty were the Uí Fiachrach, based in north Co. Mayo, but there were many other rivals. The far north of Connacht—modern Co. Sligo—was traditionally dominated by the Uí Néill, particularly the Cenél Conaill of the Donegal area. In the south was another important and practically autonomous kingdom, the Uí Máine, who occupied most of south Co. Galway and, at an early date, much of south Co. Roscommon as well. The bleaker west of Cos. Galway and Mayo was undoubtedly a peripheral zone, thinly populated by relatively unimportant groups including the Conmaicne Mara, who gave part of the region its modern name: Connemara.

There are very few ringforts in the upland areas west of Lough Corrib–Lough Conn. Those that do exist tend towards the coast; there is a particular concentration around Clew Bay, Co. Mayo. To the east, however, is probably the densest concentration of these monuments in Ireland. Despite their high numbers, bordering on congestion in certain areas, there is no published analysis of ringforts in this region. Though published more than half a century ago, Ó Ríordáin and MacDermott's excavation at Letterkeen, Co. Mayo, is still the only detailed examination in print. There are also a considerable number of crannógs in this region, concentrated around the upper reaches of the Shannon and between Lough Conn and Lough Mask. They were clearly an important settlement form. Crannógs have a very broad chronological range and in this region they range in date from the possibly late Mesolithic sites around Lough Gara to medieval ones such as Castle Hag, Lough Carra, Co. Mayo. Fredengren's detailed analysis of the crannóg structures around Lough Gara stands out as the only dedicated analysis of western crannógs in modern times.

The ecclesiastical history of the west begins with St Patrick's reference to people living near the 'wood of Foclut'—the only Irish place name recorded by the saint—located by his 7th-century biographer, Tírechán, in Co. Mayo. Liam de Paor identified Foclut with Kilmoremoy, on the outskirts of Ballina, Co. Mayo. Indeed, St Patrick's mission may well have begun here and there are numerous sites associated with him throughout Mayo. The last few stops on his journey to the summit of **Croagh Patrick** (Crochán Aigli; Mountain of the Eagle), where he fasted for forty days, are now part of an extended pilgrimage to the summit of the 'Reek' undertaken, barefoot, on the last Sunday in July. A Munster connection also features in the early Church in the West. St Brendan 'the Navigator', alleged discoverer of America, founded monasteries at Annaghdown and **Clonfert**, Co. Galway, and St Énde, with the intercession of St Ailbe, was granted land to found his church on **Aran** by Óengus mac Nadfráich, king of Munster at **Cashel**. In the 6th century St Jarlath founded the important monastery of Tuam, which ultimately became an archbishopric in the 12th century, at the place where his chariot wheel broke. In the 7th century, St Colmán of Lindisfarne founded a monastery at modern-day Mayo abbey, in south Mayo, for a community of Saxon monks. All of these churches grew in importance during the early Middle Ages, but many lost out to new, royal-sponsored foundations in the later Middle Ages. The multitude of small, isolated islands off the west coast, such as High Island and **St Mac Dara's Island**, Co. Galway, and **Inishmurray**, Co. Sligo, offered the perfect retreat from the bustle and distractions of everyday life for Christians interested in eremitic solitude. Lake islands, such as **Inchagoill**, Lough Corrib, Co. Galway, sometimes offered the same quietude. However, there was a price to pay: they were all of them susceptible to Viking attack.

During the 8th century the Uí Fiachrach were superseded by the Uí Briúin, based in Co. Roscommon, who extended their power over most of Connacht by the end of that century. Uí Briúin control over the kingship of Connacht was unchallenged for the rest of the Middle Ages, but there was considerable rivalry between various Uí Briúin dynasties, especially in the 10th and 11th centuries. Eventually the dynasty of Uí Conchobhair (O'Connor) won out and in the 12th century their greatest king, Toirdhealbhach Ó Conchobhair (d. 1156), brought Connacht right to the forefront of Irish politics, reigning as effective high-king of Ireland for over thirty years. His son Ruaidhrí might have enjoyed a similar reign and it has even been suggested that the Uí Conchobhair might have established a hereditary, feudal kingship of Ireland if Henry II of England had not intervened in 1171. The stature of the Uí Conchobhair kings ensured that the English conquest did not reach Connacht until more than half a century after it had begun in the south-east, but change was inevitable.

In 1224 Cathal Crobhderg Ó Conchobhair, the last effective king of Connacht, died and a long succession struggle resulted. Taking advantage of this Richard de Burgh, one of the most important Anglo-Irish barons (who already owned large estates in Cos. Tipperary and Limerick), obtained a grant of Connacht from Henry III in 1227. Helped by the internal Uí Conchobhair dispute, de Burgh proceeded to occupy much of Connacht, while the government built or strengthened royal castles along the Shannon, such as **Rindown**. These initial conquests were lost to an Uí Conchobhair backlash in 1233 but were regained following a major royal expedition in 1235. De Burgh kept significant

▲ **Fig. 50.** Dún Guaire tower house, Kinvara, Co. Galway (photo: Conor Newman and Eamonn O'Donoghue)

estates for himself in south Co. Galway, establishing the town of **Galway** around the castle he built in 1232, but he regranted considerable parts of Connacht to other baronial families. Thus the de Berminghams became lords of **Athenry** and the FitzGeralds lords of **Sligo**. The Uí Conchobhair retained considerable lands, including most of Cos. Roscommon and Leitrim, around their traditional heartlands on the west banks of the Shannon. A series of royal castles along the Shannon were intended to keep the Uí Conchobhair in check. These included **Rindown** and **Roscommon**, both of which suffered frequently at the hands of the Uí Conchobhair, who remained a potent force, and both had been permanently lost to English control by the later 14th century. Indeed, Connacht as a whole was effectively outside the control of the Dublin government after *c*.1350. The disturbances related to the Bruce invasion of 1315–18 seem to have had a serious effect on Anglo-Irish settlement in Connacht, even though Bruce himself did not campaign there to any great extent. Anglo-Irish families such as the de Burghs (Burkes) continued to hold substantial estates but many of these (notably the de Burghs) became so assimilated, culturally, as to be virtually indistinguishable from their Gaelic neighbours.

Anglo-Irish settlement was later and much less intensive in Connacht than in eastern and southern parts of Ireland. The de Burgh estates in south Co. Galway seem to have been heavily settled with English tenants, but elsewhere most Anglo-Irish lords seem to have been content to act as overlords to the local Irish, who were left relatively undisturbed. Apart from south Co. Galway, town foundation was sporadic, largely confined to major lordly castles such as **Sligo** and **Roscommon**. Mottes—the classic earthen castles of early English settlement—are almost non-existent, although there is a reasonable sprinkling of later moated sites across east Cos. Galway and Mayo and in north Co. Roscommon/Co. Sligo. By contrast the region is rich in the most distinctive monuments of the late Middle Ages—tower houses and the friaries of the mendicant orders, notably the Franciscans. These reflect the power of late medieval lords, both Irish and Anglo-Irish, who prospered in Connacht in the absence of centralized control.

Abbeyknockmoy, Co. Galway Abbey

Take N63 (Galway–Roscommon) to Knockmoy village; turn north in village, then turn right (east) through gateway after 500 m; signposted. Disc. Ser. 46.

This impressive Cistercian abbey was founded in 1190 by Cathal Crobhderg Ó Conchobhair, king of Connacht, with monks from the abbey of **Boyle**. Cathal Crobhderg himself was buried there in 1224 and it became an important burial place of the Uí Conchobhair and, in the later Middle Ages, of the local Uí Ceallaigh kings. The abbey was dissolved in 1542 but some form of secularized monasticism seems to have continued there for a period. Although typically Cistercian in plan, Knockmoy shows the influence of the local 'School of the West' in its architectural style and in details such as the continuous framing of windows with mouldings and sculptured capitals. The architecture is normally described as Transitional (Romanesque/Gothic), but one writer has described it as 'a last flowering of Romanesque in one of the more remote provinces of Europe'. It has been suggested that the abbey of **Boyle** had a major influence in the development of this style and at Knockmoy the parallels with the mother house of **Boyle** are particularly strong.

The surviving remains consist mainly of the church and east and south ranges of the claustral buildings. The church and the east range are both dated *c.*1210–30. The church is cruciform with a very plain aisled nave, distinguished only by some interesting carvings on the abaci of the aisle arches. The presbytery is covered by a pointed ribbed vault in two bays, very similar to the contemporary structure at the Augustinian abbey of **Ballintubber**, also founded by Cathal Crobhderg. The eastern elevation, with its triplet of round-headed lancets and a larger, pointed lancet above, is also almost identical to **Ballintubber**. In the north wall of the presbytery are the remains of the canopied tomb of Malachy Ua Ceallaigh, king of Uí Máine (d. 1401), and his wife Fionnuala (d. 1403). Note the carving of the head of John the Baptist on a plate, above the apex of the canopy. East of the tomb are faded traces of one of the few medieval wall paintings to survive in any Irish church, probably of 15th century date and containing a number of common late medieval scenes. One is the martyrdom of either St Sebastian or St Edmund, tied to a tree and being shot at by archers. Over this are figures representing three living kings and three dead ones, whose warning to the living kings ('we have been as you are, you shall be as we are') was written underneath in Gothic black letter.

Each of the transepts has two barrel-vaulted chapels on the east side, a typical feature of early Cistercian churches. High in the south wall of the south transept is the doorway which gave access to the church from the adjacent monks' dormitory for night services, via a now vanished night stair. In the east range is the once-fine chapter house of *c*.1220, lit by five decorated lancet windows but unfortunately marred by the insertion of dividing walls and vaulting in the 15th century. Overhead was the dormitory. On the south side of the cloister are the remains of the refectory, at first-floor level. Note the traces of an arch inside the door, which covered the lavabo—the basin in which the monks washed their hands before eating. There is no definite evidence for a west range, and if one ever existed it was probably a timber structure.

Aran Islands, Co. Galway

Boats to the islands leave regularly from Galway, Rossaveel, and Kilkieran, Co. Galway, and from Doolin, Co. Clare. You can also fly there with Aer Arainn from Inveran. Disc. Ser. 51.

The three Aran Islands, Inis Mór, Inis Meán, and Inis Oir, share a quite remarkable number of archaeological monuments, to which this can only be the most basic introduction. There are innumerable guidebooks ranging from the multi-author *Book of Aran*, and Carleton Jones's recently published *The Burren and the Aran Islands: Exploring the Archaeology*, to works of a more literary bent, yet still hugely informative, such as John Millington Synge's *The Aran Islands* and Tim Robinson's *Stones of Aran: Pilgrimage* and *Stones of Aran: Labyrinth*. There are also the voices of the islanders themselves, Dara Ó Conaola, Liam O'Flaherty, Máirtín Ó Direáin, and Breandán Ó hEithir. As for maps, for you will surely need one—though you could do worse than to lose yourself in the maze of fields and lanes—Robinson's *Oileáin Árann. The Aran Islands, Co. Galway, Eire: A Map and Guide* is really all that you will need. It is cartography brought to an art form.

Inis Mór

Inis Mór ('the big island') is the largest of the islands. The northern end is Iararne, the focus of which is *An Trá Mór*, a great sandy beach, whose ever-mobile dunes have covered over prehistoric field systems, and, perhaps more tangible for the visitor, *Teaghlach Éinne*. *Teaghlach Éinne*, the

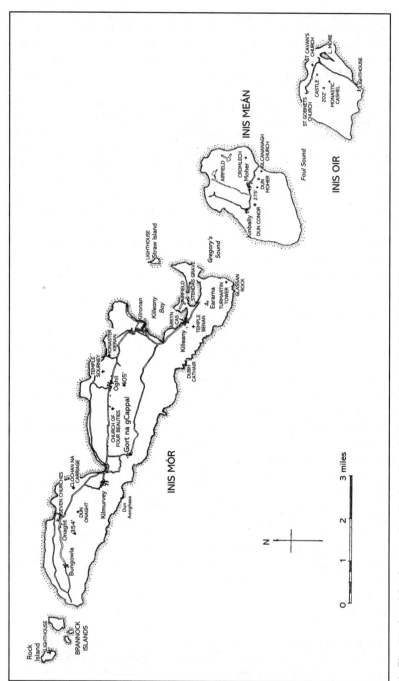

▲ Fig. 51. Aran Islands: map, showing location of principal sites (after Pochin Mould)

nearby stump of a round tower and *Teampall Bheanain*, further up the hill, are probably outliers of the monastery of *Cill Éinne*, founded by Éanna in the early 6th century. Little now survives—four of the original six churches having been demolished to build the nearby Cromwellian fort (1652–3) at Arkin (*Aircín*) on the site of an earlier castle. *Teaghlach Éinne* is a two-period church, the eastern gable with projecting antae being of early medieval date, while the western end was added in the 17th century; an early grave slab was incorporated below the window of the later portion. Further grave slabs have been incorporated for safe-keeping into the modern altar. There is also an early account of the slab-grave or founder's tomb of St Éanna (Enda) who, having trained at Candida Casa in Argyllshire, was one of the earliest monastic founders in Ireland. The graveyard is reputed to house the remains of 120 saints. Fragments of two high crosses have been found. One of these is in five pieces, two of which are mounted on a plinth near the round tower stump, the remaining three reassembled in *Teaghlach Éinne*. It is an accomplished late cross with Ringerike-style ornament. The second cross is represented only by its ringed head and was found outside the western gable during excavations in the 1980s. On the hill overlooking this is *Teampall Bheanáin*, curiously orientated north–south. It had a steeply pitched roof and inclined jambs. Charcoal from the mortar dates from the 11th century AD.

Back along Killeany Bay a path veers left at *Loch an tSáile* for the promontory fort of *Dúchathair*. Here a massive, terraced, drystone wall, fronted by *chevaux de frise*, cuts off a narrow, precipitous promontory. Access is a test of nerve between the south end of the wall and a sheer drop of over 60 m. Tucked in behind the wall is a cellular arrangement of four elongated huts. Beyond these is a comparatively slim wall creating an enclosed space, but beyond this again are traces of six or so contiguous, elongated cells opening to the east. Like the other stone forts on Inis Mór, its original architecture may have been compromised by 19th-century restoration.

As the main road around Killeany Bay veers right towards the village of *Cill Rónáin* (Kilronan), a minor road to the left leads to *Cill Charna*, a small church of which only the partial foundations survive. Kilronan may be the largest village on the island but its founding saint is an anonymous figure in the history and tradition of Inis Mór. The road turns inland after the village and about 1.5 km further on the right is *Teampall (Mainistir) Chiaráin*, a 6th-century foundation attributed to Ciarán, founder of **Clonmacnoise**. Here, on a terrace above *Port na Mainistreach*, are the remains of three churches, cross-slabs, and a burial ground to the north-east. The main church is of medieval date. It has a pointed-oval doorway and a fine but quite simple Transitional window (*c.* AD 1200) in the east wall. The perforated, cross-inscribed slab to the north–east of the church is probably a sundial. To the west is a very tall cross-slab and two others of similar size to the east and north–east may be *termon* or boundary crosses. Three cross-slabs survive in the graveyard. There is a holy well at the base of the small cliff to the south of the churches.

About 1 km further along the main road is *Dún Eochla*, a fabulous, oval-shaped cashel about 38 m in maximum diameter, walls up to 3.5 m thick and 5 m high. Built on a limestone terrace, this fortification is enclosed within another drystone wall of less regular plan. Occupying one of the highest prominences of the island, there is a great view from the top of the walls. The area to the west of this is known as *Baile na mBocht* ('village of the poor') and has a concentration of enclosures and grassy mounds. This area is difficult to access. Three of these mounds were excavated by Goulden in the 1950s (Oghil 1–3) and shown to be collapsed stone buildings of uncertain date.

About the same distance on the far side of the main road is *Teampall Asurnaí*, a small, denuded oratory, associated ecclesiastical building, cross-slabs, bullaun stone, and holy well. A sacred bush nearby is also associated with St Sourney who is said to have retired here from Kilcolgan.

Left at the next crossroads is *Teampall an Ceathrar Álainn*, a small, 15th-century church, final resting place of the 'Four Beautiful Saints', Fursey, Brendan of Birr, Conall, and Bearchán, whose tomb, or *leaba*, is a rectangular enclosure attached to the eastern end of the church containing four contiguous cross-slabs. To the immediate south-east is a holy well and to the north-east is a bullaun stone. A little further along the same road is Eochaill Wedge tomb with three overlapping roofstones and remains of outer walling surviving along the south side.

Another fine, sandy inlet, *Cill Mhuirbhigh* (Kilmurvey), lost out to Kilronan as the hub of port activity and its pier is now all but abandoned. A short distance south-west of the inlet are two churches, *Teampall Mac Duach* and *Teampall na Naomh*. Dedicated to Colmán Mac Duach (founder of **Kilmacduagh**), the larger of these two churches is a simple nave and chancel building with trabeate doorway with inclined jambs and antae. The chancel is clearly a later addition (13th century) and is approached through a rounded arch. On the outside of the north wall is a stone with a horse or fox in relief. A fine cross-slab stands a few metres to the west. Nearby is a holy well, Tobar Mac Duagh, and to the south-east is *Teampall na Naomh* ('church of the saints'), a plain rectangular oratory. To the south is a limestone bluff on which a 20 m long massive stone rampart has been built. This is all that survives of a once great enclosure about one half of which existed at the time of George Petrie's visit to the island in 1821.

The ground here rises steadily to the citadel of *Dún Aonghasa*, one of the most spectacular monuments in western Europe. Abutting a 100 m sheer drop into the Atlantic, this massive D-shaped hillfort comprises

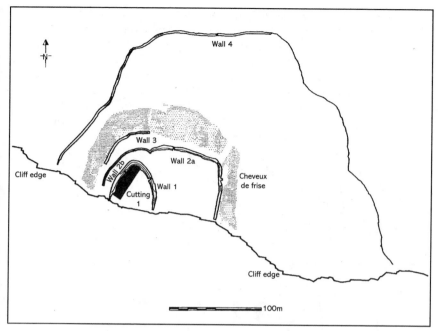

▲ **Fig. 52a.** Dún Aonghasa: plan (after Cotter)

four widely spaced ramparts and a band of *chevaux de frise*. Excavations by Claire Cotter (for the Discovery Programme) have revealed substantial later Bronze Age activity in the innermost, terraced enclosure (wall 1). The outlines of six or seven round/oval huts (approximately 6 m in diameter) have been identified and these are associated with a layer containing clay moulds (for swords, axeheads, bracelets, etc.), coarse pottery, and a faunal assemblage which reveals an adaptive strategy of sheep rearing rather than the usual emphasis on pig and cattle. This deposit extends under the wall, which is up to 5 m thick, but since it does not appear on the far side there may be an earlier enclosure wall subsumed within it. Wall 2 is shaped like the number 3 and Cotter is not alone in suggesting that the two arcs (2a and 2b) represent different phases. She postulates that the wider, eastern arc (2a) may be of later Bronze Age date and have been attached to wall 1. She further speculates that wall 4 may also date from this time. The implication here is that the fort was substantially remodelled at a later date with the construction of walls 2b and 3 and the erection of the *chevaux de frise*. This sequence is supported by an impressive series of radiocarbon dates. Waddell, on the other hand, is persuaded by the concentricity of walls 1, 2b, and 3 that *Dún Aonghasa* was originally a regular, trivallate D-shaped fort and that wall 2a is a later modification. Finally, Rynne has argued against a

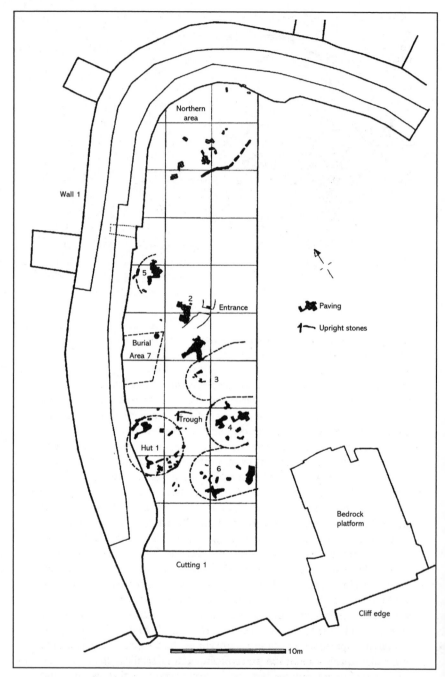

▲ **Fig. 52b.** Dun Aonghasa: detail of excavated area (after Cotter)

▲ **Fig. 53.** Dún Aonghasa (photo: Dept. of Archaeology, NUI, Galway)

military model, suggesting that the defences are excessive to the point of ostentation and that Dún Aonghasa is, first and foremost, a temple. There are two stray finds of note, one a handaxe from among the *chevaux de frise* (possibly a hoax), the other a beautiful omega-form brooch from a crevice in wall 1, dating from the first few centuries AD. Early medieval activity is represented in the excavated assemblage and there is a Viking-style crouched inhumation of 9th–11th-century date.

Continuing north-westwards across the island, to the right of the main road is *Clochán na Carraige*, an exceptionally well-preserved *clochán*. This oval-shaped, beehive hut has a rectangular floor plan with two opposing doorways. It is of unknown date. About 1.25 km north-westwards as the crow flies is *Dún Eoghanachta*, another of the great stone forts of Aran. The perfection of the walls, which are over 4 m thick and 5 m high, is no doubt the product of 19th-century restoration, but the original cannot have been too different and was certainly no less impressive. There are remains of three houses. The fort is sited on a prominent limestone ridge and below this to the north-east is an irregularly shaped enclosure (completely overgrown) known as *Cill Comhla* with two collapsed *clocháns* and a rather denuded tent-shaped founder's tomb and holy well.

On the opposite side of the main road are *Na Seacht dTeampaill* ('the seven churches'), one of the more complete ecclesiastical complexes on Aran. Here are the remains of about nine rectangular buildings, only two of which are churches, namely the largest one, which is dedicated to

Breacáin, and the most westerly building which is known as *Teampall an Phoill*. The outline of the original enclosure may be preserved in the field walls and a bluff to the west probably marks the boundary here. Various building phases can be distinguished in the architecture and masonry of *Teampall Bhreacáin*. The north-west corner preserves one of the antae and is, therefore, the earliest component. The chancel is probably a 13th-century addition and there are 15th-century modifications as well. *Teampall an Phoill* is of late medieval date. The outline of an elongated oval-shaped enclosure in front of *Teampall Bhreacáin* is a little cemetery and it contains a square *leaba* or saint's grave in which is a fragmentary slab bearing a partial inscription reading . . . *SCI BRECANI* . . . ('. . . of St Brecan . . .). There are two other *leaba*, one either side. There are a number of other interesting cross slabs in this complex, most of which are typologically quite late. Of potentially earlier date are three fragmentary, decorated high crosses positioned to the north, west, and south. The west cross stands beside one of the *leaba* and can be dated on art-historic grounds to about the 12th century. The north cross is considerably more fragmented and now stands a little distance north–east of *Teampall Bhreacáin*. The south cross is possibly a little older and is cemented together on top of the aforementioned bluff. The exposed face is entirely covered in interlace and fret patterns.

Inis Meán

Inis Meán ('the middle island') lies to the south-east of Inis Mór. The landing place is near *Cill Cheannach* on the south-east side of the island and from here the main road crosses directly to the other side. As in the case of Inis Mór, the general lie of the land is that of a gentle but steady incline towards high cliffs facing out to the Atlantic along the west side of the island. The airstrip is at the north-west point. *Cill Cheannach* is a monastic foundation traditionally associated with St Gregory. The principal remains are of a plain, rectangular church with projecting corbels on the corners and triangular-headed doorway. Nearby is a triangular stone which is possibly the gable end of a founder's tomb, and 30 m to the north-north-west is a holy well. It has a basal tenon and is perforated.

Overlooking *Cill Cheannach* from the south-west is *Dún Fearbhaí*, a sub-rectangular, drystone fort of the same massive proportions as those on Inis Mór (27 m × 23 m, with walls 3 m thick and up to 5 m high). Four sets of steps lead to a narrow parapet, and the entrance faces east. Between *Dún Fearbhaí* and *Dún Chonchúir*, on the far side of *Baile na Mhothair*, is *Teampall na Seacht Mac Rí* ('church of the seven king's sons'). Here, beside the priest's house, are the remains of a small, undistinguished church. Of interest, however, is *Leaba Chinndeirge*, grave of this otherwise relatively obscure female saint. The cross is rather modern. A holy well to the south-west also commemorates Cinndeirge.

Dún Chonchúir is another quite spectacular stone fort. It is oval-shaped (69 m × 35 m) and the walls are up to 6 m high and 5 m thick. The remains of an outer, terraced rampart survive around the western side at a distance of about 20 m. A smaller outwork is attached to the north-west side of the outer rampart and provides yet further protection to the entrance here. The outer wall does not extend around the eastern side because here a low cliff provides a natural defence. Like the other forts, *Dún Chonchúir* has been heavily restored but it appears to have had three terraces originally. The outlines of a number of stone huts/houses exist in the interior, those on the west side being cellular and broadly comparable to the huts in *Dún Dúchathair*.

There are two Wedge tombs north-east of *Baile an Mhothair*. One of them, called *Leaba Dhiarmada's Gráinne*, is a National Monument and is somewhat collapsed but evidently faced west. There is a third Wedge tomb at *Ceathrú an Teampall* on the west side of the island 1 km or so south of the beach.

Inis Oir

Inis Oir ('the east island') is the smallest and most southerly of the Aran Islands and, like the others, has beaches on the landward side, presenting a bulwark of cliffs against the ocean. At the east end of the island is *An Loch Mór*, a large teardrop-shaped freshwater lake around which is the best land. Following the main road north-westwards towards Formna the visitor comes upon a modern graveyard in the centre of which, half-buried in the sand (some of it recently cleared), is *Teampall Caomháin*. The chancel is probably a later, 13th-century, addition to an otherwise simple oratory of the 11th century. The much-venerated 'saint's bed' lies to the north-east and is now housed within a modern building. The remains comprise a rectangular setting of slabs around a fine cross-slab on which the sick used to lie in hopes of a cure.

To the south-west of *Teampall Caomháin*, commanding a prominent ridge overlooking the bay, is *Dún Formna* and *Caisleán Uí Bhriain* ('O'Brien's castle'). The castle is a two-storey rectangular tower, possibly of 14th- or 15th-century construction, of the Clann Thaidhg Uí Bhriain of Clare who had held the Aran Islands since about the 13th century. The interior is quite ruined but there is a fine trefoil-headed window in the south-west wall and two projecting stone heads on the outer wall. The castle stands within a thick-walled, sub-rectangular (52 m × 41 m) enclosure known as *Dún Formna*, which is thought to be an earlier fort modified in the Middle Ages. To the south of this, on the highest point on the island, is an early 19th-century, two-storey, signal tower, built to provide advance warning of a threatened French invasion. Further along this road and to the east is *Cill na Seacht nIníon* ('the church of the seven daughters'), the incomplete circuit of a cashel, in the southern side of which is a *leaba* or penitential altar surrounded by a number of graves. Nearby is a tall, cross-inscribed slab which was broken by vandals in the 1970s.

Back on the main road, about half a kilometre further on, is the circular burial mound of *Cnoc Raithní*. The mound is surrounded by a stone wall (21 m in diameter) and rather rudimentary excavations here in 1885 produced two cinerary urns containing cremated bone and a bronze awl buried in a small circular grave. Protruding slabs may mark the position of further graves, and towards the eastern side of the mound is a sub-square enclosure outlined with upright slabs. Waddell postulates that this is a multi-period burial mound.

To the north-west again, behind the village, is an ecclesiastical complex known as *Cill Ghobnait*, after the Munster saint associated with Ballyvourney, Co. Cork. The patron saint of bees, her connection with the island is shrouded in mystery but this does not detract from annual celebration on 11 February. The church is a simple rectangular building with inclined door jambs. There are several stone-built vaults beside the church and two bullaun stones. To the west, under a small cliff, is a ruined and substantially buried *clochán*. A nearby shell midden was recently removed for road building. About 1 km further south along this road are the remains of a possible megalithic tomb known locally as 'The Grave'.

Athenry, Co. Galway Medieval town

18 km east of Galway; take R347 or R348 off N6 (Dublin–Galway). Audio-visual presentation at castle (admission charge). Disc. Ser. 46.

Athenry is one of the better-preserved medieval walled towns in Ireland, founded by Meiler de Bermingham, who built his castle there soon after being granted the area by William de Burgh *c.*1235. The town took its name [*Áth an Rí*, 'the ford of the king'] from a ford on the Clarinbridge river, but the ultimate origins of the name are obscure. The foundation of a Dominican priory in 1241 is a good indication that the town was developing by this date. The walling of the town is said to have been funded by the spoils taken at the Battle of Athenry, in 1316, when an Anglo-Irish force under de Burgh and de Bermingham defeated Feidhlimidh Ua Conchobhair, king of Connacht. The town was sacked by Aodh Ruadh Ó Domhnaill (Red Hugh O'Donnell) in 1596.

The town

A considerable part of the circuit of town walls survives, along with five mural towers and one 15th-century gatehouse (the North Gate). One of the striking features of Athenry is that the modern town occupies little more than half of the area enclosed by the walls. It is possible that the area within the walls was never fully built up, but it is likely that the town

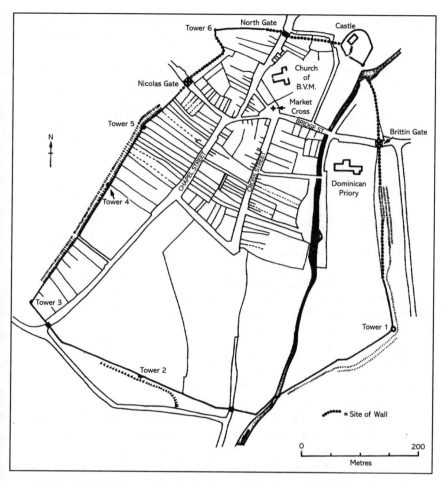

▲ **Fig. 54.** Athenry: outline map of town showing medieval features (after Bradley)

was considerably larger in the 13th/early 14th century and shrank in the later Middle Ages. This desertion of much of the enclosed area makes it difficult to reconstruct the original layout with confidence, but it seems that the town was laid out on a rough chequer pattern with two main north–south streets intersected by a series of cross-streets. The two main streets converge near the north end of the town in a small triangular market place which was possibly larger originally. In the market place is the only medieval Irish market cross still in its original position, although only a fragment of the 15th-century cross (carved with a *Crucifixion* and *Virgin and Child*) remains on its high stepped base.

Parish church

To the north of the market place is the parish church of St Mary, a 13th-century foundation which was made collegiate by the archbishop of Tuam before 1485, apparently with a staff of nine priests. Despite a papal instruction to disband in 1489 the college continued to function until suppressed in 1576. The 13th-century nave and transepts of the church survive in fragmentary form, while the modern church (now a Heritage Centre) occupies the site of the chancel.

Castle

Beyond the parish church, the castle forms a redoubt at the north-east angle of the town. It consists of a roughly quadrangular enclosure with a free-standing hall or tower near the north-west side. The curtain wall is largely rebuilt on the north-west, from the modern entrance to just east of the hall, but otherwise most of the visible structure is mid-13th-century work. On the south and south-east, facing the river, are two round towers which barely project from the line of the curtain wall, with evidence of a long rectangular building running between them, internally (note the large windows in the upper level of the curtain wall). There is no evidence of a gatehouse—unless this was located along the rebuilt section of the curtain, it appears that the entrance was a simple doorway. The rectangular hall or tower (recently restored and re-roofed) is now of three storeys, but may have been of two storeys originally. It is entered at first-floor level (via a now vanished forebuilding) through a pointed doorway with decorated capitals, near the south-east angle. This level was the lord's hall and is lit by tall trefoil-headed windows at the middle of each wall, which also have decorated capitals to their rear arches. There is a garderobe in the north-western angle but no fireplace. The fireplace must have been in the centre of the floor and this suggests that there was no second floor above, originally, although there may have been a timber gallery around the walls. The battlements at the top of the building are original, with long, plunging arrow loops in the merlons, but the gables at either end are late medieval additions. At ground level is a vaulted store or cellar, lit only by narrow loops set centrally in each of the four walls. The ground-level entrance is not original.

Priory

150 m south of the castle is the Dominican priory, separated from the rest of the town by the Clarinbridge river (*access from Bridge St., east of market place; key must be obtained from Mrs B. Sheehan, Church St.*). As with many other Irish friaries, it was quite possibly sited within its own extra-mural precinct originally, and was subsequently taken into an enlarged circuit of town walls. The priory was founded by Meiler de

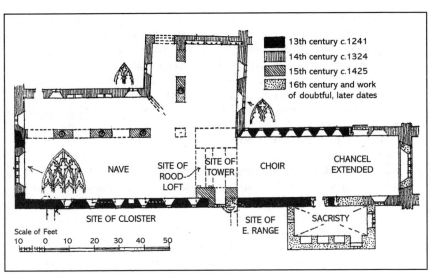

▲ **Fig. 55.** Athenry: plan of Dominican priory (after Leask)

Bermingham in 1241 and building seems to have progressed rapidly, as the church was consecrated as early as 1242. It was a high-status burial place—many de Bermingham lords, bishops of **Clonfert** and **Kilmacduagh**, and at least one archbishop of Tuam were buried in the church and this is reflected in the fine collection of tomb niches. The church was apparently enlarged by William de Burgh (d. 1324) and it was also repaired *c.*1327–45. Papal indulgences were granted to raise funds for repairs to the priory in 1400, 1423, and 1445, in the latter two cases following serious fires. The priory continued to function after the dissolution but it was seriously damaged in the wars of the late 16th century and became derelict. It was briefly reoccupied by Dominicans in the mid-17th century when it was proposed to establish a university there.

All that survives today is the priory church. The cloisters to the south have disappeared, although the roof lines of the north ambulatory and west range are visible in the south wall of the church, externally. The church consisted originally (*c.*1241) of a long, rectangular building, of which the south wall of nave and choir, parts of the west wall of the nave, and the north wall of the choir survive, lit by narrow lancet windows. The choir was lit by a row of at least seven closely spaced lancets in the north wall, a distinctively Irish arrangement also seen, for example, in the Dominican priories of **Cashel** and **Sligo** and the cathedrals at **Ardfert** and **Ferns**. In the early 14th century (*c.*1324) the choir was extended to the east by *c.*6 m and an aisle and transept were built onto the north side of the nave. The extended choir was lit by a large east window with elaborate, modified switchline tracery, and by twin-light windows with multifoiled centrepieces above in the adjacent north and south walls. The east window, in turn, was replaced by a smaller and simpler window, probably in the 16th century, but the remains of the 14th-century tracery can be seen externally. In the north wall are two tomb niches. One (probably 15th century) has an arcade of three cusped, pointed arches, beside which is a heraldic plaque recording the rebuilding of the family tomb by Walter Wall in 1682, following its destruction by Cromwellians. Next to it, to the east, is a much larger 15th-/early 16th-century wall tomb, set within a large pointed arch which was originally filled with tracery and flanked by tall pinnacles. At the base is a tomb chest divided on the frontal into five cusped, ogee-headed panels; note also the *Virgin and Child* on the eastern jamb, just below the springing of the arch. Opening off the south side of the choir is a vaulted sacristy, probably added in the 16th century.

The nave also saw substantial rebuilding. A large four-light window with elaborated switchline tracery was also inserted in the west wall; only the top of it is visible now, as the west wall suffered the indignity of being incorporated in a handball alley (externally) in the early 20th century! An unusual feature of the nave is the internal projecting window or squint in the south wall, near the west end. This is clearly designed to allow a view of the services in the church, probably from a vanished chamber in the west range of the cloisters. These windows are often described as 'leper squints', and this example may have been intended for the use of sick friars or lay people, but local tradition suggests that it was for an anchorite or hermit attached to the priory. Beneath this window is a blocked doorway, which led to the north ambulatory of the cloisters. Further east are three tomb niches. Two are fronted by arcades of three arches; that to the east also has quatrefoil openings overhead, while the western tomb niche has unusual round-headed arches. In the 14th century a north aisle and transept were added, and the north wall of the nave was replaced by an aisle arcade of five large pointed arches, carried on round columns with octagonal capitals. These arches were reduced in size during the 15th century, with even the columns largely encased in the masonry which blocked the arches.

The aisle beyond is lit by twin-light cusped windows with a pointed quatrefoil above, and continues along the west side of the north transept, ending in a 15th-century door at the north end, which is now the entrance to the church. In the north wall of the aisle are two double niches with elaborate ogee heads. The transept itself was lit by a large north window of four lights with elaborate tracery. Beneath the north window is a continuous arcade of cusped, pointed arches separated by slender columns, actually consisting of three separate tomb niches of three arches each, the northernmost squashed rather uncomfortably into the corner. These, and the niches in the north aisle, seem to be set at ground level but it is clear from blocked doorways (visible externally) near the west end of the aisle and in the east wall of the transept that the original ground level was much lower. The central tower, probably erected *c.*1425, has now vanished; it was as wide as the church but relatively shallow, from east to west. All that remains are the lowest levels of the supporting piers, on the south side—the corresponding piers on the north side must have largely blocked the transept from the remainder of the church. The partial blocking of the aisle arcade probably coincided with the erection of the tower.

Aughanure, Co. Galway Tower house

22 km north-west of Galway, on east side of N59 (Galway–Clifden), 3 km south of Oughterard. Disc. Ser. 45.

Aughanure [*Achadh na nIúr*, 'the field of the yew trees'] is one of Ireland's most impressive and best-preserved (although somewhat restored) late medieval tower houses. Built by the Ó Flathartaigh (O'Flahertys) *c.*1500, it was captured and seriously damaged by the English in 1572, but was subsequently reoccupied by the O'Flahertys in the 17th century.

The tower house stands on what is virtually a rocky island on the south bank of the Drimneen river, close to the shores of Lough Corrib, and is protected by two outer stone-walled bawns. The outer bawn is an irregular enclosure, with projecting towers at the north-east, south-east, and south-west angles and another midway along the south side. It is entered through a projecting rectangular gateway on the east. In the south-west corner are the remains of the great hall. The western part of the hall has collapsed into a dried-out river bed, but the decorated reveals of the tall, mullioned windows in the east wall are worth seeing. The inner bawn occupies the north-west corner of the outer bawn, along the river bank. To the east this was a regular, squared enclosure, most of which is now missing apart from the two-level round turret at the south-east angle. To the west the bawn is more irregular, following the contours of the natural rock, with the gatehouse at the west end, protected by an outer drawbridge.

The tower house itself, at the centre of the inner bawn, is rectangular, six storeys high, with a gabled attic behind high stepped battlements, and bartizans at second-floor level on the south-east and north-east angles. It is entered through a pointed doorway in the centre of the east wall, protected by a machicolation high overhead. Similar machicolations occur at battlement level on the other sides. A passage and steps within the east wall lead to a spiral stair in the south-east angle, which gives access to the upper floors. Each level has a single main chamber—that on the second floor has a good fireplace and may have been the lord's main chamber.

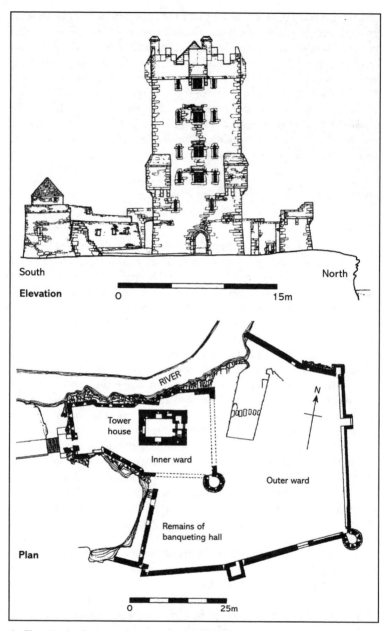

▲ Fig. 56. Aughanure: plan and elevation (OPW)

▲ **Fig. 57.** Aughris Head: promontory fort (photo: Dept. of Archaeology, NUI, Galway)

Aughris Head, Co. Sligo Promontory fort and assembly landscape

20 km west of Sligo town, off N59 (Sligo–Ballina); turn north 16 km west of Ballysadare, following signposts for Dunmoran Strand. Disc. Ser. 25.

The Aughris peninsula is on the north coast of Sligo, about midway between Ballysadare and Ballina. It has a stunning situation between the Ox Mountains and the Atlantic, with Knocknarea, Benbulben, and the Bluestack Mountains of west Donegal forming a dramatic backdrop to the east. The peninsula is peppered with interesting archaeological sites—some of which lie to the west of the pier—that may (according to Elizabeth FitzPatrick) constitute the assembly theatre of the Uí Fiachra, including the enigmatic 'Coggins' Hill' and 'Healy's Round Hill'. These are on private land and permission must be sought locally. Public access is, however, encouraged to a magnificent promontory fort on the east side of Aughris Head, by following the fenced-off path to the left of the pier. The fort is a small spur of land, halfway to becoming a sea stack, defended on the landward side by a small counterscarp bank and two quite massive sets of banks and ditches. A final counterscarp bank is constructed around the landward edge of the citadel. With no evidence surviving of an outer fosse, the possibility is that this may be an internally ditched and, therefore, somewhat uncharacteristic fort. This is one of the best examples of a promontory fort in the country but beware, it backs onto a cliff!

Ballintubber, Co. Mayo Abbey

10 km south of Castlebar, off (east of) N84 Castlebar–Galway road.

The small but elegant Augustinian abbey at Ballintubber [*Baile an Tobair*, 'the town of the well'] is said to have been founded in 1216 by Cathal Crobhderg Ó Conchobhair, king of Connacht. It was largely built by 1221, when the first abbot, Maelbrigdhe Ó Maicen, died. It was burned in 1265 but recovered and seems not to have been effectively dissolved until *c.*1585. It was reoccupied for a period in the 17th century.

The church (restored in the 20th century) was originally built in Transitional (Romanesque/Gothic) style with strong Cistercian influence. It was a cruciform building, without aisles, with a vaulted presbytery and vaulted transepts at the east end, each transept having twin chapels on the east side. The details of windows (especially the three-light east window), doorways, capitals, and mouldings are typical of the so-called 'School of the West' of late 12th-/early 13th-century Transitional architecture. A number of capitals in the presbytery have high-quality carvings of birds, beasts, and foliage in late Romanesque style. These are attributed to a skilled mason known to scholars as the 'Ballintubber Master', who had previously worked in the nave of the Cistercian church at **Boyle**. Note also the restored 13th-century altar and the early baptismal font in the south transept. The nave of the church was subsequently rebuilt, probably after the fire of 1265. The (restored) west doorway is 15th century. The claustral buildings are on the south side of the church. In the sacristy (immediately south of the south transept) are the remains of the once-grand tomb of Tiobód na Long Burke (d. 1629), Viscount Mayo and son of the legendary Granuaile (Grace O'Malley). South of this, the chapter house has a good Transitional doorway. Most of the other claustral buildings are 15th century. Excavations in the 1960s recovered evidence for two successive cloister ambulatories, which are now partially reconstructed on site.

Ballyglass, Co. Mayo Court tombs and settlement site

25 km north-west of Ballina, off R314 coastal route; 1 km north-west of Ballyglass Post Office, turning west off R314 and first right after Ballyglass Bridge; signposted. Disc. Ser. 23.

This well-preserved central-court tomb, in a lozenge-shaped cairn, is located 4 km east of the **Céide** Fields, in the area of densest concentration of Court tombs. The court area is oval shaped (11 m in length) and is accessed from the north-east. At either end are two large, two-chambered galleries. Excavation by Ó Nualláin revealed that the western end of the cairn overlays the foundations of a large, rectangular house (13 m × 6 m). Of plank-walled construction with up to three 'rooms', the central one was the largest and, as with other houses of this type, was

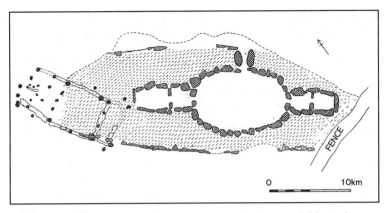

▲ **Fig. 58.** Ballyglass: plan of tomb, with pre-tomb structure visible on the west (after Ó Nualláin)

the main area of activity. Hearths, pits, and sherds of carinated bowls and flints were also found. Ó Nualláin took it to be a domestic dwelling but this has since been challenged in favour of a religious function. It is radiocarbon dated between 3690 and 2910 BC. Two other structures, one oval and the other D-shaped, were uncovered during excavation of another Court tomb (Ballyglass 14) 275 m to the south. These are regarded as being production centres.

Ballymacgibbon, Co. Mayo Cairn

35 km north of Galway, off R346 (Cong–Cross), 2.1 km from Cross; signposted. Disc. Ser. 38.

This is one of a group of impressive cairns in the vicinity of **Nymphs-field** stone circles. Most of them are associated in the antiquarian mind with the mythological Battle of Magh Tuireadh between the *Túatha Dé Dannan* and the *Fir Bolg* (an equally plausible claim on the battle ground is made by Magh Tuireadh near Lough Arrow, Co. Sligo). The cairn is about 30 m in diameter and nearly 10 m tall. A cylindrical cap is of recent date. A handful of possible kerbstones can be identified around the base of the mound, which is in turn surrounded by a wide, shallow fosse and a bank of uncertain date or function. These latter elements are heavily overgrown. It is quite possibly a Passage tomb. There are beautiful views of the Partry and Maumtrasna Mountains across Lough Mask from the top. In the field adjacent is an unusual, heavily overgrown enclosure, about 35 m in diameter, that may well be a henge. On the other side of the R346 (*on private land*) is a denuded cashel, known as 'Caher Faeter', just to the south of which is a possible three-stone alignment.

Other cairns worth visiting in the area are Carn Dáithí, about 8 km north-east of Cong (*private ownership, off the Clonbur–Ballinrobe road*), and the prominently situated 'Eochy's Cairn', about 1 km to the east, which is surrounded by a massive (140 m diameter) hengiform enclosure, comprising bank and internal fosse. This type of juxta-position between a (possible) Passage tomb and henge is repeated elsewhere in the country (e.g. **Ballynahatty**, Co. Down).

Boyle, Co. Roscommon Abbey

Off N4 (Dublin–Sligo), 13 km west of Carrick-on-Shannon; signposted. Visitor centre. Disc. Ser. 33.

The most important Cistercian abbey in western Ireland, Boyle [*Mainistir na Búille*, 'abbey of the (river) Búill'] was founded by monks from **Mellifont** in 1161, possibly on the site of the obscure earlier monastic site of *Ath-da-Larc*. The patrons were the local ruling family, the Mac Diarmata (MacDermotts), many of whom were subsequently buried there. The abbey was raided by the English in 1202 and 1235, during the attempt to establish English control of Connacht, but despite the

▼ Fig. 59. Boyle: outline plan of abbey (OPW)

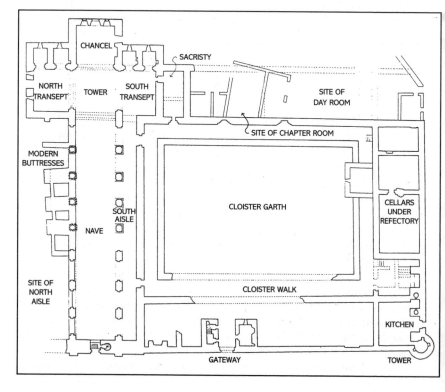

ultimate English success Boyle itself remained strongly Irish in character. The abbey had been officially dissolved by 1569 but may have continued to function for a further 20 years. From the late 16th century it was used to accommodate a military barracks and this led to serious damage, particularly to the claustral buildings.

Nevertheless Boyle is perhaps the most attractive Cistercian church in Ireland. It was built over some 60 years (c.1161–1220) and although typically Cistercian in its overall plan, it shows a number of changes of design. The earliest part (c.1161–80) is the east end, with barrel-vaulted presbytery and transepts each having twin eastern chapels, all reminiscent of Cistercian churches in Burgundy, home of the original **Mellifont** community. The tall lancet windows in the east wall are a later 13th-century addition, as is the crossing tower. Originally the east wall had two rows each of three round-headed windows, one above the other, and the stringcourses of these windows can still be seen in the external east elevation. Similar original windows survive in the transept chapels. High in the south wall of the south transept is the doorway which provided access to the church from the adjacent monks' dormitory for night services, via a now vanished night stair.

The style of the nave is quite different, and indeed displays a number of distinct phases within the eight bays of its arcade, which are clearly divided roughly halfway along. The four eastern bays are remarkably different in their arcades—the southern elevation displays round arches springing from impressive cylindrical piers, while the northern arcade has pointed arches springing from clustered piers. The southern arcade probably dates from c.1175–80 and the northern arcade c.1180–1200, but the stark difference between them is hard to understand. Finally, the four western bays were added c.1200–20 in a single operation, although even here the distinction between round arches on the south side and pointed arches on the north was maintained. The outer walls of the north and south aisles have almost entirely disappeared. The west doorway (c.1220) is a fine piece with pointed arch and two orders of continuous roll mouldings, with a large pointed window overhead. Just inside this doorway, on the south side, is a mural stair that gave access to the upper levels of the walls for maintenance purposes. The nave as a whole, despite its internal differences, is very English in character. In particular, the design of the western bays and west façade is similar to early 13th-century work at Christ Church in **Dublin** and the same mason(s) may have been involved. The latest phase of the nave also features the work of another mason, the so-called 'Ballintubber Master', who carved a number of the new pier capitals with scenes of birds, beasts, and human figures in a late Romanesque style drawing on both earlier local traditions and contemporary English style. Note especially the fifth pier from the east end, on the south side, but almost all of the pier capitals are worth examining.

Two doorways in the south wall of the south aisle provided separate access to the church for the Cistercian monks and lay brothers. The monks entered the church from the eastern ambulatory of the cloister and occupied their choir at the east end of the nave, while the lay brothers entered from the western ambulatory and sat in their own choir at the west end of the nave. The cloisters are poorly preserved. Only the inner wall of the east range survives, with the bases of elaborate door-ways to the chapter house and day room; overhead are some windows of the dormitory. A room above the sacristy (next to the south transept of the church), separate from the dormitory and equipped with a fireplace, may well have been the abbot's bedroom. The refectory, with cellars below, survives in the south range but was much modified in the late 16th/17th century. The remainder of the south range and the west range with its recently reconstructed gatehouse are entirely of late 16th/17th-century date. Beside the refectory was the kitchen, but the high stone chimney and the ovens in one of the recesses below are all post-medieval. At the south-west corner is a round turret. There are sugges-tions that it embodies the unrecognizable remains of a round tower derived from the earlier monastic foundation of *Ath-da-Larc*, but these may be discounted—it, too, is post-medieval.

Carrowkeel, Co. Sligo Passage tomb cemetery and settlement site

28 km south of Sligo town, off N4 (Sligo–Boyle). Best approached following the signs from Castlebaldwin, from where it is a steep and narrow ascent to the turn off on to the 'tarred road' that leads into the heart of the complex. Signposted. Disc. Ser. 25/33.

Carrowkeel is one of the most evocative archaeological landscapes in Ireland and, between exploring the monuments and the spectacular geography, visitors could easily spend a whole day here. Five long fingers of limestone, separated by deep, gorgelike valleys, reach out from the northern edge of the Bricklieve Mountains. On each of them are Passage tombs and on a platform below the summit of Mullagh Farna, the east-ernmost of the ridges overlooking Lough Arrow, is a 'village' of more than 150 hut circles. Most of the tombs fell foul of a team of anti-quarians led by Macalister, Armstrong, and Praeger, around 1910, whose activities here, historical circumstances notwithstanding, were nothing short of butchery. The tombs are now vulnerable and exposed and so care and respect are demanded of the visitor.

The first site you will see on a pinnacle of rock high above the right-hand side of the road is Cairn B. In the townland of Treanscrabbagh, and at 7 m high and 24 m in diameter, it is one of the largest cairns in the cemetery and its entrance faces northwards. Like all the tombs here, the entrance to the chamber is about halfway up the cairn and is typically slightly higher than the floorlevel of the chamber. The cairn consists of

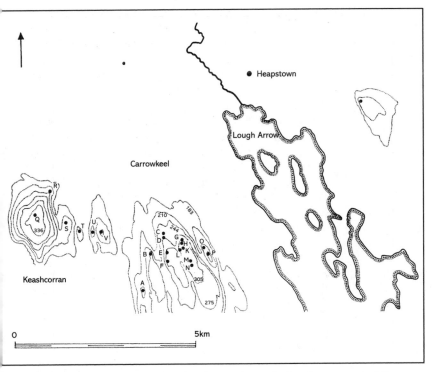

▲ **Fig. 60.** Carrowkeel: Passage tomb complex and related monuments (after Bergh)

loose, angular limestone rocks, with some evidence of a boulder kerb, and about halfway up the cairn around the south side was uncovered a vertical retaining wall. The chamber is roughly wedge-shaped and divided by sillstones into two compartments. A cist-like box is constructed with flagstones against the left-hand side of the innermost compartment. Cremated bone was found throughout, along with two potsherds. Two cists were also found in the cairn, both containing cremated bone, and one a sherd of pottery. From here one can see, to the south-west, Cairn A, a smaller tomb 2.5 m high and about 12 m in diameter. To the north-west the horizon is dominated by **Knocknarea** and Medb's Cairn.

Across the valley to the east, in Carrowkeel townland, the hill is crowned by two cairns, E and F. Below these, on a level platform on the northern side of the road, are cairns C and D. The latter two, though clearly Passage tombs, are in a somewhat ruinous state. The steep climb up the hill will bring you to two of the more enigmatic tombs in the complex. Cairn E, a long cairn (40 m in length), kerbed and orientated north–south, has been described as a curious mixture of Court tomb and Passage tomb. There is an open courtlike configuration of large slabs

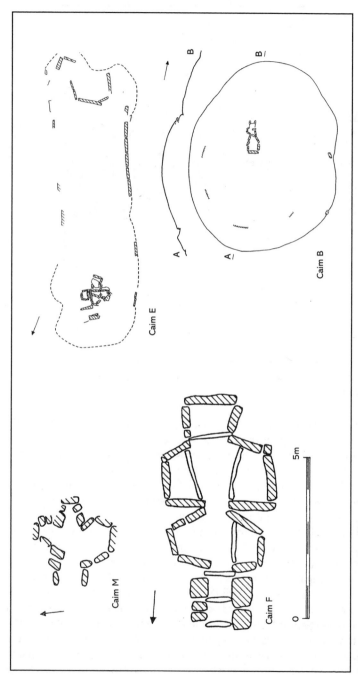

▲ **Fig. 61.** Carrowkeel: plans of cairns B, E, F and M (after Bergh)

▲ **Fig. 62.** Carrowkeel: Passage tomb cemetery (photo: Conor Newman)

at the south end, but no corresponding burial gallery. At the other end is a cruciform chamber with Passage tomb affinities. Emanating from the eastern side of this, however, are two orthostats forming a tolerable arc and thereby introducing the possibility of a court area at this end too. Is this then a dual-court tomb? Cremated bones were found in the two side chambers. Fragments of two mushroom-headed antler pins were also found, a type normally associated with Passage tomb assemblages, and a boar's tusk.

Cairn F is one of the more elaborate of the Passage tombs and is located a little further along this ridge to the south. It too is orientated northwards and comprises a rubble cairn 28 m in diameter and 8 m high. When exposed, the chamber (which is now backfilled with stones) was shown to be stalled, with two recesses on either side and one at the end. Its corbelled roof was reasonably intact and a broken stone pillar was demonstrated to have stood upright in the centre. Cremated human bone was reported and the only recorded artefact is a jasper bead.

The next ridge to the east is also in Carrowkeel townland and has six tombs strung out along its axis. The lowermost, and first encountered—and indeed also the first ransacked by Macalister and his companions—is Cairn G, a rubble cairn about 22 m in diameter and 7 m high. It has a cruciform chamber, accessed through a short passage from the north-west side of the cairn. Deposits of cremated human bone were accompanied by a range of artefacts including bone points, ten beads (including three pestle-shaped specimens and one spiroid—again all classic Passage tomb types), and sherds of Carrowkeel ware, the pottery normally associated with Passage tombs but in this case mis-identified as a Food Vessel.

A short distance further upslope is Cairn H, which has a simple undifferentiated, angled passage, expanding slightly at the end. The cairn is double kerbed, the second kerb occurring about 2 m inside the first. It is about 20 m in diameter and 3 m high. Burial deposit included cremated and unburnt bone, a small stone ball, and a perforated sea shell. Cairn K (there is no I or J!) is further up the hill and has a cruciform burial chamber in a cairn about 22 m in diameter and 6 m high. It is orientated due north. Deposits of cremated human remains occurred under the flagged floor of the chamber and recesses. Three stone beads, a bone point, and numerous small fragments of pottery were also found. Secondary use is demonstrated by the presence of an intact urn of Bowl Tradition. There is a large, open cist to the east. Little is known about Cairn L, which is slightly to the south-west and is partially enveloped in peat. It was disturbed, but not opened by Macalister and his team. The summit of this mountain is a drawn-out climb to the south-east. There are two cairns here, M and N. Both are quite small and denuded of their stones. Cairn M, about 8 m in diameter, has a small, cruciform chamber accessed via a short passage orientated north-eastwards. Cairn N, which is about 7 m in diameter, is in rather poorer condition but appears also to have been cruciform.

To the east, across a deep gorgelike valley, is Mullaghfarna and Doonaveeragh, the last of the limestone ridges. It cannot be accessed safely across the gorge, which has high vertical cliffs, but rather is approached by following (on foot!) the rough road down onto the valley floor and then crossing a few fields onto the ridge. Otherwise, it can be approached from the other side entirely along a meandering *road* off the N4 (*take the second turn after Castlebaldwin*). The highest point of this outcrop is in Doonaveeragh and here there are two cairns, O and P. Access is difficult and, in places, dangerous. Cairn O comprises a rubble cairn about 18 m in diameter and 6 m high. About halfway up on the south side is a small, two-chambered cistlike structure about 1.2 m long. This is not readily accessible. Inside, a Vase Tradition urn was found sitting on top of a small pile of burnt and unburnt bones mixed with sandstone slabs. Cairn P, to the south, is a conical-shaped cairn 10 m in diameter and 4 m high. Close examination failed to identify a chamber.

The level platform below Doonaveeragh, to the north, in the townland of Mullaghfarna, is home to scores of hut circles averaging about 12 m in diameter. Some of them have an inner and outer kerb of upright slabs, others present more as sunken, circular hollows. Stefan Bergh recently sampled a few of these and found Neolithic material, indicating possible contemporaneity with the tombs.

Castlestrange, Co. Roscommon La Tène decorated stone

7 km south-west of Roscommon town, between Athleague and Fuerty. The stone is beside the driveway of Castlestrange Demesne. Signposted. Disc. Ser. 40.

This squat, oval-shaped, granite boulder (90 cm in height) bears an elaborate design of incised La Tène ornament. It was moved to its present location as an estate ornament in the last century and its original position was not recorded. One relatively small portion is defaced but the remainder comprises an unbroken pattern of sinuous loose spirals and variations on the pelta and trumpet-curve motifs. Some of the motifs are quite similar to those on the **Turoe**, Co. Galway, stone and a similar date around the Birth of Christ is proposed. The purpose of such stones is unknown but it is reasonable to propose some sort of cultic or religious significance. If the stone is in its original position (a big assumption!) it is on a south-facing slope ultimately overlooking the river Suck. There are plenty of curious undulations in the surrounding fields.

Céide, Co. Mayo Pre-bog field system, settlements, and tombs

7 km north-west of Ballycastle on the R314 coastal route from Ballina. Award-winning visitor centre; signposted. Disc. Ser. 23.

With your back to perpetual wind whipping up over the cliffs, it is hard to imagine that the barren sweep of bog before you could ever have been a hive of farming activity. But 4 m below the bog, the Céide Fields

▼ **Fig. 63.** Castlestrange: La Tène-style decorated stone (photo: Dept. of Archaeology, NUI, Galway)

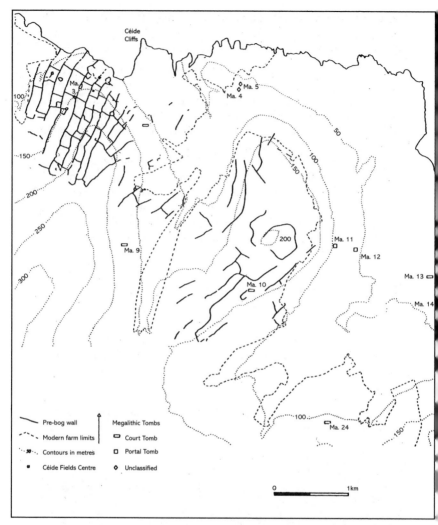

▲ **Fig. 64.** Céide: plan of field system as surveyed. The tomb marked Mayo 13 on the east is the Court tomb and house at **Ballyglass** (after Caulfield)

(stretching over the townlands of Behy and Glenulra) is an extensive and perfectly preserved coaxial field system, nearly 6,000 years old. An integrated complex of stone walls, enclosures, houses, and tombs, now known to straddle two hills, is buried beneath thick blanket bog. First recognized to be of considerable antiquity by Patrick Caulfield, to date over 1,000 ha of this system have been mapped and excavated by a team led by his archaeologist son Séamas. The fields are long and rectangular, up to 7 ha, and there can be little doubt that the system was conceived of and executed as an ambitious, communal enterprise between 3700 BC and 3500 BC, and this speaks volumes about the society of the time. Caulfield postulates that the fields were used for grazing livestock—which is borne out by pollen diagrams. The walls, however, are exceedingly low (50 cm–70 cm) for livestock control and, furthermore, palaeobotanists O'Connell and Molloy have argued that since there appears to be no peat under the stones they cannot be collapsed walls of abandoned fields. The onset of the blanket bog is dated to around 3200 BC.

An oval enclosure (22 m × 25 m) within the system was excavated in 1970–1 and postholes of a small circular hut were found, dating between 3500 and 2780 BC. Round-bottomed, western Neolithic sherds were found with a leaf-shaped arrowhead, part of a stone axe, and numerous scrapers. The transeptal Court tomb at Behy is also integrated into the system and is completely enveloped in peat. It was excavated by de Valera and radiocarbon dates from basal peat beside the tomb gave dates of 2850–1980 BC and 2860–2130 BC. Indeed this area has one of the densest concentrations of Court tombs in the country; the famous tomb at **Ballyglass** is less than 4 km from the eastern part of the field system.

Caulfield excavated another, smaller settlement at Belderg Beg 7 km to the west, near the harbour. Here was a series of conjoined enclosures dating from the first half of the 3rd millennium BC. Criss-cross ploughing was also evidenced, overlain by early lazybeds. Commencement of peat growth was temporarily arrested by afforestation, only to reappear in the earlier 2nd millennium when the site was reoccupied and a round house (9 m in diameter) was built; there were associated cultivation plots.

There is an award-winning interpretative centre at the Céide Fields, a must for anyone interested in the presentation and interpretation of prehistoric archaeology.

Clonfert, Co. Galway Cathedral

15 km south-east of Ballinasloe. Take R355 (Ballinasloe–Portumna, off N6) to Laurencetown, and take minor road east; signposted. Disc. Ser. 47.

A monastic site said to have been founded by St Brendan in the 6th century, Clonfert [*Cluain Ferta*, 'the meadow of the burial mounds'] became the seat of a bishopric in the early 12th century. A cathedral was probably built soon after this and an Augustinian abbey was founded in the mid-12th century, located to the south-east of the cathedral. In 1414 indulgences were granted to raise funds for the cathedral and abbey church, both of which needed repair. The abbey was plundered and ruined in 1541, although it continued to function (at least in theory) until 1571.

The small Romanesque cathedral was a simple rectangular structure

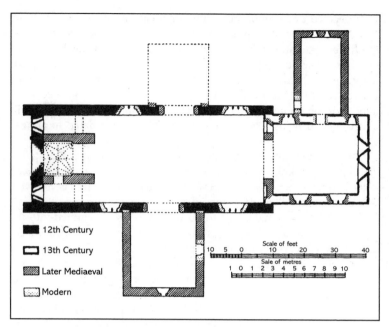

▲ **Fig. 65.** Clonfert cathedral: plan (after Clapham)

with antae on the gable walls. Its outstanding feature is its magnificent
Romanesque west doorway, perhaps the most remarkable piece of
Romanesque sculpture in Ireland, which is actually a slightly later addition, probably *c.*1160. The doorway is in six orders and preserves the
older tradition of inclined jambs. Above the doorway, rising from the
outer pilasters, is a steeply pitched gabled pediment filled with a blank
arcade of five arches, surmounted by a diaper pattern of inverted triangles. Almost the entire surface of this complex structure is covered
with decoration including interlace, foliage patterns, chevrons, and zig-
zags. The capitals of the doorway columns are decorated with a series of
animal heads, interpreted as dragons, cats, horses, and possibly asses.
Further beast heads occur on the arch over the fifth order of the doorway. The most striking feature of the entire composition, however, is the
carved human heads so prominently displayed in the pediment—seven
heads occur in the blank arcade and ten in the diaper pattern above. The
pinnacle over the apex of the pediment is also flanked by two human
heads. The heads are carved with individual character; some are
bearded, some are not. The inner doorcase is a later (15th-century)
insertion in limestone, quite different from the red sandstone of the
Romanesque work; it bears carvings, including a bishop and an abbot,
very similar to those on the west doorway erected in 1471 at
Clontuskert.

▲ **Fig. 66.** Clonfert cathedral: Romanesque doorway (photo: Dept. of Archaeology, NUI, Galway)

In the early 13th century a chancel was added to the east end of the cathedral; it is distinguished mainly for its exceptionally fine twin-light east window in Transitional style. A chancel arch of similar character was presumably inserted in the east wall of the nave, but the present arch is of 15th century Gothic style. Among its decorative features are angels, saints, and a mermaid with a mirror. As well as this arch and the inner doorcase of the west doorway, much other work was carried out on the cathedral in the 15th century. A slender tower, of the type normally found in friaries, was inserted over the west end of the nave, and north and south transepts (the former now vanished) were added to the east end. New windows were also inserted in the west front and in the north and south walls. Two early grave slabs, inscribed with the names *BECGÁN* and *BACLAT*, can be seen in the nave and south transept, respectively, while there is a medieval font in the nave.

Clontuskert, Co. Galway Priory

5 km south of Ballinasloe, north side of R355 (Ballinasloe–Portumna, off N6). Disc. Ser. 47.

Traditionally, the first monastery at Clontuskert [*Cluain Tuasceart*, 'the north meadow'] was founded by St Boedán in the late 8th century, but it is not certain that this was located on the site of the present Augustinian priory, which was probably founded in the mid-12th century. In 1413 an indulgence was granted to raise funds for the repair of the priory church, which had recently been 'totally destroyed' by fire. The surviving architecture of the site reveals extensive 15th-century rebuilding which may have continued for much of the century, as the west doorway of the church bears the date 1471. The priory probably ceased to function *c.*1550, but was later occupied by Augustinian friars (distinct from the original Augustinian canons) in the 1630s; the doorway between chancel and nave bears the date 1637.

The surviving remains consist of the church and little more than the foundations of the claustral buildings. The church consists of a nave and chancel, with a transept opening off the nave and a sacristy off the chancel, both on the north side. The chancel was, in fact, the original church of the priory, probably erected in the later 12th century. It has a later wall tomb, sedilia, and piscina in the south wall. The five-light traceried east window is a 15th-century insertion, reconstructed following excavations in the 1970s.

The nave was added in the 15th century, and the wall between nave and chancel is 17th century—note the date 1637 on the doorway. The nave has two main features: the first is the fine west doorway, outlined with multi-rolled jambs and surmounted with tall pinnacles, and with bold carvings of Michael the Archangel, St John the Baptist, St Catherine, and a bishop above. A Latin inscription on the upper frame of the doorway records its erection in 1471 by Matthew (MacCragh), bishop of **Clonfert**, and Patrick Ó Neachtain, a canon of Clontuskert. Note also the fine holy water stoup on the inner face of the north jamb, with double openings and figure sculpture above. The second feature of the nave is the remains of a vaulted rood gallery at the east end, which was three bays wide and one bay deep. The vaults were supported on polygonal pillars and responds in the north and south walls, which survive in part. The southern respond bears the name *JOHES* (short for Johannes)—presumably the mason who built the gallery. Both the west doorway and the rood gallery strikingly resemble similar features inserted in the cathedral at **Clonmacnoise** (only *c.*16 km to the east) at about the same period. A pointed arch in the north wall of the nave leads to the transept—the final major addition to the church, probably in the early 16th century.

The claustral buildings lie to the south of the church, but only the northern end of the east range survives to any height. The buildings surrounded a small cloister garth, the arcade of which has been partially reconstructed. The east range, which included the chapter house at ground level and the dormitory at first-floor level, is an early structure—late 12th or 13th century. However, it was extensively modified by the 17th-century friars, with fireplaces, chimney, and an oven inserted. The south range was erected in the 15th century and probably contained the kitchen and storerooms at ground level, and the refectory above. The east range, probably of 13th-century date, may have held further storerooms and perhaps a lay brothers' dormitory above. Surrounding the priory buildings and extending to the north are a series of earthworks, mainly low earthen banks forming roughly square or D-shaped enclosures and quite possibly representing medieval fields attached to the priory.

Creevykeel, Co. Sligo Court tomb

20 km north of Sligo on the N15 (Sligo–Bundoran), 1.5 km north of Cliffony; signposted. Disc. Ser. 16.

This very well-preserved full-court tomb was excavated by the Harvard Archaeological Mission to Ireland in 1935. The cairn is 48 m long, trapezoidal in plan, and has a drystone kerb. The large, oval court area is accessed from the wide, east end, through a 4.5 m long orthostatically defined passage. The burial gallery is two chambered and is entered between two massive jambs and a lintel stone and there are some remnants of corbelling. Small pits in each chamber contained minute quantities of cremated bone. Artefacts included carinated, Western Neolithic bowls, plano-convex knives, hollow scrapers, arrowheads, a stone bead, and two polished stone axeheads. In addition there were sherds of Early Bronze Age type and two clay balls that were considered to be of possible Iron Age date. There are three subsidiary chambers opening off the sides of the cairn behind the gallery. The best preserved of these, on the south side, comprises a sub-circular chamber accessed through a 2 m long passage, occasioning comparison with Passage tombs. A kiln of early medieval date was constructed in the court area and associated with this was iron-smelting detritus.

Hemmed in by a stone wall, the visitor is deprived of the tomb's original hillside setting and the sense of how its builders effectively turned their backs on Donegal Bay, Streedagh Point, and Mullaghmore, turning their attention towards the Dartry Mountains instead.

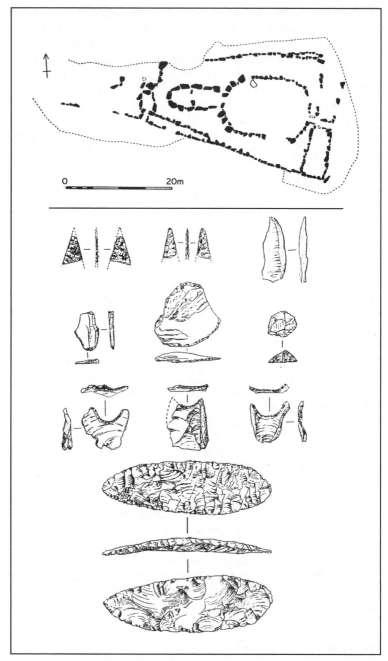

▲ **Fig. 67.** Creevykeel: plan of Court tomb with selection of excavated finds (after Hencken)

Cúil Irra, Co. Sligo Prehistoric burial landscape

This peninsula is due west of Sligo town and is approached on the R292; sign-posted. Disc. Ser. 16/25. Official brochure with map available locally (2006).

The huge mound of *Miosgán Meadhbha* ('Medb's heap', hereafter Maeve's Cairn), on the summit of Knocknarea (310 m), is the focal monument of prehistoric Cúil Irra, which includes the famous Carrowmore Passage tomb cemetery, and others on Carns Hill and Slieve Daeane to the east and south-east respectively. There are also Court tombs, barrows, and a host of hut sites.

Maeve's Cairn (Knocknarea 2, after Bergh) is flat-topped, 60 m in diameter, and 10 m high, with six kerbstones of gneiss around the northern side, and is encircled, eccentrically, by a low earthen bank, 1–6 m out from the base. Two so-called 'marker stones' occur immediately to the south and north of the cairn and there are five semicircular appendages around the base. The earthen bank deviates to incorporate the easternmost one of these and the northern marker and is, therefore, later. The interior of the cairn has never (as far as is known) been investigated and it can only be assumed that it contains a Passage tomb. There are seven satellite tombs on the summit of Knocknarea and hut circles on the flanks. Another satellite tomb occurs on an adjacent spur to the east at Grange North. Chief among the satellite tombs is Knocknarea 1, a cruciform Passage tomb in a low cairn (12 m in diameter) surrounded by a stone embankment and located about 50 m to the north of Maeve's Cairn. Site 5 is a ruined megalithic structure comprising an incomplete chamber, probably opening south-eastwards, and part of a surrounding stone circle or kerb. It was probably investigated by Richard Chambers Walker, a local landlord, in the mid-1830s. His description of this work as an 'attack' requires no further comment; that he found the tomb to have been previously 'ransacked' just proves that everything is relative! Sites 6 and 7, 30 m and 18 m south of Site 5, are both denuded megaliths. Sites 8 and 9 are low and barely distinguishable cairns. Site 10 is located near the edge of a shelf below the summit, 325 m south-south-east of Maeve's Cairn. Shrouded in heather, it comprises a 13.5 m diameter kerbed cairn, with a cruciform chamber approached from the south-east. The monument on Grange North, the eastern spur of the mountain, comprises a boulder circle, or kerb, 11 m in diameter, and four surviving chamber stones towards the east side.

Carrowmore Passage tomb cemetery, a short distance to the east of Knocknarea, has the greatest concentration of tombs in Ireland and in what follows the reader is guided to the more interesting monuments. About 60 monuments occur in an oval-shaped cluster from which a lineation of more dispersed monuments extends northwards. Notwithstanding the dominant presence of Knocknarea and its tombs, the Carrowmore cluster has its own integrity and can, on some levels, be

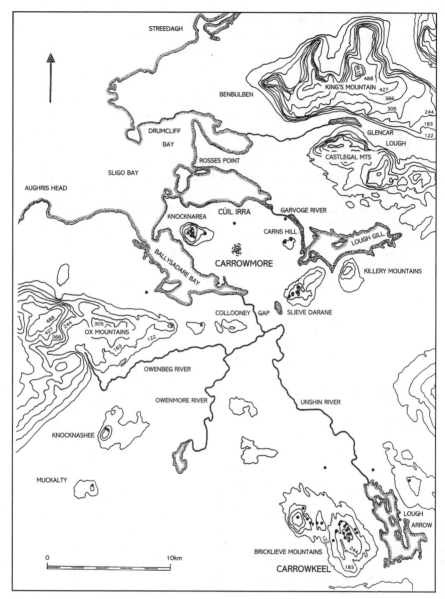

▲ **Fig. 68.** Cúil Irra: map showing location of monuments (after Bergh)

▲ **Fig. 69.** Knocknarea: 'Medb's Cairn' (photo: Dept. of Archaeology, NUI, Galway)

considered independently. There are 31 surviving megalithic structures (25 of which are Passage tombs) and evidence of a further 15 or so destroyed sites. Some of them are arranged in lineations. There are also barrows of various types and a plethora of enigmatic configurations, many of which are probably natural. The largest of the megaliths, a possible focal point in the complex, is Site 51 (Listoghil), a little to the north of centre. It comprises a large but robbed-out cairn, 35 m in diameter and 0.3 m high, kerbed with boulders. Inside this is a circular platform surrounding the rectangular megalithic chamber with extant roof slab. It appears to have been investigated by Walker and there is a report of cremated bone and a kite-shaped flint javelinhead. No less an authority than the great French archaeologist Abbé Breuil claimed to have identified lozenges engraved into the roofslab but this has yet to be corroborated—a distinguishing feature of the Passage tombs here is the absence of art.

About 100 m north-west of Site 51 is Site 52, a boulder circle (10 m in diameter) surrounding a dolmen-like structure. It was investigated by Wood-Martin, who found a cremated and an inhumed burial, the latter probably associated with a V-perforated button. Two similar sites, nos. 56 and 57, form a sort of couplet about 100 m north-east of Site 52. Again both were investigated by Wood-Martin in the 1880s. The chamber in Site 56 was figure-of-eight shaped, orientated roughly north–south, and contained a large quantity of cremated bone. Site 57 has been encroached on by a field wall and is just over 16 m in diameter with the entrance in the east. The chamber is all but gone, but while digging within the ring, Wood-Martin found a burnt hollow scraper. Sites 58 and 59 form another couplet about 50 m further north-east but both are so badly denuded as to defy classification. Parallel to this lineation is another one running from Site 1 to Site 7, among them some of the more interesting monuments in the complex.

Site 1 is a double boulder circle: the outer comprising 33 stones (12 m in diameter) is somewhat disturbed, the inner ring of slightly smaller stones is just over 8 m in diameter. The chamber(?) orthostats are difficult to reconstruct in a meaningful way. A bone pin and some sherds of a cinerary urn were found by Wood-Martin. Beside this, Site 2 is a boulder circle with no surviving internal features. Site 3, which is a few metres to the north-east, has the dubious distinction of having been investigated no fewer than three times, the latest as part of a Swedish expedition led by Göran Burenhult during the 1970s and 1980s. The site comprises a 13 m diameter boulder circle and intact, undifferentiated chamber, approached along a short passage orientated roughly southwards. Wood-Martin recovered the bulk of the associated artefacts, including an impressive range of different forms of bone pins and stone beads. Burenhult's excavations some 100 years later revealed the existence of two concentric circles of stones inside the boulder ring. There were two cists associated with the inner ring. A date of 4838–4400 BC was returned from charcoal found at the base of one of the chamber stones and another of 3306–2666 BC came from an arcuate arrangement of stones immediately outside the chamber. Burenhult argued for two distinct phases of construction and, more contentiously, that the earlier dates imply that this tomb tradition was initiated by hunter-gatherer societies of the later 5th millennium BC, thus challenging the orthodox model associating megalithic architecture with the first farmers. Support for this thesis is gained from Stefan Bergh's more recent excavations of a cairn on Croaghan Mountain on the far side of Ballysadare Bay, which yielded even earlier dates (5640–5490 and 4675–4460 BC). However, even Bergh admits that the dates create a culture-historical conundrum. There is also the problem of the absence of evidence of Mesolithic activity in this region. Burenhult's other thesis that the origins of the Irish Passage tomb series lies amongst these simple tombs has, nevertheless, found considerable support among scholars working in this area.

Between Sites 3 and 4 is an anomalous configuration, possibly a destroyed boulder circle. Site 4 is a boulder circle, about 12 m in diameter, surrounding a polygonal dolmen-like structure. It was also investigated by Wood-Martin, who found cremated bones and fragmentary bone pins. About 150 m north-east of this is Site 7, a well-preserved boulder circle (12.5 m in diameter) with a polygonal dolmen-like chamber and possible passage leading from the east. There is an inner semi-circle of stones in the northern quadrant. This site was also thoroughly disturbed by the time of Burenhult's excavations. Despite this, an interesting assemblage of bone, shells, and artefacts, including a barbed-and-tanged arrowhead, was recovered. A centrally placed posthole returned a date of 4330–3820 BC. It has been argued that the posthole related to earlier activity on the site. Site 13, which lies about 100 m to the south-east, was originally much the same but has been all but destroyed by the modern road. What survives is part of the chamber.

Continuing on this trajectory, Sites 15 to 18 (over a distance of about 400 m) are similarly badly disturbed by modern developments. However, despite some disturbance by a sand quarry, Site 19 is reasonably intact and quite striking. It comprises a boulder circle (24 m in maximum diameter), in which the boulders are set upright, surrounding some sort of megalithic chamber. Further south, around the side of the quarry, Site 22 is also a boulder circle with a central construction but it is in a sorry state. Site 26, about 100 m further south, has fared rather better. It is a boulder circle (17 m in diameter) with a paved entrance in the south-east and a destroyed central chamber. It was one of the sites excavated by Burenhult. A mushroom-headed pin and cremated bone were found in the centre but the deposits were disturbed by quite intense activity during the later Bronze Age. Still later, an inhumation burial was inserted in the centre of the circle around the Birth of Christ. Site 27 is about 100 m further south, along the quarry edge, and comprises a circle of 37 boulders, 20 m in diameter, with a cruciform chamber. It was excavated by both Wood-Martin and Burenhult, who identified an inner circle of smaller stones. Cremated and unburnt human and animal bones were found along with bone pins and ring fragments, chalk balls, sherds of Carrowkeel ware, sea shells, etc. Dates range between about 3950 and 3650 BC, but once again it has been argued that these may relate to earlier settlement activity. On the south-west side of this sand quarry are Sites 48a and b, a ring barrow and bowl barrow respectively. Site 30a lies some 500 m to the east of Site 19 in Cloverhill townland. It is an unusual construction, not just because it presents as a slab-lined oval pit dug into the side of a hill, but because three of the slabs bear decoration, not of the Passage tomb tradition but rather executed in Iron Age La Tène style.

Derryinver, Tully, Co. Galway Stone alignment

85 km north-west of Galway, off N59 (Clifden–Westport); on a ridge between Tully Mountain and Tully Lough, near Renvyle. Not signposted but visible from the link road to the south of Tully Lough between Renvyle and Letterfrack. Disc. Ser. 37.

A stone row, comprising six, or possibly seven, stones, was erected on the Tulach, a ridge between Tully Mountain and Tully Lough in north-west Connemara. The orientation of the alignment vis-à-vis solar/lunar positions is unknown. Close by is a three-stone arrangement like a denuded cist and, about 100 m to the north-east, in cut-away bog, is a small hengelike enclosure, 28 m in diameter. To the north-west and north are pre-bog field walls. One of these walls runs across the middle of the stone row. Samples from directly underneath the walls have been dated 756–360 BC and 783–355 BC. At the west side of Tully mountain is a denuded Court tomb. Further out towards Renvyle Point there is a nexus of different types of monuments including, near the sea, Renvyle Castle, a tower house (*in dangerous condition*), a Wedge tomb (*at the other side of the junction*), a possible Court tomb, and a cliff-edge fort. These latter are all on private land and permission is required. At the north-west point of the headland is the extraordinary occurrence in section of a tiny lens of lake mud and peat sealed beneath glacial till, the former representing the very last vestiges of an interstadial basin bog, the latter probably deposited during the last ice advance around 11,000 years ago.

Doonloughan, Co. Galway Shell middens, barrow

80 km west of Galway, off N59 (Galway–Clifden); take R341 (Clifden–Roundstone) to Ballyconneely, turn west for 2.25 km and north (right) at the crossroads. Disc. Ser. 44.

Differential erosion of the sand dunes at Doonloughan has led to the creation of a lunar-like landscape, where the harder shell middens rise proud of the sand and are set off with haloes of countless periwinkle and limpet shells. Excavation by Finbar McCormick in the late 1990s revealed, on one of the middens, the foundation stones of a small round hut of early medieval date (still largely visible). A fairly accomplished 9th-century bronze brooch testifies to the high status of those who dined here when the shellfish were in season. Mammalian bones, with butcher marks, are scattered throughout, as are bird and fish bones (the latter probably under-represented) revealing other dimensions to the diet. These middens are suffering badly from erosion and visitors are asked not to contribute to this!

Further along the headland (to the left of the road to Connemara Golf Course) are more dunes with middens. Behind them is a flat area with numerous small bumps or hillocks overlooked by a small but well-preserved ring barrow. Further along is a lozenge-shaped enclosure, which may be a kelp-drying mound. There is another excavated shell midden at the far end of Dog's Bay, just outside Roundstone. Here, at the far end of the beach, are midden deposits in section at the head of a miniature valley. Above and to the right of this is a five- or possibly six-stone alignment.

Galway, Co. Galway Medieval town

At junction of N6, N17, and N18. Disc. Ser. 45.

Galway, the main city of western Ireland, probably originated as a settlement on a ford at the mouth of the river Corrib; its name comes from the original name of the river, *Gaillimh* ('stoney'). A castle (probably of earth and timber, rather than stone) was erected there in 1124 by Toirdhealbhach Ó Conchobhair, king of Connacht, and functioned through most of the 12th century. In the initial English penetration of Connacht, Richard de Burgh built another castle at Galway, probably on the site of the older one, in 1232. Although this was destroyed by Feidhlimidh Ó Conchobhair, king of Connacht, in 1233, de Burgh remained in possession and had established some form of town around the castle by 1247, when both were burned by the Irish. The effective foundation of the modern town, however, can probably be credited to de Burgh's son Walter, in the period 1250–70. The medieval town was probably laid out in this period and was being walled in the 1270s, although the chronology and processes involved are not fully understood. Indeed, little is known of the town's history or development in the first two centuries of its existence. In 1396 Galway received a new, royal charter of incorporation, freeing it from the lordship of the de Burghs and paving the way for the growth of an oligarchy of merchant families who effectively ruled the town in its period of greatest prosperity (mid-15th to mid-17th centuries). This prosperity was based on trade, due largely to the opening up of the Atlantic trade routes in the 15th century. A further charter in 1484 gave Galway even greater autonomy and facilitated a period of dramatic development, in which the town seems to have been largely rebuilt after a disastrous fire in 1473. In 1485 the parish church of St Nicholas was re-established as a collegiate church effectively controlled by the civic authorities, and in the succeeding years the structure of the church was substantially enlarged. A Dominican friary was founded in 1488, and an Augustinian friary in 1500 (a Franciscan friary had existed since 1296). This period of prosperity came to an abrupt end with the Cromwellian siege and occupation of Galway in 1651, which caused serious damage to the town and destroyed the old merchant oligarchy. Ironically, 1651 also bequeathed a marvellous treasure to the city—a wonderfully detailed pictorial map, which is still the main source for the reconstruction of the medieval town.

At its greatest extent, the medieval town occupied a lozenge-shaped area of *c.*11 ha on the east bank of the river, surrounded by walls with at least six gates and 14 mural towers. Little of the town walls survives, although a substantial portion with two rounded mural towers (reconstructed on the original foundations) has been incorporated into a modern shopping centre (*south-west side of Eyre Square*). At the southern angle of the town (*Spanish Parade, off Flood St.*) is another wall fragment and the so-called 'Spanish Arch'—actually part of a projecting spur of the town wall which protected the quay. This was probably erected in the 16th century, but the two arches in the structure (there may have been four originally) may have been inserted in the 17th century, when the area outside (east of) the wall was being reclaimed.

The external face of the wall also features fine corbelled wall walks. Within the walls the town was laid out along a central street (*William St./Shop St.*) running north-east/south-west before splitting into two streets, one (*Main Guard St./Bridge St.*) leading westward to the bridge over the river and the other (*High St./Quay St.*) running south to the quay. A single street (*Abbeygate St.*) ran right across the town from north-west to south-east, and another (*Market St./Lombard St./Cross St./ St Augustine St.*) effectively mirrored the line of the town wall in a great curve around the west, south, and east sides.

Castle

The location of the original castle is, almost certainly, at the southern end of the town, in the area bounded by Cross St., Quay St., Flood St., and the Corrib. At the centre of this area, on Court House Lane (*between Quay St. and Flood St.*), in the offices of the Revenue Commissioners, were excavated the foundations of a large medieval hall-like structure. This building is clearly shown on the 1651 map, where it is labelled as 'the old castle of the most illustrious Lord, Richard De Burgo, the red Earl' (i.e. Richard de Burgh, earl of Ulster, 1271–1326). Excavation also revealed, just to the south-west of this building, traces of a substantial wall with external batter, which may well be part of the curtain wall of the castle. The combination of archaeological and cartographic evidence strongly suggests that the large structure was the great hall of the 13th-century de Burgh castle. There is considerable evidence for later modifications, including the central arcade of octagonal stone columns (of which three column bases remain), added in the 14th/15th centuries to support the roof. By 1651 the hall was a ruin and the castle had disappeared beneath later buildings, but it is interesting to note that two of the main functions of the lord's hall—collecting taxes and dispensing justice—have continued on the site, more or less uninterrupted. As the street name suggests, this was the site of the city's Courthouse (until the early 19th century) and also of the Custom House, which is still reflected in the presence of the Revenue Commissioners. If your tax affairs are safely in order, you should visit the Revenue Commissioners building to view the attractively presented excavated remains of the medieval hall.

Houses

Between the 15th and 17th centuries Galway was built up by its merchant families and many of their town houses (which were stone built) survive, at least in part. They are mostly masked behind modern façades and are not accessible to the public. However, the careful observer will find features such as doorways, window frames, and other stonework of the 15th–17th centuries in many places, especially on William St., High St., Quay St., Cross St., and Kirwan's Lane. At the south end of Quay St.

is 'Blake's castle', the (reconstructed) 16th-century fortified town house of the Blake family. No original internal features are visible, but the doorway and two windows on the north-east angle survive—one an unusual double window on the corner. At the south end of Flood St., nearby, is another house which must originally have resembled the Blake house, although it now appears quite different as a result of substantial later remodelling. Currently serving as an Indian restaurant, this building retains a well-carved 16th-century doorway (note the interlace on the chamfer stops) and, on the south façade facing Spanish Parade, a twin-light ogee-headed window.

Lynch's castle

The finest surviving house in Galway is 'Lynch's castle' (*on Shop St./ Abbeygate St.*), a large, fortified building owned by the medieval town's most prominent merchant family. Built *c*.1500 at the main crossroads of the medieval town, it was crudely 'restored' in the 1960s as a bank and little more than the façades survive. Even these are largely reconstructed as a result of previous rebuildings and many of the visible features are rearranged, out of their original positions. Despite this the elevations are superb, with finely carved window mouldings, heraldic plaques, and gargoyles overhead. The tall sash windows were inserted in the late 18th/ early 19th century, probably at the same time as the floors were raised, reducing the original five storeys to four. The ornate hood mouldings over these windows are presumably salvaged from original windows, and testify to the quality of the original architecture. The only original windows still in position are all blocked, as they now fall between floors. These are a magnificent four-light window between the present second and third floors on the Shop St. elevation, a single-light ogee-headed window between first and second floors on the Abbeygate St. elevation, and the angle loops on the corner of the building. None of the doorways and windows on the ground floor are original—the site of the original ground-floor entrance is probably indicated by a small machicolation at the west end of the Abbeygate St. frontage. However, the main entrance was at the original second-floor level (on Abbeygate St.), and must have been reached by an external stair. Two projecting corbels overhead (currently at second-floor level) probably supported another machicolation, to protect this entrance. At the same level, at the east end of the frontage, is a heraldic plaque within a roundel, bearing the arms of the FitzGeralds, earls of Kildare and effective rulers of late 15th/ early 16th-century Ireland. A similar plaque on the Shop St. frontage bears the arms of the Lynch family, while a larger plaque, situated lower down over one of the doorways, bears the arms of Henry VII of England (1485–1509).

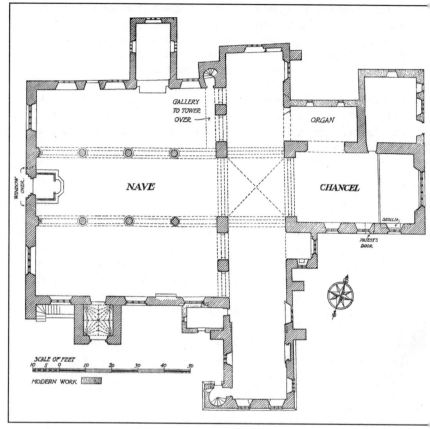

▲ **Fig. 70.** Galway: plan of St Nicholas's church (after Leask)

St Nicholas's church

Galway's most important building is St Nicholas's church (*north-west side of Shop St.*), one of the largest and certainly the best-preserved medieval parish church in Ireland. It seems to have been built *c.*1320—almost certainly on the site of an earlier church—as a cruciform structure, with chancel, transepts, and aisled nave. The church was made collegiate in 1484 and this seems to have prompted a substantial rebuilding over the following century. The nave aisles were enlarged (both are now larger than the nave itself), a crossing tower was added, the south transept was extended, and chapels were built on at various points. The church is entered via a vaulted south porch, probably added to the south aisle in the mid-16th century. The aisle itself (enlarged in the late 15th/early 16th century) is lit by three-light windows in the south wall (probably modelled on a late 15th-century window in the gable of the south transept) and a four-light window in the west wall with Decorated tracery and an external ogee-headed hood moulding with crocketed pinnacle above. The outer walls of the south aisle and transept are topped with stepped battlements, from beneath which project a fine assortment of carved gargoyles. Some uncertainty surrounds the date of the battlements and gargoyles, which may be as late as the 19th century. At the west end of the aisle is a beautifully carved baptismal font (probably late 16th/early 17th century), two sides of which bear tracery patterns apparently mimicking those of the aisle windows.

The nave clearly had aisles from the beginning and retains its original (early 14th-century) arcade of four bays on circular pillars. The large west window with Perpendicular-style tracery is, however, a late 16th/17th-century insertion. Beneath it is a late 15th-century west doorway with multi-moulded pointed arch in three orders, its pinnacles truncated by the insertion of the window above. The north aisle was enlarged in the mid-16th century, probably beginning in 1538 and perhaps continuing until 1583—the date on the four-light window in the west wall. There are three windows in the north wall; the central one seems to be a copy of those in the south aisle, and it is flanked by others with reticulated and switchline tracery, but the quality of the carving is inferior to the south aisle windows. Opening off the aisle to the north, and broadly contemporary with it, is the chapel of the Holy Sacrament. The structure built into the entrance, sometimes known as the 'Confessional', is obviously not original to this location. The twin, cusped ogee heads and 'barley sugar' column between suggest a late 15th-century date, and perhaps the best suggestion is that this is a reader's pulpit taken from the refectory of the medieval priests' college. In the aisle nearby is an unusual free-standing holy water stoup (late 15th/early 16th century).

The north transept (*now the Henry Library*) retains its original (early 14th-century) dimensions and is lit by a three-light trefoil-headed window with switchline tracery in the north wall and a simpler three-light trefoil-headed window in the east wall. Also in the north wall is an arched tomb recess and, in the gable, a small three-light window inserted when the roofs of both transepts were raised c.1561. The crossing tower is an addition, probably of the late 15th century. Externally, it has unusual chamfered angles with shallow central pilasters; the stepped parapets are a 19th-century restoration, and the spire above was added in the late 17th century. Note the 'manticora' (a mythical creature, half man, half lion) carved above the pulpit in the north-east angle of the crossing. The chancel is lit by a five-light east window with switchline tracery, probably late 15th century in date, but the three twin-light windows in the south wall are earlier—possibly original early 14th-century work. Beneath these are an aumbry and sedilia. In the north wall is the

doorway to the sacristy. At the junction of the chancel and south transept is the small chapel of Christ, containing a cross-slab with Norman
French inscription commemorating Adam Bure. This slab is probably
late 13th century, almost certainly earlier than the present church and
possibly associated with an earlier church on the site.

The south transept has been substantially rebuilt, especially in 1561
when it was extended to the south by *c*.10 m. Roughly midway along the
east wall is a three-light window similar to the north window of the
north transept, which may be the original (early 14th-century) south
window. The fine three-light window with reticulated tracery currently
in the south gable is 15th century, and probably replaced the original
window until it, too, was reset in its present position when the transept
was extended in 1561. The 1561 extension was a two-storey structure
with a stair turret in the south-west angle providing access to the (now
vanished) upper floor. This upper level was probably a private chapel or
chantry for the Lynch family, patricians of the town who built this and
many other parts of the church. In conjunction with the building of this
extension, the roofs of both south and north transepts were raised
slightly. In the east wall, at ground level, is a fine tomb chest within a
recess with Flamboyant tracery, probably early 16th century. Like other
Lynch tombs to the north and south, it shows signs of defacing, probably
caused during the Cromwellian occupation of 1652. In the west wall
opposite is the late 16th-century 'Shoemaker' grave slab, with 'Gaelic
Revival' interlaced cross.

Gleninagh, Co. Galway   Stone alignment

*55 km north-west of Galway; take R344 northwards off N59 (Galway–Clifden),
2 km west of Recess. Disc. Ser. 37.*

A long, narrow, curving lake between the *Benna Beola* (Twelve Pins) and
the Mamturks, *Gleann Eidhneach*, the Lough Inagh Valley, is one of the
most beautiful places in Connemara. At the north end of the lough,
overlooking the Gleann Eidhneach river where it turns westwards, is a
row of six quartz boulders. These are aligned north-east/south-west on a
saddle between Binn an Choire Bhig and Binn Dubh, where the sun sets
on the midwinter solstice. Two spectacularly long waterfalls tumble
down the nearly sheer face of rock below the saddle. The land is in
private ownership and access is problematic, not least because of
difficult, part-cut-away bog.

Inchagoill, Co. Galway   Church site

*In Lough Corrib, 30 km north of Galway; accessible by boat from Cong and Ough-
terard (tours also operate on the Corrib Princess from Galway). Disc. Ser. 16.*

Inchagoill [*Inse gaill*, 'the island of the foreigners'] is one of the larger
islands towards the north end of Lough Corrib and has two churches

and a small collection of cross-slabs. The first building one encounters after disembarking is Templenaneeve [*Teampull na naoimh*, 'the church of the saints'], a small 12th-century church with a fine, Romanesque-style doorway at the west end. The doorway was incorrectly reassembled around 1860 by Sir Benjamin Guinness. There are numerous solution holes in the doorway. Inside are a number of simple cross-slabs. The most interesting of the island's carved stones, however, stands in a small, rather disorganized-looking graveyard beside St Patrick's church, a nave-and-chancel building of medieval date. It is a small pillar with a vertical inscription reading, in the genitive case, *LIE LUGUAEDON MACCI MENUEH* ('the stone of Luguedon son of Menbh'). The vertical axis of the inscription, and the familiar three-word formula, has led to speculation of a connection with the ogam script, perhaps even an antecedent, but it is later and probably dates from the 7th century. There are, in addition, seven inscribed crosses on the pillar.

Inishmurray, Co. Sligo Island monastery

Accessible only by boat, which may be hired at Mullaghmore or Rosses Point, off N15 north of Sligo. Disc. Ser. 16.

Inishmurray [*Inis Muireadaigh*, 'Muireadach's island'], a small island 6 km off the coast of Co. Sligo, is often considered the classic example of an island monastery or hermitage, a characteristic feature of early Irish Christianity. Although the island is named after the 5th-century St Muireadach, who is reputedly buried there, the monastery is said to have been founded by another 5th- or 6th-century saint, Laisrén or Molaise. The island was very exposed to Viking raids, including one of the earliest recorded in Ireland, in 795. After another raid, in 807, nothing is heard, historically, of the monastery and it is possible that the monastic community abandoned the island and united with the monastery of Aughris, on the mainland. However, the surviving archaeology clearly points to continuing activity on the island—possibly related more to pilgrimage, rather than to strict monasticism.

The substantial visible remains on the site were extensively restored in the 19th century and are not easily dated. However, while they do little to clarify the history of the monastery, they are of great importance in illustrating the physical appearance of an early island monastery. The main buildings are set within an egg-shaped enclosure, located *c.*150 m from the southern shore of the island. It is surrounded by a massive drystone cashel wall, up to 4 m high and 4.5 m thick. Within the thickness of the wall are flights of steps leading to the top and several small chambers, although some of these may be 19th-century creations. At least four entrances run through the wall, with the main entrance to the north-east (the entrance on the south is probably a 19th-century insertion). Within the enclosure, three small areas in the north, south, and west are cut off from the main area by low stone walls.

In the main area are two churches. To the north-west, against the cashel wall, is *Teach Molaise* ('St Molaise's church'). This tiny church or shrine has a (reconstructed) stone roof and flat-lintelled west door bearing, on the outer face of the lintel, an equal-armed cross. A fine 12th/13th-century wooden statue of St Molaise was found in this church (*now on display in the National Museum of Ireland at Collins Barracks*) and it was probably erected as a tomb for the founder. A radiocarbon date from mortar in the masonry suggests a date as early as the 8th century for this church. To the south-east, near the centre of the area, is *Teampull Molaise* or *Teampull na bFhear* ('the men's church'), a simple rectangular church with antae and flat-lintelled west doorway. Around *Teampull na bFhear* to the east, south, and west are three stone platforms known as *leacht*, possibly open-air altars—that to the east is known as *clocha breaca* ('the speckled stones') after the water-rolled stones laid on top of it. Some of these are decorated with crosses and all were presumably used for some ritual or devotional purpose, but this is uncertain. A fourth *leacht* adjoins the cashel wall externally, on the north.

Within the western area of the enclosure is *Teach na Tine* ('the church of the fire'), a small rectangular structure with a doorway in the south wall. It was probably a church or shrine within which a perpetual fire was maintained on a stone hearth on the floor. Adjacent to it is a *clochán*, a circular structure of drystone walling with hemispherical, corbelled roof. In the northern area is a small, sub-rectangular *clochán* built against the cashel wall. Outside the enclosure, on the coast to the south-west, is a fourth church, *Teampull na mBan* ('the women's church'). To the east is a well, covered by a small building with corbelled roof, of uncertain date, while 100 m to the west is another cemetery, Relickoran. Many interesting pillar stones and cross-slabs are visible, both within the enclosure and around the shores of the island, associated with a series of *leachta*—drystone cairns marking the location of 'stations' visited by pilgrims.

Killala, Co. Mayo Round tower
12 km north of Ballina, on R314. Disc. Ser. 24.

Killala owes its name [*Cill Alaid*, 'the church of Alad'] to an early monastic site, reputedly founded by St Patrick in the 5th century, although there is no definite evidence for its existence before the 12th century. It was, however, important enough to be selected as the seat of a diocese in 1111. All that survives of the monastic site is the round tower, probably of 12th-century date. Built on a limestone outcrop, it is 26 m high with five floors and is complete, although the roof was repaired in the 19th century. The round-headed doorway is 3 m above ground and faces south-east, towards the present cathedral, which clearly occupies the site of a medieval predecessor.

Kilmacduagh, Co. Galway Monastic site

30 km south-east of Galway, off R460 (Gort–Corrofin); signposted. Disc. Ser. 52.

Cill Mic Duach ('the church of Mac Duach') bears the name of its reputed founder, Colmán Mac Duach, a little-known 7th-century saint. It became the seat of a diocese *c.*1152. The monastery was destroyed by the English in the early 13th century, but an Augustinian abbey was founded *c.*1225–50. At least five churches and a round tower survive on the site today, together with a medieval residence.

Round tower

The most striking and important building at Kilmacduagh is the beautiful round tower, the tallest surviving in Ireland at 34 m in height, with seven floors. Much of the roof was rebuilt in the 19th century. 19th-century excavations also revealed that the foundations of the tower are remarkably shallow (little more than 0.6 m) and rest on earlier burials. This has had the effect of causing a slight leaning in the tower as the underlying soil settled. The round-headed doorway faces north-east, towards the west door of the cathedral, and is set almost 8 m above ground.

Cathedral and churches

The cathedral is the largest church at Kilmacduagh and also the earliest—or, at least, the west end of the nave, with its flat-lintelled west doorway (now blocked), is. The original building is probably of 10th/11th-century date, but was extended to the east in the late 12th century. Considerable alterations took place in the 15th century, when a new chancel, sacristy, and transepts were added at the east end (the north transept may be slightly earlier than the rest). A new doorway was also inserted in the south wall of the nave, probably to replace the west door. The west gable was raised—note the corbels marking the base of the original gable, externally—and a new window was inserted into it. The carvings of the *Crucifixion* and *St Colmán* in the north transept are post-medieval folk art.

East of the cathedral, across the road, is Templemurry [*Teampull Muire*, 'St Mary's church'], a small rectangular church probably of early 13th-century date, with a 15th-century south doorway. North of the cathedral is the small church of St John the Baptist, originally a simple rectangular structure, perhaps of 12th-century date, to which a chancel was later added at the east end.

Glebe House

Further north is the 'Glebe House' (restored), a 13th-century residential hall house, probably the residence of the abbot or bishop. It was originally a two-storey rectangular building, entered at first-floor level via an external stair. The first-floor level was originally a single chamber—the hall, lit by twin-light windows. The ground floor below is lit only by narrow loops. At a later date a third storey was added to the western end, with a probable oriel window in the north-east wall.

Augustinian abbey

The small Augustinian abbey, known as *O'Heyne's church*, is located in the north-west angle of the site. The church consists of a nave and chancel of early/mid-13th-century date and is an important example of 'School of the West' Transitional (Romanesque/Gothic) architecture. This is seen most clearly in the chancel arch and the east window, which consists of a beautifully carved pair of narrow, round-headed lights, framed within bold roll mouldings with carved capitals. Externally the lights are framed within double recesses with flanking shafts and a pointed hood moulding overhead. Note also the carved pilasters at the corners of the east wall. The present north wall of the nave is a late medieval replacement, although incorporating the original 13th-century doorway near the west end. The remains of the original wall, which evidently collapsed, can be seen on the outside. On the south side of the nave is a later sacristy, part of the east range of the cloister, although it is not certain if the other sides of the cloister were ever built. Opposite this range, to the south-west, is a long, rectangular building with a doorway in the south wall and a 15th-century window overhead.

Knockma, Caltragh, Co. Galway Hilltop cairns

7 km south-west of Tuam off the R333 (Tuam–Headford). Entrance is unmarked but lies between the two formal entrances to present-day Castle Hackett House, opposite a small pointed-arched pedestrian gate. Disc. Ser. 46.

The limestone hills of Knockma, Knockcarrigeen, and Cave/Kildrum (between Belclare and Headford) dominate the north-eastern skyline of *Magh Seola*, the plains to the east of Lough Corrib. Enclosures have been identified on the latter two hills but they are not accessible. At 180 m, Knockma is the highest of the three and boasts the only potential Passage tombs in Galway. Four cairns have been identified. The largest is over 22 m in diameter and 5 m high and is known as *Carn Ceasarach*, the burial place of the mythological Cessair. According to the medieval mythological tract *Lebor Gabhála Érainn*, Cessair was a granddaughter of Noah and leader of the first settlers to Ireland, arriving at *Corca Duibne* (Dingle, Co. Kerry) forty days before the Flood. She died of a broken heart when her husband Fionntan absconded under the pressure of being the only surviving male among fifty women. The story of how he alone survived the Flood under the earth at *Tul Tuinne* (Tounthinna, Portroe, Co. Tipperary), and lived for a further five and a half thousand years, is told in conversation with a hawk from Achill, Co. Mayo, and underwrites his bona fides as the principal historical source for the *Lebor Gabhála Érainn*. The middle cairn is almost 30 m in diameter and is known as 'Finnbheara's Castle'. Finnbheara was king of the Connacht fairies and his name is a corruption of *Findbharr* meaning 'fair top', which describes not just the bright limestone flags of the hilltop, but also the cairns themselves which, viewed from the plain, seem to fairly radiate on a sunny day. This cairn has suffered considerable damage at the hands of one of the Hackett landlords who remodelled it into a cashel-like structure, in which to commune with the Fairy King. The third and fourth cairns are barely discernible among the thick hazel scrub at ground level and occur between Carn Ceasarach and Finnbheara's Castle, and at the far west end of the summit, respectively. These cairns are regarded as Passage tombs on account of their size, shape, and hilltop siting.

The long avenue to the path passes by the original Castle Hackett, a five-storey tower house and bawn, occupied until as late as 1703. This castle probably superseded a crannóg, still visible in nearby Lough Hackett, as the principal residence of the local royalty. The hilltop affords quite spectacular views over Magh Seola, later the barony of Clare, Lough Corrib, and across to Connemara. To the north, the peak of Croagh Patrick stands out. The plain is peppered with archaeological monuments of all periods with a particular concentration along the Mayo border, including the cist tumulus of Annaghkeen and the stone circles at **Nymphsfield**.

Knocknashee, Co. Sligo Hilltop enclosure and hut circles

25 km south-west of Sligo off the N17 (Sligo–Tobercurry), beside the village of Lavagh, from where it is signposted; best approached from the east side where the climb is steep but short. However, there is no public right of way up the hill, nor a path, and landowner permission is required, but well worth the effort. Disc. Ser. 25.

In shape and archaeological persona, Knocknashee is, in many ways, a miniature Knocknarea—which is visible through a gap in the mountains to the north. The summit is enclosed by an internal fosse and bank (along which the modern field wall is constructed). There are two rather disturbed but nonetheless impressive cairns on the summit. The first has an Ordnance Survey trigonometrical point erected in the centre and the other, to the north and slightly downhill, has been modified in places by the construction of wall shelters. Their size (about 20 m diameter) and location suggest that they might be Passage tombs.

Between them is a hut or enclosure circle, one of a half-dozen or so, mostly found below the summit to the east of the trigonometrical point. These are about 12 m in diameter and one of them has a definite eastern entrance. The views are excellent in all directions. To the west are the upper reaches of the Moy Valley (from which the tombs are most readily visible), while to the east are the lakes of the Owenroe river. In this direction also are some fine ringforts. Looking northwards from the second cairn one gets a bird's-eye view of Gilligan's World, a theme park in the centre of which is a very fine ring barrow. To the south-west, in the townland of Arnyara, is a 2 m high roadside mound, *Carn Uí hEadhra* ('O'Hara's Mound'). It is possibly a large bowl barrow, its top having been levelled off to serve as a ceremonial platform.

Nymphsfield, Co. Mayo Stone circles

35 km north-west of Galway, near Cong; off the R345, between Cong and Neale; signposted. Disc. Ser. 38.

The four stone circles at Nymphsfield form the core of an extended ritual complex occupying the area of Moytura, border country between Lough Mask and Lough Corrib and between Magh Seola (the plain of east Corrib) and north Connemara. Other monuments include cairns such as **Ballymacgibbon** and Eochy's Cairn and standing stones such as the one at the junction of the R345 and R334 at Neale. The more modern townland boundaries are wont to fragment these broader canvases and so, despite their close proximity to one another, two of the stone circles here are in the townland of Nymphsfield, while the other two are in Tonaleeaun and Glebe respectively. In plan they are arranged like the four points of a lozenge. The best preserved is in Glebe and is a National Monument (*signposted*). About 16 m in diameter, there remain 30 stones, some of them broken and others disturbed by tree-roots, the monument having been turned into a tree-ring (a landscape feature). There is a small, irregular mound in the interior. The other three circles are in adjacent fields to the south-east (Tonaleeaun), south, and south-west (Nymphsfield 1 and 2 respectively) and are on private land.

The two circles in Nymphsfield are of interest because they combine embankments. Nymphsfield 1 is actually the biggest, with a projected diameter of about 25 m–30 m. Although badly denuded, there seems to be a double circle and intervening bank. Many of the stones are broken or dislodged. Nymphsfield 2 is in a private garden and comprises about 22 stones (*c.*17.5 m diameter). Around the outside of the northern half of the circle is an embankment—a similar composition, therefore, to Grange stone circle at **Lough Gur**, Co. Limerick. At a mere 13 m or so in diameter, Tonaleeaun circle is the smallest. About two-thirds of the circle survives and it appears to be constructed around a slightly raised platform. Piles of small, loose stones in all the circles are of uncertain antiquity.

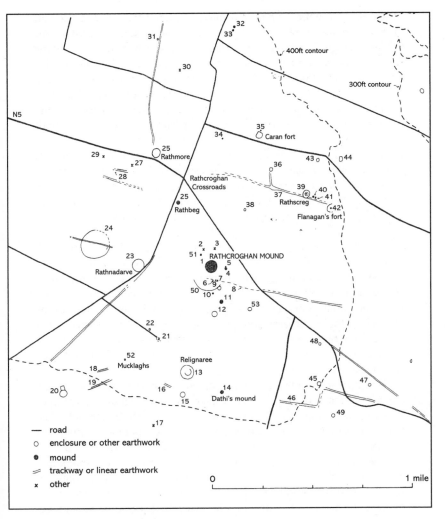

▲ **Fig. 71.** Rathcroghan: plan showing location of monuments (after Waddell)

Rathcroghan, Co. Roscommon Ritual and assembly landscape

25 km north of Roscommon town, off the N5 (Athlone–Castlebar); signposted. Disc. Ser. 33.

Known as an assembly site, hosting an *óenach* (ceremonial fair) on 1 August, Rathcroghan, or *Crúacháin*, is one of five or so great 'royal' sites of later prehistoric Ireland. It is indelibly associated with Queen Medb and the epic *Táin Bó Cuailgne* ('Cattle Raid of Cooley'). It was here that Medb and her consort Ailill quarrelled over their respective fortunes only to discover that Ailill owned a magnificent white bull, the sole equal of which was the Brown Bull of Cooley, in Co. Louth. A great cattle raid ensued and the Brown Bull, symbolizing the potency of Ulster, was defended single-handedly by the Ulster hero Cú Chulainn. Because the monuments are quite dispersed and hidden among a labyrinth of fields and bótharíns, Rathcroghan is one of the more complex of the 'royal' sites to visit and therefore a stop-over at the visitor centre in Tulsk (*4 km to the south-east at the junction of the N5 and N61*) is a must. Many of the monuments are on private land so enquire at the centre about accessibility.

Rathcroghan Mound, signposted on the N5 towards Ballaghadereen, is a good place to start. It is near the centre of the complex and commands views over the surrounding countryside. The mound (85 m in maximum diameter, 5 m high) appears to be at least partly artificial, as detailed geophysical prospection has revealed internal, buried structures. It was enclosed around its base by a fosse or palisade, approached from the south-east along a huge funnel-shaped avenue. This was in turn surrounded by a giant enclosure, *c.*400 m north–south by 360 m east–west, evidenced as a fosse. Two opposing ramps lead to the summit of the mound, where geophysics has recorded a host of successive structures, including a double circle of posts (30 m in diameter). Beyond the mound to the north-east and south-east respectively, geophysics has revealed double-ringed barrows. From the summit one can just about make out Rathbeg and beyond it Rathmore to the north-west, and Rathnadarve to the west.

The main concentration of monuments is on the south side of the N5, and to reach them you have to take the first road on the left after Rathcroghan Mound. Rathmore, however, is on the north side, just beyond this first left. It comprises a huge, flat-topped mound (*c.*60 m in diameter, 6 m high), surrounded by a 5 m wide fosse traversed by two causeways, one of which slopes to the summit through a corresponding gap in the bank around the top. A hundred metres or so down the road on the left side is Rathbeg, a possible bivallate ring barrow *c.*45 m in diameter. It has a pert central mound, which is likely to be a modified, natural rise. Further along on the right-hand side is Rathnadarve [possibly *Rath na dTarbh*—'fort of the bulls'], an unclassified enclosure *c.*85 m in diameter defined by a large bank (5 m wide and 2 m high) and external fosse and rather smaller outer, counterscarp bank. It is low-lying and quite wet. To the west of this, but only visible from the air, is a huge enclosure (no. 24 after Waddell 1983) *c.*200 m in diameter.

The next left-hand turn is a cul-de-sac, at the end of which is Oweynagat, Relignaree, and access to the Mucklaghs. Oweynagat or *Úaim Chruachan* ('the cave of Cruachu') is the traditional gateway to the Underworld of Irish mythology, from which a veritable bestiary of dark entities emerges at the festival of Samhain, and from which Mór-Ríoghain, the war goddess (also known as Anu of the *Túatha Dé*

Danann), emerged. It is a long, natural fissure in the limestone bedrock, accessed through a now-truncated souterrain. One of the lintel stones of the souterrain bears an intriguing ogam inscription *VRAICCI MAQI MEDVVI* ('of Fraich, son of Medb'). Another bears the inscription *QUREGASMA*. A short distance back along the road, on the left-hand side, is a fine ring barrow.

Relignaree, the Cemetery of the Kings, is about the same distance beyond the end of the cul-de-sac. It is a 100 m diameter univallate enclosure with a small arc of external fosse surviving on the north side only. In the centre is a smaller, more faint enclosure *c*.48 m in diameter. It is sufficiently different from the large outer bank for some to suggest that it may be an earlier monument. There are traces here of at least three rectangular houses and a souterrain in the south-western quadrant. 240 m south-east of Relignaree is Dathi's Mound. Named after the last pagan king of Ireland, who died in AD 429, it comprises a scarped natural mound surrounded by a fosse and external bank *c*.38 m in diameter. In the middle is a red sandstone pillar. Though the exact nature of the monument remains elusive, excavations in 1981 demonstrated it to have been built in the last few centuries BC/AD.

The Mucklaghs are more difficult of access but are well worth a visit. They are two fields south of Oweynagat and are probably best approached through the yard opposite the aforementioned barrow. They comprise two massive, arcuate embankments, 100 m and 200 m long respectively and sloping downhill. The shorter, northern set of banks are *c*.3 m high and 5 m wide at base. The southern Mucklaghs are *c*.6 m apart and appear to double up towards the west end, where they approach a pool known as Caldra Pool. Nearby, to the south-west, is the ruined ringfort of Cashelmanannan, *c*.58 m in diameter.

Carnfree, to the south of Tulsk, is doubtless closely connected to the Rathcroghan complex and comprises a dense concentration of interesting but equally enigmatic monuments including, at the roadside, the conjoined barrow and ringfort of Lismurtagh.

Rathra, Co. Roscommon Multivallate enclosure

3.2 km south-east of Castlerea, on the north-western flank of Mewlaghadooey Hill. Access via the link road from Castlerea to Ballintober, by taking a narrow, tertiary road uphill from the bad S-bend, c.4 km from the edge of the town. Behind the water tower at the top of the hill is a large mound and Rathra is approached by taking the next turn on the left. Not signposted. Disc. Ser. 40 (upper left-hand corner). Private land.

Rathra is arguably the most spectacular earthwork in the west of Ireland, and, though difficult to find, is well worth a visit. Four massive sets of banks and ditches, *c*.145 m in diameter, surround a comparatively small internal space dominated by a tall mound, slightly off-centre. The top of the mound is concave and surrounded by a bank. The site is virtually without parallel, but Joe Fenwick has suggested general comparisons with other multivallate sites such as Tlachtga (**Hill of Ward**), Co. Meath. A mere stone's throw from Rathcroghan, Fenwick argues that Rathra ought to be considered an outlier to that complex. Rathra surrenders the summit of Mewlaghadooey Hill to a fine mound, possibly containing a Passage tomb, and this may reveal a relative chronology. Close-set multi-vallation, so well exemplified at Rathra, continues from the Iron Age well into the early medieval period, so the date and true function of this monument remain a mystery. There are fine views from Rathra over Castlerea and north-west Roscommon.

Rindown, Co. Roscommon Deserted medieval town

15 km north of Athlone, off N61 (Athlone–Roscommon); take minor road east; signposted. Disc. Ser. 47.

Rindown, although sadly neglected, is a striking example of a deserted medieval town. Located on a strategically important peninsula in Lough Ree on the Shannon, it was first fortified by the English in 1227, when Geoffrey de Marisco built a castle there, as part of the major campaign to take control of Connacht. However, there was almost certainly an earlier fortification here—the name [*Rinn Dúin*, 'the promontory of the fort'] suggests it was probably a promontory fort. An early medieval cross-slab found in a graveyard here also suggests that there was an earlier church site. The castle was probably destroyed by Feidhlimidh Ó Conchobhair in 1232, but by 1251 the peninsula was reoccupied by the English and a town had been established beside the castle. This was fortified on the landward side by a stone wall across the width of the peninsula. Very little is known about the size or population of the town, but it was large enough to include a parish church and a hospital of the *Fratres Cruciferi*. Considerable work was carried out on the castle in the late 1270s, but by 1341 it was reported as 'lost' to the Anglo-Irish parliament. With the loss of the castle, which was permanent by the late 14th century, the town clearly would have been abandoned and was never reoccupied.

Hospital of St John the Baptist

Approaching Rindown from the landward side, the first monument met with is the Hospital of St John the Baptist, just outside the town wall on the west. This religious house may be the earliest establishment at Rindown, as it is said to have been founded under the patronage of King John (d. 1216) for a religious order known as the *Fratres Cruciferi*. It continued to function, despite the desertion of the town in the later Middle Ages, until suppressed *c.*1569. All that survives of the hospital is a graveyard with a small rectangular building, which has been heavily modified but retains some traces of 13th-century fabric. It may be a

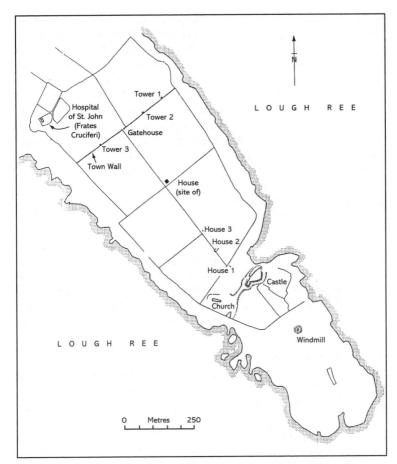

▲ **Fig. 72.** Rindown: outline map showing medieval features (after Bradley)

church, but its orientation (almost due north–south) is unusual, and it may in fact be part of the cloisters that would have been attached to the church. A fragment of an early medieval cross-slab was found in the graveyard, suggesting that the hospital was built on the site of an early medieval church.

Town

South-east of this is the town wall, a straight wall running across the width of the peninsula, cutting it off on the landward side. It was probably built shortly after a murage grant to the town in 1251. The wall is c.430 m long, survives up to 4 m high and 1.2 m thick, and has three rectangular towers for added defence. In the centre is a rectangular gatehouse, probably of two or three storeys originally, with traces of a portcullis slot on the west face of the entrance passage, 2.2 m above ground. Within the wall a long, straight field boundary runs south-eastwards from the gatehouse, along the central axis of the peninsula, and marks the line of the main street of the town. House sites—presumably medieval—can barely be made out at a number of points on the east side of this line. At its end the peninsula narrows further, with a slight inlet on the west and a more pronounced cove on the east, which clearly functioned as the harbour of the medieval town. Overlooking this are the heavily overgrown ruins of the castle, and on lower ground to the south stand the ruins of the parish church. This is a relatively simple, 13th-century nave-and-chancel structure. The chancel is clearly a later addition to the nave, but the details of the east window, consisting of two lancets, indicate that it is not later than the 13th century.

Castle

The castle was cut off from the remainder of the peninsula by a broad fosse running between the two inlets. Traces of this fosse are still vis-ible—it would have been water filled originally and also extended right around the castle. The castle was first erected by the English governor, Geoffrey de Marisco, *c.*1227, probably on the site of an earlier Irish

▼ **Fig. 73.** Rindown: plan of castle (after Bradley)

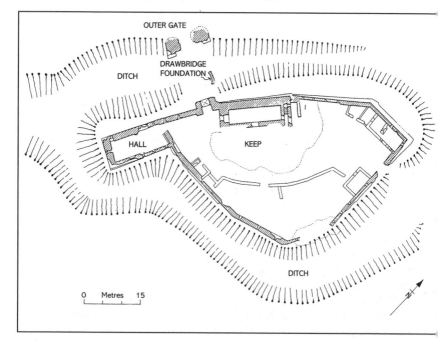

fortification. Further work is documented in the 1230s and especially in the late 1270s, in both cases following devastating attacks by the Uí Conchobhair. In 1299–1302 the building of a new hall is recorded. The present remains consist of an irregular polygonal enclosure, surrounded by a curtain wall without any mural towers. On the west side is a rectangular, two-storey hall keep, divided into two vaulted chambers at ground level and with the hall at first floor. Adjoining this on the south is the gatehouse. Only a simple arched gateway survives, but originally the gatehouse was a substantial, three-storey building with outer drawbridge and barbican—traces of which survive outside the fosse. The gate itself was defended by a portcullis (for which the slot survives) and a murder hole above.

The curtain wall originally had arrow loops for defence, but these were subsequently blocked, the walls raised in height, and wooden hoardings added (indicated by surviving beam-holes near the tops of the walls). A rectangular building was subsequently added, projecting from the south-west side of the castle. This may be the hall built in 1299–1302, although there are possible remains of another hall on the north-east. Perhaps the most remarkable feature of Rindown Castle is how poorly defended it is, despite its strategic importance. The lack of flanking towers must have greatly restricted the garrison's ability to defend it, while the hall projecting on the south-west must have been almost impossible to defend. To the east of the castle is a stone windmill tower, surrounded by undergrowth; this is probably post-medieval, but almost certainly occupies the site of a mill whose construction is documented in 1273.

Roscommon, Co. Roscommon   Medieval town

At junction of N61 and N63, 30 km north-west of Athlone. Disc. Ser. 40.

Roscommon [*Ros Comáin*, 'Commán's wood'] was originally a monastery founded by St Commán in the 6th century. It was one of the major church sites associated with the Uí Conchobhair kings of Connacht, becoming especially prominent in the 11th and 12th centuries. In 1123 Toirdhealbhach Ó Conchobhair presented the monastery with a relic of the True Cross, enshrined in the reliquary now known as the 'Cross of Cong' (*on display in the National Museum of Ireland*). Roscommon briefly became the seat of a bishopric in the mid-12th century, and adopted the Augustinian rule in the 1140s. It suffered a series of English raids in the mid-13th century but in between, in 1253, a Dominican priory was founded by Feidhlimidh Ó Conchobhair, king of Connacht. In 1269 the English governor of Ireland, Robert d'Ufford, began to build a castle on the lands of the monastery at Roscommon, in an attempt to control the Uí Conchobhair and establish a foothold in Connacht. The castle was destroyed by the Uí Conchobhair and rebuilt on several occasions in the following ten years, but was finally rebuilt in 1278 as the major royal castle in Connacht.

A town was also established alongside the castle, probably in 1278. It has the distinction of being probably the last town founded by the English in Ireland in the Middle Ages, and was also one of the shortest-lived. Already by 1281 the town had been burned and the town wall demolished by the Irish, and it had probably ceased to exist by c.1320. Even the castle was captured by the Uí Conchobhair in 1315 and again c.1340. Although it was recovered by 1344, the castle had been permanently lost to English control before the end of the 14th century. The town was probably laid out somewhere along the long linear axis of Abbey St./ Castle St., but its present layout is essentially post-medieval and no trace survives of its medieval predecessor. No trace of the early monastic site or the later Augustinian abbey is visible today, apart from a number of 12th–15th-century architectural fragments built into the tower at the west end of the Church of Ireland parish church (*on Church St.*). All that is visible of medieval Roscommon is the castle and the Dominican priory.

Castle

The castle is one of the finest examples in Ireland of a nearly symmetrical keepless castle, closely related to those being built at the same date in Wales by Edward I—particularly Harlech (*access via small lane off Castle St., c.400 m north of The Square; signposted, but easy to miss!*) Although first begun in 1269, its form is due mainly to the final rebuilding of 1278. There were few, if any, changes over the following three centuries, as the castle was mainly in Irish hands. After 1578 the castle was occupied by Sir Nicholas Malby, English governor of Connacht, and substantially remodelled. It was partly demolished in the mid-17th century, reflected in the massive blocks of masonry that still lie around, intact but prone, especially on the south side. Situated on low-lying ground beside a former lake, the castle consists of a rectangular enclosure, with projecting D-shaped towers at the angles and a large gatehouse in the centre of the east side. Originally there was a moat outside the curtain wall and, probably, further earthen defences outside this again. Unusually, there is also a projecting rectangular postern gate placed off-centre on the west side, with an external drawbridge pit. Access to the interior of the castle is now through this postern, but the original entrance was through the gatehouse on the opposite (east) side.

This gatehouse was heavily modified by Malby in the late 16th century, when most of the original windows were replaced by larger mullioned windows. Nevertheless, its main features can still be made out. It was at least three storeys high, the ground floor consisting of an entrance passage flanked by two large towers with projecting half-round fronts. At first- and second-storey level the entire gatehouse (including the area over the entrance) was available as residential accommodation. Although the original internal arrangements are now lost, it is clear that these floors provided the finest suites of chambers in the castle. Since Roscommon was a royal castle (rather than the residence of a baron or knight), these chambers were probably intended for the constable (keeper) of the castle. Further good accommodation was provided by the four angle towers, which have first-floor chambers with fireplaces and garderobes built into the angle between tower and curtain wall. No trace remains of the buildings that would have occupied the internal courtyard of the castle, including the great hall, which was probably on the west side. An enclosure visible on the north side of the castle, externally, may be a garden associated with the late 16th-century reoccupation of the castle.

▼ **Fig. 74.** Roscommon: plan of Dominican priory (OPW)

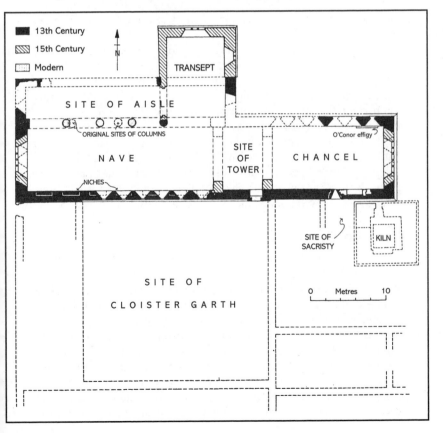

Dominican priory

The Dominican priory is now isolated *c.*300 m south of the town—although it may well have been within, or on the edge of, the medieval town (*access via a small lane off south side of N63 as it loops around south side of town*). A papal indulgence was granted to raise funds for the repair of the priory in 1445, and it seems to have been dissolved by 1573. Only the church (consecrated in 1257) survives—the cloisters to the south have almost completely disappeared. The church was originally a typical long, rectangular nave-and-choir building, but it probably had a north aisle from the beginning. A north transept was added in the 15th century and a tower (now vanished) was erected between nave and choir, probably also in the 15th century. A series of original lancet windows survive in the south wall of the nave and in the fragmentary north wall of the choir, but otherwise few 13th-century features survive. The original triple lancets in the east and west walls were replaced in the 15th century by large traceried windows that have largely disappeared, apart from their arched openings and hood mouldings with crockets and flanking pinnacles. This is particularly regrettable as the surviving fragments of tracery point to exceptional quality of work. Perhaps the most interesting feature of the priory is the fine effigy of *c.*1300, set in a tomb niche in the north-east angle of the choir, and depicting a male in a long, loose robe, holding a sceptre with fleur-de-lis head. It is traditionally said to represent the founder, Feidhlimidh Ó Conchobhair, who was buried there in 1265. Fronting the effigy are parts of a 15th-century tomb chest that is also of interest because of the armoured figures, possibly representing gallowglass, taking the place of weepers on the tomb front. The front consists of two separate parts, each with four figures set within ogee-headed niches. The two parts differ slightly in detail (note the angels over the niches on the left-hand side), but they are probably from the same tomb chest, originally. Another unusual feature is the series of seven pointed niches in the south wall of the nave.

Ross, Co. Galway Friary

2 km north-west of Headford (on N84 north of Galway). Take minor road to west in Headford and turn north after 1 km. Disc. Ser. 45.

Ross, or Ross Errily [probably from *Ros riaghla,* 'wood of the religious order'] is the largest and best-preserved medieval Franciscan friary in Ireland. Its foundation date is uncertain—suggestions range from as early as 1351 to as late as 1498—but it was certainly in existence by 1469 and a date around the middle of the 15th century seems most likely. The visible architecture seems to be mainly of late 15th-/early 16th-century date, but such a large complex was obviously not built in a single campaign, and a detailed analysis of the phases of building is still badly needed. The friary was officially dissolved *c.*1540 and granted to the earl of Clanricarde in 1562, but it continued to function more or less normally until *c.*1580, and intermittently thereafter until the mid-17th century. After that it was used mainly for burial and one of the features of the friary is the wealth of late 17th- and 18th-century memorial slabs.

The church consists of a nave and choir of roughly equal size, divided by a tower, with an aisle and large double transept on the south side of the nave. A later Lady Chapel projects from the east end of the transept, while on the south side of the nave is a 17th-century addition, the Jennings chantry chapel. It contains a variety of well-preserved windows with switchline tracery, the largest being in the east wall of the choir and the south gables of the transept. The nave is entered through a strangely off-centre—but apparently original—west doorway. The attractive tower has a rood loft over the arched ground-level opening, with two storeys above this, topped by typical late medieval stepped battlements. The choir originally had a gallery over the west end, and adjoining the east end, on the north side, is a small sacristy with a larger, three-storey building to the east. This larger building is slightly later in date and apparently provided a larger sacristy at ground level, with residential accommodation, perhaps for the guardian (equivalent of the abbot or prior), on the upper levels.

The extensive claustral buildings are on the north side of the church and unusually, are based around two courtyards rather than one. The cloisters proper lie immediately north of the church, based around a cloister garth that is very small, relative to the size of the overall complex. On each side of the garth are ambulatories that, typically for late medieval friaries, are integral parts of the surrounding building ranges, the ranges carrying over them at first-floor level, and resting on the cloister arcades. The arcades are formed of pointed arches on relatively simple pillars, in groups of five, but the east arcade is quite different, with solid walling between the arches. One arch in the east arcade is unusually small, presumably because of a miscalculation of distance on the part of the masons.

To the north of the cloister is a second courtyard of roughly similar size, again surrounded on all sides by building ranges, though without ambulatories or arcades. The main conventual buildings seem to be arranged around this northern court, rather than the cloister proper. On the east side is the refectory, with reader's niche (for reading devotional literature as the friars ate) in the north-east corner. Above this, at first-floor level, is the dormitory. A second dormitory is located on the north side of the courtyard, also at first-floor level, with a latrine building in the north-eastern angle, between the two dormitories. The ground-floor chamber of the north block has an oven at the west end, and may have been a bakery. Adjoining it, at the north-west angle of the complex, is the large kitchen, with a fireplace in the east wall and a very unusual stone fish- or water-tank in the north-east angle. Immediately north of the kitchen are the ruins of the friary mill, powered by a stream which ran along the east and north sides of the friary, and also serviced the latrine at the north-east angle, before entering the Black river just north of the friary.

Rosserk, Co. Mayo Friary

7 km north of Ballina. Take R314, then minor road to east, 3 km north of Ballina; turn east again after 4 km (signposted). Disc. Ser. 24.

Rosserk is a Franciscan friary, beautifully located on the estuary of the river Moy. Unlike the nearby friary at Moyne (*4 km to the north*) or that at **Ross Errilly**, it belonged not to the main order of Franciscan friars, but to the Franciscan Third Order. The Third Order was originally a system of confraternities for lay people that became increasingly clericalized in the later Middle Ages. It was very popular in late medieval Ireland, particularly in the non-Anglicized areas of the west and north. Rosserk is the only complete Third Order friary in Ireland, and its background is reflected in its relatively small size and simple layout. It was founded before 1441 (but probably not long before this) and continued to function until burned by the English in 1590. There are traditions of a much earlier monastic foundation here, associated with the little-known Searc, who gave her name to the site [*Ros Serce*, 'Searc's wood'], but no evidence of such a foundation is visible.

The buildings are mainly of mid-15th-century date, and consist of the usual simple rectangular church, with a central tower, a transept on the south, and a small cloister and associated buildings on the north. The choir is lit by a four-light east window with elaborate tracery, and has a sedilia and piscina in the south wall. The piscina is set within a niche with twin pointed arches, one of which has a pair of angels in the spandrels, while one of the jambs has a unique carving of a round tower—possibly that at nearby **Killala**. The crossing tower is a later addition and is typically slender, although carried on unusually wide arches. The transept has two chapels in the east wall, separated by a small mural chamber for storage of altar vessels and equipment. The southern chapel is lit by a two-light window with quatrefoil above—a much simpler version of the east window of the choir. The nave is relatively plain, apart from the west doorway, decorated with flanking pinnacles and crockets. A doorway just west of the tower leads to the small cloister garth on the north side.

The claustral buildings are very simple, consisting of three almost separate two-storeyed, gabled buildings—without ambulatories—on the west, north, and east sides of the garth. Each range contains three plain vaulted chambers at ground level and there is also a mural stair to the upper floor in each range. The ground-floor chambers cannot be identified apart from the sacristy, immediately north of the choir in the east range, and the next room to the north, which may have been the chapter house. At first-floor level, both east and west ranges consist of a single long chamber with a garderobe at the north end, both of which may have been dormitories. The north range is divided into a kitchen (to the west) and refectory, divided by a double fireplace.

St MacDara's Island, Co. Galway Island hermitage

60 km west of Galway; accessible only by boat, which may be hired from Mace (An Más), 4 km west of Carna, off R340 coastal road. Disc. Ser. 44.

This small island, 2.5 km off the west coast of Co. Galway, was the location of a hermitage associated with Sionnach Mac Dara, a little known 6th-century saint. The main visible remnant of this foundation is a small stone church that is one of the most interesting of all early Irish churches, mainly because of its stone roof. The church displays all the classic features of the early Irish church—small size and simple rectangular plan, the use of large stone slabs in the masonry, the flat-lintelled west doorway, and the antae on the gable walls. In addition, it has a high-pitched roof of corbelled stones, restored in the 1970s. The other important feature of the church is the continuation of the antae up to the apex of the gable, where they were surmounted by carved gable finials. It is suggested that the antae recall the appearance of elbow crucks in a timber-built church, with the finials mimicking the crossing of the crucks or roof beams.

Sligo, Co. Sligo Medieval town

138 km north of Galway, on N4, N15/16 routes. Disc. Ser. 16.

Sligo [*Sligeach*, 'shelly'] is an Anglo-Irish town, founded in the mid-13th century at an important fording point on the Garvoge river. The only visible trace of medieval Sligo, however, is the Dominican priory, founded in 1253 by Maurice FitzGerald, who had built a castle at Sligo in 1245, and was in the process of founding a town there. Castle and town changed hands on several occasions subsequently, being controlled by the de Burgh earls of Ulster in the early 14th century, by the local Irish dynasty, Ó Conchobhair *Sligeach*, from the mid-14th to later 15th century, and by the Ó Domhnaill of Tír Conaill in the later 15th and most of the 16th century. The town apparently continued to function throughout this period, despite repeated attacks and burnings, but its present form is largely of 18th/19th-century origin. Even the castle (destroyed in the late 16th century) has completely disappeared from the townscape.

The Dominican priory, located on the south bank of the Garvoge, at the north-eastern corner of the medieval town, continued to function until the 1580s and was reoccupied by Dominicans for a period in the 17th century. It was seriously damaged by fire in 1414, and substantially

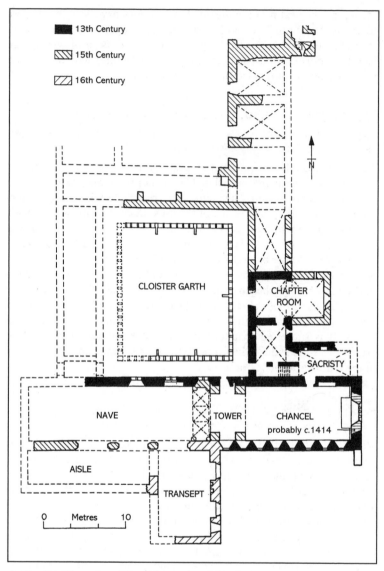

13th Century
15th Century
16th Century

CLOISTER GARTH

CHAPTER ROOM

SACRISTY

NAVE

TOWER

CHANCEL
probably c.1414

AISLE

TRANSEPT

N

0 Metres 10

▲ **Fig. 75.** Sligo: plan of Dominican priory (after Cochrane)

rebuilt in the years after 1416. However, much original 13th-century work survives, especially in the choir, with its characteristic row of eight closely spaced lancet windows in the south wall. The lancets in the east end were replaced in the early 15th century with a single window with reticulated tracery. Below this window is the only decorated medieval high altar to survive in any Irish monastic church; it is probably late 15th century, although restored in the 19th century. The altar is carved at the front with nine ogee-headed panels and foliage above. Around the upper edge is a Lombardic inscription recording the name of the donor, *JOHAN* (John), but unfortunately the surname is missing. There is also a fine monument of O'Conor Sligo, dated 1623, in the south wall.

The only 13th-century fabric in the nave is the north wall, with three pairs of lancets; the remainder is 15th century. Built into a recess on this wall is an altar tomb set within a high pointed canopy with Flamboyant tracery (much of it now missing). The tomb front is divided into nine cusped niches, each containing a figure; the central niche contains a *Crucifixion*, flanked by the Blessed Virgin and St John. On the upper border of the front an inscription records the names of those commemorated, Cormac Ó Criain and his wife Johanna Ennis (or Magennis), and the date, 1506. A later heraldic stone within the recess also bears the Ó Criain arms, and is dated 1616. In the south wall is an arcade of large pointed arches, leading to the remains of a south aisle and transept that were added in the late 15th/16th centuries. In the east wall of the transept are two recessed windows, within which would have stood altars. Between the windows are a piscina and aumbry. At the east end of the nave is a partially reconstructed rood screen and gallery that separated the laity, in the nave, from the choir (reserved for the friars). It was originally three bays wide and one bay deep, the gallery supported on octagonal pillars and three-sided responds that are still in place on the north and south walls. The rood screen was inserted, probably in the early 15th century, but before the erection of the crossing tower. This slender tower is typical of late medieval Irish friaries, but in this case not particularly tall.

A doorway under the tower led to the cloister, on the north side of the church, which had an attractive integrated arcade of pointed arches supported by well-carved pillars, of late 15th-century date. Most of the claustral buildings are also 15th century, but on the north-east side of the church the vaulted sacristy, vestry, and chapter house are largely original 13th-century fabric. The chapter house was extended to the east in the 15th century, with the line of the original east wall being carried by a stone arch in the vault. The east range is continued beyond the line of the north range, and ends in a small turret with spiral stairs, leading to the first floor that would have been the friars' dormitory. In the north range, at first-floor level, was the refectory—identified by the fine reader's pulpit in the south wall, from which devotional literature was read to the friars as they ate.

Turoe, Co. Galway La Tène-decorated stone.

Off the R350 6.5 km north of Loughrea in east Galway. Disc. Ser. 46.

The Turoe stone is undoubtedly one of the finest examples of La Tène sculpture anywhere in the Celtic world. A laterally flattened, dome-shaped, granite pillar, 1.7 m tall, the upper half is covered with an intricate curvilinear design in relief, bordered around the bottom with a comparatively tame step pattern. Duignan ascertained that this is a quadripartite composition, consisting of two D-shaped and two triangular fields, the latter being joined across the top of the stone by a wavy line. The pattern of trumpet curves, comma leaves, and triskeles (and one possible bird head) is mature Insular style, comparable with the ornament on British mirrors of the 1st century BC/AD. Comparisons with simply decorated monoliths in Brittany, notably one in Kermaria, Finistère, are unconvincing. Removed a few kilometres from its original location, beside a hill near the Rath of Feerwore, it now stands in the

▼ **Fig. 76.** Turoe: La Tène-style decorated stone (chalked up for drawing) (photo: Dept. of Archaeology, NUI, Galway)

grounds of Turoe House, Bullaun, to the north of Loughrea. Waddell has speculated that it and three small standing stones may once have stood in a cultic formation (see **Killycluggan**, Co. Cavan) on top of the hill at Feerwore. Hoards from nearby Attymon (to the north) and Somerset (south of Ballinasloe) and burials at Grannagh and Oranbeg attest to a strong and culturally influential La Tène presence in this part of Connacht and are undoubtedly connected in some way to the Turoe stone. Excavation of the Rath of Feerwore in 1938 produced, among other things, a socketed iron axe of Iron Age date in a pre-enclosure context, raising the possibility that some activity here may also relate to the decorated stone. A Bronze Age cist from the same site also pre-dates the rath.

East: Dublin, Kildare, Laois, Louth, Meath, Westmeath, Wicklow

Introduction

This region comprises a sizeable portion of Ireland's Central Plain and the flat, benign coasts of counties Dublin, Meath, and Louth. Fertile and accessible, it is one of the agricultural heartlands of Ireland and was identified as such from earliest times. The principal drainage arteries are the Boyne, Blackwater, and Liffey, but the region is bounded on the west by the Shannon and on the south by the upper reaches of the Barrow and Nore. It is dotted by fluvio-glacial features, many of which are today exploited for gravels and sands. Grey-brown podzolics and acidic brown earths predominate, with extensive bogland occurring towards the centre and west. Excavations at Lough Boora, near Birr, Co. Offaly, indicate that the central lowlands were home to hunter-gatherer communities from around 7000 BC. Sporadic finds of later Mesolithic lithics and excavated camp sites such as at Moynagh Lough, near Nobber, Co. Meath, and on Dalkey Island off the Dublin coast demonstrate continuous exploitation of mainly aquatic resources throughout the 5th and 4th millennia BC. The earliest farmers are evidenced most clearly by their tombs—mainly Passage tombs and Portal tombs. The handful of Court tombs along the northern edge of the area is, in reality, the southern edge of their distribution, while Linkardstown-type Single Burials are found across the southern part of the area. Settlement sites are, however, found with increasing frequency and suggest that the most intensely populated districts in early prehistory were across northern Co. Meath and Co. Louth. Concentrations of stone axes at fording points, such as at Castlereban, Co. Kildare, however, demonstrate increasing mobility and down-the-line trade across this area. The broader and more even distribution of henge monuments and various types of barrows and standing stones suggests general and largely spontaneous population and territorial expansion around the close of the 2nd millennium BC. The small cluster of Wedge tombs in the Dublin/Wicklow mountains may be specifically related to mineral deposits and herald the emergence of metallurgists.

The damp and boggy midlands may have been a taxing place to live in more ways than one. Control of the few passable routes across these wetlands may lie behind the impressive material wealth testified by the

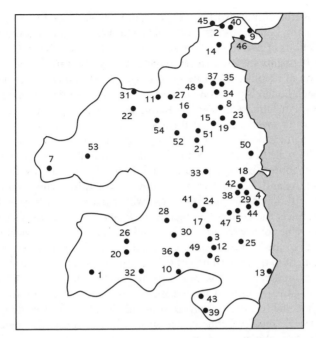

▲ Map 5

Key:

1. Aghaboe, Co. Laois
2. Aghnaskeagh, Co. Louth
3. Athgreany (Piper's Stones), Co. Wicklow
4. Ballybrack, Co. Dublin
5. Ballyedmonduff, Co. Dublin
6. Baltinglass Hill, Co. Wicklow
7. Bealin, Co. Westmeath
8. Boyne Valley, Co. Meath
9. Carlingford, Co. Louth
10. Castledermot, Co. Kildare
11. Castlekeeran, Co. Meath
12. Castleruddery, Co. Wicklow
13. Castletimon, Co. Wicklow
14. Cloughnafarmore, Co. Louth
15. Danestown, Co. Meath
16. Donaghmore, Co. Meath
17. Donard Upper, Co. Wicklow
18. Dublin, Co. Dublin
19. Duleek, Co. Meath
20. Dunamase, Co. Laois
21. Dunsany, Co. Meath
22. Fore, Co. Westmeath
23. Fourknocks, Co. Meath
24. Furness, Co. Kildare
25. Glendalough, Co. Wicklow
26. Greatheath, Co. Laois
27. Kells, Co. Meath

28. Kildare, Co. Kildare
29. Kiltiernan, Co. Dublin
30. Knockaulin, Co Kildare
31. Loughcrew, Co. Meath
32. Manger, Co. Laois
33. Maynooth, Co. Kildare
34. Mellifont, Co. Louth
35. Monasterboice, Co. Louth
36. Moone, Co. Kildare
37. Mount Oriel, Co. Louth
38. Mountpelier Hill, Co. Dublin
39. Moylisha, Co. Wicklow
40. Proleek, Co. Louth
41. Punchestown, Co. Kildare
42. Rathfarnham, Co. Dublin
43. Rathgall, Co. Wicklow
44. Rathmichael, Co. Dublin
45. Roche, Co. Louth
46. Rockmarshall, Co. Louth
47. Seefin, Co. Wicklow
48. Slieve Breagh, Co. Meath
49. Spinan's Hill/Brusselstown, Co. Wicklow
50. Swords, Co. Dublin
51. Tara, Co. Meath
52. Trim, Co. Meath
53. Uisneach, Co. Westmeath
54. Hill of Ward, Co. Meath

great hoards of metalwork retrieved from midland bogs. Excavations at Ballinderry Lough, just east of Moate, Co. Westmeath, uncovered the foundations of two sizeable houses alongside the Eiscir Riada. Comparable settlements are fewer closer to the east coast, but this is likely to be a function of visibility. The Late Bronze Age (*c.*900–700 BC) settlement at Moynagh Lough is probably connected to a hilltop settlement excavated by Newman 2 km to the south at Raffin. Stray metalwork and a veritable labyrinth of *toghers* or wooden trackways indicate continuity of settlement in the midlands into the Iron Age, though possibly on a less intensive scale than at the beginning of the 1st millennium BC. Further east are monuments on a grander scale. Three of the great 'royal' sites of ancient Ireland—**Tara, Uisneach**, and **Knockaulin** (Dún Ailinne)— occur in this region, each associated with ritual and settlement landscapes. Inlets and estuaries along the Meath and Dublin coasts facilitated considerable commerce with Roman and sub-Roman Britain during the first half of the 1st millennium AD and this established an international component in the eastern half of this region that was to endure well into the next millennium. The northern half of the region fell under the control of the Uí Néill during the 5th and 6th centuries AD and the story of the next few centuries is one of consolidation. Some of Ireland's most famous early medieval church sites, such as **Kells, Duleek, Glendalough**, and **Monasterboice**, occur here, benefiting not just from what nature had to offer in the way of natural resources but also from competing political patronages. Royal patronage manifests itself at these sites in the surviving architecture and sculpture, as well as other treasures such as the Book of Kells. The association of some of the churches with early founders such as Secundinus (Dunshaughlin, Co. Meath), Iserninus (Kilcullen, Co. Kildare), and Brigid (**Kildare**) confirms the pivotal role of the region in the development of the Christian church in Ireland.

For most of the historic period this region was divided in two, politically, between the over-kingdoms of the Uí Néill in the north and the Laigin to the south. The Uí Néill kingdom was much the more important and largely dominated Leinster to the south. Indeed, for most of the 9th and 10th centuries its kings, symbolically based at **Tara**, were the first effective high-kings of Ireland. The Uí Néill kingdom was divided into Mide in the west (roughly corresponding to modern Co. Westmeath) and Brega in the east (roughly modern Co. Meath). Early historical sources suggest that Mide—later Anglicized as Meath—was originally in the hands of the Laigin, who were driven out by the Uí Néill in the late 5th/early 6th centuries. Thereafter a reasonably stable frontier developed, corresponding roughly to the river Liffey and, further west, the boundary between modern Cos. Meath/Westmeath and Kildare. The Laigin lands, in turn, were in practice often divided between two major dynasties. The Uí Dúnlainge, based on the plains of the Liffey basin with their main centre at Naas, controlled most of modern Cos. Kildare,

Dublin, Wicklow, and Laois, while to the south the Uí Cheinnselaig controlled Cos. Wexford/Carlow. Among the few alien, subject peoples included in the Laigin hegemony were the Loígis, in the area of modern Co. Laois, who were often seen as the front line of defence against Munster aggression. They were dependent on the Uí Dúnlainge but probably fell under the dominance of the resurgent Uí Cheinnselaig in the 12th century.

This region was deeply affected by Viking activity, and this was especially true of the east coast which, throughout the early Middle Ages, was relatively peripheral, with the major power centres being inland. In the aftermath of the Viking raids the coast became the gateway to Ireland and the growth of **Dublin**, in particular, was to result in a major shift in the balance of power. After the early 11th century the power of the Uí Néill over-kings collapsed dramatically, mainly because their power centres were too far removed from Dublin and the coast. The economic and political dominance of the east coast—still a feature of modern Ireland—has its origins in the Viking period. It was cemented, however, by the English conquest. From the arrival of Henry II in 1171, Dublin has been the unquestioned capital of Ireland and this region was among those colonized earliest and most comprehensively by the English. Politically, the old divisions were initially maintained, because Henry II wanted to counter the power of Strongbow, who had effectively taken control of the Laigin kingdom. While Strongbow was confirmed in his new lordship of Leinster (including Cos. Kildare, Laois, and Wicklow but excluding Co. Dublin, which was kept in royal hands), a trusted baron, Hugh de Lacy, was given the old Uí Néill kingdom of Mide. This became the new lordship of Meath (essentially Cos. Meath and Westmeath) with its centre at **Trim**. Louth, which never formed part of Mide, was divided at the end of the 1180s between two lesser baronial families, de Verdon and Pipard—although English colonization had probably already begun in the area before this.

The two huge lordships of Leinster and Meath should have formed the main power blocs of the English colony, but a remarkable failure to produce male heirs led to them being broken up into smaller, less effective lordships. In 1241 Walter de Lacy, lord of Meath, died without a male heir and the lordship was divided between two heiresses. In 1245 the last Marshall lord died and Leinster was divided between five heiresses. Thus Cos. Kildare/Wicklow/Laois were separated from the remainder of the old lordship to the south. While the new lordships were still quite substantial—roughly equivalent to a modern county—they could never be as successful as the original entities. As centralized English control declined in the late Middle Ages the more peripheral of these lordships, especially in Cos. Laois and Westmeath, largely disappeared—most of Co. Laois was entirely dominated by Irish lords from the early 14th century onwards. The mountainous bloc of Wicklow was never fully

▲ Fig. 77. Trim Castle: aerial view (photo: Conor Newman and Eamonn O'Donoghue)

subdued and was to be a constant menace to the heavily Anglicized farmlands of south Co. Dublin and to the city itself. Even by the mid-13th century there is evidence of raiding on Dublin by the Wicklow clans, notably the Ó Broin (O'Byrnes) and Ó Tuathail (O'Tooles). In the later 14th century this raiding intensified, while Co. Kildare experienced increasing pressure from the Ó Mordha (O'Moores) of Co. Laois and the resurgent Mac Murchada of Uí Cheinnselaig to the south.

By the early 15th century only a small core surrounding Dublin remained in English control—essentially modern Cos. Dublin and Meath, with adjoining parts of Louth and Kildare. Later this area was partially fortified, with the erection of a series of earthen defences or 'pales', after which the eastern enclave was known as the Pale. Outside of this, not all was doom and gloom—both Irish and Anglo-Irish lordships were thriving, largely free from governmental control. The FitzGerald earls of Kildare, in particular, managed to increase their holdings very considerably by retaking lands formerly part of the lordship of Leinster that had reverted to Irish control. On foot of this expansion the earls emerged in the later 15th century as the most powerful magnates in Ireland. Kildare hegemony ended abruptly in conflict with Henry VIII in 1535. Thereafter Henry and his successors launched a veritable reconquest of Ireland, starting from this eastern region.

Aghaboe, Co. Laois Monastic complex, motte-and-bailey castle

20 km east of Roscrea, on R434 between Borris-in-Ossory on N7 (Dublin–Limerick) and Durrow on N8 (Dublin–Cork); signposted.

Aghaboe [*Achadh Bhó*, 'field of the cows'] was an important monastic site, one of the main churches of the kingdom of Osraige (Ossory) and said to have been founded by St Cainnech (Canice) in the 6th century. It seems that St Virgil (Irish *Feargal*), the well-known 8th-century bishop of Salzburg in Austria, was abbot of Aghaboe before departing as a missionary to continental Europe *c*.745. In the later 11th and early 12th century Aghaboe was the principal church of Osraige and the burial place of its kings, although during the 12th century it was superseded by **Kilkenny**. An Augustinian priory seems to have replaced the original monastery in the early 13th century. In the late 12th and 13th centuries Aghaboe was an important manor of the lords of Leinster, but by *c*.1300 it was already becoming an exposed outpost on the frontiers of the Anglo-Irish colony. By the mid-14th century Aghaboe was once again under the control of the Mac Giolla Phádraig lords of Osraige, who burned the settlement (including the church) in 1346 and captured the castle in 1349. They founded a Dominican priory there in 1382, which was suppressed in 1540.

No visible remains of the early monastery survive. The present Church of Ireland church (*north-west side of village*) is on the site of the

Augustinian priory. Some of the church windows are medieval, but are thought to be taken from the Dominican priory, rather than the Augustinian priory. The tower, however, may be largely medieval; it has a 15th-century doorway and 13th-century fragments, including an arcade near the top. A number of stone heads over the west door and an octagonal font, on the ground in front of the church, are also probably medieval. A short distance to the west is the Dominican priory. Only the church survives, although faint traces of the claustral buildings can be made out on the north side. The church is a plain, narrow building probably dating from the 15th century—although it could possibly be almost as early as the 1380s. On the south side is a 'transept' which is effectively a free-standing building built against the church and reached through a large arch in the north wall. However, the fact that there are two pointed arches in the south wall of the church at this point suggests that there may have been an earlier transept or aisle here. The existing transept was probably built *c.*1500 and has two aumbries with interesting carved arches. It also had some fine Perpendicular-style windows which were removed and re-erected in the 19th century at Heywood, Ballinakill, Co. Laois.

In the field north of the churches is an interesting motte, almost square and 5 m high, with a double bailey to the north. It has been dated as late as the late 13th/early 14th century, largely on the basis of its unusual squared appearance. However, this may be due to later modifications—there are stone wall footings around the perimeter of the summit—and a more conventional date in the late 12th/early 13th century may be more likely.

Aghnaskeagh, Co. Louth Megalithic tombs

7 km north of Dundalk, off the N1 (Dundalk–Newry); take minor road to west (left) at the second crossroads after the Ballymascanlan interchange, followed by the second left. Disc. Ser. 36.

Two megalithic tombs at Aghnaskeagh were excavated in the early 1930s by Estyn Evans. The first is a Portal tomb, evidenced today by three orthostats (twin portal stones and an endstone) located on the east side of an oval cairn, 17.5 m in length. In the chamber were the cremated remains of four adults as well as sherds of Western Neolithic ware, a bipartite bowl, and a blue glass bead. The cairn was subsequently enlarged to incorporate six cists during the Bronze Age. One of the cists contained three pots, including a Bowl, and traces of blackberries found under one of the floor slabs indicate an autumn funeral.

The second cairn, 40 m to the south, was originally rectilinear and revetted. It contained four small chambers accessed from the east and west sides. Finds include cremated bone, sherds of pottery, and two hollow scrapers. These chambers compare with the subsidiary chambers of Court tombs, suggesting a possible classification for this monument. The area is rich in megalithic tombs, including **Proleek**, a short distance to the south-east. Aghnaskeagh is located just outside the **Ring of Gullion**, in the shadow of Feede Mountain, and not too far from **Kilnasaggart**.

Athgreany (Piper's Stones), Co. Wicklow Stone circle

On the N81, 17.5 km north of Baltinglass and 11.5 km south of Blessington; signposted. Disc. Ser. 56.

The 'Piper's Stones' is a stone circle comprising granite blocks, approximately 13 m in internal diameter. Only five stones remain standing in their original position; another five lie close to their original standing positions. A number of other stones are evidently displaced. The entrance is marked by two tall stones on the north-east side of the circle and 40 m beyond them is the so-called 'Piper', an outlying glacial erratic. Cross-shaped grooves occur on the top of this stone as well as on a fallen stone at the south-east side of the circle.

Ballybrack, Co. Dublin Portal tomb

Between Loughlinstown and Killiney in south-east Co. Dublin, between the M11 and the R119; close to the link road with the R118. Disc. Ser. 50.

Located on the green area in a housing estate, though originally uphill from the now all-but-invisible Loughlinstown river, this is a fine, though comparatively small example of the great granite Portal tombs of the Dublin/Wicklow mountains. A second such tomb was also recorded in Ballybrack in the 19th century.

Ballyedmonduff, Co. Dublin Wedge tomb

In forestry on the south-east slopes of Two Rock Mountain, south Co. Dublin; off the link road between Glencullen (on the R116) and Stepaside (on the R117); about 0.6 km above the road, near forestry track. Disc. Ser. 50.

This is a fine example of the small pocket of eastern Wedge tombs concentrating in south Co. Dublin. The monument consists of a three-chambered gallery, opening to the west, set into a U-shaped cairn, the outline of which is preserved in a large-stone kerb. A socket in the antechamber is interpreted as representing the equivalent of that holding a small standing stone in the antechamber of the **Island** wedge tomb. Excavation produced a small quantity of cremated bone, sherds of Beaker pottery and a stone macehead. A stone on the southern side of the cairn is decorated with seven cupmarks.

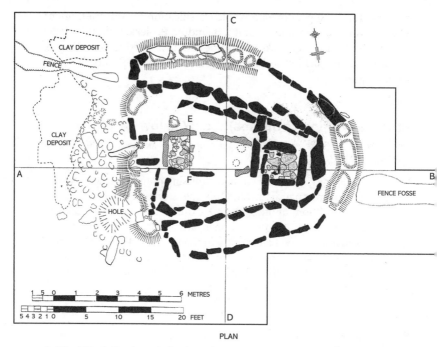

▲ **Fig. 78.** Ballyedmonduff: plan of site as excavated (after Ó Ríordáin & de Valera)

Baltinglass Hill, Co. Wicklow Passage tomb and hillfort

60 km south-west of Dublin on the N9 (Dublin–Carlow); the summit can be approached from virtually any side, but there is an established track starting behind the An Oige youth hostel in Baltinglass. Disc. Ser. 61.

Baltinglass Hill in west Co. Wicklow boasts panoramic views, particularly in the direction of neighbouring Co. Kildare. On the summit is a Passage tomb (Rathcoran), which is in turn surrounded by a cashel, and further downslope are the ramparts of an impressive bivallate hillfort that encloses the summit. The cairn (27 m in diameter), which was reused to build the massive cashel wall, was excavated between 1934–6 and two or possibly three phases of kerbstones distinguished. What may be the primary Passage tomb is located at the north side of the present cairn and has a simple, polygonal chamber with three shallow recesses and a stone basin with pecked ornament. A flint scraper was found in the chamber. A tight arc of orthostats either side of the entrance may be original kerbstones of a small 10 m diameter cairn. South-west of this is a small corbelled chamber, partly overlain by the phase 2 kerb and possibly contemporary with the primary tomb. Overlapping with the southern side of the primary kerb is a near-complete circle of kerbstones

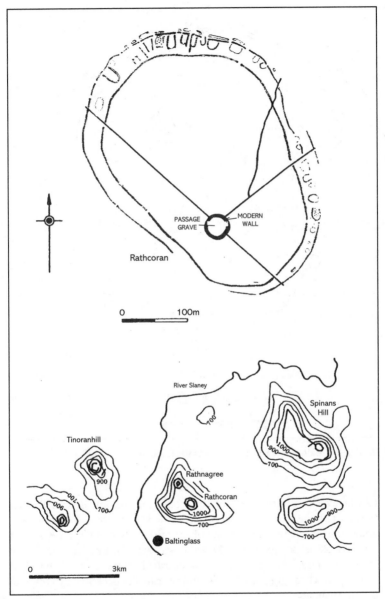

▲ **Fig. 79.** Plan of Rathcoran hillfort and map of hillforts in Baltinglass area (after Condit)

about 15 m in diameter. Towards the southern side of this is another, passageless tomb divided into three (or possibly five) compartments which contained cremated bone, fragments of white quartz, and a sherd

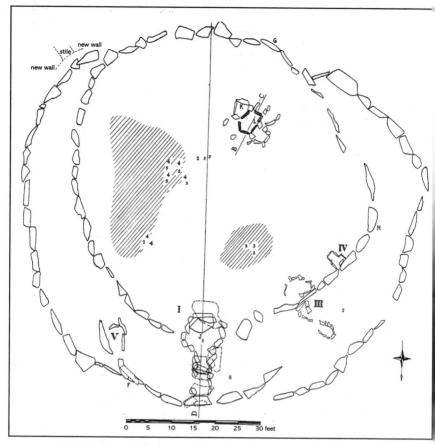

▲ **Fig. 80.** Baltinglass Hill: plan of Passage tomb as excavated (after Walshe)

of Carrowkeel pottery. Two of the stones are decorated with Passage tomb art. The third structural phase, evidenced by the outermost kerb, amalgamated the first and second phase cairns into one large monument (approx. 27 m in diameter). Material was also found under the cairn including a number of scrapers, a polished stone axehead, hazelnut shells, and wheat grains. There is another cairn approximately 100 m to the south-west.

The walls (3 m thick, 2 m high) of the cashel are comprised of cairn material and inside can be traced the outlines of two huts. Downslope of this are the ramparts of the hillfort. Set about 15 m apart, they enclose an area 380 m by 270 m. Composed mostly of stone, they are preserved best in the north and north-west. Half a kilometre to the north, on a spur of Baltinglass Hill, is Rathnagree, a trivallate hillfort.

Bealin, Co. Westmeath High cross

6 km east of Athlone; in Twyford Demesne, near Glassan, off the N55 (Athlone–Ballymahon); signposted. Disc. Ser. 47.

The original location of this high cross is unknown; **Clonmacnoise** has been mooted. It now stands in Twyford Demesne, about midway between **Uisneach** and Clonmacnoise. It is slightly damaged and is predominantly decorated with panels of bold interlace and on the north and east faces figural scenes of animals, including a hunting scene. On the west face is an inscription *OROIT AR TUATHGAIL LAS DERNATH IN CHROSSA*, which translates 'a prayer for Tuathgail who caused this cross to be made'. Henry identified this with Tuathgaill, abbot of Clonmacnoise, whose death is recorded in the *Annals of Ulster* in AD 810, but this has since been disputed. Harbison places it in his Bealin–Banagher group and suggests an early 9th-century date. The related Banagher, Co. Offaly, cross is in the National Museum of Ireland.

Boyne Valley, Co. Meath Passage tomb cemetery and archaeological complex

8 km west of Drogheda. Access to the major Passage tombs is only via the Brú na Bóinne Visitor Centre, at Donore on the south side of the Boyne, reached via Drogheda or from the N2 (Dublin–Derry) just south of Slane. Signposted. Disc. Ser. 43.

The Boyne Valley is the best-known archaeological complex in Ireland. Destined to become Ireland's first archaeological park, it is a World Heritage Zone. Although many of the monuments can be accessed individually, a visit to the *Brú na Bóinne* interpretative centre at Donore, on the south side of the Boyne, is recommended and is the *only* access to Newgrange, Knowth, and Dowth. Most of the monuments are of early prehistoric date and are concentrated in a great loop in the river Boyne, about 10 km upstream from Drogheda, where the river skirts southwards around a hard, carboniferous ridge. The earliest concerted activity dates from the Neolithic period and is characterized monumentally by a Passage tomb cemetery of about 40 tombs. The cemetery has three distinct foci—each a miniature ritual landscape—around the largest tombs at Knowth, Newgrange, and Dowth. It has been estimated that there may have been as many as 700 decorated stones in the Boyne Valley, making it the premier place in Europe to study megalithic art. The tombs continued to be the focus for religious activity well into the 2nd millennium BC. No fewer than four henges and three pit circles were built, compounding the religious significance of this area. The eastern and northern periphery of the Boyne Valley are marked by a small Passage tomb at Townley Hall and a henge at Monknewtown. It has been suggested, on the basis of a significant decline in arable farming evidenced in the pollen record from nearby Red Bog, Co. Louth, that the Boyne Valley was well-nigh deserted from around 1800 BC until the end of the 1st millennium BC. This, coupled with the absence of other typical Bronze Age features, such as cist burials, barrows, etc, suggests an abeyance of activity in the Boyne Valley during these centuries.

The river Boyne, named after the goddess Bóand (meaning 'illuminated cow' in the sense of a bountiful giver), *Buvinda* on Ptolemy's 2nd-century map, marks the traditional, and much disputed, border between the ancient kingdoms of Ulster and Tara. Overlooking an important fording point on the river (the Ford of Brow or *Brú na Bóinne*) it was inevitable that Newgrange should acquire special politico-religious significance during the later Iron Age. It was deemed to be the burial mound (*síd*) of the pagan kings of Tara and erstwhile dwelling place of the Dagda of the *Túatha Dé Danann*. A hoard of Romano-British objects, including a gold chain and two gold finger-rings, is perhaps testimony to the new role that Newgrange now played. Rosnaree (*ros na rí*), overlooking the ford from the south side of the river, means 'kings' wood', and nearby was Cléitech, one of the principal residences of the kings of Tara. At Knowth, however, the evidence is even more tangible. A large fosse, dug halfway up the mound, turned it into a formidable fortification and sowed the seeds for its early medieval transformation into the seat of the Síl nAedo Sláine kings of northern Brega. A sept of the Uí Néill, these kings bore the title Rí Cnogba (kings of Knowth) in the 9th and 10th century. Knowth was a major focus of settlement during the early medieval period. Dowth was also settled at this time.

The 12th century saw the arrival in Ireland of the Cistercians. Their first foundation was at **Mellifont**, about 6 km from Knowth. The area came under the control of the kings of Bréifne, who granted all of the land on the north side of the Boyne, between Slane and Drogheda, to the new monastery. Granges (outlying monastic farms) were established throughout this area. Dowth, on the other hand, was commandeered as a motte castle by de Lacy in 1172, and the manor of Dowth became an independent unit within a landscape otherwise dominated by these highly organized farms. Thus the agricultural landscape of the Boyne Valley changed forever, though its rural character has remained.

Knowth

Knowth is at the western end of the Boyne Valley complex and is situated on a bluff high above the Boyne. The complex began as a settlement, evidenced as spreads of occupation material, hearths and pits, and the preserved outlines of three quite substantial wooden houses. At some point during this phase, a large, double-palisaded enclosure was constructed; now disappearing beneath the main mound, it has a projected diameter of about 100 m. The construction of the Passage tomb cemetery began shortly thereafter, a little before 3000 BC, and would eventually

▲ **Fig. 81.** Boyne Valley: decorated kerbstone of main passage tomb at Knowth (photo: Dept. of Archaeology, NUI, Galway)

lead to the construction of the main tomb and seventeen so-called 'satellite tombs'. Some of the deviations in the ground plan of the main tumulus arise from the need to avoid earlier satellite tombs (nos. 8, 14, and 16), indicating that they were built before the main tomb. Others, however, were built later. The satellite tombs range in size from 10 m to 20 m in diameter and have both undifferentiated and cruciform chambers. Some appear to be aligned towards the centre of the main mound, but others have different orientations.

The main tomb (*not accessible by the public*) is not just the biggest in Europe (about 85 m in maximum diameter and 9.9 m high) but with over 300 decorated stones, it also boasts the largest collection of Passage tomb art. The lowest part of the mound comprises water-rolled stones on a bed of sods, while the upper half is of alternating layers of stone and soil. The mound has a megalithic kerb of 127 contiguous stones. Subcircular in plan, the mound flattens noticeably on the east and west sides at the entrances to the two, opposing burial chambers. The ground here is roughly paved and in front of the entrances to each tomb are standing stones (two in the case of the western tomb). Around the bases of these are stone-lined hollows that hold egg-shaped granites and mudstones, for all the world like nests. Indeed, the 'cycle of life' symbolism could hardly be any plainer. The kerbstones in front of the passages are highly ornate.

The stones of the main passages are built against a cushion of sods, stripped from grassland. Once de-sodded, these fields were virtually ruined for agriculture for the next few years, thus illustrating the level of commitment to the building of these great monuments on the part of the community. The eastern tomb is just over 40 m long and opens into a spectacular, corbelled, cruciform chamber 5.9 m high. As is often the case, the right-hand recess is the largest and contains a beautifully decorated basin stone that was placed there before the chamber was fully completed. Another such basin stone was upturned over some cremated bones in the left-hand recess. Pockets of cremated bones were concentrated in the recesses along with stone beads and pendants and large antler pins. In the right-hand recess an outstandingly beautiful flint macehead was found (*now on display in the National Museum of Ireland*). The western tomb is 34 m long (less than 5 m behind the eastern chamber) and is undifferentiated, widening only slightly at the end. The passage, however, dog-legs to the south about 6 m from the chamber and this change in direction is marked by a sillstone. A smaller sillstone distinguishes the burial chamber, which, like the passage, is roofed with lintels. The left-hand wall of the chamber comprises a highly decorated stone. Pockets of comminuted, cremated bone were concentrated in the area of the chamber.

The megalithic art at Knowth is truly exceptional. The motifs are clearly symbolic but have yet to be deciphered convincingly. The more highly decorated stones demarcate the most important parts of the tombs, such as the entrances, the passages, and the chambers. Likewise, highly decorated kerbstones around the mound are likely to mark important points. The motifs are curvilinear and geometric and are incised and pecked into the rock surface.

Later Neolithic activity is marked by the construction of a small wooden circle or temple, approximately 8 m in diameter, in front of the eastern tomb. Votive or propitiatory offerings of pottery (including Grooved Ware) and animal bones were placed in the post pits and around the posts. This event marks the beginning of secondary ritual activity at the site and a fundamental change in the role of the tombs as they moved from centre-stage to backdrop. Four discrete areas of occupation material, dating from the earlier Bronze Age, occur around the main mound. No structures have been identified, but there were numerous pits and hearths with associated flints (rounded scrapers, arrowheads, etc.) and pottery, including sherds of Beaker ware. Associated ritual activity is evidenced by the cremated remains of an adult and young child that were buried with a plain Beaker pot in satellite tomb no. 15.

Other Iron Age activity is attested to in a series of crouched or flexed inhumation burials, with diagnostic glass bead necklaces. One interesting variation was the head-to-toe burial of two decapitated adult males, with a scatter of gaming pieces between them. From such obscure beginnings, however, the importance of Knowth grew and for two centuries, from around AD 800, it became the principal residence of the Síl nAedo Sláine. A large fosse was dug about halfway up the mound and a sizeable settlement developed. The mound itself became a veritable warren of souterrains. Two fields to the south of Knowth, a splendid promontory ringfort defends this approach to the royal site. The remains of a large stone building on the top of the main mound date from the later Middle Ages and are probably connected to the Cistercian grange of Knowth.

Newgrange

Newgrange stands on a ridge, more or less in the middle of the Boyne Valley. From it the ground drops away towards the river, creating a natural amphitheatre, a pocket of ritual monuments. As at Knowth, the earliest activity appears to have been of a domestic nature, though the remains are far more ephemeral. The tomb complex is essentially contemporary with that at Knowth and comprises the main tumulus and three satellite tombs, two to the west (sites K and L) and one to the east (site Z). An irregular line of seven possible Passage tombs stretches from the river bank below Newgrange eastwards towards Dowth and, depending on one's perspective, these too might be considered satellites. The sequence of tomb construction is unclear, but site K may have been the first. The main tomb is about 11 m high and between 80 m and 95 m in diameter. Built of rounded, water-rolled stones, it has a megalithic kerb of 97 contiguous stones, two of which, the entrance stone and one on the opposite side (referred to as K52), are probably the most beautifully decorated of the Irish series. The mound subsided quite soon after completion and the kerb was buried. The front part of the mound was reinstated by Michael O'Kelly during excavations in the 1960s and early 1970s. Beneath the collapse was found a pavement-like spread of quartzite and egg-shaped granites. Erecting these stones as a façade, and then deliberately collapsing them in order to examine how they then lay, convinced O'Kelly that they once stood as the façade you see today. The semicircular recess at the entrance is, however, a modern accommodation to allow access to the tomb around, rather than over, the entrance stone. Radiocarbon dating places the construction of the tomb between around 3300 and 2900 BC.

The passage and chamber have survived remarkably intact; indeed a sophisticated 'relieving arch' in the mound was uncovered during excavation. The passage is 19 m long and opens into a cruciform chamber with a corbelled roof 6 m high. Over the entrance is a small, rectangular opening, the so-called 'roof-box'. Level with the floor of the chamber, it is through this small aperture that the rising, winter solstice sun shines on 21 December each year, illuminating the chamber for a few minutes with a warm, orange glow. There is a stone basin in each of the recesses (two in the eastern one). Megalithic art is found throughout, some of it clearly carved before the stones were fixed in place—evidently not all of the art was meant to be seen. Tiny amounts of cremated human bone, representing no more than four or five people, and a selection of stone beads, balls, and pendants were found in the chamber. There is also an early 18th-century record by the famous Welsh antiquarian Thomas Molyneux, of a stone pillar, 1.5–1.8 m long, lying recumbent in the middle of the chamber. This has since disappeared, but recalls stones in the subterranean burial chamber at Ballynahatty, the chamber of Cairn F at Carrowkeel, and the Welsh Passage tomb of Bryn Celli Ddu. Such stones may be phallic symbols and their placement in, or in front of, the womb-shaped Passage tomb might be literally and metaphorically pregnant with meaning. A miniature version of one of these stone cylinders was found in a stone-lined hollow in front of the tomb.

Newgrange remained the focus of religious activity into the later Neolithic and earlier Bronze Age. A cursus was built about 100 m east of the tomb. Comprising two parallel banks, about 20 m apart and orientated north–south, this linear earthwork can be traced running downslope for a distance of about 100 m. Insofar as the U-shaped terminus at the southern end commands a significant vantage point over the Newgrange landscape, it is a sign that the monumental aspect was being deliberately composed. It is suspected to date from the later Neolithic. A little while later, a very large pit and post circle, about 120 m in projected diameter, was built immediately to the south-east of the main tumulus, encircling site Z. Some of the pits contained votive offerings of animal bones. Inside the circle were spreads of occupation-like material, including almost 800 flint flakes and sherds of Grooved Ware and Beaker pottery. Sweetman's excavation of this monument revealed that it predated the erection of one of the 12 surviving standing stones around the mound (originally thought to number 35), thus countering O'Kelly's claim that the stone circle was contemporary with the Passage tomb. There remains a question mark over whether the stone circle was ever completed. Two embanked enclosures, or earthen henges (sites A and P), were also built nearer the river bank below Newgrange. Both are ploughed out, but originally measured about 170 m in diameter. A little while later the area around the front of the tomb became the focus of a settlement with an associated Beaker pottery assemblage. There is very little archaeological evidence for concentrated activity after this. Sometime between the 1st and the 4th century AD votive offerings of Romano-British jewellery and coins were scattered around the front of the tomb. There may even have been a temple here and this may coincide with or merely explain the appropriation, at least in legend, of Newgrange as the burial place of the pagan kings of Tara and home to the Dagda, god of druidism.

Dowth

The third focus of ritual activity in the Boyne Valley is around the massive Passage tomb at Dowth. It has not been the subject of large-scale excavation—though a very large hole was dug into the top in the 1840s—and is the least understood of the three great tombs. The mound is about 85 m in diameter and edged with 115 kerbstones. Two modest tombs open from the west side and an inward curve on the opposite side of the mound probably marks the entrance to a third tomb. The more northerly of the tombs has a passage just over 8 m long and opens into a cruciform chamber with an L-shaped annexe leading off the right-hand recess. There is some very accomplished megalithic art in this tomb. A souterrain of early medieval date leads off the left-hand side of the passage. By contrast, the chamber in the southern tomb is sub circular (about 4 m diameter) and has a large trapezoidal annexe on the south-west side. There appear to be no satellite tombs immediately around Dowth, but about 0.5 km to the east and south-west are outlying tombs. Further east again is the spectacular Dowth henge, 175 m in diameter (*land privately owned; no public access*). The well-preserved banks are 20 m wide and up to 5 m high. It probably dates from around 2500 BC.

Carlingford, Co. Louth Medieval town

21 km east of Dundalk on R173; turn east off N1/A1 (Dublin–Belfast) 3 km north of Dundalk or 2 km south of Newry; signposted.

Set between the mountain (590 m) and the Lough after which it is named [*Cairlinn*, 'bay of the hag', with Old Norse *fjord*], the town of Carlingford was founded by the younger Hugh de Lacy, earl of Ulster from 1205. De Lacy built a strong castle here *c.*1200, as the centre of his lordship. The town was probably founded shortly afterwards and occupies a long, rectangular area along the west shore of the Lough, south of the castle. It was subsequently enclosed by a stone wall—at least on the landward side—and laid out along two streets running north–south, parallel to the shoreline. It preserves an interesting range of archaeology, typical of Irish medieval towns.

Castle

The castle stands on a rock overlooking a harbour in the Lough and had been erected in some form by 1210, when it was taken by King John. It consists of a D-shaped enclosure surrounded by a massive curtain wall, with a gatehouse on the west, a projecting square tower on the south-west, and possibly others on the north, east, and south-east. The gatehouse originally consisted of two rectangular towers flanking a particularly narrow entrance passage, but only parts of the northern tower remain. Traces of a spiral stair at the north-east angle of the tower

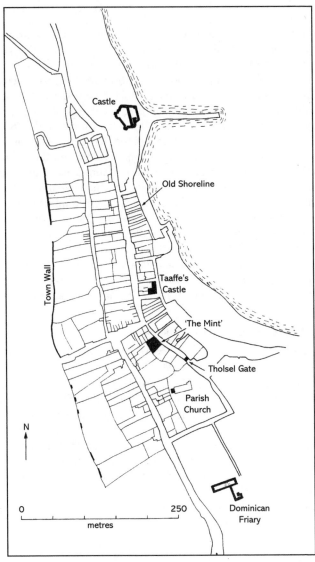

▲ **Fig. 82.** Carlingford: outline map of town showing medieval features (after Bradley)

indicate that there was at least one upper storey. The projecting tower on the south-west is square at ground level, with arrow loops in each of the projecting walls, but it becomes five sided at first-floor level, where the original entrance was. Traces of two other projecting towers can be seen in the outer face of the curtain wall on the north and on the south-east. In the curtain wall are a series of large embrasures with arrow loops—

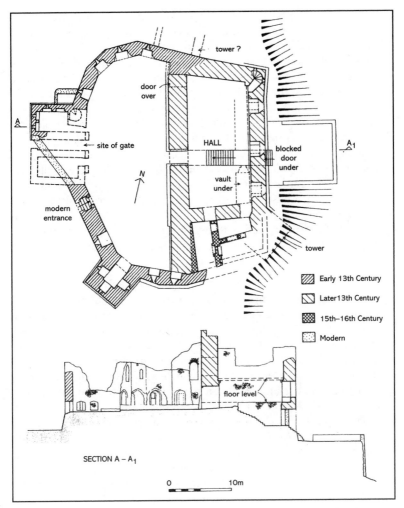

▲ **Fig. 83.** Carlingford: plan of castle (OPW)

the present entrance to the inner courtyard is through one of these embrasures. Other arrow loops occur at a higher level, implying that timber structures once existed against the inside of the curtain wall. There are also beam-holes at wall walk level, suggesting the presence of a wooden hoarding.

At the eastern side of the castle is a large rectangular block of two storeys above basements. It is clearly not original, as its massive western wall (up to 3.3 m thick) blocks window opes in the curtain wall at either end. The main ground-floor chamber (*currently not accessible to the public*) is lit by three windows (with seats) in the east wall and has a spiral stair in the north-east angle giving access to the first floor. It has been suggested that this chamber is later 13th century and functioned as the great hall, but this is not certain on either count. There are few datable features and the size of the west wall, its lack of windows, and the presence of battlements could suggest that it was built as an external wall. The stair in the middle of the chamber, leading down to the basement, is modern but the doorway in the west wall which leads to the stairs may be original. The vaulted basement leads to a smaller block in the south-east corner, which seems to have been rebuilt in the 16th century on the site of an earlier projecting tower. This block was up to four storeys high and was divided internally by a T-shaped wall displaying fireplaces and a first-floor arcade of octagonal pillars; the external wall is absent. Outside the castle to the east is a platform, accessed through a blocked doorway in the east curtain wall. The platform is probably for artillery and both it and the doorway are post-medieval, but there are traces of a medieval tower under the platform.

Town wall and 'Tholsel'

Only one gatehouse and two substantial fragments of the town wall survive and its precise line has not been firmly established. One section of wall survives at Back Lane, on the north-west side of the town, while the other is south-east of the 'Tholsel'. Both sections contain arrow loops. The 'Tholsel' is actually a rectangular gatehouse giving access to the main street, at the south-east end of the town. Originally three-storeyed, it has been much altered and is now two-storeyed with a modern slate roof. A large vaulted opening runs through the ground floor, with a small chamber to the east; there is no evidence for a portcullis or other defensive features. At first-floor level is a single chamber with much-altered openings over the doorways below and a garderobe in the south-east angle. This chamber, and the second floor above, were originally reached via a spiral stair in the north-east angle, but this is now replaced by a modern straight stair.

Fortified houses

Carlingford preserves two fine (although poorly maintained) urban tower houses which testify to the wealth of merchant families who traded here in the late Middle Ages. One, popularly known as 'the Mint', is located on the main street c.45 m north of the 'Tholsel'. It is a three-storey building with a single chamber at each level and a wall walk with stepped battlements above. Gun loops in the battlements suggest a later 16th-century date. A tall machicolation protects the main doorway. The internal features of the three floor levels are unremarkable and the main feature of the building is the ogee-headed windows, with finely carved jambs and spandrels featuring 16th-century 'Celtic revivalist' interlace.

To the east, nearer the harbour, is the second fortified house, known as 'Taaffe's castle' (*not accessible to the public*). It is a much larger four-storey building with wall walk and battlements above. A two-storey wing attached to the north side was added later, but both it and the main building are 16th century. Each level of the building is divided into a main chamber and a much narrower passage at the west end, containing the spiral stairs giving access to the upper floors. The stair is located in the north-west angle at ground- and first-floor levels but in the south-west angle above this. The original main doorway—now blocked—is on the west side and is protected by a machicolation overhead. It gave access to the stair passage and upper levels, but not to the main ground-floor chamber, which must have had a separate entrance. The ground-floor chamber and the attached wing to the north probably served as warehouses for the merchant family who built the house, while the upper floors were living chambers. There are a number of windows with well-tooled jambs in the east and south walls. At the south-east angle are traces of a projecting wall, apparently part of an enclosure to the south.

Holy Trinity church

South-east of the 'Tholsel'—outside the town wall—is the Church of Ireland parish church of Holy Trinity. This much-altered building may incorporate some medieval fabric and has a pointed doorway in the south wall, as well as a late medieval or post-medieval tower at the west end. Suggestions that this may actually be a mural tower, formerly on the town wall, seem to be without foundation.

Dominican priory

Outside the town, to the south, is the Dominican priory, said to have been founded c.1305 by Richard de Burgh, earl of Ulster. The visible remains consist of the church and part of the domestic buildings. The church is a simple, long rectangular structure, divided into nave and chancel by a three-storey tower. It is probably of early 14th-century date, but most windows and other features which might date the building are removed or blocked. The central tower is a later (but probably 14th-century) insertion. It was accessed at first-floor level through a doorway (now blocked) in the south wall, from the now-vanished domestic buildings on the south side of the church. A small projecting turret at the south-east angle contains a stairwell, giving access to the upper levels. Rectangular openings in the east and west walls of the tower, over the vault, gave access to lofts above the nave and chancel (the roof lines of which are visible above the openings). At a later date (15th/16th century) the west end of the church was fortified, possibly after an indulgence was granted in 1423 to raise funds to repair the priory 'after damage by enemies'. The west wall has battlements and a machicolation flanked by two small turrets and it is likely that battlements were added to the north and south walls also. The cloisters and domestic buildings were located on the south side of the church. In the south wall of the church, externally, are the roof line and beam-holes of the east range and north cloister walk. All that remains of the domestic buildings is the south end of the east range, *c.*20 m south of the church, with a defensive tower-like structure added on the east which is probably contemporary with the fortification of the nave. Clear traces of the northern end of this range are visible in the external wall of the chancel, as well as a blocked doorway which gave access to the chancel from this range.

On the hill slopes south of the town are the remains of a little-known monastic foundation ascribed (with no great certainty) to the Knights Templar. Only the north-west angle of the church survives above ground, with a fallen stone nearby which is probably the lintel of the west doorway. To the west and north-west of the church are extensive grass-covered wall footings, clearly the foundations of the domestic buildings. One long rectangular range extends north–south, with returns to the west at either end.

Castledermot, Co. Kildare Early church site and medieval town

10 km north-east of Carlow, on N9 (Dublin–Kilkenny).

Castledermot, as the Irish name [*Díseart Dhiarmada*, 'Diarmait's hermitage'] indicates, was originally a hermitage founded in the 9th century by Diarmait ua hÁedo Róin. Diarmait (d. 825) was from an Ulster royal family but was a leading figure in the ascetic *Céli Dé* reform movement. The land itself appears to have belonged to the monastery of Bangor, Co. Down. Diarmait's foundation developed into an important monastic site and it was plundered by the Norse in 841 and by the Irish in 1040. It is the burial place of Cormac mac Cuilenain, scholar and abbot-king of Cashel, slain in the decisive Battle of Belach Mugna (near Leighlinbridge, Co. Carlow) against Flann Sinna, king of Tara. It was sufficiently important to attract the English in the late 12th-century conquest. A castle was erected here for Walter de Ridelisford *c.*1181—probably a motte, of which no trace survives—and a borough was established, probably before 1199 when it received the right to hold a weekly market. The town was well located, on the route between Dublin and the wealthy, Anglicized south-east, and it was frequently the venue for meetings of the Irish parliament, especially in the late 14th century. Castledermot received a murage grant in 1295—perhaps a sign of growing insecurity—and was damaged in an attack by Edward Bruce's Scottish army in 1316. By the 15th century it was an exposed frontier town, subject to frequent Irish attacks, and was

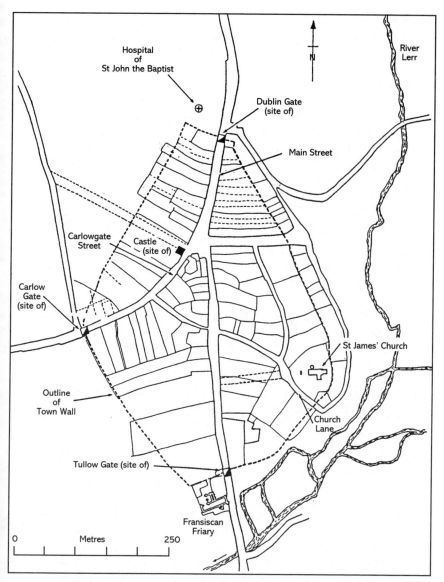

▲ **Fig. 84.** Castledermot: outline map of town showing medieval features (after Bradley)

burned on several occasions. One such burning, by Gearóid Mac Murchada in 1428, was so severe that parliament granted a special subsidy to aid the rebuilding. Further damage was caused in the wars of the 1640s, finally confirming Castledermot's decline to a minor market town.

Monastic site

The original monastic site was located on a bend in the small river Lerr, now on the east side of the town. Few traces of its layout survive, although the curve of the lane to the east and south-east of the present Church of Ireland church probably reflects an early enclosure. Around the present church, however, there are significant remains of the early monastery. The fine Romanesque doorway (*reconstructed*) to the west of the present church is all that remains of a mid-12th-century church. It has two orders with chevron decoration but a third, inner, order may be missing. The present church is largely post-medieval but the south wall of the nave is 13th century, with three arches of an aisle arcade (now blocked) and one window to the east. It seems clear that a new parish church was built in the 13th century by adding an extended nave with south aisle to the east end of the 12th-century church; there was probably a chancel also. This 13th-century church was not only considerably larger than its predecessor, but also larger than the present church. It was subsequently reduced in size, however, as Castledermot itself declined.

The round tower on the north side of the church, built of irregular blocks of the local granite, is 20 m high at present but the battlements at the top—and possibly the large windows below it—are later. With its original conical roof the tower would have been somewhat taller. Its flat-headed doorway (*only accessible through the church*) faces south-eastwards and is at current ground level and may always have been so. Internally there are currently five floors, but these do not align well with the windows and are clearly not original. Although it is currently attached to the church, this tower—like all round towers—was originally free-standing.

Two important high crosses—a South Cross and a North Cross—survive in the churchyard, along with the base of a third, West Cross. All are of granite, a difficult stone to carve, and this has given the sculpture a distinctive character, with relatively simple figures in low relief. A break in the stone on the south face of the South Cross, at the base of the cross head, provides a rare opportunity to see the mortice-and-tenon construction used to join the different pieces of many high crosses. The South Cross is also unusual in that one of its main faces (east) is decorated entirely with geometric motifs, while the west face bears a mixture of Old and New Testament scenes (from base to top):

Daniel in the Lions' Den
Temptation of St Anthony(?)
Adam and Eve
Sts Paul and Anthony(?)
Unidentified
Crucifixion [cross head]

David Playing the Harp [right arm of cross]
Sacrifice of Isaac [left arm of cross]

The narrow sides are decorated with geometrical decoration and a series of unidentified human figures, either singly or in pairs—possibly representing the twelve apostles. On the base is the *Miracle of the Loaves and Fishes.*

The North Cross bears a *Crucifixion* at the centre of the east face, surrounded by four panels each with three figures, probably representing the *Twelve Apostles.* Below this are *Sts Paul and Anthony* and an unidentified panel. On the west face are mainly Old Testament scenes, although near the base is a panel probably representing the *Temptation of St Anthony.* Above this are (from base to top):

Daniel in the Lions' Den
Adam and Eve [cross head]
David Playing the Harp [right arm of cross]
Sacrifice of Isaac [left arm of cross]

Between the Romanesque doorway and the South Cross lies a long, gabled stone which is thought to be the only Irish example of a 'hogback' stone, a type of Viking-age grave marker common in northern England and apparently based on the shape of a Viking house. On one of the gabled faces two crosses are carved, one of them ringed.

Medieval town

The medieval town was originally laid out on a Y-shaped street pattern, with the main road entering from the north and dividing into two at a market place in the centre of the town. Around this was a roughly diamond-shaped enclosed area, with the original monastic enclosure occupying the eastern angle, the Franciscan friary at the southern end, and the Hospital of St John the Baptist at the northern end. The line of the town wall can be fairly readily made out but few convincing fragments of it survive. At the north end of the town stands a lone square tower, the only remnant of the Hospital of St John the Baptist, a monastery/hospital of the *Fratres Cruciferi,* or 'crutched friars' founded in the early 13th century and dissolved in 1539.

Franciscan friary

The Franciscan friary was probably founded *c.*1240 but was extensively altered later. It was dissolved in 1539. Effectively only the church survives—the cloisters and other buildings, which were on the south side of the church, have disappeared. The church is typically 13th-century Franciscan—a long, narrow rectangular building—although the only 13th-century features still visible are lancet windows in the north and west walls. The friary was burned by Bruce's Scottish army in 1316 and it was

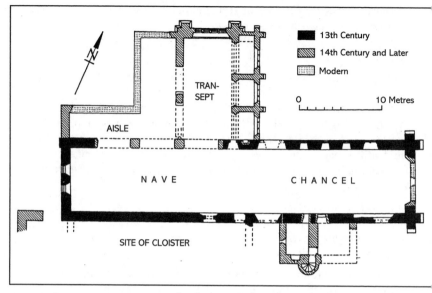

▲ **Fig. 85.** Castledermot: plan of Franciscan friary (after Leask)

probably in the wake of this (certainly in the early 14th century) that the church was enlarged—by lengthening the choir and adding an aisle and large transept on the north side of the nave. In contrast to the plainness of the 13th-century building, the transept is quite elaborate. It has three chapels on the east side and an aisle on the west, separated by an arcade with relatively elaborate mouldings. The chapels are lit by large windows with some of the earliest 'switchline' tracery known in Ireland. Even larger windows were inserted in the north wall of the transept and in the new east wall of the extended choir. Unfortunately the elaborate tracery of these windows (known from antiquarian drawings) does not survive. On the south side of the choir is an unusual three-storey 15th-century tower—built as a fortified residence rather than as a belfry—with a now vanished sacristy on the east side. The cloisters were located on the south side of the church but have vanished. The only evidence of their location is a pointed doorway (blocked) in the south wall of the nave and another doorway, *c.*3.5 m above ground level, in the south wall of the choir, which may have led to a night stair.

Castlekeeran, Co. Meath Monastic site

5 km west of Kells, approached via the R163 (Kells–Oldcastle), taking the minor road to the north (right), 2 km west of Kells; signposted, across one field. Disc. Ser. 42.

The monastic site at Castlekeeran is situated upriver from Kells on a very slight prominence overlooking the upper reaches of the Blackwater

river valley towards Lough Ramor, Co. Cavan. A hermitage outpost of
Kells, it was known as *Díseart Chiaráin* ('Ciarán's desert, or isolated
retreat'). It was plundered by the Vikings in 949 and by Diarmait Mac
Murchada and the Anglo-Normans in 1170. In the 13th century it came
under the control of the Knights Hospitallers. All that remains of the
early foundation are three mostly plain high crosses and a developed
grave slab of early medieval date. Legend has it that a fourth high cross
lies at the bottom of the Blackwater, hastily thrown there by Columba
when Ciarán caught him trying to steal it. Of particular interest is an
ogam stone bearing the inscription *COVAGNI MAQI MUCOI LUGUNI*
('of Covagni, son of the tribe of Luguni'). A late Iron Age territorial
marker in this traditional border zone, the inscription testifies to the
colonization of this area, possibly around the 5th century, by the Luigni
and the Gailenga, precursors to full Uí Néill conquest. A short distance
further along the road is Ciarán's Well, a fascinating micro-environment
of water-eroded limestone, foot-bridges, and penitential stations overlooked by a shrine behind which is a curious, possibly embanked hollow.
As with so many holy wells, the pattern day is the first Sunday in August.

▼ **Fig. 86.** Castleruddery: plan of stone circle as excavated (after Leask & Price)

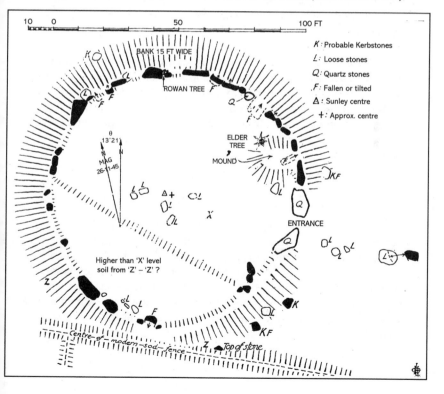

Castleruddery, Co. Wicklow   Embanked stone circle

8.5 km north-east of Baltinglass, off the N81 (Dublin–Baltinglass); take minor road east off N81 towards Glen of Imaal/Donard for 1 km; monument on south side of road, 0.5 km beyond Castleruddery Cross; signposted. Disc. Ser. 55.

Overlooking the river Slaney near the village of Donaghmore, the 'Druidical Circle' at Castleruddery is a 30 m diameter embanked stone circle comparable in many respects to Grange, Co. Limerick. Enclosed within an earthen bank, the circle of 29 or so large, contiguous stones (some fallen over, others missing) has its entrance between two massive quartz boulders on the east side. There may also have been a revetment around the outside of the bank. Another standing stone occurs a little to the east of the entrance. Aerial photographs reveal that the circle is centrally located within a larger enclosure (80 m in diameter) with a narrower, trench-size circle (50 m in diameter) between the two. The skyline to the south is dominated by **Spinans Hill** with its massive hillfort and, further along the shoulder to the east, Brusselstown hillfort.

Castletimon, Co. Wicklow   Ogam stone

13 km north-east of Arklow, off N11 (Dublin–Wexford); turn east off N11 on first minor road north of Jack White's Crossroads. Alternatively, take minor road west, toward Rathdrum, at Ballynacarrig Cross at north end of Brittas Bay, off the R750 (Wicklow–Arklow coastal route). Disc. Ser. 62.

Tucked into a roadside niche, the Castletimon ogam stone, now recumbent, is a granite slab 1.5 m long. The inscription reads *NETA-CARI NETA CAGI*. From its present location it overlooks the Potters river valley. A short distance to the south are the ruins of Castletimon church, which is of late medieval date, although the bank around the graveyard is probably from the original early medieval monastery. There is a bullaun stone near the south-west corner of the church.

Cloughnafarmore, Co. Louth   Standing stone

4.5 km south-west of Dundalk, 1.5 km north-east of Knockbridge; off the R171 (Dundalk–Louth). Disc. Ser. 36.

According to tradition, the standing stone (2.9 m high) at Cloughnafarmore [*cloch an fhir mhóir*, 'the great man's stone'] was the stone to which the dying Cú Chulainn, legendary defender of the Brown Bull of Cooley (a symbol of the honour of Ulster) tied himself in a last, desperate stand against Queen Medb's forces from Connacht. Such was their fear of the mighty Cú Chulainn that the Connacht warriors would only approach the slain hero after seeing a raven land on his shoulder and sip on his blood.

Danestown, Co. Meath Ringfort

15 km south-west of Drogheda, off the N2 (Dublin–Slane); turn west at Balrath Crossroads onto R153 (toward Navan) and take minor road to south after 3 km; signposted. Access is through a private farmyard, and permission should be sought. Disc. Ser. 43.

This fine example of a bivallate ringfort was probably a royal residence of the 7th to 10th centuries. It consists of a raised, oval-shaped platform edged by a bank, with external fosse and outer bank (maximum diameter 82 m). The entrance, comprising a gap in the banks and a causeway across the fosse, is in the south-western quadrant.

Donaghmore, Co. Meath Monastic site, round tower

2 km north-east of Navan, on N51 (Navan–Slane); signposted. Disc. Ser. 42.

The foundation of the early monastery of Donaghmore [*Domhnach mór*, 'the great church'] is attributed to St Patrick. A splendid round tower (*renovated but inaccessible*) can be seen for miles around and probably dates from the 12th century. There is a *Crucifixion* above the Romanesque-style, round-topped door and heads on either side of the arch. Nearby are the remains of a 15th-century church that incorporates a head from an earlier, Romanesque building on the site. There are some early grave slabs in the graveyard.

Donard Upper, Co. Wicklow Ogam stone

20 km south of Blessington off N81 (Dublin–Baltinglass); turn east at Merginstown Crossroads for 2 km; signposted. Disc. Ser. 56.

Relocated to the village green in Donard in west-central Wicklow, this ogam stone has been moved at least three times! 1.5 m tall, the inscription reads *IAQINI KOI MAQI MUC . . .* ('of Iaqini Koi, son of the tribe of . . .'). Also in the village, on the south side, are a possible motte (Donard was granted to Jordan de Marisco before 1190) and the nearby remains of a medieval church of 15th–16th-century date.

Dublin, Co. Dublin Medieval town

Dublin's urban origins date to 841, when Viking raiders established a *longphort* at Duiblinn—presumably a defended encampment on the banks of the River Liffey. The place name *Duiblinn* ('black pool') probably refers to a tidal pool at, or near, the confluence of the Liffey with a tributary, the Poddle. This is thought to have been located on the site now occupied by the ornamental garden on the south side of Dublin Castle, although there is no definite evidence for this. References in the annals in the 7th and 8th centuries indicate that there was an earlier monastic foundation at Duiblinn, and the curving line of Peter Row/

Stephen St. Upper/Stephen St. Lower (*south of Dublin Castle*) may preserve the outline of its monastic enclosure. Recent archaeological excavation in the area immediately west of the Liffey/Poddle confluence, north of Dublin Castle, has produced the first apparent (although unconfirmed at the time of writing) evidence for 9th-century settlement in the medieval core, suggesting that this was, indeed, the location of the 9th century *longphort*. In the 10th century Dublin developed into probably the first real town in Ireland—and certainly the most important. It was the hub of an extensive Scandinavian kingdom spanning both sides of the Irish Sea, with extensive trading connections beyond this. Dublin's political independence effectively ended in the 11th century, as it tended to be controlled by one or other of the major Irish kings, although they were wise enough not to interfere in the town's development or commercial activity.

The invading English recognized Dublin's economic and strategic importance and from the visit of Henry II in 1171 it was the effective capital of the English lordship. This was accompanied by substantial redevelopment of the town. Dublin Castle was begun *c.*1204. Christ Church cathedral was completely rebuilt, beginning in the late 12th century, and a second cathedral—St Patrick's—was built in the 13th century. Several new monasteries were added, including Franciscan, Carmelite, Augustinian, and Dominican friaries and the great St Thomas's abbey, while existing houses such as St Mary's abbey were rebuilt. Early 13th-century reclamation along the riverfront produced a substantial amount of extra building land, which was subsequently enclosed within an enlarged circuit of town walls. Extensive extra-mural suburbs developed to the north, west, and south, but medieval Dublin was never a particularly large town, even by the standards of the time. There are suggestions that in terms of overseas trade, it may have been eclipsed in the 13th century by the south-eastern ports of **Waterford** and New Ross, but its political importance was unchallenged. The 14th century brought two major setbacks—in 1317 the citizens themselves burned a considerable part of the suburbs in face of an impending siege from Edward Bruce's Scottish army, while 30 years later the Black Death caused serious mortality in the city. Dublin held its own, but hardly prospered in the late Middle Ages, and it was probably not until the 17th century that the city expanded beyond its 13th-century limits. Nevertheless, its position as Ireland's leading town was never seriously threatened, and this was the basis for its present status as Ireland's capital and largest city.

Time has not been kind to medieval Dublin. Little of its medieval fabric survived beyond the 19th century, while in the late 20th century a succession of appallingly insensitive road schemes have effectively destroyed the street pattern and layout of the medieval town. As a result it is difficult, when visiting the surviving sites, to appreciate them in relation to one another or within the context of the medieval town. In many

respects the real importance of Dublin lies in its exceptionally rich archaeological deposits, mainly of the 10th–13th centuries, which have been
revealed in a spectacular series of excavations. Deposits of the later
Middle Ages are unfortunately scanty, so that in many respects we know
more about Dublin in AD 1000 than in AD 1500. The main displays of
excavated material from Dublin are in the National Museum of
Ireland (*Kildare St.*) but smaller displays can be seen in the 'Dublinia'
interpretative centre (*beside Christ Church cathedral*).

Dublin Castle

The royal castle of Dublin was the symbolic centre of English rule in
Ireland until the 1920s. Its construction—on the site of an earlier castle
—was authorized by King John in 1204, but it was built mainly in the
period *c.*1213–30. The castle occupied the south-east angle of the walled
town and was a large keepless structure, roughly rectangular with large
drum towers at the corners and a twin-towered gatehouse in the middle
of the north side. Most of the medieval fabric was demolished in 18th-
century rebuilding and the only original feature still visible above
ground is the 'Record' tower at the south-eastern corner (now housing a
police museum). There is, however, an underground exhibition area
displaying excavated features around the north-eastern 'Powder' tower
(*accessible only by guided tour; admission charge*). The base of the medieval tower and adjoining northern curtain wall—with postern gate—are
visible, along with the foundations of the town wall carried on a large
arch over the castle moat. At the west end of the castle the bases of the
south-west and north-west towers can also be seen.

Christ Church cathedral

The church of Holy Trinity (Christ Church) was founded *c.*1030 as the
cathedral of recently Christianized Dublin—probably its first church.
Nothing is known of the early form of Christ Church, as all traces were
swept away in a complete rebuilding of the cathedral, which probably
began in the late 1180s under John Cumin, the first English archbishop.
The present form of the cathedral is based almost entirely on this late
12th-/early 13th-century rebuilding. However, this is largely due to
extreme late 19th-century restoration, which removed many later features in order to re-establish the 'original' form. Among the features lost
were the extended 'long choir' of the 14th century and the entire south
side of the nave, which had been rebuilt (admittedly rather poorly)
following the disastrous collapse of the original south side and nave
vaulting in 1562. As a result, relatively little of what is visible in Christ
Church today is original medieval fabric, but the restoration has at least
provided a reasonably accurate impression of the cathedral's form in the
13th century.

The earliest parts of the cathedral (c.1185–1200) are the transepts and choir, with the crypt below. Apart from the westernmost bay, the choir is a 19th-century restoration. The transepts and choir were built in a late Romanesque style with a clear south-western English flavour, reflecting the political changes in Dublin since 1171, when Henry II granted the city to the men of Bristol. Indeed, the very stones of the new cathedral reflected the political realities, for the architectural detailing was rendered in a fine, creamy limestone imported from Dundry, near Bristol. There was probably a crossing tower from the beginning, but the present tower is substantially a rebuilding of c.1600. The overall architectural design of this phase of building is undistinguished, but there are many well-carved capitals, especially on the north side. There is also a fine, substantially original round-headed doorway in the south transept, although it was moved here from the north transept in 1831.

The nave is later, although its date is less certain—previously dated c.1215–35, a date of c.1230–40 has recently been suggested. It is not particularly large—there are only six bays, of which the westernmost seems to be a slightly later addition. However, it contrasts with the choir and transepts, not only because it is built in Gothic style (again with definite west English influences) but because of its quality. Although the southern side of the nave is a restoration, the north elevation is almost entirely original and has rightly been described as 'the most distinguished piece of Gothic architecture in Ireland'. It is a sophisticated design with an early and very successful vertical integration of triforium and clerestory elements above the arcade, outlined by dark marble shafts. The arcade arches are deeply moulded and each bay is defined by a wall shaft running vertically from floor to vault. Again there is substantial use of imported Dundry stone for architectural detailing, and Purbeck marble (also from southern England) is used in the banded shafts which adorn the nave elevation. The upper parts of the north wall of the nave still lean markedly out of the vertical—a dramatic testimony to the lateral thrust of the original vault, which pushed the walls out and eventually led to its collapse in 1562.

One of the most interesting features of Christ Church is its crypt, which—unlike most British cathedrals—runs under the entire length of the cathedral (apart from the westernmost bay of the nave) and has recently been conserved. Its east end is almost certainly late 12th century, contemporary with the choir and transepts above, but the chronology of the west end is less clear. Most probably it was constructed after the east end, but prior to the construction of the nave overhead in the 1230s. Two other points of interest in the cathedral are the brass lectern at the east end of the nave—probably the only medieval lectern surviving in Ireland—and the so-called tomb of Strongbow under an arch of the south nave arcade. Strongbow—Richard de Clare, lord of Leinster—is thought to have been buried here on his death in 1176, but the effigy of a knight, traditionally said to be his, is at least a century later. A late 16th-century plaque on the aisle wall nearby records the destruction of Strongbow's tomb in the roof collapse of 1562, and it seems that another effigy was subsequently pressed into service as a replacement, because of the importance the original tomb had acquired in the medieval city's business life. Another monument of an important figure is in the chapel of St Lawrence (*on the east side of the south transept*)—a worn, early 13th-century effigy of an archbishop, probably the first English incumbent John Cumin (d. 1212). Outside the south transept are the remains of the 13th-century chapter house, the only visible remnant of the cloisters, which originally stood on the south side of the cathedral. The chapter house was originally a fine structure, with a three-light east window and elaborately moulded west doorway of two orders, flanked by smaller windows. There was also a ribbed vault in four bays overhead, supported by moulded wall shafts, parts of which survive.

St Patrick's cathedral

Dublin was almost unique in medieval Christendom in having two cathedrals. This was due to the first two English archbishops' desire to reduce the influence of the Augustinian canons who ran Christ Church cathedral. Archbishop Cumin established a new college of secular canons *c*.1190 at the church of St Patrick, an early church site just outside the walls of the town, to the south. Cumin's successor, Henry of London, raised this college to full cathedral status *c*.1220 and began the construction of the largest church in medieval Ireland. The cathedral was more or less complete by the time it was dedicated in 1254. Thus Dubliners of the period *c*.1230–40 would have witnessed both cathedrals being built simultaneously. Like Christ Church, St Patrick's was extensively restored in the 19th century and this work is poorly recorded, so that distinguishing original from restored fabric is difficult, even for experts. Most of the external architectural detailing is restoration—often of questionable authenticity—but the interior preserves the original 13th-century appearance reasonably accurately, and a lot of original detail survives.

The visitor enters through the south porch (a 19th-century addition), leading into the western end of the south aisle. This area is on a slightly different alignment from the remainder of the nave and has a lower, rather cruder vault. This has given rise to suggestions that it may be a fragment of Archbishop Cumin's late 12th-century collegiate church. The great belfry tower in the north-west angle is on a similar alignment and may also reflect the layout of the collegiate church, although the five-storey superstructure was rebuilt by Archbishop Minot *c*.1372, along with the adjacent north-west section of the nave. An original tower in this location, however, would explain the absence of a crossing tower in the 13th-century design—unlike the model at Salisbury.

Architecturally, St Patrick's is slightly less accomplished than the nave of Christ Church, but it has the virtue of being effectively a single-period structure with a unity and harmony rarely found in medieval cathedrals. Not surprisingly, it is very English—specifically west English—in style and has often been compared to Salisbury cathedral (built c.1220–60). Indeed, the imitation of Salisbury may well have been quite deliberate. The cathedral is cruciform, with aisled nave and choir and large aisled transepts. The internal elevations of nave, choir, and transepts are similar, strongly divided horizontally into the three orders of arcade, triforium, and clerestory. However, the architectural detail becomes less elaborate as one moves towards the west end—perhaps indicating a shortage of funds in the later stages of building. The original nave vault collapsed in 1544—as did that at Christ Church only 18 years later—and all the present vaulting is restored, apart from the crossing and fragments in the south nave aisle (east end), east aisle of the south transept (south end), and possibly the north choir aisle. The triple lancet west window is a 19th-century insertion, replacing a large, late medieval Perpendicular-style window, and the entire west front, with its flanking turrets and stepped battlements, seems to have been remodelled in typically Irish late medieval style.

At the east end, beyond the choir, is a beautiful Lady Chapel, almost entirely restored. The flying buttresses on the exterior of the choir are probably 14th/15th-century additions (although considerably repaired and restored subsequently). Among the internal features worth noting are two fine early 17th-century monuments at the west end of the nave—the Boyle monument on the south side and the Jones monument, almost opposite in the north aisle. At the west end of the north aisle are displayed two granite cross-slabs, probably of 9th/10th-century date and associated with the early church of St Patrick. Two further cross-slabs are displayed in the west aisle of the south transept. On the south wall of the choir are mounted two small, 16th-century memorial brasses—not particularly impressive, but among the very few surviving medieval brasses in Ireland. Further east, beyond a rail, is the effigy of Archbishop Michael Tregury (d. 1471, although the effigy may be slightly later). In the north choir aisle is a boldly carved, later 13th-century effigy of an archbishop, said to be Fulk de Sandford (d. 1271).

St Audoen's church

The medieval High Street widened at its west end into the Cornmarket. Both are now sadly mutilated by road widening, but Dublin's only surviving medieval parish church still stands here, on the north side of the street. St Audoen's, dedicated to a 7th-century bishop of Rouen

(France), was probably founded in the 12th century. It has recently been conserved and provided with a visitor centre in the south aisle (*admission charge*). The earliest parts of the present building are late 12th century, and there is no definite evidence of any earlier structures apart from a granite cross-slab now housed in the porch beside the tower. This slab—possibly 9th century—may be evidence for the existence on the site of an earlier church dedicated to St Colmcille (Columba), although this is unproven. Ironically, the oldest part of the church—the original nave of *c.*1190—is actually the only part still in use today (*accessible on regular guided tours from the visitor centre*). Although considerably modified, it is worth visiting for its late Romanesque west doorway (rebuilt) and font, and its fine aisle arcade, all carved in imported limestone from Dundry, near Bristol. There are also two interesting 17th-century monuments in the north wall.

The 12th-century church was greatly enlarged in the late Middle Ages, when St Audoen's was one of Dublin's wealthiest parish churches, patronized by several city guilds and a highly desirable burial place for wealthy citizens. A large south aisle, almost as large as the nave, was added probably in the 14th century; it now serves as the visitor centre. From 1430 this became the chapel of St Anne, maintained by a religious guild founded that year. Also in the early 15th century a tower was added to the west end of the aisle, although it was rebuilt in the 17th century. A modern porch connects the west end of the nave with the tower. The ground floor of the tower is dominated by the monument of Roland FitzEustace, Baron Portlester, and his wife Margaret Jenico. The monument is dated 1482, but Sir Roland did not, in fact, die until 1496 and is not buried in St Audoen's! The monument commemorates his founding a chapel—probably the aisle on the south side of the chancel—and it was presumably located there originally. This aisle and the long chancel to the north were added in the late 15th century, almost doubling the size of the church again.

A pathway running around the west and north sides of the church leads to 'St Audoen's arch'—actually the only surviving gateway of the medieval town, set within a section of the original (*c.*1100) town wall. Only the vaulted gate passage survives of the original three-storey gatehouse and it, like the adjoining town wall (best seen from the exterior, on Cook St.), has been considerably modified by later rebuilding, culminating in an inaccurate restoration in the 1970s. The pathway around the church follows the line of a medieval street, which originally ran directly uphill from the gate to High Street, passing to the east of what was then a much shorter church. When the extended chancel was added in the late 15th century this street was redirected around the west end of the church. A section of the older street is now displayed within the visitor centre. For a period it actually ran through a passage under the extended church (the blocked, arched opening in the church wall is still visible).

St Mary's abbey

St Mary's abbey was one of the great monasteries of medieval Ireland. It was probably founded in 1139 for the Benedictine order of Savigny, but became Cistercian in 1147. It was thus older even than **Mellifont** (though not as a Cistercian house) and the two abbeys frequently competed for seniority within Ireland. It was suppressed in 1539. St Mary's was unusually located (for a Cistercian house) just outside the city of Dublin, on the north side of the Liffey. This led to the destruction of most of the abbey in the late 17th century, as the city expanded. All that survives above ground is the fine rib-vaulted chapter house of *c.*1200 and adjoining slype or passage, rather incongruously buried within a 19th-century warehousing complex. Access is quite restricted (*Sundays and Wednesdays, June to September only; access from Meetinghouse Lane, off Mary's Abbey, west side of Capel St.*) but a visit is worthwhile. Displayed within are fragments of a fine 15th-century cloister arcade in Perpendicular style, probably from St Mary's.

Duleek, Co. Meath Early monastic site

8km south-west of Drogheda on R152, or take R150 west from N1 at Julianstown; signposted.

Duleek seems to be a genuinely early monastic foundation, said to have been founded by St Cianan (or even St Patrick himself) in the 5th century. It may also be the earliest recorded site of a stone church in Ireland. Indeed, its name [*Damhliag Chianan*, 'the stone church of Cianan'] preserves the early Irish term for a stone church and is recorded no later than the 7th century. It was frequently plundered by Vikings, but was still important enough to have been designated the see of a bishopric in the early 12th-century church reforms, although this was later reversed. Later in the 12th century the monastery was reconstituted as an Augustinian priory. It was raided by the English in 1171 and a daughter house of the English Augustinian abbey of Llanthony was established here *c.*1180. This house, St Michael's, functioned mainly as a grange, farming substantial estates for the benefit of Llanthony. It was dissolved before 1538.

The visible remains of the early monastic site consist of St Patrick's (or Cianan's) church, two high crosses, and unusual evidence for a round tower—in the form of a negative impression, 14 m high, in the side of the later medieval tower of the Augustinian priory. These are all located in or around the churchyard, north of the main street of the modern village. In addition, the outline of a roughly circular enclosure, up to 350 m in diameter, is preserved in the surrounding street pattern, with the main street forming the southern part. St Patrick's church (often mistakenly referred to as St Cianan's), a ruined building located north-west of the present churchyard, is later medieval in its present form but may incorporate parts of an earlier structure. Possible foundations of an earlier building are visible beneath the north and east walls, externally. Built into the north wall is an early grave slab with the inscription *ÓR DO SCANLAN*, 'a prayer for Scanlan'. Within the churchyard (north of the present church) is a small high cross of 9th/10th-century date, decorated mainly with geometric and animal ornament but with religious scenes on the west face. There is a *Crucifixion* on the cross head and the shaft has three panels which have been interpreted as scenes from the childhood of the Virgin Mary. Another high cross is represented by a base and cross head (with *Crucifixion*) now located within the ruins of the Augustinian priory. The priory church is located almost at the centre of the monastic enclosure and clearly occupies the site of the original principal church. The surviving remains consist of the large west tower, the south arcade and aisle of the nave, and part of the north choir aisle (incorporated into the modern church). The remains of the church are probably 13th century (although the east window of the south aisle is a later insertion) but the tower is late 15th/early 16th century.

Dunamase, Co. Laois Castle

5 km east of Portlaoise, off N7 (Dublin–Cork/Limerick) to south; best approached via N80 (Portlaoise–Stradbally); signposted.

This dramatic rock outcrop was already a royal site in the 840s, when it was attacked by Vikings, and its name [*Dún Máisc*, 'fort of Másc'] derives from that period. In 1170 Diarmait Mac Murchada, king of Leinster, gave the site to his ally Strongbow (Richard de Clare), from whom it passed to his successor as lord of Leinster, William Marshall. It seems that Marshall constructed much of the visible fabric of the castle in a few years from 1208, but it is clear that a castle of some form existed prior to this, when it was held by his vassal, Meiler FitzHenry. From the early 14th century, as English rule in the midlands crumbled, Dunamase came under increasing pressure from the local Ó Mordha (O'Moore) dynasty. In 1323 the castle was described as burnt and its associated manor destroyed. The Ó Mordha finally took the castle *c.*1330, but thereafter left it unoccupied for the rest of the Middle Ages. Much of the castle has been deliberately destroyed, probably with the use of gunpowder—this is usually attributed to the wars of the 1640s/1650s, but some of the damage may have happened as late as the late 18th century.

The layout of the castle is almost entirely determined by the natural contours of the rock outcrop. The only easy approach is from the southeast and here the main entrance was defended by outer earthworks, consisting of a large triangular area (the 'outer barbican') outlined by large rock-cut fosses and probably by strong timber defences. Within this is another triangular area (the 'inner barbican'), defended by a stone wall with an external bank and fosse, *c*.10 m wide. The wall is up to 1.6 m thick; it has no towers but instead relied on archery for defence—as is clear from the many arrow loops both at ground level and in the battlements. The only access through the wall was over a drawbridge and through a projecting rounded gatehouse, originally two-storeyed. The outer and inner barbicans are probably contemporary, and the inner barbican is certainly of 13th-century date—though whether early or later in the century is uncertain.

From the inner barbican, the castle proper was entered through a two-storeyed gatehouse in the main curtain wall. The gatehouse consists of two rectangular towers flanking an entrance passage, originally guarded by a portcullis and by archery loops in the walls of the flanking towers. Although the curtain wall is fragmentary, it is clearly thickest (up to 2.25 m) on the eastern side and has many archery loops on two levels along this side, as well as a small, open-backed rectangular tower at the southern end. Elsewhere, the curtain wall is a relatively thin, modest affair with no obvious defensive elaborations, apart from a postern gate on the south-west. Presumably the natural strength of the rock was felt to be sufficient defence on the north, west, and south sides, and only the east side had to be strongly fortified. The gatehouse and curtain wall replaced an earlier gatehouse—a rectangular structure with simple openings front and rear, located just to the north. The earlier gate-house and wall were probably built *c*.1180 by Meiler FitzHenry and the later gatehouse and wall by William Marshall, *c*.1208. Recent excavation has also shown that the curtain wall—at least in this area—is built along the line of much earlier (9th/10th-century?) drystone defences.

Crowning the summit of the rock is a large rectangular building resembling a keep—but it's actually a single-storey hall with a two-storey solar block at the east end, probably built *c*.1180. This building is badly damaged and was extensively modified in the late 18th century, but it seems that it originally had doorways in the north and south walls and window embrasures in the north, south, and west walls. In the 18th century both doorways were blocked and a new doorway inserted near the east end of the north wall. Along with the windows in the east wall, this doorway is dressed with late medieval stonework (apparently taken from another site), giving the false impression that the building was reused in the 16th century. The solar block was particularly heavily modified in the 18th century and most of the visible features, including the main (north–south) and smaller (east–west) cross-walls and the mural passage in the north-east corner, date to that period. Despite the thickness of its walls (almost 3 m in places), the hall as originally built was very weak, with two undefended doorways at ground level. Both doorways were therefore provided with forebuildings, for extra defence, in Marshall's works of *c*.1208. North-west of the hall are possible traces of a well or cistern, but no other buildings are visible within the castle enclosure.

Dunsany, Co. Meath Late medieval church

11 km east of Trim, off R154 (Clonee–Trim), in grounds of Dunsany Castle; turn east at Dunsany cross. Visits can be combined with a tour of Dunsany Castle, on weekday mornings between June and mid-November (excluding mid-August to mid-October).

This is one of three very similar manorial churches, all erected by a branch of the Anglo-Irish Plunkett family in the 15th century. No firm dating evidence is available but it has been suggested that Dunsany was built in the middle of the 15th century, in imitation of the slightly earlier church at nearby Killeen Castle, only 2 km to the east (*access restricted*). The third church, at Rathmore, 21 km to the north-west (*4 km north-east of Athboy, off N51*), may be the earliest of the three, although this cannot be proved. In plan and detailing, the three churches are almost identical; Dunsany (dedicated to St Nicholas) is the largest, although not necessarily the best preserved. It presents a fortress-like appearance, especially in the west façade with its two flanking towers. A spiral stair in the south-west tower led to a continuous wall walk and the walls were probably topped by battlements originally. This defensive aspect is a reflection of the insecurities of late medieval Ireland.

The internal plan is fairly simple—a nave and chancel of almost equal size, reflecting the fact that these churches were practically private, built for the use of their lordly patrons, their families, and a small number of servants. Further evidence of this is found in the large, two-level recess in the north wall of the nave, just inside the chancel arch. A doorway in the reveal of the chancel arch and a spiral stair in the thickness of the wall lead to the upper level. At this level the recess was originally continued out over the nave as a timber gallery, where the lord of the manor and his family sat, with a clear view through the chancel arch of the ceremonies at the altar. Behind the altar, the east window with its elaborate tracery is actually a 19th-century copy of that at Killeen. In the south wall is a once-fine sedilia, while opposite it, a doorway leads to a sacristy (now a burial vault) set within another tower, which contains residential chambers for a priest above. Two other features of the church are a fine baptismal font near the west end of the nave, carved around the bowl with figures of the twelve apostles, and a fine tomb set within the north wall recess. This tomb consists of a free-standing tomb chest, surmounted by the double effigies of a knight in armour flanked by his lady, dressed in a long pleated gown with horned headdress. The tomb surrounds bear the arms of (among others) the Plunketts and the FitzGeralds and this suggests it commemorates Sir Christopher Plunkett, probable builder of the church, and his first wife, Anne FitzGerald.

Fore, Co. Westmeath Early monastic site; medieval town; holy well

18 km north-east of Mullingar, off R195 (Castlepollard–Oldcastle) and R395 (Castlepollard–Delvin); signposted.

This small village is the site of an important early medieval monastic site, a later medieval priory, and a failed medieval town. The early monastic site was set in a secluded, marshy valley on the north side of Lough Lene, and is said to have been founded by St Feichín in the 7th century. The name Fore derives from *Fobhair Feichín* ('the spring of Feichín'). The monastery functioned until the late 12th century. In 1172 Hugh de Lacy, the new English lord of Meath, briefly occupied and burned the monastery. He established effective control of the area *c.*1180, and within the next few years built a motte-and-bailey castle and founded a French Benedictine priory. A borough had been established on the site by *c.*1235, and the presence of two parish churches indicates that the place thrived for a time. By the 15th century, however, Fore was an exposed frontier town at the north-western extremity of the Anglo-Irish colony. The Irish burned the priory in 1423, and the town in 1417 and *c.*1432, and it was probably in response to this that the town and priory were fortified or refortified. Grants of murage were made to the town by Henry VI in *c.*1436 and by Edward IV in 1463, but the town continued to decline into obscurity, surviving only as a small village.

Early monastic site

The early monastery was presumably enclosed, but no definite evidence of an enclosure is known—although it may be reflected in the slight curve in the line of the road, running north from the village green toward the priory. Otherwise, the only visible trace of the early monastery is St Feichín's church (*in the graveyard on the south side of the main road, c.100 m north-west of the village*). The church was originally a simple rectangular building, to which a chancel was added in the 13th century. The original structure displays the classic features of early Irish church architecture—steeply pitched gables, antae, and a lintelled west doorway with inclined jambs. The massive lintel, which tradition says could only be raised in place by St Feichín himself, bears a Greek cross in a circle. A 10th-century date for this church is quite possible. After the English conquest the church was adapted to serve as a parish church for the new town, and a chancel was added in the early 13th century to provide additional space. The chancel arch, which was inserted into the east wall of the original church, bears an interesting carved figure on the springing stone on the north side. The chancel was lit by narrow lancet windows in the north and south walls, and originally by a two-light east window, but this was replaced in the 15th century by a single-light ogee-headed window. Traces of the earlier window are visible underneath this, externally. Underneath it, internally, the base of the altar table survives, carved with two equal-armed crosses. In the south-east corner are a piscina and wall cupboard. Also in the chancel are a cross head decorated with marigold pattern and three fragments of grave slabs. These all date to the period of the early monastic site (8th–11th centuries), as does a plain high cross, reconstructed on a concrete shaft, in the graveyard east of the church. In the nave is a 13th-century font.

West of the church, at the foot of a rock outcrop, is another church-like structure known as the 'Anchorite's Cell'. Most of it is, in fact, a 19th-century mausoleum, but on the site of an earlier church, and the tower at the east end is late 15th/16th century. It may well occupy the site of an early medieval church associated with the monastic site, and in the late Middle Ages was occupied by a series of anchorites (hermits). On the east wall of the later mausoleum is preserved a wall plaque of 1616 commemorating the last of these anchorites, Patrick Begley.

Benedictine priory

350 m north of the village is the Benedictine priory of Sts Taurin and Feichín, founded in the early 1180s by Hugh de Lacy with Benedictine monks from Normandy. It was the only substantial Benedictine abbey in medieval Ireland. Like Fore itself, the priory experienced increasing insecurity in the later Middle Ages and was substantially rebuilt and fortified in the 15th century. It is located within its own defended precinct, on a natural hillock known as Knocknamonaster [*Cnoc na mainistir*, 'the hill of the monastery']. The hillock has been scarped and fortified with a large fosse and external bank on the west, north, and east sides, with traces of an entrance on the north side. At the south-west angle of the enclosure are the remains of a round-arched gateway, while the main entrance on the south-east is defended by a two-storey gatehouse with two towers on the east façade. The main priory buildings occupy the south-eastern angle of the enclosed area, but earthworks and wall footings are visible in other parts of the enclosure also. The remains of a dovecote are visible *c.*35 m north-east of the priory buildings.

The buildings follow the conventional layout, with the church on the north side of a cloister garth, which is surrounded by building ranges on the other three sides. The fabric is early 13th century with extensive 15th-century rebuilding. This rebuilding had two characteristics that are typical of many late medieval Irish churches and monasteries: Firstly, it was on a substantially smaller scale, almost certainly reflecting a reduced population, and secondly, it replaced the earlier communal arrangements with more comfortable, private residential accommodation for the monks. The church was originally a simple rectangular building, with practically no distinction between nave and choir, other than a change in floor level. There was a chapel on the north side, of which only foundations remain. There are Transitional (Romanesque-Gothic) round-headed lancet windows in the east gable, in the north wall of the choir (rebuilt in the 19th century), and at clerestory level in the south wall, suggesting a very early 13th-century date. The piscina in the south wall of the choir has similar mouldings; a doorway beside it leads to the east range of the cloister. In the 15th century a four-storey tower was built within the west end of the church, incorporating the original west gable and significantly reducing the length of the nave. This tower was a fortified residence, rather than a belfry, and was barrel vaulted over first-floor level. The upper floors were reached by a spiral stair in a turret at the north-east. At the same period other structures were built onto the outside of the church, to the west and north, but only foundations of these survive.

The cloisters to the south were originally laid out on a rectangular plan, but in the 15th-century a new south range was built within the original, reducing the length of the cloister garth by c.10 m to a roughly square plan. The kitchen at the south-west angle of the complex preserves the line of the original south range, the foundations of which survive to the east. The cloister arcade now consists only of reconstructed fragments, but is a good example of 15th-century Irish style—divided by internal piers into three bays on each side, each with four multi-cusped pointed openings. Immediately south of the church, in the east range, was the sacristy, which was rebuilt in the 15th century with another four-storey residential tower overhead. The room south of this should have been the chapter house, but in the 15th-century rebuilding both it and the next chamber seem to have been redesigned as residential apartments. On the first floor, overhead, are two further residential chambers, each with a fireplace and garderobe and clearly designed as lodgings for monks or, perhaps, as a suite of chambers for the prior. A doorway in the west wall of the southern chamber leads to the well-lit refectory, on the first floor of the rebuilt south range. At ground level underneath the refectory are three rooms, probably stores.

In the south-west angle of the refectory a mural stair leads down to the kitchen, which originally formed the west end of the south range, but is now a detached structure outside the later south range. On the south side are foundations of the large oven and, to the west of the kitchen, the foundations of a building with a sluice at the south-west angle—probably a mill. The west range was rebuilt in the 15th century as a three-storeyed structure, barrel vaulted over ground floor, with considerably thickened east and west walls. In the west wall is an original 13th-century fireplace, with a 15th-century replacement built in front of it. To the south is a projecting garderobe turret. At first-floor level was the monks' dormitory (or perhaps further residential apartments), with fragments of the second floor surviving midway along the west wall.

The town

The medieval borough was laid out along a single street, more or less on the line of the present street—although this has clearly been realigned somewhat to bypass the medieval gateways at either end. The position of these gateways, *c*.450 m apart, also indicates how much larger the medieval town was than the modern village. Near the south-eastern end of the town the street widened into a triangular market place, with a street running off to the north towards the Benedictine priory, and another to the east towards the motte-and-bailey castle. The gatehouses, which defended the main points of entry and exit, are probably 15th century. The north gate (*120 m north-west of St Feichín's church*) is the smaller and simpler of the two, consisting of a rectangular structure with a central round-arched opening. A murder hole in the soffit of the arch indicates that there was an upper floor, but no trace of this, or of the rear of the gatehouse, survives. The south gate (*south-east of the modern village*) is a slightly more elaborate structure, with a segmental-arched opening and a spiral stair to one side leading to an upper floor. On the south side of this gatehouse a bank up to 1.5 m high runs south-west for over 100 m. It has a core of stone rubble and traces of masonry facing and probably represents the remains of the town wall erected in conjunction with the gatehouses in the 15th century. Otherwise, however, no definite trace of the town defences survives and even their line is difficult to reconstruct.

To the north of the south gatehouse, in the old graveyard on the north side of the modern Catholic church, are the ruins of the parish church of St Mary. This church, with its typically English dedication, was probably founded when the new borough was being established in the early 13th century. The ruins are fragmentary, overgrown, and featureless apart from a late medieval ogee-headed window in the east gable. 400 m east of the village is the motte-and-bailey castle (*on private property*), probably erected by Hugh de Lacy in the early 1180s. Sited on a ridge overlooking the town, with commanding views to the west and south, the motte is oval in plan with a roughly square bailey to the south-west. Both are surrounded by a large fosse with outer bank, while another fosse separates motte and bailey.

There is a local folklore tradition of the Seven Wonders of Fore, some of which have their roots in the archaeology of the valley: the Anchorite in the Stone; the Stone raised by St Feichín's prayers; the Monastery in a bog; the Water that won't boil; the Wood that won't burn; the Mill without a race; the Water that flows uphill.

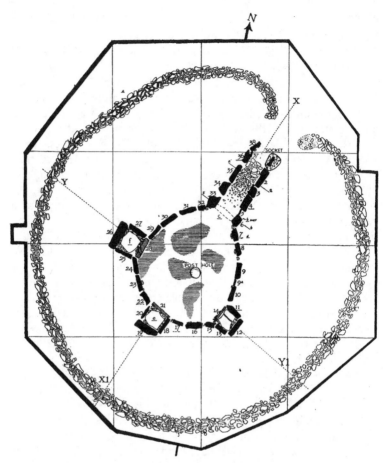

▲ Fig. 87. Fourknocks I: plan of site as excavated (after Hartnett)

Fourknocks, Co. Meath Passage tomb cemetery and prehistoric complex

26 km north of Dublin. From the village of Naul (west of M1 motorway) the site is reached via R108 (to Drogheda) to the north, taking the first turn to the west, or via R122 (to Garristown/Oldtown) to the west, taking the first turn to the north; signposted. Disc. Ser. 43.

A Passage tomb cemetery lies at the core of this complex of early pre-historic religious monuments, which also includes a number of smaller tumuli and a concentration of no fewer than three henges. Passage tomb no. 1 is the only National Monument in the complex; the remaining monuments are on private property. The Passage tombs, sited on a hill above the village of Naul, are 16 km south-east of the Boyne Valley and

18 km east of Tara, and were excavated by Paddy Hartnett 1950–2. Fourknocks I, the smaller of the two tombs (19 m diameter), comprises a mound of sods surrounded by a low, drystone kerb. The passage leads from the north-north-east into a large, oval-shaped chamber with three recesses. The roof of the chamber was partially corbelled. Estimating that the volume of collapsed roofstones was insufficient to close over the roof space, Hartnett suggested that the remainder of the roof was wooden, supported by a central wooden post. The passage may also have been unroofed. Eleven stones are decorated. Geometric patterns predominate and one of the compositions is said to be anthropomorphic. Burials were confined to the passage and the three recesses, in each of which a primary deposit of cremated bone (15 cm–25 cm thick) was sealed beneath flagstones. A combination of cremations and inhumations, the burials in the passage reached to the tops of the orthostats. Analysis of the burials suggests that adults were accorded the rite of cremation, primary location in the recesses, and were accompanied by grave goods, whereas children (often inhumed) were placed peripherally, in the passage. Grave goods included stone and bone pendants and beads, pin fragments, flints, and 13 stone balls. Cattle, sheep, and pig bones and some marine shells were also found.

Fourknocks II (50 m to the east of Fourknocks I) is an altogether more complex monument and difficult to interpret. The mound (25 m in maximum diameter) was surrounded by a penannular fosse. Off-centre, in the core of the mound, was a small cairn of soil and stones (11 m in diameter) that was also surrounded by a berm and annular fosse. Beneath the cairn was a number of concentric arcuate and C-shaped settings of stones, in the centre of which was a small pit with charcoal and cremated bone. Under the opposite side of the mound a short megalithic passage, positioned through the gap in the outer fosse, terminated in a short, deep transverse trench, interpreted as a crematorium. The trench contained some cremated burials of adults, whereas the bones (mostly unburnt and disarticulated) of children were found in the megalithic passage. Sherds of Carrowkeel Ware were found in the mound.

Both tumuli were reused as cemetery mounds during the earlier Bronze Age. Eight burials were placed into the mantle of soil over Fourknocks I. Five were contained in cists, four of which contained crouched burials of children (one was empty); one was accompanied by a Bowl. Two inverted Vase Urns were also found in pits, this time associated with the bones of adults. There were eight burials (four in cists and four in pits), including both cremation and inhumation, inserted into Fourknocks II. These too were accompanied by Bowls and cinerary urns. A small mound (15 m in diameter and 2 m high) near the two Passage tombs covered the cremated remains of a child accompanied with a Cordoned Urn. A Vase was also found in the mound. To the east of

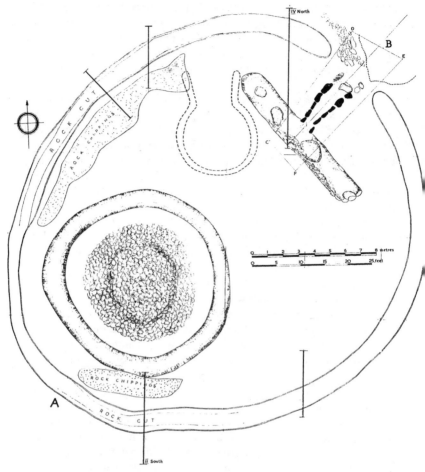

▲ **Fig. 88.** Fourknocks II: plan of site as excavated (after Hartnett)

Fourknocks II is another mound, Fourknocks III (15 m diameter and 2 m high), which proved upon excavation to cover a small pit containing soil, charcoal, and cremated bone. It may be contemporary with the Passage tomb. Two Cordoned Urn burials were later placed into the mound.

A fourth large mound (23 m in diameter and 4 m high) occurs about 1 km north of Fourknocks in the townland of Micknanstown. It is probably an outlying Passage tomb and is situated beside one of three henges (*all in private ownership*), ranging in size from around 80 m to 200 m in diameter, to be found within a short distance of the Passage tombs. Their presence emphasizes the importance of this area in early prehistory and the recurring association that exists between henges and Passage tombs in Ireland.

Furness, Co. Kildare Rock art

3 km east of Naas; marked 'Forenaughts' on maps. Take minor road north (towards Rathcoole) off R410 (Naas–Blessington), 3 km south-east of Naas, then first turn to west (left) after 2.5 km. Disc. Ser. 56.

A greywacke boulder decorated with rock art now stands in the grounds of the late medieval church of Furness, moved there following its accidental discovery in 1975 in a field some 200 m to the south-east. One face only is decorated with interesting combinations of cupmarks and concentric circles. 700 m further north is the famous Longstone Rath, a henge at the centre of which is a 5.1 m tall standing stone. Excavations here, at the beginning of the 20th century, uncovered a cist containing a stone wrist-guard. A similarly tall standing stone, also with a burial cist at the base, stands at **Punchestown**, 5 km to the south. Eoin Grogan excavated a very low-profile Iron Age barrow nearby.

Glendalough, Co. Wicklow Early monastic site

40 km south of Dublin on R756 (Laragh–Hollywood); accessible either from N11 (Dublin–Wexford) or N81 (Dublin–Baltinglass); visitor centre.

One of Ireland's most visited National Monuments, the monastic site at Glendalough is said to have been founded by St Coemhghein (Kevin) in the 6th century. At that stage it must have been a small hermitage in a remote mountain valley, but Glendalough [*Gleann dá locha*, 'the valley with two lakes'] subsequently grew into an important foundation, and was chosen as the seat of a diocese in 1111. Much of the diocese was reassigned to **Dublin** later in the 12th century, however, and in 1216 Glendalough was fully absorbed into the diocese of Dublin. The monastery continued to function—as an Augustinian priory—until destroyed by the English in 1398. There are two distinct clusters of monuments at Glendalough—one around the southern edge of the Upper Lake and a larger concentration east of the Lower Lake. The relationship between these two clusters is unclear. It is usually suggested that Kevin's original foundation was a hermitage at the Upper Lake and that the focus of the monastic site later (perhaps in the 8th century) moved further down the valley to a level area below the Lower Lake, within the confluence of two small rivers. There has been very little archaeological excavation here, however, and this sequence is by no means certain.

Upper Lake

A partly man-made cave in the rock face above the Upper Lake, on the south side, is pointed out as 'St Kevin's bed', where tradition says the

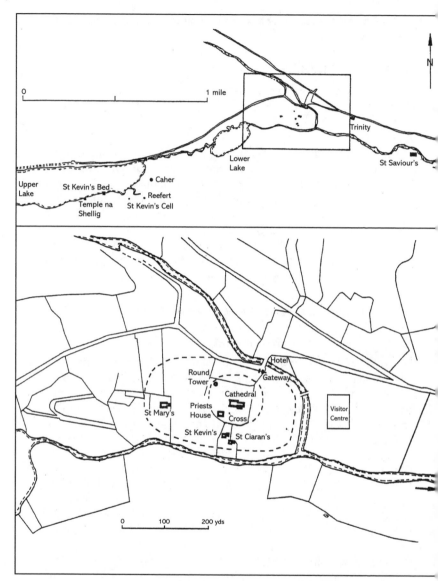

▲ **Fig. 89.** Glendalough: plan of site showing major monuments (after Bradley)

saint spent prolonged periods in prayer. It can only be approached by boat from the lake, as can the nearby *Teampull na Scellig* ('the church of the rock'), a small rectangular church with a two-light east window and a west doorway with inclined jambs. Rebuilt in the 12th century, the church was also partially reconstructed more recently. At the east gable is an inscribed Latin cross and three smaller crosses. To the west, a raised platform surrounded by stone walling may have contained domestic buildings.

At the south-east corner of the lake (*accessible from the footpath*) is Reefert [*Righ Fearta*, 'the burial place of kings']. This attractive but small nave-and-chancel church of the late 11th/early 12th centuries has a flat-lintelled west doorway and a round chancel arch of granite (reconstructed in the 1870s). Projecting corbels at the six external angles would have supported the outer beams of the timber roof. Within the enclosed area to the east of the church are two stone crosses, one with carved interlace. This was probably the burial place of a number of kings of Leinster. The foundations of another small church are to be seen across the river, to the east. To the west, on a spur overlooking the lake, is 'St Kevin's Cell', the foundations of a round building, 3.6 m in diameter, possibly of *clochán* construction with corbelled stone roof and a doorway to the east.

On lower ground at the east end of the Upper Lake is the 'Caher', a small, round stone-walled enclosure. Such structures are normally seen as stone equivalents of the earthen ringfort, an early medieval settlement site, but this enclosure is quite small and may have had another function, perhaps even as a small burial enclosure.

Lower Lake

Around the Lower Lake, traces of two concentric enclosures can be read into the surviving features, although physical remains of the enclosures (which seem to have consisted of large drystone walls) are hard to locate on the ground. The outer enclosure was bounded on the north, east, and south by the confluence of two small rivers, but the western limit is less clear. This oval enclosure measured almost 200 m from north to south, and at least 300 m (possibly much more) from east to west. A unique feature of this enclosure is the stone gatehouse on the north side, which is still the main entrance to the site from the street. Originally a two-storey structure, the gatehouse has large round-arched openings in the north and south walls, flanked by antae—a characteristic feature of early Irish church architecture. A large cross is inscribed on a stone just inside the gatehouse. The outline of the inner enclosure is more difficult to reconstruct, but its western and southern limits are probably indicated by the position of the round tower (usually on or near the line of the enclosure) and the curving south-western and south-eastern corners of the graveyard. This would indicate a roughly circular enclosure, slightly over 100 m in diameter, with the cathedral at its centre.

The cathedral consists of a simple rectangular nave with later chancel and sacristy. The nave is the second largest pre-Romanesque church in Ireland, after the early 10th-century cathedral at **Clonmacnoise**, and the Glendalough cathedral is probably of similar date, or perhaps slightly later. At first glance, it is classic early Irish church architecture, with antae at the east and west ends, a large, flat-lintelled west doorway, and—in the lower parts of the walls—masonry of large, squared mica-schist stone (actually only a thin facing over a rubble core). The upper parts of the walls are different—of rubble masonry—and it has been plausibly suggested that the large facing blocks below are reused from an earlier, smaller church and simply were not sufficient to face the entire building. The doorway, too, seems to be reused from this earlier church, with additional blocks inserted just below the lintel to raise the height. Substantial alterations were made in the later 12th century, after Glendalough became the seat of a diocese and this church became a cathedral. The chancel was added, accessed through a fine Romanesque arch inserted in the east wall of the nave, and with a small sacristy on the south side. In the south wall of the chancel are an aumbry and a piscina. A new doorway was also inserted in the north wall of the nave at this date.

*c.*50 m north-west of the cathedral is the fine round tower, which is 30.5 m high and probably had five floors internally. The roof was restored in the 19th century. The granite doorway has a rounded arch carved into the lintel stone, and is set 3.2 m above ground, facing south-east towards the west end of the cathedral. South of the cathedral is 'St Kevin's cross', a plain high cross of granite, with unpierced ring. Such undecorated crosses are difficult to date, but a 9th/10th-century date is possible.

The only other structure visible within the inner enclosure is the 'Priest's House', apparently so called because priests were interred there in the 18th and 19th centuries. It is a very small rectangular oratory or shrine with a Romanesque-style arched recess on the exterior of the east wall, suggesting a later 12th-century date. The function of this recess is uncertain. The other notable feature of the building is the gabled lintel stone over the south door, carved with a scene showing a seated figure flanked by two others, one carrying a churchman's handbell, the other a crosier. If this was a shrine, it may have been built to enclose the grave or tomb of St Kevin himself.

Within the outer enclosure are three further churches. The most interesting is St Kevin's church (*south of the Priest's House*), popularly known as 'St Kevin's kitchen' because of its distinctive attached round tower. Suggestions of the date of this church range from the 9th to 12th centuries, and there is still no certain evidence to date it, but it clearly had a relatively complex structural history. It was originally a simple rectangular church with a flat-lintelled west doorway. Unfortunately, this doorway is kept closed (*except on official guided tours*) and the interior of the church is usually not accessible, but can be viewed through the metal gate at the east end. The church has one of the finest corbelled stone roofs of any early Irish church, characteristically steep with an internal arch or vault about halfway up the slope, designed to prevent the sides of the roof from sagging inwards. A space above the vault was accessed through an opening near the west end, and this in turn provided access to the unique round tower built over the west end of the church. The tower rises to *c*.13.5 m above ground and was added later—though probably no later than the 12th century. There was another chamber (possibly residential) immediately below the vault, supported on timber beams inserted in the side walls of the church *c*.3.8 m above ground. The voids in which the beams sat are still visible. A small chancel, now reduced to foundations, was later added to the church, with a sacristy to the north; both were stone roofed. The roof line of the chancel is visible in the east gable of the nave, along with two small slit windows to light the space above the vault and the chamber below it. The present round-headed 'entrance' at the east end is actually the chancel arch, broken through the east wall of the original church to provide access to the new chancel. It cut through the original east window, traces of which can still be seen above the round arch.

Beside St Kevin's church, to the south-east, is a very small nave-and-chancel church, of which little more than the foundations survive. It is thought to have been dedicated to St Ciarán of **Clonmacnoise**, reflecting close links between Glendalough and **Clonmacnoise** in the early Middle Ages.

c.150 m to the north-west is St Mary's church, another simple rectangular church to which a chancel was later added. The chancel, and a doorway inserted in the north wall of the nave, are probably 12th century. The nave itself is obviously earlier, but cannot be dated more precisely. Its main feature is its massive flat-lintelled west doorway. On the underside of the lintel is carved a saltire cross with circular expansions in the centre and at the ends of the arms.

Outside the monastic enclosure, to the east, is Trinity church (*accessed from the main road*), another nave-and-chancel church—although in this case the chancel is original, not a later addition. There is, however, a later addition at the west end of the nave—a small, square structure originally with a corbelled stone roof, traces of which can be seen on the north wall (the other walls are reconstructed). Until 1818 this annexe supported a round tower, which was presumably built up from the stone roof much as the tower in St Kevin's church. When the annexe was built, a round-headed doorway was inserted in the south wall of the nave to replace the fine flat-lintelled west doorway, which now served only for access to the annexe. The simple round-headed windows in the east wall of the chancel and south wall of the nave, and a triangular-headed window in the south wall of the chancel, are similar to those found in many round towers and on this basis the church can probably be dated to the 11th/12th centuries.

The most distant church at Glendalough is St Saviour's priory, *c.*1 km east of the main monastic enclosure (*accessed via the 'Green road' south of the monastic enclosure, across the river*). This Augustinian priory was probably founded by St Lorcán Ua Tuathail, the most famous abbot of Glendalough (1153–62) and later archbishop of Dublin. Lorcán was a supporter of the 12th-century church reform movement and the priory may have been deliberately built at a distance from the main monastery to allow him to train followers in the new ideas of church reform and the Augustinian rule. The nave-and-chancel church has interesting Romanesque features, particularly a fine decorated chancel arch and twin-light east window with round rear arch. These, and the other windows in the church, were reconstructed in the 1870s. Adjoining the north side of the church is a rectangular building, probably a residence or dormitory. A stairway in the east wall led to a chamber above the chancel, which was originally vaulted.

Greatheath, Co. Laois Ring barrow cemetery

5.5 km north-east of Portlaoise, off M7 motorway, but best approached via Dunamase off the N80 (Portlaoise–Carlow). Disc. Ser. 55.

This ring barrow cemetery comprises nine extant specimens. The best defined is fortunately also the most accessible—at the south end of the cemetery, and nearly 16 m in diameter. There is a slight depression in the centre of the mound, which may be the result of modern disturbance.

Kells, Co. Meath Early monastic site

15 km north-west of Navan on N3 (Dublin–Cavan).

Kells was, at the dawn of history, a royal site associated with the legendary *Conn Céadchatach* ('of the hundred battles') and Cormac mac Airt. It is overlooked by a prehistoric hillfort on the Hill of Lloyd. Excavations in 1987 behind 'St Columb's House' (see below) uncovered part of a circular fosse and artefacts of early 7th-century date, but little is known of the pattern of human activity at Kells prior to the 9th century. In *c.*804 the site was granted to the community of St Columba's monastery of Iona (off the west coast of Scotland), as a safe refuge from Viking raids, following a number of attacks on Iona itself. The grant was probably part of a settlement between two rival Uí Néill dynasties, Clann Cholmáin and Síl nAedo Sláine, both of whom had territorial ambitions in this area. A further devastating attack on Iona in 806 prompted the commencement of building at Kells, and the first church was completed in 814. In 878 the relics of Columba were removed from Iona to Kells, which was becoming an important monastic site in its own right, and possibly even developing into a quasi-urban settlement. In 1007 Ferdomnach was appointed abbot of Kells and *comarba* (heir) of Columba by the Clann Cholmáin king of Tara, Máel Sechnaill, at the revived

Teltown Fair. The appointment was part of a plan to create a Columban-Clann Cholmáin alliance, to rival Brian Borumha's recent alignment with Armagh. It also marked the end of a 9th/10th-century connection between the Columban *familia* and Armagh—eloquently recorded on the South Cross at Kells, which is dedicated to Sts Patrick and Columba (*PATRICII ET COLUMBA CRUX*).

Kells was a major artistic centre in the early medieval period. This is reflected in the surviving high crosses—possibly the finest collection at any one site—and in metalwork such as the Shrine of the Cathach (*now in the National Museum of Ireland*), known to have been made at Kells in the 11th century. Kells's most famous treasure is, of course, the Book of Kells (*now in Trinity College, Dublin*), though it is uncertain whether the book was actually produced at Kells or Iona (or both) at the turn of the 8th/9th centuries. This is almost certainly the 'great Gospel of Colmcille', which was stolen from the main church of Kells in 1007. Fortunately it was subsequently recovered, although its ornate shrine had been removed. Kells retained its status into the 12th century. A separate Augustinian abbey (of which no trace survives) was probably founded in the 1140s, and Kells was the venue for the important reforming synod of 1152, at which it was designated as the centre of the new diocese of Bréifne. Nevertheless, Kells's greatest days were over by this date. At roughly the same date as the synod, it was replaced by **Derry** as the chief monastery of the Columban community, and the diocese of Kells was absorbed into the diocese of Meath in the early 13th century. The English conquest brought a further significant loss of status for Kells, effectively cutting it off both from its Columban roots and from the bulk of the Bréifne diocese, which was forced to establish a new diocesan centre at Kilmore, Co. Cavan. Hugh de Lacy, the new lord of Meath, built a castle at Kells in 1176 and the de Lacys had established a borough and founded a priory/hospital of the *Fratres Cruciferi* there, before the end of the 12th century. Whatever benefit Kells may have derived from de Lacy patronage ended, however, with the death of the last de Lacy lord in 1241 and the division of the lordship of Meath between his heiresses. It was important enough to be walled, at some point, and survived throughout the Middle Ages as an increasingly exposed frontier town.

Monastic site

Some traces of the early medieval monastic site survive at Kells. The outlines of two concentric enclosures, which originally defined the monastery, are partially preserved in the modern street pattern. The curving line of Carrick St./Cross St. reflects the northern and eastern sectors of an outer enclosure, which must have measured c.360 m (east–west) by c.280 m (north–south). Within this, Church St., Church Lane, and Cannon St. define an inner enclosure, still largely occupied by St

Columba's church and containing four high crosses and a round tower. The modern church probably occupies the site of the principal early medieval church, and beside it is the belfry tower of its late medieval predecessor (probably 15th century). Within the church are the remains a 14th-century grave slab and two medieval baptismal fonts, one from Knightstown, the other from Martry.

Round tower

On the south side of this inner enclosure, straddling the (later) grave-yard wall on Cannon St., is the round tower. It is 26 m high at present but would have been c.31 m high originally, with six floors. The round-headed doorway faces north and is 1.9 m above present ground level in the graveyard, but 4.2 m above the pavement outside the graveyard wall—which is probably closer to the original ground level. The doorway has a carved head on one jamb, with an uncarved block on the other side and an uncarved panel over the arch, probably intended to receive other carvings that were never finished. In 1076 Murchad, king of **Tara**, was murdered in this tower.

High crosses

Five high crosses of sandstone survive, in whole or in part, at Kells—four of them within the churchyard at the centre of the monastic enclosure, including a decorated cross base standing near the late medieval belfry tower. Most of the crosses have been reconstructed, to some extent, in the past and may not stand in their original locations. In some respects the most interesting of the crosses is the one on the south side of the church, because it is clearly unfinished and tells us a lot about how these crosses were carved. The ringed cross head has been fully carved, with a partially finished *Crucifixion* on the east face. To either side of this, however, and on the shaft below are blocked-out panels intended to receive further scriptural scenes, but never completed. Unlike the other crosses, which are probably 9th century, this cross may date to the 10th century.

Near the west door of the church is the shaft of what must once have been a very fine cross, known as the 'Broken Cross'. A worn inscription on the base has been read as *OROIT DO ARTGAL* ('a prayer for Artgal'). The shaft is decorated with panels of scriptural scenes from the Old and New Testaments, as follows (from base to top):

East face: *Baptism of Christ*
Marriage Feast at Cana
(?)*Christ Heals a Lame Man* (left), *Christ Blesses Samaritan Women* (right)
The Christ Child being Bathed

        The Magi Meet Herod
        Christ Enters Jerusalem (fragmentary)
West face: *Adam and Eve*
        Noah's Ark
        Moses and Aaron with Pharaoh
        Israelites led by a Pillar of Fire
        Crossing the Red Sea (fragmentary)

Near the round tower is the 'Cross of Sts Patrick and Columba', so called because of the inscription on top of the base (east face). The broad faces of the cross carry scriptural scenes but, unlike the other crosses, these are not arranged in formal, framed panels. The west face is dominated by the *Crucifixion*, with Christ flanked by the spear- and cup-bearer. Above this Christ sits in majesty or, perhaps, in judgement. The east face has a greater number of distinct scenes, as follows (from base to top):

Adam and Eve (left); *Cain and Abel* (right)
Three Youths in the Furnace
Daniel in the Lions' Den (bottom of cross head)
Sacrifice of Isaac (left arm of cross)
Sts Paul and Anthony (right arm of cross)
David Playing the Harp (top of cross head)

Outside the new Heritage Centre (*Headford Place, on the N3*) is the recently re-erected Market Cross, which formerly stood at the corner of Market St. and Cross St. An inscription on the cross records its erection in that position in 1688, and this may well have been its original location—on the line of the outer enclosure of the early medieval monastic site, to the east. The narrow sides bear a series of figured panels that cannot be confidently identified, but the broad faces carry more conventional scriptural scenes, as follows (from base to top):

South face: *Christ in the Tomb, with Soldiers*
            David and the Israelites
            Adam and Eve (left); *Cain and Abel* (right)
            Sacrifice of Isaac (left arm of cross)
            Daniel in the Lions' Den (cross head)
            Temptation of St Anthony (left arm of cross)
North face: *Christ Blesses the Children*
            Christ Heals the Centurion's Servant
            Miracle of the Loaves and Fishes
            Temptation of St Anthony (left arm of cross)
            Crucifixion (cross head)
            Sts Paul and Anthony Fight the Devil (right arm of cross)

The base is decorated with a mixture of horsemen and animals, possibly a hunting scene. The slash-like grooves around the top of the base are the same as those on the cross-slab at **Kilnasaggart**, Co. Armagh.

St Columb's House

While the principal medieval church does not survive, there is a classic example of the early Irish church with steeply pointed stone roof, located uphill to the right of the present church grounds. It is known as 'St Columb's House', but it is a church and, indeed, may be a very early one. Radiocarbon dates for the mortar suggest a date in the 9th century, perhaps soon after the foundation of the monastery in 804. The original entrance was in the west wall, but the building is now entered at a lower level, through a relatively modern doorway in the south wall. The church originally had a timber floor, but this has long since vanished and the interior ground level has been substantially reduced. The interior was divided into two floors and above the vaulted roof is a small attic accessible by ladder.

Town walls

The later medieval town was apparently walled; murage grants are known at various dates from 1326 to 1472, but the walls were ruinous by 1654 and even their location is uncertain in some respects. It seems that the walls followed the line of the monastic enclosure on the west, but enclosed a more extensive area to the north, east, and south. Five gates are referred to, located on Cannon St., Carrick St., Maudlin St., John St./Headfort Place, and Bective St./Suffolk St., respectively, but their precise locations are uncertain. The only surviving fragment of town wall is a stretch of c.70 m to the rear of the properties on the south side of Cannon St., which incorporates a small, round mural tower.

St John's priory

This priory/hospital of the *Fratres Cruciferi*, founded by Walter de Lacy c.1199, was located outside the east (Dublin) gate of the town. It was suppressed in 1539 and no standing remains are visible in the graveyard, which occupies the site on the north side of Headfort Place. Within the graveyard are a number of architectural and sculptural fragments, probably derived from the priory, including (in the north-western part of the graveyard) a crudely carved 13th-century effigial slab of a woman.

Kildare, Co. Kildare Early monastic site; medieval town
50 km south-west of Dublin, off M7 (Dublin–Cork/Limerick).

Kildare [*Cill Dara*, 'the church of the oak-wood'] was one of medieval Ireland's major monastic sites and may also have been one of the earliest—traditionally founded by St Brigid in the early 6th century. There are strong indications of pre-Christian origins as a pagan cultic site and Brigid herself may be a Christianized version of a Celtic goddess, rather

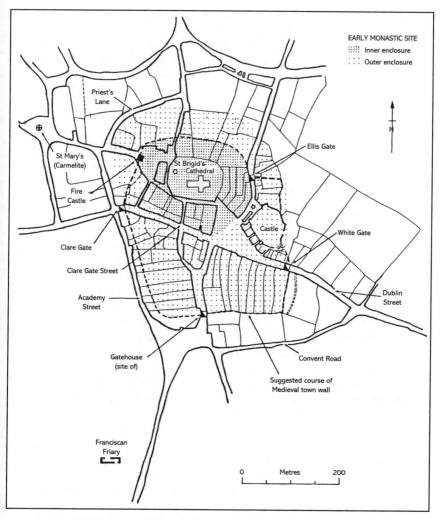

▲ **Fig. 90.** Kildare: outline map showing location of medieval features (after Bradley)

than a historical person. However, evidence that the early monastery was partly, if not entirely, for women is consistent with a female founder in the 6th century. The earliest definite historical evidence for the monastery occurs in the early 7th century and soon after this we get the first biography of Brigid. This describes an elaborately decorated wooden church on the site, divided into sections for monks and nuns, with tomb shrines of Brigid and the first bishop, Conlaed. In later centuries Kildare was closely associated with the Uí Cheinnselaig kings of Leinster and was chosen as the seat of a diocese in the 12th century reforms. It was occupied by the English very early in the conquest. By 1175 a borough had been established and a motte-and-bailey castle probably erected by Richard de Clare ('Strongbow'), the new lord of Leinster. He may even have intended to make Kildare the main centre of the lordship of Leinster, but as the lordship disintegrated in the later 13th century Kildare lost importance. From the 14th century it was little more than a small provincial town and was seriously damaged in the wars of the late 16th century and mid-17th century.

Early monastic site

The visible remains of the early monastery, in the cathedral churchyard, are a plain high cross (*west of the cathedral*) and the round tower. There are also a number of grave slabs, dating not later than the 12th century, in the cathedral. However, the boundaries of the churchyard itself almost certainly preserve much of the outline of the original inner enclosure of the early monastery. Similarly, the outline of a larger, outer enclosure is partially preserved in the street pattern to the east (Nugent St.) and west (White Abbey St.) of the churchyard. Another feature of the modern town which almost certainly has its roots in the early medieval monastery is the market place, located immediately outside the churchyard, to the south-east. The round tower is in a classic location, near the boundary of the inner enclosure and north-west of the cathedral, which its doorway faces. It is 33 m high but lacks its roof—the battlements are a later addition—and originally would have stood 34–5 m high. The lowest 3 m is built of well-coursed granite blocks, while the remainder above this is of limestone rubble masonry. This may suggest a rebuilding of the tower, or at least that it was built in two distinct stages. The doorway is 4.6 m above ground and was once finely decorated with four Romanesque orders in red sandstone, with a triangular hood moulding above; it is now much reconstructed. The windows (other than those on the top floor) are unusual, being narrow slits splaying widely internally. The tower has six floors and can be climbed to the top.

Cathedral

The cathedral is a cruciform structure with an aisleless nave and a massive central tower, probably built in the early 13th century by the first English bishop, Ralph of Bristol. Already in ruins by *c.*1600 it was further damaged in 1641 and was substantially restored in the late 19th century. The chancel, north transept, north side of the tower, and west wall of the nave are 19th-century replacements. Most of the structure is original 13th-century fabric, however, and the overall appearance is probably quite faithful to the medieval form. It is lit by lancet windows throughout, grouped in threes at the gable ends of the chancel and transepts. The architectural treatment of the windows is simple and plain. The most distinctive feature of the architecture is an arcade of wide arches running around the exterior, springing from buttresses between the windows and supporting a wall walk and parapet with late medieval stepped battlements. These have been dated to the end of the 14th century, following the granting of a papal indulgence to raise funds for the repair of the cathedral, and they strikingly reflect the growing insecurity of the times. Displayed within the cathedral is an important collection of medieval stone carving, including a rare early medieval motif piece (*mounted on the south wall of the nave*), a unique early 16th-century 'pardon stone' (*set on a window ledge in the south transept*), and a number of effigies and tomb chests. South-east of the cathedral, near the entrance to the churchyard, are the foundations of a circular structure, unfortunately 'restored' by an over-zealous local committee. This structure is called the 'fire house' but it is not certain that this is actually the structure referred to in medieval documents, within which a perpetual fire was kept burning.

Castle

A motte-and-bailey castle was probably built at Kildare by Richard de Clare early in the 1170s. No trace of this survives but its location can be established, on the eastern end of the ridge on which the original monastic enclosure and later cathedral stood. This earthen castle was replaced by a stone castle in the early 13th century. Again, little trace of this survives, the only visible remnant being a four-storey gatehouse, largely of 15th-century date, but which may incorporate parts of an earlier structure (*north side of Dublin St., behind Courthouse; private property*).

Friary

500 m south of the cathedral, now just outside the town, are the ruins of the Franciscan friary (*take R415 south from centre of town; friary is in graveyard on west side of road*). Founded c.1254 by the English lord William de Vesci, it was subsequently patronized by the FitzGerald earls of Kildare, the most powerful Anglo-Irish nobles in Ireland. The friary seems to have been the earls' main burial place in the 14th and 15th centuries and several are known to have been buried there. Unfortunately, only the friary church has survived the turbulent 16th and 17th centuries, and even this is in poor condition. It can be made out to be of the usual long, rectangular friary church type. Most original opes are either destroyed or obscured, but there seems to have been a row of at least six closely spaced lancet windows in the north wall of the

choir. The location of the cloisters, on the south side of the church, can be made out from earthworks at ground level and beam-holes in the church wall, for the lean-to roof of the north ambulatory.

Kiltiernan, Co. Dublin Portal tomb

15 km south-east of Dublin, off R116 (Loughlinstown–Glencullen); at Kiltiernan, veer right past the ruined church and on foot through private housing estate, keeping right, and across two fields. Private land, though signposted at gate. Disc. Ser. 50.

This most impressive Portal tomb overlooks the head of the Loughlinstown river valley. The enormous capstone is propped up by twin portals, in between which is the blocking or door stone. An exploratory excavation unearthed a number of hollow scrapers and a round scraper, as well as a chert arrowhead and some sherds of coarse pottery, which is generally considered to be later prehistoric, though it can be confused with Grooved Ware.

▼ **Fig. 91**. Dún Ailinne: plan of summit area as excavated (after Wailes)

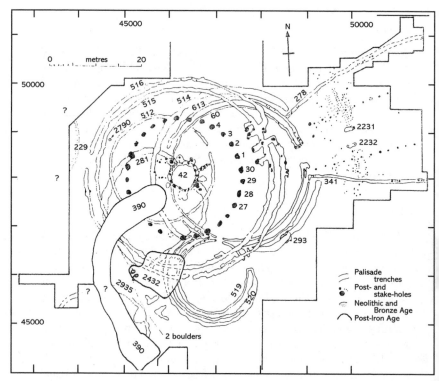

Knockaulin, Co. Kildare Iron Age royal/ceremonial site

15 km south-west of Naas, on west side of N78 (Kilcullen–Athy), 1 km south of junction with M9/N9 (Dublin–Waterford). Signposted but strictly only accessible with the permission of the landowner. Disc. Ser. 55.

Knockaulin [*Cnoc Ailinne*, 'the hill of Ailenn'] is crowned by the remains of *Dún Ailinne* ('the fort of Ailenn'), one of the great so-called 'royal sites' of late prehistoric Ireland, the cult centre and inauguration place of the Laigin, who gave their name to Leinster. The site comprises a large, oval hilltop enclosure (13 ha) with internal ditch and external bank. Apart from the impressive rampart, there are no visible features, all the structures having been of wood. Excavations on the summit by Bernard Wailes in the 1970s revealed a complex sequence of enclosures dating from the early Neolithic to around the Birth of Christ, after which there appears to have been no material investment in the site. By far the most dramatic structural remains date from the Iron Age when two massive palisaded enclosures, each in excess of 30 m (Wailes's 'Rose' and 'Mauve' phases, respectively), were constructed. The figure-of-eight 'Rose' phase structure was approached from the east by a wide, funnel-shaped, palisaded avenue. In plan it is closely similar to the phase 3(ii) structures at

▼ **Fig. 92.** Dún Ailinne: reconstruction drawing of 'Rose' phase structures (after Wailes)

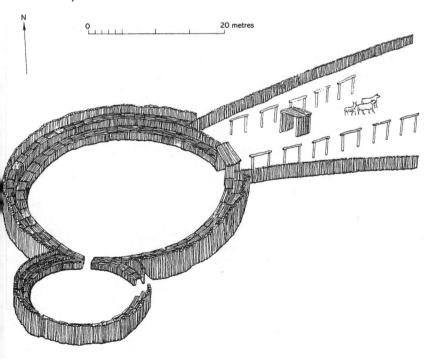

Navan Fort, albeit on a monumental scale, appropriately reconstructed as a tiered amphitheatre. The later 'Mauve' building consisted of a huge double-palisaded enclosure, inside which was a free-standing timber circle surrounding an enigmatic circular structure (approximately 9 m in diameter), reconstructed as a tall podium. It is suggested that a denuded bank evident before excavation is the remains of a ringfort.

Dún Ailinne overlooks the Curragh, or Plain of Kildare, which has numerous monuments and is clearly an important part of the associated ritual landscape. 1 km to the south is Old Kilcullen, one of the oldest Irish monasteries, probably founded by St Iserninus, a pre-Patrician saint. The juxtaposition of early Christian church and pagan cult site is a recurring pattern (see also **Tara**/Dunshaughlin and **Navan** Fort/**Armagh**) and reveals much about the strategic development of the Church in Ireland.

Loughcrew, Co. Meath Passage tomb cemetery, ritual landscape

15 km west of Kells, off R163/R154 (Kells–Oldcastle). Car park located in the saddle between Carnbane East and Carnbane West; signposted. The Passage tombs are National Monuments (key available at Loughcrew Gardens), but the remainder of the sites are in private ownership. Disc. Ser. 42.

The archaeological landscape of Slieve na Calliagh (*Sliabh na Caillí*, 'the hill of the witch') covers at least eight townlands, but the whole area is usually called after one of them, Loughcrew. Slieve na Calliagh is a small mountain with four summits over a distance of about 3 km, the three

▼ **Fig. 93.** Loughcrew: map showing locations of monuments (OPW)

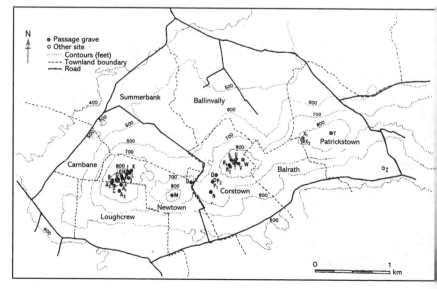

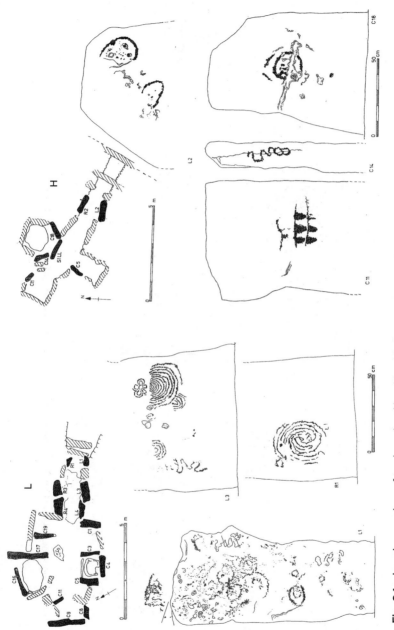

▲ **Fig. 94a.** Loughcrew: plans of tombs, cairns H and L, with decorated stones (after Shee-Twohig)

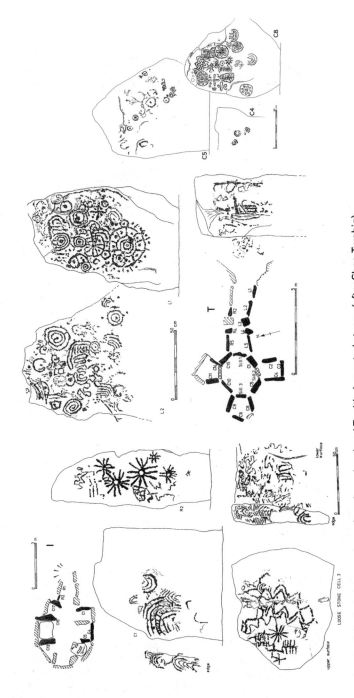

▲ Fig. 94b. Loughcrew: plans of tombs, cairns I and T, with decorated stones (after Shee-Twohig)

▲ **Fig. 95.** Loughcrew: Carnbane West (photo: Conor Newman and Eamonn O'Donoghue)

highest being (from east to west respectively) Patrickstown, Carnbane East, and Carnbane West. With a concentration there of at least twenty-five Passage tombs, it is one of the four great Passage tomb cemeteries of Ireland. Many of the tombs were excavated during the 19th century. The valley to the north is also peppered with monuments, many of Bronze Age date. Together they comprise one of the most intriguing but least explored early prehistoric landscapes in Ireland.

The densest concentration of monuments is on Carnbane West, where there are two large tombs (Cairns L and D) and twelve smaller, satellite tombs, some of which are accessible. Cairn D, on the summit, survives only as an enormous mound of rocks (about 54 m in diameter), dug into during the 19th century. It is surrounded by upwards of eight smaller tombs (A1–3, B, E, F, and G). Cairn F (15 m in diameter), to the east, has a cruciform chamber with a number of decorated stones. Underneath a stone basin in the northern recess was found part of a bone pin and a spherical, ironstone ball.

Cairn L (about 40 m in diameter) was also subjected to excavation. The passage, which was found to contain a recumbent stone pillar (2.65 m long), is approached via a funnel-shaped entrance and opens into a seven-celled chamber with eighteen decorated stones. Two basin stones survive. Under one of them was found a quantity of cremated human bone, two bone pins, two polished stone balls, and eight chalk balls. There are four satellite tombs (H, I, J, and K) concentrated around Cairn L. Cairn H (16 m in diameter) has a cruciform chamber with a number of decorated stones. A very broad range of material was recovered from this tomb, which was clearly reused time and again into the Iron Age. The finds include over 4,000 bone flake fragments (some of which are decorated in La Tène style compass curves), bone and glass beads, bronze and iron rings, and the leg of an iron compass. The purpose and chronology of this material is uncertain. Cairn I, situated on a small prominence to the west of Cairn L, has a polygonal chamber, divided into seven regular compartments.

Cairn T (35 m in diameter and 5 m high) is the focus of the tombs on Carnbane East. It has a cruciform chamber that is decorated with some very fine examples of Passage tomb art. One of the kerbstones on the north side of the mound is called the 'Hag's Chair' and may have been used as a piece of inaugural furniture during the medieval period; it, too, has Neolithic decoration. Upon excavation in 1865, a quartz wall was found standing to a height of about 1.2 m behind the kerbstones. Around Cairn T are the remains of six satellite tombs. Some have lost their covering mound and are accessible. Cairn S (17 m in diameter), to the northwest, has an unusual, Y-shaped chamber with six decorated orthostats. The recesses contained substantial deposits of comminuted, cremated bone and the finds included a leaf-shaped arrowhead, Carrowkeel ware, and some stone pendants. Cairn U (13 m in diameter), immediately to the north-east of Cairn T, has a cruciform chamber with proportionately large side recesses; the right-hand one is divided into two parts.

The remains of four more Passage tombs occur on Patrickstown, the next summit to the east. Carnbane East provides a bird's-eye view over the many monuments scattered across private land to the north (the townlands of Ballinvalley and Summerbank). In the centre foreground a fine, but very low-profile, cursus approaches in the direction of the summit. There are standing stones at various points along it and others continue its projection to the north. The northern terminus is obscured by a very thick stone wall that is actually the remains of one of the very few cashels in the east of the country. The fields to the north are dotted with standing stones, including a possible stone alignment, a stone circle, 75 m or so east of the cursus, cists, and enclosures of various dates, including a very fine bivallate ringfort.

Manger, Co. Laois Megalithic structure

18 km south-east of Portlaoise; best approached via R426 (Portlaoise–Castlecomer), taking minor road to east 4 km south of Timahoe. Disc. Ser. 61.

One of the rare megalithic structures in a county that has very few surviving megalithic tombs, this structure comprises a simple slab roofstone supported on a number of sidestones. There are a number of outlying stones and an early account suggests it may have been surrounded by a circle of stones, and contained a number of cists. It is not classifiable. It is built into a field bank in a convenient, roadside location, but on private land. The structure lies on an eastern foothill of Fossy Mountain at the northern end of the Castlecomer plateau. This foothill rises to a peak about 2 km south-east of Manger, where it is crowned by a small hillfort defined by one massive bank and external fosse. The fort is prominently situated to overlook the upper catchment of the river Douglas and, further to the east, the broad valley of the river Barrow.

Maynooth, Co. Kildare Castle

24 km west of Dublin, off M4 (Dublin–Galway); follow signs to Maynooth village— castle is located at west end of Main St., beside entrance to College.

Maynooth has, since the late 12th century, been associated with the great Anglo-Irish dynasty, the FitzGeralds. The first stone castle was probably built at the beginning of the 13th century and was the main FitzGerald stronghold for the remainder of the Middle Ages. In 1535, when it was besieged by the English during the revolt of 'Silken' Thomas FitzGerald, Maynooth became the first Irish castle to suffer a major artillery bombardment. Considerable repairs were carried out in the 1630s, but further extensive damage was caused in the wars of the 1640s. The castle is built within the junction of two small rivers and the surviving remains are dominated by a great tower, set at the west end of a rectangular walled enclosure with a gatehouse to the south. The gatehouse is a simple three-storey structure, probably late medieval with inserted 17th-century windows, and originally defended by an outer barbican. The castle was enclosed by an extensive curtain wall but practically all that survives today is the short eastern side, with the foundations of a square turret at the north end and a substantial rectangular tower (with inserted 17th-century windows) at the south end. The unusual external buttresses with oversailing arches may also be 17th century and are probably linked to a later hall built against the east curtain wall. The castle was more extensive than at present appears—beside the entrance to Maynooth College, for instance, is a Church of Ireland church (with medieval tower) on the site of a chapel which was within the castle, at least in the 16th century.

The rectangular great tower is the earliest surviving building, probably dating *c.*1200, but at least two—possibly three—phases of building are visible. The uppermost 2–3 m, including the wall walk, are clearly a later addition, but it is less certain whether the change from granite to tufa quoins at first-floor level marks a significant break in construction. The tower is accessed through a doorway at first-floor level in the east wall. Clearly there was an external stair supported on a forework, toothings for which are visible in the east face of the tower. The first-floor chamber occupies the entire interior of the tower and is well lit by large, but much restored, windows. There are mural chambers in the south, west, and east walls while a second doorway in the north wall must have led to a chamber over the stairs in the external forework. The first floor seems to have served mainly to accommodate the hall—the main public room in which the lord's business was carried out. Overhead there are joist holes, corbels, and an offset ledge in the walls, all apparently designed to hold the timbers of an upper floor. However, there are no windows to light such a floor and it is possible that there was a gallery over the hall, rather than a second floor. The first floor is supported on a twin barrel vault—a later insertion at ground-floor level, along with the spine wall, spiral stairs at the north end, and octagonal pier base at first-floor level. This late medieval wall replaced an arcade of stone piers supporting a timber floor; traces of the piers can be seen embedded in the later wall.

Mellifont, Co. Louth Abbey

8 km west of Drogheda off N51 (Drogheda–Navan); take R168 (Drogheda–Collon) and minor road to west after 3 km or 6 km; signposted. Visitor centre; admission charge.

Although not the best-preserved medieval abbey in Ireland, Mellifont [Latin *Fons Mellis*, 'fount of honey'] should not be missed because of its historical and architectural importance. It was, as far as we know, the first monastery in Ireland to be laid out on the typical European claustral plan (i.e. in ranges of buildings around a central open space). So it is, in a sense, the ancestor of all the Irish abbeys, priories, and friaries subsequently laid out in this manner. More directly, it was the mother house of the many Cistercian abbeys in Ireland, which had such an influence on subsequent religious and architectural history. Mellifont was the first Cistercian abbey in Ireland, founded in 1142 by St Malachy of **Armagh**, with a community of French and Irish monks trained at Clairvaux in Burgundy. The abbey grew rapidly—by 1147 it could send monks to found a first daughter house at Bective, Co. Meath. Seven further daughter houses had been established by the time the abbey church at Mellifont was finally consecrated in 1157, and in all at least 21 abbeys were founded directly or indirectly from Mellifont. By 1170 the abbey was said to have 100 monks and 300 lay brothers—possibly exaggerated, but still testimony to Mellifont's remarkable early success. After the English conquest a serious rift developed between those Cistercian abbeys affiliated to Mellifont, which were strongly Irish in orientation, and those founded by the English and affiliated to English abbeys. The English abbeys (with the support of the Cistercian order) tried to impose discipline on the Irish houses, whose resistance erupted in a major crisis, known as the 'Conspiracy of Mellifont', in the 1220s. The outcome, after 1228, was a reduction both in the influence of Mellifont (now firmly under English control) and in the size of its community. However, it remained one of the wealthiest Cistercian abbeys in Ireland, with extensive holdings of land in the fertile Boyne Valley. It was dissolved in 1539 and in the 1560s was converted into a fortified house by the Moore family, who occupied it until *c.*1730.

The abbey is located beside the river Mattock, a tributary of the Boyne. Extensive excavation has exposed its full ground plan, but the only buildings standing to any height are the vaulted chapter house of *c.*1220 (in the east range of the cloister) and the very fine octagonal lavabo of *c.*1200 on the south side, where the monks washed their hands before entering the refectory for meals. A short section of the late 12th-century cloister arcade has been re-erected nearby. There is also a late medieval church, known as 'St Bernard's chapel', on the hillside over-looking the abbey to the east. This may be a late replacement for a chapel provided by the abbey for the use of local people. North-east of the main abbey buildings is a ruined four-storey building, often described as the abbey gatehouse. In fact it seems to be an ordinary 15th/16th-century tower house whose end walls were later broken out, giving the barrel-vaulted ground-floor chamber the appearance of a gate passage.

Although the ruins of the abbey otherwise consist of little more than foundations, they allow some reconstruction of its structural history, which was so important in the development of Irish medieval archi-tecture. The abbey was laid out in the mid-12th century along standard Cistercian lines—a cruciform church with aisled nave, square presbytery, and transepts, each with three chapels on the east side. The cloisters lay to the south, surrounded by ranges of buildings on the east, west, and south. As might be expected, the design of the church at this stage shows clear similarities with Burgundian abbeys, but there are unusual fea-tures, notably the apsidal (semicircular) chapels in the transepts and the crypt at the west end. A feature of the original church is the small size of presbytery and transepts, relative to the large nave. This is an indication of the large number of lay brothers attached to the monastery (or at least envisaged) in the 12th century, since the lay brothers worshipped in the nave, while the presbytery was preserved for the monks proper. Between *c.*1240 and *c.*1320 the presbytery and north transept were enlarged in Early English Gothic style and at a slightly later date the south transept was enlarged in Decorated style. Much of the nave was also rebuilt, following a fire in the early 14th century.

Monasterboice, Co. Louth Early monastic site

8 km north-west of Drogheda off M1 (Drogheda–Dundalk); take minor road to west off M1; signposted.

Monasterboice [*Mainistir Bhuithe*, 'Buithe's monastery'], said to have been founded by St Buithe in the 6th century, is important mainly for two magnificent high crosses of the 9th/early 10th century. The south cross, in particular, is one of Ireland's greatest cultural treasures.

The monastery seems to have been closely allied with **Armagh** and, indirectly, with the dominant northern Uí Néill dynasty. When it apparently fell under Viking control in the mid-10th century, Monasterboice was wrested back in 968 by the Cenél nEógain high-king, Domhnall Ua Néill, killing 300 Vikings in the process. Domhnall's interests in liberating the monastery may have had less to do with devotion or altruism than with familial aggrandizement. The last recorded abbot died in 1122. What happened after this is unclear, but the foundation of the first Cistercian abbey at nearby **Mellifont** probably undermined the older establishment. Nevertheless, the presence of two late medieval churches demonstrates that the site continued to be used, perhaps as a parish church or as a place of pilgrimage, to the end of the Middle Ages.

The monastic site

Aerial photography has revealed traces of three concentric, widely spaced earthen enclosures which once surrounded the site. The outer enclosure was at least 600 m in diameter and encloses an area of at least 24 ha. An enclosure of this scale must be an indication of the status of the monastery and provides a worthy setting for the magnificent high crosses. Unfortunately, these enclosures have been levelled for centuries, although traces of the innermost enclosure are sometimes visible from the top of the round tower, in the field south of the graveyard. Four souterrains (*not accessible*) are also recorded within the enclosed area. Within the present graveyard are two churches, a round tower, three high crosses, a bullaun stone, a sundial, and two early grave slabs. Both churches are small, simple structures of late medieval date (probably 15th century). The south church, however, once had a chancel to the east and may originally have been a 12th-century structure. West of the north church is the round tower which survives to a height of 28 m but originally would have been at least 33 m high, with six floors, which can be climbed to the top. The tower was burned in 1097, when it was recorded to have contained the monastery's library and other treasures, and this may explain the loss of the roof. Its round-headed doorway, 1.8 m above ground, is on the east side and presumably faced the west door of an earlier church located on the site of the present north church, or perhaps further east. In the ground to the north of the north church is a 10th/11th-century grave slab, decorated with a large incised cross and bearing the inscription *ÓR DO RUARCAN* ('a prayer for Ruarcan').

High crosses

The three surviving high crosses are all of sandstone and are referred to as the North, West, and South Crosses, although it is not certain that they all stand in their original positions. Beside the North Cross is a rare surviving medieval sundial, marked off for the canonical hours of 9.00 a.m., 12.00 noon, and 3.00 p.m. Of the North Cross itself only the head and upper part of the shaft survive, mounted on a modern replacement; part of the shaft of another cross can be seen nearby. The cross head is mostly plain and may be unfinished, with decoration confined to the centre of the cross on each side—on the west side is a *Crucifixion*, while on the east side is a round medallion ornamented with a cruciform arrangement of C-spirals. In contrast, the West and South Crosses are entirely covered with rich decoration, generally consisting of scriptural scenes on the broad faces and abstract or animal ornament on the narrow sides. The West Cross is the tallest of all Irish high crosses, almost 7 m high, set within a pyramidal base. Like the South Cross its capstone is a model of a roof, presumably of a church, with gable timbers and shingles clearly visible. The decorative panels may be identified as follows (from base to top):

West face:	*Soldiers at the Tomb of Christ*
	Baptism of Christ in the Jordan
	Three figures, possibly women at the tomb of Christ
	Three figures, possibly Christ flanked by Peter and Paul
	Three figures, probably Thomas meeting the Risen Christ
	Soldiers Cast Lots for Christ's Garment (?)
	Judas Betrays Christ [right arm of cross]
	Crucifixion [cross head]
	Mocking of Christ (left arm)
	Peter Drawing his Sword (top of cross)
	Pilate Washes his Hands(?)
East face:	*David Kills a Lion*
	Sacrifice of Isaac
	Moses Draws Water from the Rock
	David Anointed by Samuel (right), *David Kills Goliath* (left)
	Samson Topples the Philistine Temple
	Men in chariot, probably *Elijah Being Taken to Heaven*
	Three Youths in the Fiery Furnace
	Possibly *Sts Paul and Anthony* [right arm of cross]
	Christ in Judgement [cross head]
	Temptation of St Anthony [left arm of cross]
	Christ Walking on Water [top of cross]

South Cross

The South Cross, near the entrance, is arguably the finest high cross in Ireland. It is often referred to as 'Muiredach's cross' because of an inscription at the bottom of the shaft (west side), which reads *ÓR DO MUIREDACH LAS NDERNAD IN CHROS* ('a prayer for Muiredach who had this cross made'). This Muiredach was probably one of the monastery's most celebrated abbots, Muiredach mac Domhnall, who was also abbot-elect of **Armagh** and steward of the southern Uí Néill, and who died in 923. However, there was another abbot of the same name, who died in 844, and the inscription could also refer to Muiredach mac Cathail (d. 867), the king in whose territory Monasterboice was at that time situated. The cross is c.5.5 m high and is carved from a single block of sandstone, apart from the pyramidal base and the capstone which, as on the West Cross, is carefully carved in the form of a shingled roof. Almost every surface of the cross is decorated and the carving is unusually well preserved—though it must originally have been even finer. It is particularly interesting for the level of detail of clothing, weapons, and other features which can still be made out. The base and sides are largely covered with geometric or interlace ornament, although there is a series of figures on the base apparently representing figures of the zodiac. Biblical scenes dominate on the two broad faces, as follows (from base to top):

West face: *Soldiers Mock Christ*
Thomas Meeting the Risen Christ
Christ Flanked by Peter and Paul
Resurrection of Christ [right arm of cross]
Crucifixion [cross head]
Peter Denies Christ [left arm of cross]
Ascension of Christ? [top of cross]

East face: *Adam and Eve* (left), *Cain Killing Abel* (right)
David and Goliath
Moses Draws Water from the Rock
Adoration of the Magi
The Last Judgement [cross head]; below Christ, *St Michael Weighs a Soul (with a little unwelcome interference from Satan)*; to the left, *The Saved, with David playing a lyre*; to the right, *The Damned, being driven into hell by a devil with a trident*
Sts Paul and Anthony [top of cross]

Other panels worth noting are:

North side: *Pair of beard-pullers* (bottom of shaft)
Right Hand of God (underside of cross arm)
Scourging of Christ? (end of cross arm)
Sts Paul and Anthony in the Desert (top of cross)

South side: *Pilate Washing his Hands* (end of cross arm)
Christ Enters Jerusalem (top of cross)

▲ Fig. 96. Moone: high cross (photo: Dept. of Archaeology, NUI, Galway)

Moone, Co. Kildare Early monastic site

17 km north-east of Carlow, on N9 (Dublin–Kilkenny); follow directions to Moone village and take minor road to west; signposted.

Moone [*Maoin Choluim Chille*, 'gift of Colmcille'] is the site of a monastery that was part of the Columban federation (i.e. associated with the 6th-century saint Columba), although there are no historical references to its existence prior to the 10th century. The English conquest in the late 12th century separated Moone from the Columban system. It was reassigned to the bishop of **Glendalough** and became a parish church. A substantial borough was established by William Marshall, lord of Leinster, in the 1220s but disappeared during the turbulent 14th century. The parish church, however, continued to function until the 17th century and its physical form preserves a record of the rise and fall of the medieval settlement.

The only visible traces of the early monastery are a famous high cross and parts of at least three others. All are of granite, and are located around a late medieval church, which itself incorporates a substantial part of a 10th/11th-century church. The gently curving roadway to the west of the church may also preserve part of the line of an original enclosure. The church is a long, rectangular structure, built in local slate and granite and mostly 13th century or later. However, at the east end are the remains of an earlier, probably 10th/11th-century, church. Most of the north and west walls have disappeared but the east wall and parts of the west wall survive. Antae are visible on the external face of the east wall, and also built into the south wall *c.*11 m from the east end—representing the original west end of the church. In the 13th century the church was enlarged to more than three times its original size, by extending it to the west. New windows were inserted in the east wall and adjacent ends of the north and south walls, and a chancel arch replaced the original west wall. The new church had two doorways in the south wall and at least one in the north wall. At a later date, probably in the 15th century, a wall walk protected by stepped battlements was added around the roof and a fortified residential tower erected beside the church (now vanished). Such defensive features reflect the increasing insecurity of that period.

Within the church are displayed the high cross and fragments of a second. Probably because of the difficulty of carving in granite, the sculptors of the crosses adopted a uniquely simple, geometrical style, and—whether by accident or design—produced one of the most attractive of all high crosses. The intact cross (*restored*) is over 7 m high and unusually slender, with a tall, pyramidal base. The shaft and cross head are mainly taken up with carvings of unidentified beasts, spirals, bosses, and geometric ornament, but the base contains several scriptural scenes, as follows (from base to top):

East face:	*Daniel in the Lions' Den*
	Sacrifice of Isaac
	Adam and Eve
South side:	*Loaves and Fishes*
	Flight into Egypt
	Youths in Fiery Furnace
West face:	*Twelve Apostles*
	Crucifixion
North side:	*Unidentified monster*
	Temptation of St Anthony
	Sts Paul and Anthony in the Desert

Because of its uniqueness the cross is difficult to date, but a 9th-century date is most likely. At the west end of the church are displayed fragments of another highly distinctive cross which originally had an open hole at the centre of the cross head. Unfortunately only fragments survive, but the style of decoration is so similar to the complete cross that a comparable date is likely. In the graveyard south of the church are a granite cross base and a 13th/14th-century grave slab with floriated cross. There is another cross base in the graveyard east of the church, and a third in the adjoining field to the north-east. To the south of the church, in the grounds of Mooneabbey House, is a late medieval tower house (*private property; no access*).

Mount Oriel, Co. Louth Barrow cemetery

15 km north-west of Drogheda; take the N2 (Dublin–Derry) to Collon and take minor road to west, at the north end of the village, for 2 km; a minor road to the north (right) leads to the summit. Private land. Disc. Ser. 36.

This barrow cemetery is situated on the summit of Mount Oriel, and comprises five barrows, three of which are on the summit, with the remainder located on the eastern and northern slopes respectively. Those on the summit range in size from 11 m to 22.5 m in diameter. From this prominent location the views north towards Armagh and Dundalk Bay and south over Meath are beautiful.

Mountpelier Hill, Co. Dublin Passage tombs

10 km south of Dublin, on the summit of Mountpelier (better known as the 'Hell Fire Club'); access is by forestry path from car park off the R115 (Ballyboden–Glencree); not signposted but a popular and well-known walk. Disc. Ser. 50.

On the summit of Mountpelier (226 m) are the remains of two Passage tombs located immediately behind Mountpelier House, better known as the 'Hell Fire Club' on account of the raucous parties held there in the 18th century. The better surviving of the two tombs comprises a low mound and circular kerb (26 m in diameter), with the outline of a passage leading from the north. The second tomb lies to the east and is about 18 m in diameter but is far more difficult to discern. A standing stone is recorded beside the trackway within a few metres of the car park.

Moylisha, Co. Wicklow Wedge tomb

25 km south-east of Carlow, off R725 (Carlow–Gorey) on the north slope of Moylisha Hill; best approached from the link road running northwards out of the village of Park Bridge, which is signposted from the R725 between Carnew and Shillelagh. Disc. Ser. 62.

This Wedge tomb was excavated in 1937. The sub-rectangular cairn (13 m × 10 m) is orientated north-west/south-east, with the gallery at the north end. The gallery (approx. 6 m long), preceded by a small ante-chamber and sillstone, widens towards the south-east. One displaced roofstone remains. Flagstones were uncovered beneath the cairn. Surviving burial deposits consisted of a very small quantity of cremated bone,

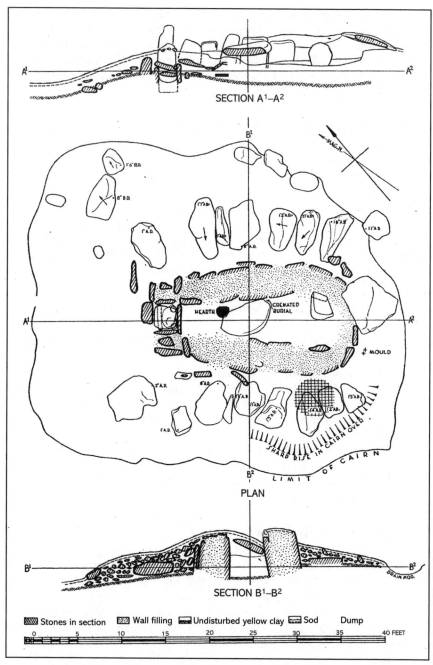

SECTION A¹–A²

PLAN

SECTION B¹–B²

▨ Stones in section   ▩ Wall filling   ▤ Undisturbed yellow clay   ▱ Sod   Dump

0   5   10   15   20   25   30   35   40 FEET

▲ **Fig. 97.** Moylisha: plan of site as excavated (after Ó hIceadha)

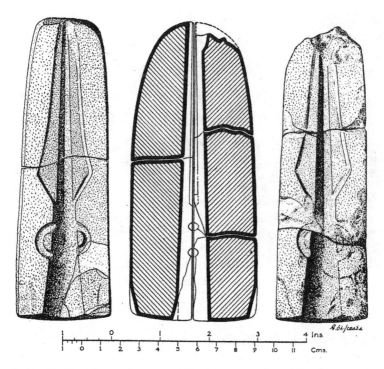

▲ **Fig. 98.** Moylisha: sandstone mould for bronze spearhead (after Ó hIceadha)

two stone discs, and some coarse pottery. A bi-valve mould for a looped, socketed spearhead of Middle Bronze Age type was found in the base of the cairn and is attributed to later disturbance. Moylisha is overlooked by Stokeen Hill to the east, on the summit of which is a circular cairn.

Proleek, Co. Louth Megalithic tombs

4 km north-east of Dundalk, off N1 (Dundalk–Newry); take R173 east off the Kilcurry/Ballymascanlan interchange, and park in Ballymascanlan Hotel. Disc. Ser. 36.

Located in the grounds of Ballymascanlan Hotel are a Wedge tomb and a Portal tomb. The gallery of the Wedge tomb is defined by large ortho-stats and measures 6 m in length. The portal tomb, 80 m to the west, is of classic tripod design, comprising two portal stones and a slightly lower back stone. The capstone is estimated to weigh between 30 and 40 tonnes. The small pile of pebbles on the top relates to a local tradition of good fortune to those who manage to land a stone on the top thrown backwards over your head!

▲ **Fig. 99.** Proleek: Portal tomb (photo: Etienne Rynne)

Punchestown, Co. Kildare Standing stone

3.5 km south-east of Naas, near the entrance to Punchestown racecourse on the link road between the R411(Naas–Ballymore Eustace) and the R410 (Naas–Blessington). Disc. Ser. 55.

This interesting little complex of standing stones and barrows, lying just to the north-west of Punchestown racecourse, boasts one of the tallest and most impressive standing stones in Ireland. A burial dating from the Bronze Age was found at the base, much as at the similar standing stone at **Furness**, 5 km to the north.

Rathfarnham, Co. Dublin Castle

In south Dublin; take roads to south from city centre towards Terenure, and continue south on Rathfarnham Road for 1 km; signposted. Admission charge.

Rathfarnham [*Ráth Fearnáin*, 'fort of the alder'] is an important building in the transition from the medieval castle to the modern large house. Located *c*.5 km south of the medieval city of **Dublin**—though now well within the modern city—it was built in the 1580s by Adam Loftus, an English archbishop of Dublin. It originally consisted of a rectangular block of three storeys over basement, with bastion-like flanking turrets at the four angles. The building was extensively modified in the 18th and 19th centuries, when many of its original features were removed, and the current conservation programme aims to present mainly 18th/19th-century interiors. Nevertheless, the castle is still worth visiting for those

▲ **Fig. 100.** Punchestown: standing stone known as 'The Longstone' (photo: Dept. of Archaeology, NUI, Galway)

interested in the end of medieval architecture. Ongoing conservation work adds to the interest of a visit.

Rathgall, Co. Wicklow Hillfort

5 km east of Tullow, Co. Carlow, off R725 (Tullow–Gorey); signposted. Disc. Ser. 61.

An important political, industrial, and ritual centre during the later Bronze Age, Rathgall is a triple-ramparted hillfort (320 m in maximum diameter) with a medieval cashel in the centre. Excavated by Raftery in the 1970s, the site overlooks to the east the town of Tullow, Co. Carlow, and the middle reaches of the river Slaney. The middle and inner ramparts are quite close to each other (between 10 m and 12 m apart) and lie about 50 m uphill from the outer rampart. The ramparts are not securely dated, though they are suspected to be contemporary with later Bronze Age activity uncovered in pre-cashel contexts on the summit.

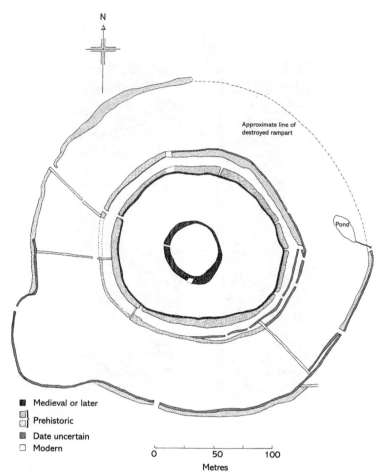

▲ **Fig. 101.** Rathgall: plan of site (after Raftery)

Here was unearthed a round building (15 m in diameter) with an east-facing entrance, surrounded by a concentric ditched enclosure (35 m in diameter; 0.5–1.5 m deep). Off-centre was a ritual pit that contained a small quantity of cremated human bone and a gold 'hair ring' belonging to the Dowris phase of the later Bronze Age. There was plenty of evidence of domestic activity within the area of the enclosure. Immediately to the east was a metalworking area with moulds for the manufacture of swords, spearheads, and gouges as well as an assemblage of more exotic, prestige items including gold and glass beads and a second gold 'hair ring'.

Just to the south was another ditched enclosure (19 m in diameter) with burial pits and a small hoard of metalwork including a small chisel

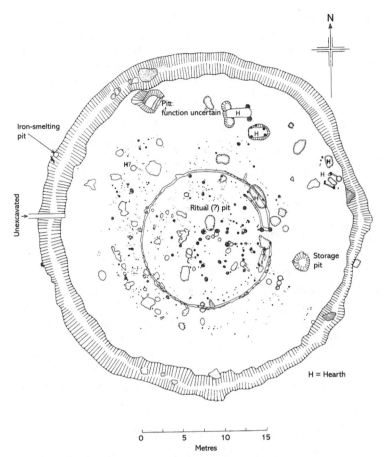

▲ **Fig. 102.** Rathgall: plan of central area as excavated (after Raftery)

and fragments of a spearhead and a sword blade. A centrally placed burial pit, surrounded on three sides by over one-and-a-half thousand stake-holes set in fire-reddened soil, contained the cremated remains of an adult. Elsewhere were other pit burials, some accompanied by coarse ware. Three fields away to the north lies the univallate hillfort of Knockeen (200 m in diameter), which has a cairn at its centre.

Rathmichael, Co. Dublin Church; cross-slabs; hillfort

East of Shankill, between the M11 and the R116. Access is from Shankill village. Not signposted. Disc. Ser. 50.

The plain, 13th-century church ruins at Rathmichael belie the former existence of an important south Co. Dublin monastery, most famous for its collection of idiosyncratic 'Rathdown slabs', which are postulated to date from the Viking period. Made of the local granite, such slabs concentrate in the barony of Rathdown and are distinguished by the abstract form of their ornamentation. A bullaun stone and two 'entrance stones' hint at the original size of the monastic enclosure, part of which is preserved as an arcuate length of stone walling to the north-west of the church. Nearby is the outline of a possible souterrain and, to the south-west, a well. A little to the east of the church are traces of a possible inner enclosure. Beside the church is the stump of a round tower. A short climb uphill (west) from the church, along a trackway, is one of Ireland's smallest hillforts, around 120 m in diameter. It is univallate with an external ditch. Denuded and a little overgrown with heather, it is worth the effort if only for the views it affords over Dublin and Wicklow.

Roche, Co. Louth Castle and deserted borough

7 km north-east of Dundalk, off N53 (Dundalk–Castleblayney); take minor road north at Hackballs Cross for 2.5 km, then east at Castle Roche crossroads.

This dramatically sited castle was probably built in the 1230s by Rohesia de Verdun, on a high rock outcrop commanding one of the passes from Co. Louth into Co. Armagh. Despite its impressive appearance, however, it had a short life—by 1331 it had been burned by the Irish and does not seem to have been reoccupied. It is one of the earliest examples of 13th-century developments in castle architecture, based on an integrated system of curtain walls, flanking towers, and a strong gatehouse. The

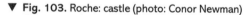

▼ Fig. 103. Roche: castle (photo: Conor Newman)

strong curtain wall encloses a roughly triangular area, with a rounded tower projecting at the northern apex, a twin-towered gatehouse on the eastern side, and a hall in the south-eastern corner. The castle is naturally defended by cliffs on all sides but the east, where there is a level plateau that was probably the site of a short-lived borough, founded alongside the castle. There are the remains of a boundary wall and a tower in the north-west corner of this area, as well as possible rectangular features in the interior. The castle was separated from this plateau by an outer rock-cut fosse over 15 m wide, with a causeway opposite the castle entrance. In the causeway is a 3 m gap, which was presumably spanned by a drawbridge, mounted in an outer barbican.

The gatehouse is poorly preserved, especially internally, but outwardly the twin D-shaped towers are still impressive—four storeys high, barrel vaulted above ground-floor level, and with several arrow loops providing lines of fire along the walls and to the front. The entrance passage between the towers—which was probably vaulted originally—leads to the interior of the castle. The two floors that originally existed overhead must have provided substantial accommodation space. A doorway in the south side, at first-floor level, leads to a passage within the curtain wall containing additional arrow loops for defence. Within the castle, the south-east corner is occupied by the hall, a rectangular two-storey building set at a lower level than the gatehouse because of the underlying rock topography. It is entered at the north-west corner, through a slightly later forebuilding; there was probably also access from the upper levels of the gatehouse. The large ground-floor chamber is lit by four narrow windows in the south wall and has a possible sally port in the east wall. A mural stair in the west wall led to the first floor—the hall proper—which was lit by three fine windows (with window seats) in the south wall. North-west of the hall are the remains of a roughly square free-standing building of uncertain date and function, although it may be a well house. At the narrow, northern end of the castle yard is the entrance to the northern tower, probably of four storeys originally, but poorly preserved. The barrel-vaulted ground floor survives intact, but only the south wall of the other floors remains. This wall has a doorway at first-floor level that gave access to and from the wall walk. In the adjacent curtain wall are the remains of a spiral stair that gave access from the wall walk to the upper levels of the tower. The full circuit of curtain walls is well preserved, with wide, regularly spaced merlons. A series of small beam-holes below these merlons probably supported a wooden hoarding that projected over the top of the wall to provide extra protection for defenders.

Rockmarshall, Co. Louth Shell middens

8 km east of Dundalk, off the R173 (Dundalk–Carlingford/Greenore), 0.8 km east of the junction with the R174, near Jenkinstown. Not signposted, permission required. Disc. Ser. 36.

These four middens are located on a raised beach, originally overlooking a lagoon on the southern side of the Cooley peninsula near Dundalk and in the shadow of Slievenaglogh. Oysters and periwinkles dominated the shellfish remains but there were also limpet, whelk, mussels and cockles, crab claws, and a variety of fish bones. The lithic assemblage is Late Mesolithic and includes blades, flakes, and cores. Midden no. 3 yielded a radiocarbon date of 4570–4040 BC. A human femur from the same midden returned a date of 4774–4366 BC.

Seefin, Co. Wicklow Passage tomb and cairn

20 km south-west of Dublin. Caution: These sites are just outside the Kilbride Rifle Range and must be approached from the south side of the mountain off the R759 from the car park near Kippure Bridge, about midway (approx. 7 km) between the Sally Gap and Kilbride. Steep climb through afforestation. Disc. Ser. 56.

At 623 m, the Passage tomb on the summit of Seefin Mountain commands one of the most spectacular vistas in north Wicklow. The cairn is sub-circular (24 m–26 m in diameter) and largely intact (3 m in height) and is surrounded by an incomplete megalithic kerb. The passage (11 m long) is on the north side of the mound and has two decorated stones. It opens into a transeptal, corbelled chamber with five compartments, two on either side and one at the rear. Excavated in

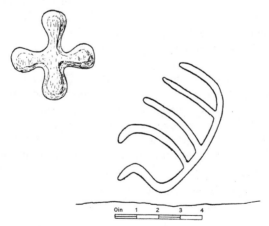

▲ **Fig. 104.** Seefin Mountain: decorated stone from Passage tomb (after Macalister)

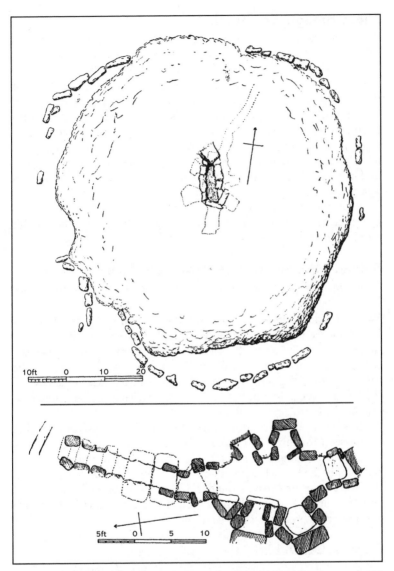

▲ **Fig. 105.** Seefingan Mountain: plans of cairn and chamber as excavated (after Macalister)

1931 by Macalister, there were neither burials nor artefacts. 1.5 km to the north-east is another cairn of comparable dimensions on the summit of Seefingan Mountain.

Slieve Breagh, Co. Meath Barrow cemetery

7 km north-west of Slane; take the R163 (Slane–Kells) opposite the entrance to Slane Castle, in the direction of Kilberry, but veer right at first junction and right at the next crossroads to top of the hill. Not signposted. Disc. Ser. 36.

Slieve Breagh is a peak with spectacular views, towards the west end of the uplands running from Collon to Rathkenny forming the northern backdrop to the **Boyne Valley**. It is the site of a barrow cemetery, comprising at least twelve specimens. The barrows are not susceptible to typological dating; however, the excavation of a nearby Neolithic settlement with two circular (?) houses and the splendid Mountfortescue hillfort immediately to the south demonstrates that the area had seen significant activity throughout prehistory. The barrows are aligned east–west. On the lower terrace, on the west side of the hill, are two small henges and it is possible that two of the larger barrows near the summit are also henges.

Spinan's Hill and Brusselstown, Co. Wicklow Hillforts

8 km north-east of Baltinglass off N81, near the west end of the Glen of Imaal. Disc. Ser. 56.

Two large and impressive hillforts on the same mountaintop. Spinan's Hill, at the west end of the ridge, is the higher and bigger hillfort of the two, measuring 550 m north–south and 320 m east–west, but its peat-covered banks are more difficult to discern. There are six cairns on the summit, comprising one large one, 27 m in diameter, surrounded by five smaller specimens (4.5 m to 8 m in diameter). They are best preserved around the north and east sides.

Known as 'Brusselstown Ring', the hillfort on Brusselstown hill comprises a roughly oval-shaped, collapsed boulder rampart (320 m × 200 m) surrounding the undulating summit. There are a number of hut sites within the hillfort. Both hillforts are in turn surrounded by a huge, double rampart and fosse around the 300 m contour, L-shaped in plan and enclosing a massive 130 ha. Revetted in places, these ramparts are best preserved on the east and west sides.

Swords, Co. Dublin Early monastic site, castle

13 km north of Dublin city centre, off N1 (Dublin–Belfast); signposted.

Swords [*Sord Cholmchille*, 'the pure spring of Colmcille'] is now effectively a suburb of **Dublin**, but its origins lie in an early monastic site associated with the great 6th-century saint Columba (Colmcille). Despite tradition, however, it is unlikely that Columba actually founded the monastery, and there is no definite evidence for its existence prior to the 10th century. The monastery appears to have been controlled by Hiberno-Norse Dublin in the 11th century, and belonged to the archbishop of Dublin by the 12th century—subsequently becoming one of

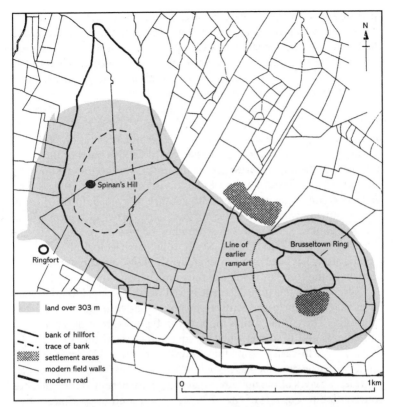

▲ **Fig. 106.** Spinan's Hill: plan of the enclosure complex (after Raftery)

the archbishops' most important manors. A substantial borough was established in the late 12th/early 13th century and continued to function throughout the Middle Ages. The archbishops' castle, probably first built *c.*1200, still stands at the northern end of the town. The borough may have been enclosed and was laid out along the linear axis of Main Street, running south from the castle gate and widening at the north end to act as a market place.

The early monastic site was located on a ridge of high ground, south-west of the modern town, at a bend in the Ward river, which bounds it to the east and south. The core of the monastic site is occupied by the Church of Ireland church (*on Church Road, west side of Main St.*), but the only visible trace is the round tower. This tower, probably of 11th/12th-century date, survives more or less intact at 26 m high but much of the upper 2–3 m, including the roof, seems to be reconstructed. There were probably six floors originally. The doorway faces east and is cur-rently at ground level, but the original ground level was probably some-what lower. Assuming that the doorway of the round tower faced the west doorway of the principal church of the monastery, this church would have been located up to 10 m north of the modern church. Beside the round tower is the late medieval square tower of the now vanished medieval parish church. This tower seems to have been attached to the north-west corner of the parish church, which must also have extended slightly further north than the modern church.

The archbishops' castle occupies rising ground at the north end of the town, its main entrance facing south onto Main St. (*access from the park adjoining the west side of the castle*). A major conservation project is currently under way, which restricts access to various parts of the castle at times—at the time of writing, only the north-western tower, known as the Constable's Tower, was accessible to visitors. There are suggestions that the castle originated in the 13th century as a small, fortified complex occupying what is now the north-eastern corner of the enclosure, and subsequently expanded in a number of phases, reaching its full extent in the later 15th century. No thorough archaeological and architectural study has been carried out at Swords, however, and so the development of the complex is still not fully understood.

Nevertheless, this unusual castle is well worth visiting. It is an irregular pentagonal enclosure with a gatehouse nearly midway along the south side. The curtain wall is topped with typical 15th-century stepped battlements and is strengthened by square towers on the west, north-west, and north-east. Despite this, Swords is not strongly defended and might better be described as a fortified manor house than a true castle. No trace survives of the buildings that must have occupied the extensive courtyard, but four sets of chambers survive around the perimeter, two of them flanking the entrance passage. On the west side of the gatehouse is a suite of chambers on three floors, possibly the constable's lodgings. The gatehouse itself is a three-storey tower, reached through a door on the east side of the entrance passage, with a single chamber on each floor. East of this is a rectangular building, possibly 14th century, with large windows in the south and east walls (now blocked up), suggesting that it was a chapel. Adjoining this, angled to the north-east, is another large rectangular chamber with a smaller chamber or tower at the northern end, projecting to the east. Excavations in the 1970s revealed a 14th-century tile pavement in the larger chamber, which may perhaps have been the archbishops' private oratory. Further north, along the curtain wall, is the probable site of the great hall. Unfortunately this, and the tower at the north-east angle of the enclosure, which together may comprise the earliest part of the castle, survive very poorly. The tower in the north-west angle, by contrast, is well preserved and has now been fully restored as the 'Constable's Tower'; it also contains residential chambers on two floors over a storage/cellar floor.

Tara, Co. Meath Royal complex

10 km south-east of Navan, off the N3 (Dublin–Navan); parking near church/coffee shop; signposted. Disc. Ser. 42 and 43.

Described by Douglas Hyde, George Moore, and William Butler Yeats in a letter to *The Times* as 'probably the most consecrated spot in Ireland', Tara emerges onto the pages of history as the pre-eminent sacral kingship in Ireland, a reputation founded on three and a half thousand years of its being a pagan sanctuary and burial ground. It is associated with the high-kingship of Ireland and a panoply of pagan deities and characters from the world of Irish legend. It is the place where St Patrick's biographers located his triumphant victory over the druids, and it became the symbol of Irish nationhood from the time of Daniel O'Connell and among Irish nationalists around the turn of the century.

Anglicized to Tara, the Irish word *Temair* shares the same root as the Greek word *temenos* and the Latin *templum*, meaning sanctuary, i.e. a sacred space cut off, or circumscribed, for ceremony. However, one 10th-century commentator opined that *temair* meant a great height from which there were fine views, and his explanation has gained popular currency. The names of the monuments themselves probably date from the early medieval period and are preserved in the 11th-century *Dindshenchas Éireann* ('lore of the place names of Ireland').

An extraordinary convergence of history, literature, and archaeology reveals the Hill of Tara to be the centrepiece of a larger ritual and settlement landscape; defined and protected by religious and military monuments, taboos, and traditions, it became the *ferann ríg* or royal estate of the kings of Tara during the early Middle Ages. In time, this estate provided the footprint for the Anglo-Norman barony of Skryne (or Skreen). The king of Tara was king of the world, and the process of his investiture, involving a lengthy procession through this landscape towards the Hill of Tara, brought together myth, monument, and history into one seamless narrative of historical and tribal affirmation.

Apart from the monuments on the Hill of Tara, most of the remaining sites and monuments are on private land and permission should always be sought before attempting to visit any of them. The remains of 25 monuments are visible (some more easily than others) on the Hill of Tara itself and at least three times that many again have been discovered through geophysical prospection and aerial photography.

While geophysical survey and excavation have revealed evidence of multiple palisaded enclosures that are now gone, most of the monuments you see today are much as they were in the past; grassy mounds and embankments, they are graves and open-air enclosures for worship.

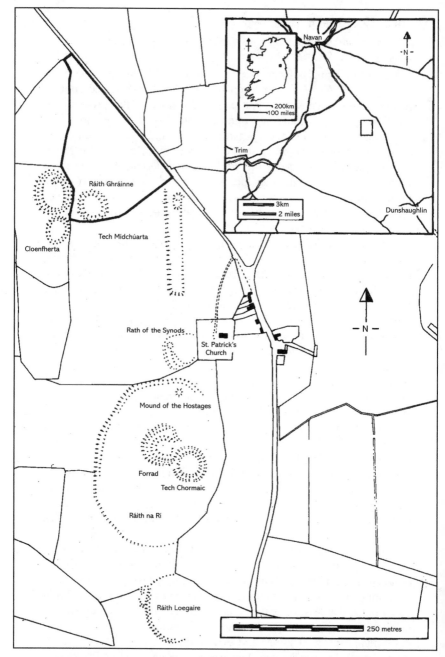

▲ **Fig. 107.** Tara: overall plan of monuments on the Hill of Tara (after Newman)

▲ **Fig. 108.** Tara from the air (photo: Conor Newman and Eamonn O'Donoghue)

The best way to visit these monuments, to get a sense of the history and sublime religiosity associated with this place, is to ascend, as our ancestors did, along the *Tech Midchúarta* or Banquet Hall, starting at the north (that is the lower) end, for this is the ceremonial avenue of Tara, the final part of the processional journey to the summit sanctuary.

The *Tech Midchúarta* is probably one of the later monuments on Tara (5th to 8th century AD) and it is designed to unite the remains on Tara into a formal, religious arena or campus. A semi-subterranean space, this is the one monument on the Hill of Tara where the views to the outside world are denied. Thus removed from the familiar, the visitor, in an almost literal sense, enters Tara. Proceeding along the avenue, glimpses of the tombs of the ancestral kings and queens of Tara are caught through the gaps on the right-hand side. Reflecting on the lives of the ancestors, they remind the royal party of the burden of responsibility that comes with World Kingship, and of the fact that in re-enacting this ceremony they are about to take their place in history. To the east, the gaze is drawn to Skreen, the mirror kingship of Tara and the limbo that awaits those who break the taboos of kingship or fail to live up to the principle of *fír flathemon*, the ideal justice of a ruler. Cormac mac Airt, one of the legendary kings of Tara, lost his kingship and was banished to Skreen after being blinded, and thus physically blemished, by a bee sting. Emerging from the *Tech Mídchúarta*, the Mound of the Hostages looms large over the embankments of the Rath of the Synods. Ten centuries ago your way forward would be blocked by the fosse of a massive enclosure built around three and a half thousand years earlier, forcing you around to the right, in accordance with the rules for entering Tara righthandwise. This would bring you counterclockwise around the ramparts of *Ráith na Ríg* and thence into the inner sanctuary through its entrance in the east. The climax of the inauguration ceremony took place beside the Mound of the Hostages, when the king placed his foot on the *Lia Fáil*, which according to tradition cried out to announce his rightful reign.

The monuments, of course, date from all periods and this is the enduring legacy of Tara. Each one, however, represents the contribution of a former generation and tells its own story. What follows is, therefore, a chronological travelogue across the hilltop.

Mound of the Hostages

The oldest visible monument is the Passage tomb of *Dumha na nGiall* ('the Mound of the Hostages'), dating from the 3rd millennium BC. Excavations between 1955 and 1959 revealed pre-tomb activity, including part of a small enclosure centred to the north of the mound, as well as a ring of fire pits around the mound itself. The monument was fully restored after the excavation. The Passage tomb is of modest proportions (about 20 m diameter) and is one of very few such tombs lacking a kerb. The 4 m long passage is undifferentiated and divided by sillstones into three compartments. These were originally filled with cremated bones and a typical Passage tomb grave assemblage of pottery, beads, and pins. An intricately decorated stone occurs on the left-hand wall. Two propitiatory burials in small cistlike compartments were constructed behind the orthostats. In one of them a Carrowkeel pot was filled with cremated bone, an antler pin, and a bone bead necklace. These and the burial chamber were covered with a cairn of stones and a mantle of soil.

The original *Lia Fáil* ('stone of destiny'), upon which the king placed his foot, reclined beside *Dumha na nGiall*. Though there is a documentary account of its removal to Teltown sometime during the early medieval period, the local tradition is that the white granite pillar standing on the Forrad is the *Lia Fáil*, and that it was moved from near *Dumha na nGiall* in 1824 in commemoration of the 25th anniversary of the 1798 rebellion.

Dumha na nGiall is the most southerly of five very similar mounds stretching in a line north-eastwards towards the Boyne Valley. It is possible that these, too, are Passage tombs and thus document the catchment area of Tara in early prehistory, which may have stretched down towards the confluence of the Boyne and Blackwater at Navan. During the earlier Bronze Age 40 burials were interred in the soil mantle and further burials were placed in the passage itself. All but one of the 40 burials in the mantle were cremations, many under inverted Collared and Encrusted Urns. Some were in cists; most, however were in pits. One burial contained two pots, a riveted bronze dagger, and a stone 'battleaxe'. The inhumation burial was of a young man with a necklace of jet, amber, bronze, and faience, and at his feet a dagger and a bronze awl. Evidently, he was a person of considerable social standing. The Bronze Age burials in the passage were a mixture of inhumations and cremations and they disturbed considerably the original, Neolithic burials.

Later, around 2500 BC, the Mound of the Hostages was incorporated into the orbit of a huge pit or timber circle, 250 m in diameter. A very slight dip in the ground to the south-west of *Tech Midchúarta* is all that can be seen of its 4 m wide fosse which was originally surrounded on both sides by approximately 300 2 m wide pits. This monument drapes over the eastern side of the hill and surrounds both the Rath of the Synods (which was built in the centre of it) and the present church grounds. It was designed to be viewed from the east, thus emphasizing once again the importance of the Gabhra (or Gowra) Valley between here and Skreen. And around the same time, two great henges were built just off the hill. 1.5 km to the south is Rath Meave, named after the female deity of Tara. This henge is one of the largest in the country, measuring a massive 270 m across its north-east/south-west axis. The entrance is in the western quadrant, at which point the bank towers 5.5 m above the surrounding ground level. The footprint of a smaller, circular monument is preserved in the S-shaped curvature of a field boundary running across the henge. 1 km to the west is an unnamed henge in Riverstown. Only about one-third of the earthwork survives; originally it had a diameter in excess of 120 m. Monuments like these are really open-air temples. In the case of the one on the Hill of Tara, all the soil from the fosse was removed elsewhere and an entire woodland of trees was felled to create the double circle.

Later prehistoric activity

Over 25 barrows and ring-ditches of various forms occur on Tara. Most probably date from the Bronze Age when Tara was effectively a cemetery. Many of them form linear strings across the hill. Stray finds of tools and weapons are further evidence of 2nd-millennium activity around Tara. Two massive gold torcs of Middle Bronze Age date were found on Tara in 1810 (*now on display in the National Museum of Ireland*). Some of the barrows were deliberately incorporated intact into the fabric of the large ring barrows, which were probably built during the Iron Age. Bowl barrows were incorporated into both the northern and southern *Clóen-fherta* ('sloping trenches') and into *Rath Ghráinne* ('Gráinne's fort') and the *Forradh* ('the "royal" seat'). Between them these four ring barrows are among the largest in the country (the northern *Clóenfherta* is 80 m in diameter) and it is no surprise that they have attracted their own folklore. It is believed, for example, that the *Clóenfherta* collapsed over the side of the hill as a result of calamity—in the case of the northern *Clóenfherta* as a result of a false adjudication meted out there by Lughaidh Mac Con. The southern *Clóenfherta* is said to have collapsed after the murder of virgins by a king of Leinster and *Rath Ghráinne* is reputed to be one of the refuges used by Gráinne and Diarmaid during their flight from Fionn Mac Cumaill. The *Forradh* is the inauguration mound of Tara.

The Iron Age, thus, saw a revival in monumental religious architecture at Tara and elsewhere and this is nowhere better exemplified than in the case of *Ráith na Ríg* ('the fort of the kings'), a huge hengiform enclosure, 1,000 m in circumference, encircling the crown of the hill and radiocarbon dated to around the 1st century BC. The internal ditch is V-sectioned and 3 m deep. The bank seals the remains of a metal workshop. 2 m inside the ditch is a palisade trench, but there are reasons to suspect that it and the three entrances to *Ráith na Ríg* are all later modifications. A high concentration of dog and horse bones, as well as human burials in the fosse, remind us of the more arcane ceremonies associated with pagan cults, totemism, and the long-standing Indo-European association of horses and inauguration.

Ráith Lóegaire, immediately to the south of *Ráith na Ríg*, is a bivallate circular enclosure, around 125 m in diameter. It has a more military character and compares with sites such as Ringlestown Rath (2 km to the south-west) and Rath Lugh (to the north-east), both strategically sited, bivallate earthworks. A few fields due north of Ringlestown Rath are the remains of a bivallate linear earthwork, stretching for at least 1.5 km (much of it is now destroyed) which defends Tara's western flank. It is tempting to see these earthworks as a defensive ring around Iron Age Tara. Later in the Iron Age *Ráth na Senad* ('the Rath of the Synods') was constructed. The earthwork, which is quadrivallate, represents the fourth use of this site—twice a burial ground and once a series of wooden enclosures. Excavations in the 1950s revealed quantities of Romano-British material and conventional domestic refuse suggesting possible occupation sometime between the later 1st and 4th centuries AD. The site had been quite badly mutilated at the turn of the 20th century during a rather misguided search for the Ark of the Covenant.

There is no doubt about the authenticity of some of the pagan sacral kings of later Iron Age Tara. The existence of others, such as the 3rd-century Cormac mac Airt, who is credited with a great revival in monumental architecture at Tara, is less easily verified. It is their exploits, however, that comprise the core of the huge corpus of medieval literature associated with Tara. One text describes the inauguration of Conaire Mór. While wearing a cloak that should normally have been too big for him, he had to steer a chariot harnessed to two unbroken horses between the magical stones *Blocc* and *Bluigne*. Though one could normally only slide a hand sideways between them, these druid-stones parted before the king's chariot, allowing him to pass over the *Lia Fáil*, which then screeched out against his axle, declaring him king. In this way, the king mated with Tara in her female manifestation, and became truly sacral.

Medieval activity

Unlike most of the great 'royal' sites, material investment in Tara did not end with the coming of Christianity. In spite of the story of Patrick's battle with the pagan druids of Tara, the premier cult site of prehistoric Ireland did not yield so quickly or easily to the new order. On the contrary, the position occupied by Tara in literary and documentary sources is indication of its enduring *de facto* and symbolic importance, symbolism that was used to bolster the political ambitions of the rising stars of early medieval Ireland. *Tech Chormaic* ('Cormac's house'), a bivallate ringfort, was built within the sanctuary and the fact that it conjoins the *Forrad*, the inauguration mound of Tara, speaks volumes about the aspirations of the person who had it built. Likewise, the construction of *Tech Mídchúarta* demonstrates that Tara continued to fulfil a very real purpose in the ceremony of kingship and was still in use as a political arena well into the later 1st millennium AD. However, as always, people did not live on the Hill of Tara. A few kilometres to the south a new royal residence had been established on the shores of *Loch Gabhair* (Lagore) beside the important monastery of Dunshaughlin, founded by Secundinus in the 5th century. Another was established at Rossnaree, overlooking the Boyne opposite Knowth.

Skreen, recognizable by the tall, elegant belfry of the 14th century Augustinian church, is associated with the early medieval church, *Scrín Coluim Cille* ('the shrine of Colmcille'), which possessed a relic of St Columba. The original name of the hill was *Achall*, after the burial mound of Achall, daughter of a mythical king of Tara. The earliest reference to the Columban church is in 976, when it was plundered by Domhnall Ua Néill, during a period of conflict over the kingship of Tara between two rival branches of the Uí Néill. Allying with the early kings of south Brega (Meath), and recognizing its symbolic importance as a counterpoint to Tara in the claim of territorial ownership, the Norse king of Dublin, Amlaíbh Cúarán, commissioned a poem associating himself with Skreen. However, Hiberno-Norse expansion was halted with the defeat of Dublin and her allies (including the Leinstermen) in the decisive Battle of Tara in 980. This battle probably took place in the valley between Tara and Skreen.

The barony of Skryne (which may have been co-terminous with the older *túath*) was granted to Adam de Feypo around 1174 by the new lord of Meath, Hugh de Lacy. Behind the church, further down the hill, is Skryne Castle, now completely incorporated into an 18th-century house (*private*), and, in the grounds of the house, a very impressive motte, which was probably built by, or for, de Feypo soon after 1174. There are some interesting memorial slabs, including an effigy of an unidentified bishop, in the remains of the church. A key to the late medieval belltower can be borrowed from the proprietor of O'Connell's pub in the village and the view from here is wonderful (*warning: belfry is tall and completely open at the top*). The mullion of the north light is actually a reused cross-slab with part of an inscribed Maltese cross. This is one of the few tangible remains of the pre-Norman church that is otherwise amply demonstrated in documentary sources analysed recently by Edel Breathnach.

Tara, on the other hand, was granted to Ralph de Repenteni, and the earliest reference to a church here is in a charter dating from around 1191–2. It was administered by the Knights Hospitallers. The present church on Tara, now serving as the visitor centre, dates from 1822 and incorporates a number of features from the 15th-century church (of which only a stump of wall survives), including the fine west window. Inside is a late 16th-century memorial plaque to Robert Dillon and his wife Katherina Sarsfeld. There are two standing stones in the church-yard; one has a sheela-na-gig carved on one side and may originally have been part of the 15th-century church. The other, more squat, rounded stone has potentially far greater antiquity. Neither is likely to be in its original position.

Trim, Co. Meath Medieval town

45 km north-west of Dublin; take R154 off N3 at Clonee; signposted.

Trim is the site of the largest and most impressive medieval castle in Ireland. As the Irish name [*Áth Truim*, 'the ford of the elder trees'] suggests, Trim was an important fording point on the river Boyne and it became the site of an early monastery—said to have been founded by St Patrick himself. It was never a very prominent monastery, however, and little is known of its subsequent history. The community adopted Augustinian rule, probably in the 1140s, and tradition suggests that the abbey was rebuilt by Hugh de Lacy, the new English lord of Meath, *c*.1180. The turning point in Trim's history was de Lacy's decision to make it the centre of his new lordship, in the early 1170s. A castle was already in existence by 1174, when it was destroyed by the high-king,

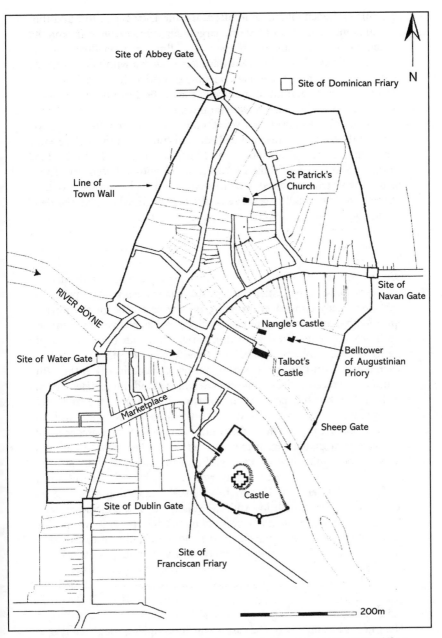

▲ **Fig. 109.** Trim: outline map of town showing medieval features (after O'Keefe)

Ruaidhrí Ó Conchobhair. Soon afterwards de Lacy began to build the present stone castle, the oldest and largest surviving castle in Ireland. A substantial town was also established, straddling the river Boyne north and west of the castle. The town was later enclosed within a circuit of stone walls with at least five gates, possibly erected at the end of the 13th century, following a grant of murage in the 1290s. Dominican, Franciscan, and Augustinian friaries were founded in the 13th century and two fine late medieval houses survive, demonstrating the continuing prosperity of the town. The original de Lacy lordship passed through several major English families including the Mortimers in the 14th/early 15th centuries and Richard, duke of York, in the mid-15th century. They ensured that Trim survived, albeit as an increasingly exposed frontier town, in the late Middle Ages. The castle was refortified and bombarded during the wars of the 1640s.

Town

Only fragments of the town walls survive, mainly around Castle St. and Emmet St., west of the castle. The only surviving gate is the Sheep Gate, a small, originally two-storey structure on the east bank of the Boyne, opposite the castle. Within (north of) this gate is a group of monuments on the site of the medieval Augustinian friary. The only obvious trace of the friary is its belfry tower, known as the 'Yellow Steeple'—once a fine seven-storey 14th-century structure, but partly demolished in the 17th century. No trace survives of the church which stood immediately south of the tower, but fragments of the claustral buildings of the friary are incorporated in the two late medieval fortified houses, Nangle's castle to the west and Talbot's castle to the south-west (*both private property, not accessible to the public*). Further north (*off St Lomond St.*) is St Patrick's parish church, mainly 19th century but with medieval remains. The plain tower has on its west face the arms of Richard, duke of York (lord of Trim and viceroy in Ireland from 1449), suggesting a mid-15th-century date. The church incorporates fragments of the medieval nave. Beyond it, to the east, are the remains of the medieval chancel with a fine three-light ogee-headed window in the south wall, also mid-15th century. There are several loose fragments of medieval stonework within the church.

Castle

The town is dominated by the castle, which occupies a roughly triangular area on the west bank of the Boyne, surrounded by a strong curtain wall with many flanking towers. The curtain wall was an impressive structure, surrounded by a large rock-cut fosse and built against the exposed rock face for added stability. Where the wall walk survives arrow

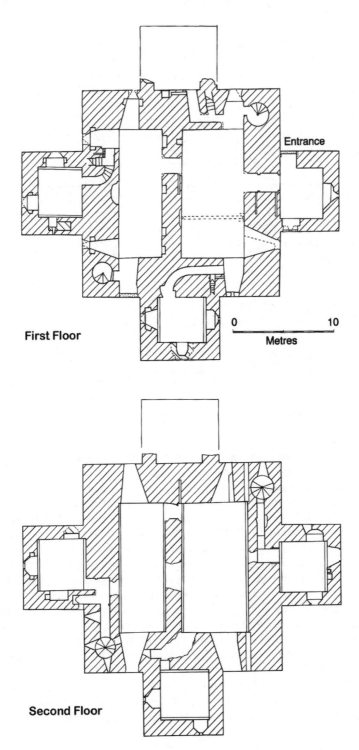

First Floor

Entrance

0   10
Metres

Second Floor

▲ **Fig. 110.** Trim Castle: plans of keep (after McNeill)

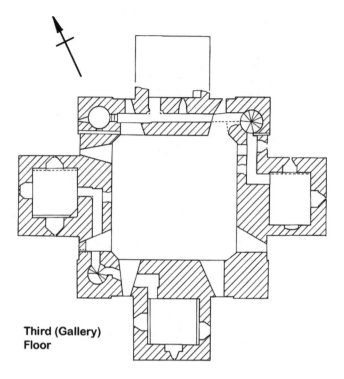

Third (Gallery) Floor

▲ **Fig. 110.** (cont.)

loops can be seen both at ground and wall walk level. The fosse could be flooded from the Boyne to create a moat. There is a clear difference between the towers and gatehouse on the north and east sides of the castle and those on the south. The former are rectilinear in plan, suggesting a late 12th-century date, but the latter are rounded or D-shaped externally, indicating a slightly later date. There are two gatehouses—on the south, facing the road from **Dublin**, and on the north-west, facing the town. The town gate is two storeyed, rectangular at ground level but changing to polygonal above. Its gateway was defended by a portcullis, a murder hole above, an outer drawbridge across the fosse, and an external barbican (now vanished). The entrance passage was flanked by a single chamber, only accessible from the first floor above. The Dublin gate, to the south, consists of a three-storey rounded tower defended by a portcullis and murder hole, with a drawbridge over the fosse and a surviving external barbican.

Near the centre of the enclosure is the massive keep. Recent excavations revealed a large fosse with evidence for an internal palisade, surrounding the keep, with evidence of burnt structures within it. These are probably the remains of the original ringwork castle that was burnt in 1174. The great stone keep that replaced this is basically square in plan but with square turrets projecting from the centre of each side, producing a unique 20-sided plan (*access by guided tour only*). It is now three storeys high with higher turrets at the angles, but was built in a number of stages. The first two storeys are perhaps as early as 1175–180. The walls were raised slightly in the late 1190s, but the building remained at two storeys until the upper storey and turrets were added c.1205. The keep originally contained the main domestic accommodation for the lord and his household—presumably including the great hall, although its location is problematic. It is entered through a round-headed door at first-floor level in the north wall of the eastern projecting tower. This entrance was defended by a drawbridge, lowering onto a forebuilding to the north, and by a timber gallery overhead. The entire north-east sector of the keep was further defended from the mid-13th century by an outer rectangular enclosure, with rounded turrets at the north-west and south-east corners, accessed over a drawbridge across the old ringwork fosse.

From the eastern tower, the main inner space of the keep was accessed via a passage in the intervening wall protected by two substantial doors, the bar-holes of which are visible in the south side of the passage. The keep seems to be divided into two zones. There is a public zone on the north and east sides including the entrance, the chapel at second-floor level in the east tower, and a stair in the north-east angle which gave access to the hall above. On the south and west sides were the lord's private chambers, largely contained within the south and west projecting towers which (unlike those on the north and east) have fireplaces and relatively high ceilings. A separate—and presumably private—stair in the south-west angle also leads to the hall above. The main first-floor chamber is now divided by a large north–south spine wall, but excavation has revealed a large stone pillar, apparently designed to support the floor above, which may indicate that the spine wall is a later addition. Without it, the first-floor chamber may well have functioned as the hall. When the second floor was added a large chamber with a large fireplace was provided which presumably functioned as the hall until, in the later 13th century, a new hall was erected in the north-east angle of the castle. This new hall adjoined the large square corner tower, which was modified to provide a solar. The hall is poorly preserved, but was single storeyed, aisled, and lit by large windows opened in the curtain wall. The kitchen was attached to the south-east end and beyond this was a riverside gate, with external slipway for the unloading of provisions from boats on the river. A vaulted storage chamber was incorporated under the hall at this end.

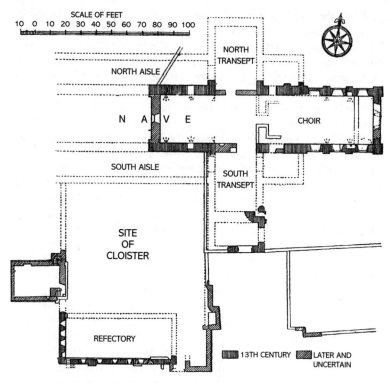

▲ **Fig. 111.** Newtown Trim: plan of cathedral (OPW)

Newtown Trim

Some 1.5 km downriver (east) from Trim is Newtown Trim (*off R154 from Trim towards Dublin; take minor road to north after 1 km; signposted*). It is the site of a failed attempt by the first English bishop of Meath, Simon de Rochfort, to set up his own town in rivalry to de Lacy's. In 1202 de Rochfort moved his diocesan seat from Clonard (recently burned by the Irish) to the 'new town of Trim', which can only have been in formation at this date. A priory of Augustinian canons, dedicated to Sts Peter and Paul, was set up soon afterwards to run the new cathedral of the diocese. A priory and hospital of the *Fratres Cruciferi* was also founded at some date in the early 13th century. The new town was a failure, however, losing out to the older town of Trim in the battle for survival. The Augustinian priory was dissolved in 1537, when it was noted that part of the church could be used as a parish church, while the remainder of the church and other buildings of the priory had already been demolished.

The *Cruciferi* priory of St John the Baptist is sited on the south bank of the Boyne. The surviving buildings are fragmentary, and were much altered in post-medieval times. The east end of the church, with its lancet windows, is clearly 13th century but the fortified tower at the west end is probably 15th century. Across the bridge (which is partly medieval), on the north side of the river, is the cathedral. Although not impressive today, it was originally one of the largest churches in medieval Ireland, *c.*70 m long with transepts and side aisles that, along with most of the nave, have disappeared. The west end of the nave, the aisles, and the transepts were abandoned and became derelict in the later Middle Ages, when the choir alone was found to be adequate for the declining population of Newtown Trim. The choir has tall, early 13th-century lancet windows. At the west end—which is part of the original nave—is a niche containing a once-fine early 13th-century effigy of an ecclesiastic, quite possibly of Simon de Rochfort himself (d. 1224). Both choir and nave were originally vaulted—the springings for the vaulting ribs can still be seen at the heads of wall shafts between the windows, especially on the south wall of the nave. To the south of the cathedral are fragments of the claustral buildings of the priory, probably the chapter house in the east range and the refectory with vaulted undercroft below, in the south range. East of the cathedral is another small medieval church, probably 13th century with inserted 15th-century window. Within it is the late 16th-century tomb of Sir Luke Dillon and Jane Bathe, his wife.

Uisneach, Co. Westmeath   Royal complex/meeting place

On the north side of the R390 from Athlone to Mullingar, near Loughnavally; signposted. Disc. Ser. 48.

Uisneach is one of the great 'royal' or cult sites of late prehistoric Ireland and, according to tradition, is located at the meeting place of the five ancient provinces. Here stood a sacred ash tree. The actual point of intersection is marked by the 'Cat Stone', halfway up the south-west flank of the hill. An extraordinary glacial erratic perched on quite a steep incline, its five faces are said to point towards the five provinces or *coiceada*. It has been surrounded by a low circular embankment. Uisneach is associated with druidical fire ceremonies celebrated during the festival of Beltaine (1 May). As at the other 'royal' sites, there is a panoramic vista from the top, which is deceptively rangy and undulating. There are two ponds, one about halfway up the southern slope (which appeared quite recently), the other more or less on the summit. Anomalous in this hilltop context, there can be little doubt that the summit pond contributed to the attraction of the place for prehistoric ritual. More or less between the two is a fenced-off well called 'St Patrick's Well'.

There are a few recognizable monuments, as well as a host of

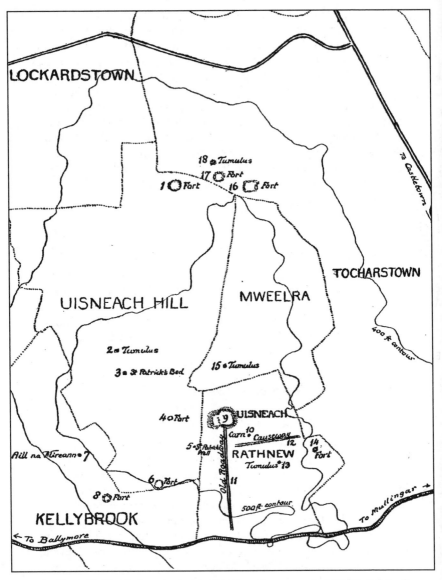

▲ Fig. 112. Uisneach: map showing location of monuments (after Macalister & Praeger)

intriguing bumps and hollows. On the eastern summit, and approached from the south by an avenue, is a denuded and overgrown figure-of-eight earthwork, excavated early in the 20th century by Macalister. A 4th-century Roman coin and a Roman-style key were found but the

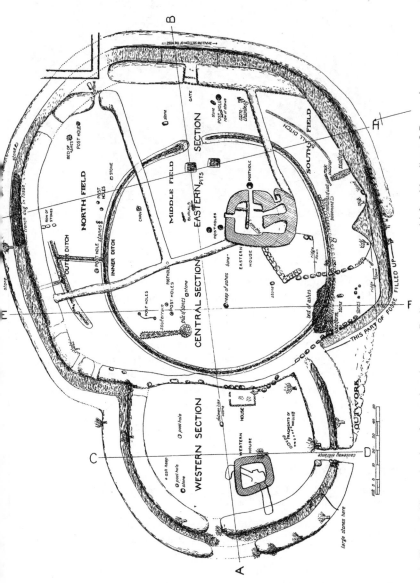

▲ Fig. 113. Uisneach: plan of central enclosure at Rathnew as excavated (after Macalister & Praeger)

▲ **Fig. 114.** Uisneach: the 'Cat Stone' (photo: Conor Newman)

contexts inadequately recorded. The smaller element may have been added later and incorporates a standing stone. North-west of this is one of the ponds and north-east of this are three or four small burial mounds or barrows. North-west again, near the edge of a small spur, is a beautifully preserved ring barrow. Some of the better-preserved monuments lie at the northern foot of the hill, including three interesting enclosures, one of which has a fine souterrain. Again, select excavations by Macalister have yielded the only information thus far. There are more barrows on the south side of the Mullingar road, emphasizing the fact that the Hill of Uisneach is merely the focal point of an extensive but largely unexplored archaeological landscape.

Ward, Co. Meath Ceremonial enclosure

2 km east of Athboy, off N51 (Athboy–Navan), at the crown of the hill, adjacent to waterworks; signposted. Disc. Ser. 42.

Slightly to the east of the summit of the Hill of Ward is the hugely important *Tlachtga*, a quadrivallate earthwork associated with the festival of Samhain. The monument is about 149 m in diameter and incorporates a small, flat-topped barrow and a now prostrate standing stone. Samhain (1 November) was the start of the Celtic year and all the druids of Ireland were reputed to assemble at Tlachtga to celebrate this fire ceremony and make offerings. The monument looks across the middle reaches of the Boyne towards **Tara** and in early Irish cosmology symbolizes Munster, the primeval world of demons, witches, and serfs.

Tlachtga was the daughter of the sorcerer Mug Ruith of Valentia Island, in west Munster. At the eastern foot of the hill a small standing stone (*not signposted*) marks the boundary between farmland and bogland and in the nearby townland of Dressoge was found a Dowris-phase hoard of gold dress fasteners.

Shannon: Clare, Limerick, Offaly, North Tipperary

Introduction

Physically, this region is for the most part relatively low lying, with few mountains, drained primarily by the river Shannon and its tributaries and bordering the Atlantic to the west. Most of Co. Tipperary and east Co. Limerick have fertile soils, with few serious use limitations. West

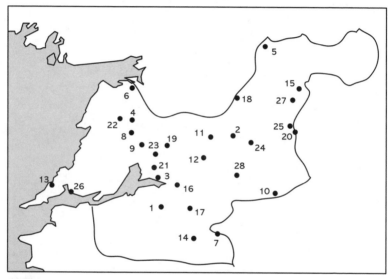

▲ Map 6

Key:

1. Adare, Co. Limerick
2. Ashleypark, Co. Tipperary
3. Bunratty, Co. Clare
4. Cahercommaun, Co. Clare
5. Clonmacnoise, Co. Offaly
6. Corcomroe, Co. Clare
7. Duntryleague, Co. Limerick
8. Dysert O'Dea, Co. Clare
9. Ennis, Co. Clare
10. Holycross, Co. Tipperary
11. Inishcaltra, Co. Clare
12. Killaloe, Co. Clare
13. Kilkee, Co. Clare
14. Kilmallock, Co. Limerick

15. Kinnity, Co. Offaly
16. Limerick, Co. Limerick
17. Lough Gur, Co. Limerick
18. Lorrha, Co. Tipperary
19. Magh Adhair, Co. Clare
20. Monaincha, Co. Tipperary
21. Mooghaun, Co. Clare
22. Poulawack, Co. Clare
23. Quin, Co. Clare
24. Rathurles, Co. Tipperary
25. Roscrea, Co. Tipperary
26. Scattery, Co. Clare
27. Seirkieran, Co. Offaly
28. Shanballyedmond, Co. Tipperary

Limerick and most of Cos. Clare and Offaly, however, are dominated by poorly drained soils with considerable areas of bog. These areas also experience relatively high rainfall. In antiquity Munster was to some extent physically cut off from the rest of Ireland by the Shannon, the bogs of Co. Offaly, and the Slieve Bloom Mountains to the east. Clare, west of the Shannon, belongs more logically with Connacht and, indeed, may have been ruled by western kings prior to the 7th century. Since then, however, it has consistently formed part of Munster. A feature of the northern boundaries of the ancient province of Munster is the concentration of important monastic sites, such as Birr, **Clonmacnoise**, Durrow, Rahan, and **Seirkieran** (Co. Offaly), and **Lorrha, Roscrea**, and Terryglass (Co. Tipperary).

An Early Mesolithic site on the shores of present-day Lough Boora, near Birr, Co. Offaly, constitutes the oldest human settlement in the Shannon region. The site came to light during drainage and was excavated by Michael Ryan. Both the lithic and faunal assemblages were broadly comparable with those from **Mount Sandel**, Co. Derry. There were no structures and the site was occupied between about 7000 and 5500 BC. The location of this settlement, deep in the Irish midlands, indicates that our first inhabitants were not confined to coastal areas. Direct evidence that the Shannon was being used, not just as a means of communication but also as an exploitable ecosystem, from the later Mesolithic onwards, has emerged from Aidan O'Sullivan's survey of the intertidal zone on the Shannon and Fergus estuaries.

Evidence of early farming activity comes from both settlement and burial sites, the former representing some of the most important sites in the historiography of Irish archaeology. The spectacular tomb at **Poulnabrone**, Burren, Co. Clare, with its surprisingly impressive burial assemblage, lies towards the southern fringe of the Portal tomb range. The bare limestone around Poulnabrone belies the probability that this was one of the more densely populated areas in early prehistoric Ireland, a theory that is supported by the pollen diagram from Gragan West which records strong evidence of early Neolithic clearance. Pollen diagrams from south Clare, on the other hand, remain curiously silent about early farming activity. Further inland, the megalithic tradition is represented by Linkardstown-type burials at **Ashleypark** and Ardcrony, Co. Tipperary, and an unusual one in a cave at Annagh, Co. Limerick. Further south again, the enclosures and houses at **Lough Gur**, Co. Limerick, indicate the existence of a sizeable, closely knit, and permanent Neolithic community in this immediate area. Settlement at Lough Gur endured well into the Bronze Age and the settlement landscape here is matched by an equally impressive ritual landscape, with which it is integrated.

The Shannon region generally has been an important focus of Bronze Age studies. It is here that some of the largest and most significant finds of later Bronze Age metalwork have been made, including the great gold gorgets from Gleninsheen in the Burren (Co. Clare) and Ardcrony, Co. Tipperary, the **Mooghaun**, Co. Clare, gold hoard and the Dowris, Co. Offaly, hoard of bronzes that lends its name to the latest Bronze Age industrial phase. **Mooghaun** hillfort in south Clare was evidently a seat of regional power, presiding over a settlement and social hierarchy that included wetland sites like Knocknalappa, Co. Clare. Further to the east, wetland sites like Ballinderry and Cloonfinlough, Co. Offaly, were strategically located alongside communications routes, such as the Eiscir Riada (or Slígh Mór). An important aspect of the Bronze Age archaeology of the region is the Wedge tombs (which are most numerous in Co. Clare) as well as fulachta fiadh and barrow cemeteries.

Eamonn Kelly's excavations on Aughinish Island in the Shannon estuary are of critical relevance to the question of the beginnings of the Irish Iron Age. The modest assemblages associated with two adjacent enclosures included Coarse ware, a Dowris-type bronze chisel, and part of an iron horsebit. The context is radiocarbon dated to the first half of the 2nd millennium BC. Etienne Rynne has proposed that the lower Shannon region was a primary area in the introduction of La Tène culture to Iron Age Ireland. Indeed, the incidence of La Tène material along the Shannon basin is indicative of how the river was capable of sustaining a regional cultural province of its own. Rynne marshals as evidence a selection of great stone forts, such as **Cahercommaun** and Ballykinvaraga, Co. Clare, though many would argue that these are early medieval constructions. **Cashel** emerges as the prime centre of power in the south-eastern part of this region, although the only archaeological evidence of prehistoric activity is a 1st-century AD Roman dolphin-type fibula. At this early period its sway is unlikely to have extended across the Shannon into Clare or northwards across the Bog of Allen into Offaly, and one must look to sites like Knockainey, Co. Limerick, and Croghan Hill, Co. Offaly, as sacro-political foci during later prehistory. That the Shannon was also a point of exit is evidenced by a hoard of late Roman hack silver found on the south side of the estuary at Balline, Co. Limerick. It has been suggested that this, and hoards like it, represent secreted booty from Irish raids on later 4th- and early 5th-century Roman Britain.

The region is rich in Early Christian remains (including place name evidence). **Clonmacnoise**, Co. Offaly, and St Senan's foundation on **Scattery Island**, in the middle of the estuary, stand out as the most important early monasteries along the Shannon. The early Columban foundation at Durrow, Co. Offaly, was also of considerable standing. The wealth of the Church in the region is amply illustrated by the magnificent chalices and brooches found at Ardagh, Co. Limerick, and the equally superlative ecclesiastical hoard from Derrynaflan to the north-east of Cashel. Most of the region was included within the early

▲ Fig. 115. Blackhead, Burren, Co. Clare: cashel and field system (photo: Dept. of Archaeology, NUI, Galway)

medieval province of Munster (*Muma*), ruled from **Cashel** by one or other of the several Eóganacht dynasties distributed around the province. Among the most important of these were the Eóganacht Chaisil, based around Cashel itself, and the Eóganacht Áine, based at Knockainey in east Co. Limerick. Across the Shannon, most of east Co. Clare was controlled by a relatively obscure subject group, the Déis Tuaiscirt. In the mid-10th century the ruling dynasty of this group, the Dál Cais of **Killaloe**, rose to prominence and captured the kingship of Cashel itself. Their greatest leader, Brian Ború, established himself as effective highking of the entire island in the early 11th century. Brian's rise was helped by his realization of the value of the Shannon and the new Viking town of **Limerick**, which he was quick to control. Brian's grandson Toirdhealbhach went a step further by making Limerick his capital. The Dál Cais—subsequently known as *Uí Briain* ('descendant of Brian')—were unable to maintain this national dominance after Brian's death. Their decline led to the effective partition of Munster, in the early 12th century, with Uí Briain control limited to Thomond (*Tuadmuma*, 'north Munster')—mainly Cos. Limerick, Clare, and North Tipperary.

Even in Thomond, the Uí Briain grip was weakened by English colonization in the 13th century. English attempts to capture Limerick in 1175 proved abortive because of the power of King Domhnall Mór Ó Briain. In 1185, however, a considerable part of Thomond was granted by the English Prince John to Theobald Walter, ancestor of the Butler family. He seems to have begun actively colonizing north Co. Tipperary and south Co. Offaly soon afterwards, though there was no serious

▲ **Fig. 116.** Turlough Hill, Burren, Co. Clare: hut circles (photo: Conor Newman and Eamonn O'Donoghue)

attempt to penetrate the Ó Briain heartlands in Cos. Clare and Limerick. Co. Offaly bears the name of the Uí Failgi, a Laigin dynasty who were pushed westwards from the Liffey plain by their cousins, the Uí Dúnlainge. Following the English conquest much of their territory in east Co. Offaly was taken over by the FitzGeralds. The extensive bog lands further west were a physical impediment to conquest and in any case made it unattractive to English lords.

After the death of Domhnall Mór in 1194, Uí Briain resistance collapsed. Limerick was quickly taken and most of Co. Limerick was occupied by English lords by the early 13th century. Little more than Co. Clare was left to the Uí Briain and even that was threatened in the 1270s, when Thomas de Clare (brother of the earl of Gloucester) established a lordship in south Co. Clare, based on **Bunratty**. This marked the high point of Anglo-Irish control in the region, but decline followed quickly. The de Clare lordship was destroyed after the Battle of **Dysert O'Dea** (1318) and Ó Briain rule in Co. Clare was unchallenged after this. By the

later 14th century the Uí Briain were reasserting control over much of
Co. Limerick and beyond, and Anglo-Irish settlement was crumbling,
outside of walled towns such as **Limerick** and **Kilmallock**. In Co.
Tipperary the earldom of Ormond was created for the Butlers in 1328
but by *c*.1350 most of northern Co. Tipperary was controlled by Irish
lords such as the Uí Cinnéadaigh (O'Kennedys). Further north, the Uí
Conchobair Failge increasingly threatened Anglo-Irish lands, not only in
east Co. Offaly but also in Cos. Kildare and Meath. Their erstwhile
conquerors, the FitzGeralds, had progressed to greater things as earls of
Kildare, with a consequent eastward shift in their focus, which allowed
the Uí Conchobhair to recover much of east Co. Offaly. In the 1550s,
however, the Uí Conchobhair were dispossessed following a renewed
English campaign and their lands were planted with English settlers.

Adare, Co. Limerick Medieval town

16 km south-west of Limerick, on N21 (Limerick–Tralee/Killarney). Disc. Ser. 65.

The picturesque village of Adare disguises one of Ireland's most interesting shrunken medieval towns. The layout of the modern village dates to
the 19th century and bears little relationship to the town founded in the
early 13th century, probably by Geoffrey de Marisco, at a fording point
[*Áth Dara*, 'the ford of the oaks'] on the river Maigue. The new settlement received the right to hold an annual fair in 1226, and in 1310 it
received a grant of murage—clear evidence of the existence of a substantial town. A castle, a Trinitarian abbey, and a parish church already
existed by this date and an Augustinian friary was soon added. A Franciscan friary was founded in the 15th century. From the early 14th century the manor of Adare belonged to the powerful FitzGerald earls of
Kildare, but with the resurgence of Irish power in Thomond, Anglo-
Irish towns like Adare became less secure. The town was burned in 1376
and although it recovered, this possibly marked the beginning of a long
decline. By the end of the 17th century it had declined so much that even
the layout of the medieval town is difficult to reconstruct. The creation
of Adare Manor demesne in the 18th century and the replanning of the
village in the 19th century have added to the confusion. The concentration of the castle, parish church, and Franciscan friary on the north side
of the river Maigue suggest that the main focus of settlement may
have been in this area, but the presence of the Augustinian friary and
Trinitarian abbey on the south bank, near the modern village, indicates
medieval settlement here, also.

Castle

The castle (*east side of N21, north of Maigue bridge; conservation work
may restrict access*) was probably first built by Geoffrey de Marisco in the

early 13th century. It is situated on the bank of the river Maigue—probably to control traffic on the river—and consists of a roughly rectangular enclosure with a rounded inner ward at the north-western angle. The outer ward was defended by an external moat, fed by the river. On the west side is a simple gateway, with a later two-storey gatehouse built onto the rear, containing a chamber to one side of the gateway and another overhead. Along the southern (river) side of the outer ward are two rectangular structures—apparently two successive halls. The earlier, set in the south-west angle beside the gatehouse, is a two-storey building with the hall on the first floor. The two-light windows in the north, east, and south walls are framed by continuous roll mouldings in 'School of the West' style, indicating an early 13th-century date. This hall was replaced by the larger, single-storey, aisled building further east, with a porch on the north side and a kitchen to the east, and large twin-light windows in the north and south walls. This aisled, ground-floor hall is similar in many respects to the hall at **Trim**, and like it may be of later 13th-century date.

Surrounding the inner ward is a deep fosse, possibly a survival from an earlier earthen fortification preceding the stone castle. Access to the interior was through another gatehouse—originally defended by a drawbridge—on the south side. On the east side is a four-storey tower or keep, of which only the northern half survives to full height. It was originally (presumably in the early 13th century) a two-storey structure—note the roof line in the internal north wall over first-floor level. Later, probably in the 15th century, it was raised to four storeys. A spine wall was also inserted to support new vaulting over the ground floor, replacing the original wooden floor. The keep was probably entered at first-floor level—the ground-floor doorway on the west side is a later insertion. Very little can be said about the internal arrangements of this tower, and some of its features (especially at the upper levels) may be the result of 19th-century restoration.

Parish church

North of the castle (*in the grounds of the golf club, near the clubhouse*) is the ruined parish church of St Nicholas. This nave-and-chancel building is apparently of 13th-century origin, judging by the lancet windows in the chancel, but it has been much altered in late and post-medieval times. The gabled cross-wall, *c.*5 m from the west end, is probably a late medieval insertion—indicating that the church was reduced in size because of declining population. On the north side of the church is a smaller, but better-preserved chapel. It is a simple rectangular building with single-light, cusped pointed windows, suggesting a 13th-century date. A series of beam-holes in the side walls at the west end indicate that there was an overhead gallery here, and there is also an underground vault. West of these churches and north of the castle is a ruined masonry wall aligned north–south, over 1.5 m thick with an external batter at each end and traces of a barrel vault internally. This is traditionally identified as part of the 'Kilmallock gate' and may well be part of a medieval town gate, although this has not been confirmed.

Franciscan friary

The well-preserved Franciscan friary is now rather unfortunately surrounded by the local golf course (*access through Adare Manor Hotel; take care while crossing the golf course!*), but it must originally have been located at the edge of the medieval town, if not actually within it. It was founded by the earl of Kildare in 1464 and officially dissolved in 1539, but probably continued to function until *c.*1580. The church and one side of the cloister were built in the 1460s. The large aisled south transept, the tower, and the remainder of the cloister are almost

▼ Fig. 117. Adare: plan of Franciscan friary (after Dunraven)

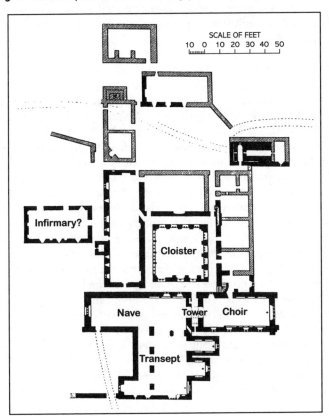

contemporary, certainly added before 1500. The church displays a variety of window types, including a triple lancet-type west window and large four-light windows with switchline tracery in the east gable and south gable of the transept. It was entered through a doorway in the south wall of the nave, or from the cloisters through a doorway under the tower. The tower is a fine example of the typical friary type—tall (five storeys) and slender, with high stepped battlements. In the north wall of the choir are three pointed tomb niches with ogee-headed hoods and shafted pinnacles, built as a unit. Opposite them is a finely carved sedilia flanked by two further tomb niches, although the eastern niche (which contains a piscina) may have been intended as another sedilia.

The cloisters are on the north side of the church. Only the west range is reasonably intact, but the cloister arcade survives on all sides. This consists of bays of three pointed openings, each set in a wide, three-centred embrasure, on the north, east, and south sides. On the west side the arcade is of more conventional design, with groups of openings between buttressed piers. Beyond the cloister are the ruins of further buildings, probably including a guesthouse and kitchens (to the north) and an infirmary (to the west). To the north-west are the ruins of a mill, fed by a covered millstream running across the northern side of the extra-claustral buildings.

Augustinian friary

Two further monasteries occur on the south side of the river Maigue, closer to the modern village. The Augustinian friary (*west side of N21 immediately south of Maigue bridge*) was founded before 1316 by the earl of Kildare and officially suppressed in 1539, although it probably continued to function until *c.*1580. The church was restored for use by the Church of Ireland in the 19th century, and is one of the few to preserve something of the atmosphere of a medieval Irish friary church. It was built in the early 14th century and is divided into a nave and choir, both almost equal in length. In the 15th century the original south aisle was widened, a typical friary tower was erected between the nave and choir, and a small cloister was built to the north of the church. The present entrance, through a modern porch, leads into the south aisle, which is lit by windows with switchline tracery in the east and south walls, and a twin-light window with Flamboyant tracery in the west wall—all 15th century. In the south wall is a tomb niche with ogee-headed canopy, flanked by shafts. The aisle is separated from the nave by an arcade of three large pointed arches, but the eastern arch is a replacement—originally this space was spanned by two arches. The nave has a 15th-century west doorway below a three-light window with switchline tracery. At the east end of the north wall, above a wall tomb, a twin-light trefoil-headed window was partly blocked when the tower was inserted.

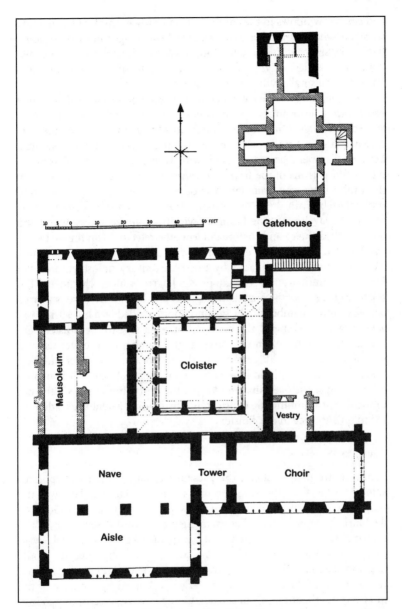

▲ Fig. 118. Adare: plan of Augustinian friary (after Dunraven)

The tower had six floors with a wall walk and stepped battlements above, and a sedilia between the piers at ground level—presumably for priests saying Mass in the nave. Another sedilia and piscina are more conventionally located in the choir, which is lit by a five-light east window and smaller windows in the south wall—all early examples of switchline tracery. In the north wall are two wall tombs with ogee-headed canopies, flanked by shafts with crocketed finials. West of these is a round-headed doorway that led originally to the east range of the cloisters, now replaced by a small, 19th-century vestry.

Outside, the attractive cloister arcade consists on each side of three bays, each a deep pointed embrasure with three multi-cusped round-arched openings. Only the openings on the north and east sides are original (the others are modern) and these have, in the spandrels between the openings, small shields with saltire crosses—the arms of the FitzGerald patrons of the friary. The ambulatories are vaulted, but only the vault of the west ambulatory is definitely original; the others were probably rebuilt in the 19th century. Midway along the north ambulatory is the lavabo, a stone basin set within a pointed recess, where the friars washed their hands before entering the refectory (on the first floor overhead) for meals. The east and west claustral ranges have vanished. The west range was replaced by the 19th-century mausoleum of the Dunraven family—apart from an original barrel-vaulted chamber at the north end. The north range is well preserved, however. There is a large barrel-vaulted chamber on the ground floor (divided by a modern cross-wall) and at the east end, the main entrance passage to the cloisters. On the first floor is the refectory, a large single chamber restored for use as a school in the early 19th century. To the north-east is another building range extending north, in line with the missing east range. It is mainly occupied by a 19th-century building in the centre but at the south end, immediately adjoining the cloisters, is a two-storey gatehouse leading to the main entrance to the cloisters.

Trinitarian abbey

In the centre of the village, the present Catholic church incorporates substantial parts of the 13th-century Trinitarian church. This was the only Irish abbey of the Trinitarian order, probably founded by Geoffrey de Marisco before 1226. The main medieval feature surviving is the crossing with its tower, but parts of the medieval south nave wall (with twin-light window and piscina) also survive—although heavily modified—in the south aisle of the modern church. The cloisters were located to the north of the church and are largely occupied by the nave of the modern church, but much of the north range survives incorporated into the 19th-century convent building, with towers at east and west ends. In the extreme north-west corner of the church grounds is a rebuilt dovecot, probably belonging to the medieval abbey.

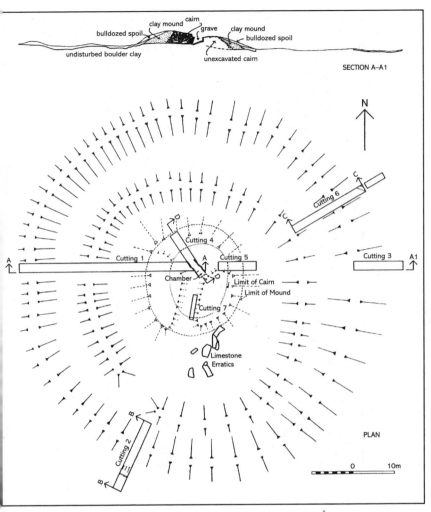

▲ **Fig. 119a.** Ashleypark: plan of site (after Manning)

Ashleypark, Co. Tipperary Neolithic burial mound

6 km north of Nenagh off the N52 (Nenagh–Birr); take second turn to west (left) north of Lough Eorna; signposted. Disc. Ser. 59.

This Linkardstown-style burial, dating from around 3500 BC, was found in an open-ended stone chamber under a large mound, which was surrounded by two concentric banks with internal fosses (about 90 m in total diameter). The disarticulated remains of an elderly man and a child were accompanied to the grave by three bipartite bowls and a selection of cattle, sheep, and pig bones. In the mantle of soil over the cairn were

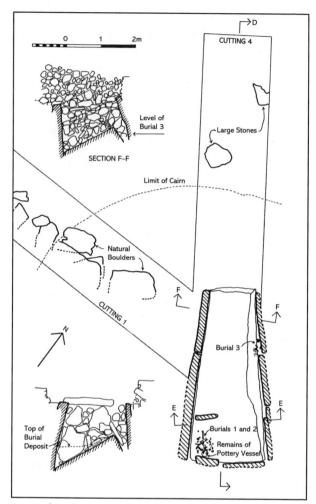

▲ Fig. 119b. Ashleypark: plan of burial chamber (after Manning)

the bones of three mature cattle and a pig femur. Butchery marks were in evidence and some of the bones had been split for their marrow. These were covered over with soil from the fosses and are considered to be contemporary with the burial and to represent a funeral feast.

Ashleypark is on the side of a slight rise, topped by a tumulus, over-looking Lough Eorna, to the south. The horizon to the south-west is dominated by Knight Hill with its double summit, on each of which is a cairn (to the south-east) and a barrow (to the north-west). Another such burial was found just up the road (2 km) at Ardcrony. Here was a burial of two men accompanied by a highly decorated bipartite pot. Tradition that there was once a surrounding bank and fosse has not been confirmed.

Bunratty, Co. Clare Castle, medieval borough

9 km north-west of Limerick, on N18 (Limerick–Shannon-Ennis); signposted. Disc. Ser. 58.

The impressive late medieval castle at Bunratty is a major tourist attraction, but what is less well known is that Bunratty was the site of a 13th-century English borough settlement, traces of which still remain. In fact, it is even possible that a Viking fortification was established here in the 10th century, but this has yet to be confirmed. In 1248–51 a castle was erected at Bunratty by Robert de Muscegros, as part of the first English attempt to settle the Uí Briain kingdom of Thomond. In 1276 de Muscegros was replaced by a more powerful English baron, Thomas de Clare, who established a substantial borough settlement at Bunratty, as well as building a new castle. De Clare's enterprise came to a disastrous end in 1318 when his son Richard was killed at the Battle of **Dysert O'Dea**. The settlement seems to have been abandoned by its inhabitants before being destroyed by the Irish. Although the castle of Bunratty was briefly reoccupied by Anglo-Irish garrisons in the 1320s and again in the 1350s, English settlement in Thomond effectively ended in 1318 and the region reverted to the control of the Uí Briain kings.

The settlement at Bunratty was sited on an area of slightly raised ground, originally surrounded by marshy ground on the west, south, and north, and bordered on the east by the Owenogarney river—originally known as the Ráite, hence the name *Bun Ráite* ('the mouth of the Ráite'). Remains of substantial earthworks surrounding this area were traced in the early 20th century, but are no longer visible. These were presumed to be the medieval borough defences, but recent archaeological excavation suggests that they may (at least in part) be of 17th-century date. Roughly in the centre of the enclosed area are the ruins of the parish church, first established in the 1250s, although the present simple structure is an early 17th-century rebuilding by Donnchad Ó Briain, earl of Thomond.

Castle

To the east, beside the river, is the castle—presumably on the site of de Clare's castle, which must have fallen into ruin or been destroyed after the last Anglo-Irish garrison abandoned it in 1355. The present castle is of 15th-century date and seems to owe nothing to any earlier structure, although excavation in the 1950s revealed traces of an outer curtain wall that may be earlier. Tradition states that the castle was built by the local lords, the Mac Conmara (MacNamara), in the mid-15th century, but it may have been built directly by their Uí Briain overlords, who were certainly in possession by the early 16th century. Bunratty was the main residence of the Uí Briain lords of Thomond until 1646, when the castle was besieged and damaged in the wars. It subsequently fell into ruin but was heavily restored in the 1950s and 1960s. The present furnishings, although authentic and very important, are not original to Bunratty.

▼ **Fig. 120.** Bunratty: plan of castle at upper hall level (after Leask)

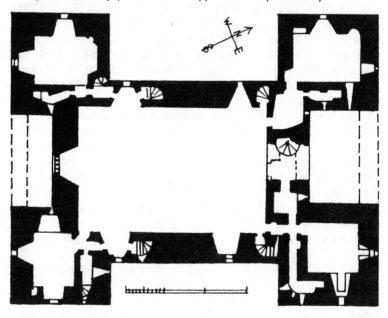

The castle is essentially a very large rectangular tower house with projecting square turrets at each angle, which are linked by high arches on the narrow (north and south) ends. The deeper arch on the north side helped to defend the original entrance below. The internal arrangements are quite complex, as the main bloc has three storeys, while the turrets have six storeys and rise above the central block. There are also a warren of chambers, passages, and stairways built within the massively thick walls. The main entrance, in the north wall at first-floor level, gives access to a hall that rises through two floors and has a pointed barrel vault. This hall was the main reception area and probably the living quarters of the lord's retinue. Below it, at ground-floor level, is another vaulted chamber that was essentially a cellar for storage. All four corner turrets can be accessed from the first-floor hall and the ground-floor chambers of these turrets can only be reached from first-floor level. The turrets also have second-floor chambers, at the level of the vault of the first-floor hall.

Above this, at third-floor level, is the great hall, the lord's main public chamber, which preserves fragments of late 16th-century decorated plasterwork—very rare in Ireland. There is further plasterwork of similar date in the chapel, located in the south-east turret at this level. At fourth-floor level, above the great hall, there are chambers in the turrets and another, larger chamber carried on the arch between the northern turrets. Now known as the 'north solar', this was probably the main chamber of the lord's private apartments, and is equipped with a very large fireplace (probably not original) and a peep-hole allowing a view of the great hall below. Another peep-hole looks into the north-east turret—probably the lord's private chapel. Originally there was direct access from the main chamber into the turret chambers at either end, although the doorway to the north-eastern turret (the chapel) is now blocked. The north-western turret chamber may have been the lord's bedroom. The main chamber rises through two storeys, and high in the west wall is a blocked doorway leading to the north-west turret at fifth-floor level. This was presumably reached by means of a now-vanished wooden gallery, carried on the corbels in the north and west walls. At fifth-floor level, carried on the arch between the southern turrets, is a true solar (the 'south solar'), lit by a fine six-light window, with direct access to the adjacent turret chambers. Outside the turrets is the reconstructed roof of the main block. The stepped parapets are entirely modern, although not inappropriate for the period of the castle.

Cahercommaun, Co. Clare Stone fort

10 km north-east of Kilfenora; take R476 (Corrofin–Kilfenora) north from Killinaboy for 1 km, then turn north (right), keeping left at fork after 500 m; continue straight through crossroads after 3 km, to the next right turn where a pathway, to the right of the large house, leads to the fort; signposted. Disc. Ser. 51.

This multivallate stone fort stands dramatically on the edge of a cliff overlooking a steep valley. It is the most impressive of hundreds of stone forts in the Burren area of Co. Clare, and was clearly an important site— quite possibly a royal residence—but despite this, almost nothing is known of its history. It has recently been suggested that the name [*Cathair Chommáin*, 'Commán's fort'] is derived from Commán mac Maínaich, a 7th-century sub-king of the Uí Fidgeinti, the dominant force in the Co. Clare area until superseded in the 9th century by the Dál Cais. Although it was excavated by the Harvard Archaeological Expedition to Ireland in 1934, the archaeological sequence of the site was far from clear. A fine silver penannular brooch, found in a souterrain within one of the internal buildings, was the main reason for Hencken's conclusion that the site was built and occupied in the 9th century. This conclusion has been questioned by some archaeologists, however, who have suggested that the site might be considered a prehistoric hillfort,

▼ Fig. 121. Cahercommaun: plan (after Hencken)

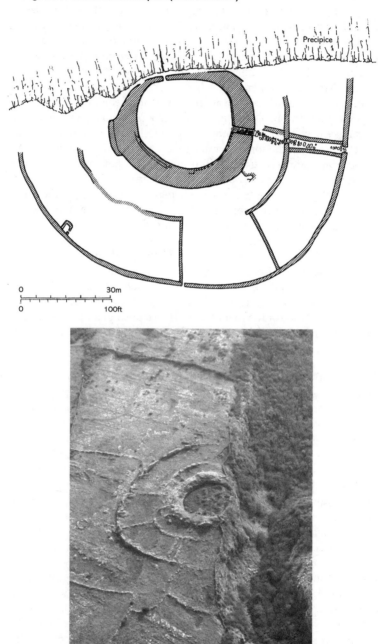

▲ Fig. 122. Cahercommaun (photo: Conor Newman and Eamonn O'Donoghue)

rather than an early medieval cashel, or even that it might represent a late prehistoric progenitor of the cashel.

A recent reappraisal of the excavated evidence (both structural and artefactual) broadly confirms Hencken's interpretation, although it suggests the settlement history of the site was slightly more complex than he realized. There is clear evidence for prehistoric activity on the site, but this cannot be related to any structural features and the evidence favours an early medieval date for the major phase of construction and occupation. Three phases of early medieval occupation have been recognized. The first is dated sometime between the 5th and 8th centuries, the second is dated to the 9th century and the third, possibly, to the late 9th/10th centuries. The construction of the fort, as it exists today, probably took place during the second phase (i.e. in the 9th century) but it is possible that there was an earlier fort or enclosure contemporary with the first phase, at some period between the 5th and 8th centuries.

The fort today consists of three roughly concentric, widely spaced drystone walls defending an oval inner space measuring *c*.32 m by 28 m. The maximum dimension of the outer enclosure is 116 m. The innermost wall is by far the most massive, up to 4.3 m high and 8.5 m thick, and is the only full enclosure. The two outer walls are C-shaped, rather than round, with their open sides against the cliff edge. These outer walls are linked by radial walls and in general, much of the masonry of the enclosures has been rebuilt at various periods. The inner enclosure was clearly intensively occupied. A paved entranceway to the east passes through all three enclosures and was flanked, just inside the inner enclosure, by two rectangular structures. In all, the stone foundations of at least 11 structures—two of which had souterrains—and 22 hearths were exposed by excavation within the inner enclosure. There were also a number of niches or chambers within the inner enclosing wall itself, which was also terraced internally. All of these internal features are no longer visible, however, having been back-filled by the excavators and subsequently overgrown. Although a number of small structures were found within the areas enclosed by the two outer walls, the excavator felt these spaces were used primarily for keeping cattle, which was clearly the mainstay of the site's economy.

Clonmacnoise, Co. Offaly Early monastic site

10 km south of Athlone on river Shannon; take R444 (Moate–Shannonbridge) to south off N6 (Dublin–Athlone), 3 km west of Moate; signposted. Visitor centre; admission charge. Disc. Ser. 47.

Clonmacnoise [*Cluan Moccu Nóis*, 'the meadow of the sons of Nós'] is probably the most famous early monastic site in Ireland, and was one of the most important. Founded by St Ciarán in the mid-6th century, it was

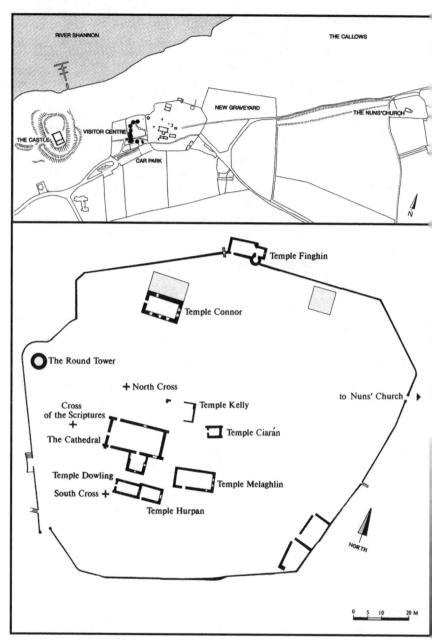

▲ Fig. 123. Clonmacnoise: plan showing location of monuments, with detail of central area (after Manning)

▲ **Fig. 124.** Clonmacnoise: South Cross (photo: Dept. of Archaeology, NUI, Galway)

strategically located at the very heart of the island, on the junction of two of early medieval Ireland's main routeways—the river Shannon and the east–west land route known as the *Slighe Mhór*. The monastery prospered under the patronage of several royal dynasties—the kings of Connacht from the late 7th to early 9th centuries, the Uí Néill kings of Mide from the mid-9th to early 11th centuries, and the Uí Conchobhair kings of Connacht for most of the 12th century. Largely as a result of this, it was perhaps the most important centre of artistic and literary production in early medieval Ireland. No fewer than three of the main Irish annals—the *Annals of Tighearnach*, the *Chronicon Scottorum*, and the *Annals of Clonmacnoise*—were produced here, along with several important surviving manuscripts. Many of Ireland's major surviving pieces of medieval metalwork were also produced at Clonmacnoise. These include the 11th-century shrine of the Stowe Missal and the Crosier of the Abbots of Clonmacnoise, and possibly also the two finest surviving pieces of 12th-century Irish metalwork—the Cross of Cong

▲ **Fig. 125.** Clonmacnoise boasts the largest single collection of cross-slabs in the country (photo: Dept. of Archaeology, NUI, Galway)

and St Manchan's Shrine (*all but the last are now in the National Museum of Ireland*). Clonmacnoise also has the finest collection of early medieval stone carvings in Ireland, including three important high crosses and some 700 grave slabs, datable from at least the 8th to 12th centuries.

The status of the monastery is reflected in the visible remains on site, which include eight churches, two round towers, two holy wells, and the crosses and grave slabs. As impressive as the visible remains are, however, Clonmacnoise in its heyday was much larger and more complex. There is historical evidence for an enclosure around the site, part of which was found behind the present national school. Within it there were a series of distinct precincts (*trians*), probably surrounding the ecclesiastical core where the visible remains survive today. There is also evidence for streets, houses (105 houses are recorded as having been burnt in an English raid in 1179), craft workers, and markets. Clonmacnoise is a prime example of what is sometimes referred to as a 'monastic town', having expanded far beyond its original ecclesiastical functions and taken on quasi-urban attributes. The historical evidence for these activities concentrates on the 11th and 12th centuries, but recent archaeological excavations in the New Graveyard, immediately east of the ecclesiastical core, produced evidence for houses, workshops, and other activities from at least as early as the 8th century. The remains of a major wooden bridge, dating the beginning of the 9th century, have also been found in the river Shannon opposite the later castle.

Unlike many other 'monastic towns', however, Clonmacnoise failed to develop into a modern town, and became one of the real victims of the English conquest. It was cut off from its Uí Conchobhair patrons (who in any case rapidly declined in importance) following the English advances of the late 12th century. No significant new patrons were found to replace the Uí Conchobhair and Clonmacnoise found itself stranded on the frontier between the new English- and Irish-controlled zones. While a royal castle was erected here in 1214, the English chose to promote Athlone, 15 km upriver, rather than Clonmacnoise, as a town and major crossing point on the Shannon. Even in church affairs, the English-controlled bishopric of Meath began to expand at the expense of the diocese of Clonmacnoise. The monastery continued to function, but its greatest days were over, and an English raid in 1552 seems to have led to the final abandonment of the site.

A visit to the site should begin at the visitor centre, where many grave slabs and the high crosses are on display (replicas stand in their original locations). Pride of place goes to the West Cross, or 'Cross of the Scriptures', one of the finest of all the Irish high crosses which originally stood opposite the west door of the cathedral. It bears a damaged inscription, apparently recording its erection by the abbot Colmán under the patronage of Flann Sinna, Uí Néill king of Mide (879–916). The cross was probably erected c.909, when the same pair are known to have built the cathedral. It is decorated on the broad faces with scriptural scenes, as follows (from base to top):

West face: *Christ in the Tomb*
             Three figures, possibly the Scourging of Christ?
             Soldiers Casting Lots for Christ's Clothing
             Crucifixion
East face: *Two figures, probably Moses, Aaron, and the Brazen*
             Serpent
             Two figures, unidentified
             Christ with Peter and Paul
             Christ in Judgement

Other scenes on the sides and base of the cross are more difficult to interpret. The South Cross is earlier in date—mid-9th century—and is decorated mainly with panels of interlace and geometric ornament, although there is a *Crucifixion* scene on the west face.

The cathedral

Eight churches are visible at Clonmacnoise. Of these, the most important is the cathedral (*directly in front of the replica Cross of the Scriptures*). Despite the appearance of the early Gothic west doorway of *c*.1200, or the even more elaborate 15th-century north doorway, the cathedral is substantially the *daimliag* ('stone church') recorded as having been built in 909 by Abbot Colmán with the patronage of the high-king, Flann Sinna. It is thus the earliest precisely dated church surviving in Ireland and was also the largest pre-Romanesque church. It was originally much wider than at present, as the south wall was rebuilt some 2 m inside (north of) its original line in the late 13th/early 14th century. Around 1200 a new west doorway was inserted and the sacristy added on the south side. The height of the north wall (and presumably also of the south wall) was also raised by *c*.1.6 m, probably in order to lower the pitch of the roof. This may have taken place in 1207 when the remains of Ruaidhrí Ua Conchobhair, the last high-king of Ireland, were interred in a new stone shrine in the cathedral. About a century later the south wall was rebuilt. Further substantial alterations took place in the mid-15th century, when first-floor chambers were added above the east end of the church and the sacristy, presumably as a priests' residence. The chamber over the church was built on a vaulted canopy, supported by engaged and free-standing columns, while the chamber above the sacristy was provided with a fireplace and chimney. The perpendicular Gothic doorway in the north wall, erected by Dean Odo O'Malone in the 1450s, and the two-light window at the east end of the south wall were also inserted at this period.

Temple Dowling

South of the cathedral and beside the South Cross is a two-part structure, of which the western part is the earlier. Known as Temple Dowling (after Edmund Dowling who rebuilt it as a mausoleum in 1689), it preserves a substantial part of a relatively early church characterized by large masonry blocks, antae at the east end, and a round-headed east window. The west end of this church was extended and rebuilt (complete with antae) in the 17th century. The structure added to the east of the church, now known as Temple Hurpan, is also probably of 17th-century date.

Temple Melaghlin

East of Temple Hurpan is Temple Melaghlin, also known as *Teampull Rí* ('the king's church'). This simple rectangular church has a two-light round-headed east window of Transitional style, probably late 12th century. The lancet window in the south wall is slightly later, while the doorway further west is late medieval, and there is evidence of a gallery at the west end of the church.

Temple Ciarán

North of Temple Melaghlin is Temple Ciarán, a very small, partly collapsed church with antae, traditionally said to be the location of St Ciarán's grave. A sample of mortar from the wall of this church was radiocarbon dated to AD 660–980, and the similarity of the sandstone masonry to that in the cathedral has led to suggestions that this church was also built in the early 10th century. The south wall, and southern end of the west wall, are modern.

Temple Kelly

Nearby, to the west, are the fragmentary remains of another church, Temple Kelly, probably erected in 1167 by Conchobhar Ua Ceallaigh. Between this church and the round tower, to the west, stands the shaft of the North Cross, a weathered cross decorated on three sides with interlace panels, including human and animal interlace. It dates to the beginning of the 9th century.

Round tower

The round tower, known as 'O'Rourke's tower', is presumably the *cloigtheach* whose completion is recorded in 1124, and which lost its roof when struck by lightning in 1135. The present parapeted top with eight openings was probably rebuilt after this, and the diameter at the base, 5.6 m, suggests that the tower may have been considerably taller originally. The present height is 19.3 m and there are four floors internally. The round-arched doorway, 3.5 m above ground, faces south-east towards the west end of the cathedral.

Temple Conor

North-east of the round tower, near the graveyard wall, is Temple Conor, the only church at present roofed and in use (by the Church of Ireland). The west doorway and the window at the east end of the south wall are of Transitional style, suggesting a date of *c*.1200. To the north is a small enclosed burial area.

Temple Finghin

Further north-east, on the graveyard wall, are the remains of another church, Temple Finghin, a nave-and-chancel church distinguished by an attached round tower on the south side. Although little remains of the nave, the chancel is relatively complete with a fine Romanesque chancel arch, indicating a mid-12th-century date. The base of a similar doorway is visible in the south wall of the nave. The round tower is complete and 16.8 m high, finely built with unusual herring-bone coursing in the masonry of the roof. It is clearly of the same date as the church, and its position at the junction of nave and chancel recalls the towers in a similar location on Cormac's Chapel at **Cashel**.

The Nuns' Church

The Nuns' Church, c.500 m east of the graveyard, is reached by the Pilgrims' Way, an ancient roadway (now partly covered with a modern surface) running eastwards from the centre of the graveyard, near Temple Ciarán. Despite its apparently remote location, there is evidence for houses and settlement around the Nuns' Church in the 11th century, and it may have been the focus of a suburban settlement. The completion of the Nuns' Church is recorded in 1167, although there is evidence for an earlier church on the site. The 1167 date is in keeping with the details of the present nave-and-chancel church, particularly the Romanesque west doorway and chancel arch (both reconstructed in the 19th century). The patroness of the 12th-century building was the renowned Dearbhforgaill ('Dervorgilla'), wife of the king of Bréifne, whose abduction by Diarmait Mac Murchada in 1152 was one of the events that led ultimately to the English invasion of Ireland.

The castle

An exceptional, non-ecclesiastical monument lies at the extreme western end of the Clonmacnoise complex—an English royal castle, probably built in 1214 and positioned to dominate both the monastery and the bridging point on the Shannon. The monument today consists of the shattered ruins of a stone castle, surrounded by a massive rectangular earthwork with a fosse that was probably designed to fill with water. The stone castle may not be contemporary with the earthwork—it has been suggested that the earthwork represents an earlier ringwork or motte-and-bailey castle, the motte being located under the present stone castle. However, the stone castle cannot be much (if at all) later than the earthwork, as the entire structure seems to have been abandoned soon after the 1230s. The castle consists of a hall or keep with a rectangular courtyard to the north-west, entered through a gate in a three-storey tower in the western angle. The hall was entered at first-floor level from the southern angle of the courtyard, via a laterally set drawbridge mounted on a forebuilding, which in turn was accessed from the wall walk of the courtyard walls. In the western angle of the hall a spiral stair provided access to the ground floor.

Corcomroe, Co. Clare Abbey

7 km east of Ballyvaughan, off N67 (Galway–Kilkee coastal route); take minor road to south at Bealaclugga and turn to east after 300 m; signposted. Disc. Ser. 51.

Located in a green valley on the northern edge of the stony Burren region, this Cistercian abbey was appropriately called in Latin *Petra Fertilis* ('the fertile rock'). It was probably founded *c.*1195 by Donnchad Ó Briain, king of Thomond, and dissolved *c.*1554, although it continued to function in some sense for a significant period after this. The community was always small and poor and this is reflected in the surviving buildings. Effectively only the church survives—of the claustral buildings, little more than fragments of the east range survive, while the remains of a gatehouse survive in the outer precincts.

The church was built *c.*1210–25 along normal Cistercian lines, but is unusually small, with a short vaulted presbytery, shallow transepts with only a single side chapel, and a relatively short nave. There is some good quality stone carving of the 'School of the West' in the mouldings, capitals, and bases of the presbytery and transepts. The presbytery also has a fine ribbed vault and an imposing east window of three tall lancets. In the south wall are an early 13th-century sedilia (missing its seat) and a tomb recess containing an effigy—probably of Conchobhar Ó Briain, king of Thomond (d. 1268). Mounted in the wall above this is a low-relief effigy of a bishop or abbot, set within an architectural canopy. It, too, probably dates to the 13th century. In contrast to the presbytery, the nave is very poorly built, possibly reflecting a downturn in the abbey's fortunes. Although it is aisled, the aisle arcades are very rough and not symmetrically arranged. There is even some doubt about whether there was ever a north aisle. As small as it was, the church was further reduced in size in the late Middle Ages by the insertion of a new west wall, near the east end of the nave—a sure sign of a declining community. The tops of the walls and the roof were also modified at the same time.

Duntryleague, Co. Limerick Archaeological landscape

27 km west of Caher, Co. Tipperary, off R663 (Bansha–Kilmallock); take minor road to north 3 km west of Galbally. The barrow cemeteries are around the western fringe of the hill. Disc. Ser. 73. Private land.

Duntryleague Hill (Deerpark townland), immediately to the north-west of Galbally, Co. Limerick, is the focus of an important complex of prehistoric monuments. Marking the west end of the beautiful Glen of Aherlow, the summit cairn on Duntryleague commands panoramic views of the Galtees to the south-east, Slievereagh with its summit cairn to the south-west, and, in the distance to the north-west, Knockainy, which boasts a hillfort, barrows, standing stone, and cursus. On a platform below the summit of Duntryleague is a very fine Passage tomb, which has a lintelled, cruciform chamber with an elongated end recess. The passage has an unusual, funnel-shaped entrance and there are the remains of a round cairn (27 m in diameter). Duntryleague is overlooked by a third cairn on the summit of Slievenamuck (Shrough townland) on the north side of the Glen of Aherlow, and together these three monuments constitute a probable Passage tomb cemetery. The low-lying wetlands between Duntryleague and Knocklong are peppered with barrows, many of which have been excavated (e.g. Lissard; Duntryleague; Mitchelstowndown; Knocklong). In general these ones seem to range in date from the Neolithic to the Middle Bronze Age. The barrows on Knockainy are very much part of this broad concentration.

O'Donovan identified Duntryleague with *Cnoc Claire*, burial place of Ailill Olum, father of the eponymous Eogan Már and molester of Áine, one of the mother goddesses of the *Túatha Dé Danann*, at Knockainy. In later times, this became the territory of the Eóganacht Áine Cliach, whose seat was at Knockainy. This area is also connected with St Ailbe of Emly, one of the pre-Patrician saints. St Patrick himself is brought, with some political expediency, as far south as Ardpatrick (at the foot of Seefin Mountain to the south-west) in *Acallam na Senórach*. Nearby, at Kilfinnane, is the great stepped, inaugural(?) mound of *Treada na Ríg*, enclosed behind three ramparts.

Dysert O'Dea, Co. Clare Early monastic site; tower house

9 km north-west of Ennis, off R476 (Ennis–Corrofin); take minor roads to west at 4 km or 6 km north of R476/N85 (Ennis–Ennistimon) junction; signposted. Disc. Ser. 57.

This monastery is said to have been founded by St Tola in the early 8th century, but little is known of its history. Its correct name, *Dísert Tóla* ('the hermitage of Tola') suggests that it was originally a simple hermitage, but it clearly had become significantly wealthier by the 12th century. The site preserves a once-fine suite of church, round tower, and high cross, all probably erected in the 12th century and possibly closely contemporary. There is, however, some uncertainty about the integrity of the surviving remains, especially of the nave-and-chancel church, which has been considerably altered. Its most important feature is a highly decorated Romanesque doorway, now in the middle of the south wall. This is clearly a reconstruction and is probably not in its original location, which was more likely in the west wall. In the outer order of the arch are a striking series of human and animal heads, but unlike the human heads, the animal heads bite roll mouldings and probably formed a separate arch originally. The doorway may even be reconstructed from fragments of more than one doorway—perhaps even from more than one church, though this is not certain. One of the windows in the west gable is also clearly reconstructed from fragments, probably of more than one 12th-century round-headed window. The lancet windows in the gable of the east wall are 13th century. The belfry over the chancel arch is probably late medieval.

The ruined round tower is 15 m high at present and is unusual in its relatively wide base, almost 6 m in diameter, and in an external offset 8.6 m above ground, above which the tower narrows abruptly. On the north-west side there is a large opening, 1.3 m above ground—probably the site of a later, inserted doorway. This may be related to other later features (now fragmentary), including an inserted ogee-headed window near the top and the parapet above. The original round-headed door-way—which suggests a 12th-century date—is also unusually large and is 4.5 m above ground, facing east. Interestingly, the doorway does not face the present church, immediately to the south, raising the possibility that there may have been a church just to the north of the present one, when the round tower was built. Some distance east of the church is one of the classic examples of the 12th-century series of high crosses. In its present form it is a re-erection of 1683, on a base largely composed of archi-tectural fragments taken from the church. Carved of local limestone, the cross is dominated by two large figures of Christ (above) and a bishop or ecclesiastic (below) on the east face. The other surfaces are decorated with panels of Scandinavian-derived animal interlace, geometric pat-terns, and human figures. To the north of the church and cross is a late medieval tower house that has recently been restored and houses a local museum.

Ennis, Co. Clare Friary, County Museum
40 km north-west of Limerick on N18 (Limerick–Galway).

Clare's lively and interesting county town is a 17th-century creation, but owes its existence to the presence of a Franciscan friary, founded in the 13th century by the Uí Briain kings of Thomond. The friary, in turn, is clearly linked to the establishment of the main Uí Briain residence nearby (at Clonroad, on the north side of the modern town), after their other residences at **Limerick** and **Killaloe** fell under English control in the early 13th century. No trace of the castle of Clonroad survives today. The Franciscan friary was founded either in the 1240s or the 1280s. The later date seems more likely and the earliest surviving buildings point to a late 13th-century date. The friary flourished under Ó Briain patronage throughout the Middle Ages, and was the main burial place of the kings of Thomond, before being finally suppressed *c.*1570. In the late 16th century it became the effective centre of English government in Thomond, and from the early 17th century the church was used as the Church of Ireland parish church.

The earliest surviving building of the friary is the church, particu-larly the choir, which is late 13th century. Its main feature, the fine east window, shows an early stage in the development away from groups of single lancet windows to larger openings—in this case the three central lancets have become a single opening, with the lights separated by slender mullions. Much of the nave (especially at the east end) is basically 13th century, but the original features are mainly removed or obscured by later rebuilding, and the west end was entirely rebuilt in the 15th century. One of the original windows can still be seen, high up in the north wall just west of the tower. The crossing tower was inserted in the 15th century, and the large transept on the south side of the nave is of roughly the same date. The Gothic pinnacles on the top of the tower are an 18th-century addition. The cloisters, north of the church, are mainly 15th century, but the barrel-vaulted sacristy on the north side of the choir is 13th century (the two upper floors, and the tower to the rear, are probably 15th century). A feature of the friary is its collection of late medieval figure carvings, an all-too-rare survival in Irish churches. These include depictions of the Virgin and Child, and of St Francis on the piers of the tower. In the choir, fragments of an elaborately carved altar tomb, with overhead canopy, have been incorporated into a 19th-century reconstruction. The original tomb is said to have been erected *c.*1470 by More Ní Bhriain for her husband Terence MacMahon. On the south and east sides of the tomb are a series of fragments with scenes from the Passion of Christ, which are particularly interesting as they are clearly local copies of alabaster tables produced in the English midlands (especially Nottingham) in the mid-15th century.

The Clare County Museum is located a short distance south of the friary, at Arthur's Row, off O'Connell Square in the heart of the town. Its displays include excavated material from the **Poulnabrone** Portal tomb, **Cahercommaun**, and **Inishcaltra**.

Holycross, Co. Tipperary Abbey

6 km south-west of Thurles on R660 (Thurles–Cashel), or take minor road to west off N8 (Dublin–Cork) 1 km south of Littleton; signposted. Disc. Ser. 66.

This Cistercian abbey is one of the finest surviving complexes of 15th-century church architecture in Ireland, and since its restoration as a parish church in the 1970s it also provides possibly the best experience of the atmosphere of a medieval church. It was probably founded in 1180 by Domhnall Mór Ó Briain, king of Thomond, who also presented it with a relic of the True Cross—hence the abbey's name. The abbey struggled to survive for the first two centuries of its existence, but by the 15th century it had become a major centre of pilgrimage focused on the relic. This, together with the patronage of the powerful Butler earls of Ormond, led to a remarkable transformation in the fortunes of the abbey, which was largely rebuilt after 1430. The community avoided dissolution in 1540 by turning itself into a college of secular priests, and

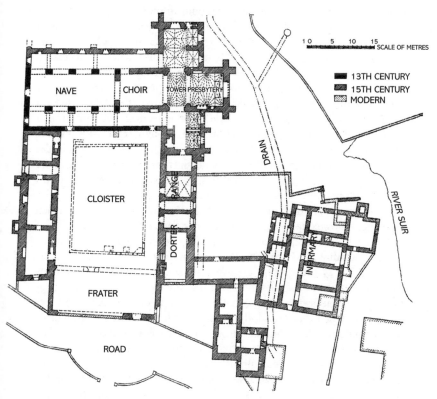

▲ **Fig. 126.** Holycross abbey: plan (after Leask)

even after this was suppressed in 1561 the church continued to function as a parish church and a centre of pilgrimage. The Cistercians briefly reoccupied the abbey in the early 17th century but the Cromwellians finally brought its life to an end.

The abbey follows the conventional Cistercian plan. The church has an aisled nave, a short presbytery, a crossing tower, and transepts, each with two chapels on the east side. On the south side of the church are the claustral buildings, arranged around a cloister garth that is rectangular, rather than square. This may indicate that the 15th-century cloister was extended further south than its original predecessor. Both church and cloisters are almost entirely of 15th-century date, apart from some fragments of the original late 12th-/early 13th-century church in the nave. This consists of severely plain work, especially in the nave arcades, characterized by rough rubble masonry. There are traces of the original lancet windows in the west wall—but the large traceried window is early 16th century—and at the east end of the south aisle is a late 12th-century round-arched doorway, leading to the cloisters. In contrast, the east end and transepts were entirely rebuilt in the later 15th century to provide a better setting for the famous relic, which probably provided the funding for the rebuilding through pilgrims' offerings. The 15th-century fabric displays a remarkable range of late medieval curvilinear window tracery, both reticulated (netlike) and Flamboyant or flowing. There is also very fine ribbed vaulting over the presbytery, crossing, and especially the north transept. Most of these are ultimately based on 14th-century English Decorated style but the immediate inspiration is probably Irish, rather than English. The six-light east window, for example, resembles and may be based on a much earlier window in the Dominican priory at **Kilmallock**. The north transept contains one of the few surviving medieval wall paintings in Ireland, a hunting scene in unfortunately poor condition.

The overall architectural form of the rebuilding has been described as a 'motley collection . . . lacking in unity and coherence' and its chief glory lies in the exceptionally fine carving seen on much of the architectural detailing. The sedilia in the south wall of the presbytery and the shrine in the south transept are especially accomplished. The sedilia is the finest example in Ireland, with three fine ogee-headed arches supporting an elaborate canopy. In the spandrels of the arches are five shields, of which the second, third, and fourth represent the royal arms of England, and the arms of Butler and FitzGerald, respectively. The shrine, located between the two chapels of the south transept, features a canopy with exquisite rib vaulting (internally), supported on arcades of pointed arches with spirally fluted columns, below which is a decorated base. Although sometimes described as a tomb, it was almost certainly built to display the relic of the True Cross. Other details worth noting are the owl on the north-west pier of the crossing, and the two crowned angels flanking a corbel head on the south-east pier. On the north side of the presbytery is a round-arched tomb niche containing a 16th-century cross-slab commemorating Donagh O'Fogarty and his wife Ellen Purcell.

There are residential chambers above the vaults of the presbytery and transepts—that over the south transept was possibly the abbot's chamber. The south transept also retains its night stairs, by which the monks entered the church from their dormitory (at first-floor level in the east range of the cloister), for night offices. Only the ground floor survives of the east range, comprising sacristy, chapter house, slype, parlour, and undercroft, all barrel vaulted. The doorway of the chapter house, with billet decoration, is very unusual. The refectory block on the south is fragmentary, but the west range is well preserved, with three large residential chambers (probably monks' apartments) above a vaulted undercroft. The cloister arcade, which has been partially reconstructed, had elaborately cusped pointed arches, set within a Perpendicular frame, on three sides and plainer round-headed openings on the west. To the east of the cloisters are further buildings, linked at the south-east angle. That immediately to the south-east may well be the abbot's lodging, a two-storey residential building with a fine upper chamber containing a good fireplace, garderobe chamber, and two fine windows with seats. The buildings further east probably include the monastic infirmary. To the east again is the river Suir, spanned by a fine late medieval bridge.

Inishcaltra (Holy Island), Co. Clare Island monastery

12 km north of Killaloe in Lough Derg; accessible only by boat, which may be hired at Knockaphort Pier or Mountshannon on R352 (Ennis/Killaloe–Portumna). Disc. Ser. 58. Note: Boats should stay well out from the rocky shore and land only at the island piers.

A monastic site was apparently established on this small island [*Inis Cealtrach*, 'island of churches'] in Lough Derg in the 6th century, which functioned until the end of the 12th century. The early history of the site is obscure, but excavations in the 1970s revealed evidence for the existence of a small, probably monastic, settlement from the 7th century. From the later 10th century the monastery enjoyed the patronage of Brian Ború and his descendants, the Uí Briain kings of Munster, and most (if not all) of the visible buildings on the site are probably products of Uí Briain influence. The later history of the site is obscure, and it is not entirely clear when the monastery, and the various buildings associated with it, ceased to function. It seems certain, however, that all the churches on the island were permanently ruined and abandoned by the end of the 17th century.

The monastic site was located on the east side of the island, where the remains of five churches and a round tower are visible, surrounded by extensive later medieval earthworks. The principal church is St Caimin's, originally a rectangular nave with antae that is traditionally—and not implausibly—attributed to the patronage of Brian Ború himself. The church was enlarged in the 12th century—when a small chancel with an altar was added, along with a Romanesque-style chancel arch and west doorway. Within the church are a number of carved stones, including a stone cross bearing two inscriptions: *ÓR[OIT] DO ARDSENOIR HER-ENN. I. DO CATHASACH* ('a prayer for the high senior of Ireland, for Cathasach') and *Ó[ROIT] DO THORNOC DO RINGNI IN CROIS* ('a prayer for Tornoc who made the cross').

To the south-west is the round tower, now 22 m high with at least five floors—the top is missing and was possibly never completed. The round-headed doorway, some 3 m above ground, faces north-east towards the west door of St Caimin's church. Near the round tower is the base of a high cross, probably 9th century, the head of which is in St Caimin's church. In the graveyard to the east of St Caimin's are the ruins

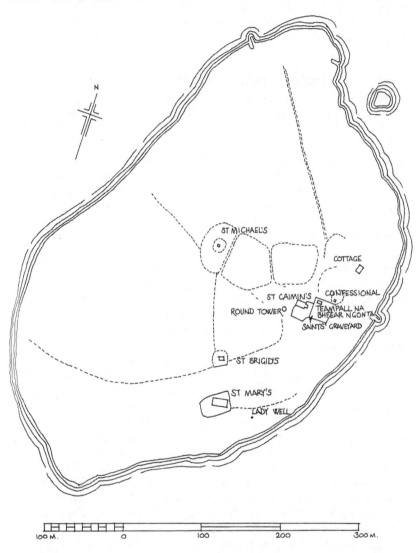

▲ **Fig. 127.** Inishcaltra: plan of island showing location of monuments (after de Paor)

of *Teampull na bhFear nGonta* ('the church of the wounded men'). This rectangular building, with three doorways, is possibly of late 12th-/early 13th-century date originally, but was rebuilt as a mortuary chapel for the O'Grady family in the early 18th century. The unusual name may derive from the O'Grady motto, 'wounded but not vanquished'.

Just outside the north-east corner of this graveyard is the 'Confessional' or 'Anchorite's Cell', a tiny rectangular building divided into two small chambers—probably an early tomb shrine that also was frequently rebuilt. To the east is a stone slab carved with a ringed cross in relief, and the base of a high cross.

Some 120 m west of St Caimin's church, near the highest point of the island, is St Michael's church, a small ruined oratory within an earthen enclosure. *c.*130 m to the south are the ruins of St Brigid's church, also known as the 'Baptism Church', a simple rectangular church with an (incorrectly) reconstructed Romanesque-style west doorway, dating to the mid-12th century. South of this is the largest and probably latest church on the island, St Mary's—a plain, early 13th-century church with later rebuilding. This served as a parish church for the small community which remained on the island after the monastic site had ceased to function.

Kilkee, Co. Clare

50 km south-west of Ennis, on N67 coastal route. Disc. Ser. 63.

A lot of the monuments around this beautiful but sadly over-developed seaside resort are in private ownership. A walk along the spectacular cliffs around George's Head (at the east end of the bay) and on towards Chimney Bay, however, brings the visitor upon the much-depleted ramparts of the promontory fort of George's Head itself and, on the fairway of the golf course to the left of the path to Chimney Bay, two beautifully preserved ring barrows. But watch out for golfers who have right of way! On the opposite side of the bay, behind the County Council car park, is one of the numerous St Senan's wells. This one is housed in a little, roofless, oratory. Senan is virtually the county saint and had his most famous monastery on **Scattery Island**.

Killaloe, Co. Clare Early monastic site; borough

22 km north-east of Limerick; take R494/R496 west off N7 (Dublin–Limerick); signposted. Disc. Ser. 58.

Killaloe is a small, picturesque town at the head of Lough Derg on the river Shannon—but if history had run differently, it might be the capital of Ireland. It is inextricably linked with the Dál Cais dynasty, later known as Ó Briain (O'Brien) after its most famous member, Brian Ború. The principal residence of the Dál Cais rulers, *Ceann Coradh* [Kincora, 'the head of the weir'], was located beside the monastic site of Killaloe [*Cill Dálua*, 'the church of Dálua'], and as the Dál Cais progressed from local rulers to kings of Munster in the 10th century, so too Killaloe rose from obscurity to prominence. The monastic site may have been founded by St Flannan in the 8th century, at an important fording point on the river Shannon, but almost nothing is known about Killaloe before the 10th century. Indeed, it was probably an obscure, unimportant foundation until the late 10th century, when it was brought to prominence by the rise of Brian Ború and the establishment of his residence at *Ceann Coradh*. In the reforms of the early 12th century (when Muirchertach Ó Briain was the most powerful king in Ireland), Killaloe became the seat of a large diocese. The combination of the diocesan centre, the Ó Briain residence, and the crossing point on the Shannon—where a bridge existed from 1071, and possibly earlier—made Killaloe a very important settlement that probably took on an increasingly urban aspect. It seems to have become a borough before the English conquest of the 1170s—the first non-Scandinavian settlement in Ireland to do so. With the gradual decline of Ó Briain power after the English conquest, however, Killaloe lost its prominence. An initial English attempt to seize Killaloe and build a castle there in 1208 was repulsed (see Béal Ború, below), but in 1217 a castle was erected and an English bishop of Killaloe was appointed, symbolizing the reality of the takeover. Although this attempt to establish English control of Killaloe was again a failure, its finest hour had already passed. The Ó Briain were never a major national force after the late 12th century and, in any case, seem to have abandoned Killaloe as a residence in the 13th century.

No visible trace remains of the Ó Briain residence of Kincora, but it is thought to have been on the high ground overlooking the river, at the west end of the town. This suggests that the secular settlement was in existence before the church site, which was relegated to the lower ground at the foot of the hill. Beside the modern Catholic church at the top of Main St. stands St Molua's Oratory, a small, early nave-and-chancel church that originally stood on Friars' Island in the river Shannon, but was moved to its present location when the level of the Shannon was raised in 1929. Its most interesting feature is the chancel, with its massive, high-pitched stone roof, which was added onto the timber-roofed nave, probably in the 10th or 11th centuries.

The core of the monastic site of Killaloe is clearly indicated by the location of the 13th-century cathedral and an adjacent 12th-century church. The curving line of Bridge St. and John St. probably reflects the line of an original enclosure on the west, and the enclosed area probably backed onto the Shannon, measuring some 250 m north–south and 200 m east–west. North of the cathedral stands St Flannan's Oratory, an early 12th-century church with a fine high-pitched stone roof, propped by a barrel vault over the nave, and Romanesque-style west doorway. A plain, round-headed chancel arch gave access to the now-vanished chancel. Built into the south wall of the nearby cathedral, at the west end (internally), is another Romanesque-style doorway, dating to the late 12th century and far more elaborately decorated. In fact, it is probably the most highly decorated Romanesque doorway in Ireland, with four orders and every surface covered with a profusion of foliage and animal ornament. Almost certainly this was the west doorway of the cathedral that preceded the present structure—probably built by Domhnall Mór Ó Briain c.1180, but destroyed by a Connacht army soon afterwards. At the base of the doorway is laid an early cross-inscribed grave slab, traditionally said to be that of Muirchertach Ó Briain (d. 1119), the last Ó Briain to be effective high-king of Ireland. Outside of this is another, more elaborately decorated cross-slab, quite possibly of early 12th-century date.

The present cathedral was probably built in the early 13th century by Donnchad Ó Briain, king of Thomond, perhaps after the enlargement of the diocese following the dissolution of the dioceses of **Scattery** and **Roscrea**. It is a simple but attractive cruciform structure without aisles or side chapels, unfortunately divided at the crossing by relatively modern screens. The windows throughout are tall, acutely pointed lancets, with an unusual and striking east window of three lights, flanked by piscinae. The central light of the east window is round headed but the others are pointed, and they are set within a large embrasure with a rear arch of three decorated orders. The lights are separated by attached shafts that end in carved capitals, while forming a continuous moulding around the sides and base. This framing of the window is typical of the 'School of the West'—a style of Transitional Romanesque/Gothic architecture found in many western churches of the early 13th century. Killaloe may have been influential in the development of this style. Other features typical of this style include the carved corbel capitals seen at the cornice of the chancel and under the arches of the crossing. The south transept has a good Transitional two-light window in the east wall and a medieval font. The north transept, closed off from the crossing by a screen wall, is largely a late medieval reconstruction—as is much of the west end of the short nave. The west gable itself, however, with its good moulded doorway, is original. The crossing tower is also original, but was raised in height in the early 19th century, when the stepped battlements were added. Near the west end of the nave is a fragment of a stone cross bearing inscriptions in both Norse runes and Irish ogam script, asking for prayers for the patron of the cross, Thorgrimr, who may well have been a Christianized Viking serving the Ó Briain kings. Beside it is another 12th-century high cross, moved from Kilfenora in the 19th century.

Béal Ború

2 km north of Killaloe (*on the R463 to Scarriff; signposted*) is Béal Ború. This is the name given to an earthen enclosure, strategically located on a gravel spur overlooking the point where the river Shannon issues from Lough Derg—formerly an important river crossing. The enclosure is two phase, beginning as a conventional ringfort that was later heightened, probably in an attempt to construct a motte. The site is distinguished for two reasons; firstly, it may provide the latest date currently known for the construction of a ringfort, and secondly, it is traditionally identified with the site called Borumha in medieval documents, and ultimately with Brian Ború, the greatest Irish king of the late 10th/ early 11th centuries. There is no definite evidence to support any association between the king and the site, but limited excavation in 1961 demonstrated that a house within the enclosure was occupied in the 11th century, and the ringfort itself was almost certainly constructed in the 11th century also. This house was rectangular, with walls probably of wooden posts, measuring 4 m × 2.5 m internally with a central hearth and south-facing doorway with external porch. The earthen bank of the ringfort was originally faced with wooden posts externally, and with stone internally. After a period of abandonment (the annals record the destruction of the Borumha in 1116), a much larger earthen 'bank', up to 17 m wide, was constructed over the primary enclosure. A large outer fosse was also dug, but the excavator felt that the second phase monument was never completed, and no evidence for contemporary occupation was discovered. He suggested that the monument might be an unfinished motte, associated with an English raid on Killaloe in 1208, when it was recorded that the English intended to build a castle 'near the Borumha' but were 'frustrated'. This still seems the most likely interpretation of the monument.

Kilmallock, Co. Limerick Medieval town

30 km south of Limerick on R512 (Limerick–Fermoy), or take R515 east off N20 (Limerick–Cork) at Charleville; signposted. Disc. Ser. 73.

Kilmallock takes its name [*Cill Mo-Cheallóg*, 'Mo-Cheallóg's church'] from a monastic site said to have been founded by the 7th-century St Mocheallóg. The only visible traces of this early monastery are the scarcely recognizable remains of a round tower, built into the 13th-century parish church. This later church is dedicated to Sts Peter and Paul, rather than Mocheallóg, which suggests that the earlier monastery may already have ceased to exist prior to the foundation of the latter. Kilmallock, like **Cashel** and **Swords**, is an episcopal town, probably founded by the bishop of **Limerick** in the early 13th century. In the later Middle Ages it was effectively controlled by the FitzGerald earls of Desmond and was one of the most important towns in south-west

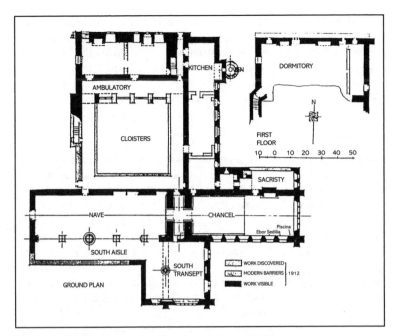

▲ **Fig. 128.** Kilmallock: plan of Dominican friary (OPW)

Ireland. The town was laid out along two intersecting main streets, with the market place on the north–south High Street (*modern Sarsfield/ Sheares/Lord Edward St.*). A number of 16th/17th-century houses survive in Sarsfield St., mostly hidden behind apparently modern façades. The side walls of one, with three chimneys and a limestone mantelpiece, survive on the site of the modern cinema.

Town defences

Kilmallock received a grant of murage before 1300 and further grants in the late 14th and early 15th centuries. Much of the town wall survives, especially on the west side of the town, and appears to be mainly of late 14th/15th-century date. Two of at least five original gatehouses also survive. 'Blossoms Gate', on the west side of the town, is a three-storey structure (missing much of its upper floor and parapet), with a partly modernized round-arched gate opening. It is fairly typical of 15th-century Irish urban gatehouses, quite similar to those in **Athenry** and **Fore**. In Sheares St. is a much larger, atypical gatehouse known as the 'King's Castle', of 15th/16th-century date. It has three storeys with a pointed-arched gateway over the street, a ground-floor chamber beside it, and a projecting stair turret on the north-east. On the first and second floors are large chambers, now lit by large, pointed 18th-century openings—the only original windows are small and rectangular. Over-head are typical late medieval stepped battlements. This impressive gatehouse must have been the entrance to the town on the north-west until at least the 15th century, and Sheares St. must represent a later extension, probably dating to the 16th century. Only after this did the gatehouse acquire the name 'King's Castle'.

Parish church

The parish church (*in Orr St., on the north of the town; access restricted*) was built in the 13th century, apparently on the site of the earlier monastery, of which the round tower was adapted to serve as a belfry in the north-west angle of the new church. Only the lowest 3 m of the tower are definitely original—a doorway at ground level, opening into the nave of the church, is a later insertion. So too is the sill of another doorway, 2.8 m above ground, at the head of a set of stone steps built into the west wall of the nave. However, this probably marks the position of the original doorway, facing south-east towards a long-vanished earlier church. The later, collegiate church has a nave, chancel, and south transept, all 13th century. It was substantially rebuilt in the 15th century when the nave aisles and arcades, south porch (now missing), and inner pointed doorway with ogee-headed hood mould were added. The west doorway of the nave is also 15th century, ogee headed, and flanked by tall pilasters. Overhead are the original three graduated lancets. At the west end of the south aisle is a large window with switchline tracery. Most other windows are smaller twin lights, apart from the 13th-century east window of the chancel, composed of five graduated lancets. This is very similar to the east window of the nearby Dominican friary, but which came first is uncertain.

Dominican friary

On the opposite bank of the Loobagh river from the town stand the ruins of one of the finest Dominican friaries in Ireland (*access via a footpath from Sarsfield/Sheares St., opposite 'King's Castle'*). It seems the friary was originally established in 1291 within the town, but without the consent of the bishop of Limerick, who promptly had the friars expelled. It was subsequently agreed that the friary could be re-established, but on the far bank of the river. It was suppressed in 1541, although friars continued to use it into the 17th century. The friary consists of a nave-and-choir church of *c.*1300, with a slightly later south aisle and south transept, a later crossing tower, and cloisters on the north side. The nave has a three-light west window with switchline tracery, probably a 15th-century insertion. The south transept and, presumably, the south aisle were added in the 14th century—possibly *c.*1320, judging by the ball-flower ornament on the capital of the pillar separating the transept from its west aisle, and on the fine gabled tomb niche nearby. The great south window, of five lights with reticulated tracery, is one of the finest early 14th-century windows in any Irish church. The typically slender crossing tower, of three storeys with stepped battlements, was inserted between nave and choir in the late 14th/15th century.

The choir retains its marvellous east window of five graduated, pointed lights. Dating to *c.*1300, it illustrates an early stage in the development away from grouped, but distinct lancets towards a single large window filled with tracery. The south wall is almost entirely filled with six closely spaced twin-light windows, below which is a sedilia with six openings. In the north wall is an inserted 14th-century ogee-headed tomb niche, presumably for the tomb of a major benefactor or even the founder. Beside it, a doorway leads to the two-storey sacristy. At the west end this sacristy communicates with the east range of the cloisters. Only the east and north ranges of the cloister survive, and there may never have been anything other than an ambulatory in the west range. Both surviving ranges may be original work of *c.*1300, but were much modified in the 15th century and are now ruins. There are indications, however, that the north range may have had an integrated ambulatory— i.e. incorporated within the footprint of the building overhead— whereas the east range had the more conventional lean-to ambulatory. At the north end of the east range is the kitchen, with a large fireplace and oven on the east side. Overhead, on the first floor of the north range, was the dormitory. This upper floor of the north range appears to be a later addition to the vaulted ground floor, which has windows similar to those in the aisle of the south transept and is therefore, presumably, early 14th century.

Kinnity, Co. Offaly High cross

13 km east of Birr, at the junction of the R440 (Birr–Mountrath) and R 421 (Roscrea–Tullamore). Castle Bernard Demesne is 2 km to the east off the R421 in the direction of Cadamstown. Disc. Ser. 54.

The monastery of Kinnity (*Cennettig*), at the western edge of the Slieve Bloom Mountains, was founded in AD 557 by St Finan *Cam* ('the crooked'), who was apparently a pupil of St Brendan the Navigator. Nothing survives of the original foundation, which is now occupied by the Church of Ireland church and graveyard. There is an early cross-slab in the porch of the church.

2 km away to the east, in Castle Bernard Demesne, is the 'Kinnitty' high cross (alternative claims are made for an origin at another nearby monastery, Drumcullen). This mid-9th-century monument bears eroded inscriptions on the north and south faces identifying Máel Sechnaill Mac Maelruanaid, king of Tara (*RIG HERENN*) 846–62, as the

patron and attributing the erection of the cross to Colmán who had the cross made for his royal sponsor. Máel Sechnaill, of the Clann Cholmáin branch of the Southern Uí Néill, may be legitimately claimed as the first genuine high-king. The cross is decorated with figural and ornamental motifs. De Paor has convincingly demonstrated that the inscription, at least, is by the same hand responsible for the dedication on the West Cross (Cross of the Scriptures) at **Clonmacnoise** to Máel Sechnaill's son and successor Flaind.

Limerick, Co. Limerick Medieval town

200 km south-west of Dublin on N7, N20 (from Cork), and N24 (from Waterford). Disc. Ser. 65.

Limerick originated as a Viking settlement, founded *c*.920 on an island (now known as 'King's Island') between the river Shannon and a side channel known as the Abbey river. By the late 10th century, this settlement had probably developed into a town, but had also come under the effective control of the emerging Dál Cais dynasty from modern Co. Clare, across the Shannon. Control of Limerick was a significant factor in Brian Ború's successful drive for overall power in Ireland in the late 10th/early 11th centuries, and the town in turn prospered under Uí Briain patronage. From the later 11th century Limerick was actually the main residence of the Uí Briain kings. With the Christianization of the Hiberno-Norse inhabitants a church would presumably have been built, and a bishop of Limerick was consecrated in 1107. In the early 12th-century church reforms Limerick became the seat of a diocese and the present cathedral of St Mary was built in the late 12th century by Domhnall Mór Ó Briain, possibly on the site of an earlier royal residence. The cathedral was probably begun shortly after an abortive occupation of the city by the English in 1175. Limerick was finally captured by the English in the mid-1190s and thereafter colonized. It continued to flourish under English control and expanded, both on King's Island and on the south bank of the Abbey river, where a large suburb was established. This was known as the Irishtown—in contrast to the Englishtown on the island—and may have originated in the expulsion of the original Hiberno-Norse inhabitants following the English capture of the town. A major royal castle was begun in the early 13th century and the town received a grant of murage from 1237 to 1243. Dominican and Franciscan friaries were also founded in the 13th century. From the later 14th century the town in many respects reverted to the indirect control of the Uí Briain kings of Thomond, although within its walls it remained a bastion of Englishness and was relatively prosperous.

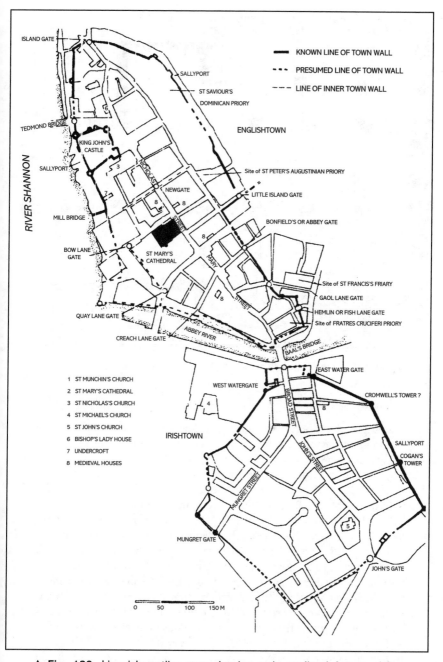

▲ **Fig. 129.** Limerick: outline map showing main medieval features (after O'Rahilly)

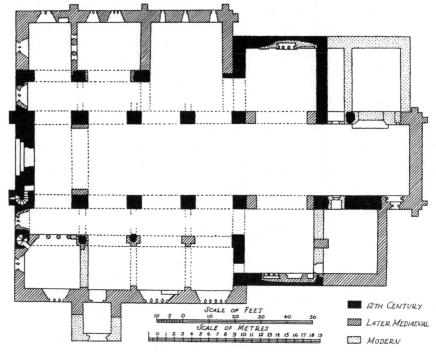

▲ **Fig. 130.** Limerick: plan of St Mary's cathedral (after Clapham)

The town

The Englishtown occupied a long, oval-shaped area, fronting the river Shannon on the west and the Abbey river on the south, and was laid out along a single main street (Nicholas St./Mary St.) with bridges at either end. Thomond Bridge, at the north end, spanned the Shannon, while to the south Baal's Bridge, over the Abbey river, connected the Englishtown with the Irishtown. Both are now represented by modern replacements. The Irishtown occupied a squatter, lozenge-shaped area and was laid out along a main street (Broad St.) that divided into two (Mungret St. and John St.). Both parts of the town were walled by the 14th century and good stretches of the town walls, including traces of mural towers, survive on the north and north-east sides of the Englishtown (*west side of N7 Island Road, north of Athlunkard St.*) and the east side of the Irishtown (*visible from St Lelia St./New Road*). None of the original gates survive, but a large early 17th-century gatehouse survives, now built into St John's Hospital (*east side of John's Square; not accessible*). This controlled the main entry to the Irishtown from the south-east and replaced a medieval gatehouse. On the west side of Mary St. (*between Matthew Bridge and Baal's Bridge*) are the remains of a late medieval urban tower house known as 'Fanning's Castle'. The fine four-storey façade facing the Abbey river survives, but the site is poorly kept and not accessible. On the south side of Athlunkard St. is the much-altered façade of another large late medieval stone house, known as 'Bourke House'.

Of the Dominican priory founded in 1227, only the north façade of the church survives (*Dominic St.; not accessible but visible from car park of nursing home at north end of Bishop St.*). The priory occupied its own precinct outside the town walls originally, but was later incorporated within an expanded circuit of walls. South-west of the medieval town, the 18th-century Customs House (*on Rutland St.*) now houses the Hunt Museum, an outstanding if rather eclectic collection of archaeological, historical, and artistic treasures. Although it contains little from medieval Limerick (or Ireland), apart from the beautiful mitre and crosier of Cornelius O'Dea, bishop of Limerick 1400–25, it should not be missed.

Cathedral

St Mary's cathedral (*entrance on Bridge St.; donation requested*) presents an almost entirely late medieval face today, but internally the late 12th-century building is largely intact. This was a large (for its time), but relatively simple building, strongly influenced by Cistercian architecture in both its plan—cruciform, with an aisled nave—and lack of ornamentation. A series of late medieval chapels was built onto the outer sides of the nave aisles and these, together with a series of monuments internally, are evidence of the enduring prosperity of late medieval Limerick. The chapels obscure the original form of the building but, as in so many Irish churches, original fabric is often indicated by the presence of sandstone mouldings, in contrast to the grey limestone of the later medieval work. The cathedral is now entered through a south porch, partly late medieval and partly modern, which leads into a range of later 15th-century chapels. These are divided into bays corresponding to those of the original south aisle (to the north) and lit by a series of large, traceried windows. At the west end an upper floor has been provided above the chapel, presumably for priests' residences.

At the east end of the chapels is the original south transept, in the south wall of which are a trefoil-headed piscina and the sedilia erected by John Budstone *c.*1400 (see his name in the spandrel of one of the openings). Also in this wall is the roughly contemporary Galwey–Bultingfort tomb, which has a low, cusped pointed opening with a strongly moulded, crocketed gable over, flanked by pilasters with carved finials. Within the gable are the arms of Richard Bultingfort (d. *c.*1406) and overhead are the arms of the Galwey family, into which he married. Recent excavations suggest that both transepts were originally longer (north–south) than at present and may have been shortened in the late medieval period. The original nave aisles have been modified beyond recognition, their outer walls replaced by arcades of arches and their roofs raised—the original lean-to roof lines are visible at the west ends of each nave. The aisles originally had vaulting supported on transverse ribs springing from the nave piers—the sandstone corbels that supported these ribs can still be seen. The four-bay nave arcade has pointed arches rising from massive square piers but the west door (restored) and clerestory windows are round arched, in late Romanesque style that matches the scalloped capitals of the piers. Recent excavations revealed 13th-century burials truncated by the west wall immediately outside the west doorway, indicating that the doorway, at least, is not in its original location. The nave itself is relatively unchanged by later work, apart from the high arch inserted between the westernmost piers to support the east side of the tower. The tower (*not usually accessible*) was erected over the west end of the nave, probably in the 14th century, although the upper storey with battlements and turrets is 16th century. There was never a tower at the crossing.

In contrast to the transepts, the choir was extended in the later medieval period. In the north wall are the reconstructed remains of the once-fine monument of Donough O'Brien, earl of Thomond (d. 1624). Below this is a grave slab said to be that of his ancestor Domhnall Mór Ó Briain, the founder of the cathedral. It is carved with a cross and the three lions of the Ó Briain arms. In the north transept, set in a trefoil-headed tomb niche, is a wall memorial to Walter Arthur, treasurer of the cathedral (d. 1519). St Mary's boasts the only surviving set of medieval misericords in Ireland (*at time of writing housed in the Jebb chapel, west of the north transept*). These late 15th-century wooden choir stalls are carved with animals, real and imaginary, typical of medieval bestiaries, as well as plant ornament. Also connected with the cathedral are the early 15th-century O'Dea mitre and crosier, now displayed in the nearby Hunt Museum.

Castle

The royal castle is located near the northern end of the Englishtown, controlling the vital crossing point over the Shannon at Thomond Bridge. Considerable recent excavation and restoration have made it a popular visitor attraction (*entrance through visitor centre on Nicholas St.; admission charge*), but it is also of great archaeological importance. Both the castle and the adjoining bridge were built in the early 13th century, within a few years of the English takeover. The castle occupies the site of an earlier fortification—excavation has revealed traces of a stone-faced earthen bank with a large external fosse, probably an English earthwork of *c.*1175 or an earlier Ó Briain fortification. The castle was designed as a rough quadrangle with large drum towers at each angle and a twin-towered gatehouse on the north side—similar to the roughly contemporary royal castle in **Dublin**. It seems, however, that the south-east angle and adjoining parts of the curtain wall may not have been completed until a rectangular bastion was built there in the early 17th century. The gatehouse, flanked by rounded towers, is probably the earliest example of its type in Ireland and was originally defended by a drawbridge over the external fosse, by a portcullis, and by a high machicolation overhead. To the rear of this façade was a narrow vaulted passage (no longer standing) rather than a true gatehouse.

The upper levels and battlements of the gate towers, and of the curtain wall generally, have been rebuilt in recent centuries. The drum towers at the angles were higher originally, but were lowered in the 16th century, when new vaulting was inserted to support artillery platforms. The towers display fine plunging arrow loops—especially the north-west tower, overlooking the river and the bridge. On the west side of the castle is a projecting rectangular turret that defends a water gate in the curtain wall on the river bank. Within the castle enclosure excavation has revealed a number of buildings, notably the great hall, dating to the later 13th century, on the western side. Also on display beneath the visitor centre are the excavated remains of late 12th-century sunken-floored houses, the sole archaeological evidence to date for Hiberno-Norse Limerick. Beside the castle is Limerick City Museum—in a fine location and with some interesting archaeological material, but the displays are, frankly, disappointing.

Lorrha, Co. Tipperary Early monastic site; medieval borough

14 km west of Birr; take minor road south off R489 (Birr–Portumna) or north off N65 (Nenagh–Galway); signposted. Disc. Ser. 53.

Lorrha is a good example of an early monastic site (associated with the 6th-century St Ruadán) that was taken over by the English in the late 12th century and subsequently developed into an Anglo-Irish borough. A stone church at Lorrha is referred to in 1037, and the important 9th-century decorated manuscript the Stowe Missal—and its later 11th-century shrine (*now in the National Museum of Ireland*)—were produced for this monastery. The monastery became an Augustinian priory in the 12th century and was burned in 1154, 1157, and in 1179. Although officially dissolved by 1552, the priory probably continued to function until after 1578. Following the English conquest, a castle was erected at Lorrha no later than 1208, when it was destroyed by the king of Thomond, Murchad Ó Briain. English control was subsequently restored and a borough was established—first documented in 1333, but probably in existence well before this. A Dominican priory was also founded *c.*1270. The manor and borough belonged to the bishop of **Killaloe**, although they seem to have been actually held by the powerful de Burgo family for much of the 13th century. With the resurgence of native Irish power in the later 14th century the borough undoubtedly declined and may well have been abandoned. No physical trace of the borough survives, other than the churches, but the modern village is its direct successor.

Monastic site

The visible remains of the early monastery include fragments of a church, much altered in later centuries, and some stone crosses. These are in a graveyard east of the present village, whose east and south sides preserve the line of the original inner enclosure of the monastic site. The entire south side of this enclosure is reflected in the curving line of the street as it runs past the graveyard, and it would have been c.120 m in diameter originally. Outside of this, traces of a much larger, slightly oval enclosure also survive in a field boundary to the north and north-west of the graveyard. The enclosure has been levelled to the north-east and east, but is clearly visible from the air and its original diameter can be calculated as c.400 m, with the early church at its centre. This early church is now incorporated in the modern parish church. The original parts of this church display antae at each gable end and a high-pitched east gable, and may well be the church referred to in 1037. Later features include the vaulted two-storey structure attached to the west end—probably a late medieval residential building—and the doorway in the south wall, which has decorated 15th-century mouldings but is set within a larger 13th-century doorway, with a stone head above. Both doorways may be relatively late reconstructions, as is the window to the east. Parts of two high crosses, probably of 8th/9th century date, stand to the west of the church. One, near the south-west corner of the church, has a very worn base and a fragment of the shaft with interlace decoration on all sides. The other, located further west, has only a small fragment of the shaft, but a well-carved base in the form of a stepped pyramid. Most of the base is covered with panels of interlace and geometric decoration, with a frieze of horses above.

Augustinian priory

Outside the graveyard, to the north-east, are the remains of the Augustinian priory. The church is a simple rectangular structure, with an ornate 15th-century Perpendicular west doorway, below a window consisting of two trefoil-headed lights with quatrefoil above. The east window is a small, two-light ope with modern mullion. In the north wall is a blank arcade of two large arches, with two windows to the east. Adjoining the church on the south are fragmentary remains of conventual buildings, now partly reused as a handball alley—a blocked round-headed doorway and projecting corbels can be seen in the south wall.

Near the east end of the church an ornate doorway in the south wall leads to a vaulted two-storey structure, probably a sacristy with a residence overhead, with a stone chimney in the south gable.

Motte

The motte is presumably the castle destroyed by Murchad Ó Briain in 1208 and rebuilt no later than 1221. It stands on the south-eastern perimeter of the outer enclosure of the early monastic site, bounded on the east by a river. It is some 5 m high and was just under 10 m in diameter at the summit, but much of the eastern half has been removed. A possible bailey lies on the west side.

Dominican priory

South-west of the modern village, beside the Catholic church, are the ruins of the Dominican priory, said to have been founded in 1269 by Walter de Burgo, earl of Ulster and a major local landowner. In 1401 a papal indulgence was granted to raise funds for the repair of the priory. It was dissolved in 1552, but the Dominicans seem to have returned to the site in the 17th century—which accounts for the fine 17th-century memorials in the church. The church is a long, rectangular structure, with the choir undistinguished from the nave, except for the presence of six pairs of tall lancet windows in the south wall. There may, however, have been a stone screen across the church, dividing nave from choir, originally. Below the easternmost window in the south wall is an aumbry with cinquefoil arch, containing a double piscina. In the east wall is the base of a five-light window, while a doorway in the north wall presumably led to a sacristy that no longer survives. At the west end of the choir a large block of masonry projects from the south wall, with a small altar on the west side. Adjoining this in the south wall are a piscina and sedilia, but the masonry block is clearly a late addition. The nave was lit mainly by a series of lancet windows in the north wall, of which only two survive intact. The south wall has only two windows—a late three-light square-headed window to the east and a single lancet near the centre. The cloister and conventual buildings may have been on the south side of the nave. The west wall and gable are reconstructed, following a collapse in 1939. On the north side of the graveyard, north-east of the modern church, are the overgrown ruins of a building sometimes described as a mill, but which is more likely to be a residential tower house, perhaps the prior's residence. It is of three storeys and is probably of 15th-century date.

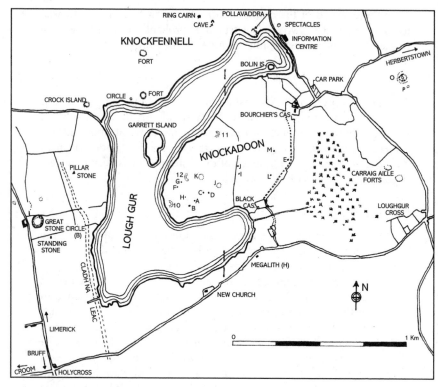

▲ **Fig. 131.** Lough Gur: map showing location of monuments (after O'Kelly)

Lough Gur, Co. Limerick   Prehistoric landscape

15 km south-south-east of Limerick city. Off the R512 to Bruff, turning left at Holycross for Lough Gur itself. Visitor centre; signposted. Disc. Ser. 65.

Lough Gur occupies a uniquely important position in Irish archaeology. Excavations here by Séan P. Ó Ríordáin between 1936 and 1954 created a watershed in the study of Irish prehistory and in particular of Neolithic settlement, pottery sequences, and early landscape analysis. Ó Ríordáin's untimely death in 1957 left many of the reports unfinished and their subsequent publication, as well as ongoing excavations into the 1980s, have sustained active interest in the complex. Lough Gur itself is a horseshoe-shaped, spring-fed lake enclosing a headland known as the Knockadoon peninsula. Across the lake to the north is the high ground of Knockfennell; to the west is Grange and to the east is the hill of Carraige Aille, all familiar names to students of Irish archaeology. In the Neolithic period Knockadoon was probably completely surrounded by water. Drainage, resulting in a 3 m drop in water level, led to the discovery of a great number of artefacts along the foreshore, some of which were, doubtlessly, votive offerings. The lake issues into Pollavaddra, a swallow hole on the north-eastern shore which is overlooked by a configuration of monuments known as the 'Spectacles'. Adjacent to this is the Interpretive Centre. Modelled on two of the Neolithic houses excavated on Knockadoon, the photographs, audio-visuals, and maps are an essential introduction for the first-time visitor.

Knockadoon

The greatest concentration of monuments is on Knockadoon and this is a good place to start. The headland is divided in two by a north–south running valley and most of the monuments are towards the western end. The landward side of the peninsula is guarded at each end by a castle—Bourchier's castle at the north end and the older but ruinous 13th-century Black Castle at the south end. The pathway to Knockadoon passes to the right of Bourchier's castle and near the shore of the lake here is Bolin Island, a crannóg, trial trenched in 1938 but not published. Excavations near Bourchier's castle (15th century) in 1977/8 revealed the foundations of two 13th-century houses that may have been part of a village, clustered around an earlier castle or manor house of the FitzGerald earls of Desmond, on the site of the tower house.

Overlooking the next broad left-hand turn of the path is a natural cave in the limestone cliff, in front of which is a crescent-shaped platform. The climb is difficult and the cave is not readily accessible. Parts of both cave and platform were excavated by Rose Cleary between 1985 and 1988. Protracted habitation on the platform was associated with a succession of wooden buildings of differing ground plans (round, square, and oval respectively), radiocarbon dated to the later Bronze Age. There were also some burials, ranging from the later Neolithic to the later Iron Age; all but one were infants. A different aspect to religious behaviour is evoked by the burial of an infant's head in a pit. At least 26 coarse pottery vessels of Ó Ríordáin's Lough Gur Class II, which is a flat-bottomed, slightly convex-sided, plain-rimmed ware, were found. A locally produced domestic pot, Lough Gur Class II seems to have continued in use from the Neolithic to the later Bronze Age and is the most common type throughout Knockadoon. Van Wijngaarden-Bakker's analysis of this and all other available faunal assemblages concluded that pig, and not cattle as previously thought, was the most common domesticate on the menu, and was bred for the purpose. Even so, some of the humans displayed evidence of malnutrition.

A couple of hundred metres further along, on the 100 m contour, is site 11, an irregularly shaped habitation enclosure. It has not yet been excavated (*pace* O'Kelly) but compares in form with site 12 (below). Following this contour westwards we come upon (OR) G, a D-shaped hut, with a north-facing entrance, built in quasi-lean-to style against a vertical rock outcrop. (The monuments are referenced according to separate alphabetical schema worked out by Windele and Ó Ríordáin, with the result that there is some potentially confusing duplication. In their excellent little guidebook to Lough Gur, Claire and Michael O'Kelly devised a solution to this according to which duplicate letters are distinguished by the prefixes WIN and OR and this is adopted here. In addition, there are also sites referred to by numbers.) Associated pottery is Lough Gur Class II. Above and slightly east of (OR) G is site 12, a D-shaped enclosure excavated in 1954. While there were no structures, flint and chert tools, pottery, and animal bones are ample testimony of habitation during the Neolithic. The pottery assemblage was a combination of Class II ware and Western Neolithic (or Lough Gur Class I) pottery, namely round-bottomed, carinated vessels, known also from other sites in Ireland.

Retracing your steps and continuing a further 80 m or so around the headland, along the foot of the vertical rock face, will bring you to (OR) F. This is a sub-rectangular rubble-walled building, again constructed against the cliff face. Ó Ríordáin argued for three distinct phases of activity: (1) a primary Neolithic habitation, (2) the construction of the building as a metal workshop, and finally (3) its partial demolition during the early medieval period, for the construction of a field bank and ditch that emanates from the north-east corner and runs downhill for about 25 m. The casting moulds, which were not directly associated with the building, bear matrices for objects such as looped spearheads and rapiers, thus dating phase 2 to the Middle Bronze Age (c.1700–1400 BC).

Site 10 occupies a level platform overlooking the end of the peninsula. It is an enclosed habitation of later Neolithic/Early Bronze Age date. The earliest, pre-enclosure, activity is represented by three generally arcuate lines of postholes, possibly part of a structure. Later the platform was cut off from the rest of the peninsula by a double-kerbed wall. There is a very fine lithic assemblage from the primary habitation layer, as well as 32 stone and bone beads and sherds from up to 35 Class I pots, 15 Class II, and at least 24 Beaker pots. The enclosure wall has a double facing of boulders. Associated habitation layers yielded the same range of artefacts, but in different proportions: there was less Class I pottery, comparatively more Beaker, and, for the first time, Bowls. There was no real break in habitation between the open and enclosed phases and this is a pattern reflected at other sites [(OR) J, K, and L]. (OR) H is directly uphill from site 10, but has no visible trace. Excavation shed little light on the jumbled remains of this sub-rectangular house. Two phases were identified. Phase 1 deposits returned a little Class I ware and comparatively more Class II and part of a human skull, while Beaker sherds were found at a late level pertaining to phase 2.

To the south-east of (OR) H are Neolithic houses (OR) A and B. Downhill and closer to the shore, site B is less well preserved. At least two successive buildings and three habitation surfaces were evidenced, the earliest of which compared, structurally, to site A. The ceramic assemblage was nearly exclusively Class I (with a notable absence of Class II), including a decorated version referred to as Class Ia. (OR) A is probably the best-preserved Irish Neolithic house. The walls of this rectangular house (over 9 m long and 5 m wide) comprised a basal rubble core with paired posts on either side. It is assumed that the walls were wattled and the space between filled with organic insulation. There were also internal roof supports and a central hearth. The entrance was in the south-west corner. Class I and II pottery were present, as well as a lithic assemblage including scrapers, arrowheads, and blades, fragments of four polished axeheads, and an unusual slate spearhead.

(OR) C is about the same distance further uphill to the north-east, and though there is nothing to be seen here today, one must walk over it to get to (OR) D. (OR) C is one of the more important sites on Knockadoon and in fact was one of the largest areas opened for excavation over two seasons (1940 and 1949). A cluster of three, or possibly four, contemporary round houses was identified with associated occupation deposits, pits, trenches, and postholes. A secondary burial, accompanied by a Class 1a pot, was placed in pit 24. The houses ranged from 5 m to 6 m in diameter. In this case part of the settlement was enclosed at some point early in its history by a wall, similar in plan to Lough Gur itself. Over 14,500 sherds of pottery were found, mostly of Classes I and II, with a small amount of Beaker and Bowls. Ó Ríordáin reported that the stratigraphic sequence suggested that although both types were coextensive, Class I was gradually supplanted by Class II ware. There was a huge variety of lithics, including a fragmentary mace and a selection of beads, axeheads, arrowheads, blades, and scrapers, as well as bone points. Eclectic material of later date includes a bronze socketed axe and knife or dagger blade, part of a La Tène rod-bow fibula, and two 10th-century silver pennies. In addition to the usual domesticates, the faunal assemblage included brown bear, wild cat, red deer, hare, wolf, 14 different species of birds, oysters, and fish.

(OR) D is located on the rocky terrace above and immediately east of (OR) C and is a good vantage point from which to view the west end of the peninsula. To the east it overlooks a small, sheltered valley. The remains comprise a succession of houses and terracing of the valley floor, the latter having taken place relatively late in the sequence. The earliest activity is represented by two wooden huts, one oval, the other D-shaped. Beside the former were the burials of two young children in pits, one with Class I pottery. The latest house was of stone and is later than the terracing. The ceramic assemblage was much the same as site C but there was substantially more Beaker. The stone building had mainly Class II wares, and associated crucibles, a stone mould for a palstave, and clay mould for a socket-looped spearhead date this latest activity to the middle Bronze Age and suggest an industrial function. A number of bronze tools were also found. The pottery sequence is the same, though differently proportioned, as at (OR) C.

Across the little valley to the north-east, yet below the top of the hill, is (WIN) Circle J. First investigated by Harkness in 1869, it was excavated by Ó Ríordáin in 1946–7 and published by Grogan and Eogan in 1987. It derives its name from its pre-excavation appearance as a double ring of stones (29 m diameter) projecting from the ground. There were three phases of activity, the first an apparently open habitation of Neolithic date, which was badly disturbed by later activity. Pottery included Classes I and II and (possibly intrusive) fragments of a Beaker pot. Deposits relating to the enclosure were also badly disturbed by later burials within it. Finds include leaf-shaped, hollow-based, and barbed-and-tanged arrowheads, a variety of scrapers and knives, a complete axehead and fragments of others, bone points, beads, and, of course, pottery. Sometime probably between the 5th and 7th century AD, the enclosure was commandeered as a burial ground. 58 burials were excavated, including more than 20 slab-lined graves. These were generally orientated east–west. A standing stone in the south-eastern quadrant was probably erected at this time. 30 per cent of the dead were children under the age of 5, and only two were over the age of 50.

(WIN) Circle K lies less than 100 m to the north-west. Constructed in the same manner as Circle J, it is 31 m in diameter and has its entrance facing south-east. The outline of a stone building (House 1) was visible off-centre before excavation and postholes and wall footings of another, pre-enclosure building (House 2) were found outside the circle to the north-east. A number of inhumation burials were uncovered but their stratigraphic position was not always clear. Four of the burials occurred in House 2 but their relationship with the building is uncertain; the material assemblage is domestic and Neolithic. All but one of these burials were of children, the exception being the crouched burial of a woman and her unborn (near-term) child and a 2-year-old infant. More children were buried within the enclosure, two of them, virtually neonates, in shallow pits in the floor of House 1. A deep fissure occurs in the rock to the north-east of House 1 and was used for a time as a shelter and possibly a place of burial before being blocked off to level the interior of the enclosure. Two further burials near this were of a youth and a neonate. That the enclosure was used also for habitation is evidenced by a huge and diverse corpus of Neolithic and Early Bronze Age lithics and ceramics, with increasing amounts of Beaker pottery at higher levels. Paste-trail glass beads were also found.

Two house sites, (OR) I and J, in the north–south valley across Knockadoon were excavated in 1945. Site J was a 17th-century farmhouse, under which were Neolithic deposits. Site I was a crudely built, sub-rectangular stone hut with hearth pit and associated Class I ware. It appears to be associated with the terracing or little fields across the valley.

By descending the valley southwards to the 100 m contour and turning east past Black Castle, the next site you will encounter is (WIN) Circle L. Built on level ground at the base of a vertical outcrop, the circle comprises a double-walled enclosure 25 m in diameter. From here the ground drops steeply to the lake. Pre-enclosure occupation centred around three possible houses and associated occupation deposits including Class I, Ia, and II pottery (comprising at least 40 pots), Beaker at higher levels, and a cache of 47 bone and stone beads, some with a distinctly anthropomorphic shape, presumably a complete necklace. In the centre was an oval-shaped house, outlined by large rocks and stakeholes around a clay and cobblestone floor. A refuse pit outside contained Class I sherds. On the east side of the house was a paved yard and near the edge of this was an extended, adult inhumation of uncertain date. As with the other sites that were eventually enclosed, there appears not to have been any break in occupation. Indeed, the oval house evolved directly from one of the earlier houses, and the material culture remained unchanged.

About midway along the path between Black Castle and Bourchier's castle, on the left-hand side, is (OR) E. Here, on a level platform about 10 m above the path, Ó Ríordáin excavated one of a number of identifiable, quasi-lean-to structures like sites G and F on the other side of the hill. A leaf-shaped arrowhead of chert was embedded in the floor. High above (OR) E, and best approached from the less precipitous Bourchier's castle side, is (WIN) Circle M, unexcavated but by far the best vantage point from which to view the whole landscape. The high ground to the east across the marsh is Carraig Aille.

Carraig Aille

Three sites (two cashels and a hut) were excavated here in 1937–8, and are accessible from the road leading into Lough Gur. Carraig Aille I, to the north, is an oval-shaped cashel, with wall walk and east-facing entrance. This, coupled with the relatively high quality of the artefact assemblage of ringed pins, a hand-pin, knives, bone combs, and rotary querns, jars somewhat with Ó Ríordáin's conclusion that the occupants merely squatted in rock hollows. Carraige Aille II is a well-preserved, sub-square cashel with stairs giving onto a wall walk. The walls of two elliptical stone huts were uncovered and a paved pathway led from the entrance to one of them. These were later replaced by rather more substantial rectangular houses. Finds included some fine decorative bronzes from which two distinct assemblages can be identified. The earlier material includes an ibex-headed pin, a hand-pin, a Roman-style grattoir, and an imitation Roman coin of the 350s. The later assemblage includes two 9th-century ring brooches and an ornithomorphic drinking horn terminal. A hoard of early 10th-century Viking armlets was also found. This late activity is associated with extensive occupation in the area between the two cashels that eventually led to the partial dismantling of the north range of cashel II to facilitate access.

(WIN) Circles O and P are closer to the Herbertstown road out of Lough Gur. They were the first sites excavated by Ó Ríordáin in 1936 but are not yet published. A henge-type monument, Circle O is a stone-faced embankment with internal fosse about 56 m in diameter. In the centre is a 15 m diameter contiguous stone circle. Circle P is a flat-topped cairn, 10 m in diameter, surrounded by a stone kerb. There were two urn burials but neither appears to have been diagnostic.

Returning past the Interpretive Centre, a tarmacadam path leads to a viewing spot with information panel and on to the 'Spectacles', so named because of the figure-of-eight configuration, before excavation. In fact the remains consist of four small, rectangular fields and associated buildings, including two quite substantial houses and two huts or animal pens. The northernmost house was square with rounded corners. Postholes on either side of the stone wall footing suggest that the upper part of the wall was of wood or even sod. The house nearest the Interpretive Centre was rectangular and was stone built. The associated material assemblage suggests an 8th- to 10th-century AD date for this settlement.

Knockfenell

Continuing westwards around the lake past Pollavaddra, one begins to ascend Knockfenell which rises to just over 160 m and is a fabulous viewing place. About two-thirds of the way up the south-eastern side is Red Cellar Cave, a narrow crevice in which was found only animal bones. Further up, on the eastern summit, is a ring-cairn, about 15 m in diameter, in which was found cremated human bone. Across the saddle, on the western summit, is a denuded, oval-shaped, cashel with associated field system. Again, it was excavated but remains unpublished. Directly below this near the lakeshore is yet another excavated but unpublished ringfort, this time a raised earthen ringfort, a modest 23 m in diameter. It too has an associated field system. 50 m to the west of this is (WIN) Circle T, an irregular oval of widely spaced, small stones of uncertain function.

Grange stone circle

Though relatively close, Grange stone circle cannot be approached from this side. Instead you have to retrace your steps to Lough Gur cross, turn right and right again onto the Limerick–Kilmallock road (R512) at the next crossroads (at Holycross). The stone circle is signposted less than

1 km on the right-hand side. However, before you get there, about half-way between Lough Gur Cross and Holycross is an excellent example of a Wedge tomb (H), excavated by Ó Ríordáin in 1938. The double-walled gallery, opening to the south-west, has an antechamber and main chambers separated by a septal stone. A cist was built into the antechamber. The primary deposits were disturbed and removed when the chamber was used as a habitation. At least eight adults and some children were buried in the main chamber, others were found outside it. A young ox was also buried nearby. Most of the associated pottery is Beaker ware, but there were also fragments of Encrusted Urn, Vase, and Bowl Urns. Recent radiocarbon dating of some of the bones confirms the protracted use implied by the pottery range and indicates that the tomb was built around 2560–2040 BC and saw burials over the next few centuries.

A near perfect ring of 113 contiguous stones, 45.7 m in diameter, and surrounded by a bank 9 m wide and over 1 m high, Grange stone circle is undoubtedly the most majestic monument in the Lough Gur complex. A cobbled, orthostat-flanked entrance passage facing east opens to the interior, which was carefully levelled off, relatively late in the site history, with 45 cm of redeposited soil. The entrance to the circle is marked by the tallest stones and these are mirrored on the opposite side, creating an alignment on the midsummer moon. The site was excavated in 1939 by Ó Ríordáin, who found the outlines of up to five shallow, annular trenches in the interior. He considered these to be of 17th-century date, possibly bell-tent drainage gullies. A comparable annulus was uncovered in the Monknewtown henge, Co. Meath, which must call into question Ó Ríordáin's dating. Artefacts included flint arrowheads and scrapers, axe fragments, and thousands of sherds of pottery including Lough Gur Classes I and II ware, Beaker and Bowl Tradition wares. Two hearths and a small scatter of human bones were also found. The circle was probably built during the last few centuries of the 3rd millennium BC.

There are two further stone circles nearby. About 100 m to the north is Circle C, which is about 16 m in diameter and surrounds a small mound. Only half (i.e. a semicircle of nine stones) of Circle D survives. Nearer the road, and partly incorporated into a field boundary, originally it would have been a very impressive 55 m in diameter. A line drawn from the centre of Circle D through the centre of the Grange Circle and out the same distance again brings us to a standing stone known as Cloghavilla. A second one, known as the Pillar Stone, is about 250 m to the north-east of Grange Circle. Finally, across the road opposite Circle D, is a denuded megalith, possibly a Court tomb.

Magh Adhair, Co. Clare Inauguration site

10 km east of Ennis; take minor road south off R352 (Ennis–Scarriff) 9 km east of Ennis; signposted. Disc. Ser. 58.

The mound of *Magh Adhair* ('the plain of Adhar') is an unexceptional earthen mound, almost 30 m in diameter and 4 m in maximum height, surrounded by a shallow fosse with low external bank. Historically, it was the inauguration place of the Dál Cais, later the Ó Briain kings of Munster. Several Irish inauguration places are known, and accounts survive in historical documents of the ceremonies surrounding the inauguration of kings. Unfortunately no such details survive for Magh Adhair but the site does preserve some of the classic features of inaugur- ation places. A sacred tree apparently stood here, but was cut down in 981 as a deliberate insult by Brian Ború's rival for the high-kingship, Máel Sechnaill king of Meath. Another sacred tree was destroyed in 1051 by Aed Ó Conchobhair, king of Connacht. The mound itself may be prehistoric in origin, but was probably modified subsequently to serve its inauguration purpose, with the addition of an entrance causeway on the west, and the flattening of the top of the mound. Around the mound, to the north-west, north, and east is a natural terrace that could have accommodated a large crowd assembled to watch the ceremonies, and may have been one of the factors in the choice of this location. Immedi- ately to the west is a small river, which may also be significant as cere- monial bathing seems to have been a part of some inauguration rituals. There are also two prominent stones—one a large conglomerate block located to the north of the mound, with at least one man-made depres- sion on the upper surface, the other a limestone standing stone located on the opposite side of the river, to the west. While there is no definite evidence that either stone was used in inauguration ceremonies, stones were clearly important in such ceremonies elsewhere, such as at **Tullaghoge** and most famously at **Tara**, where the stone known as the *Lia Fáil* would, according to legend, cry out under the feet of the rightful king.

Monaincha, Co. Tipperary Early church site

3 km south-east of Roscrea; take minor road to south-east off easternmost round- about on Roscrea Bypass (N7); signposted. Note: the final 400 m of access is via an unpaved road. Motorists should not attempt to drive this road in wet conditions. Disc. Ser. 60.

The monastic site of *Móin na h-inse* ('the bog of the island') stood on an island surrounded by bog, which once formed the lake of Loch Cré. It probably began as a hermitage in the 6th/7th century. By the 10th century a community of *Céli Dé* was in existence, which seems to have continued to function for some time after an Augustinian priory was established in the 1140s. The present Romanesque-style church was probably built by the Augustinians. The site was described by the writer Gerald of Wales in the 1180s, who claimed that any female (human or animal) that set foot on the island would die instantly. In 1397 the priory had to be released from paying church dues because of its poverty, and the site seems to have been abandoned by the Augustinians c.1485. It continued as an important centre of pilgrimage well into the 17th century.

The priory church sits on a small, roughly circular, raised enclosure, c.40 m by 35 m, which itself lies at the eastern edge of a larger oval-shaped enclosure measuring c.110 m by c.90 m. At the west end of the church is a restored high cross consisting of a decorated base, perhaps of 9th-century date, and fragments of a 12th-century shaft with a figure of Christ in a long robe on one face. The church itself is a simple but attractive nave-and-chancel structure, built of good-quality masonry in warm red sandstone. Unfortunately, the interior is somewhat marred by a clutter of recent gravestones. The Romanesque west doorway and chancel arch have slightly inclined jambs and round arches of three orders, decorated with chevron and foliage ornament—all of which indicate a date perhaps in the 1170s. The most easterly of the three windows in the south wall is original—the other two are mid-13th-century insertions with angle-shafts on the jambs, having small human heads on the capitals. The east window, in the chancel, was of the same form and date. Over the west doorway is an even later, ogee-headed window of 14th-, or even 15th-century date. On the north side of the church is a later, cruder two-storey building. The vaulted ground-floor chamber was possibly a sacristy but the upper chamber was apparently residential, judging by the seats in the north window.

Mooghaun, Co. Clare Hillfort and archaeological landscape

2.5 km north-east of Newmarket-on-Fergus; access via link road at north-west edge of the town, 0.25 km beyond the national school on the N18 (Limerick–Ennis); signposted. Disc. Ser. 58.

Mooghaun is a massive, triple-ramparted hillfort (enclosing more than 11 ha) overlooking the Fergus estuary—and, further away, the Shannon—in south-east Co. Clare. It was probably the 'capital' of this region in later prehistory and was the focus of excavations and landscape analysis in the Discovery Programme's North Munster Project. Arising from this, an archaeological trail has been established and a guidebook published.

The widely spaced ramparts are constructed in revetted stacks, or skins, of otherwise loose limestone rubble, the course of the walls having first been outlined with large rocks. The outer rampart comprises a double bank with intervening, 2 m deep, fosse. Charcoal from beneath this produced a date of 1260–930 BC, one of the rare scientific dates for

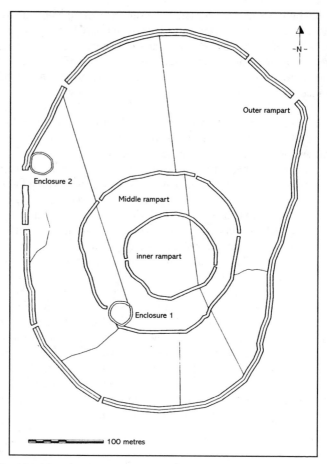

▲ **Fig. 132.** Mooghaun: plan of hillfort (after Grogan)

hillforts employing widely spaced ramparts. There are a number of entrances through all three banks, though they are not all easily found as the site is very heavily forested. Habitation occurred between the ramparts, the foundations of a number of round houses having been found on the south side of the middle enclosure. In addition to these, a number of possibly contemporary stone banked enclosures have been identified in the north-west quadrant. Two cashels (enclosures 1 & 2) were built on the ramparts during the early medieval period; three contemporary house foundations lie to the north of the upper cashel.

A pollen diagram from nearby Mooghaun Lough records intensive agriculture during the later Bronze Age. This is the site of the 'Great Clare Find' of over 200 gold collars and bracelets, unearthed in 1854 during drainage work for the Limerick–Ennis railway line. The largest known votive offering in western Europe, it is a striking testimony to the wealth and status of the occupants of Mooghaun hillfort.

A regional hierarchy of monuments has been proposed, according to which the second order of settlement is represented by nearby hilltop enclosures like Clenagh, to the south-west, Langough to the south, and Knocknalappa crannóg on the shore of Rosroe Lough. Associated in some way with these are scores of fulachta fiadh, barrow cemeteries, standing stones, and a host of ceremonial enclosures. The area is also rich in hoards of later Bronze Age date. Economic strategy extended onto the intertidal mudflats of the Fergus estuary where, among other things, fish-traps have been found. Craggaunowen, one of the first archaeological parks in Ireland, lies to the north-west, in the grounds of Craggaunowen Castle, and **Magh Adhair** is to the north-east, near Quin.

Poulawack, Co. Clare Multi-period cemetery cairn

10 km east of Lisdoonvarna; take the R480 (Ballyvaghan–Kilfenora), turn west (right) at the first crossroads south of Poulnabrone, and veer south-west (left) at the first Y-junction. This tertiary road ascends the northern flank of a hill, on the summit of which is the cairn. Disc. Ser. 51.

This complex cemetery mound was excavated by O'Neill Hencken, of the Harvard Archaeological Mission to Ireland, in 1934 and remains one of the more important monuments in the Burren. Since then no fewer than three reassessments have been published, the most recent arising from the generation of a series of ten new radiocarbon dates, which confirm three distinct phases of burial over a two-and-a-half-thousand-year period.

The earliest burials, dating to around 3350 BC, were of a middle-aged man and woman, an adult woman and an infant in a double-chambered Linkardstown-style cist, centrally placed in a drystone-revetted cairn (approx. 10 m in diameter, the revetment 2 m high). Grave goods comprised a hollow scraper, a boar tusk, an oyster shell, and two tiny sherds of pottery. Around 2000 BC the cairn was converted into a cemetery mound with the insertion of three cists containing the remains of up to seven individuals, adults and children, inhumed and cremated. With one of these was found a sherd of Beaker pottery. The earliest of these (no. 4 after Hencken) was built into the north side of the revetment wall. The third phase of activity refers to the heightening and enlargement of the cairn by some 2 m all round and the construction of a new, flagstone revetment. Dating of the four or so burials relating to this phase suggests protracted use, or even two distinct periods between 1610–1554 BC and 1486–1452 BC. One of these burials (no. 2) was an adult female accompanied by an end scraper and a bone point.

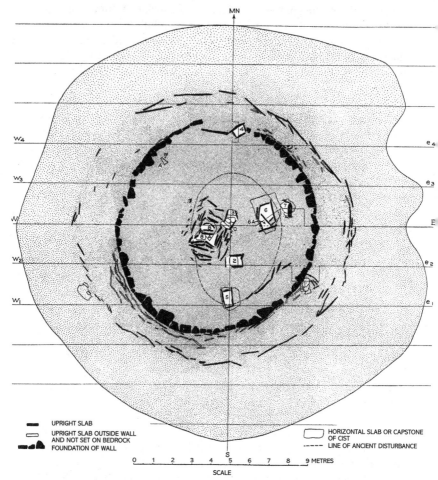

MN

W₄   e₄

W₃   e₃

W   E

W₂   e₂

W₁   e₁

UPRIGHT SLAB
UPRIGHT SLAB OUTSIDE WALL
AND NOT SET ON BEDROCK
FOUNDATION OF WALL

HORIZONTAL SLAB OR CAPSTONE
OF CIST
LINE OF ANCIENT DISTURBANCE

S

0 1 2 3 4 5 6 7 8 9 METRES
SCALE

▲ **Fig. 133.** Poulawack: plan of site as excavated (after Hencken & Movius)

Quin, Co. Clare   Castle, friary

8 km south-east of Ennis on R469; signposted. Disc. Ser. 58.

The Franciscan friary at Quin [*Cuinche*, 'arbutus grove'] is not only an extremely well-preserved example of a late medieval friary, but also preserves a remarkable visual record of the changing balance of power in late medieval Co. Clare. The friary, founded *c*.1433 by MacCon Mac Conmara, stands literally on the ruins of a castle built in 1278–80 by the English baron Thomas de Clare, as part of his attempt to take control of the Ó Briain kingdom of Thomond. The castle was destroyed by the Irish soon after de Clare's death in 1287. Ironically, the castle itself may have been erected on the site of an earlier church, although there is no visible evidence for this. However, the remains of the castle can clearly be seen on the south and east sides of the later friary. It was roughly square, with strong curtain walls up to 3.3 m thick and large circular towers at the angles. Little more than the foundations survive and the interior is obscured by the friary, but the details of the north-east angle tower, in particular, can still be made out.

The friary was probably built in its entirety between c.1433 and 1450 and was carefully designed to fit within the outline of the castle. The massively thick south and east walls of the church are founded on the curtain walls of the castle, and as a result the windows in the east, west, and especially the south wall have exceptionally deep embrasures. North of the church are the cloisters, whose northern and western boundaries also rest on the underlying curtain walls. The church consists of a nave and choir, separated by a tall central tower. A south transept, opening off the nave, is the only part projecting beyond the line of the castle. The windows in the west wall and south wall of the choir look like lancets, strangely archaic for the 15th century, but the main windows in the east gable and in the south gable of the transept have more typical switchline tracery. In the north-east angle of the choir is a Mac Conmara tomb of c.1500. West of this a doorway leads to the sacristy, and in the south wall is a good sedilia. The well-preserved cloister is of the integrated type— that is, the ambulatory is set within the surrounding ranges of buildings, rather than being an attached lean-to structure. The cloister arcade consists of pairs of pointed openings, separated by high raking buttresses that help to break up the blank wall faces above, as well as supporting the weight of the high pointed vaults over the ambulatories within. The east range contained the dormitory at first-floor level, with vaulted chambers below. At the north end of the range a bridge leads to a detached latrine building set outside the perimeter of the castle. The north range contained the kitchen, with the refectory above.

On the opposite bank of the river Rine is the 13th-century parish church of St Finghín, a simple rectangular structure with three graduated lancets in the east gable and the remains of a more elaborate window in the south wall. The buttresses on the east wall and the tower at the south-west are later additions.

Rathurles, Co. Tipperary Ringfort and assembly site

5 km north-east of Nenagh, on a hilltop off the R491 (Nenagh–Cloghjordan); signposted. Disc. Ser. 59.

Rathurles is a trivallate ringfort, identified as an assembly or *oenach* site. A few metres to the north-east of the rath are two quite massive conglomerate stones. Each has a recessed ledge at the top, from which protrudes a rounded tenon, evidently to secure in place a lintel stone. In the centre of the rath are the ruins of a 15th-century church. To the south of the hill flows the Ollatrim river and 1.25 km to the north is Lough Duff, which has two crannógs.

Roscrea, Co. Tipperary Early church site, castle, friary

40 km south-west of Port Laoise on N7 (Dublin–Limerick); signposted. Disc. Ser. 60.

Roscrea [*Ros Cré*, 'the wood of (Loch) Cré'] originated in a monastic site, said to have been founded by St Crónán in the 7th century. An important 8th-century gospel book, the Book of Dimma (*now in Trinity College, Dublin*), was produced there. It became the seat of a bishopric, briefly, in the 12th century and adopted the Augustinian rule around the same time. This was a period of profound developments at Roscrea, reflected physically in the erection of a new, Romanesque-style church, a

▼ **Fig. 134.** Roscrea: map of town showing medieval features (after Manning). A: monastic site; B: castle; C: Franciscan friary

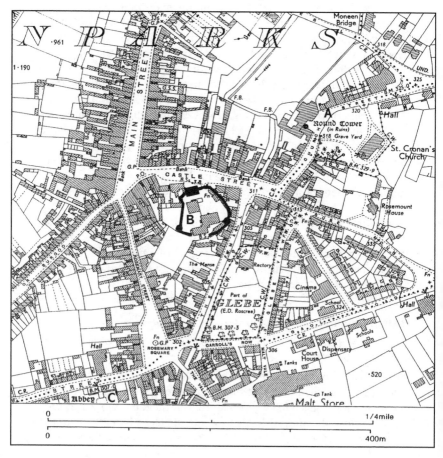

high cross, and a round tower, and in the creation of a richly decorated metal shrine for the Book of Dimma (*now in the National Museum of Ireland*). Before the end of the 12th century, however, Roscrea was incorporated into the diocese of **Killaloe** and the church seems to have declined in importance. It had probably fallen under English control even before 1213, when a castle with a wooden tower was erected by the English as part of a campaign against the Ó Briain. The castle was built on church lands, presumably where the stone castle was built later in that century, and was possibly one of the last motte-and-bailey castles erected in Ireland. A borough, first documented in 1305, was probably established during the 13th century, but there is no evidence that Roscrea developed into a town during the Middle Ages. Indeed, by the time a Franciscan friary was founded there *c.*1477, even the borough had probably ceased to exist.

Monastic site

The oldest surviving building at Roscrea is probably the round tower (*north side of Church St.*), which is recorded as having been struck by lightning in 1135. It is 20 m high at present and was probably 5–10 m higher originally, with five floors. The round-headed doorway is 2.2 m above present ground level—which was probably somewhat lower originally—and faces south-east towards the west doorway of St Crónán's church. A carving of a ship is visible on the north jamb of the second-floor window, which faces east. St Crónán's church is 20 m to the south-east of the round tower, but unfortunately separated from it by a busy road. Built probably around the middle of the 12th century, it must have been very fine originally, with an elaborate Romanesque west front, but little more than this survives. The west front is a typical 12th-century combination of traditional and imported elements, the antae and high-pitched gable being traditional (although the apex of the gable, with belfry, is clearly rebuilt). Between the antae is a blank arcade of four round arches, surmounted by steep tangent gables, with a centrally placed doorway. The doorway is of three orders, projecting like a porch, with chevron-decorated arches above. Over the arches is a high-pitched tangent gable with the worn figure of an ecclesiastic (presumably St Crónán) in the centre. Just outside the wall of the church is a high cross that is typical of the 12th-century revival of cross carving, in having large figures of Christ on the west face and of a bishop or abbot on the east face. Unusually it also has worn figures, perhaps one male and one female, at the bottom of the north and south sides. The conjunction of church, cross, and round tower clearly marks the core of the early monastery, but no evidence survives for the extent of the site, or for any enclosing features.

Castle

The castle (*on Castle St.; admission charge*) was built *c.*1278–85 and has recently been restored. Originally a royal castle, it soon passed to a branch of the Butlers of Ormond. It occupies an area of raised ground on the west bank of the river Bunnow, and consists of a polygonal enclosure with a massive gatehouse on the north and projecting towers at the south-west and south-east angles. The gatehouse is rectangular and three storeys high. The ground floor was divided into three parts by the central vaulted gate passage, which was protected by a portcullis, drawbridge, and external fosse, with machicolations high above. A spiral stair on the eastern side of the building gave access to the upper levels. The first floor consists of a fine hall with groin-vaulted roof, a fireplace in the south wall, and a garderobe chamber—set within the adjoining curtain wall, but reached via a mural passage opening off the north-west corner. Another fine chamber occupies the second floor, but this was considerably modified in the 16th century, when the fireplaces and

▼ **Fig. 135.** Roscrea: plan of castle (after Manning)

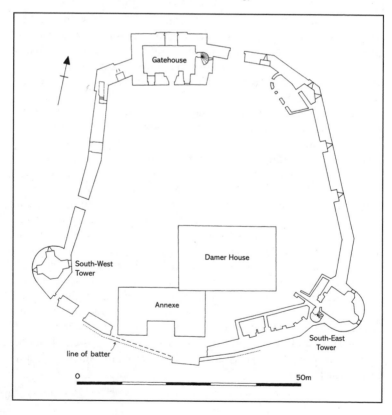

chimney stacks were added. A series of mural passages and stairs on the west side of the building lead out onto the wall walk of the curtain wall, to the west, and up to the wall walk over the gatehouse. Both mural towers on the south side have been extensively modified in recent centuries. The south-western tower is roughly D-shaped and three storeys high, with cross-slit loops at ground- and first-floor levels. In the first-floor chamber are traces of the duke of Ormond's coat of arms in plaster over a fireplace, dating to the 17th century. The south-eastern tower is larger, more regularly D-shaped, and is two storeys high, although possibly of three storeys originally.

Franciscan friary

The Franciscan friary, located on the southern side of the modern town (*south side of Abbey St.*), was founded *c*.1450–70 by the local Uí Cearbhall lords, who had regained control of the area. It was formally dissolved by 1568 but probably continued to function until *c*.1580. Its main feature is the attractive belfry tower (actually a late 15th-century addition to the church), but the east and north walls of the choir and part of the north wall of the nave also survive. The nave wall has two arched openings (now blocked) which presumably led to a north transept. Unusually for a late medieval friary, the cloister was located on the south side of the church, but no trace of it is visible.

Scattery, Co. Clare Island monastery

Access by boat, available from Kilrush, Co. Clare. An interpretative centre devoted to Scattery is located at Merchants Quay, Kilrush (admission charges). Disc. Ser. 63.

The monastery on Scattery, an island in the estuary of the river Shannon, is said to have been founded by St Seanán (Senan) in the 6th century. Like many such sites, it was raided by Vikings on several occasions in the 9th century, but it also appears to have been occupied by Vikings for a period in the late 10th century, until 'liberated' by Brian Ború. Indeed the name 'Scattery' is a Norse version of the Irish name, *Inis Cathaig* ('the island of the Cata'). The monastery seems to have briefly been the seat of a diocese in the mid-12th century, but was soon incorporated into the diocese of **Killaloe**. It was raided by the English at least twice in the 1170s, but continued to function, becoming a collegiate church in the 14th/15th centuries, before being finally dissolved in the late 16th century.

The visible remains of the monastery include five churches, a round tower, and a castle, all located on the eastern part of the island, near the best landing point. This landing place was protected by a small castle at the foot of the pier, built probably in the 1570s, although little of it remains. A short distance to the south, on the strand, stands *Teampull na*

Marbh ('the church of the dead'), a simple, rectangular, later medieval church. The most important buildings occur *c*.150 m inland, due west of the landing point. The principal church, which was the 12th century cathedral and later the collegiate church of Sts Mary and Senan, is a simple, rectangular structure with antae and a flat-lintelled west doorway. It may be quite early (10th/11th century), but has been considerably altered and extended to the east. The present east window and other windows in the south wall are 13th/14th-century insertions. Immediately north of the cathedral is a smaller nave-and-chancel church with Romanesque features—notably the ruined chancel arch—indicating a late 12th-century date. Traces of a drystone cashel wall which enclosed the core of the monastery can be seen to the north. *c*.150 m north of the cathedral is *Teampull Sheanáin* ['St Seanán's church'], a small, plain nave-and-chancel church, probably later medieval. Inside is an early grave slab with the inscription *OR DO MOENACH AITE MOGROIN* and *OR DO MOIN-ACH* ['a prayer for Moenach, tutor of Mogróin'; 'a prayer for Moinach'].

West of the cathedral is the round tower, 26 m high with six floors originally. The roof appears truncated, and indeed it is incomplete externally (and may always have been), but is complete internally. The round tower is unusual in having its doorway at ground level, as well as unusually small windows. The doorway faces south-east toward the west door of the cathedral, and is corbelled, rather than arched at the top. *c*.30 m west of the round tower is *Tobar Sheanáin* ['St Seanán's well']. *c*.250 m south-west of the cathedral is the church of *Cnoc na nAngail* ['the hill of the angels'], a small, probably relatively early church. It is poorly preserved, with a later medieval addition on the south side. At the southern tip of the island is an artillery battery, part of the defences of the Shannon of the Napoleonic period.

Seirkieran, Co. Offaly Early church site, motte, borough

12 km north of Roscrea, off R421 (Roscrea–Kinnitty); take minor road east 200 m south of Clareen; signposted. Disc Ser. 54.

This church site is important primarily for its well-preserved earthen enclosure and other earthworks, which often do not survive on early Irish church sites. Historic interest in Seirkieran stems from the very early date of its foundation, which is attributed to St Ciarán the Elder, traditionally first born of the saints of Ireland and one of the pre-Patrician saints, in the 5th century—hence the name [*Saighir Chiaráin*, 'St Ciarán's fresh well']. A tradition of a perpetual fire having been kept there may indicate that the monastery occupied the site of an earlier pagan sanctuary. It was the principal church of the kingdom of Osraige (Ossory) and the burial place of its kings until the mid-11th century, when it was supplanted by **Aghaboe**. The monastery became an Augustinian priory in the late 12th century and was dissolved *c*.1540. The church and its lands were probably taken over by the English baron Theobald Walter in the late 12th century, but were apparently acquired (or more likely, regained) from his Butler descendants by the bishop of Ossory, Geoffrey St Leger, in a duel in 1284! A borough was established at Seirkieran, probably in the 13th century and, surprisingly, was still in existence in the 15th century when most Anglo-Irish settlement in this area had collapsed. Its subsequent history is obscure, but it presumably disappeared after the burning of Seirkieran in 1548, if it had not already vanished.

The earliest surviving building is the round tower, which now stands only as a ruined base, 3 m high, just outside the north-west corner of the graveyard. Possible traces of a doorway are present at ground level on the south-east. Just to the west are the scant remains of the Augustinian priory church—little more than the north wall, with foundations of the south and east walls. Its 14th/15th-century triple-light east window is now built into the east wall of the modern church. Other decorated stonework is built into the gable ends of the modern church, and it is possible that part of its structure is actually medieval. At the south-east angle of the priory church is a two-storey round tower, a late medieval defensive structure with a number of gun loops. Within the present churchyard, to the west, are the bases of two high crosses—one of which is decorated and probably of 10th-century date—as well as an early grave slab. Within the modern church are four other early grave slabs, including one bearing the fragmentary inscription *OR DO CHE* . . . ('a prayer for Ce . . .'), which has been suggested to be the grave slab of Cearball mac Dúnlainge, a famous king of Ossory (d. 885).

Surrounding the churchyard at some distance is a substantial earthen enclosure, roughly round and composed of two earthen banks with a fosse in between. The enclosure is over 300 m in diameter and 7 ha in area, and the earthworks survive best on the north, west, and south sides. It is possible that the earthworks were restored or rebuilt as late as the 17th century, but they undoubtedly preserve the line of the early medieval enclosure. A probable entrance occurs on the north side while on the south-west, at the highest point of the enclosure, is a small, roughly square earthen mound. This is probably a motte or ringwork castle erected by Theobald Walter in the late 12th/early 13th century, although it may be a late 13th-century fortification of Bishop Geoffrey St Leger. A series of internal earthworks may well relate to the later medieval borough, rather than the earlier monastic site.

Shanballyedmond, Co. Tipperary Court tomb

28 km east of Limerick; accessed via the village of Rear Cross, on the R503 (Limerick–Thurles); take the link road south from the village, which skirts around the eastern flank of Shanballyedmond Hill. Disc. Ser. 66.

This is one of the most southerly Court tombs in the Irish series and is of interest for this reason alone. It is located on Cullaun, a south-eastern

▲ **Fig. 136.** Shanballyedmond: Court tomb, conjectural reconstruction (after O'Kelly)

spur of the Slievefelim Mountains, on the Limerick–Tipperary border, just south of the village of Rear Cross and overlooking the middle reaches of the river Bilbao. It was excavated by O'Kelly in 1958. The U-shaped cairn, which is demarcated by upright slabs and drystone walling, has a funnel-shaped court area at the north-east end, opening into a two-chambered gallery. Outside the slab walling was a low 'hem' of cairn material, which was formally demarcated by posts (now marked by stones). The carbonized remains of one of these posts returned a date of 3940–3540 BC, although a contradictory date of 1930–1680 BC came from charcoal under the 'hem'. Four smaller stones form an arcade around a cobbled area at the front of the cairn and court. A young teenager had been cremated and placed in a sub-rectangular, stone-lined pit in the end chamber. The pit seems to have been fire cleansed prior to the burial. A secondary cremation burial, probably a child, was accompanied by a coarse pot (Lough Gur Class II) and the partial, unburnt remains of an adult female were found outside the front chamber. Sherds of round-bottomed bowls (Lough Gur Class I) were found and five fine leaf-shaped arrowheads were recovered from below the cobbling in the forecourt.

1.5 km to the north is the fine Wedge tomb and multiple cist cairn of Baurnadomeeny, which was also excavated by O'Kelly. It is to be found on Skrag Hill (a south-west spur of Mauherslieve) 1 km north-east of Rear Cross.

South-east: Carlow, Kilkenny, South Tipperary, Waterford, Wexford

Introduction

The south-east is blessed with the sunniest and driest climate in Ireland, combined with generally good, fertile soils. The landscape is for the most part open and low-lying, apart from the Blackstairs Mountains on the Cos. Wexford/Carlow border and the Galtee/Knockmealdown/Comeragh Mountains in south Tipperary and west Waterford. The region is drained by two main river systems—the Nore/Suir/Barrow system to the west, discharging into Waterford Harbour, and the Slaney and its tributaries to the east, issuing into Wexford Harbour. There is comparatively little indication of a Mesolithic presence, the evidence being confined to a handful of late Mesolithic flint scatters in coastal and riverine locations. The presence of early Mesolithic sites in east Cork, however, suggests that there was no *a priori* obstacle to early colonization of this part of Ireland. The Nore, Barrow, and Suir rivers were key communications arteries, and polished stone axes dredged from them during the last century attest to their use during early prehistory. Nevertheless, evidence of Neolithic activity is also quite restricted, but this may be a question of visibility; this region is really outside the main distribution of megalithic tombs, which are the most tangible footprints of the first farmers elsewhere. The Portal tomb tucked between Bree Hill and Raheennahoon Hill at Ballybrittas (just east of Clonroche) is Wexford's only upstanding, classifiable, megalith. Waterford fares rather better with an interesting selection of Portal, Court, and Passage tombs as well as a handful of Wedge tombs. Four tombs (**Gaulstown**; Ballynageeragh; Knockeen; Matthewstown) to the south-west of Waterford city are National Monuments, while **Harristown** is the most south-easterly Passage tomb in Ireland. In truth, all these specimens are outliers to the main areas of concentration further north, and their existence here raises very interesting questions. However, the majority of Linkardstown-style tombs (or Single Burials) occur in this region, and a visit to the Linkardstown-style grave at **Baunogenasraid** should convince anyone that there is a unique and regional megalithic tradition, even if the chambers in such tombs are too small to have been accessible. It has been argued that the males buried in such tombs were elites among their kin and that this is evidence of social hierarchy in the 3rd millennium BC. Although there are

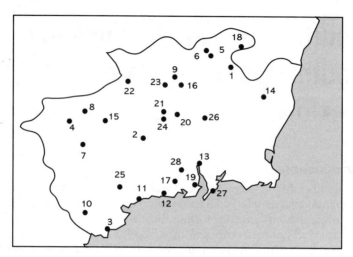

▲ **Map 7**

Key:

1. Aghade, Co Carlow
2. Ahenny, Co. Tipperary
3. Ardmore, Co. Waterford
4. Athassel, Co. Tipperary
5. Baunogenasraid, Co. Carlow
6. Brownshill, Co. Carlow
7. Caher, Co. Tipperary
8. Cashel, Co. Tipperary
9. Clara, Co. Kilkenny
10. Dromore, Co. Waterford
11. Drumlohan, Co. Waterford
12. Dunabrattin Head, Co Waterford
13. Dunbrody abbey, Co. Wexford
14. Ferns, Co. Wexford

15. Fethard, Co. Tipperary
16. Freestone Hill, Co. Kilkenny
17. Gaulstown, Co. Waterford
18. Haroldstown, Co. Carlow
19. Harristown, Co. Waterford
20. Jerpoint, Co. Kilkenny
21. Kells, Co. Kilkenny
22. Kilcooly, Co. Tipperary
23. Kilkenny, Co. Kilkenny
24. Kilree, Co. Kilkenny
25. Monavullagh Mountain, Co. Waterford
26. St. Mullin's, Co. Carlow
27. Slade, Co. Wexford
28. Waterford, Co. Waterford

a number of specimens, the area is also well outside the national distributional range of Wedge tombs.

The great variety and number of potentially Early Bronze Age monuments in the south-east, such as barrows and standing stones and circles, raises the visibility of human populations living here during the later 3rd and 2nd millennium BC. There is a particularly high concentration of Bronze Age cemeteries, both along the coast and to the immediate west of the Wicklow and Carlow uplands. As usual, however, this biases the picture in favour of funerary monuments and comparatively little is known about settlement of the period. It has often been surmised that at least some of the gold ornaments of the Middle and Late Bronze Age are made from gold panned from the granite beds of mountain streams in Wicklow, but this does not square with the general dearth of gold, or indeed bronze, objects from this region. A notable exception to this is the relatively recent discovery of a Dowris-phase gold hoard at Ballin-esker, Co. Wexford, which comprised two dress fasteners, a bracelet, and four spool-shaped objects thought to have been worn as very large earrings. And while 'hair rings' are also known from the south-west, there is a notable scarcity of Middle and Late Bronze Age hoards. Against this is the concentration of extraordinarily large hillforts overlooking **Baltinglass**, Co. Wicklow, that can only have been built for ostentation.

Raftery's reassessment of **Freestone Hill**, Co. Kilkenny, has demon-strated that this univallate hillfort dates from the later Bronze Age. But there is also a late Iron Age presence here that Ó Floinn argues comprises a Romano-British-style sanctuary. This is of particular interest because, while the south-east region is somewhat outside the La Tène province (as defined by art style), and is therefore *terra incognita* for much of the Iron Age, there is a genuine concentration here of Romano-British material. This, and coastal north Leinster, are likely to have been the areas best known to the outside world during, and immediately after, the Roman occupancy of Britain. Ptolemy's mid-2nd-century placement here of the Brigantes, Coriondi, and Manapii may contain more than just a germ of truth. The discovery of a Roman glass-urn burial at Stoneyford, Co. Kilkenny, not far from **Freestone Hill**, has been taken to imply immigration and at least semi-permanency. In this context, the finding of a Romano-British dolphin fibula on the Rock of **Cashel**, traditionally regarded as the pre-Christian seat of the Mumu, is of con-siderable importance. A Roman occulist's stamp was found near a holy well at Golden, a short distance to the west.

The late 4th/early 5th century AD saw the tide change to the other direction, as the Déisi and Uí Liatháin spearheaded migrations into south Wales, where they carved out an independent kingdom and erected bilingual ogam stones. The jury is still out as to where exactly ogam was invented but there is no doubt about its concentrating along the south-east coast, and this is an excellent place to study this arcane cipher. This is also a good area in which to study promontory forts. Kieran O'Conor has recently argued that Raymond le Gros refortified the smaller of the two promontory forts at Baginbun Head in 1170, used it as the base from which to attack the Irish and Waterford Norse, and thereafter constructed, *de novo*, the larger one. Although the date of the older fort is not known, some would argue that this form of earthwork defence was introduced in the later Iron Age, possibly even from as far afield as Brittany.

Connections with western Britain were also instrumental in the introduction of Christianity to Ireland. It is reasonably certain that Pal-ladius, the first bishop appointed to Ireland by Rome in 431, operated in the south-east. There were other so-called pre-Patrician saints here also, including St Declan of **Ardmore**, Co. Waterford, St Abbán at Moyarney, Co. Wexford, and St Ibar of Beggerin, on the outskirts of Wexford town.

According to his genealogy, St Declan was of royal stock associated with **Tara**. He was patron saint of the Dési and the extensive remains at **Ardmore** are ample testimony of the regional importance of his church into the Middle Ages. Although there may be virtually nothing to be seen today at Clonmelsh, Co. Carlow, Fanning and Ó Cróinín have postulated that this was the Saxon monastery of Rathmelsigi. It was to this place in 656 that the infant Merovingian prince Dagobert, heir to the kingdom of Austrasia, had been secreted/exiled, only to return twenty years later to claim his throne (he was murdered three years after that). Paradoxically, in spite of such close connections, there are virtually no finds of imported, European wares, notably in particular E ware, from the south-east. There can be little doubt, however, that this is once again a question of visibility. It is fair to say that, with some notable exceptions, pre-Viking south-east Ireland is generally understudied.

There is an even, but light scatter of ringforts in the region that becomes slightly more dense towards the west, across north Kilkenny and south Tipperary. Generations of mechanized agriculture on these good lands have been blamed, but the contrasting densities of ringforts in either side of the Pale line should not be dismissed so readily, as they may mean that this settlement form came to a premature end in areas most affected by Anglo-Norman control. Apart from the chance discovery in 1879 of an eroding crannóg on the beach at Ardmore Bay, Co. Waterford, there are effectively no crannógs in this region.

Historically the region included parts of two of the great early medieval provincial kingdoms—Leinster (*Laigin*) to the east and Munster (*Muma*) to the west and south. From the 7th century the Cos. Wexford/ Carlow area was dominated by the Laigin dynasty of Uí Cheinnselaig, based on the great monastic site of **Ferns** and substantially autonomous of the Laigin overkings of the Kildare area. To the west, **Cashel** was the symbolic centre of the over-kingdom of Munster (most of which lay outside this region), usually held by one or other of a number of related dynasties known as the Eóganacht. Sandwiched between Munster and Leinster was the kingdom of Osraige, centred on modern Co. Kilkenny. Traditionally part of Munster, Osraige emerged as a significant entity in the 9th and 10th centuries. Later Osraige kings had real aspirations to the kingship of Leinster, a goal that was briefly achieved in the mid-11th century, before they were eclipsed by the Uí Cheinnselaig.

The Viking period brought changes, especially in the coastal area. Recent discoveries at Woodstown, near **Waterford**, have raised the prospect of an important Viking riverside site, whose relationship with Waterford remains to be established. **Waterford** and Wexford were probably established in the 9th century as raiding bases on the estuaries of the two main river systems. Both seem to have been re-established on a more permanent basis in the early 10th century and **Waterford**, in particular, was to become a major town. Wexford may not have been as successful, but its presence was an important factor in the rise of the Uí Cheinnselaig in the later 11th/12th centuries. Diarmait mac Maíl-na-mBó (d. 1072) not only achieved overlordship among the Laigin for the Uí Cheinnselaig, but was a credible claimant to the high-kingship of Ireland. His family retained the kingship of Leinster until it was effectively extinguished on the death of his great-grandson Diarmait Mac Murchada in 1171. Diarmait's son-in-law Richard de Clare ('Strongbow') was subsequently confirmed as feudal lord of Leinster by Henry II of England. Wexford and **Waterford** were the first places occupied by Strongbow's forces and it was at **Waterford**, in 1171, that Henry II became the first English king to set foot in Ireland.

Inevitably, this region experienced earlier and more intensive English colonization than most parts of Ireland. Leinster (including modern Cos. Carlow, Kilkenny, and Wexford) was one of the two initial English lordships established under Henry II's authority in 1171. On Strongbow's death in 1176 it passed to his son-in-law William Marshall, one of the most powerful figures in England. In 1185 much of south Co. Tipperary was granted to two English barons, William de Burgh and Philip de Worcester, and along with Co Waterford it saw substantial English settlement by 1200. In Leinster, too, considerable settlement had probably taken place by 1200, but massive progress was made in the years 1207–13, when Marshall was almost continually present. Most of this area was intensively settled by tenants, brought mainly from England and Wales, and a network of towns and villages established. The region is liberally sprinkled with motte castles, probably erected between 1171 and c.1225, and has an especially dense distribution of moated sites—rectangular earthworks thought to reflect a secondary phase of Anglo-Irish colonization, often on more marginal lands, in the later 13th century.

In 1245 the last Marshall lord died and the lordship was divided between five heiresses and their husbands; Cos. Carlow, Kilkenny, and Wexford were now separate lordships. This inevitably weakened the Anglo-Irish position, and even before the chaos of the Bruce invasion (1315–18) there are indications that Irish lords such as the Mac Murchada were beginning to reassert themselves. By 1328 Domhnall Mac Murchada was reviving the family's claim to the kingship of Leinster. By the end of the 14th century Art Mac Murchada effectively controlled most of south Leinster—so much so that Richard II of England personally led two campaigns in 1394 and 1399, which were largely (and unsuccessfully) aimed against Art. The Carlow/Wexford area continued to be dominated by the Mac Murchada until the late 15th century, when the earl of Kildare mounted a veritable reconquest of much of Co. Carlow. Kildare, however, was acting primarily on his own behalf (much in the manner of an Irish lord) and this did not lead to any Anglo-Irish resettlement of the area. To the south, much of Co. Waterford had found its way into the hands of the FitzGeralds, future earls of Desmond, by the mid-13th century. At a somewhat later date south Co. Tipperary came under the control of the Butler earls of Ormond. The hegemony of these two great baronial families (often bitter rivals) was to last until the end of the Middle Ages.

Aghade, Co. Carlow Standing stone

15 km south-east of Carlow town, east off N81 (Tullow–Bunclody), 3.5 km south-west of Tullow; signposted. Disc. Ser. 61 (marked Cloch an Phoill).

This reclining standing stone, 2.4 m long, was one of a pair in this area— the other one, sadly, is now missing. Known as Cloghaphile [*Cloch an phoill*, 'the stone of the hole'], it is perforated at the top with a round hole (0.32 m in diameter), through which sick infants were passed by way of a folk cure. Legend associates it with Niall Noígiallach (Niall of the Nine Hostages) and Eochaidh of the Uí Cheinnselaig.

The name Aghade derives from *Áth Fhádhad* or *Áth Fithot*, a fording point on the river Slaney near where Iserninus founded a church. Iserninus (d. AD 468), known as Fith in Irish, is referred to as a contemporary of St Patrick, and elsewhere as a disciple of the great saint. He also founded Kilcullen, Co. Kildare.

Ahenny, Co. Tipperary High crosses

7.5 km north of Carrick-on-Suir, off R697 (Kilkenny–Carrick-on-Suir); take minor road to west 7.5 km north of Carrick-on-Suir, then turn south; signposted.

At Ahenny is a neat little graveyard on the site of the church of Kilclispeen [*Cill Criospín*, 'St Crispin's church']. While it may not look particularly imposing, it was clearly an important early monastic site, but nothing is known of its history—probably because the original name of the site has been lost and replaced by a later dedication to St Crispin. No traces of early buildings are visible, apart from the ruins of a late medieval church north of the graveyard (*not accessible to the public*). What makes the site so important are two decorated high crosses and the base of a third, which are of major significance in illuminating the chronological and technological development of Irish high crosses. Certain features of the crosses make it clear that these are 'metalwork crosses translated into stone'. Practically the entire surface is covered in panels of interlace, spirals, and geometrical patterns, much of which imitates cast chip-carved ornament seen in early metalwork. Around the edges of the cross is a slightly raised, cable pattern moulding, clearly imitating the metal binding strips which would have held in place the various decorated panels on a metalwork cross. Most revealing of all is the arrangement of five rounded bosses on each face of the cross head. These imitate the glass or enamelled studs used to conceal structural rivets on early metalwork. The details of the ornament indicate an 8th-century date for the Ahenny crosses, and they may form a vital link in the development of the great 9th/10th-century scripture crosses from early metal prototypes.

Other distinctive features of these crosses include their relatively widely spaced rings and the manner in which the main shaft rises well above the ring, giving the cross a slightly stumpy appearance. The North Cross has a peculiar conical capstone, although it is not certain that this is an original feature of the cross. Figure carving is rare, effectively confined to the cross bases, and difficult to interpret. On the base of the North Cross are scenes that may be tentatively interpreted as *Christ and Apostles* (west face), *Adam Naming the Animals?* (east face), *Chariot procession—translation of relics?* (north side), and *Procession with a headless corpse?* (south side). The scenes on the base of the South Cross are more weathered but include *Daniel in the Lions' Den* and *Christ and Apostles?* (east face) and *Temptation of Adam and Eve* (south side).

Another group of crosses, of similar style and date, can be seen at Kilkieran, 2 km to the south (*go straight at crossroads where R697 turns right*). Among the crosses here is a tall cross with short arms and no ring, which may possibly reflect influences from Anglo-Saxon England—links that are well supported in historical sources of the 7th and 8th centuries.

Ardmore, Co. Waterford Early monastic site

15 km east of Youghal, off N25 (Waterford–Youghal); signposted.

Ardmore [*Ard Mór*, 'the great height'] is a beautifully located monastic site associated with the 5th-century saint Declan, who allegedly ministered in this part of Ireland even before the time of St Patrick. It seems to have briefly achieved the status of a bishopric in the later 12th and early 13th centuries, and much of the surviving Romanesque-style building work probably relates to this period. In 1203 the death is recorded of Mael Etuin Ó Duib Ratha, a priest who completed the building of the church of Ardmore, and this seems to confirm the late 12th-century date suggested for the most significant phase of surviving building on the site (see below). The visible remains consist of the 'cathedral', a smaller oratory and a round tower. These originally stood within a roughly circular enclosure *c.*200 m in diameter, the outline of which is partially preserved in the line of the road west and south-west of the graveyard and in the boundary of the rectory, to the north-west. There is possible evidence confirming an early date for the church site, in the form of two ogam stones, now kept in the cathedral. One of these carries the inscription: *LUGUDECCAS MAQI . . . COI NETA-SEGAMONAS* ('[the stone] of Lugaid, grandson of Nia-Segmon').

Cathedral

The cathedral is a long, narrow nave-and-chancel building in which three main phases of construction are visible. The earliest structure, characterized by large masonry blocks with an external batter, is represented by the western ends of the north and south walls of the chancel. This was probably a small, simple rectangular building that was greatly enlarged in the second phase, when a long rectangular nave was added at the west end, with the original church becoming the chancel. The architectural details of the chancel arch and the round-headed windows and doorways in the north and south walls of the nave belong to the Transitional (Romanesque/Gothic) period, and indicate a late 12th-century date for this second phase of building. The pointed chancel arch may be slightly later in date—the capitals supporting the arch have clearly been rebuilt. A striking feature of the cathedral is the virtual absence of later medieval work. Apart from the rebuilt chancel arch, two tomb niches at the east end of the nave, and a doorway in the south wall of the chancel, all probably 13th century, there is no evidence of work from c.1200 until after 1600. This is testimony to the obscurity into which Ardmore sank from the early 13th century, when it lost its status as a bishopric. The third main phase of building probably dates to the 17th century, when the chancel was enlarged to the east and massive buttresses were applied to the external north-west, north-east, and south-east corners and internally to the west side of the chancel arch. The buttress at the external south-east corner bears a stone with the date 1630, and this seems a reasonably reliable date for all the work of this period.

It was probably also at this period that the west end of the nave was either rebuilt or extended. This is significant because the west gable contains the cathedral's most important feature—a frieze of sculpture panels set within Romanesque arcading, with two large semicircular panels below, containing further panels. Whether the west gable is a later extension to the original, or was simply rebuilt on the original foundations, it seems clear that the current arrangement of the arcading and sculpture dates to the 17th century—many centuries after they were originally carved. It is uncertain whether the sculptures were originally carved for display within the arcading, or were part of another arrangement. The sculpture is extremely worn, but some panels can be tentatively identified, as follows (reading from north to south): *Unidentified figure laying hands on another* (arch 4), *Two processing figures* (arch 5), *Unidentified ecclesiastics with crosiers* (arches 6 and 8), *Christ in Majesty?* (arch 7), *The Weighing of Souls* (arch 10), and *Enthroned figure with kneeling figure holding a ?scroll* (arch 11). In the northern of the two semicircular panels below, a central panel with *Adam and Eve* is clearly visible, flanked by an *Equestrian figure* to the left and *Two figures, one kneeling* to the right. In the southern lunette is a panel depicting the

Judgement of Solomon above, with the *Adoration of the Magi* set in an arcade of five arches below.

St Declan's House

South-east of the cathedral is 'St Declan's House', a small, rectangular oratory with boldly projecting antae, in which St Declan is traditionally said to be buried. A long cavity in the floor is said to be his burial place, and may well mark the site of a tomb or shrine. The original west doorway is now blocked and the present north doorway is relatively modern. The oratory probably had a stone roof originally, but all trace of this was destroyed when the building was re-roofed in the 18th century.

Round tower

Due south of the cathedral is the round tower. Described as the 'most unorthodox of all the Round Towers', it is also perhaps the most attractive. The tower is 29 m high and is distinguished by its strongly tapering profile, and by its three external stringcourses, at each of which the wall is slightly inset. The roof was rebuilt in the 19th century and the present capstone with cross is modern. There are six floors and several projecting corbel stones internally, five of which are carved as human and animal heads of 12th-century character. The round-arched doorway is 4 m above ground and faces north-east. This is significant—doorways of round towers generally face the west end of the principal church, but at Ardmore the doorway of the round tower does not address the west end of the cathedral, which is clearly later than the tower. It is possible that the tower addressed the earlier church represented in the chancel of the cathedral, but this appears very small to have been the main church of an important monastery. In any case, the doorway of the round tower does not address the west end of this structure either, and it may be that the principal church in the earlier 12th century was located slightly to the south-east of the cathedral, between it and 'St Declan's House'. Fragments of earlier Romanesque-style carving built into the nave of the cathedral may have come from this church, of which no other trace is visible.

Athassel, Co. Tipperary Priory

8 km south-west of Cashel, off N74 (Cashel–Tipperary); take minor road to south on west side of Golden village; signposted.

The Augustinian priory at Athassel [*Áth Íseal*, 'low/shallow ford'] is one of the largest surviving monastic complexes in Ireland. It was founded *c.*1200 by William de Burgh, ancestor of the great de Burgh (Burke) family, and lord of extensive areas in south Tipperary and Limerick. De Burgh himself and several of his descendants were buried there, including Walter, earl of Ulster (d. 1271), and Richard, the 'Red Earl' of Ulster (d. 1326). There was also a town at Athassel, probably founded at much the same time as the priory. Town and priory were burned by both Irish and Anglo-Irish nobles in the 14th century and the town had probably been deserted by the middle of the century. The priory survived, however, enduring another particularly severe attack in 1447 before being dissolved in 1541.

The remains of the priory occupy a roughly rectangular area enclosed by a stone wall, bounded by the river Suir on the east and a smaller channel of the river on the west. In the north-west angle is a vaulted gatehouse, approached via an external bridge, probably medieval, which spanned the river channel. An outer barbican, defended by a portcullis, stood over a mill race within this. The opening of the gate passage proper was originally a large round-headed arch, but this was later reduced to a smaller, pointed opening. The main buildings of the priory occupy the eastern half of the enclosure.

The large church is cruciform, with aisled nave, choir, and Cistercian-style transepts, each having two chapels on the east side. Another large chapel projected eastwards from the north transept. It must once have been an extremely impressive building but is poorly preserved—especially the nave, which was added to the church *c.*1280. Little of the side walls of the nave survive, and the large west window and doorway are gone. There was also a belfry tower at the north-west angle of the nave, a feature also seen at the Augustinian priory of **Kells** (Co. Kilkenny). On the north aisle wall a number of shafts survive (or have left vertical scars marking their former locations), from which vaulting originally sprang. Thus the aisles, at least, were originally vaulted but we cannot say whether the nave itself was. Unusually, the aisles did not lead directly into the transepts, which were cut off by side walls. The nave is also separated from the crossing by a screen wall pierced only by a very fine doorway of *c.*1260, with pointed arch of four orders, flanked by trefoil-headed niches which probably held statues originally. The large pointed arch or recess over the doorway was probably open, originally, containing the great rood (crucifix), but was blocked when the crossing tower was rebuilt in the 15th century.

The choir and transepts form the earliest part of the church, probably *c.*1220–30. The choir is lit at the east end by rows of closely spaced lancet windows in the north and south walls, beneath which, presumably, would have been stalls for the canons. The three-light east window is a 15th-century insertion, probably much smaller than the 13th-century original. The niches flanking it probably held statues. In the south wall was a recess containing a fine late 13th-century altar tomb, now on display in the Vicars Choral hall at **Cashel**. Several other pieces of sculpture are still visible, including a late 13th-/early 14th-century effigy of a nobleman, possibly Walter de Burgh, earl of Ulster, and an attractive early 14th-century incised grave slab of a man and woman. There seems to have been an original crossing tower but practically all trace of it has been removed by the insertion of a later tower in the 15th century. The arch to the south transept is, however, part of the original crossing. Its piers rest on a screen wall, separating transept from crossing. In the south transept are the night stairs, leading to the dormitory (over the sacristy) and through which the canons entered the church for night services. Substantial alterations were made to the church in the 15th century, possibly in the wake of the 1447 attack. The east window was replaced and a large new tower inserted over the crossing, the upper levels of which were partially used for residential chambers. Access to the upper chambers was via a spiral staircase located in the angle between the south transept and the sacristy. Most importantly, the absence of any roof line in the western face of this tower indicates that the nave was abandoned and left unroofed at this point. The greatly reduced church, now consisting merely of choir, crossing, and transepts, is a clear sign of serious decline both in the priory itself and in the community that it served.

The cloisters lie to the south of the church, with a large garth surrounded by an ambulatory. The arcade is late 14th/15th century, consisting of groups of three ogee-headed openings, splaying widely internally with rounded rear arches, and separated by internal buttresses. The surrounding buildings are not particularly well preserved but give a good idea of the original scale and layout. In the east range, at ground level, was the sacristy (nearest the church), the slype or passage, the chapter house with a later eastward extension, and cellars. All of these chambers were vaulted, to support the long dormitory overhead, which had access to the church (via the night stairs) at the north end and a projecting latrine building at the south end. A projecting chamber over the chapter house may have been the prior's apartment. The south range was entirely occupied by the refectory, at first-floor level, with vaulted cellars below. The west range probably consisted largely of cellars, at ground level, with perhaps guest accommodation above, reached via a mural stair in the wall dividing the west range from the church. Traces of further buildings survive against the southern boundary of the enclosure, south-west of the claustral ranges.

Baunogenasraid, Co. Carlow Neolithic burial

7 km south-east of Carlow, south off the R725 (Carlow–Tullow; marked 'Tumulus'). Disc. Ser. 61.

This Neolithic Single Burial (sometimes referred to as a Linkardstown-style tomb) was reused as a cemetery cairn during the earlier Bronze

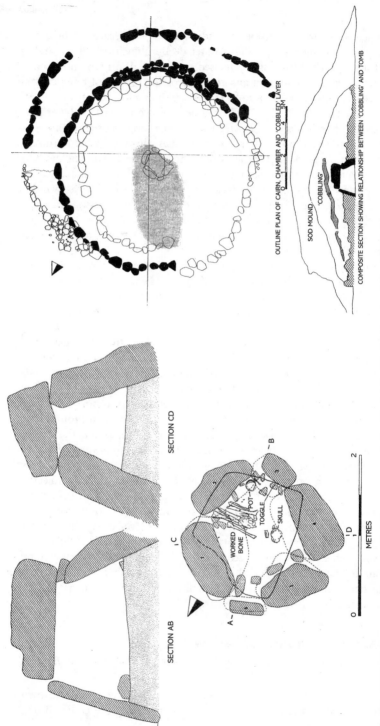

SECTION CD

SECTION AB

B

WORKED
BONE
POT
TOGGLE
SKULL

A

C

D

METRES

0   1   2

OUTLINE PLAN OF CAIRN, CHAMBER AND 'COBBLED' LAYER

0 1 2 3 4 5M

SOD MOUND

'COBBLING'

COMPOSITE SECTION SHOWING RELATIONSHIP BETWEEN 'COBBLING' AND TOMB

▲ Fig. 137. Baunogenasraid: plan and section, as excavated, with detail of burial chamber (after Raftery)

▲ **Fig. 138.** Baunogenasraid: decorated Neolithic pot (after Raftery)

Age. Located on a gentle, west-facing slope, it consists of a round cairn (20 m in diameter), at the centre of which, on a fairly level platform of stones (0.3 m high), lay a polygonal, granite chamber and capstone and, on one side, a removable limestone block. The chamber contained the inhumed remains of an adult male accompanied by a distinctive, Linkardstown-type, round-bottomed, ornate bowl, a bone point, and a toggle. The burial was radiocarbon dated to 3632–3376 BC. Arcuate, 'retaining' walls or settings, identified in the cairn, are compared with similar settings in cairns of Passage tombs such as at **Carrowmore** (nos. 3 and 7) and at Townley Hall, Co. Louth, suggesting some common ground between the two monument types. The cairn was covered by a mound of turves (2 m in maximum height) and this was later enlarged and used as a burial mound during the earlier Bronze Age, with the insertion of at least ten pit burials. Comprising both cremated and inhumed burials, one of them was accompanied by a Bowl. Two of the pits had evidence of organic linings.

Browneshill, Co. Carlow Portal tomb

3 km east of Carlow town, off R726 (Carlow–Baltinglass); signposted from junction of N9 (Dublin–Carlow) with ring road on north side of Carlow; Disc. Ser. 61.

Reputed to have the heaviest capstone of any portal tomb—estimated at around 100 tonnes—Browneshill (in Kernanstown townland) is the sole survivor of three megaliths recorded in this area in the late 1800s. The downslope, eastern end of the huge capstone is propped on two portal stones and a door stone. Beside the north portal is another free-standing orthostat that may be the remains of a façade.

Caher, Co. Tipperary Medieval town

At junction of N8 (Dublin–Cork) and N24 (Limerick–Waterford); signposted. Visitor centre at castle; admission charge.

Caher [*An Chathair*, 'the stone fort/castle'] is best known for one of the largest and best-preserved castles in Ireland, but it also preserves the ruins of an Augustinian priory and a parish church. Castle, priory, and church all seem to have originated in the 13th century, probably because the centre of the extensive de Worcester lordship, originally based in Knockgraffon (see below), was moved there. There was a borough here in the 13th and 14th centuries but it seems never to have been walled or to have achieved the status of a true town, and no trace of it survives. The present layout of the town is post-medieval and even the location of the original borough is uncertain.

Castle

The architecture of the castle (*off Castle St.*) suggests that it was initially constructed in the mid-13th century but the historical background to this has never been satisfactorily explained. It may, however, have replaced the motte-and-bailey castle at Knockgraffon (see below) as the centre of the de Worcester lordship. Caher was acquired by the Butler earls of Ormond in the late 14th century and this led to a major extension of the castle in the 15th century. Although it was involved in the wars of the late 16th and mid-17th centuries, the castle remained in Butler hands and was heavily restored c.1840.

The castle is sited on a rocky island in the river Suir. The original 13th-century structure is at the north end of the island, with a large, rectangular 15th-century extension to the south. The entrance on the east side leads into the north end of this extension, which is cut off from the remainder by a large inserted wall (probably 16th century) just south of the entrance. This is the Middle Ward, and both it and the Outer Ward to the south are largely featureless, apart from two round turrets at the angles of the south end. North of the Middle Ward, on the highest part of the island, is the Inner Ward, which effectively is the original

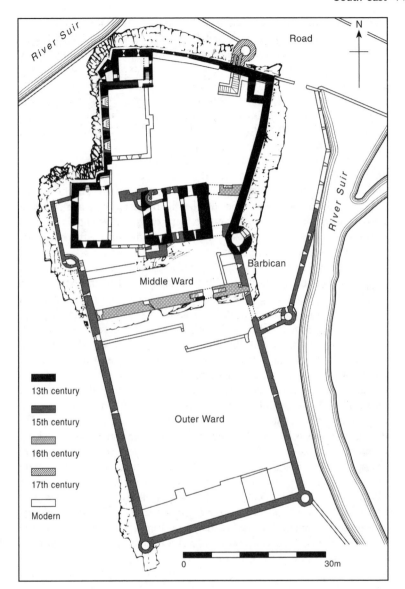

Road

N

River Suir

River Suir

Barbican

Middle Ward

13th century

15th century

16th century

17th century

Modern

Outer Ward

0   30m

▲ Fig. 139. Caher: plan of castle (OPW)

13th-century castle, much modified in the late Middle Ages. It was roughly square in outline, with towers or turrets at each corner (each very different from the others) and a large, three-storey gatehouse on the south side, similar to that at **Roscrea**. Just outside the gatehouse to the south are the foundations of a large cross-wall, probably 13th century, which may represent the original curtain wall on this side. The original gate passage in the centre of the gatehouse was blocked in the 15th century—the outline of the arched opening is still visible—and replaced by a new opening on the east side of the gatehouse, within a new wall crossing from the east curtain wall. The arch of this opening, with its portcullis slot, may be reused 13th-century masonry, while the machicolation overhead is 19th century. Further north is a second gateway, within a wall built onto the gatehouse in the 16th century, leading into the inner courtyard.

Around this courtyard are the main buildings of the castle—the hall on the west side with an attached tower in the north-west angle, a domestic tower in the south-west angle, and smaller towers in the north-east and south-east angles. Beside the north-east turret are rock-cut steps leading under the curtain wall to a projecting external tower, which contained a well. The present tower is mainly 17th century but may have replaced an earlier feature. The large, three-storey tower adjoining the hall in the north-west angle was originally a solar that was entered from the hall, at ground level. It was substantially rebuilt in the late Middle Ages and now resembles a tower house, with a gabled attic behind high battlements. The hall itself is almost entirely a 19th-century rebuilding. The only original feature is the west wall—the curtain wall—with 15th-century windows within 13th-century embrasures. The hall may originally have extended as far south as the gatehouse, where there is a fragment of wall with a large fireplace. The gatehouse was also altered in the late Middle Ages, when it was no longer used as a gatehouse but as a form of keep. The ground floor consists of three vaulted chambers—the original gate passage in the centre, flanked by two guardrooms. Access to the upper levels is by a spiral stair in the north-west angle which, along with the doorway in the north wall, was probably inserted after the gate passage had been blocked. The first-floor chamber contains a large, late medieval fireplace which may have been inserted into the original slot for the portcullis of the gateway below. The mullioned windows are also late medieval and probably replace earlier opes. The second-floor level, as well as the gabled attic and battlements above, are almost entirely of late medieval construction. So, too, is the latrine tower built onto the south-western side of the gatehouse.

Priory

A priory of Augustinian canons was founded in Caher *c.*1220; it was dissolved in 1540. The ruins of the priory (*east side of Abbey St.*) consist of the choir and tower of the church, and parts of the east and south claustral ranges. The choir has an unusual 15th/16th-century window that is almost a hybrid between switchline tracery and earlier lancets. Traces of earlier windows, carved in sandstone, indicate that the core of the fabric is 13th century. The tower at the west end is also somewhat unusual, quite wide but very shallow (from east to west), and was modified for residential use after the suppression of the priory. The cloisters are to the south of the church. The east range contains a series of small, vaulted chambers of uncertain function and a larger chamber to the south, probably the chapter house. Also at the south end is a four-storey residential tower and to the west of this are traces of a long chamber forming the south range of the cloister. This may have been the refectory, and has a series of sandstone windows (modified after the suppression) suggesting a 13th-century date.

Parish church

The medieval parish church (*on Old Church St., off The Square*) is a simple rectangular building, probably first built in the 13th century. The original work is characterized by the use of sandstone mouldings, seen in the blocked door in the south wall and the windows in the east wall. The main east window (only one jamb of which survives) was replaced by a late medieval four-light window with transom and mullions. Like all the late medieval modifications, this was in limestone.

Knockgraffon

4 km north, at Knockgraffon (*take minor road to north-west at junction of N8 and R670, 2.5 km north of Caher*), is the original centre of the de Worcester lordship. There is no trace of the borough which was established there in the 13th century, but there is an interesting collection of monuments. The fine motte-and-bailey castle was erected by Philip de Worcester in 1192, as part of the initial English advance into the Ó Briain kingdom of Thomond. The entire earthwork is surrounded by an external bank and fosse. The fosse also separates the motte from the bailey, which has a slight internal bank and traces of a rectangular stone tower on the north side. To the north are ruins of the 13th-century parish church, a nave-and-chancel structure with a 15th-century east window set within the embrasure of the original window. Beside it is a late medieval tower house, probably erected by a branch of the Butlers in the 16th century.

Cashel, Co. Tipperary Ecclesiastical site; medieval town

At junction of N8 (Dublin–Cork) and N74 (Cashel–Tipperary); signposted. Visitor centre on Rock; admission charge.

Cashel is rightly famous for the spectacular group of buildings on the Rock north of the town, but it is also a medieval town, boasting a Dominican priory, a Cistercian abbey, a fortified urban tower house, and

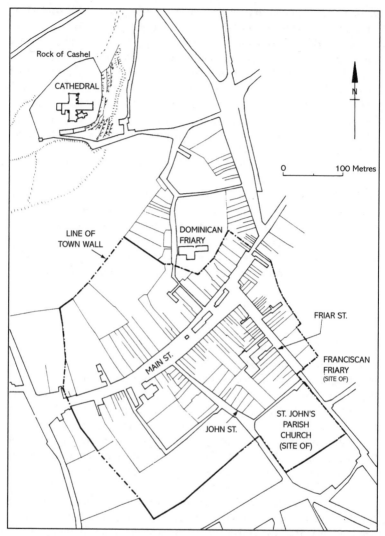

▲ **Fig. 140.** Cashel: outline map of town showing main medieval features (after
Bradley)

fragments of town wall. The Rock of Cashel, one of the most striking
and important archaeological sites in Ireland, is a large limestone outcrop rising 60 m above the surrounding land. Although traditionally
associated with St Patrick, it was primarily a secular site, as the name
[*Caiseal*, 'stone fort'] indicates—the chief residence of the Eóganacht
kings of Munster. In 1101 Muirchertach Ó Briain, king of Munster (of
the Dál Cais dynasty, rivals of the Eoghanacht) gave the Rock to the

Church. Ten years later, because of the strength of Ua Briain influence, Cashel became the seat of one of Ireland's two archbishoprics (the other being **Armagh**). Although recent archaeological excavation has found evidence of burials and church buildings pre-dating 1101, possibly of the 9th/10th century, the events of the early 12th century transformed the nature of the Rock. A major building campaign took place, for which evidence survives in a suite of structures dating to the first half of the 12th century—a high cross, a round tower, and most importantly a church, known as Cormac's Chapel after its patron Cormac Mac Cárthaig, king of Munster. This is the finest surviving Romanesque church in Ireland and was consecrated in 1134, probably for one of the first communities of Benedictine monks in Ireland. It is clear from the layout of the buildings, however, that Cormac's Chapel was not the focal point of the 12th-century site. Rather, this must have been a church in the area now occupied by the choir of the cathedral, but nothing is known of this church, which was replaced by the present cathedral in the 13th century.

The town

The town at the foot of the Rock was founded by the archbishop before 1218 and had probably reached its full extent by c.1265, when a Franciscan friary was founded just outside the south-eastern corner of the town. A Dominican priory had been founded in 1243, just outside the north-eastern angle of the town. The town walls were probably erected in the late 13th/early 14th century. Some reasonably good fragments survive, especially on the south and east sides of St John's churchyard (*off John St., south of Main St.*). Mounted on the inner face of the wall at this point is a series of 13th-century effigies, presumably from the medieval parish church. The town was laid out on a linear pattern with a single main street—widening near the east end to form a market place—and a number of smaller side streets. On the south side of Main St. is a fine late medieval tower house, known as 'Quirke's Castle'. Now incorporated into a hotel (the large arched opening at the front is not original), it is six storeys high with a pronounced wall batter at the base.

Dominican priory

The Dominican priory (*in Moor Lane, off the north side of Main St., at the east end*) was founded by the archbishop in 1243 and dissolved in 1540. The church is reasonably complete but the cloisters to the north have vanished. The long rectangular church is original mid-13th-century work and the row of nine closely spaced lancet windows in the south wall of the choir may be the earliest example of a feature also seen in Dominican priories at **Athenry** and **Sligo** and in the cathedrals at

Ardfert and **Ferns**. The original triple-lancet east window was replaced in the mid-15th century by an attractive five-light window with reticulated tracery. The same also happened, at the end of the 15th century, to the south window of the south transept (although the tracery in this case is flowing rather than reticulated) and to the window in the west gable. As in many Irish churches there is a clear distinction between the yellow sandstone used for 13th-century architectural features and the grey limestone used in later medieval work. The transept, with its west aisle, and the adjoining south nave aisle were added to the church *c.*1270— one of the earliest examples of the 'preaching transepts' which were added to so many friaries in the later Middle Ages. The crossing tower is also a later medieval addition.

The Rock

Visitors enter the Rock through the restored 15th-century dormitory and hall of the Vicars Choral of the cathedral. Among other items on display in the vaulted undercroft of the hall are a fine 13th-century tomb front from **Athassel** priory, a 13th-century effigy and sarcophagus from the Franciscan friary in Cashel, and the high cross erected on the Rock in the 12th century. A replica stands on the previous location of the cross, between the Vicars Choral and the cathedral, but excavation has revealed that it was only set in that position in the late Middle Ages. Although now very weathered and incomplete, this was clearly one of the most unusual of Irish high crosses. In typical 12th-century style, it is dominated by large figures of Christ (*west face*) and a bishop or abbot (*east face*). Like several other crosses of this period it lacks a ring, but unlike any other cross it had vertical struts (one of which survives) to support the relatively long cross arms. On the base are panels of Scandinavian-derived interlace and geometric motifs, now extremely worn.

Cormac's Chapel

Emerging from the Vicars Choral, the next stop should be Cormac's Chapel, generally regarded as the earliest and finest example of Romanesque architecture in Ireland. In fact it is a unique mixture of elements that are traditional to early Irish church architecture, and others that are new. In plan and proportions it is essentially a traditional nave-and-chancel structure but with opposed north and south doorways near the west end, instead of a west doorway, and squared towers at the east end of the nave. The two towers could probably only be entered from within the church, originally—the blocked doorway in the east wall of the north tower was actually a window, which was later enlarged, and the upper levels of the tower were reached from the croft over the nave.

The flat parapet at the top of the south tower may be an addition, and the tower may originally have had a pyramidal roof similar to the north tower. To some eyes these towers appear exotic, perhaps of German inspiration, but an alternative suggestion is that they are, in effect, squared versions of the traditional Irish round tower. The chancel is set off-centre with respect to the nave, possibly because the builders decided to widen the nave after the chancel had been laid out. The high-pitched stone roof is a traditional feature (but exceptionally large and well built), as are the crofts or spaces between the roof and vaults. The scarcity of windows is also characteristic of early Irish church architecture. The nave was apparently lit only by a window in the west wall (the large openings in the south wall are not original) and the chancel by two small opes within the recess at the east end. Other small opes in the roof and gables lit the crofts above the vaults. On the other hand the ribbed vaults, especially the groined vault over the chancel, are probably the earliest in Ireland.

The most striking features of Cormac's Chapel are the decorative elements, which include the earliest known fresco painting in Ireland, in the chancel. On the exterior walls of the nave, chancel, and towers are striking rows of blank arcading, separated by stringcourses, while similar arcading occurs internally, especially in the chancel. The elaborate north and south doorways and chancel arch are boldly carved with Roman-esque roll mouldings, chevrons, and human and animal heads. The north doorway has a large gabled porch, reflecting the fact that it was originally the main entrance to the church. Unfortunately, the building of the 13th-century cathedral against the north side of the church has completely destroyed the setting of this important entrance. The gable of the porch has three vertical bands rising from a horizontal band, all decorated with zigzag chevron ornament, which were probably intended to mimic the effect of beams in a timber-framed structure. Beside the porch, to the east, is a stone tomb within a round-arched recess. An external location for a tomb is unusual, but this may be the tomb of the founder. At the west end of the nave, internally, is a stone sarcophagus with a finely carved front decorated with interlaced beasts and serpents in the Hiberno-Scandinavian Urnes style of the early 12th century. This might also be the tomb of the founder, Cormac Mac Cárthaig, or per-haps of his brother and predecessor as king of Munster, Tadhg (died 1124), although it is not in its original position. It was brought into the chapel in the 19th century, having been discovered in the north transept of the cathedral, but as the sarcophagus is up to a century older than the cathedral, this cannot have been its original position either. It may well have come from the long-vanished principal church which stood at the east end of the present cathedral.

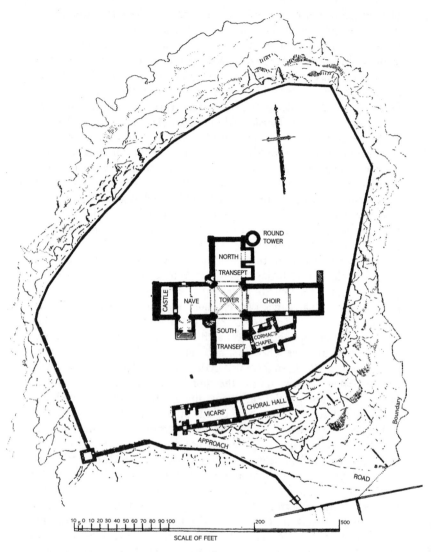

▲ **Fig. 141.** Rock of Cashel: plan (OPW)

Cathedral

Surrounding Cormac's Chapel to the west and north is the cathedral, erected in the 13th century on the site of the principal church of the 12th century. The cathedral is a strangely lopsided structure, with a remarkably short nave relative to the large choir and transepts. Clearly, circumstances never allowed the nave to be completed on the scale originally intended. The choir dates to the first half of the 13th century, the transepts and crossing are slightly later, and the nave is later again—but still probably 13th century. The crossing tower and the five-storey tower house at the west end of the nave were probably added in the early 15th century. The choir is lit by rows of high, narrow lancets in the north and south walls and, originally, by a triple lancet in the east wall. Above the lancets are unusual clerestory windows with small quatrefoil openings externally but much larger internal openings flanked by moulded jambs. All of the original architectural mouldings are in sandstone, whereas limestone is used elsewhere in the cathedral. In the south wall are recesses for the piscina and sedilia, beside which is the wall tomb of the controversial late 16th-century archbishop Miler McGrath. A series of grave slabs, mainly 16th century, has been assembled on the floor of the choir. The transepts, probably built *c.*1270, are lit by majestic triple lancets in the gable ends, partially blocked in the 15th century. Above the lancets in the north gable is a small, unusual rose window, with a central quatrefoil opening surrounded by blind tracery. On the east side of each transept are Cistercian-like twin chapels, three of which have piscinae, while three also have tomb niches. Another collection of late medieval tomb sculpture has been assembled in the north transept. Externally, the transepts have fine angle buttresses with niches for statues and (on the south transept) octagonal turrets above. The crossing, with its fine arches with multiple mouldings, is contemporary with the transepts, but the tower itself is later, probably 15th century. In the external angles between the crossing and the nave are polygonal turrets containing spiral staircases.

The remarkably short nave was built in the late 13th century, with a stone vaulted porch on the south side. A north porch was clearly also intended but it is not certain if it was ever built. The outer doorway of the south porch was inserted in the 15th century. The nave was origin-ally slightly longer than at present, but was reduced in the early 15th century when the tower house at the west end was erected—note the angle buttress of the nave, still visible at the south-west corner of the tower house. The tower house was residential—for the use of the arch-bishop himself. It was of five storeys, barrel vaulted over the second floor, and could be accessed at second-floor level directly from the mural passage in the nave walls. When the tower house was built, the south porch was also raised in height to provide an extra chamber overhead, which contains a fine fireplace. The nave was also modified, with an upper floor inserted to act as a hall attached to the archbishop's tower house. This may have been done at a slightly later date, perhaps even in the early 16th century.

Round tower

Attached to the north-east angle of the cathedral's north transept is the round tower, probably erected in the early 12th century. It is 28 m high, with six floors, and is complete (although the roof was rebuilt in the 19th century). The original doorway is round arched, set 3.3 m above ground, and faces south-east. It clearly faced the west end of a 12th-century church, on the site of the east end of the present cathedral. When the cathedral was built in the 13th century another doorway was opened in the east side of the round tower, to allow access from the triforium passage of the cathedral, suggesting that the tower was being used, probably as a belfry.

Hore abbey

Hore was the latest Cistercian abbey in medieval Ireland, founded in 1272 by David Mac Cearbhaill, archbishop of Cashel, with monks from **Mellifont**. Apparently the Cistercians were a replacement for the Benedictine monks based in Cormac's Chapel, whom the archbishop expelled. Unusually for the Cistercians (who generally favoured remote settings), the new abbey was built just outside the town of Cashel. It was dissolved in 1540, although parts of the church continued in use as a parish church, while others were converted for residential use. The church was built soon after 1272 and is reasonably complete (with considerable late medieval modification) but the claustral buildings survive mainly as foundations. The architecture throughout is typically Cistercian, both in its plan and in its austere lack of decoration. It is also quite archaic for the late 13th century—note, for instance, the tall simple lancets in the gable walls—but there are similarities to the cathedral on the Rock and the same masons may have worked on both churches.

The nave is aisled with a simple arcade, although the quatrefoil clerestory windows are unusual. It was extensively modified in the 15th century, when the tall lancet in the west wall was blocked and replaced by several smaller windows, most of the nave arches were also blocked, and a new wall was built across the nave between the second and third bays. The rather low, squat crossing tower was also added at this date. The transepts had two chapels on the east side, although those in the south transept have vanished. The presbytery, lit by three graded lancets (subsequently partially blocked), was never vaulted. In the south wall is an attractive piscina with an aumbry alongside. Hore is the only Irish Cistercian abbey with its cloister on the north side of the church, but apart from the projecting chapter house (*c.*1280) on the east side and a reconstructed fragment of the cloister arcade, little survives above ground. After the suppression of the abbey the chapter house was converted into a two-storey chamber and was lived in by a tenant of the earl of Ormond. The same also happened in the south transept and at the west end of the nave.

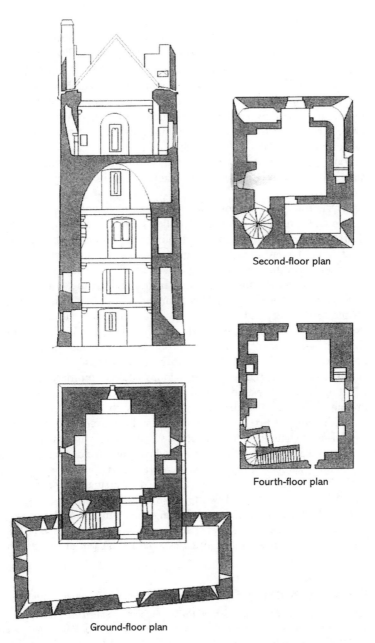

Second-floor plan

Fourth-floor plan

Ground-floor plan

▲ **Fig. 142.** Clara: Floor plans and cross-section of tower house (after O'Keefe)

Clara, Co. Kilkenny Tower house

7 km east of Kilkenny, off N10 (Kilkenny–Carlow); take minor road to north at Clifden (6.5 km east of Kilkenny) and follow for 3 km; signposted. Disc. Ser. 67.

The well-preserved 15th-century tower house at Clara [*Clárach*, 'plain/ level place'] is often presented as typical of the entire Irish series. It is a simple rectangular tower of five storeys with a gabled attic chamber above, surrounded by a wall walk defended by high stepped battlements. There is a high barrel vault over the third floor. The other floors are of timber and, unusually, in Clara these are original, or at least of some antiquity. The flooring structure is typical of many tower houses—the main joists rest on large beams set against the walls and supported on corbels.

The entrance, on the north side, is a well-carved pointed doorway. It is defended externally by a small walled forecourt with gun loops— clearly a later addition—and internally by a murder hole overhead. Inside the doorway a small lobby gives access to the spiral stairs to the upper levels (in the north-east angle), to a small dark chamber, perhaps for a doorkeeper (in the north-west angle), and, to the south, to the main ground-floor chamber. This chamber is lit only by narrow loops on the south, east, and west sides and was presumably used only for storage. Overhead, at first-, second-, and third-floor levels there are two chambers—the main chamber to the south and a smaller room in the north-west angle. The smaller chambers served partially to defend the entrance below, by means of arrow loops and the murdering hole at first-floor level. At second- and third-floor levels these chambers were probably also used as bedchambers. The larger chambers were residential, although the first-floor chamber is still relatively poorly lit. The second-floor chamber was probably the lord's private apartment and is distinguished by its large fireplace, a good two-light window in the south wall, and a garderobe reached via a mural passage in the south-west angle. The fourth floor is entirely occupied by a single, large chamber with a large fireplace, good windows, and several wall cupboards. This was clearly the lord's hall, the main living and eating space. A feature of Clara is the presence of a secret chamber within the west wall, accessible only through an opening disguised as a garderobe seat at fourth-floor level.

Dromore (Kiltera), Co. Waterford Enclosure, ogam stones

18 km north of Youghal, Co. Cork, off R671 (Youghal–Clonmel); best accessed via Villierstown, turning west (right) at the first crossroads south of Villierstown. Signposted. Disc. Ser. 81.

This circular enclosure (36 m in diameter), located on the south bank of the Goish river, is of uncertain date. Excavations by Macalister in 1934 revealed two parallel trenches (possibly the remains of a building) and a pit containing iron slag, overlain by a cemetery. The majority of burials adhered to the orthodox Christian modus, but others appear to have been crouched. Some were overlain by the enclosing stone wall, into which three ogam stones had been built. One of the them is now in the National Museum of Ireland, the other two are *in situ* and can be read as follows:

1. *COLLABOT MUCOI LUGA MAQI LOBACCONA* ('of Collabot of the tribe of Luga, son of Lobaccona')
2. *MEDUSI MAQI LUG MUCOI LUGA* ('of Medusi, son of Lug of the tribe of Luga')

Drumlohan, Co. Waterford Ogam stones

14 km north-east of Dungarvan, off N25 (Dungarvan–Waterford); take minor road south off N25, 1.5 km south-west of Kilmacthomas. Disc. Ser. 82.

Disturbances to part of the *vallum* surrounding this early monastery resulted in the discovery of a rectangular souterrain chamber, ten of the lintel and sidestones of which were reused ogam stones. These have since been erected along either side of the now-exposed souterrain. There is also a bullaun stone and a millstone. Slightly different readings have been advanced over the years for some of the inscriptions, but the most likely readings are as follows:

1. *MANU MAGUNO GATI MOCOI MACORBO* ('of Manu Maguno Gati of the tribe of Macorbo')
2. *CALUNOVIC[A] MAQI MUCOI MACORBO* ('of Calunovica, son of the tribe of Macorbo')
3. *MAQIINI [. . . MAQI QE]TTEAS* ('of Maqiini, son of Qetteas')
4. *CUNALEGEA MAQI C . . . SALAR CELI AVI QVECI* ('of Cunalegea, son of C . . . salar, follower of the grandson of Qveci')
5. *BIGU MAQI LAG . . .* ('of Bigu, son of Lag . . .')
6. *BIR MAQI MUCOI ROTTIS* ('of Bir, son of the tribe of Rottis')
7. *. . . MAQI NE[TACUN]AS* ('. . ., son of Netacunas')
8. *DENAVEC[A MU]COI MEDALO* ('of Denaveca of the tribe of (?) Medalo')
9. *BRO[INION]AS* ('of Broinionas')
10. *SOVALINI/DEAGOS MAQI MUCO[I . . .]NAI* ('of Sovalini/Deagos, son of the tribe of [I . . .]nai')

Dunabrattin Head, Co. Waterford Promontory forts

20 km south-west of Waterford city, off the R675 (Tramore–Dungarvan coastal route), 2 km west of Annestown. Disc. Ser. 82. Private land.

The coast between Annestown and Bunmahon boasts no fewer than four promontory forts, including one on the point overlooking Corcoran's Island, 0.5 km west of the beach at Annestown and accessible along the cliff path. 2 km further west, as the crow flies, is Dunbrattin Head. This small peninsula boasts two promontory forts, one more or less contained within the other. The larger, covering an area of about 6 ha, is defended by a 105 m long fosse and internal bank (now denuded). Three hut sites have been recorded behind the bank. Along the west side of the promontory is a far smaller citadel-like promontory, cut off by a well-preserved fosse and internal bank. Two enclosures have been identified nearby. The first appears only as a circular crop-mark (40 m in diameter) just outside the main promontory fort, the other (15 m in diameter) near the landward edge of the 'middle finger' of the promontory.

Dunbrody abbey, Co. Wexford Abbey

12 km south of New Ross, off R733 (New Ross–Ballyhack/Arthurstown); signposted. Visitor centre; admission charge. Disc. Ser. 76.

The Cistercian abbey at Dunbrody was a daughter house of St Mary's abbey in **Dublin**, and was founded in 1182 by Hervey de Montmorency, Strongbow's seneschal of the new lordship of Leinster. It was always a strongly Anglicized community and was among the first abbeys to be dissolved, in 1536. The church is a large cruciform structure in Gothic style of *c.*1210–40 and is a fine example of Cistercian austerity, being practically devoid of ornamentation. The presbytery, lit by three plain lancets in the east wall, was never vaulted and originally had little to distinguish it from the nave. The piers of the crossing tower, which now constrict the view from the nave, are a 15th-century addition, like the tower itself. The transepts are particularly large, each containing three rib-vaulted chapels on the east side. The low, barely pointed arches to the transepts are ornamented with banded masonry of yellow limestone and darker sandstone. The south transept retains its night stairs, used by the monks to enter the church from their dormitory for night services. The appearance of this transept is greatly altered by the construction over it of a three-storey manor house in the mid-16th century, to which the mullioned windows, fireplaces, and chimney stacks belong.

The nave has five bays but the arches of the easternmost bay (which was blocked when the tower was added) are narrower and more steeply pointed than the rest—similar to the arches leading from the transepts to the nave aisles. This may indicate a break in construction, with the first bay of the nave contemporary with the presbytery and transepts (*c.*1210–20), and the remainder of the nave slightly later, *c.*1220–40. The clerestory windows of the nave are, in typical Irish fashion, sited over the piers rather than over the aisle arches, an arrangement which ruled out the use of vaulting. The second window from the east is more elaborate than the others, with a double trefoil rear arch ornamented with dog-tooth and engaged shafts. This probably marks the division between the

monks' choir (to the east) and the lay brothers' (to the west). The south
arcade of the nave collapsed in 1852, unfortunately taking with it most
of the west façade—perhaps the most interesting feature of the church.
Antiquarian drawings show a very large west window with an early form
of plate tracery, but only one of the original three lancets survives, with
no trace of the roundels above them and only fragments of the fine
doorway underneath.

The cloister, to the south, was unusually large but is not particularly
well preserved. Only fragments of the 15th-century cloister arcade survive but there are possible traces of a circular lavabo on the south side of
the garth. In the east range there are substantial remains of the sacristy,
chapter house (originally vaulted), slype or passage, and, at the south
end, a vaulted undercroft or cellar. Overhead was the monks' dormitory.
The south range was almost entirely occupied by the refectory, which is
well preserved, with lancet windows in the south wall indicating a 13th-
century date. There is no definite evidence of a west range, which normally housed the lay brothers, but there are traces of the main gateway
to the cloisters, near the south-west angle. Further south, beyond the
claustral buildings, are the ruins of a gatehouse and another structure,
possibly a chapel.

Ferns, Co. Wexford Medieval town

*On the N11, between Gorey and Enniscorthy. Small visitor centre at castle; admis-
sion charge. Disc. Ser. 69.*

Ferns [*Ferna Mór*, 'the great plain'] is today a small market town, but it
originated as a church site, said to have been founded by St Aidan
(Maedhóg) in the 7th century. It seems to have become the main political centre of the local Uí Cheinnselaig (later Mac Murchada) kings of
Leinster from the 11th century. In the early 12th-century reforms,
because of Uí Cheinnselaig influence, Ferns was chosen as the seat of a
diocese. The most famous Uí Cheinnselaig king, Diarmait Mac Murchada, founded an Augustinian abbey at Ferns *c.*1150, rebuilt it in 1169,
and was buried there in 1171. With his death Leinster passed into the
hands of Richard de Clare (Strongbow) and subsequently of his son-in-
law William Marshall. Marshall (or his son) probably built the fine stone
castle at Ferns *c.*1220 and may have founded a town around the same
date. A new cathedral was also erected, probably by John St John, the
first English bishop (1223–43). All of this indicates that Mac Murchada's
former capital was still an important centre of the new lordship of
Leinster. After the Marshall male line failed in 1245, however, Leinster
was divided between five female heiresses, which resulted in a loss of
importance and prosperity for Ferns. By the late 13th century the Anglo-
Irish town was under pressure from the Mac Murchada, the resurgent
descendants of Diarmait Mac Murchada, who eventually regained

control of much of southern Leinster. The town was plundered and burnt by the Scottish army of Edward Bruce *c.*1317, and for most of the later Middle Ages the castle, at least, was held by the Mac Murchada. It is not clear if the town still functioned in the later medieval period, and the modern village seems to be considerably smaller than the 13th-century town. The abbey was dissolved in 1538 and the cathedral was burned in 1577.

Monastic site

The core of the early monastic site is now occupied by the Church of Ireland church, which itself incorporates substantial parts of the chancel of the 13th-century cathedral (*beside the N11 at the east end of the town*). Within the graveyard are the heads of four high crosses of granite with solid rings and little decoration, the base and shaft of another high cross with fret-pattern decoration, and a cross-inscribed grave slab. These cannot be closely dated, but are all probably of 10th–12th-century date. The cathedral was built in the early/mid-13th century, probably by the first English bishop, John St John (1223–43), and was apparently a large structure with nave and choir, both aisled, transepts, and a crossing tower. It must have been quite similar to the contemporary cathedral of St Canice in **Kilkenny**, but all that survives today is part of the aisled choir, forming the eastern end of the modern church. The lancets flanking the central (19th-century) window in the east wall are original 13th-century work, as are the smaller windows above. At the chancel arch of the 19th-century church are surviving 13th-century piers with carved capitals and bases, which mark the eastern responds of the arcades opening onto the north and south choir aisles. No trace is visible of these aisles, or of the transepts, crossing tower or nave, which must have extended considerably further west than the present church. In a niche in the south wall of the present church is a mid-13th-century effigy of a bishop with mitre and (restored) crosier, which may be the effigy of John St John, the builder of the cathedral. Due east of the present church are further remains of what was once a fine building, with arcades of closely spaced lancet windows (originally seven in both the north and south walls) having carved capitals and banded shafts internally. This building is of early/mid-13th-century date, contemporary with the remainder of the cathedral, but its function is uncertain. It was clearly not part of the cathedral, but must have been associated with it in some way. One suggestion is that it was a separate choir built for the canons of the nearby Augustinian abbey.

South-east of the cathedral (but still within the site of the early monastery) is the Augustinian abbey, founded in 1150. The only visible remains consist of the northern side of the church, which was a nave-and-chancel structure with an unusual belfry tower at the west end, a two-storey sacristy on the north, and (originally) a cloister on the south. The tower at the north-west angle is the most interesting feature. Currently 17.5 m high (but higher originally), the tower is square in plan up to the roof level of the church, above which it changes to a circular plan. It contains a rising stair and three doorways in the east wall, which gave access to the nave of the church, to a gallery over the west end of the nave, and to a wall walk on the roof of the church. The upper part of the tower inevitably recalls the traditional round towers of other church sites, and although this is definitely not a round tower, some relationship is possible. It may even represent a form of transition between the detached round tower and the squared belfry, attached to the church, which is typical of later medieval churches. In the external angle between the tower and what remains of the west wall of the church are the bases of columns from the now-vanished west doorway. At the north end of the north wall of the nave a doorway leads into a two-storey annexe on the north side of the chancel. The barrel-vaulted ground floor of this annexe was presumably a sacristy. A stair in the south-east angle rises to a room above (probably residential) and to a chamber which once stood over the chancel. The springings (with ribs) of a barrel vault over the chancel are visible in the wall, below which is a round-headed window flanked by two round-headed niches. The features of the chancel indicate a mid-12th-century date. A cloister stood on the south side of the church, but only foundations survive.

To the north, on the opposite side of the road, is the ruined St Peter's church, a nave-and-chancel church now missing its west end. It is usually suggested that this church is of post-Reformation date (although this is not certain) and that most of the architectural features are taken from elsewhere. Thus the window in the south wall of the chancel, with Romanesque embrasure, may be from the parish church of Clone (c.3 km to the south) or possibly from the Augustinian abbey, while the lancet windows in the east wall may be taken from the cathedral.

Castle

The castle was built in the first quarter of the 13th century by William Marshall, lord of Leinster. Archaeological excavations revealed a pre-castle earthwork and fosse on the east and south-east, probably the remains of a late 12th-century castle. The 13th-century castle was partially built on top of the flattened earthworks of this earlier fortification and originally consisted of a square block with large round corner towers (only half of which now remains). A small group of early 13th-century castles share this distinctive form, all located in Marshall lands, mainly in south-eastern Ireland. Excavations in the 1970s also revealed evidence for a drawbridge and outer barbican on the south side of the castle, now the site of the modern bridge across the fosse. As no evidence for internal walls was revealed, the interior of the castle must have contained wooden walls and floors, but the internal layout is not fully understood. The main structure was entered at first-floor level, which was probably the lord's hall, to judge by the fine fireplace in the east wall and the large two-light windows—also found on the second floor—probably inserted in the mid-13th century. The ground-floor level was only accessible from above and was lit only by narrow loops. It was probably used as cellars for storage. Of the two surviving angle towers the most complete (the south-east tower) has a vaulted basement only accessible from above, which may have served as a prison. At second-floor level this tower contains a fine circular chapel with ribbed vault and trefoil-pointed windows of later 13th-century date.

Fethard, Co. Tipperary Medieval town

15 km south-east of Cashel; take R692 from Cashel or R689 north from Clonmel; signposted. Disc. Ser. 66.

One of the better-preserved medieval towns in Ireland, Fethard [*Fíodh Ard*, 'high wood'] may have been first established by Philip de Worcester in the late 12th century, although it is first documented *c.*1208. It subsequently passed into the hands of the archbishops of **Cashel**. The town received a grant of murage in the 1290s and much of the surviving fabric of the town walls may date to this period. The walls were clearly strengthened in the 15th century, probably through the proceeds of a series of further murage grants made from the late 14th century onwards. This was a period of growing insecurity, and the town was attacked and burned by the earl of Desmond in 1468. The circuit of

▼ **Fig. 143.** Fethard: outline map of town showing medieval features (after Bradley)

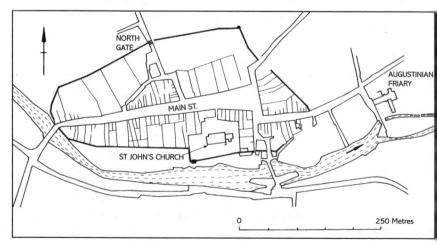

town walls is still almost complete (over 1,100 m in total length) and encloses a roughly oval-shaped area of *c*.5.5 ha on the north bank of the Clashawley river. The internal layout of the town is almost entirely medieval in origin, based on a single Main St. which widens at the east end to form a market place. Other minor streets diverge from this to the north, north-east, east, and south-east. An Augustinian friary, founded in 1306, is located outside the town walls to the east.

The town walls survive up to 6 m high and 1.4 m thick. One of the five original gateways, the 15th-century North Gate survives (*on Sparagoulea, off the north side of Main St.*) as well as two mural towers—a rectangular tower on the south side (see below) and a round turret at the north-east angle (*north side of Barrack St.*). In the external face of the town wall, facing the river near Watergate St., is a sheela-na-gig, a late medieval female exhibitionist figure. The best view of the walls is to be gained by taking the Kilsheelan road (R706) around the south side of the town, from which a new footbridge over the river gives access to a riverside walk outside the parish church. The churchyard is enclosed by the recently restored town wall on the south and south-west, and at the south-west angle is a fine 15th-century mural tower, much like a three-storey tower house and topped by stepped battlements.

Immediately east of the churchyard an urban tower house, probably 15th century, has been built onto the town wall (*interior not accessible*). It is of three storeys—possibly four originally—and barrel vaulted above first-floor level. It has doorways on the north and west sides, traces of fine, large windows in the east wall, and smaller, well-carved cusped ogee-headed windows in the south wall. Also on the south wall is a later garderobe chute. This building is referred to as the 'Bishops' Palace' and although there is no definite evidence for this, it may have been built as a residence for the archbishops of **Cashel**, who were lords of Fethard in the later Middle Ages. Just north-east of this building (*west side of Watergate St.; interior not accessible*) is another large urban tower house known as 'Fethard Castle'. Little is known of its background, but it appears to be a late 15th-/early 16th-century structure of four storeys, which was substantially modified about a century later.

Fethard, typically for English towns in Ireland, had a single parish church—the church of St John, now Holy Trinity Church of Ireland church, located on the south side of Main St. (*key to churchyard available from Whytes Foodstore on Main St.; church usually inaccessible*). It is practically invisible from the street, being hidden by a much-modified 17th-century building known as the Market House, which is possibly the Tholsel (Town Hall) known to have been erected following the reincorporation of the town in 1608. The church is basically of 13th-century date, although much altered subsequently, and consists of a nave-and-chancel structure with a belfry tower at the west end. Only the aisled nave is still roofed and it has been suggested that this shows

Cistercian influence, particularly in the transverse arches over the aisles springing from the arcade piers. The ruined chancel was extensively modified in the late 16th/17th centuries, when the present windows with hood mouldings were inserted and a southern extension was added. The belfry tower is a very attractive late 15th-century addition, crowned by striking parapets and turrets with stepped battlements. The elevations are distinguished by stringcourses and well-carved ogee-headed windows, and the west elevation has a pointed doorway with moulded jambs at ground level, and a large four-light window with flowing tracery above.

Outside the town to the east (*on Abbey St.*) are the ruins of the Augustinian friary, founded in 1306 and dissolved in 1540. The friars continued to occupy the friary periodically until the mid-17th century and returned in the early 19th century, when the church was substantially rebuilt. Although the 19th-century restoration significantly altered the appearance of the church, it still provides a good idea of the feel of a typically long, narrow medieval friary church. Most of its fabric probably dates to the early 14th century, including the two large windows near the east end of the north wall, which display some of the earliest examples of Decorated and switchline tracery in Ireland. Just east of these is a late medieval two-light ogee-headed window with well-tooled mouldings. To the north of the church are the remains of a chapel which formerly opened off the north side of the nave. On the south side of the choir is a large chapel or aisle, accessed through a series of three round arches with fine, late medieval carved mouldings. The friary does not seem to have had a formal cloister, but instead all the domestic chambers were concentrated into a single long range on the south side of the church, which was unusually high at three storeys with an attic storey above. The ground floor was entered through an ogee-headed doorway in the west wall and is divided into three barrel-vaulted chambers, each lit (originally) by two-light ogee-headed windows in the east wall. Smaller, single-light windows replace these at first-floor level; the second-floor windows are mainly missing.

Freestone Hill, Co. Kilkenny Hillfort, cairn, Iron Age sanctuary

7 km east of Kilkenny, on north side of N10 (Kilkenny–Carlow). In private ownership and permission should be sought. Not signposted. Disc. Ser. 67.

Freestone Hill is a somewhat isolated prominence (140 m) marking the southern tip of the Castlecomer plateau, 7 km east of **Kilkenny**. It boasts fabulous views over the middle reaches of the Barrow around Bennetsbridge and south-eastwards past Gowran towards the Barrow Valley. The site comprises a hilltop enclosure (bank and outer fosse) of about 2 ha surrounding, slightly off-centre, a denuded cemetery cairn (23 m in diameter) and later cashel-like, drystone enclosure. Arcuate traces of

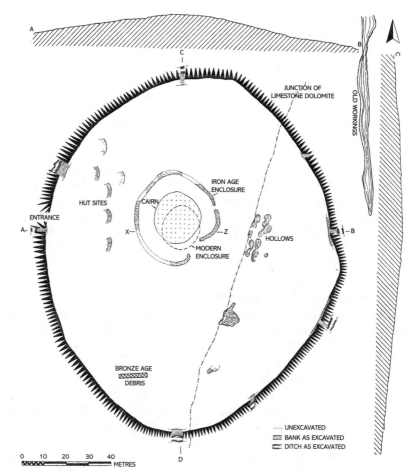

▲ **Fig. 144.** Freestone Hill: plan of site as excavated (after Raftery)

huts can be seen in the north-west quadrant. The site was excavated in 1948–9 by Bersu, after whose death it was published by Raftery (1969). It has recently been reassessed by Ó Floinn (2000). Seven cuttings were placed through the ramparts and the central area was totally excavated.

At least eighteen burials were found in the cairn (fifteen of them cremated), loosely associated with vessels from the Bowl and Vase Traditions, two bone pins, a plaque, and flint and chert implements. An exploratory trench in the south-western quadrant revealed contemporary settlement evidence. The drystone enclosure (about 32 m in diameter) was built around the cairn and the associated habitation layer covered over the now-denuded mound. Coarse ware from this layer matched sherds from under the rampart, implying general contemporaneity and a date in the later Bronze Age.

The recovery of provincial Roman bronzes from the habitation layer is evidence of a third phase of activity when, Ó Floinn argues, the drystone enclosure was used as a shrine, or *temenos*, at which votive offerings (e.g. bracelets) were made in accordance with Roman–British custom. Ó Floinn has further postulated that the area overlooked from Freestone Hill was, in early historic times, a contested boundary between the Laigin and the Osraige, and that this is reflected in ogam inscriptions, of which there are no fewer than ten. Two of these are built into the wall of **Clara** church at the foot of the hill, and a third, reading *MAQI ERACIAS MAQI DIMAQA MUCO[I]* . . . ('of the son of Eracias, son of Dimaqa of the tribe of . . .'), is in Gowran churchyard. Physical manifestation of the boundary is found in the Rathduff linear earthwork (the 'Gripe of the Pig'), which follows the present Carlow–Kilkenny border and can be traced for about 11 km from between Whitehall and Royal Oak to the top of the plateau.

Gaulstown, Co. Waterford Portal tomb

7 km south-west of Waterford city, off N25 (Waterford–Cork). Take R682 towards Tramore, 5 km west of Waterford; site is located roadside off the track leading up Gaulstown Hill near Lisnakill Cross, 2 km south from N25. Disc. Ser. 76.

One of ten Portal tombs in the county, this excellent specimen comprises a thick rectangular capstone resting on two portal stones and a backstone. There are, in addition, two sidestones and a sill or doorstone. It is situated at the bottom of a slope, in the shadow of Sugar Loaf Rock, and is orientated south-east. There is a cist with a large, rectangular roofstone, some 8 m to the south-west of the megalith, which may originally have been inserted into the cairn of the Portal tomb. At the top of the hill is a modest ringfort and another, slightly larger one lies to the southwest of the tomb. Across from this is a motte, overgrown. Knockeen Portal tomb is 3.5 km to the east.

Haroldstown, Co. Carlow Portal tomb

8 km by road north-east of Tullow, on R727 (Carlow–Hacketstown) just after Tobinstown Crossroads; signposted. Disc. Ser. 61.

This excellent example of a Portal tomb comprises two overlapping capstones resting on two fine portal stones and a number of sidestones. The rear capstone inclines to ground level and here is a pile of small stones, possibly the remains of a cairn. The chamber is orientated north-north-west/south-south-east.

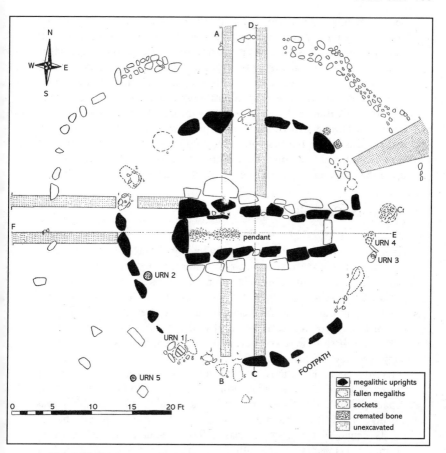

▲ **Fig. 145.** Harristown: plan of site as excavated (after Hawkes)

Harristown, Co. Waterford Passage tomb

12 km south-east of Waterford city, off R684 to Dunmore East; take the link road (east of the R684) 4.5 km north of Dunmore East, turning east (left) at first cross-roads; signposted. Disc. Ser. 76.

One of a small collection of Passage tombs concentrated in the general area of Tramore Bay, this small specimen is situated on the summit of the highest (127 m) of three modest hills, each commanding beautiful panoramic views, particularly to the south and west. The tomb comprises a near-complete megalithic kerb (9.5 m in diameter) with undifferentiated passage (6.1 m long), accessed from the east-north-east. A small sillstone marks the beginning of the passage, which rises towards the back. There are two surviving lintel stones. The remains of a low mound, 15 m in diameter, surround the tomb.

Excavation by Jacquetta Hawkes in 1939 revealed the tomb to have been previously disturbed. All that remained of the original burial deposit were the cremated bones of two individuals and a stone pendant. The site was used as a cemetery during the earlier Bronze Age when seven secondary burials were inserted into the mound. It is possible that the primary mound was enlarged at this point. All these burials, with one possible exception, appear to have been in pits. Three were accompanied by Cordoned Urns (one with a bronze knife, a quoit-shaped faience bead, and a perforated bone pin) and one had a fragmented, decorated Bowl. In the base of another pit were two partially cremated young adult males, accompanied by a perforated bone pin, and higher up in the same pit another more thoroughly cremated adult male.

Jerpoint, Co. Kilkenny Abbey

On N9 (Dublin–Waterford), 2 km south of Thomastown. Disc. Ser. 67.

Jerpoint was probably founded *c.*1160 by Dónal Mac Gilla Pátraic, king of Ossory. There are suggestions that it was a Benedictine abbey, rather than Cistercian, until 1180. However, the architecture of the earliest parts—the presbytery (chancel) and transepts, built *c.*1160–80—suggests that Jerpoint was Cistercian from the outset. After the English conquest Jerpoint was seen as a centre of resistance to English control within the Irish Cistercian community. In 1228, however, it was made subject to the English abbey of Fountains, its abbot was deposed and forced to go to Fountains, and an adjacent monastery for nuns was closed. A papal indulgence was granted in 1442 to raise funds for the repair of the cloisters, belfry, and other buildings. The abbey was dissolved in 1540, although the nave continued in use as a parish church.

The plan of the abbey is classically Cistercian, with a cruciform church and cloisters to the south. The church is entered through a door in the north wall of the nave. As you enter, look up at the projecting machicolation overhead—a defensive feature added in the turbulent late Middle Ages. The aisled nave is later than the presbytery and transepts, probably built *c.*1170–1200, although the easternmost bay has decorated capitals similar to the presbytery and is probably contemporary with it. The arcade of six bays consists of pointed arches and round-headed clerestory windows. The arches rest on alternating round and square piers, themselves rising from low perpyn walls, which formed the backs of the monks' and lay brothers' stalls. Across the middle of the nave are the foundations of a screen wall which separated the monks' and lay brothers' choirs.

The square, barrel-vaulted presbytery and the transepts, each with two vaulted chapels, are typical of the earliest Cistercian churches and reminiscent of the Burgundian abbeys from which the first Cistercians came to Ireland. The characteristic Cistercian plainness is somewhat relieved, however, by several decorated capitals. The traceried east

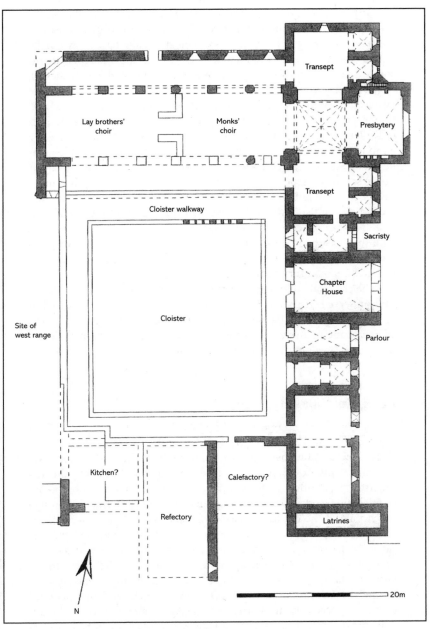

▲ **Fig. 146.** Jerpoint abbey: plan (after O'Keefe)

window is an early 14th-century replacement—originally there were three Romanesque round-headed windows (and probably at least one more over them), the stringcourses of which can still be seen externally. Similar round-headed windows still survive in the transepts. In the south wall of the presbytery is a fine Romanesque sedilia with chevron ornament; in the opposite wall are tomb niches with traces of late medieval wall painting above. Two effigies of bishops or abbots are mounted in the presbytery. The earlier (to the east) is said to represent Felix O'Dullany (d. 1202), first abbot of Jerpoint and later bishop of Ossory, although the effigy itself may be 20–30 years later. The other effigy may be considerably later, perhaps late 14th century. In the southern chapel of the south transept are two incised grave slabs, an early 14th-century slab of an abbot holding his crosier, and a very unusual late 13th-century incised slab of two armoured knights. In the chapels of the north transept are two 16th-century tomb chests with images of the apostles, each with their distinctive attribute, set within niches. The impressive crossing tower, with its corner turrets and typically Irish stepped battlements, is a later 15th-century addition.

The claustral buildings, especially the south and west ranges, are not well preserved. However, the reconstructed cloister arcade of c.1400 is unique, not only in Ireland but in the Cistercian world generally. The rich pageant of lively sculptured figures, human and animal, found mainly on the piers of the arcade, is quite at odds with Cistercian austerity.

Kells, Co. Kilkenny Priory

13 km south of Kilkenny; take R697 (Kilkenny–Carrick-on-Suir) to Kells village and take minor road to east in village for 600 m; signposted. Disc. Ser. 67.

Kells [*Cealla*, 'churches'] is probably the most impressive medieval monastic complex in Ireland. The priory was founded c.1193 by the new English lord, Geoffrey de Marisco, for Augustinian canons from Bodmin in England. Geoffrey also built a motte castle and established a borough on the site of the modern village of Kells, a short distance west of the priory. The church was probably constructed by c.1220, and the east range of the cloister soon after this. The remainder of the cloister was built by the early 14th century, by which date the church had already been substantially enlarged. Kells (probably including the priory) was burned by Edward Bruce's Scottish army in 1316 and this heralded increasing insecurity in the later Middle Ages, as English control gradually broke down. The response at Kells was the construction, in the late 15th century, of a large walled enclosure, fortified with large towers, to the south of the priory. The immediate precinct of the priory was already defended, and the purpose of the new enclosure seems to have been to provide refuge in case of attack for the local population,

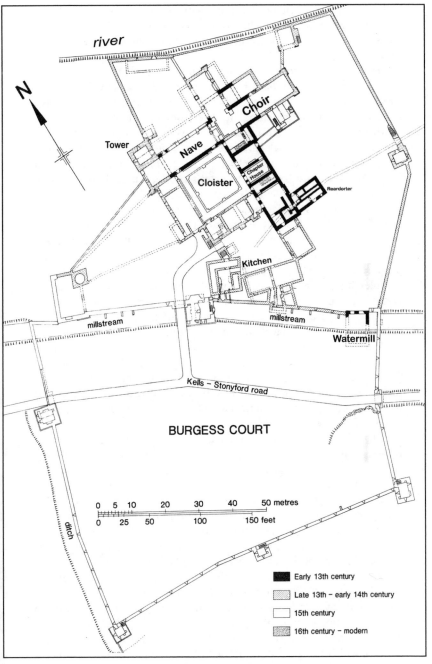

▲ **Fig. 147.** Kells priory: plan (after Tietzsch-Tyler)

including monastic tenants and the inhabitants of the borough—hence the name 'Burgess Court'. The priory was dissolved in 1540 and some parts were subsequently occupied, but gradually the buildings fell into disuse.

The priory is sited on low-lying ground on the banks of the King's river, and may actually have been on an island originally, if the mill-stream which ran around the southern side of the priory buildings was a natural channel. Approaching the site from the high ground to the south-east, the walls of Burgess Court are first met with. This is an irregular rectangular enclosure, c.95 m by c.75 m and c.0.7 ha in area. The curtain wall is up to 6 m high and 1 m thick, with regular arrow loops, and there are traces of an external fosse, especially on the west side. The wall is strengthened by rectangular mural towers at the south-west and south-east angles, midway along the north and south sides, and near the north end of the west side. The western and south-eastern towers are large five-storeyed structures—effectively like tower houses—and are equipped for residential use, but they obviously had a defensive purpose also. The south-east tower occupies the highest point in the complex and, in a sense, overlooks it. The western tower guarded a gateway at the entry point from the village of Kells. Curiously, another gateway on the east side was apparently not defended by any tower, although there is a machicolation overhead and the curtain wall is thickened around the vaulted gate passage to provide additional space for defenders overhead. No internal features are visible within Burgess Court, but there are the remains of a watermill—possibly 13th cen-tury—in the north-east corner, sited over a millstream (now vanished) which ran along the southern edge of the priory precinct, adjoining Burgess Court on the north.

The priory precinct is also walled, apparently at an earlier date than Burgess Court. Midway along its southern side is a gateway providing access to and from Burgess Court via a bridge over the millstream. It is guarded by a particularly large, five-storey tower to the east, which also spans the millstream. The western side of the precinct is poorly defended, although there seems to have been a wall running from the south-west angle of the precinct towards the west end of the church. The tower attached to the north-west angle of the church may well have functioned as a belfry, but its location suggests that it also had a defen-sive function as part of the monastic enclosure, particularly in guarding a small gateway attached to the north side. From here the enclosure ran north to the river and returned eastwards along the river bank. Near the east end of this section, along the river bank, is another tower, while midway along the east side, a three-storey tower guards a postern gate, beneath which the great drain flowed out of the precinct. Much of the precinct was occupied by the large church and the extensive cloister and associated buildings to the south.

The church and cloister are not as well preserved as the enclosure of Burgess Court, but their layout and main features can be easily reconstructed. The early 13th-century church was cruciform, with nave, choir, and transepts. It is now rather lopsided in plan, as it was considerably extended on the north side but not on the south, because of the presence of the cloister. North of the nave an aisle ran between the transept and the belfry tower at the north-west angle. The transept itself was greatly enlarged, probably in the late 13th/early 14th century, with a considerable extension to the north and the addition of aisles on both east and west sides (only the western aisle arcade survives). In the north gable is an inserted 16th-century window. Opening off the north transept, on the north side of the choir, is a large Lady Chapel. Both this chapel and the choir itself were extended considerably to the east—the footings of the original east wall can be seen running across the choir. Similarly, the nave was extended to the west, probably when the north-west tower was erected. All told, the combined nave and choir were enlarged by more than 50 per cent, while the north transept was enlarged to an even greater degree. Such a massive enlargement is very unlikely in the troubled later Middle Ages, and can probably be dated to the late 13th/early 14th century. The lancet windows in the west wall of the nave and south wall of the extended choir (where the later tower was built on) suggest a 13th-century date for these extensions.

The pointed door beneath these lancets was inserted to provide access to the four-storey tower erected on the south side of the choir, probably in the later 15th century. The tower has a fireplace at first-floor level and windows with seats at first and second floors and is clearly designed for residential use, possibly for the prior. The low, rather squat crossing tower is an addition, probably of the 15th century. It rests on masonry piers built onto the original openings of the crossing. The opening to the south transept was almost entirely blocked, and this has helped to preserve the sandstone mouldings of the original opening. In contrast to the north transept, this transept remains at its original size. Against the south wall can be seen the base of the night stairs, which provided access to the church from the canons' dormitory (at first-floor level in the east range of the cloister) for night services. As in many monastic churches, the nave has doorways in the south wall facing the east and west cloister ambulatories. That to the east was the ceremonial doorway, through which the Augustinian community entered the church in procession on formal occasions. The other doorway was probably used on less formal occasions and by laypeople, although there is also a late, inserted doorway in the west wall that may have been for the laity.

The cloister, on the south, is not well preserved, although its ground plan is complete. Only fragments survive of the 14th-century cloister arcade with trefoil-headed openings. The ambulatories surrounding the cloister garth have also disappeared, but their roof lines and the corbels which supported their lean-to roofs can be seen in the walls of the surrounding buildings. In the west and north ambulatories there are stone benches built into the adjoining walls, as well as two tomb niches in the north ambulatory (in the church wall). The east range is probably early 13th century, to judge by the surviving doorway and round-headed windows at the entrance to the chapter house. A single window from the dormitory (which occupied the entire first floor of the range) also survives overhead. The building projecting to the rear of the east range, at the southern end, was probably the reardorter—the latrine attached to the dormitory, sited over the main drain for sanitary purposes. The south range is the best-preserved part of the cloister. Like the west range, it was probably built in the late 13th/early 14th century. The ground-floor chambers were probably used mainly for storage but the western chamber contained a stair to the refectory overhead. It also has a good doorway to the ambulatory and the lavabo (a stone trough in which the canons washed their hands before eating) in the external wall. The refectory was lit by five twin-light pointed windows in the south wall and a larger (and probably later) traceried window in the west wall. At the east end of the south wall is the projecting *pulpitum*, from which devotional literature was read to the canons as they ate. A doorway (blocked) in the west wall gave access to the refectory from the outer precinct, via an external stone stair. Another doorway, in the south wall nearby, gave access from the kitchens located in a free-standing block to the south. The west range was probably used largely for storage, at ground-floor level, while the upper floor may have been used as guest accommodation.

The kitchen block and the south range form the west and north sides of another courtyard, south of the cloisters. The kitchen block is divided into three rooms—the middle room is the kitchen proper, with a large fireplace against the west wall and two stone-lined drains running through it. The western boundary of this courtyard is formed by a later chamber, built onto the south end of the east range. This was apparently a workshop—excavations in the 1970s found evidence for lead working, probably connected to the repair of windows or roofing. The south side of the courtyard was formed by a rectangular block divided into two chambers, possibly the infirmary. A passage runs south from both chambers to a doorway in the precinct wall, beyond which there is evidence for a structure sited over the millstream, most likely a latrine.

Kilcooly, Co. Tipperary Abbey

Between Kilkenny (21 km) and Thurles (16 km); take N8 (Dublin–Cork) to Urling-
ford, then R689 towards Killenaule; 3 km south of Urlingford take R690 towards
Ballingarry for 2 km, then minor road to east; signposted. Disc. Ser. 67.

The origins of the well-preserved Cistercian abbey of Kilcooly [*Cill Cúile*, 'the church of the nook'] are somewhat uncertain. In 1182 Domhnall Mór Ó Briain, king of Thomond, granted the lands for a new Cistercian monastery to the abbot of the early medieval monastic site of *Daire Mór*. It is possible that the new monastery was Benedictine until 1184, when it was affiliated to the Cistercian abbey of **Jerpoint**. Aerial photography has revealed a large circular crop-mark, *c.*70 m in diameter, located *c.*120 m east of the ruins of the abbey. This may be the site of the earlier monastery of *Daire Mór*, but this has not been confirmed. As at **Jerpoint**, the abbot of Kilcooly was deposed when English control over the order was enforced in 1228. The abbey was burned in 1418 and by 1444 it had apparently been largely destroyed by wars, but it was sub-stantially rebuilt in the later 15th century, probably with the patronage of the Butlers of Ormond. It was dissolved in 1540 but the church continued in use as a parish church, and seems to have been reoccupied by Cistercian monks in the later 16th and early 17th centuries.

Kilcooly is inevitably compared with **Holycross**, another Cistercian abbey in Tipperary which was rebuilt in the 15th century. There are many points of comparison, and **Holycross** was clearly an important source of inspiration, but Kilcooly is neither as well built nor as ornate as its wealthier sister house. Although the church, as it currently exists, is largely of late 15th-century construction, some of the original late 12th-/early 13th-century fabric remains in the nave and presbytery, especially at the west end of the nave. The west window is early 16th century, however. The original church had nave aisles but the plain arches of the aisle arcades were blocked in the 15th-century rebuilding—a reduction in the size of the church which suggests a smaller monastic community in the late Middle Ages. The rebuilt east end has barrel-vaulting over the presbytery and ribbed lierne vaults over the crossing and transepts. The presbytery is lit by a large, six-light window with curvilinear tracery, inserted into the larger opening occupied by the original windows. Over the crossing is a typically low, massive 15th-century tower—the lowest of any Irish Cistercian church. Note the unique stone stalls for the abbot and prior, built into the western piers. The transepts are entirely of 15th-century construction and are of a fairly standard two-bay plan with a chapel at the east end of each bay. The north transept is noticeably larger than the southern one and has more elaborate vaulting, supported on a central pier. The south transept is mainly distinguished for the elaborate sculptured wall dividing it from the sacristy to the south. The doorway to the sacristy has elaborate mouldings in five orders and is surrounded by several carved panels, including a mermaid with comb and mirror, an abbot, St Christopher carrying the infant Christ, a *Crucifixion*, and two heraldic shields bearing the arms of the Butlers of Ormond. Beneath the shields is a piscina, confirming that the transept was used as a chapel, and perhaps the best explanation for the presence of this elaborately carved wall in an obscure corner of the church is that this was a private chapel of the Butler family.

Among the funerary monuments in the church is the fine effigy of Piers Fitz James Oge Butler (d. 1526), in a wall recess in the presbytery. It shows the Butler nobleman in typical late medieval Irish armour and is signed by the sculptor, Rory O'Tunney. The front of the tomb consists of two slabs, with a series of ogee-headed niches containing figures of ten of the twelve apostles, their names carved above the niches. The last three figures—Bartholomew, Simon, and Thaddeus—are on a separate slab, which probably formed one end of the tomb originally. Nearby, in the floor of the presbytery, is the grave slab of Abbot Philip O'Molanayn (d. 1463), who went to England after the destruction of the abbey in 1445 to seek food and clothing for his monks, and may have begun the subsequent rebuilding of the abbey. The grave slab shows the figure of the abbot, holding his crosier and book, in false relief. Above him, on a heraldic shield, are the symbols of the Passion (cross, crown of thorns, hammer and nails, ladder, etc.).

The night stairs, which provided access to the church for the monks from their dormitory, for night offices, are unusually located in the thickness of the south wall of the transept. Overhead is a large residential chamber, possibly the abbot's. The claustral buildings have been considerably modified for post-medieval occupancy, and few definitely original chambers remain. The most interesting conventual building is not in the cloister at all, but located just to the south-east of it. This is a large two-storey structure with vaulted undercroft and hall-like chamber above, approached by a mural stair in the west wall. Although it, too, has seen considerable post-medieval modification, it probably dates to the late 15th/early 16th centuries and may have been the abbot's lodging. Some distance to the north-east of the church is a small round building with a vaulted roof. The small recesses in the internal wall face identify it as a *columbarium* or dovecote, where pigeons were kept as rare delicacies for the monks' table.

Kilkenny, Co. Kilkenny Medieval town

On N10, 40 km south-west of Carlow. Disc. Ser. 67.

As the name indicates, Kilkenny [*Cill Cainnigh*, 'the church of Cainnech'] owes its origins to a monastic site associated with the 6th-century St Cainnech (Canice), although the earliest contemporary reference is in 1085. Kilkenny was overshadowed by Cainnech's other foundation at

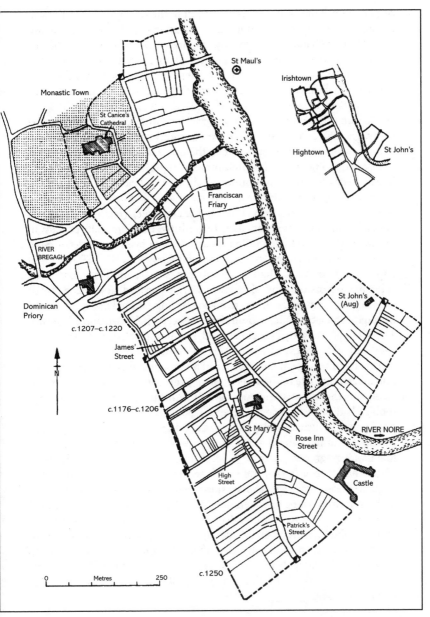

▲ **Fig. 148.** Kilkenny: outline map of town showing main medieval features (after Bradley)

Aghaboe until the early 12th century, but in the reforms of 1111 the seat of the diocese of the kingdom of Osraige was assigned to Kilkenny, rather than Aghaboe. The growing importance of Kilkenny—indicated by the fact that the 12th-century kings of Ossory had a residence there— was confirmed after the English conquest when Strongbow, as lord of Leinster, established a castle and town there *c.*1173. The monastic site (now marked by St Canice's cathedral) was located on a slight knoll overlooking the confluence of the river Nore with a small tributary, the Breagagh. The castle was located on another knoll, *c.*700 m downriver, and the new town grew up between the castle and the Breagagh. It was subsequently known as the Hightown or Englishtown, to distinguish it from a separate borough around the monastic site, under the bishop's control and known as the Irishtown.

The new town developed along a main street (High St.) running parallel to the river from the castle towards the cathedral. The properties of the burgesses stretched in long, narrow plots from the street back to the town wall, separated by laneways now known as 'slips'. The Butter Slip, running between High St. and Kieran St., is a good example. Considerable expansion took place after 1207 when William Marshall, the new lord of Leinster, acquired from the bishop all the land south of the Bregagh, which became the boundary between Hightown and Irishtown. The establishment of Franciscan and Dominican friaries, immediately south of the Bregagh, by *c.*1225–30 indicates that the town had expanded to this boundary by then. The Franciscan friary occupied the north-eastern angle of the walled town, while the Dominican priory was on the north-west, just outside the walls. An Augustinian monastery (St John's) had been founded on the opposite (east) bank of the Nore by 1211 and a suburban settlement developed around it. Kilkenny received a series of murage grants from 1248 to 1460 and most of the surviving town wall fragments seem to be 13th century, with some evidence of 15th-century repairs. The wall enclosed three sides of a roughly rectangular area—there was no riverside wall—and had four mural towers and seven gates (none of which survive). The Irishtown also had its own wall. In the late 14th century Kilkenny passed into the hands of the powerful Butler earls of Ormond, who provided an enduring source of patronage. This, and Kilkenny's location at the heart of the only area in which the Anglo-Irish colony continued to thrive in the late Middle Ages, ensured the continuing prosperity of the town, reflected in the surviving buildings.

St Canice's cathedral

The original monastic site is largely occupied by St Canice's cathedral and its churchyard. The cathedral is a 13th-century structure, and the main visible trace of the earlier monastic site is the round tower beside

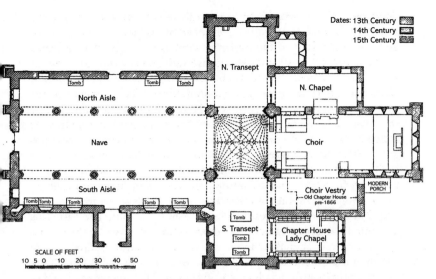

▲ Fig. 149. Kilkenny: plan of St Canice's cathedral (after Leask)

the south transept, erected in the 11th/early 12th century. Some loose carved stones, apparently from a Romanesque-style building of *c.*1150–75, have also been found. The round tower is 30 m high at present, but the battlements at the summit are a later medieval addition and with its original conical roof the tower would have been somewhat higher. There are seven floors, which can be climbed to the top. 19th-century excavations revealed that the foundations of the tower are remarkably shallow (little more than 0.6 m) and rest on earlier burials. This has had the effect of causing a slight leaning in the tower as the underlying soil settled. The round-headed doorway, 2.8 m above ground, faces south-east, away from the present cathedral, which suggests that the principal church of the monastic site may not have been on the site of the cathedral.

The cathedral is one of the most important and attractive medieval churches in Ireland, and is unusually coherent and harmonious for such a large church (by Irish standards). It is cruciform, with an aisled nave, transepts, crossing tower, and a relatively long choir. Its fabric is also remarkably intact—although considerable restoration took place in the 19th century, this was far less drastic than in the **Dublin** cathedrals and most of the architectural detail is original. The present building was probably begun by Hugh de Rous, the first English bishop of Ossory (1202–18). Parts of the choir seem to be of this period, notably the fine array of triple lancets at the east end, with trefoil-headed rear arches, banded shafts, and low-relief stiff-leaf capitals. The round-headed lancets in the north and south walls of the choir and the round-headed doorway of the north transept can hardly be later than Bishop Hugh's time. The entire eastern half of the cathedral, including choir, crossing, and the lower parts of the transepts with their chapels, was probably built c.1210–30. The style is rather conservative and broadly English, but not as clearly focused as the south-western English style of the **Dublin** cathedrals. There are some later medieval features. The original crossing tower fell in 1332 and was replaced c.1350 by the present low tower. Over the crossing is the largest medieval ribbed vault surviving in Ireland, added in the mid-15th century. In the north wall of the north transept is a fine trefoil-headed recess, probably inserted while the nave was being built (c.1245–60) to house the tomb of a bishop—most likely Hugh de Mapilton (d. 1256). The tomb front beneath the niche is 16th century. The Lady Chapel, at the south-eastern corner of the south transept, was added in the 1280s (and restored in the 1860s). Its south and east walls are entirely occupied by lancet windows, in groups of two or three.

The nave is later than the choir, c.1245–60, and displays a more common use of limestone dressings, in contrast to the sandstone of the earlier work. Its aisle arcades are of five bays with large pointed arches carried on pillars of quatrefoil plan. There is no triforium and the quatrefoil-shaped clerestory windows are placed above the arches, rather than over the piers—which ruled out the use of vaulting. The present ceiling and roof (like those of the transepts and choir) are restored. In the west wall is a graduated triplet of tall lancet windows. Beneath these, internally, is an unusual arcade, effectively a scaled-down version of the west doorway below; its purpose is uncertain. The west doorway itself (probably c.1260) may be a simplified version of the west doorway of Wells cathedral, in England. It has twin openings with pointed, cin-quefoiled heads and with a quatrefoil recess above, all set within a large pointed arch of two orders. The quatrefoil over the doorways probably held a carving, perhaps (as at Wells) a *Virgin and Child*. Flanking it are smaller, shallower recesses retaining worn carvings of angels. The cathedral is normally entered through the south porch, an original (mid-13th-century) feature. Note the heads of tonsured clerics and mitred bishops among the foliage on the capitals of the outer arch.

While much of the interior furnishing was lost to Cromwellian iconoclasm, St Canice's retains the finest collection of medieval funerary monuments in Ireland. The most important is the tomb of Piers Butler, earl of Ormond (d. 1539), and his wife Margaret FitzGerald, in the south transept. Also worth seeing are the effigy of Bishop Richard de Ledrede (d. 1360), in a niche in the north wall of the chancel (not its original position); the effigy of James Schortals (1507) near the west end of the north aisle; an early 16th-century altar tomb with the effigy of an unidentified lady, in the south aisle just west of the porch; the tomb of Richard Butler (d. 1571), in the south aisle just east of the porch; and the very archaic tomb of Honorina Grace (d. 1596), near the west end of the south aisle.

Franciscan friary

The Franciscan friary was founded *c.*1231 by Richard Marshall. It was officially dissolved in 1540 but probably not effectively suppressed until 1559, and was reoccupied by Franciscans for a period in the 17th century. Its remains now stand rather forlornly within the busy yard of Smithwick's brewery (*north-east side of Parliament St.; not generally accessible*). What survives is the mid-13th-century choir of the church, with an east front of *c.*1320 featuring a window of seven graduated, conjoined lancets. This is the largest lancet window in Ireland, where lancets continued to be used even after more advanced forms of traceried windows were introduced. The tower at the west end of the choir was probably added in the 1340s, although not completed until the 15th century. It is probably the earliest known example of the typically slender towers which were inserted in so many friaries in the later Middle Ages.

Dominican priory

The Dominican priory, known as the 'Black Abbey', was founded *c.*1225 by William Marshall (*on Abbey St., south side of Dean St.*). It was dissolved in 1540, but was reoccupied by Dominicans for a period in the 17th century. Much of the church survives and is still used as a parish church, although the choir was demolished in the 18th century. The nave and south aisle are probably 13th century and the fine south transept was added *c.*1300. It has several good 14th-century windows, particularly the magnificent south window of five lights with Decorated switchline tracery, probably erected *c.*1340. The crossing tower was erected in 1527. A memorial to the builders, James Shortall and his wife Katherine Whyte, is inscribed on the north side of the choir arch. It is not a typical friary tower, being closer to the stout Cistercian model seen, for instance, at nearby **Jerpoint**, and has particularly striking stepped battlements (also seen on the nave and transept) and turrets at the angles. At the west end of the church is the lower part of another tower, of 15th-century date. Part of the west range of claustral buildings survives to the north.

St Mary's church

St Mary's church (*between High St. and Kieran St.*) was founded before 1205 as the parish church for the town. Although heavily modified, enough survives to show that the 13th-century church was a substantial cruciform building, with transepts and an aisled nave. The much-restored tower at the west end is probably 15th century and the graveyard contains some interesting medieval monuments.

St John's church

St John's church (*John St., on the east side of the Nore*) was completed in 1220 for the Augustinian priory and hospital of St John, probably founded in 1211. The priory was dissolved in 1540 but the church continued in parochial use. The earliest part of the surviving fabric is the mid-13th-century choir, distinguished by its very fine east window of two triple lights within moulded rear arches, with foiled circular window above. In the south wall are two twin-light windows with a very early form of switchline tracery. The Lady Chapel, now in use by the Church of Ireland, dates from *c.*1280 and is famous for its magnificent run of continuous windows in the south wall. These consist of five triplets of close-set trefoil pointed lights, but the second and fourth triplet are now blocked, spoiling the intended effect of a continuous wall of glass. A small fragment of vaulted claustral building survives on the north side.

Secular buildings

Midway along Parliament St. is Rothe House, now the museum and bookshop of the Kilkenny Archaeological Society. It was the town house of one of Kilkenny's most important merchant families, and is the finest surviving example of such a house in Ireland. The complex actually consists of three distinct houses separated by two courtyards, running back along the burgage plot. The fine house on the street, with its arcaded front, was built first, in 1594, while the third house, at the rear of the complex, was the latest, built probably in 1610.

The Shee Almshouse, on Rose Inn St., was built in 1582 by Sir Richard Shee to house six male and six female paupers. Restored in 1978–81, it now houses a Tourist Office and a fine scale model, which serves as a good introduction to the medieval town. Also worth visiting is Kyteler's Inn on Kieran Street. This substantial medieval building was apparently the residence of the Kyteler family whose most famous member, Dame Alice, was burned as a witch in the 14th century. The building was much altered in later centuries and very crudely restored in the 1970s, but it retains many of its original features, including a fine vaulted undercroft or basement, now used as a restaurant.

Castle

The southern end of the town is marked by the castle which, although substantially modified in eight centuries of occupation, still retains a substantial medieval core. The present structure was begun by William Marshall, probably *c.*1192, on the site of Strongbow's castle. Recent excavations revealed traces of a large circular fosse under the west side of the castle, probably the fosse of a ringwork erected by Strongbow. As finally built the castle was a trapezoidal enclosure with large drum towers at the four corners. One of these, the east tower, is now missing, as is the curtain wall on the south-east side, where the original gatehouse was probably located. The present entrance, on the south-west side, is a late 17th-century insertion. The castle was continuously occupied throughout its history and as a result has been greatly modified on several occasions, particularly in the late 17th and mid-19th centuries. As presented today the castle interiors are mainly Victorian in aspect, but nevertheless well worth visiting. The castle is now in state care (*admission generally by guided tour only; note that this is a very busy site and visitors may experience delays during summer months*).

Kilree, Co. Kilkenny Early church site

*15 km south of Kilkenny; follow directions to **Kells Priory** and take minor road to south from car park there for 2 km, keeping right at fork after 1 km; signposted. Disc. Ser. 67.*

Kilree [*Cill Ruidhche*, 'the church of Ruidhche'] was clearly an early monastic site of some importance, as the presence of an early high cross, church, and round tower indicate, but nothing is known of its early history. It preserves the name of a little-known female saint, Ruidhche, although the church is now associated with St Brigid. The visible remains span the period from the late 8th to 12th centuries, and the monastery passed into the hands of the nearby Augustinian priory of **Kells** in the early 13th century.

The church, typically small and simple, displays antae on the gables and a flat-lintelled west doorway, suggesting a 10th–12th-century date. The chancel, with its round chancel arch, is a later addition. The round tower, 11 m north of the church, is almost intact, although its original roof has been replaced by battlements of uncertain date. It is *c*.27 m high with seven floors, but would have been somewhat taller with its roof intact. An interesting feature of the tower is the squared plinth visible at the base (from the outside of the graveyard). There are single windows at the second-, third-, and fourth-floor levels and four evenly spaced windows at the top floor. The round-headed doorway, *c*.2.5 m above original ground level, faces south towards the west end of the church.

The high cross stands *c*.50 m west of the present churchyard and may well mark the western edge of an original enclosure, the other edge of which is reflected in the curved line of the graveyard wall on the east. If so, this would indicate an original oval enclosure measuring *c*.90 m east–west and *c*.65 m north–south. The slight curve in the road east of the graveyard may also reflect the presence of a larger outer enclosure. The cross is probably of late 8th-/early 9th-century date and belongs to the early Ossory group of crosses best exemplified by those at **Ahenny**—although it may be slightly later in date than the Ahenny crosses. Most of the decoration covering the cross is abstract and geometric, consisting of fret, step, and chequer patterns, spirals, and some interlace. Figure scenes are relatively rare but, unlike Ahenny, at Kilree these are found on the cross itself and not just the cross base. The figure scenes are badly weathered, but probably include *Daniel in the Lions' Den* (west face, top of shaft), *Jacob Wrestling with the Angel* and *David/Samson Killing a Lion* (north side, end of cross arm), and *Hunting scenes?* (east face, cross arms).

▼ **Fig. 150.** Monavullagh: map showing locations of monuments (after Moore)

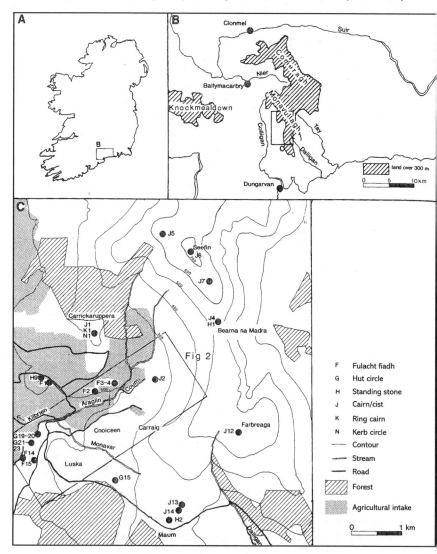

Monavullagh Mountains Prehistoric complex

11 km north of Dungarvan, east of the R672 to Clonmel and overlooking Kilbrien. Most of the sites are accessible off the mountain paths. Disc. Ser. 82.

An intriguing array of monuments awaits the dedicated fieldwalker on the western slopes of Coumaraglin Mountain, at the south-western tip of the Monavullagh Mountains, in south-central Co. Waterford. Here Michael Moore has identified an upland prehistoric complex, covering an area of 2 km². The remains occur in the headwater valleys of the Araglin and Monavar rivers, north of Dungarvan Harbour and over-looking the village of Kilbrien. Hidden by heather and ferns (in summer), they are more easily found during the winter months. Regrettably, most of the monuments on Scartnadriny Mountain (overlooking the Araglin Valley from the north) have been damaged or destroyed by forestry. Those that survive include three fulachta fiadh and a stone pair. The commanding positions of standing stones in the complex suggest that they demarcate the periphery of the complex, excellent examples being the 2.3 m tall stone (and nearby cist) in the Beara na Madra pass overlooking the valley from the north and the 1.95 m tall conglomerate at the top of Maum Pass.

The major concentration of monuments is on the south side of the valley, on the slopes of Coumaraglin Mountain. Here Moore in addition to numerous, small field-clearance cairns and features associated with transhumance grazing (booleying), are four prehistoric enclosures, 12 fulachta fiadh, 23 hut sites, 12 standing stones, stone rows, cairns, and cairn circles, nine kerb circles, a ring barrow, and a possible embanked enclosure. None of the sites has been excavated.

St Mullins, Co. Carlow Early monastic site

11 km north of New Ross, off R729 (New Ross–Borris); take minor road to west at Drummin Bridge; signposted. Disc. Ser. 68.

St Mullins [*Tech Moling*, 'the church of Moling'] bears the name of its 7th-century founder Moling, one of the first of the *Célí Dé* (an ascetic reform movement prominent in the 8th/9th-century Irish Church). Located on a promontory above the confluence of the river Barrow and a tributary, it was an important monastery, closely associated with **Ferns** and **Glendalough**, and was a burial place of the kings of Leinster. Even after it was annexed to the Augustinian abbey at **Ferns** *c.*1160, it was used as a burial place of the later medieval Mac Murchada kings. The important 8th-century Book of Moling (*now in Trinity College, Dublin*) is associated with this monastery and was quite possibly produced there. After the English conquest in the late 12th century, St Mullins came under the control of William de Carew, who presumably had the motte-and-bailey castle built. A borough was also established by the early 13th century and the rebuilding of the town is recorded in 1347, but it had probably ceased to function before the end of the 14th century as St Mullins reverted to Mac Murchada control.

The visible remains of the monastery (*in the graveyard of the Church of Ireland parish church*) include five churches and a round tower. Immediately south of the 19th-century church is the oldest church, the *Teampull Mór* ('great church')—a nave-and-chancel structure, of which only the chancel and the gable ends of the nave survive. There are indications that the gable ends of the nave had antae originally, which would suggest an early—perhaps 10th/11th-century—date for the nave. The pointed west doorway, the chancel arch, and the chancel itself are later additions, probably 15th century. The chancel arch is now blocked and above it is a later double belfry. Just outside the *Teampull Mór*, to the east, is the upper portion and base of a granite high cross with solid ring. The base is probably 9th/10th century, but the cross head bears a large *Crucifixion*, suggesting a 12th-century date.

South of the *Teampull Mór* is the largest church, known as the 'Abbey', dating to the late Middle Ages. It was a simple rectangular structure, divided into nave and slightly narrower chancel, but most of the walls survive to only a few feet above ground. The chancel had a stone vault with a chamber (probably residential) above, which was accessed by a spiral stair built into the north-west corner. In the chancel are an original altar, piscina, and sedilia. The nave was modified for residential use, probably in the 16th century, when a fireplace was inserted into the chancel arch and corbels were built into the north and south walls. In the south-west angle is the base of a spiral stair that provided access to the raised doorway of a round tower, immediately to the south of the church. Only the base of this round tower survives. The wall, *c*.1 m high and *c*.1.2 m thick, shows the nature of the fabric usually used in such structures—a rubble core sandwiched between two faces of coursed granite masonry. Although now physically attached to the 'Abbey', the round tower is older (probably 11th/12th century) and was originally free-standing. Its north-facing doorway was almost certainly intended to face the west doorway of an earlier church on the site of the *Teampull Mór*.

To the east of the 'Abbey' is a tiny shrine or oratory dedicated to St James. Its date is uncertain. South of the 'Abbey' are two further structures with lintelled west doorways and lintelled windows. Both are possibly churches, but probably of post-medieval date. The smaller structure is now a mausoleum for the Kavanagh family (descendants of the Mac Murchada kings of Leinster) and had annexes to the north and east, only foundations of which remain. The larger building displays two niches and an unusual diamond-shaped window in the east wall and a fireplace in the north wall.

The graveyard contains a fascinating collection of 18th- and

19th-century gravestones. Outside it, to the north-west, is a fine motte-and-bailey castle. The motte is *c*.40 m in diameter and 9 m high, surrounded by a fosse with outer bank. To the north-west is the rectangular bailey, *c*.46 m long and 24 m wide, enclosed by a low bank with outer fosse. Much of the west side of the bailey has been quarried away. Both the summit of the motte and the bailey preserve traces of wall footings.

Slade, Co. Wexford Tower house and fortified house

2 km north of Hook Head; take R734 (New Ross–Fethard), off R733; from Fethard, follow minor road south for Hook Head; signposted. Disc. Ser. 76.

By the pier of the small fishing village of Slade [*Slaod*, 'falling/sloping ground'] is a tower house, probably of the late 15th century, with an

▼ Fig. 151a. Slade Castle: Cross-sections (after Leask)

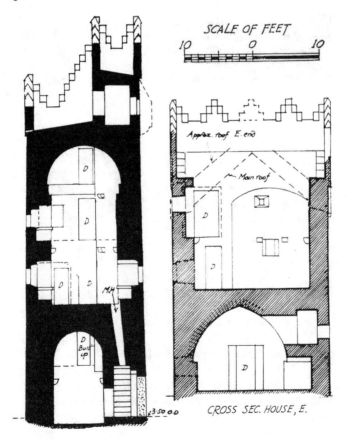

SCALE OF FEET

CROSS SEC. HOUSE, E.

CROSS SEC. TOWER, N-S.

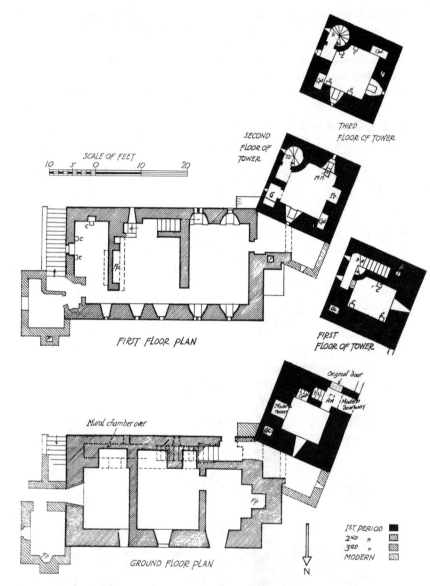

THIRD
FLOOR OF TOWER

SECOND
FLOOR OF
TOWER.

SCALE OF FEET

FIRST
FLOOR OF TOWER

FIRST FLOOR PLAN

Mural chamber over

Original door

GROUND FLOOR PLAN

N

1ST PERIOD
2ND „
3RD „
MODERN

▲ **Fig. 151b.** Slade Castle: floor plans (after Leask)

attached 16th-century house. Probably built by the Laffan family, it represents the home of a reasonably wealthy Anglo-Irish family of the late Middle Ages. The tower house is *c*.18 m high, with three main storeys, each of which has a single chamber, with a turret and stepped battlements above. The original entrance is at the west end of the south wall, protected by a machicolation at parapet level—the opening in the adjacent west wall is modern. From the entrance lobby (protected by a murder hole from the first floor above) a mural stair leads to a loftlike chamber, over the ground floor and under a barrel vault. Thereafter access to the upper floors is by a spiral stair in the southern angle. Both the ground-floor chamber and the loft above are small and poorly lit, and were probably used only for storage. The main residential chamber is on the first floor, identified by a fireplace, a garderobe chamber, a wall cupboard, and two windows with seats. Note also the opening of the murder hole in the south-west angle. The second-floor chamber was also residential and has windows with seats and wall cupboards. Above this is another loftlike space within an upper barrel vault, and over the vault is a turret occupying the southern side of the tower.

Attached to the north-east angle of the tower—but with no direct communication with it—is a rectangular house of two storeys, again with high stepped battlements and a turret at the east end. The ground floor is vaulted and each floor is divided into three chambers. The ground-floor chambers are largely featureless, apart from a large fireplace in the west wall, and are accessed through doorways in the north and east walls, neither of which is definitely original. Curiously, the only clearly original doorway—in the south wall, near the tower house—leads only to the upper floor, via a mural stair in the south wall. On the first floor are two substantial chambers. The central one has a large fireplace and the western one is lit by four windows with seats, two of which are two-light ogee-headed windows. Later extensions built onto the east and west ends of the house are possibly associated with 18th-century salt works nearby.

Hook Head

At Hook Head (*2 km south-east*) is a unique monument—a medieval lighthouse, still functioning and claimed as the oldest operational lighthouse in Europe. It was probably erected in the early 13th century for William Marshall, lord of Leinster, to facilitate passage of ships into Waterford Harbour and upriver to his new town of New Ross. It was actually built and maintained, however, by the monks of Rinndeuan, whose ruined church can be seen at Churchtown, 1 km to the north (*on west side of road*). The original tower is almost 25 m high and in two parts; first, a three-storey cylindrical structure 13 m in diameter, and above this a smaller turret, 6.5 m in diameter. Presumably beacon fires were lit on the top of the turret in the medieval period, but the modern light chamber was subsequently built over it. Each floor of the main tower has a single circular chamber, vaulted overhead. Each has a fireplace and the two upper floors have a number of mural chambers opening off them. It was originally entered at ground level, through a pointed doorway (now closed) in the east end of the buttress-like annexe on the north side of the tower. From here a mural stair ascends anti-clockwise through the thickness of the wall to the upper floors. Hook Head, incidentally, is (in part) the origin of the saying 'by hook or by crook'. The phrase was allegedly coined by Oliver Cromwell in 1649, announcing his intention to attack **Waterford**, whether from the east side of Waterford Harbour (guarded by Hook Head), or from the western side of the Harbour (guarded by Crook Castle).

Waterford, Co. Waterford Medieval town

Junction of N9 and N24. Disc. Ser. 76.

Waterford [Old Norse *Vedra-fjordr*, 'windy fjord'] was one of Ireland's most important medieval towns. It was established as a Viking *longphort* in 914, although this probably replaced a mid-9th-century fortification. The original fortification was located on a triangular promontory bounded on the north by the river Suir, and on the east and south by a tributary, the St John's river, and a marshy area adjacent. From this core area (now occupied by Reginald's Tower, the cathedral of Holy Trinity, and the Franciscan friary) the town seems to have expanded westwards in a number of stages. A major expansion of the town, more than doubling its area, has been dated to the 11th century by excavated evidence. The expanded town was enclosed on the western side by an earthen bank with a timber palisade and outer fosse in the 1080s. This was replaced by the first stone wall *c.*1120–40. The extended area was laid out on a rough chequer pattern, with three east–west streets (High St., Peter St., and Lady Lane) intersecting several smaller north–south streets.

The 11th century probably also saw the full adoption of Christianity, and the first bishop of Waterford was consecrated at Canterbury in 1096. The cathedral of Holy Trinity (Christ Church) must have been established around this date, although there may have been a church on the site from earlier in the century. Two other churches within the 11th century expansion—St Olaf's and St Peter's—can hardly be much later. Waterford was captured by Diarmait Mac Murchada and Strongbow in 1170, apparently with great slaughter, but was kept as a royal city by Henry II in 1171. The original inhabitants of the town were expelled soon after this, but allowed to remain in a suburban settlement immediately west of the town. This suburb, based on the long north–south axis of John St./Michael St./Broad St./Barronstrand St., was subsequently walled and incorporated into the town proper. Waterford prospered as a seaport under English rule, especially in the 13th and early 14th centuries, because of its position at the closest point to Bristol and south-western England, and at the head of the great Nore–Suir–Barrow river system.

Churches

This prosperity was reflected particularly in the patronage of the Church. A new cathedral was erected in the early 13th century—the only church to rival the two cathedrals of **Dublin** as the finest Gothic building in medieval Ireland. Tragically, this building was demolished, for no very good reason, in the late 18th century and replaced by the present attractive but unexceptional classical structure. It is worth visiting, if only to see the remarkable late 15th-century tomb of James Rice, a prominent Waterford merchant, in which the deceased is represented, not by the conventional effigy, but by a decomposing corpse. This is the finest Irish example of a 'cadaver' effigy of this type. Aside from the cathedral, several religious houses were founded. An Augustinian priory (*on the site of the Courthouse, Catherine St.*) was probably founded in the mid-12th century, before the English conquest. In the early years after the conquest two hospitals were founded. No medieval remains survive of the Hospital of St Stephen, founded *c.*1185, but there are some ruins of St John's church, part of a hospital also founded *c.*1185, which later become a Benedictine priory. The church ruins (*on John St./Manor St.*) are largely featureless, consisting of a nave and choir of 13th-century date with a late medieval chapel or sacristy on the south-east. A Dominican friary was founded in 1235 and parts of the church survive (*north side of High St., west end*). The main surviving feature is the late medieval belfry tower, but the north and south walls of the original, undifferentiated nave-choir structure also survive in part, with traces of a south aisle off the nave.

A Franciscan friary was founded *c.*1240, of which a substantial part of the church remains (*on Greyfriars, between the Quay and Cathedral Square; key available at the Granary*). In 1395 Richard II received the submissions of a number of Irish lords here. The church consists of a long, undifferentiated nave-and-choir structure of mid-13th-century date, with a later south aisle and south transept (probably 14th century) and an inserted tower dividing the choir (for the friars) from the nave (for the public). The sacristy also survives, on the north side of the choir, but now cut off from the church. A number of original lancet windows survive in the church, most notably the great triplet of lancets in the east wall of the choir. The bluntly pointed west doorway is also original and, like the other original features, its mouldings are of lighter coloured stone, imported from Dundry near Bristol. The south aisle has largely vanished but the blocked aisle arcade can still be seen from within the nave. The tower, unusually bulky for a friary, was added probably in the 15th century and has typically late medieval stepped battlements and two-light transomed windows at the belfry stage. The cloisters were located on the north side of the church, but no visible trace survives. The friary was suppressed in 1540 and in 1544 the nave of the church was adapted, by the addition of an upper floor, to serve as a charity for the old and infirm—the Hospital of the Holy Ghost. The Hospital occupied the nave until the late 19th century and traces are still visible of the modifications made to the nave walls to receive the upper floor.

Waterford also possessed at least seven parish churches, of which fragments survive of three. St Olaf's (*on Olaf St.*) was probably established in the late 11th/early 12th century. The present church was rebuilt in the 18th century, but a medieval doorway is visible in the west wall. St Peter's (*on Peter St.*) was shown by excavation to have been first built in stone in the early/mid-12th century, but quite possibly on the site of an earlier wooden church. The foundations of the 12th-century church, with apsidal east end, are rather incongruously displayed within the shopping centre which now occupies the site. St Michael's church (*east side of Michael St.*) is today represented by unremarkable fragments of the medieval church and an adjoining priest's residence.

Town defences

Waterford was clearly walled before 1170 but during the 13th century the defences were substantially rebuilt, beginning with a murage grant in 1215. The walls of the Hiberno-Norse town were strengthened, particularly by the addition of gates and mural towers, and the extensive suburb to the west was eventually enclosed—although probably not until the 15th century. By the late Middle Ages the town walls included at least 15 gates and 23 mural towers, and substantial sections of the walls and several towers survive. Particularly good stretches of wall may be seen on the west and south sides of the suburban extension (*west side of Mayor's Walk, north side of Castle St. and Railway Square*). Two interesting mural towers on the southern stretch have recently been restored—the rectangular 'Double Tower' (*Castle St.*) and the round 'Watch Tower' (*Railway Square*). Both are probably 15th century. 300 m north (*north side of Spring Garden Alley, beside school*) are the excavated foundations of a twin-towered gatehouse, apparently part of a new north–south wall erected to defend the western side of the original town in the early 13th century. Further stretches of the wall may be seen to the rear of properties along Spring Garden Alley, between The Mall and the cathedral, and (rather colourfully displayed) within the pub immediately south of Reginald's Tower (*north end of The Mall*).

Pride of place in the defences of Waterford, however, must go to Reginald's Tower, the largest and finest surviving tower of any Irish town's walls. Sited to defend the town against attack from the river or sea, it has played a significant role in Waterford's history. It is probably named after Ragnall mac Gillemaire, the last Hiberno-Norse ruler of Waterford, who was captured in 'Reginald's tower' in 1170. In 1174 a revolt of the original townspeople failed, only because the English garrison were able to hold out in Reginald's Tower until reinforcements arrived. Almost certainly, however, the 'tower' referred to in these accounts is not the present structure, which was probably erected as part of the early 13th-century rebuilding of the defences. The tower probably housed a mint in the late 13th century, as it certainly did in the late 15th century. In 1495 it was the scene of the first effective use of artillery in Ireland, when cannon mounted in the tower played a significant role in repelling a seaborne attack by Perkin Warbeck, the pretender to the English throne.

The tower, over 15 m high, has four storeys with a wall walk above. Each floor consists of a round main chamber with a series of embrasures opening off it in the thickness of the walls. There are suggestions that only the lower half of the tower dates to the 13th century, while the upper half is late medieval in date. The masonry changes, from predominantly shale in the lower levels to mainly limestone higher up, but it is difficult to imagine that the tower was left for any great period as a two-storey structure, wider than it was high. The upper storeys must surely be replacements for—or more likely, a rebuilding of—original floors. It is at present entered at ground level through a doorway on the north-east, but this was inserted only in the 16th century, when an artillery bastion was added outside the tower. The original entrance is diametrically opposite, on the south-west. Opening off its embrasure is the spiral stair which gives access to the upper floors. At first-floor level, another embrasure directly over the entrance contains a doorway that gave access to the wall walk of the (now vanished) adjoining town wall. Although it is clearly defensive, there is evidence that the tower was also designed for habitation—garderobe chambers (on the north-west at ground and first floors), fireplaces (on the south-east at first and second floors and on the north-west at third floor), window seats (at second and third floors), and a possible sleeping chamber (on the west at second floor). Most of the original arrow loops in the embrasures have been replaced by larger rectangular openings, but a few remain, along with some important early gun loops, probably inserted in the 15th century.

Waterford Treasures

200 m west of Reginald's Tower, at the restored Granary building on the quayside, is *Waterford Treasures*, an exhibition on the town's history which should not be missed. It features the extremely important collection of archaeological artefacts recovered in excavations in Waterford in the 1980s and 1990s, an incomparable collection of civic regalia including the unique 14th-century Great Charter Roll, and a fine collection of late medieval sculpture from the Holy Ghost Hospital, almost certainly derived from the medieval Franciscan friary.

South-west: Cork, Kerry

Introduction

Much of the western part of this region consists of a series of rugged, mountainous peninsulas jutting out into the Atlantic. The remainder can be divided into relatively poor land to the north and extensive areas of fine agricultural land to the south and east. The north and west, in addition to poor soils and extensive uplands, are prone to high rainfall but enjoy relatively mild temperatures. The south and east have relatively lower precipitation and higher levels of sunshine.

Mesolithic activity in the region has been unearthed through a successful fieldwalking programme initiated in 1984. As elsewhere in the country, the distributional trend is towards riverside and coastal contexts. Early Mesolithic sites have been found along the middle and lower reaches of the Blackwater Valley in east Cork. At Kilcummer Lower (about midway between Castletownroche and Ballyhooly) Liz Anderson excavated a site on a cliff overlooking the confluence of the Blackwater and the Awbeg rivers. The lithic assemblage included nine microliths and over 200 struck flint flakes. Later Mesolithic sites are rather more rare, and with the exception of the 6th-millennium BC shell midden site at **Ferriter's Cove**, in Dingle, excavations at lithic scatter sites have yielded little additional information.

Pollen analysis of a core extracted from Cashelkeelty, Co. Kerry, records a marked pre-elm decline drop in arboreal taxa between 4950 and 4470 BC. A single pollen grain from *Triticum*, a type of wheat, was found at the same level, introducing the possibility of pre-elm decline farming activity. While it is inadvisable to place too much reliance on just one pollen grain, particularly at such an early date, the discovery of cattle bone in a 5th-millennium context at **Ferriter's Cove** supports the notion of an established, early Neolithic presence in the south-west. Lying outside the general distribution of Neolithic megalithic tombs, however, the activities of these first farmers are well-nigh invisible.

Not so the early Bronze Age. With more than 120 surviving Wedge tombs, over 600 standing stones, 100 stone pairs, dozens of alignments, 90 stone circles, 68 boulder burials, numerous examples of rock art and copper mines, the south-west is the primary region in which to study the earlier Bronze Age in Ireland. William O'Brien's seminal work on copper mines and Wedge tombs in the region explains at least some of this wealth. A decorated copper axe and two pieces of raw copper at **Toormore** Wedge tomb reveal a very direct association between tomb builders and copper mining, between about 1900 and 1600 BC. Dating from 300–500 years after the first use of metal in the region, however,

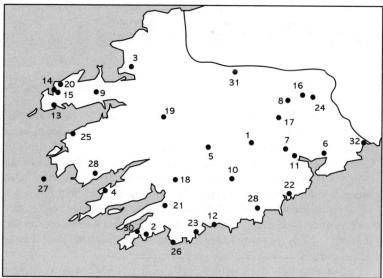

▲ Map 8
Key:

1. Aghabullogue, Co. Cork
2. Altar, Co. Cork
3. Ardfert, Co. Kerry
4. Ballycrovane, Co. Cork
5. Ballyvourney, Co. Cork
6. Barryscourt, Co. Cork
7. Blarney, Co. Cork
8. Bridgetown, Co. Cork
9. Caherconree, Co. Kerry
10. Cappeen West, Co. Cork
11. Cork city, Co. Cork
12. Drombeg, Co. Cork
13. Dunbeg, Fahan, Co. Kerry
14. Ferriter's Cove, Co. Kerry
15. Gallarus, Co. Kerry
16. Glanworth, Co. Cork

17. Island, Co. Cork
18. Kealkill, Co. Cork
19. Killarney, Co. Kerry
20. Kilmalkedar, Co. Kerry
21. Kilnaruane, Co. Cork
22. Kinsale, Co. Cork
23. Knockdrum, Co. Cork
24. Labbacallee, Co. Cork
25. Leacanabuaile, Co. Kerry
26. Sherkin Island, Co. Cork
27. Skellig Michael, Co. Kerry
28. Staigue, Co. Kerry
29. Timoleague, Co. Cork
30. Toormore, Co. Cork
31. Tullylease, Co. Cork
32. Youghal, Co. Cork

these dates put paid to the theory that coastal Wedge tombs represent the landfall sites of the first immigrant metallurgists traveling from Europe. Beaker pottery associated with the earliest copper mines at **Ross Island**, Killarney, reveals an international aspect to the first exploitation of copper but is not proof of population movement.

It could be argued that the centre of power in Munster switched to the lower Shannon basin during the later Bronze Age, as it is here that most of the major hoards, and in particular accomplished gold objects, are found. Gold aside, distribution maps show a preference in Cork and Kerry for sheet bronze pieces, such as Eogan's Class II, end-blown bronze horns and cauldrons. Finds such as the bulbous-terminal bracelet of Hallstatt C/D type from Kilmurry and the wooden Hallstatt C sword from Cappagh, also in Co. Kerry, indicate contact with iron-using communities in Europe. They are harbingers of the beginning of the Irish Iron Age.

The Iron Age in the south-west remains something of an enigma. With a general absence of La Tène-decorated artefacts, or undecorated yet recognizable types, Iron Age material is very rare. Rather than contemplating a materially retarded, lingering Bronze Age in the south-west, recent commentators have emphasized instead the privileged status of La Tène metalwork as the property of an elite minority elsewhere in the country. What is missing from the south-west, they argue, is not so much an Iron Age *per se* but this elite, La Tène stratum that renders it more visible elsewhere. Therefore, insofar as La Tène refers to a province with a culturally distinguished aristocracy, Cork and Kerry were outside it and it is likely that social hierarchies surviving from the later Bronze Age endured for some centuries in this region.

Observing how the mythological character of the region emerges into the light of history associated with women, witches, musicians, and the dead, the historian Francis John Byrne described Munster as a world to itself. The name Munster derives from *Mumu*, or *Leth Mug*, meaning the 'Slave's Half' (the counterpoint to *Leth Coinn*, 'Conn's Half', the northern half of Ireland; Conn being the eponymous ancestor of the Connachta). The early history of Munster is particularly opaque. Manipulated by the so-called 'synthetic historians', surviving texts portray its early historic inhabitants as a mixture of older groups, such as the Muscraige and Corcu Duibne, and their later masters, the Eóganachta. In the early Middle Ages the entire Munster region was theoretically ruled by the Eoghanacht kings of **Cashel**. This kingship passed between various Eoghanacht dynasties, one of which, the Eóganacht Glendamnach, was based at **Glanworth** in north Co. Cork. The first historically verifiable Eóganacht king was Feidhlimidh mac Tigernaig (d. 590–3) of the Eoganacht Raithlind, who had their inauguration site near Bandon. Munster is a large and geographically diverse area, however, and while overlordship traditionally rested with **Cashel**, various political subdivisions of the province have been advanced. According to some sources an early division of the Eóganacht hegemony was between *Iarmuma* (west Munster) and *Aurmuma* (east Munster), based on **Cashel**. Most of the Cork–Kerry region was effectively controlled by another Eóganacht branch, the Eóganacht Locha Léin, based in the **Killarney** area, who were practically autonomous rulers of *Iarmumu*. The eastern groups came to dominate from the 8th century onwards and around the beginning of the 9th century the Eoganachta Loch Lein were defeated by the Ciarraige, a subordinate kingdom that gives its name to Kerry.

This region has two significant concentrations of ogam stones, one on the Dingle peninsula in Co. Kerry and the other south of the Boggeragh Mountains in Co. Cork. Nearly twenty of the latter are associated with ecclesiastical foundations and six of these date, linguistically, from the early 5th century. These associations, demonstrating as they do connections with Latin literacy, may have some bearing on the early ecclesiastical history of south-west Munster and the existence in this region of a 'pre-Patrician' Church. Liam de Paor has postulated that the colonization of parts of Wales by the Déisi and Uí Liathain of east Munster led in turn to the establishment of later 4th- and early 5th-century Christian communities in south Munster. Between them, Cork and Kerry have some of the best-known early church sites in Ireland, from the spectacular **Skelligs** to the relative quietude of Reask and Killabuonia. Excavations in the 1950s by Michael O'Kelly at **Church Island, Ballyvourney,** and **Beginish** still represent a watershed in our knowledge of church archaeology.

Likewise, some of the most important excavations of settlement sites

▼ **Fig. 152.** Reask: cross-inscribed slab (photo: Dept. of Archaeology, NUI, Galway)

of the early medieval period were undertaken in the south-west by O'Kelly and Seán P. Ó Ríordáin during the 1940s and 1950s. These include the great ringforts at Garranes and Garryduff 1 and 2. Impressive material assemblages at both of these sites attest to the elevated rank of their residents. It has been postulated that the triple-ramparted rath at Garranes (over 100 m in diameter), known as Lisnacaheragh, is Raithliú, a royal site of the Uí Echach Muman of the Eóganacht Raithlind. The original date of occupation, in the second half of the 5th and earlier 6th century AD, is probably about a century too early and is, therefore, no longer an impediment to associating the fort with Feidhlimidh mac Tigernaig. There is a solid and quite even spread of ringforts throughout Cork and Kerry and there is a particularly dense concentration of souterrains, possibly among the earliest in the country. Crannógs, on the other hand, are extremely rare.

Changes during the Viking period were not as significant as on the east coast, but there were new developments. From the middle of the 9th century there was a permanent Viking settlement on the estuary of the river Lee, which eventually developed into the town of **Cork**. There may also have been Viking settlements on the future sites of **Kinsale** and **Youghal**, but these never amounted to true towns. One of the indirect effects of the Viking wars was the rise of the Dál Cais (later Ó Briain) dynasty of the Co. Clare area, to supplant the Eóganacht in the kingship of Munster after 950. Ó Briain dominance in the south lasted little over a century, however. In the 1120s Toirdhealbhach Ó Conchobhair, king of Connacht, divided Munster into Thomond (*Tuadmuma*, 'north Munster'), controlled by the Ó Briain, and Desmond (*Desmuma*, 'south Munster'), controlled by the Eóganacht dynasty of Mac Cárthaig (McCarthy). **Cork**, although probably not as large or wealthy as other Hiberno-Norse towns such as **Dublin** and **Limerick**, benefited in the 12th century from the patronage of the Mac Cárthaig kings of Desmond, who may even have had their principal residence here.

In 1177 Henry II of England granted the kingdom of Desmond to two barons, Robert fitz Stephen and Miles de Cogan. Within 30 years most of the coast and river valleys of east Co. Cork were taken and settled by English barons. The town of **Cork** (which was kept in direct royal control) was developed and enlarged and new towns were founded, such as the important ports of **Youghal** and **Kinsale** and inland market towns such as Buttevant, **Glanworth**, and Mallow. In the early 13th century much of north Co. Kerry, including the Dingle peninsula, was occupied by the English as part of the colonization of the Limerick area. Towns were established at the ecclesiastical centre of **Ardfert** and at the ports of Tralee and Dingle. Today, the region is almost entirely lacking in mottes and, for the most part, has few moated sites. There is, however, a striking spread of moated sites across east Co. Cork, which has been interpreted as marking the western limit of the Anglo-Irish colony.

South Kerry and the western peninsulas of Cork remained largely in Irish hands, and even before the end of the 13th century resurgent Irish power threatened the security of the Anglo-Irish colony. The Mac Cárthaig and other Irish lords were never able to destroy the colony completely, but they inflicted serious damage and regained considerable territories. In the more unstable conditions of the late Middle Ages, the big winner was actually an Anglo-Irish magnate family, the FitzGeralds, who gradually gained control of the holdings of many other Anglo-Irish lords and established themselves as earls of Desmond. From the early 14th to late 16th centuries they controlled most of this region, but their supremacy ended in rebellion and defeat in the 1580s. This was followed by a renewed English plantation of Munster, which foreshadowed the more extensive plantation of Ulster and radically changed both the demographic make-up and settlement patterns of the region.

Aghabullogue, Co. Cork   Holy well, ogam stone

25 km west of Cork city, off the R619 (Coachford–Mallow); St Olan's Well is located 1 km north of Aghabullogue, which is to the north-west of Coachford; turn west off R619 at Larchfield Cross Roads, 2 km north of Coachford. Disc. Ser. 80.

St Olan, whose feast day falls on 5 September, is especially associated with childbirth and female illness. Situated near the ruins of Aghabullogue parish church, this roadside holy well is housed in a circular stone canopy. Beside it is an ogam stone, relocated here from a nearby ringfort in 1851, and bearing an inscription that reads *MADORA MAQI DEGO* ('of Madora, son of Dego'). The holy well is part of a 'round' (penitential circuit) which also takes in St Olan's Stone and St Olan's Cap (the latter an ogam stone), both of which occur in the grounds of the ruined parish church, a few hundred metres to the south-east. The church appears to be situated within an earlier enclosure about 160 m by 130 m, which is bisected by the present road. St Olan's Stone is a small boulder bearing two depressions on the upper surface, reputed to be the saint's knee-prints. Moved to the north-east corner of the graveyard in 1985, it originally stood outside the early enclosure. St Olan's Cap gets its nickname from a removable capstone (possibly like those found on high crosses). It bears an ogam inscription reading *ANM CORRE MAQVI UDD . . . METT* ('the name of Corre, son of Udd . . . mett'). Yet another ogam stone was removed from the graveyard in 1838 and is now part of the University College Cork collection.

Altar, Co. Cork   Wedge tomb

25 km west of Skibbereen, on the R592 between Skull and Toormore, about 1.5 km east of Toormore; signposted. Disc. Ser. 88.

This small Wedge tomb is picturesquely situated overlooking the entrance to a small inlet and strand on the north-east side of Toormore

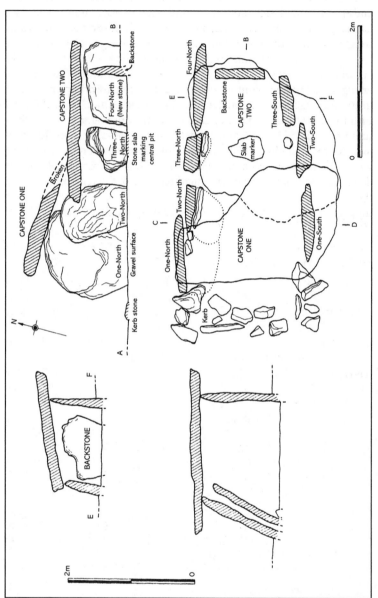

▲ Fig. 153. Altar: plan and elevations of Wedge tomb (after O'Brien & Duggan)

Bay. Restoration followed excavation by O'Brien and Duggan in 1989. The trapezoidal gallery is orientated east-north-east/west-south-west and there are two large roofstones. Excavation revealed the sockets for a backstone and fourth stone on the northern side, into which new stones were inserted during restoration. An entrance kerb of smaller stones was also found. An oval-shaped pit at the east end of the gallery saw secondary use during the later Iron Age, with the possibly ceremonial deposition of marine molluscs and fish. Nearer the entrance were fragments of cremated and unburnt human bone of later Neolithic/early Bronze Age date. A number of worked flints were also found in disturbed contexts in front of the tomb. The radiocarbon sequence provides a unique insight into the protracted history of the site, attesting to episodic activity between about 2300 BC and the medieval period. Pit deposition and burning events in the later Bronze Age and Iron Age bear the hallmarks of ritual activity, thus extending the life of the tomb into the 1st millennium AD. The tomb may simply have been used as a shelter after this.

It has been suggested that this tomb is aligned on Mizen Peak to the south-west, behind which the sun sets in early November, around the festival of Samhain. North-westwards across the inlet is another Wedge tomb at **Toormore**. Southwards across the bay is Castle Head where there is a restored O'Mahony tower house known as Black Castle. It is situated in what may have been a promontory fort.

Ardfert, Co. Kerry Shrunken medieval town

10 km north-west of Tralee on R551 (Tralee–Ballyheigue); signposted. Visitor centre; admission charge. Disc. Ser. 71.

Ardfert, now little more than a village, is the site of an early medieval monastery and a failed medieval town. The monastic site is said to have been founded by the 6th-century St Brendan, traditionally regarded as a great navigator of the north Atlantic, who may even have reached America. Little is known of Ardfert's history before the 11th century, but the place name [*Ard Ferta*, 'the hill of the burial mounds'] may preserve the memory of a pre-Christian burial site. An ogam stone displayed beside the cathedral may also pre-date the monastic site. A stone church was in existence at Ardfert by 1046, when it was destroyed by lightning. Ardfert was not selected as the seat of a bishopric at the reforming synod of Rathbreasail in 1111, but seems to have become one soon afterwards. Its importance in the 12th century is indicated by the remains of two churches with fine Romanesque-style ornament, one of which was incorporated into a larger 13th-century cathedral. Another church, although of later medieval date, may well occupy an earlier site, and two other churches are recorded on the site in the late 17th century. A round

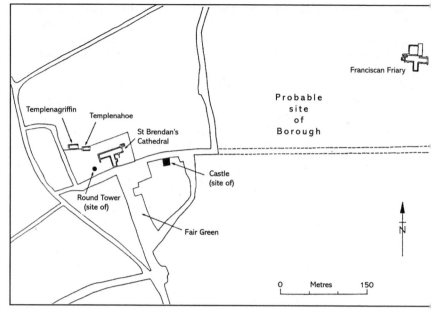

▲ **Fig. 154.** Ardfert: outline map showing main medieval features (after Bradley)

tower also stood to the south-west of the cathedral until the late 18th century.

From the early 13th century Ardfert fell under Anglo-Irish control, particularly of the FitzGeralds, future earls of Desmond. A town was founded, probably early in the 13th century, and a Franciscan friary was also founded before the end of the century. Ardfert's status as the seat of the bishopric was confirmed and the present cathedral was built, replacing a mid-12th century structure. It appears that much of the physical development of the town took place at a relatively late date, at the end of the 13th century. The new cathedral may not have been built until after c.1280 and the friary may be equally late. In 1286 a grant of murage suggests that the enclosure of the town was planned, if it had not already been begun. The later history of the town is obscure, but it seems to have survived until the rebellion and defeat of its patron, the earl of Desmond, by the English in the 1580s. The cathedral was burned, and never rebuilt, and the town probably never recovered, gradually declining until only a village remained. Without excavation, almost nothing can be said about the form and layout of the town and even its precise location is uncertain, although it probably occupied the area between the cathedral and the Franciscan friary, c.450 m to the east.

Cathedral

The cathedral was built over many centuries, from the 11th to the 17th. The west wall of the nave incorporates the west front of an earlier, mid-12th-century cathedral. The red sandstone façade features a round-arched doorway flanked by blank arcading and decorated in Roman-esque style, mainly with chevrons. This building had clearly been built by 1152, when the Synod of **Kells** noted that it was 'the finest and largest church in the united diocese and therefore most suitable for Cathedral purposes'. It functioned for slightly over a century, before being replaced by the present larger cathedral *c.*1280. When the new cathedral was built, its north side was for some reason aligned on the north wall of the earlier chancel, rather than the wider nave. As a result, the 12th-century west front projects beyond the later nave on the north side. The 12th-century chancel in fact incorporated the last remnants of an even older, 11th-century church. The masonry of the original church's north wall can still be seen near the east end of the 13th-century nave, and founda-tions of the other walls were discovered in excavations in the 1990s.

The 13th-century cathedral was a simple rectangular structure, although considerably larger than its 12th-century predecessor. Origin-ally it had a short aisle on the south side of the nave, but this is now largely vanished. At the junction of nave and choir are pairs of corbels in the side walls, which probably supported a rood screen and loft, dividing the two parts of the church. The choir may be slightly later than the nave and is lit by a fine triple-lancet east window and a striking row of nine lancets, with trefoil-headed rear arches, in the south wall. Two late 13th-/ early 14th-century effigies of bishops or abbots are mounted in niches on either side of the east window—their original positions are unknown. The cathedral must have closely resembled contemporary friary churches, and the resemblance was strengthened in the 15th cen-tury when the long south transept—similar to those found in many friaries—was built onto the nave. At the same period a long sacristy or chapel was built onto the north side of the choir, and the recently restored high stepped battlements were added to the main walls. The cathedral seems to have been largely derelict since the destruction of the 1580s, and certainly from 1641, although the south transept was restored for use as a parish church after 1670, and has recently been re-roofed as a visitor centre.

Templenahoe, Templenagriffin

North-west of the cathedral is a small church known as Templenahoe [*Teampull na hÓighe*, 'the Church of the Virgin']. This is also a 12th-century Romanesque building, but is probably somewhat later than the original cathedral. Its chancel has vanished, leaving only the simple nave with its high-pitched gables and two windows in each side wall. The west doorway is round arched and plain apart from animal head stops on the hood moulding. The chancel arch was originally of three orders (the inner order is now missing) and is decorated on the arches and imposts. Only one original window is intact and it is framed, internally, with a decorative border. The most distinctive feature of the church is the presence of engaged columns at each corner, possibly in place of the traditional antae, which rise to meet an eaves course decorated with bosses and animal head corbels, running along the side walls. West of this is another small church, a plain 15th-century structure known as *Templenagriffin*, probably from the carving of a griffin or wyvern (both mythological beasts) on one of the windows.

Friary

The Franciscan friary, founded in the later 13th century, was probably located in the north-east angle of the town, or just outside it. The church strongly resembles the nearby cathedral and may have been inspired by it—although the relative sequence of cathedral and friary is uncertain. The friary church is a simple, rectangular 13th-century nave-and-choir structure. The choir is again lit by a row of nine lancets with trefoil-headed rear arches in the south wall, and by an east window of five graduated lancets. A south aisle was probably added in the 14th century—it has now vanished but its location is indicated by the arcade of pointed arches in the nave. A south transept was added in the 15th century, lit by a fine south window with switchline tracery. A tower was also added in the 15th century but unusually, is located at the west end of the church, rather than in the middle between the nave and choir. It seems to have been designed mainly to provide secure residential accommodation. The cloister on the north is of late 15th-century date. Only the east range survives, with an integrated ambulatory and cloister arcade with triple openings set within deep, segmental-pointed embrasures.

Ballycrovane, Co. Cork Ogam stone

Overlooking Ballycrovane Harbour, 2.5 km north of Eyeries; signposted. Disc. Ser. 84.

A very tall ogam stone (5.1 m), possibly a reused standing stone, bearing the inscription *MAQI-DECCEDAS AVI TURANIAS* which translates as '[the stone] ... of the son of Decceddas of the grandson of Torrainn ...'.

Ballyvourney, Co. Cork St Gobnait's House and pilgrimage trail

55 km west of Cork city, on the N22 between Macroom and Killarney; signposted. Disc. Ser. 79.

The patron saint of beekeepers, Gobnait, who may have lived in the 6th century, is one of the few celebrated Irish women saints. According to tradition, St Abban founded a nunnery for Gobnait at Ballyvourney, around which a pilgrimage route has become established (pattern day is 11 February), which includes a range of very interesting archaeological sites located, generally, to the south of the village. The area is, in fact, quite densely populated with archaeological sites of all periods.

Excavated by O'Kelly in 1951, 'St Gobnait's house' is a round, thick-walled, stone house about 10 m in diameter, with its entrance facing south. It is the first station on St Gobnait's pilgrimage and a well outside the entrance has, since the excavation, been venerated as a holy well. The building was used as an iron workshop, resulting in numerous pits, furnace bottoms, and tuyere fragments. Objects of a less industrial nature, including a jet bracelet, were also found. The excavation revealed traces of earlier activity, when one or possibly more rectangular houses may have stood here. There appears to have been little or no interval between the two phases and, interestingly, iron smelting was also associated with this phase, which may date from around the 9th or 10th centuries AD. 30 m to the east is Ballyvourney graveyard, where stand the ruins of St Gobnait's church (*Teampall Ghobnatan*). In the south wall of the building is a possible sheela-na-gig; a badly worn carved head on the internal face of the east gable is probably a voussoir from an earlier, Romanesque church. This church is also part of the pilgrimage route and around it are five stations. One of them, 'St Gobnait's grave', occurs between the church and the aforementioned house site and comprises a small sod-covered mound, on top of which is a cross-inscribed slab. Nearby are two bullaun stones. Some 60 m to the south of the graveyard is another holy well, 'St Gobnait's Well', which is the last station of the pattern.

About midway between this complex and Ballyvourney Bridge is one of two fulachta fiadh excavated by O'Kelly in 1952. Here was found a wood-lined trough, a number of hearths, and a pile of heat-fractured stones immediately to the north of a temporary wooden shelter. It was here that O'Kelly carried out his famous re-enactment of a fulacht fiadh in action, bringing 450 litres of water to the boil with hot stones in about half an hour and tucking into a leg of Ballyvourney mutton about four hours later!

To the south-east of St Gobnait's well, in Shanacloon Wood, is a penitential station traditionally referred to as 'St Abban's Grave'. It is a small cairn surmounted by a bullaun stone and flanked by three ogam stones. Clockwise from the north-east, these read *VAITEVIA, LITUBIRI*

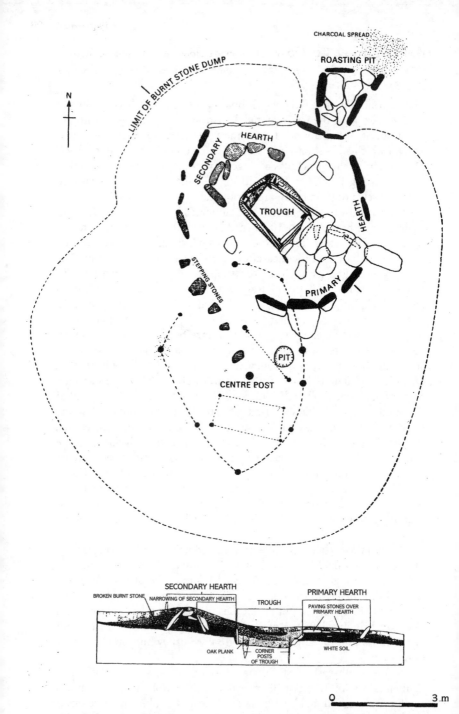

▲ Fig. 155. Ballyvourney: plan of fulacht fiadh as excavated (after O'Kelly)

Labels on plan:
CHARCOAL SPREAD
ROASTING PIT
LIMIT OF BURNT STONE DUMP
N
SECONDARY HEARTH
TROUGH
HEARTH
STEPPING STONES
PRIMARY
PIT
CENTRE POST

Section labels:
SECONDARY HEARTH
PRIMARY HEARTH
BROKEN BURNT STONE
NARROWING OF SECONDARY HEARTH
TROUGH
PAVING STONES OVER PRIMARY HEARTH
OAK PLANK
CORNER POSTS OF TROUGH
WHITE SOIL

0   3 m

MAQI QECIA ('of Litubiri, son of Qecia'), and *LACAVAGNI* respectively. There are a further two bullaun stones nearby. 70 m to the east is 'Tobar Abban', a holy well dedicated to the saint and visited on 16 March. It is uncertain whether the Ballyvourney saint is one and the same as the pre-Patrician Abban associated with Moyarney, Co. Waterford.

Off the other side of the Ballyvourney–Macroom road, to the south-east of the village, is 'St Gobnait's Stone', a fine Early Christian grave slab with an encircled Greek cross, on top of which walks a small, beguiling figure with crosier and tonsure akin to that of St Matthew in the later 7th-century Book of Durrow.

Barryscourt, Co. Cork Castle

15 km east of Cork off N25 (Cork–Youghal/Waterford); take minor road south at Carrigtohill; signposted. Visitor centre; admission charge. Disc. Ser. 81.

Barryscourt is named after the de Barry family, who built the castle and lived here probably from the 13th to 17th centuries. The present remains are 15th/16th century and consist of a large tower house, with a probable hall to the north and a roughly rectangular courtyard to the east, enclosed by a strong, late 16th-century curtain wall with square turrets at the angles. The courtyard has two simple entrances, one on the north side and the main one on the south, beside and defended by the tower house. The interior of the courtyard is featureless, apart from the north-western side, where the west wall retains window embrasures, a mural stair, and a projecting garderobe turret (at the north-west angle). These features clearly indicate the former presence of a hall, attached to the north side of the tower house.

The tower house itself is rectangular, with projecting turrets on the south-west, south-east, and north-east angles. The turrets are of five storeys, whereas the central block is of three storeys, barrel vaulted over first-floor level. The entrance is a 16th-century doorway at the north-east angle, leading into the main ground-floor chamber and to a mural stair in the east wall. A doorway in the north wall of the ground-floor chamber (probably a later insertion) now gives access to the north-east turret; it is protected by a murder hole above. The stairs in the east wall rise to the first- and second-floor chambers. The first-floor chamber, like that below, is lit only by narrow slit windows but a fireplace in the west wall identifies it as a residential chamber, probably for the lord's household. The rounded barrel vault appears to be a replacement for an earlier, pointed vault, the outline of which can still be seen in the end walls. All three turrets are accessible from this chamber. The south-west turret contains a garderobe and the south-east turret a small chamber, but the north-east turret contains a larger chamber with a musket loop overlooking the main entrance below. An adjoining mural chamber provides access to the top of the murder hole over the entrance. The main second-floor chamber was clearly the lord's hall, lit by two- and three-light mullioned windows in wide embrasures with seats, and with a fireplace in the east wall. This fireplace is dated 1588 and is a later insertion, as it blocks a window. One of the windows in the west wall is also dated, in this case 1586. A doorway in the north-west corner leads to the turret chamber, which at this level is a chapel—a feature not commonly found in tower houses. The sill of the east window projected as an altar, while the sill of the window in the south-east angle originally incorporated a piscina. An adjacent spiral stair rises to a fine private chamber above the chapel, with good windows, a latrine, and a fireplace dated 1596. Above this the stairs rise to the parapets. Further stairs in the south-west and south-east angles of the hall give access to the adjoining turrets (each at three levels) and to the parapets above.

Blarney, Co. Cork Castle

7 km north of Cork off N20 (Cork–Limerick); take R617 into Blarney village and minor road to south, off the Square; signposted. Admission charge. Disc. Ser. 80.

Blarney [*Bhlárna*, 'the plain'] is rivalled only by **Bunratty** as Ireland's best known and most photographed castle. This is due mainly to a stone in the parapet—the so-called 'Blarney stone'—reputed to bestow eloquence on those who kiss it. Despite the pseudo-historical schmaltz surrounding it, however, Blarney is well worth visiting as one of the largest and finest examples of a late medieval Irish tower house. Strongly sited on a rock outcrop overlooking the junction of two small rivers, it was supposedly built by Cormac Mac Cárthaig (McCarthy), lord of Muscraige, in the mid-15th century and was the chief stronghold of the Mac Cárthaig until the end of the 17th century.

The main building (fragments of the bawn wall also survive) is L-shaped in plan and was built in two phases. The earlier phase was a relatively slender tower of four storeys, which may well date to the mid-15th century, although there is no definite evidence for this. Subsequently, probably in the early 16th century, a much larger five-storey block was built onto the east side of the original tower. This main block has massively thick walls (up to 3.9 m) at ground- and first-floor levels and is vaulted over the first floor. Above this the walls become progressively thinner and the rooms larger. It is lit throughout with relatively small square-headed windows of one, two or three lights. Overhead are impressive battlements carried on unusually large corbels, forming a continuous machicolation around the top.

To the east of the tower house are fragmentary remains of later buildings, through which one reaches the entrance to the tower house—a double doorway defended by a murder hole over the entrance lobby. A doorway on the north side of the lobby leads to a spiral stair, which gives

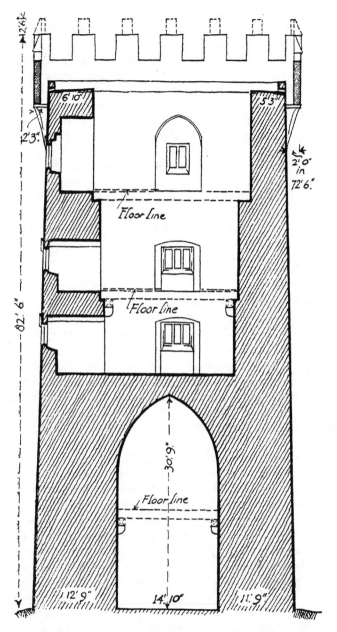

▲ Fig. 156. Blarney: cross-section of main tower house (after Leask)

access to the upper floors. The internal plan of the tower house is complex and confusing, but essentially consists of a main chamber to the south, with a warren of smaller chambers and passages on the north-west, north, and north-east sides, at all levels. The first-floor chamber is described as the 'Great Hall', but this is based mainly on the presence of a fine fireplace in the east wall, which is clearly a post-medieval insertion. A hall in this location, beneath the vault, would be very unusual and it is likely that this chamber was originally used for storage or servants' accommodation. A chamber on the north side, also at this level, is described as the 'Earl's Bedroom' and this may have some justification in view of the fine oriel window in the north wall. It is clear that the upper three floors, above the vault, were the main reception and residential areas—they are better lit and get progressively larger as the external walls get thinner. The main chamber at fourth-floor level is described as the 'Chapel' but since this is actually the largest chamber in the building and has a kitchen adjoining on the north-west, it is more likely to have been the lord's great hall.

Bridgetown, Co. Cork Priory

12 km west of Fermoy off N72 (Fermoy–Mallow); take minor road to west at Kilcummer (2 km south of Castletownroche) and road to south after 500 m; signposted. Disc. Ser. 80.

This well-preserved Augustinian priory, on the west bank of the river Blackwater, was founded in the early 13th century by Alexander Fitz-Hugh Roche, with monks from **Dublin** and **Trim,** and dissolved in 1540. The church and claustral buildings survive reasonably completely, although the architectural mouldings are often missing and the quality of the masonry is generally poor. The church is an early 13th-century rectangular structure, with nave and choir distinguished only by an internal cross-wall. The choir is actually slightly longer than the nave—a clear sign that the church was intended mainly for the use of the Augustinians, rather than a lay congregation. The west end of the nave was substantially modified in the late Middle Ages when a two-storey residential tower was inserted. The tower, in turn, was largely redesigned in the post-medieval period. The nave itself is entered through two doorways near the west end—a doorway in the south wall gave access from the cloister, whereas a doorway in the north wall gave access from outside the monastery and was probably used by the laity. Further east is another (blocked) doorway in the south wall, in line with the eastern ambulatory of the cloister. This was the processional doorway through which the community entered the church on formal liturgical occasions. All three doorways lack their original mouldings, as do most of the windows. The tall window with transom and mullion in the north-east angle of the nave is a late rebuilding, but the twin-light window immediately east of the doorway in the north wall has some original 13th-century jambs.

In the choir, the large, triple-lancet east window was almost entirely rebuilt, on a reduced scale, in the 15th century. All that survives, however, is the central twin-light window of the later rebuilding and fragments of the shafts which framed the much taller 13th-century lancets—these are in red sandstone, quite different from the limestone of the 15th-century window. An original twin-light window at the west end of the north wall gives an idea of what most of the windows would have looked like in the 13th century. In the south wall, near the east end is a twin-light window of *c.*1300 with cusped pointed heads and a quatrefoil above. Beneath it is a good early 15th-century tomb niche with a tall, pointed canopy, probably for a later Roche patron. There are three doorways in the south wall—that to the west gave access from the east range of the cloisters and that to the east led into a chapel on the south side. A two-storey tower was built onto the external north-eastern angle of the choir, probably in the 15th century.

The cloisters, south of the church, are surrounded by ranges of buildings on the east and south, but merely by a wall on the west. This wall and the south range are early 13th century, while the east range (aligned at an unusual angle to the church) may have been added later in the 13th century. The arcade surrounding the cloister garth has disappeared, although fragments of a decorated late 15th-century arcade can be seen. The only evidence for the ambulatories to the north, west, and south are projecting corbels and the roof line of the lean-to roof, preserved in the adjoining walls. On the east side, however, the ambulatory survives in a quite different form—a heavy vaulted passage built onto the east range in the late Middle Ages. Three large openings, flanked by sloping buttresses, faced the cloister garth and a large pointed arch gave access to the south ambulatory. A similar arrangement probably existed at the junction with the north ambulatory, but this no longer survives. The well at this end is a later insertion. Three pointed doorways in the inner wall of the ambulatory led to the ground-floor chambers of the east range. In the centre was the chapter house, lit by three lancets in the east wall. The chamber to the north may have been a sacristy, while that to the south was probably the day room—a kind of parlour where the canons could meet and talk. Overhead, the dormitory occupied the entire length of the range and somewhere at the north end there must have been a night stair, giving direct access to the church for night services. Over the chapter house is an apparently original twin-light window with cusped, pointed heads, of later 13th-century form, which suggests a date for the entire range.

In the south range the first-floor refectory was lit by a fine row of early 13th-century lancets in the south wall. A projecting turret alongside them contained the *pulpitum* or reader's desk, from which devotional writings were read to the canons as they ate. Beneath the refectory, at ground-floor level, was probably a space for storage, divided into three by two cross-walls and divided longitudinally by an arcade of six arches (now missing) springing from the cross-walls and from three intervening piers. The main purpose of this arcade was probably to support the floor of the refectory above. Both it and the cross-walls are later (possibly later 13th-century) insertions into the original building—note the window partly blocked by the south end of the eastern wall. The ground floor was lit by seven rectangular windows in the south wall, two of which were later enlarged into doorways. The original entrances to this building are at the north-east and north-west corners. The latter was the main entrance and beside it, in the outer face of the wall, is a recess for the lavabo, the basin for washing hands before entering the refectory to eat. A mural stairs in the internal west wall of the building probably gave access to the refectory above. The kitchen, naturally enough, was usually located close to the refectory. At Bridgetown its location is not obvious, but it may have been the chamber at the southern end of the east range, in line with and next to the refectory block. Further east is another complex of buildings, effectively a continuation of the south range. There are the remains of a good residential apartment at first-floor level, with a fine cusped window with seats in the south wall, beside an attached three-storey tower that also contains residential chambers. This area may be the late medieval apartments for the prior.

Caherconree, Beehehagh, Co. Kerry Promontory fort

*Overlooking the Finglas river valley, near the neck of the Dingle peninsula. Can be approached from the link road southwards from Curraghduff, on the N86. **Only attempt in fine weather and with appropriate hiking clothing and footwear and taking all of the usual precautions associated with mountain hiking.** Disc. Ser. 71.*

At over 600 m, Caherconree, at the west end of the Slieve Mish range, is the highest promontory fort in Ireland. Those brave enough to attempt the steep and poorly signposted climb will be rewarded, weather permitting, with a spectacular view over the south-west coast and back into the Macgillycuddy Reeks on the Iveragh peninsula. A 110 m long stone wall, up to 3 m high, 4.5 m thick, and tiered on the interior face, cuts across the east side of a triangular-shaped area of land which is otherwise naturally defended on all sides by steep cliffs. About 10 m in front of the stone wall is a denuded bank and fosse which once traversed the full width of the spur. Several D-shaped huts can be discerned inside the main, stone wall, which has two entrances. The fort is named after Cú Raoi Mac Daire, who stole away Cú Chulainn's wife Blathnad, who later betrayed him by signalling the right time to attack the citadel by pouring milk into the mountain stream.

Cappeen West, Co. Cork Ringfort

45 km west of Cork city, off N22 (Cork–Killarney); take R585 to Dunmanway, 23 km west of Cork; Cappeen is 20 km further west; signposted. Disc. Ser. 86.

Known as Cahirvagliair Fort, this bivallate ringfort occupies the head of a slight spur overlooking the west end of a small river valley. It is approximately 39 m in diameter and the entrance is in the east-south-east. The outer rampart is quite denuded and survives best around the north side of the enclosure. The monumental, lintelled stone entrance has been reconstructed following excavations. Behind this, Manning uncovered remains of two further wooden gates. The inner face of the inner bank shows traces of stone revetment. The entrance is likewise flanked with a stone facing. An earthen souterrain occurs in the south-east quadrant and was first investigated by Windele *c.*1856. Several chambers were revealed, some with flagstone roofs. Bones, including some from humans, were reported. The possibility of there being a second, collapsed souterrain, near the entrance, is raised by a longitudinal hollow. Manning dated the site to the 10th–11th centuries AD.

Cork city, Co. Cork Medieval town; County Museum

At junction of N8, N20, and N25. Disc. Ser. 87.

In the 6th century St Finbar founded a monastic site here, on a ridge overlooking an area of marshes and islands in the estuary of the river Lee, and from this the city of Cork [*Corcaigh*, 'marshy place'] ultimately developed. Little is known of this monastery until the 9th century, when it became the object of Viking raids. A fortified Viking settlement was probably established in the 840s and re-established *c.*915 on an island (the 'south island') just north-east of the monastic site. This settlement grew into a prosperous town and may well have expanded onto a neighbouring island to the north (the 'north island'). The north island was certainly developed soon after the English captured the town in 1177, and substantial suburbs grew up on the north and south banks of the mainland, opposite the two islands. Little remains of the medieval town today and the original topography has been altered beyond recognition. However, the original main street that formed the spine of the two islands survives as North and South Main St., and fragments of the town wall survive to the rear of the properties opening off this street. The medieval cathedral, which occupied the centre of the original monastic site, has been replaced by a 19th-century Neo-Gothic building (*on Bishop St./Dean St.*). A round tower formerly stood in the cathedral grounds, but was removed in the 18th century. The only surviving medieval building in the city is the tower of the Augustinian friary, known as the 'Red Abbey' (*off Douglas St.*) on the south bank of the river. Important collections of material from archaeological excavations in Cork city and county are on display in the Cork Public Museum (*Fitzgerald Park, off Western Road/N22*).

Drombeg, Co. Cork Stone circle

15 km south-west of Clonakilty, off the R597 (Ross Carbery–Glandore); take minor road to south 2 km east of Drombeg village; signposted. Disc. Ser. 89.

Midway between Glandore and Ross Carbery and standing on a river terrace overlooking the Atlantic ocean, Drombeg is one of the most picturesque stone circles and archaeological complexes in Ireland. The centrepiece is a 17-stone circle (two are missing and one has fallen over), 9.3 m in diameter, excavated by Fahy in 1957. The 2 m high entrance or portal stones are on the east side and opposite them is the recumbent or axial stone, thus aligning the circle on the midwinter sunset. There are two cupmarks on the recumbent stone. Fahy suggested that two of the stones on the northern side (the second and third stones to the left of the entrance looking 'out') represent male and female forms and imbue the monument with fertility significance. The interior was covered with a layer of stones and gravel and beneath this were five pits; the one in the centre of the circle held a cremated adolescent and a broken, coarse, charcoal-encrusted pot which yielded a date of 1124–794 BC. Several pieces of worked flint were also found.

40 m to the west are two conjoined huts and a fulacht fiadh which Fahy excavated in 1958. The fulacht fiadh comprises a horseshoe-shaped mound surrounding a slab-lined cooking pit, a U-shaped hearth, and a

▼ **Fig. 157.** Drombeg: plan (after Ó Nualláin)

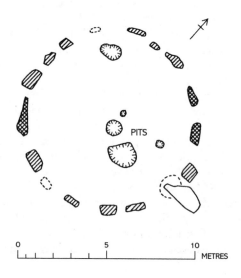

well and drain for water. Two radiocarbon dates were obtained, of 994–814 BC and 766–410 BC. A protracted period of use is suggested by the calculation that the volume of stones represents at least 300 cooking events and three phases of associated houses/huts. The first phase saw the erection of an impermanent, C-shaped shelter, which was succeeded by a larger, circular stone hut. This latter was replaced by a figure-of-eight-shaped stone house that commandeered the doorway of the phase 2 house. Later still, a causeway was built between this and the fulacht fiadh. 1st-century AD dates for the hut complex are susceptible to revision. A second, slightly nondescript fulacht fiadh lies to the east and the complex itself is overlooked from the north by a large ringfort.

Knockarudane (160 m), behind the village of Drombeg, provides the upland backdrop to the stone circle and it is more or less encircled with standing stones, which probably define the broader ritual landscape to which the circle belongs.

Dunbeg, Co. Kerry Promontory fort

15 km west of Dingle, on the seaward side of the R559 coastal route; 5 km south of Ventry; signposted. Disc. Ser. 70.

This spectacular but complicated coastal promontory fort, one of 19 in Dingle, was excavated in the late 1970s by Terry Barry, and remains one of the very few dated promontory forts. A small, triangular area of land is defended from the mainland by four banks and five intervening fosses, behind which is a massive stone rampart wall. This latter partly overlies an early fosse with a *terminus ante quem* of 802–534 BC. Stone tumble in the bottom of this fosse may have derived from a putative contemporary wall on the seaward side. There may also have been a wattle fence along this early fosse. Charcoal from the base of fosse 1, on the other hand, produced a radiocarbon date of AD 680–1020, which is probably closer to the true date of the monument we see today. The wall, which is only about half its original length and was built in two stages, is breached by a narrow, lintelled entrance, on either side of which are mural chambers, from which the draw-bar was controlled. From this a flagged pathway leads to a large *clochán* or corbel stone house, which saw two phases of occupation during the 10th or 11th centuries AD. A souterrain was discovered leading from near the entrance in the rampart wall, extending underneath the innermost rampart.

Ferriter's Cove, Co. Kerry Mesolithic settlement, middens, medieval castle

17 km north-west of Dingle, off R559 coastal route; 3 km north-west of Bally-ferriter. Disc. Ser. 70.

A series of shell middens in the cliff face beneath the dunes at Ferriter's Cove, near the tip of the Dingle peninsula, has been dated to the first half of the 4th millennium BC. The lithic assemblage, however, is of Mesolithic character and is, therefore, important evidence of hunter-gatherer presence in the south-west. Knapping occurred *in situ*, using a variety of stone types including rhyolites and volcanic ashes, which out-crop at Dunquin to the south; the products included Bann flakes, blades, axes, points, and choppers. Quantities of marine molluscs, fish, wild pig, and red deer were found associated with pits, hearths, and general occu-pation debris, and reflect very localized, episodic exploitation during the summer and early autumn; there is a noteworthy absence of marine mammals and sea birds from the assemblage. The presence of domestic cattle and sheep bones raises interesting questions about the integration of hunter-gatherer and agrarian subsistence strategies. The partial remains of at least one adult human were also found. It is unclear whether or not these represent a type of burial. It is interesting to note that isotopic analysis suggests that up to 78 per cent of the dietary protein was marine derived.

Doon Point, at the north end of Ferriter's Cove, has a fine promon-tory fort comprising two distinct sets of cross-banks and fosses, about 250 m apart, which have the effect of creating two distinct areas. A series of hut sites has been identified in the longer, western area. A tower house, known as 'Ferriter's Castle', was built on the first set of cross-banks during the 15th or 16th century. It is in poor condition. The ground floor has a vaulted ceiling and is lit by a double-splayed loop. The last resident, the poet Piaras Feirtéar, was executed in 1653.

Gallarus, Co. Kerry Church

6 km north-west of Dingle off the R559 coastal route, between Murreagh and Ballyferriter; signposted. Disc. Ser. 70.

Of all the Dingle peninsula's remarkable wealth of archaeological sites, perhaps the best known is the 'oratory' of Gallarus. This tiny, simple church is notable both for the quality of its distinctive construction and because of the debate about its age. In plan, it is a small rectangle, absolutely plain apart from a flat-lintelled west doorway with inclined jambs and a tiny, round-headed east window. Above the doorway, internally, are two projecting stones with perforations that presumably held a door of some form. The building's most important feature is its corbelled drystone roof, which rises almost imperceptibly from the walls, giving the whole structure an appearance somewhat like the upturned hull of a boat. This roofing technique is plausibly explained as an adaptation of the *clochán* ('beehive hut') tradition, from buildings of round to rectangular plan. It has also been seen as the first step in the development of the distinctive Irish high-pitched stone roof with internal propping arch, as seen for example at **Glendalough**, **Kells**, **Killaloe**, and ultimately at Cormac's Chapel in **Cashel**. On this basis a

▲ Fig. 158. Gallarus oratory (photo: Dept. of Archaeology, NUI, Galway)

date as early as the 8th century was proposed for Gallarus, but more recently a date as late as the 12th century has been suggested, albeit on no better evidence. The true date of Gallarus undoubtedly lies somewhere between the 8th and 12th centuries, but without archaeological excavation or historical information, closer dating is practically impossible. Whatever its date, the church is a remarkable piece of drystone construction and a memorable sight. Outside the church is an early cross-pillar with the Latin-letter inscription *LIE COLUM MEC GR . . .* ('the stone of Colum, son of Gr . . .').

Glanworth, Co. Cork Medieval borough and castle

9 km north-west of Fermoy on R512 (Fermoy–Kilmallock); Disc. Ser. 73.

Historians tell us that in the early Middle Ages Glanworth was the main residence of the Eóganacht Glendamnach, sometime kings of Munster, but no archaeological evidence for this residence has been found. The origins of the modern village lie in a 13th-century borough, probably established by the first English lords, the de Cauntetons, around their castle. Late in the 13th century the castle and borough passed to the Roche family, who held it until the Cromwellian confiscations of the mid-17th century. A Dominican friary was founded by the Roches in 1475. The village is located on the west bank of the river Funshion and is laid out along a linear main street, with three side streets to the east, converging on the disconcertingly narrow bridge over the river, which is probably 17th century. It is uncertain whether the layout of the village reflects that of the medieval borough. The castle, parish church, and friary are all located to the north of the bridge, which suggests that the borough was also confined to this area. The only medieval monument further south (c.*400 m south of the bridge, behind a grain store on the east side of the street*) is the small church known as 'Templealour' [*Teampull an labhair*, 'the leper's church']. This was probably the church of a leper hospital, which would normally be sited some distance away from a medieval settlement. Excavations in the 1980s revealed traces of a wall running westwards from the external south-west angle of the castle, which was interpreted as a 13th/14th-century town wall. If this was so, it must have enclosed an area to the north of the castle, rather than to the south.

The major monument at Glanworth is the castle, strongly sited on a rock outcrop overlooking the crossing point on the river (*access either through the grounds of the Glanworth Mill, or from the Mitchelstown road, to the west*). It's a complex structure dating probably from the 13th to 17th centuries, and currently presenting itself as an irregular four-sided enclosure with a rectangular hall keep in the south-eastern part and a complex of ruined buildings in the western half. Excavation has shown, however, that the original early 13th-century castle was smaller but was extended to the west and south, mainly in the 15th century. The most obvious element of the original castle is the hall keep, a two-storey rectangular building with walls up to 2 m thick. It was entered at first-floor level on the north side, where there is now a ragged opening, via an external wooden stair. The ground floor was accessible only from the first-floor chamber above—the present opening in the north wall is not original. The first floor was originally of timber supported by wooden beams (note the sockets in the side walls) but this was later replaced by a stone floor, supported on a double vault inserted over the ground floor. There was clearly an attic above the first floor, lit by a narrow slit window in the north wall. The first-floor chamber would have been the lord's hall, but it was poorly lit by small windows in the side walls and not surprisingly, it was soon replaced by a larger hall. This was built onto the north-east angle of the enclosure but nothing is now visible apart from the modified curtain walls themselves.

The least obvious part of the early castle is the gatehouse, now incorporated in the building complex to the west of the hall keep. The original gatehouse consisted of two rectangular towers flanking an entrance passage, located in the middle of the western side of the enclosure. The return of the curtain wall north of the gatehouse is still standing, but only the foundations of the south-west angle survive, revealed by excavation. The redesign of the castle began probably in the 14th century, when the gatehouse was extended as far as the north curtain wall and converted to residential use. A new gateway was opened in the curtain wall, immediately south of the former gatehouse. The major phase of modification probably dates to the 15th century, when the enlarged gatehouse block was unified by the addition of a battered external wall face on the east and south sides and a tall, four-storey turret on the west. The castle itself was significantly enlarged to the west and south, with a new curtain wall erected on these sides. The new enclosure had square or round turrets at the angles, including one added to the north-east angle, which had not been extended. A new hall was erected along the eastern side of the castle, but as with the earlier hall, all that survive are the window openings (considerably modified) in the curtain wall. Relatively minor modifications took place in the late 16th/early 17th centuries, when a kitchen was added in the north-west corner, with a large fireplace inserted into the curtain wall, and a bakehouse with a large bread oven was built in the south-west corner.

At the north-western end of the village, c.200 m from the castle, the ruined Church of Ireland church occupies the site of the medieval parish church. On the south side of the graveyard are fragments of a medieval wall with a doorway and, at the south-west corner beside the road, the base of a medieval tower with a vaulted ground-floor chamber. The stepped masonry structure to the east, on the riverbank, marks a holy well. The Dominican friary is now quite isolated from the village, c.350 m north of the castle, but it may indicate that the medieval borough extended this far. Only the church survives; the cloisters to the north have vanished, apart from the roof line of the south ambulatory, in the external north wall of the church. The church is of the usual simple, rectangular plan, with nave and choir separated by a crossing tower, pierced at ground level by rather narrow arches. The fine east window, of four lights with switchline tracery, has only recently been re-erected, having been moved to the Church of Ireland church in the 19th century. Apart from some good ogee-headed windows in the south wall and a tomb niche near the south-east angle, there are few interesting features visible in the rather neglected remains.

Island, Co. Cork Wedge tomb

8.5 km south-east of Mallow (as the crow flies), off the N20 (Cork–Mallow); take link road to Burnfort, 9 km south of Mallow, and turn north-east (right) in village towards Island; signposted. Disc. Ser. 80.

This excellent example of a Wedge tomb was excavated by O'Kelly in 1957. A series of kerb sockets around the megalithic structure indicate that the cairn was originally D-shaped (11.5 m long), with the entrance to the burial gallery at the wider, south-west side. The tomb itself (5.7 m long) is twin-walled and U-shaped, decreasing in height from front to rear. It is orientated south-west/north-east. There was a semicircle of small stones in front of the entrance. A small pillar stone (the 'sentinel stone') occurs near the entrance and the antechamber is separated from the gallery by a lintel stone. Behind this was a shallow pit containing the

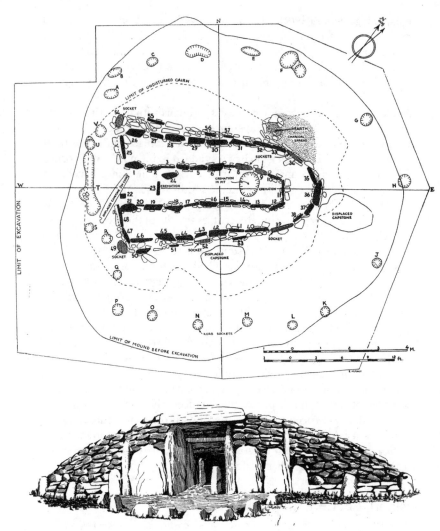

▲ **Fig. 159.** Island: plan of site as excavated, with reconstruction drawing (after O'Kelly)

remains of an elderly woman. A circular pit near the back of the gallery contained comminuted cremated bone, charcoal, and a fragmentary burnt flint implement. A small hearth just outside the gallery originally yielded dates of 1730–1000 BC but more recent dates of 1412–1226 BC and 1430–1274 BC (from one of the kerb sockets) have further refined the range. This very late dating has led to the suggestion that the cairn, which seals the hearth, was enlarged or added centuries after the tomb was built.

Kealkill, Co. Cork Stone circle, standing stones

70 km south-west of Cork city, at the junction of the R584 (Macroom–Bantry) and R585 (Cork–Bantry); signposted. Disc. Ser. 85.

This is an intriguing little complex comprising a stone circle, a pair of standing stones, and a radial stone cairn. It is located on level ground on a western shoulder of the Maughanaclea Hills and was excavated in 1938 by Sean P. Ó Ríordáin. The five-stone circle is complete and a mere 2.8 m in diameter. Two shallow trenches intersecting in the middle of the circle were thought to have held horizontal timbers with an upright at the crossover. Immediately to the east is a pair of standing stones. The south-west stone originally stood at 5.3 m high but was broken and only the upper portion re-erected by the excavator. The radial stone cairn is about 2 m to the north-east and was also excavated. Here were eighteen radially set stones (6 m in diameter) under the remains of the cairn. An enigmatic arc of stones between two larger stones, as well as fragments of three scallop shells, were also found under the cairn.

Numerous other stone circles, standing stones, and other monuments occur within the immediate vicinity, particularly around the northern and western flanks of the Hills. A markedly similar arrangement of stone circle, standing stones, and radial stone cairn occurs at Knocknakilla on the north-western side of Musherabeg Mountain, between Macroom and Millstreet.

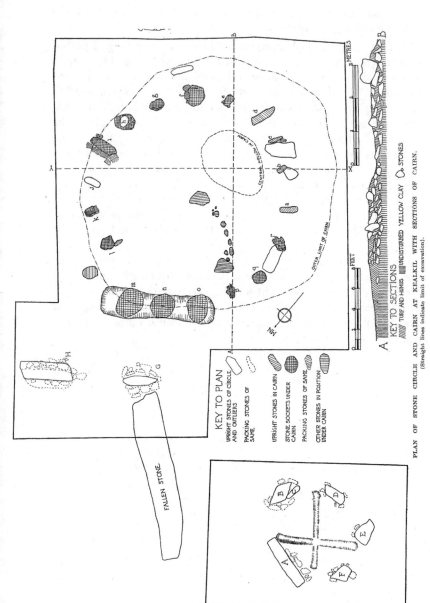

KEY TO PLAN

UPRIGHT STONES OF CIRCLE AND OUTLIERS

PACKING STONES OF SAME

UPRIGHT STONES IN CAIRN

STONE SOCKETS UNDER CAIRN

PACKING STONES OF SAME

OTHER STONES IN POSITION UNDER CAIRN

FALLEN STONE

CENTRAL HOLLOW IN CAIRN

OUTER LIMIT OF CAIRN

NM

3 METRES

FEET

KEY TO SECTIONS

TURF AND HUMUS   UNDISTURBED YELLOW CLAY   STONES

SECTIONS OF CAIRN.

PLAN OF STONE CIRCLE AND CAIRN AT KEALKIL, WITH SECTIONS OF CAIRN.
(Straight lines indicate limit of excavation).

▲ Fig. 160. Kealkil: plan of site as excavated (after Ó Ríordáin)

Killarney, Co. Kerry Castle; monastic island; friary

30 km south of Tralee on N22 (Cork–Tralee). Disc. Ser. 78.

Killarney [*Cill Airne*, 'church of the sloe-tree'] is Ireland's foremost tourist resort, situated in an area of great natural beauty. The town itself is of modern origin, but there are several archaeological monuments in the vicinity, well worth visiting while one is enjoying the scenery.

Ross Castle

2 km outside the town to the south-west, overlooking Lough Leane, is Ross Castle (*signposted; admission charge*). Sited on what was originally an island in the lake, this typical 15th-century tower house was the residence of the local O'Donoghue Ross lords. It is an impressive four-storey rectangular structure, with a wall walk and machicolations above, and was originally surrounded by a fortified bawn with round angle towers—two of which remain. Characteristically for such tower houses, the lord's hall is located at the top of the building, with a reconstructed wooden screen and minstrel's gallery. Below this, the second-floor level was probably the main bedchamber for the lord's family. A three-storey barrack block was attached to the south side of the tower house in the mid-18th century. The recently restored castle contains 16th- and 17th-century furniture (not original to the castle).

Inisfallen

From Ross Castle boats can be hired to Inisfallen [*Inis Faithlen*, 'Faithlen's island'], *c.*1.5 km offshore. A monastic site was founded on this island in the 7th century, either by St Finian or by a local king, Faithlen, or a combination of both. The monastery functioned throughout the Middle Ages, adopting Augustinian rule probably in the early 13th century, and was not finally suppressed until the 1580s. It is perhaps most famous as the site where the *Annals of Inisfallen* were compiled in the early 13th century. Three early churches survive in the north-eastern corner of the island, one of which has been incorporated into the later Augustinian priory. Near the landing pier, on the lake edge, is a small 12th-century church or oratory with a Romanesque-style west doorway, decorated with chevrons and animal heads, and a simpler round-headed window in the east gable. To the south is an even smaller oratory, probably of earlier 12th-century date, with a plain round-arched west doorway. 20 m to the west are the ruins of the Augustinian priory. Most of the western part of the priory church is early—probably 10th/11th century—with antae and a flat-lintelled doorway in its western façade. This early church was extended in the 13th century and a chancel added, which has two simple, narrow lancet windows in the east gable. On the north side of the church are the claustral buildings, with traces of a separate block (perhaps a kitchen) to the north.

Ross Island

Excavations by William O'Brien at Ross Island on the eastern side of Lough Leane, between Killarney and Muckross House, uncovered the oldest-dated copper mines in western Europe. A mining trail with information panels is provided, but old mineshafts (some flooded) are hazardous and *children should be supervised at all times*. Between 2400 and 1800 BC early miners, living in an adjacent, industrial camp, set about pounding and picking away veins of mineralized copper creating a series of low-vaulted mineshafts that look for all the world like caves. The ore-bearing limestone was first made brittle by fire and rapid quenching with cold water from the lake. Cattle scapulae were used as crude shovels. Further refining of the ore took place in the camp and involved a considerable amount of crushing, grinding, and, eventually, smelting in charcoal-fired pits. The smelted copper was made into pancake-shaped ingots. Of particular interest is the associated Beaker pottery, confirming the postulated connection between the users of this pottery and the earliest metallurgy in Britain and Ireland. The high arsenic content of the **Toormore** copper hoard suggests that the ore was mined at Ross Island. Mining continued here during the 8th century AD and involved the exploitation of lead, tin, and iron ores, and possibly also of silver. A poem dating from around this time acclaims the mythological smith Lén *Línfíaclach* ('Lén of the white teeth'), after whom the lake is named. Mining was recommenced once again in the early 18th century by two local families, the Brownes and the Herberts, and continued in fits and starts until the beginning of the 20th century.

Muckross friary

4 km south of Killarney, in the National Park, is Muckross friary (*off N71 (Killarney–Kenmare); signposted*), an attractive friary with perhaps the most complete cloister of any Irish monastery. This Franciscan friary was probably founded *c.*1440 by Domhnall Mac Cárthaig, king of Desmond, possibly on the site of an earlier monastery. A papal indulgence was granted in 1468 to raise funds for the completion of the buildings. Thus the buildings, which are unusually well preserved, can be dated quite closely to the middle of the 15th century. The friary was dissolved *c.*1586 but reoccupied by friars for a period in the 17th century. The church is divided by a central tower into a choir and a relatively short nave. The transept on the south side of the nave was probably added *c.*1500. The church is lit by large windows with switchline tracery in the east gable and in the south gable of the transept. Elsewhere the windows

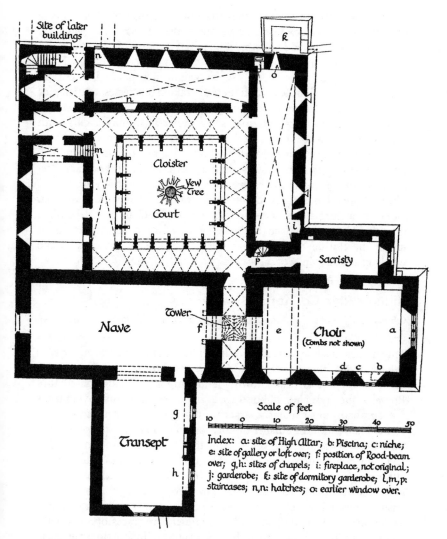

▲ **Fig. 161.** Killarney: plan of Muckross friary (after Leask)

are groups of two or three single lights, mainly round headed, or single ogee-headed lights. The choir has a piscina in the south wall, a later sedilia in the north wall, and originally had a gallery over the west end. The tower was added after the church was built and is unusually broad for a Franciscan church, with a ribbed vault under the central opening. On its west wall are corbels that would have supported a rood beam.

The small cloister and its associated buildings, on the north side of the church, are reached through a doorway under the tower or through the sacristy from the choir. The claustral buildings are practically complete, with an ancient yew tree in the centre of the garth, which is surrounded by an arcade of arched openings—round on the south and west sides and bluntly pointed on the north and east. As in many Franciscan friaries, the ambulatory is integrated, or incorporated within the ranges at ground-floor level, and there are raking buttresses on each pier of the arcade to help support the upper floor. A side-effect of this is that the remaining ground-floor spaces are rather narrow and dark, and these vaulted chambers were probably used largely for storage. By contrast, the first-floor chambers are well lit and comprised the dormitory (in the east range), the refectory (in the north range), and probably the residence of the guardian or superior of the friary (in the west range). The refectory has a niche or *pulpitum* for the reading of devotional literature at meals and is separated from the kitchen by a large, late fireplace. There is evidence (in the wall joints) for the sequence of building of the cloister ranges—the east range is earliest, followed by the north and finally the west range.

Kilmalkedar, Co. Kerry Early church site

6.5 km north-west of Dingle off R559 (Dingle–Ballyferriter); signposted. Disc. Ser. 70.

This monastic site is named after its reputed 7th-century founder [*Cill Mhaolcethair*, 'the church of Maolcethair'], but little else is known of its history. It is best known for an important mid-12th-century Romanesque-style church, but there is also a ruined oratory of **Gallarus** type, probably older than the larger church, and some interesting carved stone. The roof of the smaller oratory has collapsed, illustrating a structural weakness inherent in transferring the corbelled roof from round to rectangular buildings. The larger church is of nave-and-chancel form, although the chancel is a slightly later (*c.*1200) enlargement of the original chancel or altar recess. The nave has several elements of traditional Irish church architecture—antae on the east and west ends, high-pitched gables with a 'whale-tail shaped' gable finial, and traces of a corbelled stone roof. The chancel also had a stone roof originally. However, there are also elements of the new Romanesque style which was reaching Ireland in the 12th century—the west doorway and chancel arch have decorated round arches of three and two orders, respectively, while the north and south walls of the nave are ornamented internally with flat-headed blank arcading. The decoration of the nave seems closely related to that at Cormac's Chapel in **Cashel**, suggesting a similar date (*c.*1140). Inside the church is a cross-inscribed stone and another stone, unusually inscribed with the Latin alphabet. Outside is an ogam stone inscribed *ANM MAILE INBIR MACI BROCANN* ('the soul of Mael-Inbir, son of Brocán'), a stone cross, and an attractive early sundial. 120 m to the north-east is 'St Brendan's House', a two-storey house, probably a priests' residence of the 15th century.

Kilnaruane, Co. Cork Cross shaft

1 km south-west of Bantry, off N71 (Bantry–Skibbereen); signposted. Disc. Ser. 85.

The faint circular outline of this early monastery (*Cill Ruáin*) overlooking Bantry Bay is visible from the air, with low-profile topographical remains surviving to the north of the cross shaft, which is the principal item of interest here. The shaft is 2.15 m tall and only the upper parts of the stone are decorated. The west face is divided into four panels. The lowermost contains two seated figures on opposite sides of a table, on which a bird is depositing a round object, interpreted by Harbison as the feeding of bread to the hermit saints Paul and Anthony. Above this is an equal-armed cross and over this again an unidentified figure in an orans (praying) pose, arms raised, palms outwards but possibly holding a circular disc in the left hand. The uppermost panel contains an interlaced animal, profiled head upside down at bottom right. The scenes on the west face are divided into just two panels and, apart from the interlace knot of the top one, are to be read vertically. The second panel has four profiled animals, heads abutting. Beneath this is an intriguing scene interpreted by its many admirers as a boat (pointing skywards) with four oarsmen and possibly as many as three other figures, one at the stern and (according to Harbison) two at the prow, one, with a raised hand, interpreted as Christ quelling the storm. Beneath the stern are two simple crosses. The shaft is grooved on both narrow sides and these may be to take a head or arms. This monument can be dated to the 9th or 10th century.

Nearby are four deeply grooved boulders of uncertain function. Could they be the corners of a composite, sarcophagus-like founder's tomb? There is a small burial ground within the enclosure and adjacent to this is a bullaun stone. To the east and south-east are the moorlands of Knocknaveagh and Spratt Hill respectively where there is an important complex of prehistoric monuments.

Kinsale, Co. Cork Medieval town

22 km south of Cork off N71 (Cork–Bandon); take R607 south at Halfway or R605 at Inishannon; signposted. Disc. Ser. 87.

Kinsale is a marvellously picturesque town, very popular with tourists for its shopping and restaurants, but it is also a medieval town. It is located, as its name [*Cionn tSáile*, 'head of the salt water'] suggests, at the head of a natural harbour where the Bandon river enters the sea. The parish church is thought to be located on the site of an early medieval monastic church, founded by the 6th-century saint Multose. There are also suggestions that Vikings used the site as a base in the 9th/10th centuries. The town itself, however, is an English creation, probably of the early 13th century. The new town was granted the right to hold a market in 1226 and was already walled before a grant of murage was made in 1348. A Carmelite friary was founded in 1334. Kinsale was not a particularly important medieval town, but was the scene of one of the defining moments in Irish history when in 1601 a Spanish force landed there to assist the Irish lords (led by Ó Néill and Ó Domhnaill in the far north-west!) in their war against the English. The Spaniards were besieged in Kinsale by the English, and Ó Néill and Ó Domhnaill, having marched south in midwinter to raise the siege, were defeated. The medieval town occupied an irregular, sub-triangular shape with a later extension (the 'base town') along the shore to the south-east. The town was walled from at least the 14th century and the base town was also enclosed, but probably not until the 16th century. Eventually the walls had up to fifteen mural towers and seven gates, but because of damage in the 17th century and later development, little remains of the walls or towers. The medieval quay, too, has been reclaimed and built over.

Parish church

The medieval parish church of St Multose, located at the heart of the medieval town (*Church St., off Church Place*), is one of the few Irish churches to have been in continuous use, effectively from its foundation to the present. Because it is still in use, access can be difficult—it is best visited immediately after services, on Sunday mornings and Wednesdays at midday. The church is said to be on the site of the 6th-century foundation of the local saint Eilte, whose name, passing through the Irish form of endearment *Mo Eilte óg* (literally 'my little Eilte'), was corrupted into Multose. The antiquity of the site, and the suggestion that the curve of Church St., to the north, reflects the line of an early monastic enclosure, has not been proved, however. The present church is a 13th-century structure, although much altered subsequently. Indeed, there may have been two 13th-century churches or building phases. The top of a window in early Gothic style, now built into the north wall of the belfry (at the west end of the north aisle), suggests the existence of an early 13th-century church. However, other architectural features such as the west window of five conjoined lancets suggest a later 13th-century date.

The medieval church was a nave-and-chancel structure, which had side aisles (to the nave) from the outset; it may also have had transepts, but this is uncertain. The north aisle arcade was rebuilt in the 18th century and only the western arch remains of the original arcade, which had seven pointed arches extending almost to the east end of the chancel. The chancel is probably a late medieval addition and was originally separated from the nave by a cross-wall with chancel arch, but this was removed in the 18th century. There is a north transept, which is generally regarded as medieval, and almost (but not quite) opposite it, on the south, are what appear to be the ruins of a south transept. It is generally thought that this is actually a late 16th-century chapel, but some of the architectural details suggest that it may indeed represent the remains of an early south transept. The belfry, at the west end of the north aisle, is apparently an original feature, although the upper storey and spire are modern. Over the doorway in the west wall is a niche with a worn late medieval statue, said to represent St Multose. The present roof, spanning nave and aisles, is relatively modern. The original roof was clearly much higher over the nave, presumably with lower, lean-to roofs over the aisles.

'Desmond Castle'

On the north side of Cork St. is a three-storey urban tower house known as 'Desmond Castle' or the 'French Prison' (*National Monument; admission charge*). It was probably built *c.*1500 as a town house for the lords of Kinsale—the FitzGerald earls of Desmond—and possibly also as a Custom House for the town. It now houses a Museum of Wine but is worth seeing as an example of the fortified houses once found in many medieval Irish towns. The original structure is a roughly square, three-storey tower house, with extensive later outbuildings to the rear, which were used in later centuries as a gaol. The tower house was entered through a well-carved pointed doorway in the centre of the south-east façade, fronting the street. Overhead are the Desmond arms while higher up, between the second and third floors, are the arms of Henry VII of England (1485–1509). Internally, the tower house consists of a single main chamber at each level, although some details, such as the original stairs to the upper levels, have clearly been removed. The ground-floor chamber was poorly lit—the windows in the south-east wall and the present entrance in the south-west wall are not original—and was probably a storage area. The principal chamber is at first-floor level, well lit by four twin-light mullioned windows, with internal seats, in the south-east wall and another in the south-west wall. In the rear (north-west) wall is a large fireplace. All the windows, which are ogee headed or round headed, have good dressed limestone mouldings with hoods and this fine chamber must have been the earl's hall. The second-floor chamber is simpler, although it has good two-light windows in the south-east and south-west walls, and a mural stair in the north-east wall leading to the wall walk above.

The attractive market house (*on Market Square*) may have been originally erected *c.*1600 but the gabled front is early 18th century. It now contains a local museum. Immediately outside the north-east corner of the medieval walled town (*west side of Abbey Lane*) are the remains of the medieval Carmelite friary, founded in 1334 and dissolved in 1541. The friary was seriously damaged in the siege of 1601 and only poorly preserved fragments of the choir and south transept survive today. The approach to Kinsale Harbour is guarded by two large 17th-century forts, both of which can be visited. On the west shore is 'James Fort', built in the aftermath of the Battle of Kinsale in 1602, and linked to a 16th-century artillery blockhouse at the tip of the peninsula (*take R600 south, towards Ballinspittle; cross the bridge just outside Kinsale and turn left immediately*). Opposite it, on the east shore, is the larger and later 'Charles Fort', built in the late 1670s. Charles Fort, in particular, is a superb piece of early modern military architecture and well worth visiting. It is a National Monument with a visitor centre (*admission charge*) and can be reached by road (*R600 east from Kinsale and follow coast road to Summercove*) or on foot along Long Quay, on the north side of the harbour, through the village of Scilly, and via a pedestrian walk along the east shore of the harbour.

Knockdrum, Co. Cork Rock art, cross-slab, souterrain, cashel

1.5 km west of Castletownsend off the R596 towards Skibbereen. Private land, permission should be sought. Disc. Ser. 89.

This interesting juxtaposition of rock art, cross-slab, souterrain, and cashel is known as 'Knockdrum'. The rock art occurs just outside the entrance to the cashel, and was turned over in 1869 to reveal a dense pattern of twenty-five cupmarks and an interesting 'dumb-bell' motif and penannular circles. A further 10 or so cupmarks occur on a fragmentary pillar-like stone in the interior of the cashel. The cashel itself is about 22 m in diameter and the walls (restored sometime before 1860) are an impressive 2 m high and 3 m thick. The entrance is flanked to the right by a sentry niche. The foundations of a rectangular stone building are traceable slightly off-centre. The souterrain was discovered in 1875 and excavated by Somerville in 1931. The passage is both earth- and rock-cut and there are three chambers. In one of them is a tabular stone hearth, above which is a chimney. The cross-slab bears a Greek cross on one face and a simple, incised cross on the other.

Labbacallee, Co. Cork Wedge tomb

*2 km south-east of **Glanworth** on the link road to Labbacallee; signposted. Disc. Ser. 73.*

This fine Wedge tomb is located between Fermoy and **Glanworth** in north-central Cork and, with a chamber nearly 14 m long, it is one of the largest in the country. Labbacallee Wedge tomb was excavated in 1934 by Harold Leask and Liam Price. The tomb is orientated south-east/north-west and the burial chamber is divided into two parts, a long

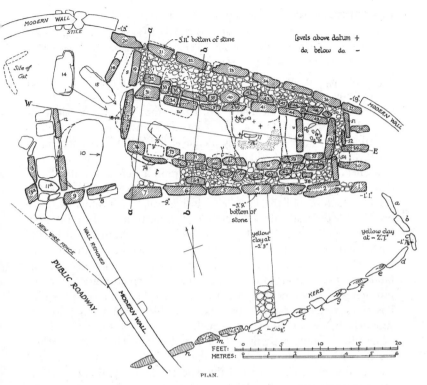

▲ Fig. 162. Labbacallee: plan of site as excavated (after Leask & Price)

western gallery and a small, boxlike compartment at the eastern end, which was accessed by sliding aside the third capstone. The floor of the chamber had been dug out to a depth of 0.6 m and the deposits, which included human and animal bone (the former inhumed and cremated) and pottery, may have been disturbed. The eastern compartment contained cremated bone midway through the deposit and below this was found a partially articulated adult female skeleton, minus the skull. Analysis at the time suggested that the missing skull was that found in the western compartment near an adult male and a child. A skewer-like pin found with the skeleton raises the possibility that the body was contained in a pinned-up bag. The pottery ranges from thin, well-baked incised vessels to coarser wares and classification has proven difficult. Recent radiocarbon dates place the headless skeleton at 2456–2138 BC and the adult and child at 2458–2038 BC and 2202–1776 BC respectively. These are considered the primary burials and the coarse pottery (concentrated at the eastern end) and cremated bone intrusive. A cistlike arrangement of stones at the front of the tomb contained inhumed long bones and a sherd described at the time as 'Food Vessel'.

Leacanabuaile, Co. Kerry Cashel (stone fort)

3 km north-west of Cahersiveen, off N70 ('Ring of Kerry' scenic route); cross Cahersiveen Bridge to north side of Valencia river, take road to west after 500 m and minor road to north after 2 km; signposted. Disc. Ser. 83.

The stone-walled ringfort at Leacanabuaile [*Leaca na Buaile*, 'hillside of the milking place'] was excavated in the 1940s, after which the visible features were partially reconstructed. These stone forts are usually considered to be versions (adapted to stony areas) of the earthen ringfort, the common housestead of early medieval Ireland. At Leacanabuaile a roughly circular area of *c.*30 m diameter is enclosed by a stone wall over 3 m thick, with an entrance to the east. Within it were substantial foundations of four stone-walled buildings, two of which were clearly subsidiary structures built against the enclosing wall, but the other two were presumably domestic houses. Adjoining the enclosing wall, on the west, is a round house of *clochán* type. A souterrain runs from just inside the entrance of this house westwards to a chamber within the thickness of the enclosing wall. At a later date a larger, roughly square building was built onto the east side of the round house, with an entrance to the east through which a stone drain ran out through the entrance of the fort. Postholes were found within both houses, which presumably held roof supports, but views differ as to whether these roofs were of corbelled stones throughout, or partly of timber and thatch. The excavators suggested a 9th/10th-century date for the fort, but some of the material recovered seems to be later and the date of the occupation of the fort remains uncertain.

*c.*400 m to the south-east is **Cahergal** [*Cathair Geal*, 'bright fort'], a large circular stone-walled fort with stairs built into the internal wall faces, similar to the better-known fort at **Staigue**. In the interior of the fort are remains of two drystone buildings, one a rectangular house built against the fort wall and the other a *clochán* ('beehive hut').

Sherkin Island, Co. Cork Promontory fort, Wedge tomb

15 km south-west of Skibbereen; accessible by boat from Baltimore. Disc. Ser. 88.

At Slievemore, near Sherkin Point at the south-south-west end of the island, are the remains of a possible promontory fort, comprising a rectangular area cut off by a pile of large rocks. Immediately to the east is a denuded Wedge tomb, three surviving gallery stones creating a space about 2.5 m long opening to the south-west. A few metres away is a tall, rectangular standing stone orientated north-north-east/south-south-west.

Skellig Michael, Co. Kerry   Monastic island

25 km west of Waterville; accessible by boat (only in suitable weather), available from Waterville, Ballinskelligs, or Valentia. This is a physically demanding site to visit; those less than fully fit might confine themselves to a cruise around the island, available from Valentia. Disc. Ser. 84.

Dramatically perched on a jagged rock outcrop *c.*12 km out in the Atlantic ocean, Skellig Michael [*Sceilig Mhichíl*, 'St Michael's rock'] is the ultimate expression of the eremitical ideal within the early Irish Church, which led to the setting up of hermitages and monastic sites in many remote and isolated places. Skellig is said to have been founded by a St Fionán, of whom almost nothing is known. Despite its remoteness, it was plundered by Vikings on at least two occasions in the 9th century and was subsequently abandoned by the community in favour of a site at **Ballinskelligs**, on the mainland. The date at which this happened is uncertain, but probably sometime between the late 9th and mid-11th centuries. The new monastery at Ballinskelligs retained the dedication to St Michael but the original site was apparently maintained in some form.

The main monastic enclosure is reached via a long series of stone steps, ascending from a landing place over 160 m below, on the east side of the island. Within the enclosure, on a series of paved terraces at the cliff edge, are six *clocháin* (corbelled drystone cells), two rectangular oratories of **Gallarus** type, and a small church dedicated to St Michael. Most of the buildings have probably undergone restoration over the last two centuries, the extent of which is not always clear. The *clochán* cells are somewhat unusual in being roughly square at the base, becoming more rounded as they rise to a domed top. The two oratories seem to be a development of the *clochán* tradition on a rectangular plan. They are tiny, simple structures with a doorway at the west end, a small window at the east, and distinctive corbelled roofs. One is located among the *clochán* cells, while the other is a short distance to the north-east. Immediately south-west of the first oratory are the ruins of St Michael's church, the only mortar-built building. It is usually regarded as later in date than the other buildings, but radiocarbon dates from the mortar suggest a date as early as the 8th century for its earliest phase. Although still very small, it is larger than the other oratories and, unusually, has its doorway in the north wall. A number of stone-lined cisterns for collecting rainwater are built into the terraces, reflecting the fact that practically all necessities of life would have had to be brought onto the largely barren island, which does not even have a regular water supply. Several *leachta* (outdoor altar-like structures) occur, the largest of which—known as the 'Monks' Graveyard'—lies at the east end of the main terrace and contains over 20 early grave slabs. Stone crosses also survive at various points on the island. Just below the South Peak, the highest point of the island (215 m), are the ruins of a second, smaller hermitage (*access is difficult and is recommended only for the dedicated and fit*).

At **Ballinskelligs** on the mainland (*7 km west of Waterville; take R566 or R567 west off N70*) are the remains of an Augustinian priory where the monks of Skelligs are said to have re-established their monastery when they abandoned the island. The priory, however, is probably an early 13th-century foundation from the Augustinian abbey at Rattoo, in north Kerry. It was apparently dissolved in the 1570s. The visible remains are mainly 15th century and have suffered from coastal erosion, which has removed the eastern part of the chancel of the church and the adjoining claustral buildings to the south. Unusually, the chancel is wider than the nave of the church and is possibly earlier than it, but the absence of datable features makes it impossible to be sure of this. Above the pointed chancel arch is a late medieval bellcote. Part of a wall of a sacristy survives north of the chancel. In the north and south walls of the nave are simple pointed windows, probably 13th/14th century. Three doorways (one now blocked) in the south wall gave access to the cloister garth, which was surrounded by an ambulatory with a now destroyed range of buildings to the east. The two-storey building still standing on the south side was probably the refectory. Further south other lengths of walling survive only as foundations. Adjoining the north-west angle of the church is a two-storey 15th-century residential building, known as the Prior's House. North-east of this are traces of two rectangular dry-stone buildings.

▼ **Fig. 163.** Staigue Fort (photo: Dept. of Archaeology, NUI, Galway)

Staigue, Co. Kerry Stone fort

11 km south-east of Waterville, off N70 ('Ring of Kerry' scenic route); take minor road to north at Castle Cove, 5 km east of Caherdaniel; signposted. Disc. Ser. 84.

This imposing stone fort or cashel is prominently sited at the head of a river valley with good views south-westwards down the valley to the sea at Kenmare Bay. It consists of a circular space *c.*27 m in diameter, enclosed by a massive drystone wall, which in turn was surrounded by a fosse and external bank. The enclosing wall is over 4 m thick and 5.7 m high and is built of a rubble core with facings of good quality drystone masonry. The wall is terraced internally and X-shaped flights of steps give access to the top at ten points around the circumference. Two chambers are incorporated within the thickness of the wall on the north-west and south-west, entered from the interior of the fort though lintelled openings. The main lintelled entrance runs through the wall into the interior, on the south. Some reconstruction of the wall is known to have taken place in the 19th century, but its extent is not always clear. The fosse surrounding the wall is *c.*3 m wide and 1.5 m deep, with a causeway opposite the entrance on the south. Outside the fosse is an external bank, *c.*5.5 m wide but only surviving to 0.5 m in height; almost certainly it was much higher originally.

The size and quality of the enclosing rampart at Staigue and a few similar structures, such as **Grianán Ailech** in Co. Donegal, have led to suggestions that these are a distinctive type of monument, unrelated to the general body of stone forts, which in turn are seen simply as stone versions of the ubiquitous early medieval ringfort. Unlike Grianán Aileach, which has medieval historical associations, there are no known references to Staigue in medieval documents. This has contributed to suggestions that it may be prehistoric, but it is most likely that Staigue—like Grianán Aileach—is merely a particularly impressive example of an early medieval stone-built ringfort. It is quite possibly a royal site that has yet to be identified in historical sources, perhaps because it was known by a different name.

Timoleague, Co. Cork Friary

11 km south of Bandon off N71 (Cork/Bandon–Clonakilty); take R602 south at Oldchapel (1 km west of Bandon) or R600 east at Scartagh (1 km north-east of Clonakilty). Disc. Ser. 89.

Overlooking the sea, where the Argideen river enters Courtmacsherry Bay, are the extensive but rather irregular remains of the Franciscan friary of Timoleague. The village itself takes its name [*Tigh Molaga*, 'St Molaga's church'] from a much earlier monastic foundation of St Molaga, of which no remains are visible. In the 13th century it was a borough, market, and port—the most westerly Anglo-Irish borough in what is now Co. Cork. The friary's origins are uncertain, but it was probably founded sometime between the mid-13th and early 14th centuries, either by the Anglo-Irish lords (the de Barrys) or by the resurgent Mac Cárthaig of Cairbre. Edmund de Courcy (d. 1518), a Franciscan bishop of Ross, apparently added the tower, a dormitory, library, and infirmary in the early 16th century. Although dissolved at the Reformation the friary was reoccupied by friars in the early 17th century, with many alterations. It was burned by the English, and finally abandoned, in the 1640s. The surviving remains are of many periods and consist of the normal long, narrow nave-and-choir church, with a south aisle, south transept, central tower, and extensive claustral buildings on the north side. Considerable later remodelling and the lack of excavation or conservation work make it difficult to tease out the building history, but this in a sense adds to the interest of the place.

The church is entered by a fairly simple pointed doorway in the west wall of the nave, with a tall twin-light window over. Despite its early appearance, this window and the entire west end is late medieval. The six-bay nave arcade is clearly of two periods—the smaller, western bays belong to a late medieval extension of the nave. The three larger bays to the east are contemporary with the south aisle and transept, which themselves are probably somewhat later than the church. Little remains of the south aisle. The south transept is also aisled and is rather crudely attached to the nave arcade by a half-arch. Again, it is lit by a deceptively early-looking south window of three tall, pointed lights, probably modelled on the original window in the east gable of the choir. The central tower is clearly a later addition—probably early 16th century—inserted into the west end of the choir. It dramatically increases the sense of separation between the choir (reserved for the friars) and the nave/transept, which accommodated the laity. The choir itself is mainly original 13th/14th-century work. Its main feature—and the most unusual architectural feature of the friary—is the internal arcade of tall, pointed arches, originally framing twin-light pointed windows in the north and south walls and a similar window of three lights in the east gable. The arches also contained a mural passage around the sides of the choir. Buildings such as this were usually paid for by wealthy lay benefactors, who in return received certain privileges, including the right of burial in the church. There are two once-fine late medieval tomb niches, possibly for the tombs of such benefactors, in the north wall of the church—in the choir is a pointed niche with remains of a traceried canopy, while the other is at the east end of the nave.

Doorways in the north wall of the choir and under the tower lead to the south ambulatory of the cloisters. Another doorway led from the choir to the sacristy, in the east range of the cloister. Little of the cloister arcade survives, but a reconstructed section at the north-east angle displays a series of wide openings each with three pointed lights. The surrounding buildings are reasonably intact, but have been much modified—especially the east range, which had two separate extensions added to the north. The east, north, and west ranges each consist of single, long chambers at ground level, although the east and west range were probably subdivided originally. Overhead, the first-floor spaces are tentatively identified as the chapter room (in the east range), a dormitory (in the west range), and a library (in the north range). The ground floor of the west range is identified as the kitchen, on the basis of a large fireplace and chimney at the north end, but these are probably post-medieval additions—although perhaps on the site of the original fireplace and kitchen. The building projecting north of the east range can be more reliably identified as a refectory, based on traces of the *pulpitum* (from which a friar read devotional literature to the community as they ate) in one of the east-facing windows. Above this may have been a dormitory and beyond it, to the north, a single-storey block with double garderobe tower on the east side may be the infirmary. The sequence of building is clearly visible in the external elevation along the east side of the friary: first the church, then the east range was added, followed by the refectory building, and finally, the single-storey infirmary building. This side of the friary was originally washed by the river estuary and at the base of the east range are two openings, reached by steps internally, which were probably for unloading provisions from boats.

Toormore, Co. Cork Wedge tomb

30 km west of Skibbereen, off the R592 Mizen peninsula coastal route; on the seaward side of the village of Toormore. Disc. Ser. 88.

Like its companion across the bay at **Altar**, this Wedge tomb has been restored following excavation by O'Brien in 1990. Forgoing sea view in favour of shelter, it is situated in a longitudinal depression near the top of a rock outcrop above Toormore Strand. It comprises a gallery just over 4 m long, orientated north-east/south-west, represented by two stones on each side and one extant capstone, restored to its original position following the replacement of the endstone with one newly quarried from the adjacent rock face. Four flagstones were placed across the gallery, 1 m in from the entrance, close to the period of construction, and charcoal from beneath one of them is dated 1870–1450 BC. This is contemporary with a stone-lined pit or cist beside the middle orthostat on the south side, which may have been robbed out in antiquity. A hoard comprising a decorated flat axe (*c.*1900–1700 BC) and two pieces of raw copper is known from Toormore. In spite of the proximity and contemporaneity of the Mount Gabriel copper mines it has been speculated that the axe, and the raw copper pieces, came from **Ross Island**.

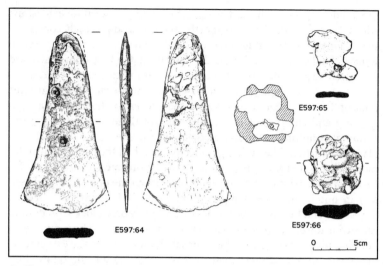

E597:65

E597:64

E597:66

0   5cm

▲ **Fig. 164.** Toormore: metal hoard (after O'Brien)

Tullylease, Co. Cork   Cross-slabs

18 km west of Charleville, Co. Cork, off the R579 (Kanturk–Broadford); signposted. Disc. Ser. 72.

According to tradition, this monastery was founded by St Berichter or Berihert, whose death is recorded in the *Annals of the Four Masters* on 6 December 839. If the entry is correct, then it is incompatible with the story that Berihert was the son of a Saxon prince who came to Ireland with his retinue and St Colmán of Lindisfarne, in protest against the Northumbrian king Oswiu's declaration in favour of the Roman Easter at the Synod of Whitby in AD 664. A more plausible explanation is that he was a grandson. Here are located around 18, mostly fragmentary, cross-slabs (five of which are inscribed) and what is perhaps the most accomplished and well-preserved cross-slab in the country. Dominated by a large cross, which has been compared with one in the early 8th-century Book of Lindisfarne, the slab bears a Latin inscription reading *QUICUMQUELEGERIT HUNC TITULUM ORAT PRO BERECHTU-INE* ('whosoever reads this inscription, let him pray for Berechtuine'). It has been postulated that the slab commemorates the founder saint and dates from around the time of his death.

Youghal, Co. Cork   Medieval town

45 km east of Cork on N25 (Cork–Waterford). Disc. Ser. 81.

Youghal [*Eochoill*, 'yew wood'] was established by Maurice FitzGerald in the early 13th century—possibly on the site of an earlier Viking base—

and became an important port under the protection of the FitzGerald earls of Desmond. Ireland's first Franciscan friary was founded there in 1224. There are no visible remains but its site, known as the 'South Abbey', is well known, outside the town to the south (*immediately south of Devonshire Arms Hotel, Friar St.*). A Dominican priory (the 'North Abbey') was founded on the north side of the town in 1268. Youghal was granted the right to hold a market in 1234 and received its first murage grant in 1275. It was badly damaged during the rebellion of the earl of Desmond in the late 16th century, but was fortunate to acquire powerful new patrons among the English adventurers who colonized the defeated earl's territories. Among these was Sir Walter Raleigh, but the most important was Richard Boyle, later earl of Cork, who controlled the town for most of the early 17th century.

The town was located on the estuary of the river Blackwater and occupied a sub-rectangular walled area, laid out along two streets running parallel to the shoreline (North Main St. and Nelson Place/Beau St./ Mouse St.), with several smaller streets intersecting at right angles. A small extension to the south, known as the 'Base Town' or 'Irishtown', was also walled in the late Middle Ages. The medieval docks (now built over) were located immediately outside the walls on the south-east. The main town was probably walled by the end of the 13th century and the entire circuit eventually included four gates and up to thirteen mural towers. Substantial parts of the town wall survive on the landward side of the town, including the remains of six mural towers. Along the north side of the town the fabric is slightly different from that on the west and may be a little later in date. The upper levels of the wall also show considerable evidence of rebuilding, especially in the section adjoining St Mary's graveyard. None of the medieval gates survive, but a large 18th-century structure known as the 'Clock Gate' occupies the site of the South Gate (*Main St.*) and a rebuilt arch spans the site of the Water Gate in the 'Base Town' (*on Quay Lane*). Beside the Clock Tower are steps leading up to a well-preserved section of the town wall.

At the corner of North Main St. and Church St. are early 17th-century almshouses, erected by the earl of Cork to house 'six poor widows'. These are essentially a terrace of two- and three-storey buildings with four pointed doorways at ground level and the arms of the earl of Cork at the centre of the elevation. Almost opposite the almshouses, on the eastern side of North Main St., is 'Tynte's Castle', a late medieval urban tower house (*not publicly accessible*). Although poorly maintained and sadly disfigured in the front elevation, it gives some impression of the type of fortified residences erected by prosperous merchants in embattled late medieval Irish towns. It has three storeys with attic above, vaulted over ground and first floors. The battlemented parapet is original and a small machicolation indicates the position of the original entrance on the street front below. Roughly midway along North Main

St., on the west side, is the site of the small Benedictine priory and Hospital of St John, possibly founded *c.*1185. Two much-modified buildings on the site appear to be of medieval origin. One is now a shop—a two-storey gable-fronted building which preserves several late medieval features in the front elevation. There is a doorway with pointed arch, moulded jambs, and decorated spandrels, an ogee-headed window, and the decorated drip moulding of another window (now replaced by a modern window). To the north of this building is a three-storey, three-bay building which has a base batter on its northern side and seems to incorporate the remains of a late medieval tower house, probably associated with the priory.

In the north-west angle of the walled town is the parish church of St Mary, one of the best surviving medieval parish churches in Ireland. It was probably founded in the early 13th century—possibly on the site of an earlier church—and became collegiate in 1464. The church (especially the chancel) was damaged in the late 16th-century Desmond rebellion and has been substantially restored in recent centuries. It is basically of 13th-century date and is cruciform, with an aisled nave. The present entrance leads into the south transept, which is dominated by the Boyle monument (1619) on the south side. Opposite this is the 13th-century tomb of Richard Benet and his wife Ellis Barry—the founders of St Saviour's chantry which was originally located in this transept. This tomb was restored by Boyle, who had the 17th-century effigies added. The nave has slightly asymmetrical aisle arcades of five bays and is lit by an original three-light lancet window in the west gable. The west doorway has decorated jambs with attached piers, similar to the chancel arch at the east end of the nave. North of the west doorway, internally, are traces of a round-headed doorway that led to a vanished external belfry tower. The north transept has a west aisle and at the north-west angle, externally, is a large four-storey tower of uncertain date that served partly as a belfry and partly as a residence. Under the south-east window of the transept is a double piscina. The chancel is mainly late 15th century, rebuilt by the earl of Desmond when the church became collegiate, but the chancel arch is 13th century. Immediately in front (west) of it were two spiral stairs—only one remains—that led to a vanished rood loft. The chancel has a fine traceried east window, a sedilia and piscina in the south wall, and opposite it, the 15th-century altar tomb of Thomas Fleming. Unusually, there is a doorway in the south wall with an external porch. Opposite this is a blocked doorway in the north wall that led to a now vanished sacristy. The chancel, aisles, and transepts display similar double- and triple-lancet windows but only those in the transepts are original 13th-century work—those in the aisles and chancel are 15th-century imitations.

To the east of the church is the College (*now a private nursing home*), originally the residence of the college of priests founded by the earl of

Desmond in 1464 to serve St Mary's. It was practically destroyed in the late 16th-century Desmond rebellion, but rebuilt in the early 17th-century as a residence for Richard Boyle. Even the 17th-century building has been largely replaced by later work but the enclosing wall with its circular turrets dates to the 1640s. Beside St Mary's, to the north-east, is Myrtle Grove, a late 16th-century mansion associated with Sir Walter Raleigh, although there is no evidence that he ever lived there (*private residence; not accessible*). It is a two-storey Tudor-style house with a three-bay gabled front, dating to the 1580s although much modified in later centuries. Just outside the town on the north-west are the scant ruins of the Dominican priory or 'North Abbey' (*access from Tallow St.*), founded in 1268 and said to have been destroyed by Walter Raleigh in 1585. Little more than the west end of the church survives, with a pointed doorway and a traceried window in the gable. Some 30 m east are the remains of a pier that probably marks the end of the nave at its junction with the choir.

Museums

The primary archaeological collection, which must not be missed, is the **National Museum of Ireland** at Kildare St., in the centre of Dublin. Exhibitions cover the full range of Irish prehistory and history, up to the end of the Middle Ages, and include most of the iconic artefacts of Irish archaeology. Other National Museum of Ireland venues include Collins Barracks (also in Dublin) and Turlough Park, Castlebar, Co. Mayo (the award-winning Museum of Country Life). The **Ulster Museum** (Botanic Avenue, Belfast) has much smaller archaeological displays, but these include some important material and should not be missed.

Ireland's museums sector has traditionally been quite centralized, with comparatively few good local museums. There are, however, a growing number of County Museums whose archaeological displays (although usually relatively small and mainly on loan from the National Museum of Ireland) help complete the picture of their respective regions. Their exhibitions tend to be stronger in the areas of more recent social, economic, and political history, which will also be of interest to most visitors. Most of these museums are referred to in the main text (under the towns in which they are located) and need only be mentioned again here. All are worth visiting.

Armagh County Museum, The Mall, Armagh.

Cavan County Museum, Virginia Road, Ballyjamesduff. Displays include the important Iron Age decorated stone from Killycluggin.

Clare County Museum, Arthur's Row, Ennis.

Cork Public Museum, Fitzgerald Park, Mardyke, Cork.

Corlea Trackway Visitors Centre, Kenagh, Co. Longford (*signposted off the R397 between Lanesborough and Ballymahon*). This is the only place to see a real, fully preserved Iron Age (mid-2nd-century BC) wooden trackway, or *togher*. Exhibition includes 20 min. audio-visual. April–Sept. 10.00–18.00. Adm. free.

Donegal County Museum, High Road, Letterkenny.

Down County Museum, The Mall, Downpatrick.

Fermanagh County Museum, The Castle, Enniskillen.

Galway City Museum, The Spanish Arch, Galway

The Hunt Museum, The Customs House, Rutland St., Limerick.

Kerry County Museum, Ashe Memorial Hall, Denny St., Tralee. Good displays on the archaeology of the county, as well as interesting temporary exhibitions. The same building houses *Geraldine Tralee*, a reconstructed visitor 'experience' of the late medieval town of Tralee.

Limerick City Museum, Castle Lane, Nicholas St.

Louth County Museum, Carroll Centre, Jocelyn St., Dundalk.

Monaghan County Museum, Hill St., Monaghan.

Tipperary South Riding County Museum, Emmet St., Clonmel. A good County Museum located in what was an important medieval town.

Tower Museum, Derry, Shipquay St./Guildhall Square, Derry.

Waterford Treasures, The Granary, Waterford.

Chronology

BC

*c.*8000	Arrival of first Mesolithic hunter-gatherers.
*c.*4300	Transitions to Neolithic technology and agricultural subsistence; first megalithic tombs erected.
*c.*2500	Earliest copper mining in south-west Ireland; beginnings of copper-based metalworking.
*c.*900–600	'Dowris' phase climax of Late Bronze Age, marked by profuse production of gold ornaments, bronze tools and weapons, and construction of hillforts.
*c.*400–100	First use of iron technology in Ireland and first appearance of Celtic material (indigenous and imported) decorated in La Tène style. Climax of the so-called 'royal' sites of late prehistory.

AD

*c.*100–400	Ireland not part of Roman Empire but receiving influences from Roman Britain. Social upheaval and migrations from Ireland into western Britain following withdrawal of Roman forces from Britain.
*c.*400–600	Christianization of Ireland, emergence of monasticism; appearance of complex early medieval society and independent polities based on tribal groupings called *túatha*. Agricultural revolution, e.g. use of coulter plough and horizontal mill.
*c.*650–800	Cementing of bonds between religious and secular power; appearance of 'monastic towns'; 'Golden Age' of Irish artistic achievement in metalwork (e.g. Tara Brooch), manuscript illumination (Book of **Kells**), and stone sculpture (**Ahenny** crosses).
795	First recorded Viking raid on Rathlin Island, Co. Antrim.
841	Establishment of Viking *longphort* at Duiblinn, ultimately developing into town of **Dublin**.
914	Beginning of new wave of Viking attacks; settlements established or re-established at **Dublin, Waterford, Limerick, Cork**.
980	Defeat of army of Dublin at **Tara** by Uí Néill king Máel Sechnaill, after which Dublin was effectively controlled by the main Irish provincial kings.
*c.*1000	Brian *Borumha* recognized as effective high-king of Ireland.
1014	Battle of Clontarf: Brian defeats revolt by **Dublin** and Leinster but dies in battle.
1112	Synod of Rath Bresail: first attempt to impose regular diocesan structure on Irish Church; finalized at Synod of **Kells** in 1152.
1171	Henry II brings army to Ireland and claims overlordship; beginning of English conquest.
1315–18	Edward Bruce, brother of Scottish king Robert, campaigns in

	Ireland, causing long-term damage to English colony.
1534	Fitzgerald rebellion marks beginning of Tudor campaigns to reassert English control in Ireland. Imposition of Reformation legislation (from 1536) and first dissolutions of monasteries (*c.*1540) form part of this process.
1594	Outbreak of Nine Years War; Ulster lords, led by Ó Néill and Ó Domhnaill, resist expansion of English control with surprising (and, to English eyes, shocking) effectiveness.
1601	Defeat of Ulster lords at **Kinsale** marks beginning of the end of Nine Years War. Ó Néill and Ó Domhnaill flee Ireland in 1607.
1609	English respond to trauma of Nine Years War with plantation of Ulster. Large numbers of English and Scots settlers brought in, transforming landscape, society, and economy of Ulster.

Glossary

ambulatory: a passage for walking, especially the covered walkway around the cloister of a medieval monastery.

antae: vertical projections of the side walls beyond the east and west gables in early Irish churches. They probably supported the end beams of overhanging roofs, and may represent translations into stone of the corner posts of timber buildings.

architrave: a decorative border around a doorway or window.

aumbrey: a wall cupboard, frequently found in medieval churches, usually close to the altar.

barbican: an external structure attached to the gate of a castle or walled town as an additional protective feature.

barrow: originally meaning a mound, the term is also applied to small, annular and penannular enclosures, many of which are for burial, comprising various combinations of banks and fosses, either alone or in combination.

bartizan: an overhanging corner turret, usually carried some distance above ground level, on a castle or fortification.

batter: a sloping external wall face on castles, churches, and towers; this feature may have originated in drystone construction, where it would have provided extra stability.

bawn: a fortified enclosure surrounding or attached to a castle, much like a bailey or ward. Probably from the Irish *bó dhún* ('cattle enclosure').

bullaun: a basin-like depression carved in natural rock or a boulder, often at church sites.

cashel: stone-built enclosure, usually considered to be the stone equivalent of earthen ringforts, or raths.

chancel: the eastern end of a church, where the high altar was located; usually separated from the nave (the main body of the church) by screens or *cancelli.*

chantry chapel: a chapel or side altar in a church, specifically endowed by a donor to support a priest saying masses for the donor's soul.

chevaux de frise: a defensive feature found on certain sites, usually consisting of large numbers of upright stones set in a band across the approaches to the site.

choir: in a monastic church, the area reserved for the monks or friars near the east end.

cist: boxlike, stone burial chamber. Typically earlier Bronze Age.

crannóg: a habitation site based on an artificial (or partly artificial) island in, or at the edge of, a lake or wetland area. Classically a settlement type of the early medieval period; similar monuments of prehistoric date have also been recognized.

cusp: in Gothic tracery (*see below*), a projecting point between the small arcs forming a window head, panel, or arch.

dendrochronology: a dating technique based on counting the annual growth rings of trees. It can provide extremely accurate dates, but only if suitable pieces of wood are available.

eustatic: movements in sea level in response to the expansion and contraction of ice masses.

flamboyant: literally 'flamelike', a term used to describe flowing, curvilinear window tracery of the 14th–16th centuries.

fulacht fiadh (pl. fulachta): prehistoric (mainly Bronze Age) installations in which water was heated in large wooden troughs by adding fire-heated stones, possibly for cooking, ritual bathing, or other purposes. They usually survive today as mounds of fire-cracked stones, close to a stream or pond.

gallowglass: armoured warriors, originally from western Scotland, who served as mercenaries in the retinues of many Irish lords during the later Middle Ages.

garderobe: a latrine, usually built into the wall of a medieval castle or church building and exiting via a chute to the external ground below.

hengiform: large enclosure comprising bank and *internal* fosse.

isostatic: depression or elevation of land surface in response to the expansion and contraction of ice masses.

La Tène: abstract, curvilinear art style of the European and Insular Celts, named after a site in Switzerland.

lavabo: from the Latin for 'I will wash', a term used for the wash basins or troughs usually located at the entrance to the refectory or dining hall of medieval monasteries.

longphort: an Irish term (literally 'ship fort'), originally given to a series of fortified encampments, usually on river junctions or islands, established by Viking raiders in the mid-9th century.

machicolation: a structure, carried on corbels or arches, projecting from a wall top; usually sited over a doorway or gate, it allowed defenders to drop missiles etc. on anyone attacking the entrance.

motte: an early form of castle, probably introduced by the English in the late 12th century. The motte (in archaeological terms) was a relatively tall earthen mound constructed as the base for a tower; there might also be a larger enclosure known as a bailey.

murage: a tax levied to pay for building or repairing the walls of a town.

mural stairway: a stair built within the thickness of the wall of a castle or church.

murder hole: an aperture in the vault or ceiling inside a doorway or entrance, through which missiles etc. could be dropped from the floor above on intruders.

nave: the main body of a church, from the west end entrance to the chancel or choir.

ogam: the earliest form of script known in Ireland, probably developed in the early centuries AD, and consisting of a series of horizontal or diagonal strokes crossing a central line, usually inscribed on the edges of standing stones.

oriel: a window or windowed recess projecting from an upper storey, usually supported on corbels.

orthostat: literally applicable to any standing stone, in Irish archaeology to term generally applied to the upright elements of megalithic tombs.

piscina: a stone basin, usually built into the wall of a church, in which priests washed their hands and the communion vessels during mass.

rath: the main Irish-language name for the monument type known in English as a ringfort (q.v.). The Irish term is also frequently used in English-language archaeological literature and it survives as a very common place name element.

reticulated: literally 'netlike', a term used to describe certain forms of late medieval window tracery.

ringfort: elliptical or circular settlement enclosed by bank(s) and fosse(s). The most common field monument in Ireland, dating from the 6th to the 10th century. Some are later.

rood screen/loft/gallery: the rood was the main crucifix of a medieval church. It was generally displayed as part of a rood screen of wood or stone, which divided the nave and choir. In larger churches a loft or gallery might be incorporated over the rood screen.

sedilia: a seat within the wall of a church, where the priest sat during mass.

slype: a covered passageway through the claustral buildings of a monastery, usually running between the church and the chapter house.

solar: a private upper chamber in a medieval house or castle.

souterrain: an underground passage, with or without chambers, usually stone built, found in association with ringforts or church enclosures, and used for storage and/or refuge.

spandrel: the space between the arch of a door or window and its surrounding frame.

termon: boundary of a monastery in early medieval Ireland.

togher: wooden trackway across boggy or marshy ground.

tracery: openwork stone ornament, especially in medieval windows and arches. The tracery filled the larger window opening or arch, and was itself often filled with glass.

túath: the basic socio-political unit of early medieval Ireland comprising an independent tribal group united by blood relations and ruled over by a king. At any moment in time there were about 100–50 *túatha* in existence.

urn: ceramic vessel used to contain cremated or unburnt human remains.

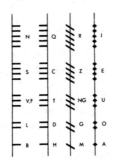

▲ **Fig. 165.** Ogam alphabet

Further Reading

Barry, T. B. 1987. *The Archaeology of Medieval Ireland*. London: Methuen.

Charles-Edwards, T. 2000. *Early Christian Ireland*. Cambridge: Cambridge University Press.

Cooney, G., and Grogan, E. 1994. *Irish Prehistory: A Social Perspective*. Dublin: Wordwell.

Cosgrove, A. (ed.). 1987. *Medieval Ireland 1169–1534*. A New History of Ireland, vol. 2. Dublin: Royal Irish Academy.

Duffy, P., Edwards, D., and FitzPatrick, E. (eds). 2001. *Gaelic Ireland: Land, Lordship and Settlement c.1250–c.1650*. Dublin: Four Courts Press.

Edwards, N. 1990. *The Archaeology of Early Medieval Ireland*. London: B. T. Batsford.

Eogan, G. 1986. *Knowth and the Passage Tombs of Ireland*. London: Thames and Hudson.

FitzPatrick, E. 2004. *Royal Inauguration in Gaelic Ireland c.1100–1600: A Cultural Landscape Study*. Woodbridge: Boydell and Brewer.

Harbison, P. 1992. *The High Crosses of Ireland: An Iconographical and Photographic Survey*. 3 vols. Bonn: Rudolf Habelt Gmbtt.

Henry, F. 1965. *Irish Art in the Early Christian Period (to AD 800)*. London: Methuen.

— 1967. *Irish Art during the Viking Invasions (800–1020 AD)*. London: Methuen.

— 1970 *Irish Art in the Romanesque Period (1020–1170 AD)*. London: Methuen.

Hunt, J. 1974. *Irish Medieval Figure Sculpture 1200–1600*. Dublin: Irish University Press/Sotheby Parke Bernet.

Kelly, F. 1997. *Early Irish Farming: A Study Based Mainly on the Law-Texts of the 7th and 8th Centuries AD*. Dublin: Institute for Advanced Studies.

Leask, H. G. 1951. *Irish Castles and Castellated Houses*. Dundalk: Tempest.

— 1955–60. *Irish Churches and Monastic Buildings*. 3 vols. Dundalk: Tempest.

McNeill, T. 1997. *Castles in Ireland: Feudal Power in a Gaelic World*. London: Routledge.

Mitchell, F., and Ryan, M. 1997. *Reading the Irish Landscape*, rev. edn. Dublin: Town House.

Moody, T. W., and Martin, F. X. (eds). 1984. *The Course of Irish History*, rev. edn. Cork: Mercier Press.

O'Conor, K. 1998. *The Archaeology of Medieval Rural Settlement in Ireland*. Discovery Programme Reports 3. Dublin.

Ó Cróinín, D. (ed.). 2005. *Prehistoric and Early Ireland*. A New History of Ireland, vol. 1. Dublin: Royal Irish Academy.

O'Keeffe, T. 2000. *Medieval Ireland: An Archaeology*. Stroud: Tempus.

Ó Ríordáin, S. P. 1979. *Antiquities of the Irish Countryside*. 5th edn. rev. R. de Valera. London: Methuen.

O'Sullivan, A. 1998. *The Archaeology of Lake Settlement in Ireland*. Discovery Programme Reports 4. Dublin.

Otway-Ruthven, A. J. 1968. *A History of Medieval Ireland.* London: Ernest Benn.

Raftery, B. 1994. *Pagan Celtic Ireland.* London: Thames and Hudson.

Ryan, M. (ed.). 1991. *The Illustrated Archaeology of Ireland.* Dublin: Country House.

Sweetman, P. D. 2000. *The Medieval Castles of Ireland.* Woodbridge: Boydell Press.

Waddell, J. 2000. *The Prehistoric Archaeology of Ireland.* Bray: Wordwell.

Wallace, P. F., and Ó Floinn, R. 2002. *Treasures of the National Museum of Ireland: Irish Antiquities.* Dublin: Gill & Macmillan.

Index

Numbers in **bold** refer to main site entries.